THE UNITED NATIONS SERIES

ROBERT J. KERNER, GENERAL EDITOR

SATHER PROFESSOR OF HISTORY IN THE
UNIVERSITY OF CALIFORNIA

✧

CZECHOSLOVAKIA
EDITED BY ROBERT J. KERNER

THE NETHERLANDS
EDITED BY BARTHOLOMEW LANDHEER

POLAND
EDITED BY BERNADOTTE E. SCHMITT

BELGIUM
EDITED BY JAN-ALBERT GORIS

✧

Other volumes in preparation

BELGIUM

TOWN HALL, BRUSSELS

BELGIUM

Chapters by George W. Carpenter, James P. Chapin, B.-S. Chlepner, Shepard B. Clough, Frans van Cauwelaert, Victor J. Dossogne, Jan-Albert Goris, Baron de Gruben, Max Gottschalk, Henri Grégoire, Jan Greshoff, Melville J. Herskovits, René Hislaire, Max Horn, Jan Frans Hostie, Charles Leirens, E. G. Misner, Felix A. Morlion, Georges Philippart, Henri E. A. M. Rolin, Georges Theunis, R. Stanley Thomson, Jean Timmermans, Albert de Vleeschauwer, Arthur Wauters, Benjamin Mather Woodbridge, Constant van de Wall, Paul van Zeeland

L'UNION FAIT LA FORCE · EENDRACHT MAAKT MACHT

EDITED BY JAN-ALBERT GORIS

UNIVERSITY OF CALIFORNIA PRESS

BERKELEY AND LOS ANGELES · 1945

UNIVERSITY OF CALIFORNIA PRESS
BERKELEY AND LOS ANGELES
CALIFORNIA

❖

CAMBRIDGE UNIVERSITY PRESS
LONDON, ENGLAND

PRINTED IN THE UNITED STATES OF AMERICA
BY THE UNIVERSITY OF CALIFORNIA PRESS

TO THE PIOUS MEMORY OF
SO MANY THOUSANDS OF BELGIANS WHO GAVE
THEIR LIVES IN THE WAR OR WHO
FELL VICTIMS
TO THE OCCUPATION OF THEIR COUNTRY

The United Nations Series

THE UNITED NATIONS SERIES *is dedicated to the task of mutual understanding among the Allies and to the achievement of successful coöperation in this war and in the coming peace. In the measure that the United Nations understand one another they will march triumphantly through total victory to lasting peace.*

The University of California offers this series as a part of its contribution to the war effort of this state and nation and of the nations united in the greatest conflict known to history, and it heartily thanks the editors of the respective volumes and their collaborators for their devoted service in this cause and for their effort to present an honest, sincere, and objective appraisal of the United Nations.

ROBERT J. KERNER
General Editor

Editor's Preface

IT HAS BEEN SAID *that those who wrote the Treaty of Versailles, confronted as they were with the opposing claims of national groups in many corners of Europe, learned much about geography. Lloyd George is reported to have been astounded when he heard about such an impossible country as the Banat of Temesvar. Even in our day Chamberlain referred to Czechoslovakia, which he could reach easily by airplane in six hours, as "that far-away country about which we know so little." It seems therefore not altogether useless, but indeed most opportune, to provide, for all those desirous of knowing the characteristics and problems of their allies, a series of books which will give objective, and thus reliable and scientific, information. Professor Robert J. Kerner is to be commended very highly for having initiated this most useful project. His solid advice and his resourcefulness, interpreting and reflecting the generous help of the University of California Press, have a great deal to do with the publication of this book on Belgium.*

There is no other general book of recent date on Belgium. A great number of books have been written about Belgium by American authors in recent decades. They describe essentially her scenic attractions or her art, with certain comments on her history and her social structure. Other more scholarly publications include only specialized, restricted subjects. This volume has been written by a number of American and Belgian scholars and writers, with the exception of Mr. Greshoff, whose contribution gives the view of a friendly Dutch neighbor on a sector of Dutch literature, Flemish letters. Through good fortune, at least eight American scholars who know Belgium or the Belgian Congo consented to write chapters for this volume. They have done so often in difficult circumstances and, like the other contributors, they have submitted generously to the general discipline the editor was obliged to impose upon them as to the length of their contributions. The other chapters are written by Belgian specialists. These authors, too, worked under handicaps, cut off from their sources and material; in some cases their contributions have had to be considerably condensed, and, notwithstanding the devoted care on the part of the translators, they lost some of their directness and poignancy.

I have striven for objectivity, and I met with understanding. I feel particularly grateful to those contributors who, although they had personal grievances to express or criticism to offer, did so in a spirit of fairness and open-mindedness which is as much a credit to themselves as a compliment to Belgium and the Belgian Congo. For instance, although education in the Belgian African territory has been mainly conducted by Catholic missionaries, I feel grateful to the Reverend George W. Carpenter, Educational Secretary of the Congo Protestant Council in the Congo, for having objectively stated achievements in the entire mission field.

Let me reserve for this final paragraph my sincerest gratitude for that excellent and intelligent friend of Belgium, Mrs. Frances Stillman, for her unerring devotion in the editing of the manuscript of this book.

JAN-ALBERT GORIS

Contents

PAGE

The Belgian National Anthem, *The Brabançonne* . xxiii
English Version by LORRAINE NOEL FINLEY

PART ONE: THE SCENE

CHAPTER I

Land and People 3

By JAN-ALBERT GORIS, D.S.H.

Professor of Comparative Literatures, National Higher Institute of
Fine Arts, Antwerp; Professor of Economic History, Louvain University, 1928–1931; Chief of the cabinet of the Mayor of Antwerp, 1928–
1932; Chief of the cabinet of the Minister of Economic Affairs, 1933–
1937; Deputy Commissioner General of Belgium at New York World's
Fair, 1939–1940; Commissioner of Information for Belgium in the
United States, 1941–. Under his own name or his pen name, Marnix
Gijsen, he has published, among others: *Het Huis* (1925); *Etude sur
les colonies marchandes méridionales à Anvers de 1488 à 1567* (1925);
Ontdek Amerika (1927); *Antwerp 1918–1928* (1929); *Odusseus achterna*
(1930); *Ons Volkskarakter* (1932); *Lierre* (1935); *De Literatuur in Zuid-
Nederland sedert 1830* (1939); *Hans Memling te Brugge* (1939); *Peri-
patetisch Onderricht* I, II (1940); *Lof van Antwerpen* (1940); *Du Génie
flamand* (1943); *Belgium in Bondage* (1943); *Strangers Should Not
Whisper* (1945). Editor of *News from Belgium,* New York, 1941–1945.

PART TWO: HISTORICAL BACKGROUND

CHAPTER II

From Caesar to 1814 15

By THE REV. VICTOR J. DOSSOGNE, S.J., Ph.D.

Formerly Professor of History, Faculté Notre Dame de la Paix, Namur, Belgium; member, Société d'Histoire Moderne and Société
d'Histoire du Droit, Paris and Brussels; traveled extensively throughout Europe on scientific missions; Professor of European History,
Loyola University of the South, New Orleans; United States Army
chaplain since 1943; collaborator with the Rev. L. Willaert on a
handbook of Belgian history.

CHAPTER III   PAGE

The Dutch Regime (1814–1830) and the Kingdom of Belgium (1830–1840) . . 25

By BARON DE GRUBEN, J.D.

Graduate in law at Louvain University; enlisted as volunteer and served in the Belgian army during the First World War; entered Belgian Foreign Service in 1923; Secretary of the Belgian Cabinet, 1937; Counselor of the Belgian Embassy in Washington, 1938; author of *Les Belges sur le Rhin* (1924); *La Crise allemande et l'occupation rhénane* (1925); *La Politique économique de l'Allemagne* (1937); and numerous articles on contemporary problems.

CHAPTER IV

Consolidation and Expansion of the Kingdom (1840–1914) 37

By BARON DE GRUBEN

CHAPTER V

In the First World War 53

By GEORGES THEUNIS, E.E.

Belgian Ambassador-at-Large in United States for special economic and financial questions, since 1939; Electrical Engineer, University of Liége; officer in artillery; after service in 1914 at front, organized ammunition supply for Belgian army in Paris and London, 1915; expert attached to Belgian Delegation at Peace Conference; Belgian High Commissioner for Reconstruction in England, 1919; First Belgian Delegate, Reparations Commission; Minister of Finance, 1920; Prime Minister (with portfolio of Finances), 1921–1925; President, Economic Conference, Geneva, 1927; President, International Chamber of Commerce, 1929–1931; also president of numerous economic commissions in Belgium, 1925–1939; Prime Minister for second time, 1934–1935; Governor of the National Bank of Belgium (1942–1944); Minister of State.

CHAPTER VI

Belgium between the Two World Wars . . 66

By JAN-ALBERT GORIS

Contents

PART THREE: POLITICAL AND CONSTITUTIONAL DEVELOPMENT

CHAPTER VII   PAGE

Constitution and Political Structure . . .   81

By HENRI E. A. M. ROLIN, J.D.

Professor, University of Brussels, where he taught Political Science
and Law, 1900–1940; President, Ecole des Sciences Politiques et
Sociales (Brussels University); Judge since 1903; President, Belgian
Supreme Court of Appeal, 1939–; devoted much study to Congo Free
State; member, Belgian Royal Academy of Sciences and Letters; author of *Théorie du beau; Vie et philosophie de Thomas Carlyle; Histoire d'un siècle d'efforts pour améliorer la condition des travailleurs;
Les Institutions ouvrières des charbonnages de Mariemont et de
Bascoup* (1904); *Le Droit de l'Uganda* (1910); *Les Vices de l'administration du Katanga, les remèdes* (1911); *Les Lois et l'administration de
la Rhodésie* (1913); and of numerous articles on legal, colonial, and
social topics.

CHAPTER VIII

Political Parties   93

By RENÉ HISLAIRE, Ph.D.

Veteran, First World War, 1914–1918; editor of the monthly, *Belgium,*
New York; editor, later editor in chief, *La Nation Belge,* 1919–1934;
head of the press and propaganda service of the Cabinet of the Prime
Minister in 1934–1935; since 1935, director of *L'Indépendance Belge;*
author of *Jacques Bainville et son œuvre* (1936); *Huit jours à Berlin*
(1937); *Le Redressement français* (1938); contributor to *Revue des
Deux Mondes, Revue Belge, Revue Catholique des Idées et des Faits,
Europäische Revue,* and *Echo de Paris.*

CHAPTER IX

The Flemish Movement   108

By SHEPARD B. CLOUGH, Ph.D.

Student at Colgate University, Sorbonne, University of Heidelberg,
Columbia University; research and writing in Belgium, France, and
Italy, 1926–1928; Instructor in History in Columbia College, 1928–
1937; member, Department of History, Columbia University, since
1937; Secretary of the Faculty, 1938–1942; member of the research staff
of the Mutual Life Insurance Company of New York, 1941–1942; member of the Division of Economic Studies, Department of State, 1942–
1943; lecturer, School of Military Government, Charlottesville, Vir-
ginia, since 1942, and for the Office of Foreign Relief and Rehabilitation since 1943; member of the Historical Service Board, the Advisory
Council on War History, and the Social Science Research Council;
author of *History of the Flemish Movement in Belgium* (1930); *Out-*

line of Modern European History (1933); *The Objectives of Education in Fascist Italy* (1935); *France: A History of National Economics* (1939); (with H. W. Schneider) *Making Fascists* (1929); (with Charles W. Cole) *An Economic History of Europe* (1941); and of articles in *University of Pennsylvania Bulletin* (1931), *Harvard Business Review* (1932), *Columbia University Quarterly* (1934), *The Social Studies* (1935), *Revue d'Histoire Moderne* (1936), *Social Education* (1938), *Political Science Quarterly* (1944).

PART FOUR: ECONOMIC AND SOCIAL DEVELOPMENT

CHAPTER X   PAGE

Foreign Policy, 1918 to 1940 129
By FRANS VAN CAUWELAERT, J.D., Ph.D.
President of the Belgian Chamber of Representatives; Minister of State; Professor of Experimental Psychology and Pedagogy at Fribourg University (Switzerland), 1907–1910; member of the Flemish Academy; member of Belgian Parliament since 1910; Mayor of Antwerp, 1921–1932; Delegate to League of Nations (1925–1927); Minister of Economic Affairs, 1933–1934; and author of *Verhandelingen en Voordrachten,* 2 volumes (1906–1908); *Vrij België* (1918); as well as contributor to European and American reviews on politics and economics.

CHAPTER XI

The Agriculture of Belgium 148
By E. G. MISNER, Ph.D.
Professor of Farm Management, Cornell University; American Fellow in Belgium from the C. R. B. Educational Foundation, Inc. (1934–1935); author of several bulletins of Cornell University Agricultural Experiment Station.

CHAPTER XII

Economic Development of Belgium . . . 167
By B.-S. CHLEPNER
Member of the Research Staff of the Brookings Institution, Washington, D.C.; Professor of Economics (General Economics, Money and Banking), University of Brussels, 1919–1940; member of the Staff of the Sociological Institute, Brussels (1913–1940); author of *Le Prélèvement sur le capital dans la théorie et la pratique* (1923); *La Banque en Belgique* (1926); *Le Marché financier belge depuis 100 ans; L'Etranger dans l'histoire économique de la Belgique* (1932); *Belgian Banking and Banking Theory* (1943); and of numerous articles in scientific publications among which are *Encyclopedia for Social Sciences,* New York University; *Revue d'Economie Politique; Revue Economique Internationale; Revue d'Histoire Economique et Sociale,* Paris; and *Renaissance,* New York.

CHAPTER XIII   PAGE

Social Structure and Development 187

By MAX GOTTSCHALK, J.D.

Legal studies at the universities of Liége, Berlin, and Paris; expert on
labor problems; President, Belgian Association for Social Progress;
Research Professor, Solvay Institute of Sociology, University of Brussels; Belgian correspondent, International Labor Bureau, Geneva;
author of articles on social research; contributor to the *Revue de l'Institut Solvay, Revue du Travail, Revue Internationale du Travail, La
Belgique Restaurée* (edited by E. Mahaim), and *L'Encyclopédie Belge.*

CHAPTER XIV

Communications and Transportation . . . 198

By JAN FRANS HOSTIE, J.D.

Official, in the Ministry for Marine, Posts and Telegraph, and in the
Belgian Foreign Office; enlisted in the Belgian army in 1914; when
invalided, resumed his official duties with the Belgian Government
in exile; represented Belgium in the Ports, Waterways, and Railways
Commission at the Peace Conference; member of the Communications section of the Economic Council; Plenipotentiary for the Rhine
and Elbe; member, Committee for the Study of Freedom of Communications and Transit; member of the Permanent Legal Committee for
the Organization of Communications and Transit, League of Nations;
Chairman of the Trail Smelter Arbitral Tribunal, United States and
Canada, 1937–1941; member of the Académie Diplomatique of Paris;
Lecturer, University of Michigan, 1942, also University of Illinois;
author of *Tendances nouvelles dans le droit des voies d'eau interna-
tionales* (1935); *L'Activité de l'organisation des communications et du
transit de la Société des Nations en matière de droit comparé* (1936);
and of many articles on maritime law, on economics, and on public
international law of communications, including transportation; contributor to the *International Law Digest.*

PART FIVE: CULTURAL ASPECTS

CHAPTER XV

The History of Christianity in Belgium . . 217

By FELIX A. MORLION, O.P.

Founded, in 1931, the DOCIP, a Catholic press service on film topics,
which published a movie guide and film sections in newspapers of
various countries; founder of the Catholic Press Center of Brussels;
escaped from Belgium and founded, in July, 1940, in Lisbon, the International Center of Information Pro Deo (CIP); since 1941 traveled
through North and South America establishing CIP agencies; author
of articles on current topics, among them, *Offensive for God, Spirit
and Practice; Film and Conscience; Liberty in Practice.*

CHAPTER XVI   PAGE

Education in Belgium 226

By HENRI GRÉGOIRE, Ph.D., Dr.h.c.

Professor at the University of Brussels; Ph.D., Classical Philology,
University of Liége; Secretary to the Commission d'Enquête au Congo
Belge (1904–1905); member of the Ecole Française d'Athènes (1906–
1909); Dean of the Faculty of Letters of the University of Cairo (1925–
1927) and of the University of Brussels (1929–1932); since 1932,
Vice-President of the Institut de Philologie et d'Histoire Orientales
et Slaves of the Brussels University. Missions to Mount Sinai, in Asia
Minor (1906–1907), and in many other countries; Visiting Professor of
History and Classics at Stanford University, 1931; Sather Lecturer on
the Classics at the University of California, Berkeley, 1938; Associate
Professor at the New School for Social Research since 1940; honorary
degrees conferred by the universities of Athens, Algiers, and Sofia;
member of the Royal Academy of Belgium; correspondent of the
Académie des Inscriptions et Belles Lettres, Paris, 1936, and of many
other scholarly institutions in Europe; corresponding fellow of the
Medieval Academy of America; co-founder and director of *Le Flambeau,* a clandestine newspaper under the German occupation of 1914–
1918; director of *Byzantion* since 1930; co-director of *L'Antiquitè
Classique;* founder and director of *L'Annuaire de l'Institut de Philolo-
gie et d'Histoire Orientales;* author of many contributions to Greek,
Byzantine, and Medieval history, among them: *Saints Jumeaux et
Dieux Cavaliers* (1905); *Recueil des inscriptions grecques chrétiennes
d'Asie Mineure* (1922–1923); translator in the Budé collection of:
*Héraclès, Les Suppliantes, Ion, Les Troyennes, Iphigénie en Tauride,
Electre,* and *Vie de Porphyre* of Marc le Diacre.

CHAPTER XVII

Science in Independent Belgium 239

By JEAN TIMMERMANS, Sc.D.

Professor of Physical Chemistry and former President of the Faculty
of Sciences at the University of Brussels; member of Fourth Committee of the National Fund for Scientific Research; secretary of the National Belgian Commission of Chemistry; director of the National
Bureau of Physical and Chemical Standards; author of *Les Solutions
concentrées; Théories et applications aux mélanges binaires de com-
posés organiques* (1936); *La Notion d'espèce en chimie* (1928); *Chemical Species* (1940); contributor to the *Bulletin de la Classe des Sciences
de l'Académie Royale de Belgique; Bulletin de la Société Chimique de
Belgique; Comptes Rendus de l'Académie des Sciences* (Paris), *Journal
de Chimie Physique; Revue de l'Université de Bruxelles; Archives
Néerlandaises; Travaux du Congrès Jubilaire Mendeleef* (Leningrad);
Actes du VII Congrès International du Froid* (The Hague); *Recueil
des Travaux Chimiques,* and *Journal of Chemical Education.*

CHAPTER XVIII PAGE

Art in Belgium 256

By CONSTANT VAN DE WALL

Dutch-American artist, Assistant Professor of Fine Arts, Hofstra College, Long Island; formerly lecturer in Fine Arts at New York University; authority on Dutch and Flemish art; instrumental in establishing summer courses in Belgian art in Brussels for advanced students in the History of Art; Fellow of the Belgian-American Education Foundation; translator of Carel van Mander's *Schilderboeck* under the title, *Dutch and Flemish Painters* (1936); author of articles in *Bulletin of the College Art Association*, New York, and *Belgium*, New York.

CHAPTER XIX

Architecture 274

By GEORGES PHILIPPART

Secretary of the National Association of Belgian Museums and of the National Committee of Fine Arts, Belgium, associated with Committee of the American Council of Learned Societies on Protection of European Cultural Material; manager of art exhibitions in Belgium, France, and the United States; art and literary writer and editor; journalist; translated from Dutch into French a number of works, including *Lettres de Vincent van Gogh à son frère Théo* (1937).

CHAPTER XX

Belgian Literature in the Dutch Language . 286

By JAN GRESHOFF

Poet and essayist; with the Netherlands Information Bureau; journalist and correspondent for Dutch and Netherlands Indies newspapers at Brussels for fifteen years; author of many works of poetry and prose, including a biography of Arthur van Schendel, four volumes of aphorisms, three volumes of essays and poems, and an anthology of Dutch poetry in two volumes. A collection of his poems was published in Maastricht in 1936.

CHAPTER XXI

French Literature in Belgium 301

By BENJAMIN MATHER WOODBRIDGE, Ph.D.

Professor of Romance Languages, Reed College; Ph.D., Harvard University; Elève titulaire de l'Ecole des Hautes Etudes, the Sorbonne, 1911; Fellow, Belgian-American Education Foundation, 1927–1928, and Director, since 1932; author of *Gatien de Courtilz, Sieur du Verger* (1925); *Le Roman belge contemporain* (1930); consulting editor and

author of studies on French literature in Belgium in *Columbia Dictionary of Modern European Literatures* (in press); contributing editor, *Books Abroad,* and contributor to American, Belgian, French, and
English periodicals.   PAGE

Note on Walloon Literature 314
By JAN-ALBERT GORIS

CHAPTER XXII

Belgian Music 318
By CHARLES LEIRENS
Professor of the History of Music, New School for Social Research,
New York; Director, Palais des Beaux Arts, Brussels, 1929–1931; Director, Maison d'Art, Brussels, 1932–1939; Professor, until the war, in
the National Institute for Architecture and Applied Art, Brussels;
author of *Belgian Music* (1943); former editor of *Revue Internationale
de Musique,* Brussels; Belgian correspondent for *Musical America;*
and contributor to *Revue Nationale de Musique.*

PART SIX: BELGIAN CONGO

CHAPTER XXIII

Geography 337
By JAMES P. CHAPIN, Ph.D.
Ornithologist; Associate Curator, American Museum of Natural History, New York; participated in field expeditions to Canadian Rockies,
1915; Panama, 1923; East Africa and Belgian Congo, 1926–1927; Galapagos Islands, 1930; Belgian Congo, 1930–1931; Polynesia, Juan Fer-
nandez, Galapagos Islands, 1934–1935; Belgian Congo, 1937 and 1943;
and author of *Birds of the Belgian Congo,* Part I (1932), Part II (1939).

CHAPTER XXIV

Peoples and Culture 353
By MELVILLE J. HERSKOVITS, Ph.D.
Professor of Anthropology at Northwestern University; Guggenheim
Memorial Fellow, 1937–1938; leader of expeditions to Dutch Guiana,
1928–1929; West Africa, 1931; Haiti, 1934; Trinidad, 1939; Brazil,
1941–1942; member of the permanent Council of the International
Anthropological Congress; author of *The American Negro: A Study
of Racial Crossing* (1928); *Anthropometry of the American Negro*
(1930); *Outline of Dahomean Religious Belief* (with Frances S. Herskovits) (1933); *Rebel Destiny: Among the Bush Negro of Dutch Guiana* (with Frances S. Herskovits) (1934); *Suriname Folklore* (with
same) (1936); *Life in a Haitian Valley* (1937); *Dahomey* (1938); *Accul-
turation* (1938); *The Economic Life of Primitive Peoples* (1940).

CHAPTER XXV   PAGE

Historical Development 366

By R. STANLEY THOMSON, Ph.D.

Professor of History, Russell Sage College; engaged in research in Brussels, Belgium, 1927–1928, 1930, and 1937, as Fellow of the C. R. B. Educational Foundation, Inc.; research on Indo-China in Paris, 1936–1937, as Fellow of the Social Science Research Council; and author of *La Fondation de l'Etat indépéndant du Congo* (1933).

CHAPTER XXVI

Administrative Structure 380

By ALBERT DE VLEESCHAUWER, J.D.

Belgian Minister of Colonies since 1938; Professor of Commercial Law at Louvain University and of Economics at its Agricultural Institute, since 1929; member of Parliament since 1923; visited the Belgian Congo in 1941–1942; and author of *Belgian Colonial Policy* (1944).

CHAPTER XXVII

Economic Development 386

By MAX HORN, J.D.

Counselor for the Congo Government in the United States and Canada; closely connected with the Belgian Congo for over thirty years as Counselor to the Belgian Government for the Ministries of Transport, Interior, and Finances, and Government Commissioner to the Congo Central Bank and other chartered corporations.

CHAPTER XXVIII

Health, Education, and Social Welfare . . . 400

By GEORGE W. CARPENTER, Ph.D., D.D. (hon.).

Educator and missionary; teacher, Kimpese Institute, Belgian Congo, training school for African missionaries and teachers, two terms, 1926–1935; and Educational Secretary, Congo Protestant Council, since 1938.

PART SEVEN: SECOND WORLD WAR AND AFTER

CHAPTER XXIX

Belgium under the Occupation 415

By ARTHUR WAUTERS, D.R.E.

Professor of Agricultural Economics, University of Brussels; member of the Belgian Government Consultative Committee in London since 1940; Senator, 1932–1936; Member of the House since 1936; Minister of Public Health (1937), of Labor (1938), of Information (1939); member, Executive Committee, Belgian Labor party and Political Director of socialist newspaper, *Le Peuple;* member, Executive Committee, Belgian Colonial Institute and University; Chairman, League of Nations Committee on Rural Life, and representative of Belgian Government in labor conferences at Geneva; High Commissioner for organization of famine relief in the Volga area (1921–1922); and author of *Le Procès des socialistes révolutionnaires* (1922); *L'Evolution du Marxisme* (1923); *La Réforme agraire* (1927); *La Réforme du réformisme* (1927); *Guerre et politique sociale* (1939).

CHAPTER XXX   PAGE

Belgium in the Postwar World 429
By PAUL VAN ZEELAND, J.D., D.R.P., LL.D., D.C.L.
Chairman of the Belgian Commission for the Study of Postwar Problems; Prime Minister, 1935–1937; Minister of Foreign Affairs, Minister of Foreign Trade, interim; President, Assembly of the League of Nations; former Vice-Governor, National Bank of Belgium; Director, Institute of Economic Sciences, University of Louvain; delegate or economic adviser of the Belgian Government at many international Conferences since 1921; charged by the French and British Governments with Special Mission on "Possibility of Obtaining a General Reduction of Obstacles to International Trade" (1937); lectured in many countries in Europe and in the United States; received honorary degrees from Princeton, Brown, and Wesleyan universities; author of *La Réforme bancaire aus Etats-Unis d'Amérique de 1913 à 1921* (1922); *Réflexions sur le plan quinquennal* (1931); *Regards sur l'Europe, 1932* (1933); *Report to the Governments of the United Kingdom and France on the Possibility of Obtaining a General Reduction of the Obstacles to International Trade* (1938); *Economics or Politics?* (1939), and of numerous articles in political and economic reviews.

BIBLIOGRAPHY

A Selected Bibliography 445

INDEX

Index 457

List of Illustrations

FACING PAGE

Town Hall, Brussels iii

Kings of Belgium 38

Flemish Landscape: Canal to Damme 54

Walloon Landscape: Panoramic View of
    Vresse-sur-Semois 54

The Port of Antwerp 170

Coal Mines and Industry, Charleroi 170

School, Léopoldville, Belgian Congo 178

Wild Life, Congo Jungle 178

MAPS
PAGE

Belgium 5

Agricultural Regions of Belgium 157

Belgian Congo 339

BELGIAN NATIONAL ANTHEM

The Brabançonne*

At last the Belgian resurrection
After long years of slavery came;
Courage restored to them protection
Of their rights, their flag and of their name.
Then your hand, bold in its reliance,
Proud Belgians, strong henceforth in might,
Upon your flag inscribed with defiance:
For King, for Liberty and Right,
Upon your flag inscribed with defiance:
For King, for Liberty and Right,
For King, for Liberty and Right,
For King, for Liberty and Right.

---

* Words by Charles Rogier, music by François van Campenhout. English version by Lorraine Noel Finley. The official text dates from 1860, the earlier version by Janneval having been superseded.

NOTE ON NAMES IN BELGIUM

BELGIUM being a bilingual country where Dutch and French are spoken in approximately equal proportions, there exist a number of names of cities, villages, and rivers which have either a Dutch or a French translation: the port of *Antwerpen* is called *Anvers* in French; the city of *Liége* is called *Luik* in Flemish. English-speaking writers, especially since the First World War, have often used the French version of names of Flemish towns, unfortunately without much logic: they write *Bruges* for *Brugge*, but they keep *Zeebrugge* as it is. Officially, on all maps and documents, the names of Belgian towns are given in the language of the region, without translation either into French or into Flemish.

Additional confusion has been created in the last decade by the fact that the spelling of many of the names of Flemish places and of a few French ones have been modernized. As a result, some of them have become scarcely recognizable. Archaic forms were discarded for a more logical spelling: *Audenaerde* became *Oudenaarde*, etc. However, this modernized spelling has not yet been completely adopted.

In this book the official Belgian regulations on the subject have been followed; but whenever an English translation of a place name was available, it was used: *Ghent*, not *Gent; Antwerp*, not *Antwerpen*. Only one exception was made, for *Leuven*, which is universally known in the English-speaking world under its French name, *Louvain*.

On the assumption that the foregoing explanation, necessary though it may be, cannot clear up the matter entirely, a list is appended of the principal place names in English and the two languages of Belgium. The official version of each name is printed in italics.

ENGLISH USAGE	FLEMISH NAMES	FRENCH NAMES
Antwerp	*Antwerpen*	Anvers
Arlon	Aarlen	*Arlon*
Audenaerde	*Oudenaarde*	Audenarde
Bruges	*Brugge*	Bruges
Courtrai	*Kortrijk*	Courtrai
Dixmude	*Diksmuide*	Dixmude
Furnes	*Veurne*	Furnes
Gheel	*Geel*	Gheel
Ghent	*Gent*	Gand
La Panne	*De Panne*	La Panne
Le Zoute	*Het Zoute*	Le Zoute
Liége	Luik	*Liége*
Louvain	*Leuven*	Louvain
Mechlin	*Mechelen*	Malines
Mons	Bergen	*Mons*
Namur	Namen	*Namur*
Ostend	*Oostende*	Ostende
Roulers	*Roeselare*	Roulers
St. Trond	*St. Truiden*	St.-Trond
Tongres	*Tongeren*	Tongres
Ypres	*Ieper*	Ypres

NAMES OF RIVERS		
Scheldt	Schelde	Escaut
Meuse	Maas	Meuse
Lys	Leie	Lys

Part One

THE SCENE

CHAPTER I

Land and People

BY JAN-ALBERT GORIS

AT FIRST SIGHT, so many centrifugal forces appear to be at work in Belgium that her existence as a political unit seems paradoxical. Geologically, her northern as well as her southern regions prolong the territorial characteristics of Germany and France. Linguistically, nearly half her population lies in the orbit of France, which country possesses a strongly radiating cultural attraction, whereas the majority of her inhabitants speak the language of her northern neighbors, the Dutch. There are no national boundaries to protect the country from incursions or invasion, and the North Sea coastline is absolutely flat. Thus, throughout her history, technically as well as spiritually, Belgium has been exposed to intermittent pressure from without. Within her boundaries, local linguistic nationalism in recent times has become a problem, but neither the attraction from outside nor the disrupting influences from within have ever endangered her destiny or led to downright dissension. The Belgian people throughout history therefore have supported strongly, and often fought for, the country's national existence. Moreover, it has been the consensus of all observers for centuries that the Belgians have, as a national heritage, a high degree of common sense which they constantly apply in their affairs, and which sometimes is considered a regrettable deficiency that prevents the nation from achieving true greatness. This quality, however, is valued by the majority as a guarantee of stability, justice, and order.

The location of the country, its size, its political adventures in the past, all have contributed to the establishment of a close contact between the two ethnic groups of people, the Flemings and

the Walloons, who live in contrasting scenery but who, nevertheless, have bowed to the same economic exigencies, who have been
influenced by the identity of their social concepts, and who have
experienced with a sense of solidarity the same successive foreign
dominations.

About one-fifth of the country was reclaimed from the North Sea
between the eighth and thirteenth centuries. Salt marshes, in which
more than 40,000 people were drowned in a great flood at one time,
became rich ploughland behind a barrier of dikes for which Dante
himself expressed admiration in the *Inferno*. A coastal strip of a
depth of almost thirty miles was thus added to the country; at the
same time, rivers like the Scheldt (Schelde), which had spread out
in broad, shallow deltas, were reduced to navigable proportions.
Behind this fringe that touches Bruges (Brugge), and Dixmude
(Diksmuide), lies the great northern plain comprising Flanders,
the Kempen, Limburg, and part of Hainaut. It is flat country
with rich loam and strong vegetation, except for the Kempen, a
region of heaths, dunes, and pine woods. In the Flemish plain rise
a few mounds which attain no more than fifty feet in height. In
the flat regions of the north, the best agricultural terrains are the
polders, land reclaimed from the sea and from the Scheldt. The
low plateau of Waes in the province of East Flanders has some
features which, because of the clay-rich soil, distinguish it from the
rest of Flanders.

The central part of the country is a slightly higher plateau which
covers part of Hainaut, of Brabant, of Namur (Namen), and borders on Liége (Luik). There the land is undulating, the soil is
rich, the climate milder than in the rest of the country. A great
number of wide valleys appear, and to the north of this region one
finds the last impressive remnants of the expansive Coal Forest
which was a dividing line between the Franks and the Celts at the
beginning of the Christian era. Toward the west of the central part
is located the Hesbaye region, an accentuated, fertile terrain consisting of a crevassed plateau covered with a thick layer of clay soil.

The southern part of Belgium is a comparatively high plateau;
it begins at some 600 feet on the right bank of the Meuse (Maas),
and rises to about 2,100 feet at the plateau of Botrange. In this section there are regions of marked individuality, like the Condroz,

the Famenne, the Ardennes, and Belgian Lorraine. These very picturesque parts are among the oldest settled regions of Europe; in the many grottoes and caves, relics of prehistoric habitation are to be found. A great number of streams cut deeply through the limestone rocks and rush through subterranean labyrinths. Woodlands are best preserved in the Famenne and on the Ardennes plateau.

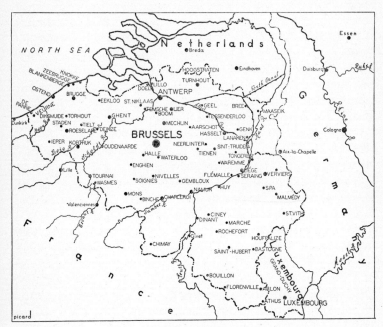

BELGIUM

The romantic though humane beauty of the landscape, together with its relative isolation, have made the Ardennes region the summer playground of Belgium. To the south, Belgian Lorraine comprises the tip of Luxemburg Province and its capital, Arlon (Aarlen). It is a country of weathered rocks and weird hills.

As a whole, Belgium's physical aspect presents no extremes. The lines of its horizon are calm, the slopes of its hills soft, the terrain depressions spread out gently. It achieves really romantic beauty, almost frightening, in the underground grottoes of Han and in its subterranean lakes. Never is there anything excessive in the proportions of the scenery. Nowhere does nature offer insurmountable obstacles to man.

At the beginning of the Christian era, Belgium was inhabited for the most part by Celts who, like nearly all peoples in Europe, had come from beyond the Rhine. The Celts, who were organized in small, warlike tribes—the Menapians, the Eburons, the Nervii, the Aduatici, and others—were once a challenge for Caesar, but rapidly became Romanized. For two centuries they suffered Germanic infiltrations into their territory until finally, in the third and fourth centuries, the avalanche of Salian Franks covered the northern part of the country and was stopped only by the great Coal Forest, a rampart of wood, which did not appeal to the agricultural invaders, and which, furthermore, was organized as a Roman frontier zone. For fourteen hundred years, the two ethnic groups inhabiting Belgium today, the Romanized Celtic Walloons and the Germanic Flemings, have lived in the territory they occupied at the end of the fifth century. The language frontier has remained practically unchanged, and if the French language gained influence in Flemish territory it happened not through frontier contacts but through administrative channels and for reasons of social prestige.

The dangers of the study of national characteristics are well known. Generalizations strongly presented in simplified form often take the place of research and factual information. But, undoubtedly, the fact that the Latinized part of Belgium, especially Liége, was in close contact with Germany and with German institutions and culture for many centuries, whereas the political and cultural impacts of France were many in Germanic Flanders, has had something to do with making Belgium a national unit and giving it a stamp of its own. The most penetrating appreciations of the Belgians as a people are attributable, of course, to foreign observers. Since few of them knew Dutch, the language of the Flemings, their contacts with them were generally slower and their knowledge of the people less complete than in the Walloon parts. That accounts, to some extent, for the reputation the Flemings have of being more reserved, and even suspicious, in their contacts, contrasting with the more vivid, expansive, gay Walloons. Physically, only very few Belgians can be identified as typical of either group. The flaxen-haired, blue-eyed, tall dolichocephalic Fleming is as rare as the stocky, dark, brown-eyed brachycephalic Walloon of the conventional anthropological descriptions. Outstanding Flemish leaders have genuine French names, whereas aggressive Walloon politicians very often go by typical Flemish names. However, it is easy to find among the Belgian people types which correspond exactly to the models who sat for the Flemish Primitives or for the painters of the school of Rubens. Located at the crossroads of western Europe, having lived since the times of the Romans in a commercial and industrial center of foremost importance, the population of Belgium has undoubtedly undergone a great number of changes; these finally have created, especially in the last one hundred years because of the attraction of the capital, Brussels, a melting pot which has produced a population neither specifically Flemish nor Walloon, but an amalgamation of the two.

History has proved that both groups have been highly gifted in the field of art. Although the Walloons are known at present for their finely developed sense of music, most of the great composers who dominated Europe in the sixteenth century were of Flemish stock. In the field of plastic art, the Walloons have contributed in good measure to one, at least, of the two great schools of Belgian painting, the Primitives and the school of the Renaissance. Since Belgium became an independent country, literary expression in French has profited from the fact that it is used as a world language, although Flemish writers, confined within their little-known tongue, have certainly been equals of the Walloons. To compare the achievements of both groups in the intellectual as well as in the artistic field would scarcely do, since the situation is complicated by the fact that some prominent Flemish authors chose to write in French. Literary and plastic expression in Belgium is characterized by a highly lyrical quality. Philosophy has always been a stepchild in Belgium, and the major part of Belgium's contribution to scientific and intellectual progress is to be found in the practical fields of applied physics, chemistry, law, and moral theology, revealing thus an underlying tendency to the rational and the useful.

The country constitutes the most densely populated area in Europe. It has 710 inhabitants per square mile compared with 340 in Germany and 270 in France. Therefore, the basic problem for Belgians has always been the production of sufficient food. Agriculture was, and still is, Belgium's chief industry.

About 17 per cent of Belgium's active inhabitants are engaged in agriculture, and more than 73 per cent of the total population live in communities which comprise no more than 25,000 persons. Life in Belgium is, therefore, with the exception of a few large towns—Brussels, Antwerp (Antwerpen), Liége and Ghent (Gent)— essentially provincial in aspect and character. This provincialism is accentuated by the fact that the majority of the small towns have succeeded in keeping almost intact part of the setting of four or five centuries ago. In these districts the influence of Catholicism is strong and deep, but seldom makes itself felt in a narrow clerical sense. It unites moral conservatism with strong democratic feeling, and is sustained by a highly developed coöperative spirit, in Flanders as well as in Wallonia.

Close to one-tenth of Belgium's population lives in the capital, Brussels (839,000 inhabitants in 1930), which was the last of the Belgian cities to mature. Having become the administrative center, as well as the financial and business hub of the country in the course of the nineteenth century, Brussels profited from the urbanistic tendencies of the sovereigns as well as from the striking beauty of the rural outskirts, or boroughs, which it absorbed and transformed into residential sections. It has varied charm, combining, with graceful transitions, the perfect loveliness of its old market place with wide boulevards and stately roads radiating to the four corners of the land. The people of Brussels are renowned for their easygoing way of life, their urbanity, and their highly developed, although sometimes slightly coarse, sense of humor.

The rival of Brussels in economic importance and architectural beauty is Antwerp (600,000 inhabitants in 1930), the third or fourth largest seaport in the world and the capital of Flemish culture and art. Although Antwerp possesses the most audacious and beautiful Gothic spire in northwestern Europe, its architectural atmosphere is definitely Baroque. The spirit of Rubens' grandiloquent expression prevails in most of the buildings, ancient as well as modern. The confidence in life which is derived from great wealth and from daring, successful enterprise, to which Antwerp merchants and seafarers are addicted, breathes through the physical aspect of the town as well as through the moral and intellectual life of its people. There is something boastful and energetic in the attitude of the people of Antwerp, something forcefully rhetorical in their mentality and their expressions. This basic self-confidence is tempered only by their daily contacts with the foreign patrons of their harbor, especially the French and the British. The existence of the port is responsible for a definitely cosmopolitan atmosphere in an otherwise medieval and baroque town.

Whereas Antwerp has always been cleverly opportunist and liberal in its policy, Liége, the spiritual capital of Wallonia, for ages has been a fighting town. At the conjunction of the international river Meuse and the Ourthe, its location and atmosphere remind one of Lyons in France. More than six hundred years ago, its inhabitants forced their overlords to consult, in all-important decisions, what they called *le sens du pays* (the opinion of the country). Liége has a great number of gunsmiths and glassmakers and is the natural center for the coal-mining and metallurgical industries in her neighborhood. It is the gateway of the tourist region of the Ardennes. Liége is also the birthplace of André-Ernest Grétry and of César Franck, the musicians.

In Flanders, Ghent, the second largest port of Belgium, is heavily laden with memories. Throughout the past, Ghent's fate has always swayed between revolt and revenge. Its topographical layout, the shape of its buildings give testimony of a bloody history. The churches, castles, and belfry are all grouped together in a profusion that gives an extremely dramatic effect of sturdiness and even of gloom. Although the city and its suburbs are a flower-growing center where tulips, hyacinths, azaleas, and orchids abound, the living quarters of the textile workers offer a rather discouraging contrast of drabness. Of all the Belgian cities, Ghent is by far the most tormented, physically and mentally. It is not by pure accident that it was the birthplace of the two greatest Belgian authors since 1830—the French-writing Maurice Maeterlinck, and the equally great Flemish poet, Karel van de Woestijne.

The other towns of Belgium are definitely provincial—Mechlin (Mechelen), the ecclesiastical capital of Belgium; Louvain (Leuven), the Catholic scholastic center; Bruges, perfect in quaint medieval charm; Tournai, the oldest town in the land; Namur, Mons

(Bergen), Lier, and scores of others. Nearly all have had their period of power and great prosperity. Their public buildings clearly affirm a desire for greatness which is still an inspiration to their people.

Whereas for many centuries the textile industry has been a predominant influence in the prosperity of Flanders, modern heavy industry developed in the Walloon part of the country because of the availability in that region of the only raw material Belgium possesses—coal. But Wallonia has to import steel and copper, just as Flanders traditionally has depended and still depends on wool and even flax imports for her major occupation. The mechanization of industry has transformed a considerable part of the population of the southern provinces into an industrial proletariat. The social crisis provoked by this hasty adaptation has subsided, but, together with the dockers of Antwerp and the textile workers of Ghent, the coal miners and the wage earners of the metallurgical plants of Wallonia constitute the most socially conscious element in Belgium.

The discovery of rich coal mines in Limburg has given rise to a rapidly increasing group of Flemish industrial wage earners, whereas on the coast the traditional industry, fishing, has never absorbed more than about 3,000 workers. All these workers, even the industrial proletariat, are heavily individualistic in the organization of their lives. Most of them supply part of their livelihood by maintaining a small vegetable garden on which they depend in times of stress. The more than 100,000 Flemish seasonal workers who go to France for the harvest do the same. This accounts for the relative stability of the population within the social framework.

On the whole, Belgians are essentially stay-at-homes. In the past, a considerable number devoted themselves to overseas trade, and agricultural groups emigrated; since then, however, steadily increasing numbers have taken up commercial occupations. This trend was accentuated from 1920 to 1930 to the extent that the percentage of people engaged in trade grew from 10.7 per cent to 14.5 per cent.

From 1841 to 1939 emigration withdrew no more than 1 to 3 persons per 1,000. The majority of those who left the country were Flemings; in fact, the proportion was 2 to 1 over the Walloons. These emigrants were recruited less and less among the agricul-

turists, more and more among those who had already abandoned
the land to become industrial laborers. The largest group of Belgians who left their home country for good have settled in the
United States and in Canada; together they number about 100,000.
Emigration to the Congo, which is not a settlement colony, is not
significant. No more than 30,000 Belgians live in Belgian-African
territory and, as a rule, they stay there only a few years, whereas
the emigrants to the Western Hemisphere sever completely their
connection with Belgium.

The Belgian population has increased from 3,785,000 in 1831
to 8,330,000 in 1936. The death rate has diminished constantly,
descending from 14.2 per 1,000 in 1913 to 12.2 per 1,000 in 1936,
whereas the birth rate, although higher than in several other European countries, has shown an alarming decrease from 22.4 per
1,000 in 1913 to 15.1 per 1,000 in 1936. This decrease reduces it to
the level of France's birth rate and leaves it but slightly above that
of Great Britain.

Since illiteracy is rare in Belgium, the political awareness of
the inhabitants is highly developed. Since the Middle Ages, the inhabitants have, after liquidating the reactionary influence of the
nobility and of the oligarchs, taken a great interest in public affairs;
but their experience as subjects of four foreign powers (the Spaniards, the Austrians, the French, and the Germans), as well as their
brief, forced reunion with Holland, has trained them in the habit
of evading laws which do not appeal to their sense of justice. In
1942 the president of the German Military Administration of Belgium, General Reeder, said: "The Belgians refuse to submit to
discipline and always try to evade the law. In Germany everybody
submits to discipline, even when the people do not like it." It is
apparent that not all of this elusive attitude is attributable to opposition to the German regime but that some of it goes back to a
solidly established tradition.

As a rule, the Belgians take more pride in their past glories than
in their remarkable achievements. They carefully perpetuate a
number of picturesque folklore traditions, based on history, legend,
and religion. Once a year in Binche, the townspeople dance for a
whole day, wearing huge plumed bonnets and dressed as the Conquistadores told them the Incas dressed; in Veurne, a procession of

penitents stumbles over the cobblestones, wrapped in the hooded cloaks of the Spanish monks. Every fair-sized community in Belgium organizes a promenade of at least a couple of dancing giants, the trolley lines having been dismantled for the occasion. At Geeraardsbergen, once a year, the mayor solemnly quaffs a cup of champagne in which panicky little fish swim. Everywhere the scene of the genre painters, Teniers and Brouwer, is constantly revived.

Such is the land, such are the people of Belgium. When they go out into the world, in which they are known everywhere as thrifty, industrious, reliable, they do so to return home, home to the drizzling rain on their old monuments, home to their cozy cafes where endlessly they discuss politics and the never-changing, but always astonishing, conduct of man, home to the few days a year when the sun shines gloriously on the golden harvests of Flanders, on the lovely primeval forests of the Ardennes, on gay and carefree Brussels, ever-scorned by national sarcasm, but so well-beloved.

Part Two

HISTORICAL
BACKGROUND

CHAPTER II

From Caesar to 1814

BY VICTOR J. DOSSOGNE

THE ORIGIN OF THE first inhabitants of Belgium is not known. It is certain that cave men and lake dwellers lived in this region which now comprises modern Belgium. Human bones, fossils, and tools are the only evidence of a long evolution. It is believed that the people inhabiting the area between the North Sea and the rivers Waal, Rhine, Marne, and Seine reached there about 300 B.C. Before the Christian era, Belgium became known through Greek and Roman writers, particularly Julius Caesar, who called it *Gallia Belgica*. The people were either of Celtic or Germanic stock, and their courage was known to be superior to that of their neighbors, the Gauls and the Aquitani. "Of all these tribes," says Caesar, "the *Belgae* are the most courageous." They did not have sufficient strength to resist the onslaught of the Roman invaders, however, because they were not politically united.

After seven campaigns, Caesar broke the stubborn resistance of the Belgians. He then organized the tribes, established a solid administration, and permitted them to maintain their former political divisions. Economically the Belgians profited by this contact with the genius of Rome. Along the routes that led to Gaul, agricultural estates were developed. The Latin language began to take root. Roman law was adopted or imposed by force, and the Christian faith was brought in by merchants and preached by missionaries.

While this civilizing process was taking place, Germanic tribes were infiltrating the Roman Empire. By the beginning of the third century of this era they had penetrated the frontiers of the Rhine, burning, plundering, and raiding. The Frisians took possession of the coastline of the North Sea, whereas the Franks moved into the Isle of Batavia and into the Kempen. In 406 the Huns, coming from the East, drove the Germans back across the Rhine. Like a devastating wave, the retreating hordes flooded the lowlands of Belgium.

The last of the invading groups, the Franks, brought specific characteristics. It is these characteristics, more than any others, that have remained with the Belgians until the present day. Clovis, the greatest of their leaders, was converted to Christianity in 496. He founded a state on the ruins of Roman Gaul and established his capital in Paris. At his death in 511, in accordance with Germanic tradition, he divided his possessions among his sons.

The Frankish invasion of the fifth century was the last notable influx of peoples into Belgium. Both the Flemish and the Walloons of the present day trace their ancestry to the inhabitants of this period. The only distinguishing mark remaining between these two groups is their language. Otherwise, to all intents and purposes, they seem to be of one stock.

It was during the Frankish reign that political power passed to the mayors of the palace and into the hands of the Carolingian dynasty. The founder of the line was Pippin of Landen, in Brabant. His son, Pippin II, a zealous supporter of missionary enterprise among the Germans and Frisians, was the grandfather of Charles Martel and the great-grandfather of Charlemagne. Charlemagne's forty-six years of rule, his fifty-three campaigns, his conquests, his imperial title, and the influence which he left upon the civilization of his era, mark him as one of the great rulers of all time. At his death in 814, however, his empire began to disintegrate.

By the Treaty of Verdun (843), Charlemagne's three grandsons divided Belgium between two neighboring states. Louis the German received the Germanic territories to the east; Lothair, the eldest, Francia Media, or Lotharingia, the middle region; and Charles the Bald the regions to the southwest, including mainly what is now France and Flanders.

By the last half of the ninth century feudalism was well established. Kings were weak, whereas the nobility was strong. Belgium, like the rest of Europe, naturally was broken up into a number of small autonomous units, each unit forming a separate principality.

These principalities were to become the future Belgian provinces of Flanders, Brabant, Liége, Hainaut, Limburg, Namur, and Luxemburg.

The first princes of these provinces are the real founders of modern Belgium. Their struggle to break the yoke of French and German domination began early. Finally, John I, Duke of Brabant (1261–1294), achieved a brilliant victory at Woeringen, on the banks of the Rhine, and German power was forced beyond the river where it was held in check for some time.

In Flanders, victory was not so easy. The struggle against France was long and bitter. The kings of the Capetian dynasty, in their compact and homogeneous domain, were more powerful than the Holy Roman emperors. They were also better able to follow a constant policy because of their system of hereditary succession. Furthermore, in Flanders they saw not only enormous economic wealth, but also a commercial and military base facing England. It was said that "He who holds Flanders holds the North Sea."

With the defeat of the princes of Flanders by France, at the Battle of Bouvines in 1214, the struggle for liberty was taken over by the people. As early as the eleventh century, however, the Flemish burghers had assumed the right of self-government in their towns. Thriving communities like Bruges, Ypres (Ieper), and Ghent had grown in wealth and power. Town life, and the commerce that supported it, was the moving force in the evolution from the Middle Ages to the modern era.

During the struggle with Philip the Fair, Count Guy of Flanders, although supported by the guilds and by Edward I of England, was made a prisoner. In retaliation the people of Bruges massacred all Frenchmen in the city. Philip sent in a strong army to subdue the rebels. On July 11, 1302, in the Battle of the Golden Spurs at Courtrai (Kortrijk), however, the French were defeated by the Flemish militia. The result of this victory was the emancipation of Flanders. It also barred the road to the Rhine, so far as France was concerned.

France now tried to bring about, through a policy of matrimonial alliances, that which she had not been able to achieve by force. To this end Charles V of France secured for his brother, Philip the Bold, Duke of Burgundy (1384–1404), the hand of the rich heiress,

Margaret of Maele, Countess of Flanders. The plan, however, did not work out, and the House of Burgundy instead of becoming a vassal became a rival; instead of binding France and Belgium together, it tore them apart.

John the Fearless, son of Philip and Margaret, had already adopted the Flemish slogan, *Ick Hou* (I hold). At his death, his son, Philip the Good (1419–1467), heir of Burgundy, Flanders, and Artois, conceived the plan of rebuilding the "middle kingdom" of Lothair. In this attempt he almost succeeded. For the first time since Charlemagne, one ruler governed the entire country. In the interior, Philip, "Founder of Belgium," sought to unify the provinces through weakening the power of the communes and the nobility. At his death the country was in a prosperous condition. Philip's son, Charles the Bold, even more than himself, was determined to establish a powerful kingdom. But in striving to unite Burgundy and the Low Countries, by annexing Lorraine and Alsace, he met a formidable foe in Louis XI, King of France. Charles the Bold died before the walls of Nancy in 1477. His daughter and successor, Mary of Burgundy, without experience and without strength, was surrounded by enemies. Belgium's fate depended upon the marriage of Mary. She chose Archduke Maximilian of Habsburg, son of Emperor Frederick III of the Holy Roman Empire. Mary's reign was short. She died on March 25, 1482, leaving a son, Philip the Handsome, who inherited the provinces at the age of four. Philip married Joanna (the "Mad"), daughter of the sovereigns of Aragon and Castile, and in consequence became king of these two great kingdoms of the Iberian Peninsula in 1504. Two years later Philip died. It was because of this marriage that the destiny of the Belgian Provinces was to be linked to that of Spain for an eventful century and a half.

Philip's son, Charles of Habsburg, born in Ghent in 1500, was recognized as sovereign by the States-General of the provinces; he became King of the Spanish countries and Holy Roman Emperor as Charles V. His immense possessions encircled France and, after the Battle of Pavia, in 1526, he forced the French King, Francis I, to sign the Peace of Madrid by which the latter renounced all claims to overlordship of Flanders and Artois. Francis I assented, also, to the cession of Tournai; and the Seventeen Provinces were transformed into a solid group called the "Circle of Burgundy." The "Transaction of Augsburg" (1548), as this centralizing act was called, was followed the next year by the "Pragmatic Sanction," which declared the Circle indivisible. Charles V had his capital at Brussels, and the provinces that were later to become modern Belgium became the heart and nucleus of his vast empire. A native of these regions, Charles chose to make them his real center, and under his rule the Belgian Provinces had one of their best periods. The case was to be quite different when Charles' son, Philip II, born in Spain and spiritually a Spaniard, succeeded him. The state conceived by Charles V could live only on the condition that it be governed according to the directions of its founder—a strong authority tempered by a respect for traditional liberties and by a collaboration of its citizens.

Charles V returned to Brussels in 1555 to lay down the scepter with which he had ruled half the world. In a remote monastery, he retired from life, and the sovereignty passed to his son, Philip II of Spain. The Low Countries now became a tool for the carrying out of Spanish power politics. Philip governed Belgium with the aid of foreign officials, maintained Spanish troops within its borders, and used Belgian resources to wage his wars and discharge his personal obligations.

The nobility and the communes found themselves in opposition to this foreign rule; all groups united in a revolutionary and national effort. Even the Calvinists, in 1565, united with the other groups in the Compromise of the Nobles. Philip II, however, decided to act. He sent the "bloody" Duke of Alva to chastise the rebels, and triumphed over William the Silent. Thereupon William withdrew from the south and declared himself protector of the Northern Provinces (the modern Netherlands). In 1576 the States-General of the Southern Provinces (Belgium) met with the northern delegates in a sovereign assembly and signed the Pacification of Ghent, by which all the provinces united to drive out the Spaniards. The revolution at first appeared successful, but internal religious strife soon created discontent in Hainaut and in Artois. A new party, called the "Malcontents," was formed. Civil war started anew. The break between the Catholic South and the Protestant North was complete.

The Southern Provinces, remaining true to the principle of a legitimate government, as well as to their religion, rallied around Alexander Farnese, the Spanish Governor. This was in accordance with Philip II's plan to keep them servile to Spain.

In 1598 Philip gave the provinces to his daughter, Isabella, who shortly afterward married the Archduke Albert of Austria. Belgium, for the first time, was recognized as a separate sovereignty by the Powers of Europe. This independent status, unfortunately, did not last long. In 1621 the Archduke Albert died, leaving no children, and the provinces reverted to the King of Spain, Philip IV.

War broke out again. Belgium was now squeezed between Holland and France. Richelieu made known his policy by stating that wherever ancient Gaul had existed a new Gaul must be set up. In conformity with his natural boundary theory, he was determined to extend the borders of France to the Rhine. This would necessitate the annexation of Belgium—the country that stood between him and his objective. The Treaty of Westphalia in 1648 left Belgium in the possession of Spain, and cut her off from the sea by severing the mouth of the Scheldt.

Shortly after this, Louis XIV launched his imperialistic policy. In England he found his strongest opponent. The great commercial island began to look upon the Belgian Provinces as the cornerstone of her European policy.

Spain, after having refused to sign the Treaty of Westphalia, was defeated by France in 1659. As a result, she lost Dunkirk—which was turned over to England—a part of Artois, and eleven strategic cities of the Belgian Provinces. Twelve more cities of the Southern Provinces went to France following the Treaty of Aix-la-Chapelle in 1668. Louis XIV, not yet satisfied, decided to go to The Hague in search of the "keys to Brussels." All Europe once more became involved. At the Treaty of Nijmegen (1678), the King of France took thirteen additional cities and what was left of Artois. He also fixed the southern border of Belgium to suit himself, leaving all roads open to invasion. Until 1684 he went on, in spite of treaties, arbitrarily helping himself to whatever territory he desired. In that year, Spain acknowledged the situation as a *fait accompli* and signed the Truce of Regensburg.

This, however, was not the end. The war went on. Belgium was
the principal theater of operations. The French General, François
Villeroy, bombarded Brussels, destroying the magnificent buildings of the town square, and burning some 3,800 houses. In the
meantime, Louvois, Louis XIV's Minister of War, inaugurated his
barbarous system of destruction by ordering that "Flanders be put
in a position whereby she would be unable to contribute anything
to Spain for a long time to come." In 1697 universal weariness led
to the Treaty of Rijswijk, and the menace of French annexation
was temporarily brought to an end. It is worth noting, at this point,
that the "bloodless revolution" of 1689 in England put William of
Orange and Mary on the English throne, and the ties between
England and the Low Countries were thereby drawn closer.

Charles II, King of Spain, died in 1700. Louis XIV claimed the
Low Countries for his grandson and, by force of arms, moved in.
The English general, John Churchill Marlborough, however, met
him at Ramillies and drove him back to the frontier. In 1709 the
Battle of Malplaquet appeared to have put an end at last to French
domination in Belgium. But Charles of Habsburg, who, as King
of Spain, had been the tool of the English and the Dutch, now
became Emperor—and, hence, ruler of the Germans. If he were
permitted to keep the Low Countries, the English Channel would
be opened to Germany. The British could not tolerate this. So
England, following her established balance-of-power policy, swung
over to the side of France.

This was in 1713. The Treaty of Utrecht followed. England,
playing the Continental Powers against each other, easily permitted the Low Countries to go back to Charles of Habsburg, but
obtained for Holland the right to occupy eight cities of the Southern Provinces as barriers against France. The Scheldt River was
to remain closed—thus keeping these provinces shut off from the
sea. By a clause of utmost importance, the new sovereign was
forced to respect the rights of the Belgians, the indivisibility of
the territories, and the unity of the country. One hundred and fifty
years of struggle were behind them, and the Belgians found themselves still condemned to a languishing economic and political life.
They continued to be exposed to the ambitions of France.

The Southern Provinces as a unit had passed to the Habsburgs

of Austria. In 1715 Emperor Charles of Habsburg became Charles
VI of Belgium. Following the philosophy of the "Enlightened
Despots," he ruled until 1740. The wheels of the new government,
with its numerous councils and committees, acquired momentum.
In 1740 the remarkable and energetic Maria Theresa inherited her
father's crown. Her admirable qualities, together with favorable
circumstances, made her reign over Belgium a very satisfactory and
gratefully remembered period. Joseph II, her son, called "the phi-
losopher on the throne," succeeded her. Imbued with progressive
ideas of the French school, he outlined for himself a definitely
liberal policy—a political blueprint which he was determined to
put into effect. He lacked, however, the knowledge of his subjects
and the art of adapting himself to circumstances. Convinced that
great things must be done at once, he set out to destroy all that was
contrary to his doctrine, without taking into consideration the
deep roots of religious habits and national traditions. His reforms
among the Belgians failed. When he died, February 20, 1790, the
French Revolution was already under way.

On January 11, 1790, the States-General of Belgium had founded
the Confédération des Etats Belgiques Unis; for the second time
since Charles V, the provinces tried to establish an independent
union. The first Congress met on February 20th, the day that
Joseph died. Joseph's brother, Leopold II, succeeded him as Emperor, and the Austrian army soon put an end to the incipient
United States of Belgium. The menace of French annexation once
more was at the frontier.

Under the Directory, in 1797, the two French generals, Charles
François Dumouriez and Jean Baptiste Jourdan, conquered Belgium. On October 17, 1797, weakened by Napoleon's victories, the
Emperor of Austria at Campo-Formio formally renounced his sovereignty over the Low Countries.

After centuries of effort France had solved "the Occidental question" in her own favor by making the Rhine her eastern frontier.
Belgium in turn, however, had suffered the worst setback to independence in her history. Like France, Belgium had experienced
a variety of regimes, but all were inspired by the same principle—
administrative centralization. Each had left its stamp on the religious and social life of the country.

From 1804 to 1814, under the Napoleonic Empire, the Belgian Provinces, although thoroughly unified and centralized, were unscrupulously robbed. In no other period of her history had Belgium been so drastically transformed. Her government was radically modified. Her communal and provincial institutions were unified. Equality of rights among citizens of the various provinces was acknowledged and upheld. Class distinction was abolished, and the development of commerce and industry paved the way for the ascent of the "bourgeoisie." The proletariat, however, fell into increasing misery.

After 1809 grudges against the Emperor began to multiply until, in 1814, the French were forced to evacuate. The success of the Belgians in casting off the yoke of France was followed by abuses from their liberators, the Allies. Desirous of making Belgium a buffer state, they planned an "extension of territory" in favor of Holland. At the London Conference of June 20, 1814, it was decided that Belgium should be reunited with Holland. The following year, at the Congress of Vienna, the United Provinces and the Principalities of Liége were handed over to William I, King of Holland. The Grand Duchy of Luxemburg, as well as the territories which make up the present Grand Duchy, also was given to William in compensation for his losses to Germany. The Allies further despoiled Belgium of the counties of Eupen-et-Malmédy and St. Vith in favor of Prussia—thus, by a disastrous imprudence, establishing the latter in the Rhineland. Prussia would have liked to have obtained, if not the whole country, at least the right bank of the Meuse. England opposed this, and Lord Castlereagh pronounced these prophetic words: "The Prussians at Aix-la-Chapelle! What madness! Before a hundred years they will be in Antwerp."

In the meantime, having escaped from Elba, Napoleon again seized control in France. He immediately substituted force for diplomacy; but then came the great Battle of Waterloo, fought on Belgian soil, and the fate of Belgium, as well as that of Europe, was fixed for a century to come.

The Congress of Vienna would not take into consideration Belgium's long struggle for unification and independence. It thought only of using Belgium as a means of checking the power of France.

Belgium must be annexed to Holland and made a sort of European
Boulevard—a line of demarcation beyond which the French could
not expand.

Material resources were not lacking in the new state. The Belgians had fertile lands, a well-developed agriculture, some mineral
wealth, and had exceptional skill for manufacturing. The Dutch,
on the other hand, possessed a large fleet, colonies with a bright
future, and commercial interests that had been established for
centuries. But from a national point of view there existed no soul
in that robust body. Since the time of Philip II, the Hollanders in
the north and the Belgians in the south had been developing along
divergent lines. Differing in temperament, religion, customs, and
political habits, the two groups did not mix. Walloon Catholics
disliked and feared the Calvinist tendencies of the Netherlanders,
and Flemish merchants, also Catholics, were apprehensive of their
competition. Both groups resented the humiliation of having been
turned over to a Protestant power less extensive in range of territory and much less thickly populated. A broader and more understanding government would perhaps have realized the difficulties
inherent in placing the Southern Provinces of the Low Countries
under the dominion of the Northern Provinces. However, William
I, the King of Holland, in spite of his qualities as organizer, like
Joseph II, failed because he insisted on imposing his authoritarian
ideas on a people whom he did not understand. He did not realize
that Belgians could not be treated as though they were Dutch.

The news of the July Revolution in France aroused the Belgians.
On August 25, 1830, disturbances began in Brussels. Within two
months the Dutch were driven out of the territory. On November
10th, a National Congress was assembled under the presidency of
Erasme Surlet de Chokier, a lawyer. A Belgian Constitution was
drawn up, and was ratified on February 17, 1831.

CHAPTER III

The Dutch Regime (1814-1830) and the Kingdom of Belgium (1830-1840)

BY BARON DE GRUBEN

WHEN THE NEWS of the revolt of the people of Brussels reached the European courts in September, 1830, it touched the sensitive nerves of international organization and of political philosophy which were woven together in the history of the preceding forty years. Thus it is necessary to turn back to the year 1790 in order to grasp the exact character and the effect of this event, for the antecedents of the period of Belgian political independence show plainly the play of the forces which were to influence the course of the entire century to follow. The intellectual, social, and political movement known as the French Revolution had upset the ideas and the political order of Europe during a quarter of a century before its final collapse at Waterloo—in the heart of Belgium—on June 18, 1815. The coalition of England, Prussia, Austria, and Russia, not to mention other European states, prevailed over France and drove back her armies to Paris, crushing the revolutionary ardor which had inspired her conquests.

From about 1814 the Allies had agreed on certain fundamental principles. France was to be limited to the boundaries which she had held before her revolutionary expansion and placed again under the sovereignty of her legitimate dynasty. The region situated between the French boundary of 1790 and the Rhine—which river the French considered their natural and historic limit—was to be fortified as strongly as possible to serve as a bulwark against an

eventual recurrence of invasion by France. Finally, the Allied
Powers were to conclude a permanent alliance with a view to maintaining the political order, domestic and international, which they
proposed to inaugurate.

It has been a constant principle of British policy that the territory at the mouths of the rivers Scheldt, Meuse, and Rhine, which
empty into the North Sea opposite the mouth of the Thames,
should never be incorporated into France or Germany. For this
reason London has supported, during the whole course of modern
history, the "independence" of the Low Countries—the low-lying
rich lands of these river basins. During the Napoleonic Wars, British policy was directed toward the formation of a state which would
include both Belgian and Dutch territory. A secret clause of the
treaty signed at Paris on May 30, 1814, provided that "the establishment of a just balance in Europe demands that Holland be so
situated as to make it possible for her to maintain her independence
unaided." With this in view, the clause gave to Holland the territory included between the sea, the French frontiers, and the left
bank of the Meuse—that is to say, the greater part of Belgium.

Many circumstances favored this disposition. England wished to
recompense Holland for certain colonial territories which had come
under English rule and which England intended to retain. Austria,
whose Emperor had been sovereign of the Low Countries since
1714, had always considered the Belgian Provinces as a burdensome
charge and so wished to be rid of them in order to direct her ambitions toward Italy and the East. There remained Prussia, whose
desires were insatiable. Her generals had taken over the administration of the territory located between the Rhine and the Meuse
and, showing for the first time a tenacious ambition, had laid claim
to a permanent position on the latter river. On his side, however,
the Prince of Orange, Stadholder of Holland, had lost his states of
Nassau and wished to extend his domain as far as the Rhine. The
Powers imposed a compromise: the eastern boundary of Belgium
was drawn approximately along the linguistic frontier and the
Prussians established themselves on the left bank of the Rhine,
thus becoming the immediate neighbors of the Belgians. In 1815
the Treaty of Vienna sanctioned the existence of the Kingdom
of the Netherlands and recognized the sovereignty of the Prince

of Orange who had proclaimed himself king under the name of William I. In exchange for his Duchy of Nassau, annexed by Prussia, William was given the Grand Duchy of Luxemburg. The Duchy, however, became a member of the German Confederation, and Prussian troops were permitted to garrison its capital city.

Annexed thus to Holland, Belgium was established within her present territorial boundaries as far as they border on France and Prussia. The Powers had not even considered it possible to make the country autonomous. It must be said that, wearied of the frequent changes of regime, Belgium's mood appeared to be completely apathetic. However, with a view to the consolidation of the new structure and in hope of truly unifying it, King William had been obliged to pledge himself before the Powers, by the Treaty of the Eight Articles, to grant to Belgium political liberty, respect for her religious beliefs, and complete equality within the union. Furthermore, the new state was compelled to accept certain obligations which would sharply remind it of the role for which it had been cast by its founders. Wellington directed the construction of fortifications in 18 Belgian cities, and in 1818, by the Convention of the Fortresses, the Allies "recommended" that William permit the occupation of these defenses by English and Prussian troops in the event of impending danger from France.

It is of some significance to examine briefly this Dutch-Belgian union, for it reveals the outline of the national structure and the movements of thought which are visible throughout the century. The Powers had imposed on William the obligation of modifying the Dutch Constitution in order to adapt it to the needs created by this extension of territory. In 1813 the King had granted to Holland a Fundamental Law (*Grondwet*), the almost purely autocratic character of which was slightly tempered by some concession to the propertied classes. Two years later, the King seems to have believed that he could satisfy his obligations and the exigencies of policy by accepting the amendments made necessary by the Treaty of the Eight Articles—that is to say, provisions for freedom of religion and equality of right for the Belgian Provinces in national representation. Immediately, however, the Belgian clergy unleashed a violent campaign against the new constitutional arrangements regarding religion. Prominent representatives of Belgian opinion, who were consulted on the Constitution by the King, rejected it by a large majority, even though they had been chosen by the King's own agents. The opponents who came from the Flemish districts were men linked to the Dutch language, race, and geography, but were entirely devoted to the Catholic Church. The Walloons of the south, however, were less hostile to a regime which promised peace and material prosperity. Support for the regime developed, curiously enough, among those bourgeois elements which had been in sympathy with the ideas of the French Revolution, and which had also done very well for themselves both in industry and in administration, as had like groups in France under the Empire. By supporting the King, the Walloons hoped to stem the clerical reaction which threatened to compromise their gains.

However, a young liberal generation which did not share the anticlerical prejudices of its fathers was more aware of the political implications of the problem. It set the idea of popular sovereignty in opposition to the practice of royal absolutism, and, chafing under the restraint of arbitrary power, its enthusiasm was aroused by the hope of civic liberty. Young believers, on their side, were attracted by the liberal Catholicism which had been spread through the preaching of Lamennais. These parallel developments, remote from the causes of past discord, united men's spirits under the banner of the ideal of the century—liberty. The edifice built by the Treaty of Vienna began to crumble. It was difficult to make the Belgians agree that they could have only the same number of delegates in the States-General as the Dutch, although they were twice as numerous. The coexistence in the same state of two peoples equally advanced, though profoundly differentiated as a result of their religious cleavage in the sixteenth century, might have been possible, strictly speaking, if the King had not attempted to govern his new subjects in the interest of Holland and with Dutch functionaries, as though he were governing a conquered country. His despotism, exasperated by the resistance of the Belgians, found expression in annoying regulations and reluctantly yielded concessions. By 1828 he had succeeded only in binding together in the Union of the Opposition the two chief sections of opinion. Political agitation spread over the whole country and was not to be appeased until its final triumph.

During the "Three Glorious Days" (July 27 to 29, 1830), the people of Paris overthrew the "legitimate" dynasty of the Bourbons, which had been reëstablished by the Allies, and thus cast down one of the pillars of the Restoration. The popular character of the revolution in Paris had alarmed the Belgian conservatives. Though there was calm for a time, and the Union of the Opposition had intended to limit its activity to a "legal, peaceful, and serious" resistance, still the spirit of agitation was at work.

On August 25th, after an uproarious demonstration at the Brussels Opera House, a revolt broke out. As though they had been expecting such a signal, the provincial towns also rose in revolt. The Dutch authorities did not dare to order out troops to suppress the violence. In their alarm at the street disorders, the bourgeoisie of the towns spontaneously organized themselves into Commissions of Safety and armed Civil Guards. The King made no move in the presence of this popular insurrection; he did not wish any bloodshed. He sent his two sons, the Prince of Orange and Prince Frederick, to Brussels at the head of a few thousand men, but immediately the populace threw up barricades in the streets. The Prince of Orange, whose good nature had won him hitherto a certain popularity, decided with considerable courage to enter the city alone. He traversed it in the midst of a noisy crowd, through streets that were decorated with the colors of Brabant—black, yellow, and red—which soon were to become the colors of the nation.

At the same time, the organizations which had been improvised for the maintenance of order were gradually transformed into agents of the national will. This will shaped itself upon an exact program: complete political separation of Belgium and Holland "leaving no point of contact except through the reigning dynasty." The Prince of Orange abandoned Brussels to the insurgents and left with a promise to support this program before the King. On September 11th the Civil Guard of Brussels proceeded to elect a new Commission of Safety—the first orderly creation of the popular will. The first act of the Commission was to proclaim the necessity of "directing the opinion and the efforts of the citizens toward their one patriotic aim, so that they should not be turned aside from this just purpose by any foreign influence." The momentum of the July revolution became plainly perceptible; adventurers had drifted in from Paris, and from both sides of the border agitators inspired the rumor that the frontier should be abolished. To gain time and to safeguard legal forms, the King summoned the States-General, and on September 29th the Assembly voted for the separation of the two parts of the state. It was too late—the revolution had already triumphed in Brussels. The city was full of volunteer bands which had come from other towns. Prince Frederick arrived at the gates of Brussels with 14,000 troops. He sent 4 columns against the city, but they were stopped by the volleys which came from the houses and from the barricades. With practically no preparation, the Belgians put up an insurmountable resistance. The Dutch took refuge in the Park of Brussels, whence they fired on the insurgents who, by now, were besieging them. On September 27th the Dutch retired under the cover of night, leaving the insurrection triumphant.

"The Belgian Revolution," says a contemporary, "was a surprise to everyone." That is not true, however, to a historian of the provinces. Its immediate origin was traceable, in great part, to the lack of vision and the blundering of King William's government. It cannot be denied, however, that French influence was very strong, due to the impression left upon the provinces by twenty years of political domination (1795–1815) ; to the fact that French was the common language of the educated classes; to the spread of new ideas; and, to a slight extent, to the activity of some individuals who had come from Paris. But this revolution was essentially national in its cause and in its character. Its roots were deep in the tradition of public spirit which had already shown itself in the urban democracy of the Belgian cities in the Middle Ages, in the constitutions of the feudal principalities of the Low Countries, and in the institutions of law in the modern period. The reaction against foreign despotism asserted itself with a power and with arms that were characteristic of the Belgian people throughout the course of their history. Foreign influences were refracted through the national temperament. The insurrection burst into flame simultaneously over the whole land. In every town it appeared in the bold and familiar features which the ebb and flow of servitude and liberty had molded throughout the centuries; but it stopped exactly at the frontiers and kept the foreigner at a distance.

On September 25th, a Provisional Government was constituted at Brussels, composed of men representing the most conflicting of tendencies, and uniting the ancient Catholic nobility with the young bourgeois Liberals. It faced with courage and skill the appalling task which confronted it: to reëstablish order in the capital, to direct the armed revolt, to rally the provinces, to channel, in a word, the whole current of the popular insurrection. On October 4th, the Provisional Government issued a decree which declared that the Belgian Provinces, having been separated violently from Holland, constituted an independent state. Commissioners sent into the provinces found complete loyalty to the new government. Small groups of Belgian revolutionaries pursued the demoralized Dutch troops. The Prince of Orange, whose headquarters were at Antwerp, offered the Belgians greater and greater concessions. His proposals were in vain, and on October 26th he left the city. Two days later the Dutch General, Baron Chassé, signed an armistice with Charles Rogier, a member of the Provisional Government. All the Belgian territory was freed except the citadel of Antwerp, the forts on the Scheldt, and the strong points of Maastricht and Luxemburg—the last of which was still held by the Prussians.

The Provisional Government realized that its powers and the decisions which it had taken during the crisis had to be endorsed in due form by the national will. On October 10th it asked the people to elect a National Congress. For this election it introduced three reforms in political organization. The first of these was embodied in a decree that replaced the complicated electoral college system of the Dutch Constitution by direct ballot. Another decree established a new category of electors to be chosen solely on their presumed capability, in addition to those whose voting rights were based on a minimum tax payment; and, lastly, the age requirement for eligibility was lowered to twenty-five years. In addition, and anticipating the decisions of the Congress, the Provisional Government promulgated in a series of decrees the fundamental liberties demanded by public opinion—liberty of teaching, of association, of the press, of the exercise of religion. At the same time, the Provisional Government abolished the state police, secrecy of the budget and of public accounts, and of judicial proceedings.

On November 3, 1830, some 30,000 electors, of a population of about 4,000,000, chose 200 deputies for the National Congress. There had been no contest among the candidates, and their political opinions were sometimes difficult to distinguish. Unanimity had been reached concerning the independence of the country and its liberal Constitution. The members of the Congress were not bound by any mandate from their electors, and they were not split into parties. Nevertheless, the two fundamental tendencies which divided public opinion in the country between Catholic-Conservatives and Liberal-Progressives were reflected in the debates and resolutions.

The National Congress met on November 10th in the Hall of the States-General in Brussels, and made a number of basic political decisions. On November 18th, it unanimously reconfirmed the independence of Belgium. Considering the circumstances of the time, the birth of the new state was certainly remarkable; it upset and defied the arrangements that had been made for her by the whole of Europe; it asserted the autonomy of Belgium after centuries of association with different foreign powers. However, there was one danger to this complete autonomy of the country—a more or less open return of the former dynasty. Europe desired this in order to preserve as far as possible the work of 1815, and business interests in Belgium were not hostile to it. Cutting to the quick of the matter a second time, the National Congress, by a resolution of November 24th, declared the members of the family of Orange-Nassau ineligible for all time to exercise any power in Belgium.

The principal work of the National Congress was the Constitution which was promulgated on February 7, 1831, after three months of work. It is, perhaps, the purest specimen of the organization of a state according to principles of nineteenth-century liberalism. Its ideal was that society leaves to the individual, in the moral order as well as in the economic, a full measure of liberty whose only limit is the liberty of others. By virtue of a kind of natural harmony, according to its devotees, liberty alone could assure both individual happiness and social progress. In accord with this doctrine, Title II of the Constitution recapitulates all the liberties proclaimed by the Provisional Government in order to ratify and define them. The Belgian Constitution does not merely express the ideal of an epoch by its liberalism, the equal of which is not to be found in any other state on the European Continent; it translates this ideal into fact by its democratic character. "All powers have their source in the nation," are the words of Article 25. And this was literally true, for the people had overthrown the established authority; it was not hindered by respect of any tradition regarding sovereignty, for it had lost contact with the national dynasty which had been embodied in the Habsburgs since the sixteenth century.

Belgium had no prejudices in principle, whether in favor of a principality or against a republic; it found before it a clear field. The institutions which the country established had no other origin and no other power than what it bestowed on them. It is true, however, that the Republic, born of the Revolution of Brabant in 1790, and of the French Revolution, had left disagreeable memories. On the other hand, the autocracies of Napoleon and of King William were no less unpopular. The result was that the Congress decided, almost unanimously, in favor of monarchical government—but a monarchy whose powers were to be strictly limited by a constitution. It saw in royalty an element which would moderate popular passions and interests, and a guarantee of wise government offered to Europe; nevertheless it meant to place monarchy under popular safeguards. The sovereign was to be chosen by the representatives of the people. He would have no authority beyond what they would give him. The essential organ of the popular will would be Parliament, which would be responsible to the people by means of direct, secret, and frequent elections.

It is true that the voting privilege was granted only to those who paid taxes of a certain sum. However, to the mind of those who wrote the Constitution, as well as to the mind of all democrats of the period, this restriction was necessary for the proper functioning of democracy, for its protection against the impulses of the masses; their ignorance, it was believed, was at the mercy of any influence, and their poverty a prey to any pressure. A regime of political and civic liberty was, in their opinion, the surest guarantee of enfranchisement. As a matter of fact, however, the property qualification written into the Constitution was destined to insure the reign of the bourgeoisie in Belgium for sixty years. Sovereignty, though divided between the permanent authority of the King and the flexible powers of the Chambers, was not ruled by the classical formula of the separation of powers but rather was shared in such a way as to demand compromise. The executive power in theory was the proper sphere of the King; he could not, however, exercise it without the assent of a minister, and this minister could not remain in power without the support of Parliament, which kept the executive in check by the annual vote of the budget for public expenses. The legislative power was exercised by the King jointly with the Chambers, the ministry serving as a common bond between them. Judges were irremovable, but were appointed by the sovereign.

This political regime translated into a written legal document the political aspirations of the time, and the Belgian Constitution was considered by European Liberals as an ideal which inspired practically all the constitutional reforms of the Continent. It assured to Belgium a long period of peace and stability. The two parties had constructed, in all good faith and in a spirit of accord, this Constitution which resulted from an almost miraculous combination of modern liberalism and progressive conservatism.

Both sides considered the Constitution their common work and placed it above all their disagreements. They were satisfied that it offered them the possibility of existing without any arbitrary restraint, and of developing in an orderly fashion, each according to its own vital principles.

The success of the Belgian Revolution and the daring of its leaders confronted the Powers with a dangerous situation. The Northern Courts—Russia, Prussia, and Austria—would have wished nothing better than to nip in the bud a revolution which was a challenge to their authority and security. They were apprehensive regarding the attitude of France, where the *Parti du Mouvement* wanted to seize the occasion to reopen the whole question of the basis of the Treaty of Vienna. However, the prudence of the French King, Louis Philippe, succeeded in making the principle of non-intervention prevail, whereas the British Government, although ill-disposed toward the Belgian Revolution, rejected the request of King William to send troops to reëstablish order in Belgium, and called a conference to protect European peace. With considerable ill grace, the Northern Courts accepted the invitation to be present. The Powers at this time did not envisage anything beyond a modification of the internal government of the Low Countries and the maintenance of the sovereignty of King William.

The Conference of London met November 4, 1830. It learned that the Belgian National Congress in successive strokes had proclaimed the independence of the country and had excluded forever the reigning dynasty, undermining the basis for the solution which the Conference had expected to impose. A gale of liberty was blowing across Europe; Poland and Italy were beginning to stir, and the Tory party was overthrown in England when Palmerston succeeded Wellington. Under these conditions, the Conference recognized the principle of Belgian independence on December 2, 1830. At this moment French diplomacy made a final effort to wrest new gains—if necessary, even through the dismemberment of Belgium—at the expense of the authors of the Treaty of Vienna. The Powers, however, unanimously replied by the protocol of January 21, 1831, which proclaimed that "Belgium forms a perpetually neutral state."

Political rivalry thereafter centered on the choice of a sovereign for the new state. On February 3d, the National Congress had elected the Duc de Nemours, the son of Louis Philippe, but the Conference vetoed this nomination. Finally, on June 4th, the Congress proceeded to elect Prince Leopold of Saxe-Coburg-Gotha. On July 21, 1831, Leopold took oath to maintain the Constitution, and became Leopold I. Several days later, however, the new King was compelled to lead his army against the Dutch troops who had invaded his territory. The Belgian forces were defeated in a campaign of ten days. France took advantage of the situation to send an army onto Belgian soil, and the Dutch retired. The London Conference then decided to step in and regulate Dutch-Belgian relations. By the Treaty of the Twenty-four Articles, it established the frontiers of Belgium as they exist at present, and the Belgian plenipotentiary signed the document on November 15, 1831. But the King of Holland refused to agree, and his troops continued to occupy the citadel of Antwerp, while the Belgians, on their side, occupied the territories of Limburg and Luxemburg which had been taken from them by the treaty.

The London Conference had pledged itself to insure the execution of the Treaty of the Twenty-four Articles. The Guaranteeing Powers, however, were divided on this capital point, following the line of their own interests and sympathies as they had done up to that moment, and as they were frequently to do in the following period. England and France blockaded the coast of Holland, and proclaimed an embargo on that country's shipping, while a French army laid siege to the citadel of Antwerp and compelled it to capitulate. But the Northern Courts supported Holland, and refused to participate in coercive measures against her. This crisis led to the adjournment of the Conference. It was settled by the *modus vivendi* established in a convention of May 21, 1833. Belgium and Holland each continued to occupy certain territories which the Conference had awarded to the other party. The blockade was lifted. Suddenly, in 1838, the King of Holland declared his intention of accepting the Treaty of 1831, thus provoking a new crisis; for the Belgians, by the terms of the treaty, were then obliged to evacuate certain provinces which had made common cause with them—German-speaking Luxemburg and Limburg east of the Meuse, the latter being regarded as compensation for the French part of Luxemburg which remained in Belgian hands. These two districts were incorporated in the German Confederation, Luxemburg as a Grand Duchy under the personal sovereignty of the King of Holland.

At last, on April 19, 1839, after years of tension and diplomatic negotiation, the treaties establishing the international status of Belgium were signed at London by all the interested parties. A new State, created by the popular will, was admitted into the European community. Its territory was small and ill-protected. Its sovereignty was encumbered with the obligation of abstaining from any active intervention in international politics, and of maintaining complete impartiality should disagreements develop between other Powers. But in return for all this, the Great Powers promised to protect Belgian integrity and independence, and each Great Power pledged itself to guarantee Belgium against violation by any other. After their age-long struggles over the narrow strip of land that is Belgium, these Powers had contrived a truce in a new form: permanent neutralization of the territory, and its corollary, the perpetual neutrality of the state which was there established. During eighty-three years, Belgium lived peacefully under this arrangement.

CHAPTER IV

Consolidation and Expansion of the Kingdom (1840-1914)

BY BARON DE GRUBEN

LEOPOLD I WAS forty years old when he ascended the throne of the new kingdom. The youngest son of a petty German prince, the Duke of Saxe-Coburg-Gotha, he had served as a page at the Court of Napoleon and as a general in the Russian army. His handsome appearance had brought him, by good fortune, to the very steps of the English throne, the heiress to which—Charlotte—he had married in 1816, his unsuccessful rival having been the Prince of Orange, a future opponent on other battlefields. In 1830, Leopold was a widower, leading the life of an English prince.

Through his lineage and the atmosphere in which he had lived, Leopold was of the eighteenth century. He belonged to the class of the ruling families of Europe, which governed the nations of the Continent as one administers a heritage—a possession which one fights for and enlarges by sharp dealing, and by observing, at all times, the rules of propriety prevailing among people of noble birth. Leopold might have appeared to feel nothing but antipathy for the revolutionary, nationalistic spirit of 1830. However, he had known the humiliation and vicissitudes of the revolutionary period, and, as a close observer, he had watched the most highly developed political system of the period—the British parliamentary regime. He was passionately interested in the game of high politics. He believed himself predestined for it by birth; he knew that he was gifted for that career by experience and by character. A careful observer, a cautious schemer, and a patient player, he moved about with ease and obvious delight amid the court intrigues which formed the political pattern of the period. He had refused the Greek throne because of his apprehensions regarding its stability; he only accepted that of Belgium when common agreement among the Powers guaranteed its stability as well as that of the new State. All Europe was united in its approval of this mature and reserved Prince, who immediately gave proof of his wisdom, political skill, and sense of international equilibrium by his marriage into the French royal family, in 1831, taking Louise Marie, the eldest daughter of Louis Philippe, as his wife.

Leopold bestowed invaluable gifts on Belgium in its infancy. To the small revolutionary country, he brought a kind of pardon from the courts which had accepted him into the family of kings; he was, for them, the sign and the condition of reconciliation. To the fiery and inexperienced nation, he was to devote his wisdom, his prestige, and his freedom from passion and local interests. His line of conduct was clear and firm from the beginning; he was intent on insuring the welfare of the country, especially its unity, strength, and independence. The Constitution had given him supreme command of the army, and foreign relations were his domain. Leopold I immediately showed particular interest in military and diplomatic affairs, which were the means and the field for the realization of his designs.

In domestic politics, his position as a constitutional monarch, combined with his inclination, kept him above the fray in the role of counselor and arbiter. Nevertheless, he made such skillful use of the restricted power granted him by the Constitution that he acquired considerable influence in the direction of the affairs of the kingdom. His reign established definitely and firmly, through several crises, the autonomy of the kingdom of Belgium in the assembly of nations. He cemented the foundations of the internal political system. The country was grateful to the King for these outstanding services. The people and the dynasty entered, so to speak, into a cordial alliance which permitted the development of one of the most interesting and fruitful experiments of modern political history—the Belgian Monarchy.

The first century of the independent existence of Belgium is covered by three long reigns, quite different in character, but sur-

LEOPOLD I
(1831–1865)

LEOPOLD II
(1865–1909)

ALBERT I
(1909–1934)

LEOPOLD III
(1934–)

KINGS OF BELGIUM
(With dates of their reigns)

prisingly adapted to the necessities of the period. This combination of diversity and permanence was for Belgium an unequaled blessing, which dominates, illuminates, and explains all her history. The Belgian dynasty was not only the symbol of the unity and the permanence of the nation. It furnished the country a line of public servants whose worth was unquestioned, whose preparation for their task was specialized, and who could not be removed from office. Unperturbed by fluctuations of opinion and sheltered from the turmoil of the period, these public servants were able to devote themselves to the essential demands of the security, order, and prosperity of the State, with a continuity of plans, an experience and authority in the task, which gained the loyalty of the Belgian people, not only to the person of their King, but to the monarchic regime itself.

The foreign relations of Belgium, during the century that followed the establishment of her independence, bear out the constant characteristics of her history. The country occupies a small area coveted by neighbors and too indefensible to resist their encroachments alone. Thus, it has been Belgium's fate to bear the brunt of schemes for conquest, varying from direct threat and plans for partition to attempts to dictate laws to her and to bring her within respective spheres of influence. If Belgium's neighbors failed to agree on dividing her, they suspected each other of developing plans for her annexation. Foreign powers watched Belgium closely for signs of complicity with their rivals, and sought to find pretexts for complaints and interference. In sum, the mutual jealousies and greediness of the Great Powers were neutralized during the entire nineteenth century and always stopped on the brink of the abyss of a general war. The compromise ratified by the Powers in 1830 was maintained because of, and by the exercise of the same balancing factors that had favored its inception.

Belgium coöperated skillfully and faithfully in the maintenance of a situation in which her independence and peace were the stakes. Her ideal blended with her interest in the maintenance of her independence. It was by firmly resisting external requests and pressure that she gave herself the best possible protection against the suspicions originating in other countries from these very demands. After all, her immunity to the ambitious designs of one power

or another was in the interest of all. It was only necessary, therefore, to stand unflinchingly by the principle of independence in
order finally to obtain the approval and coöperation of the others.
To this the foreign policy of Belgium was devoted with persistence
and success. This policy was put into effect, sometimes by a clear
and courageous attitude in the gravest crises, notably by military
demonstrations, and, at other times, by cautious and astute moves
in the international chess game, calling on certain guarantors,
especially the soundest and most disinterested—England—against
the maneuvers of the other nations. Belgium's second rule of conduct was the honest practice of neutrality which demanded of her
a strict impartiality in relations with powerful and haughty neighbors. Finally, Belgium had a primary concern for the maintenance
of general peace in western Europe, for her geographic position
could have made her, as had so often been true in the past, the
battlefield of Europe.

During this period, Belgian foreign policy was crowned with
success; not only did it assure the peace and independence of the
country, but it acquired for that country, by its political propriety,
the esteem of sincere persons and universal respect. A brief survey
may be made here of the principal events of this prolonged drama
which sometimes placed Belgium in mortal danger. The Powers
that had presided at the formation of Belgium believed themselves
authorized to interfere continually in her affairs, under pretence
of making her neutral status respected. In reality, however, they
aimed at halting developments that they judged opposed to their
interests. Thus, Great Britain opposed the ratification of the treaty
of commerce and friendship concluded in 1833 with the United
States, because the treaty contained certain clauses concerning the
rights of neutrals in time of war which displeased that Power. The
interference of the Powers took place principally in two fields:
military preparations of the country, and freedom of the press.

France had tried to make the best of circumstances, taking advantage of the presence of her troops in Belgium to obtain the
dismantling of some of the Belgian fortresses that had been erected
against her. France, however, was blocked by the refusal of the
Powers, and especially of England which, by a treaty dated November 15, 1831, imposed on King Leopold, with due regard to the

neutral status of Belgium—the obligation of renewing the pledge subscribed to in 1818 by King William—that is, to maintain the Belgian fortresses and to allow them to be occupied in the event of French aggression. It will be seen that similar incidents occur many times: each power is offended at precautionary measures taken by Belgium to defend her soil, if that power fears that such precautions might hinder its possible future operations. With a cynicism that was hardly disguised, the large states did not hide the fact that Belgian territory was to remain open to their armies, either to serve as a passage in the course of operations against their adversaries, or for them to conquer at their convenience.

In 1835 the Belgian Government projected the creation on the northern frontier of a defensive line against Holland. Prussia objected so strenuously that the program was finally reduced to the construction of a single fortress. When, toward 1852, Belgium conceived the project of surrounding the city of Antwerp with a system of forts and of raising the effective strength of the army to 100,000 men, the government of Napoleon III opposed it. It was only in 1860 that work on the fortifications of Antwerp could be begun.

The Constitution had guaranteed the freedom of the press. The newspapers stretched this freedom to the point of relentlessly criticizing the policy of the Great Powers. These Powers were annoyed by the adverse comments of Belgian opinion, and demanded that the Belgian Government put an end to them. The latter was caught between the threatening representations of the Powers and a respect for the constitutional principles aroused by the feeling of national independence. With Prussia such difficulties rose with regard to religious questions in the Rhineland. With France they took a most serious turn during the reign of Napoleon III. Belgium had received the French refugees after the *coup d'état* of December 2, 1851. These refugees carried on a campaign without respite against him whom they called the "tyrant." On the other hand, the Emperor—upheld on this occasion by Austria—took such a threatening tone that twice the Belgian Government was forced to have laws passed suppressing the worst verbal excesses of the newspapers.

The great density of the Belgian population made the country particularly vulnerable in its economy. It could live and prosper only if commercial relations with foreign states could be freely developed. The two continental neighbors of Belgium saw in this situation an opportunity for drawing her into their spheres of influence. Prussia attempted, in 1842, to absorb Belgium into the Zollverein, and France made repeated and pressing attempts at economic domination. The government of Louis Philippe—and that of Napoleon III later on—knowing that Belgium could not dispense with France as a commercial outlet, made every endeavor to impose upon her a customs union. The Belgian Government, in agreement on this point with the advice of other Powers, saw in this arrangement a form of indirect vassalage and obstinately rejected these advances.

It was inevitable that each crisis in international politics should have its effect in Belgium. On every such occasion, the susceptibilities of the Great Powers were aroused concerning the attitude and fate of neutralized Belgium. This was true in 1840, when Europe was divided on what was called the "Eastern Question." The alarm was renewed again in 1848, after the downfall of Louis Philippe. Europe feared at that moment that France might touch off a general war. During the entire reign of Napoleon III, Belgium moved through a series of the gravest possible dangers to her independence and neutrality. Each of the international adventures of that ambitious and intriguing monarch revealed again the delicate structure of the country. Such was the situation in 1852—at the time of the Crimean War—an especially serious crisis since England and France were on the same side. Nevertheless, Belgium clung firmly to her neutrality, although Russia had consented to establish diplomatic relations with her only a short time before. A new crisis rose out of the Italian War in 1859. At that time, Napoleon III conceived the project of assembling a European congress to settle all unsolved problems; in his mind, Belgium was to be used as a mere makeweight in this settlement. From 1866 on, events took a grave turn for Belgium. For imperial France, the Battle of Sadowa and its outcome amounted to a political catastrophe and prompted the Emperor to assure himself of compensations. Bismarck pretended to play Napoleon's game, and the two accomplices carried on talks in which Belgium and Luxemburg served as territories to be bartered. For Bismarck the only consideration was the gaining of time by misleading his opponent with vain hopes. He succeeded in having the

French Ambassador at Berlin, Count Vincente Benedetti, submit to him a plan in manuscript of a partition treaty, which he published at the time of the crisis of 1870. This incident and this document merely resulted in revealing the craftiness of the two protagonists, and the permanent danger of Belgium's situation. The only compensation Napoleon obtained was the creation, in 1867, of an independent state out of the Grand Duchy of Luxemburg, which until then had been linked with Holland under a common sovereign.

Each of these crises forced the Belgian Government to play a close game, in seeking support from the faithful Powers without unduly arousing the potential aggressor. On each occasion it sought to obtain reaffirmation of the engagements of 1839. In all these difficulties it was always in London that Belgium found the most faithful coöperation and the most effective support. That support was most clearly and firmly manifested at the time of the Franco-Prussian War of 1870. At that time the British Cabinet obtained the signatures of the two belligerents to a treaty by which they formally renewed their engagements of 1839. England, on the other hand, pledged herself to bring her naval and military power to bear against any violator of Belgian independence.

The formula of unionism, which had been the parliamentary basis of the Revolution, was likewise that of the first governments of the Kingdom of Belgium. Although public consciousness of the fragility of the new edifice tended to eliminate doctrinal differences and to bridge the gap separating the various parties, nevertheless the political problems which faced the new State did not offer any material for party quarrels. Rather, opinion was divided on a question of method in external negotiations, between the boldness of those who affirmed the rights of Belgium in the face of the Powers and the prudence of those who saw the danger of defying them. The latter won by a small majority in the crisis of 1839. When the storm had passed, and as the country became aware that its international status gave promise of solidity, the internal cohesion of unionism began to weaken. Its breakup was the work of the radicals of the Liberal party, who were the most active agents of the Revolution and who had been carried away by the prevailing current of political ideas toward the separation of the State from all influence of the Church. However, unionism survived for about ten years, with the help of the Catholic-Conservatives and of the King himself, who naturally favored the unity and harmony of all the elements in the nation's life.

This period was devoted to the internal organization of the State. Parliament passed a law on the organization of local government, and another on primary education. About 1846, however, the Liberals had adopted an independent attitude, although their program was a moderate one. They won a strong majority at the elections, and the King called on them to form a party government for the first time. For about forty years they were to dominate the political life of Belgium, in spite of unionism's timid attempts at revival and the intermittent return to power of the Catholics. Their chief support lay in the bourgeoisie of the cities, to whom the electoral system assured certain advantages. The Catholics were in the majority, but their conservative attitude, their fidelity to unionism and their lack of a definitive program paralyzed them.

During the first fifty years of the independent existence of the country, the fundamental political problem, which created a cleavage in public opinion, was the question of the relation between the Church and the State. This fact can only be understood in the light of the influence exercised by the Catholic Church for centuries in the Belgian Provinces, where its doctrinal authority had never been challenged. After the religious crisis of the sixteenth century, Belgium was, so to speak, monolithic in its religious unity, and the Catholic clergy exercised control not only of the religious life of the country but also of education and public welfare. The Church in Belgium had entered into an alliance with the State, which assured its undisturbed hegemony at the price of docile submission to the behests of the Sovereign. One after another, Joseph II, Napoleon, and King William gave the Church to understand that this association meant subservience on its part. At the same time there developed, especially in France, a strong movement of ideas which not only undermined the temporal power of the clergy, but seemed to shake the very foundations of the Catholic faith on the intellectual and moral plane. In Belgium, this second tendency was slow to reveal itself. The adversaries of the Church appeared to be respectful—and often really were—of its spiritual domain. They avowed the intention merely of preventing the interference of the Church in temporal matters, in the name of the sound organization of civil society. Catholics, for their part, were conscious of the paralyzing influence on the Church of too close an association with the State and were not unwilling to acquire renewed strength through a regime of freedom. It has been seen that the coöperation of the Catholics and the Liberals in 1830 was effected in this spirit; and the Constitution translated it into public law, through the principle of the separation of Church and State, by a compromise to which no serious objection was raised. Freedom of opinion, including religious opinion, and its public expression in the exercise of various cults, was guaranteed. The Church appointed its ministers, and the State paid them a salary as an indemnity for the confiscation of church property under the French regime.

It is strange, therefore, that the quarrel should have been so bitter and so prolonged. Primarily, it was because the fight was waged upon the vaguely defined territory of education, of freedom of association, and of public morals. Furthermore, the issues in the struggle were beclouded by an atmosphere of equivocation, partly unconscious and partly deliberate. On the liberal side, the fight against the strictly religious influence of the Church became more and more violent under the pretense of defending the rights of the State. On the Catholic side, such unusually clever use was made of constitutional liberties that there were grounds for apprehension lest the supremacy of the Church might reappear in a much more active form than that maintained under the old regime.

The crisis of 1848 plainly manifested the strength of the Belgian State and the wisdom of its political leaders. A tempest blew over Europe and swept away many a crowned head. Louis Philippe fled from Paris, Frederick William IV abdicated his throne at Berlin, and Metternich sought refuge in Belgium. A general war almost broke out. At Brussels, the Chambers enacted several moderate reforms—in particular the lowering of the property qualification for voting to the minimum called for under the Constitution. But that was all. In the face of peril from abroad and from social upheaval, the parties reformed their Union, while the government took steps to cope with all dangers. The country remained astonishingly calm, and the prestige of the Sovereign increased to such a point that men could call him the "Mentor of Europe."

Leopold II ascended the throne of Belgium in 1865 at the age of thirty, following the thirty-four years' reign of his father. The prince was characterized by a restless intelligence and purposeful enthusiasm which presaged a new era. He had traveled much. When he became king, his vision did not cease to turn toward all corners of the world which exploration had discovered. He was one of the race of "empire builders" of his period. He had a feeling and a taste for bold enterprise in which scientific curiosity, territorial conquest, and national prestige moved hand in hand. He directed and took part in the extraordinary economic expansion of a small, weak, and pacific people which, nevertheless, was to spread its activity over the entire world; and he endowed his people with an empire almost in spite of its own wishes. He is the symbol of a period in which material wealth was fabulously increased and took shape in venturesome and complicated forms, extending the branches of its power in every direction—scientific, social, and political. Leopold II was a business promoter and a leader in financial enterprises. He was never exactly in harmony with the temperament of his people. The territorial and psychological limits of his small country were too narrow for the vaulting intelligence and imperious character that he possessed; yet certain incidents of his private life shocked the moral standards of his subjects. In his later years he became more and more aloof. He appeared to be wholly absorbed by distant projects which the more timid regarded as fantastic. At the same time, he set an example and led the way for his subjects. Like his father, he conscientiously worked at his trade as king. If, perhaps, he felt himself constrained by his royal office, still he put forth every effort to stimulate the forward march of the country. When this great, solitary old man died in 1909, his entire work, and all his material profits, were willed to his people.

As it appears in the chapter on the early exploration and development of the Belgian Congo,[1] the history of that vast territory is the history of the enterprise of a single man, carried through in spite of the ill will of most of the European Powers, and with no enthusiastic response by the people in whose interest it had been projected. Yet, both by its methods and its results, this enterprise

---

[1] See Chapter XXV, "Historical Development," by R. Stanley Thomson.

is characteristically Belgian. In 1885 the independent state of the Congo was inaugurated under the sovereignty of Leopold II; the constitutional King of Belgium became the absolute monarch of an empire. The two states had no juridical connection except that of personal union through the same sovereign, but by a peculiar trick of fate they both had a central position in the heart of a continent, and both were surrounded by powerful and jealous neighbors. Here, however, as with Belgium, a like set of circumstances contributed to the birth of an independent state and imposed an international status founded on neutrality. The character of the new state envisaged a regime of freedom which is the very essence of the economic and moral constitution of Belgium; yet, although more and more Belgians took part in the colonization of the Congo, public opinion at home remained prejudiced against the colonial idea.

When, by 1889, the King had declared his intention of making Belgium the sole legatee of his sovereign and patrimonial rights over the Congo, he was yet reluctant to renounce his absolute authority over an empire in which his imperious character was subjected to no restraint, and where the plans of his farseeing genius had free play. Financial difficulties, however, and the increasing opposition of the Anglo-Saxon world to the methods of his administration accelerated his decision to bring his responsibility to an end. On their side, the Belgian people felt that their responsibility and their future were involved in the King's venture. Yet it was not until 1908 that the Belgian Parliament incorporated the Independent State of the Congo into the Kingdom, and only from that date has the whole country given a devoted concern to the tasks of empire, achieving in a few years a work of civilization which can well be compared with that of states whose colonial experience is much longer.

The Liberal government which came to power in the important year of 1878 entered upon a policy of militant anticlericalism, which—particularly in the matter of education—provoked so violent a reaction on the part of Catholics that the political struggles of the period are called "The War of the Schools." The elections of 1884 brought the Catholic party back to power, and it remained in office for thirty years without interruption. After a brief period

of reaction, this party was wise enough to embark upon a program colored so slightly by religious interests as not to arouse
complaints by its adversaries. Its policy was characterized by that
moderation which has always been the fundamental political
instinct of Belgian public opinion and to which opinion it has
always returned whenever it departed from its normal equilibrium. During this period it tended more and more to become a
sort of national party, uniting the most diverse shades of political
opinion on the common ground of a Christian faith. Because of
the party's composite character, all the problems of the day were
at the same time problems which affected its own essence; the solutions which it worked out within itself were sufficiently temperate,
mature, and, at the same time, progressive to satisfy all the demands
of the common good. The three fundamental problems which absorbed political activity during this period were—apart from foreign policy and its corollary, military measures—the social question,
the development of which is treated elsewhere in detail in this volume, the question of suffrage, and the Flemish problem.

The Constitution had made the right to vote conditional on
the payment of a certain amount of taxes, and thus the country,
for electoral purposes, consisted of a definitely limited number
of citizens, a condition that made it in effect a kind of bourgeois
oligarchy. From its very beginning, the Labor party had waged a
campaign in favor of extending the right of suffrage to all citizens
without any distinction. The workingmen, deprived of any means
of expressing their grievances legally, resorted to the general strike.
The Government and the two traditional parties realized that they
could not oppose a reform which had already been introduced
in most European countries, and in 1893 the Constitution was
amended in order to grant the right to vote in elections for the
Chamber of Representatives to all male citizens twenty-five years
of age. This concession to unqualified democracy was tempered
by granting supplementary votes to the heads of families, to the
educated classes, and to the most highly taxed classes—a system, in
short, of plural voting. The change in the electoral system multiplied by 10 the number of electors, who hitherto had numbered
138,000. This modification of the electorate preserved the relative
preponderance of the Catholic party, and eliminated almost com-

pletely the Liberals—the representatives of the urban bourgeoisie—who thenceforward were able to appear in Parliament only because of the system of proportional representation. The Socialists gained admission to Parliament in considerable numbers, and as time went on their position there became ever stronger. The restrictions governing the right to vote and eligibility for the Senate were no obstacle to the momentum of democracy.

Belgium is composed of two ethnic elements, different in race and tongue, but united by their religion, by their complementary economies, by their culture, and by their common political traditions. French, the language of the Southern Provinces, was imposed throughout the whole country as the official public language during the period of French domination. Higher education was completely French, and French became the customary language of the upper classes in the Flemish part of the country. During the fifteen years of Dutch rule, the language of Holland was restored to its rightful position; but the very fact that it had been reintroduced by the Government of The Hague precipitated a reaction against it after the Revolution of 1830. The French language became once more the sole official tongue and the vehicle of higher education, as it had been under the Napoleonic regime. Nevertheless, the Flemish language remained alive among the people and gradually gave birth to a literature which was more and more prolific. From 1873 onward, the Government began, through legislative measures, to restore to Flemish its status as a national idiom. Those who agitated on behalf of the Flemish language looked for assistance from the power of law, and sought to impose their point of view by pressure on the political parties. In 1914 they were still far from achieving their end.

The permanent ascendancy of a single party, through so long a period, was the beginning of the twilight of the classical parliamentary regime—a regime founded on the alternating tenure of power by two parties. Many factors contributed to this decline or, if one prefers, to this development. First of all, there was the presence of a third party, the Belgian Labor party, the mouthpiece of the socialist doctrine. Later, in 1899, the inauguration of a system of proportional representation—dividing seats among the parties in accordance with the votes each had obtained—made much more difficult the overthrow of the majority; at the same time, it encouraged the division of national representation into small groups. Again, the large increase of the electorate tended to break the contact between the elector and his deputy, and consolidated the position of organized political parties.

Differences regarding policy, instead of being decided frankly by the electorate and settled by the shift of majorities, became more and more the object of deals by professional politicians who employed all the resources of their powerful groups to get the best of any bargain and to profit by private agreements between the parties. Moreover, divisions of public opinion were reflected almost exactly inside each of the three political parties. Each had a conservative wing and a progressive wing; each represented all shades of opinion regarding the linguistic question; even the various attitudes regarding foreign policy had a vigorous representation in each. In general, however, the Catholic party shifted more and more in the direction of the peasant population of the Flemish part of the country, whereas the Socialist party was pointed toward the proletariat among the Walloons, and the petty bourgeoisie of the cities remained faithful to the Liberals. Thus, the public life of Belgium presents a confused pattern, and resembles a very complicated mosaic. Yet, it must be remembered that this regime contributed to the maintenance of national unity, avoiding sectional divisions and violent changes.

King Leopold II had been on the throne for only five years when the Franco-Prussian War of 1870 provoked the greatest crisis Belgian independence had thus far experienced. This time, however, Belgium remained unharmed by the conflict of her two neighbors, because of the energetic intervention of England and, above all, because of the fact that the armies of that period did not need a very large sphere of operations. Yet, the entire reign of the second King of the Belgians was dominated by the foreign problems that flowed from the defeat of France. For a few years, the notion of using Belgium to serve as "compensation" for France's losses was entertained by the vanquished, who were in search of a *revanche,* as well as by the victorious Germans, who were anxious to maintain peace. Actually, Bismarck had little sympathy for his small neighbor state, where Catholic sentiment had shown opposition to his *Kulturkampf*. During this time, the Belgian Government energetically maintained the rights of freedom of opinion in neutral Belgium, just as it had done in relation to Prussia fifty years earlier and in relation to France during the reign of Napoleon III.

Beginning with 1875, Germany, fearing French aggression, insistently requested the Belgian Government to fortify the valley of the Meuse in order to prevent the swift passage of French armies. This plan corresponded exactly with the policy of the Belgian Government. In 1887, it was decided to construct fortifications at Liége and Namur, which were destined by the irony of fate to delay considerably the advance of the German armies in 1914. Although the French Government, for its part, officially approved the new fortifications, it allowed an anti-Belgian campaign to be started in the press, instigated by the fears and suspicions which Belgian military measures have always provoked. And the German press did not fail to reprimand the "Francophile" attitude of Belgium.

Yet German strategy was passing from the defensive to the offensive. The Chief of the General Staff, General Schlieffen, had included Belgian territory in his invasion plans. Kaiser William II attempted, in 1904, to win King Leopold to his side, by dazzling him with the prospect of the resurrection—to Leopold's profit—of the power of the fifteenth-century Burgundian dukes. In order to hide the plans that were already maturing Berlin employed, in turn, brutal threats and beguiling promises. The King saw the storm coming. During his entire reign he had advocated the reinforcement of the army, and on his deathbed in December, 1909, he signed the law introducing compulsory military service for one son of each family.

King Leopold II of Belgium died at the age of seventy-four, after forty-four years on the throne. The succession went to a shy nephew, Albert, who was born in 1875, the son of the Count of Flanders who had been kept apart from any participation in public affairs by the great solitary monarch. Albert had led a studious and retired life. Like the other princes of his family, he had the insatiable curiosity of the traveler. It was thought that he did not have the breadth of view of his predecessors, but the people were pleased to have a prince who was devoted to his family and to his career, just like an ordinary person. Yet destiny willed that this peaceful and retiring man should be confronted with the most serious decisions and the most exhausting tasks that could ever be imposed on a king. He was to see the invasion of his country, defeat in battle, a long and dark conflict on the last remaining strip of the national soil, and all the troubles of the postwar period. But he measured up to all these trials. At the moment when it was demanded of him, he showed the wisdom and the courage that circumstances required in the head of a state. He never uttered an inept word or made an inappropriate gesture; he possessed the clear perceptions of the humble. Boastfulness was utterly foreign to him; referring to the courageous deeds of his people, this hero said simply: "We have been compelled to be heroic."

From the beginning of his reign the storm hovered on the horizon. In 1911, as once before in 1905, the two camps into which the great European Powers had divided barely escaped armed conflict. Not a moment too soon, the Parliament in 1913 voted the law which instituted general military service. In July, 1914, the British Government asked of France and Germany—as it had done in 1870—a confirmation of the terms of the Treaty of 1839. Germany attempted to temporize, but on August 2d, the German Minister at Brussels handed to the Belgian Government the famous ultimatum which asked for free passage for the German army, while guaranteeing the maintenance of Belgian sovereignty. During a night session of the Council, the King and his Ministers decided that the country's fidelity to its pledges, to its traditions, and to its destiny demanded that it reject this infamous offer. On August 4, 1914, the German army, treacherously invading Belgian soil, opened the era of the great calamities of modern times.

CHAPTER V

In the First World War

BY GEORGES THEUNIS

THE NUMEROUS WORKS which have been written on the First World War very justly allot a relatively important role to the Belgian army. It is not necessary to dwell at length on the tragic period beginning August 4, 1914, with the violation of Belgian territory, and ending on the morning of November 11, 1918, with the signing of the Armistice. The consideration here is limited to some of the principal developments of the war in which Belgium played a part.

The violation of neutral Belgian territory was an important factor in Great Britain's decision to join France in resisting German aggression. During the four years of the war, the task of the Belgian army was to hold the extremely important pivot of the Allied line which extended to the sea, thus protecting the Channel ports.

Finally, the cynical violation of Belgian neutrality by one of its guarantors was also one of the factors which made the Allied cause that of the defense of international law against brute force. Even before the intervention of the United States in the war, Belgium's cause aroused a sympathy so deep and abiding that it made possible the establishment and maintenance of the Commission of Relief in Belgium to the end of hostilities.

It should be remembered, if only to emphasize once more the perfidious character of German diplomacy that, in 1914, the diplomatic status of Belgium was still determined by the Treaty of 1839 which had put an end to the Belgian-Dutch conflict of 1830–1831. The Treaty had been signed by all the European Powers, including Prussia. Article 8 of the Treaty in reality stated: "Belgium will form an independent and perpetually neutral State." Moreover, the Treaty was guaranteed by Austria, France, Great Britain, Prussia, and Russia.

In 1913, during a debate in the Reichstag, the German Minister of Foreign Affairs declared that Belgian neutrality had been established by international covenants and that Germany was determined to respect these agreements. In the course of the debate, the German Minister of War also declared that Germany would not lose sight of the fact that Belgian neutrality was guaranteed by international treaties. Forty years ago, Germany did not hesitate to make the most solemn declarations of fidelity to her victims while busily preparing, in minute detail, the assault which would betray her pledges.

Fortunately, King Albert, at the suggestion of his uncle, Leopold II, had already begun a complete reorganization of the Belgian army. In 1913 the King received confidential information which left no doubt as to Germany's intentions toward Belgian neutrality in the event of war. The political storm which was instrumental in starting the First World War threatened toward the end of July, 1914. Accordingly, on July 29th, the Belgian Government decreed military mobilization.

On Sunday evening, August 2, 1914, the German Ambassador in Brussels handed to the Belgian Minister of Foreign Affairs a note accusing France of intending to violate Belgian territory in order to attack Germany. Under the circumstances, the note indicated, it was necessary for Germany to protect herself. The German Government therefore asked permission for the German army to march through Belgian territory.

The Crown Council, presided over by the King, indignantly refused the German proposition, declaring that if Belgium were to acquiesce in the German demand, the nation's honor would be sacrificed and international treaties violated; moreover, if the German army crossed the frontier, the Belgian army would attack. The whole country approved the Council's courageous reply.

On August 4, 1914, in the early hours of the morning, German troops crossed the Belgian frontier. A few hours later the German Chancellor, Bethmann-Hollweg, attempted to excuse Germany's violation of Belgian territory by the celebrated phrase: "Necessity knows no law" (*Not kennt kein Gebot*). He finished by terming the

FLEMISH LANDSCAPE: CANAL TO DAMME

WALLOON LANDSCAPE: PANORAMIC VIEW OF
VRESSE-SUR-SEMOIS

Treaty of 1839, guaranteeing Belgian neutrality, a "scrap of paper." Parliament assembled at ten o'clock in the morning. The King, accompanied by the Queen and the royal children, went to the Palace of the Nation and in his address to Parliament affirmed the country's decision. When he left the Palace to take command of the army, an enormous and wildly enthusiastic crowd acclaimed him.

Liége and Namur.—What action could the Belgian army take, considering the limited forces at its disposal? The fortifications of Liége and Namur, built twenty-five years earlier, were situated exactly on the line of invasion, whether from France toward Germany or from Germany toward France, and had been built precisely to discourage eventual aggressors from crossing the country. The purpose of the Liége position was to detain, on the first favorable lines of defense, any army that might violate neutral territory for strategic reasons and to stop it long enough to prevent its reaching its goal.

Knowing that on the European Continent Germany would have to face a Franco-Russian coalition, the German General Staff had decided that the crossing of Belgian territory represented an important advantage. The plan first was to conquer, by a rapid march, the small Belgian army as well as the French. Then, when this had been accomplished, the German army planned to turn toward the east and direct its attack against the Russian army which Germany believed would be slow in mobilizing, in view of the scarcity of means of communication and the enormous distances to be covered.

Between Aix-la-Chapelle and Alsace, on one side, and the Seine around Paris, on the other, Belgium, with her plateaus and plains rich in variegated resources, where roads and railways abound, was perhaps the only region in the world where an army of more than 1,000,000 men could advance rapidly. The river Meuse was the only natural obstacle from Verdun to Maastricht. On that line were two points of passage important as road and railway junctions: Namur and Liége. Liége, with its twelve bridges over the Meuse, one day's march from the German frontier, was the gateway to Belgium, and, as has been said, the key to Paris.

It would have required several days to transport the Belgian army, which was then in process of mobilization, to the banks of the Meuse. It was decided, therefore, to concentrate the main body of the army in a zone situated some thirty miles behind Liége and to employ two divisions, one at Liége and one at Namur, for the supreme defense of the two fortified positions.

The plan of the German army—one brigade of the vanguard was commanded by General Ludendorff, who later became Chief of Staff of the Kaiser's armies—was to seize Liége and its bridges before they could be destroyed. Accordingly, a strong detachment of German troops launched a brutal surprise attack. The Belgians repulsed the enemy's numerical superiority in spite of heavy losses. The Germans, however, had decided to pass at any cost and brought up heavy artillery, of a hitherto unknown caliber. Although German detachments penetrated the town, the forts held until August 17th. The Germans had lost 42,000 men—more than the total strength of the opposing Belgian divisions. For ten days the 4,000 Belgians, stationed in the forts and buried under the steel and concrete of gun turrets, immobilized the 100,000 Germans assigned to the surprise attack on the Liége position. Military authors agree unanimously that the delay occasioned by the resistance of Liége influenced considerably the subsequent development of military operations. It permitted the strategic reshuffling of the French armies.

Apart from its military aspects, the resistance of Liége symbolized Belgian resistance. The echo of Liége's cannon spread around the world. It was the cry of "Right" violated by "Force," the proof that Belgium had loyally taken up the part which she was to carry during the whole of the war, that of a soldier of civilization. The Liége garrison, cruelly tried by the losses sustained during repeated attacks by superior German forces, succeeded in rejoining the main body of the Belgian army which had taken up a defensive position between Liége and Brussels.

The fortified position of Namur which, like that of Liége, had been established neither to undergo regular siege nor to resist a protracted blockade but to prevent enemy utilization of an important railway and highway junction, soon suffered the same fate as that of Liége. The forts were crushed by the fire of 12-inch and 13½-inch howitzers, calibers of that size previously having been unknown.

The Fourth Belgian Division, which was charged with the defense of the Namur position and had received the support of a part of the French Fifth Army, succeeded in retiring toward the French border. A few weeks later it rejoined the main body of the Belgian army which, after arduous combat against the bulk of the German armies, had been obliged to abandon Brussels and fall back to Antwerp, the national citadel.

Before their entry into Brussels, the Germans burned the town of Louvain, including its famous library and, as in a number of other Belgian towns and villages, massacred large numbers of civilians. In 1916, a committee, presided over by Viscount Bryce, the former British Ambassador at Washington, published the findings of its investigations which proved that the Germans had committed a series of outrages throughout Belgium.

Antwerp.—From time immemorial, the town and the port of Antwerp had been a fortified position. As early as the ninth century, Antwerp was surrounded by ramparts. The town has endured numerous sieges, especially during the wars against the Spanish at the end of the seventeenth century. In 1914 it possessed a double belt of forts, of which only a few were really modern. Some were unfinished and none was capable of withstanding projectiles of a caliber larger than 7.88 inches. The range of the heavy guns was insufficient to counter Germany's ultramodern artillery. Under these conditions, the presence of the field army was necessary for the defense of the entrenched camp of Antwerp.

Antwerp, one of the great ports of Europe, had always had an abundant supply of food and had materials of every kind. There the army had stored food and heavy reserves of munitions, had built arsenals and hospitals. The town was, in reality, the actual base of the Belgian army. Antwerp was the port at which an English army of assistance could have disembarked most easily and been most effective. Unfortunately, at that moment the War Office had only a few battalions at its disposal.

It was evident that the Belgian field army, which had been reduced to approximately 80,000 men, could not check the 500,000 men of the German army whose chief aim, moreover, was the destruction of the French army and who, for that reason, had changed the direction of its advance toward the south and the southwest.

On August 25th and September 9th, the Belgian army, finding itself on the German flank, undertook two important offensive operations which coincided with the offensives launched by the French near Charleroi and by the English near Mons. However, the considerable numerical superiority of the German army soon forced the Allies to abandon their offensives, after which it was both useless and dangerous to prolong the sortie. Once more the army withdrew to the forts of Antwerp.

The famous Battle of the Marne was soon to begin. The French High Command, which at the beginning of August had launched an offensive toward Alsace and Lorraine, now corrected its error and reorganized its forces before Paris. On September 6th, General Joffre decided upon a general counteroffensive. King Albert resolved to coöperate energetically with the Allied effort and ordered a new sortie by the Antwerp garrison to begin on September 9th. After three days of combat, the army suffered considerable losses and was again obliged to retire to Antwerp. By its intervention, however, the Belgian army succeeded in immobilizing more than 150,000 German troops in the country and thus contributed, within the limits of its modest means, to the victory of the Marne.

Having transported the war material of the fortress of Maubeuge from the north of France, the German General Headquarters had at its disposal considerable artillery, the same, in fact, that had ruined the forts of Liége and Namur. The siege of Antwerp began. It was a repetition of what had happened at Liége, Namur, and Maubeuge; the forts were successively destroyed by the power of German artillery, but the range of the Belgian guns did not allow a reply. The Belgian army so far had fought alone. It had been furnished with some arms and ammunition, but not a single French battalion or squadron had come to its aid. Two thousand British Royal marines had arrived in Antwerp. Three-quarters of Belgian territory was occupied. The whole army would have been lost had it been kept at Antwerp after the destruction of the first lines of defense. The Belgian Staff decided, therefore, to fall back toward the coast, and the "race to the sea" began.

The Belgian army's retreat to the sea was difficult and exhausting. During the last days of the defense of Antwerp, the troops, which had long been under fire, were harried by the Germans, who realized the importance of preventing a junction of the Belgian troops with the English and French troops converging upon Ypres.

On October 18th, when the famous Battle of the Yser began, the Belgian army numbered no more than 48,000 men. Realizing the importance of the stake involved in the battle soon to be joined, King Albert issued his celebrated appeal to the soldiers, in which he said that anyone who pronounced the word retreat without specific orders would be dealt with as a traitor. The line of the Yser constituted the last line of defense in Belgium; its conservation was necessary for the development of the general plan of operations. It must, then, be held at all costs.

The Yser formed a natural obstacle some sixty feet in width. It was difficult to construct trenches of sufficient depth because of the low-lying ground which was below sea level at high tide. From the sea, the Belgians had the advantage of being supported by an English cruiser and three monitors, and by a few French destroyers. The Belgian army had just been reinforced also by a brigade of French marines and another of Moroccan scouts.

General Foch, who was in command of the French armies of the north, had asked the Belgian army to hold out for two days. The days passed and no French reinforcements arrived. On the contrary, the German attacks became more and more violent.

For the same reasons which made the holding of the Yser positions important to the Belgians and the Allies, the Germans hoped to break through the pivotal points of the Allied front in order to reach Boulogne and Calais, which also were to be their objectives in the heavy offensive of 1940. After eight days of fighting, which cost the Belgian army approximately 15,000 casualties, the situation appeared desperate. Although hard-pressed themselves, the French held out a hope of their coming to the aid of the Belgians with two battalions of Senegalese infantry and a regiment of cavalry.

Marshal French, the chief of the English army, declared that it was impossible for him to furnish a single battalion of reinforcements. It was then that the Belgian High Command decided to seek assistance from the sea. Belgian engineer officers in coöperation with an expert in the handling of the canal locks, let the waters of the sea into the plains of the Yser Valley. At the end of four or five days, the entire area was flooded.

On October 30th, the German High Command ordered five divisions, including the volunteers of the Imperial Guard, to attack the Belgian front. At the same time, six other divisions were to assault the British front in the neighborhood of Lessines. After a few hours of fighting, the Germans realized that it was impossible to continue the attack, as their soldiers were in water up to their knees and unable even to throw themselves down for protection from Belgian fire. That evening the German High Command had to order a retreat. Hemmed in by the sea, by the Belgian army, and by the floods, the Germans tried to break through the front farther to the east. The Battle of Ypres, celebrated in English annals, began and the Straits of Calais were saved.

When the Belgian army retired to the Yser, it was able to take, with its arms and ammunition, only a minimum number of motor lorries. An important quantity of railroad stock had been saved in France and had rendered signal service to the Allies. The chief problem was the supplying of cannon and ammunition. The personnel of the Belgian factories moved to Havre, where large shops were soon improvised for the repairing and manufacture of material for the artillery and for the engineers corps. The use of these shops made possible the accumulation of supplies of ammunition which were indispensable to the final heavy offensive and, therefore, greatly increased the number of batteries of all calibers. Other factories, with Belgian personnel, were installed in England for the manufacture of large caliber shells, explosives, and guns. The functioning of these factories was made possible by the employment of technicians from the Belgian army and of workers recruited from among the refugees in England and France. Supply commissions were organized in Paris, London, and in New York. These commissions succeeded in furnishing the Belgian army with complete equipment and armament.

Then the army needed more men. The Belgian Government passed decrees in 1915, 1916, and 1917 which drew into the army, apart from the many volunteers, every able-bodied man to be found among the Belgians, whether in England, France, or in the tiny unoccupied corner of the homeland. Because of these measures, in 1918 the army in the field numbered more than 175,000 men and possessed equipment of a quality equal to that of the other Allies.

During the years 1915, 1916, and 1917, the war along the front became one of position. On both sides the armies clung to their battle lines. Trenches were dug everywhere, shelters were built, and barbed-wire entanglements set up. Thousands of men were killed during these years in the various offensive movements. Machine guns and barbed wire conquered even the most courageous of troops.

At different times the Germans tried to break through the Allied line in the sector held by the Belgian army. One of the most dangerous attacks was that which marked the beginning of the second Battle of Ypres in April, 1915. Here poison gas, a new German weapon of combat, made its first appearance. Stunned by the blow, the Allied lines were temporarily breached for a distance of three miles at the junction of the French, English, and Belgian troops. However, the enemy was so surprised at the extent of its success that it failed to follow up. At the end of three days of hard fighting, the Allies recaptured their positions and closed the breach.

The year 1915 ended calmly, but it had cost the small Belgian army 12,000 casualties. The following year did not witness any important events on the left wing of the Allied front.

A heavy Anglo-French offensive was launched in April of 1917, with the intention of dislodging the Germans from the Belgian coast where their submarines were based. The Belgian army lent full support to the offensive which was, nevertheless, unsuccessful. The Yser front was constantly active, in spite of its apparent calm. Nowhere else was the war in the trenches as difficult for the soldiers as in this water-logged area. The German military account recognizes, moreover, that in this region "the front was never calm."

The beginning of the year 1918 was a particularly tragic period for the Allies. Russia no longer counted as a combatant power, Rumania was completely disabled, and the Italians had suffered disastrous defeats. The American army was still in process of organization, and in March, 1918, the English army had met with heavy reverses at Amiens and its Fifth Army no longer existed. Following these events, however, a united command was formed which enabled the Allies to halt the offensive which William II had launched in an attempt to decide the outcome of the war before the American troops could arrive in the field in sufficient force. The second Battle of the Marne was another setback for the Germans. By the end of August, 1918, the initiative had passed to the Allied Command. Two hundred and fifty thousand American soldiers disembarked each month on the soil of France. Their first action was crowned with success. Nearly 1,000,000 men, under General Pershing's command, occupied the Meuse sector, and Marshal Foch organized a triple offensive at the beginning of August. A joint Belgian-British offensive was to be launched on the Allies' left flank in Flanders.

At last, on September 26th, the Belgian divisions left their billets and their trenches to launch the attack which was to free the country. They had to attack German defense positions which had been prepared over a period of almost four years. Nevertheless, they advanced five miles in the first few days. On September 30th, the Belgian army occupied the dominant positions in the region, although their wounded in this action exceeded 10,000 in number. They had taken 5,000 prisoners, captured 250 cannon, and wrested from the enemy a position ten miles in depth. A few days later, simultaneously with the British advance, the battle was resumed and continued to the eve of the Armistice. The total number of Belgian casualties, including some 35,000 missing and prisoners, amounted to 93,000 and represented 35 per cent of the men mobilized during the war.

On November 22, 1918, the Belgian Royal Family made its triumphant reëntry into Brussels.

The African campaign, 1916–1917.—While the Germans in Europe attacked the national territory of Belgium, German troops from the East African colony attacked the Belgian coast of Lake Tanganyika. As early as 1914, an expeditionary corps of 10,000 men was organized in the Belgian Congo. Its forces were rapidly increased. Officers, commissioned and noncommissioned, were sent from Europe as were considerable provisions of food, medicine, clothing, ammunition, tools, and other supplies.

The colonial army had to face experienced, well-equipped German troops who were reinforced by the crews of German warships which had been destroyed or scuttled off the east coast of Africa, and these troops were commanded by competent, energetic officers.

In 1915, the Germans repeatedly took the offensive against the

British possessions and against the Belgian Congo frontiers. The Belgian colonial army, in agreement with the English, decided upon an offensive against the German East African colony. Some time was required for its organization, but it was finally launched in the spring of 1916, its troops under the command of General Tombeur.

In February, the British expeditionary corps arrived in Mombasa on the Indian Ocean. The corps comprised numerous white troops, of which two South African brigades were commanded by General (now Marshal) Jan Smuts.

The eastern and western extremities of the German colony were attacked simultaneously: from the Belgian side by Congolese troops under the command of Belgian officers, using rather primitive means of transport; from the west by the English, employing white troops and modern transport material.

In three months of arduous fighting, the Belgian troops, starting from Lake Tanganyika, had reached Lake Victoria, where General Smuts congratulated them upon their successes. However, their task was not ended. The Allied Command requested General Tombeur to undertake an offensive south of Lake Tanganyika and to sweep that territory clean. A new Belgian campaign then began, ending in the victory of Tabora, a relatively important town situated on the German railroad linking Lake Tanganyika to Dar-es-Salam on the coast of the Indian Ocean.

During this time, the English expeditionary army had won several expensive victories. The white troops not only had suffered severely from the climate, but also had lost several thousand men. Furthermore, a large number of animals in their train (cattle and draft animals) had perished. As important German detachments continued the fight in the center of the German colony, a Belgian column was called upon to coöperate in the Allied effort of August and September, 1917, and scored important successes at Mahengé.

The Belgian colonial army proved its worth in the First World War and demonstrated the loyalty and courage of its troops. Thus the Belgians reaped the rewards of the humanitarian policy they had followed in Africa, which had won for them the affection of the natives. As has been seen, similar results were achieved in the Congolese army's victorious campaign of 1940 in Ethiopia.

The Belgian Government during the war.—King Albert remained with his army at all times and had his headquarters at De Panne, where he was located in 1914. Near the Yser front, this small seaside resort was under constant gunfire.

The Belgian Government reëstablished its headquarters in France at St. Adresse, a suburb of Havre. The Prime Minister was then Charles de Broqueville. Before the end of the war, the Catholic Government of 1914 had been enlarged to include a Liberal member, Paul Hymans, who was later to become the first President of the League of Nations, and a Socialist, Emile Vandervelde, who was to become President of the Second International.

Occupied Belgium.—While the Belgian army stood guard for four years on the Yser, the Germans occupied the greater part of Belgium, bringing with them a reign of terror. They continually violated the international conventions of The Hague and arrested many Belgian patriots on the flimsiest of grounds. They did not hesitate even to shoot women. Their outstanding victims were Edith Cavell, an English nurse, and a Belgian girl, Gabrielle Petit. Many distinguished Belgians were arrested. Among them Adolphe Max, the Mayor of Brussels, and several university professors, including the famous historian, Henri Pirenne, were sent to German prisons. Von der Goltz was the first German Governor; the second was General von Bissing.

Moreover, the Germans plundered the country to such an extent that soon most Belgians were reduced to near starvation. However, their plight was greatly alleviated by American relief. In 1916, the Germans started deporting Belgian workers for compulsory labor in Germany. Altogether, 120,000 men were deported in violation of international law and in spite of an official note published by the German military government of occupied Belgium, in which it was stated that there was no question of sending Belgians to Germany, either to serve in the German army or for compulsory labor. Systematic plundering of Belgian finance was also a part of the German occupation army's program. As of December, 1914, Belgium had to pay a monthly tribute of 40,000,000 gold francs. In November, 1916, the amount was increased to 50,000,000, and in June, 1917, to 60,000,000 gold francs. Moreover, the Belgian National Bank and the Bank "Société Générale" were compelled to invest 650,000,000 marks in Germany. German destruction in Belgium amounted to 5,000,000,000 gold francs and the daily requisitions of the Germans amounted to some 7,000,000 marks.

Notwithstanding their suffering, the Belgians organized their resistance. An underground paper called *La Libre Belgique* was published regularly. Many underground papers in French or in Flemish were published in Brussels and in other towns. With great courage, several prominent Belgians, among them Cardinal Mercier, protested repeatedly against the exactions of the Germans.

The Germans tried hard to win the Flemish-speaking part of the Belgian population to their cause. A Flemish administration was set up and the University of Ghent was made into a Flemish university. However, the few traitors who accepted the favors of the Germans were not followed by the mass of Flemings.

The Belgian Court of Appeals arrested two members of the German-appointed Flemish administration. The Germans retaliated by arresting the Chief Justice and two presiding judges of the Court and by sending them to Germany. Whereupon all of the courts in Belgium went on strike in protest against such interference in Belgian justice.

This short account will have shown how Belgium accomplished her duty in the First World War, not only in Europe but also in Africa where she played an important part in the occupation of German East Africa. Inside Belgium, resistance to the occupation was exemplary. The position of the clergy, the judiciary, the communal authorities, and the entire population was admirable.

Historians of the Second World War will recognize the Belgians of 1940 as worthy of those of 1914. The fortunes of war turned against them this time and their initial reverses gave rise to unfavorable comments which all Allied authorities later agreed were completely unjust. Belgium, once more attacked without even an ultimatum, and notwithstanding the hypocritical protestations of Hitler's Pan-Germans—the successors of the Kaiser's Pan-Germans—did her utmost. The Belgian people's heroic resistance to German oppression is one more proof that a free people may be momentarily overrun but never conquered.

~.

CHAPTER VI

Belgium between the Two World Wars

BY JAN-ALBERT GORIS

O
N NOVEMBER 22, 1918, King Albert entered Brussels at the head of his victorious troops. All Belgium was in a
sad state, materially at least. The
euphoric feeling of deliverance and regained freedom could not
entirely atone for the enormous damage to the population and to
the country's equipment wrought by four years of warfare and
destructive German exploitation.

King Albert gave a sober account of his conduct of the war to the
Legislative Assembly. Immediately he began to lead the country
back to normal political life. Strictly loyal to his constitutional
oath, he refused to solve Belgium's many problems through recourse to a temporary authoritarian regime.

The war had destroyed, totally or partially, more than 100,000
private dwellings. More than 300,000 acres of arable land had been
devastated and, through lack of care, the entire Belgian soil had
been weakened, in places even exhausted. The cattle stock had
been reduced by half; 560,000 horned cattle, 250,000 pigs, 35,000
sheep and goats, 92,000 valuable horses, and close to 2,000,000
small poultry had been taken to Germany.

The railroad system had been disrupted by the demolition of
2,400 miles of track, and only 81 locomotives out of 3,470 were left
in the country. Heavy industry had suffered most; in the last
months preceding the evacuation of Belgium, the Germans had
shipped more than 50,000 tons of scrapped machinery a month to
the Reich. Textile factories had been wantonly destroyed. Of 2,554

coke ovens, 1,192 were damaged, and 369 entirely destroyed. Of 51 steel mills, 26 were destroyed and 20 others were damaged. Valuable forests had been plundered, the country and its economic assets had been ruthlessly exploited, regardless of the future, with the sole desire for immediate production.

But, above all, the people had suffered; about 46,000 Belgian soldiers and civilians had lost their lives; 50,000 had been invalided. The deficiency of births amounted to 340,000, the total normal number of births for two full years. Half a million Belgians, 6.5 per cent of the population, were outside the country; 100,000 had to be repatriated from Holland, 110,000 from England, 325,000 from France. Tremendous shifts of population had taken place within the borders; over 1,000,000 Frenchmen had emigrated or had been evacuated to Belgian territory in the course of four years. At the end of the war, 280,000 still lived in Belgium through the aid of relief agencies. More than 83,000 inhabitants of the coastal regions had been moved to the interior. Although the Belgian army had mobilized up to 20 per cent of the male population, the Germans had abducted more than 120,000 able-bodied men for slave labor in Germany, in some districts (Arlon, for example) requisitioning as many as 23 per cent of the male inhabitants. Belgium had been cut off from her markets, her industrial equipment was depleted, stocks and raw material were lacking, and of a population of 7,465,000 inhabitants more than 800,000 people were unemployed.

Although the country's moral prestige in the world was high, its financial situation was far from brilliant; before 1914 the public debt was 4,277,000,000 francs (it rose to 21,800,000,000 in 1919). The fiscal system was antiquated, 47.5 per cent of receipts being derived from excises and duties, direct taxation accounting for no more than 24.6 per cent. The Government bought back the German marks in circulation (7,638,000,000 francs); it endorsed the tremendous expenses in war contributions which the Germans had exacted from the provincial governments, and also paid the extraordinary expenses to which those bodies had been put during the occupation.

Morally, the vast majority of the Belgians realized that perfect "unity of the hearts and wills" for which King Albert in his speech to Parliament had asked. There was no social revolution, there was no nationalist uprising. For a number of questions the King and the Government promised a prompt solution: universal suffrage, the necessary justice to the Flemings, social equality were on the program. The development of these points accounts for a great deal of Belgium's history between 1918 and 1940. There is no doubt, however, that once the last shot had been fired and the flag of triumph had been waved to satiety, the moral atmosphere in Belgium felt the repercussion of the universal disenchantment which was the result of the Treaty of Versailles for almost every nation except Germany. Belgium had not been out for territorial aggrandizement. She wanted the damage done to the country to be repaired, the culprits punished, and a small territory returned to the motherland. She did, in fact, regain Eupen-et-Malmédy and was entrusted with the mandate of Ruanda-Urundi, a German territory, part of which the Belgians had conquered.

When the Treaty of Versailles was signed and it became clear that Belgium's great expectations would not materialize, a real moral uneasiness came over the Belgians. Writing to Prime Minister Léon Delacroix, on June 29, 1919, King Albert expressed public sentiment as follows: "Peace is signed. It does not yet bring to Belgium the full satisfaction which the achievements of her soldiers and the indomitable resistance of her population seemed to give her the right to expect." As a matter of fact, this "full satisfaction" was never given, and the Belgians, although pursuing at the same time an international policy that favored complete reparation and security, turned their main efforts to the restoration of their country.

A coalition cabinet formed under Delacroix was confirmed by the elections of November, 1919, the most striking change since 1914 in that the socialist group in the second chamber nearly equaled the number of Catholics, who for forty years had enjoyed an absolute majority. The three traditional parties profited by their coalition for quite some time, the Catholics retaining a strong position, the Liberals acting as arbiters between the two other parties, and the Socialists seeing to it that everybody should vote the social legislation promised in the *discours du trône* of 1918. By the spring of 1919, the railroad system was so far reëstablished that traffic, both passenger and freight, was almost normal. By 1921 the flooded and devastated areas were again under cultivation. Progressive inheritance taxes were voted, old-age insurance became obligatory, old-age pensions were increased, the eight-hour day became legal in 1921. Already, general suffrage had been introduced; Article 310 of the Penal Code was abolished, thus removing the last hindrance against strikes as a means of defense for the workers. Socialist unions grew from 120,000 members in 1914 to 720,000 in 1920; Catholic unions increased proportionately. Membership of socialist mutual insurance companies went up from 150,000 to 400,000. The increase in membership in similar Catholic organizations was even greater.

The relative harmony of the period was upset only by the refusal of Antwerp dockers to load weapons for the Poles at the time of the Soviet march on Warsaw, and by the popular campaign which found endorsement by all parties, except among the Liberals, for a reduction of the military burden, which was merely an expression of a general reaction against militarism and a manifestation of humanitarian optimism prevailing in most parts of the world. When in 1921 a broken gun, the symbol of the disarmament tendency, was displayed on a socialist flag, the cabinet broke up.

The main problem of the succeeding Theunis Cabinet, which relied on a reinforced Catholic group and on the unaltered liberal group (83 Catholics, 68 Socialists, 33 Liberals after the November, 1921, elections), was, however, economic; this government knew that Germany would not repair the damage done in Belgium and that the country would have to help itself. The solemn declaration of the Allies in December, 1916, that no peace could be signed unless Belgium was "largely indemnified for the damage she had suffered" had to be classified as rhetorical. Exports were still only 70 per cent of imports, and the national currency followed the downward trend whereas the cost of living steadily increased.

Although Belgium received little reparation from Germany, her debts persisted. The Treaty of Versailles freed her from a war debt of 7,000,000,000 francs, but the United States refused to accept the substitution of Germany for Belgium as a debtor. In 1925 a debt of $171,800,000 to the United States was settled by an arrangement permitting payment in 62 annuities without interest. The country still owed $246,000,000 for advances which had permitted the restoration of the devastated land. Debts to Great Britain and to France were subsequently liquidated.

By means of loans, the Theunis Cabinet succeeded in settling conditions and in accomplishing the country's reconstruction. By 1925 the scars of war were practically no longer visible; by 1926, the number of houses rebuilt numbered 120,000. Important public works had been completed: the enlargement of the Charleroi-Brussels Canal, maritime installations at Antwerp, and great harbor works at Ostend, the enormous railroad yards of Schaerbeek and Antwerp-Docks had been built.

Although social legislation progressed normally and without great difficulty during this period—the Rightist government being anxious to outdo the opposition on this point—it was far more difficult to find a satisfactory solution to the most serious internal problem—the Flemish question. The debate centered around the creation of a Flemish university. The Flemish population agreed that the State University of Ghent, where teaching was in French, should be changed to the use of Netherlandish. The opposition felt that the disappearance of a center of French culture, wherever it was located, would be a loss. The Flemish leaders, however, could not accept the fact that in the most typically Flemish town of Flanders an important cultural institution should exist which was alien in spirit and in language to the people of Flanders. After a cabinet crisis, a transitional formula was voted.

The Theunis Cabinet underwent another crisis when its majority failed to approve a trade treaty with France. Belgium, by logical tendency devoted to free trade, had always found it difficult to establish harmonious trade relations with her neighbor, one of Europe's strongest believers in protectionism.

Following the election of April, 1925, the Cabinet moved to the Left; a Catholic-Democratic-Socialist combination was established by the Catholic premier, P. Poullet, and the Socialist leader, E. Vandervelde. It lived on short-term loans (25 in two months), and did not receive the support of the bankers it had frightened, the most extreme members of the majority proclaiming that—if need be—they would resort to "confiscatory financing."

It was replaced by a coalition cabinet under H. Jaspar in May, 1926. With the energetic, often chirurgical help of a financier,

E. Francqui, who acted along the general lines laid down by his less fortunate predecessor, A. E. Janssen, the franc was stabilized at 175 francs to the pound at one-seventh of its original value. Belgium, through the creation of the belga—a measure of controversial utility—returned to the gold standard; taxes increased by leaps and bounds, but the trade balance was again equalized and imports, which in 1926 represented only 77 per cent of exports, went up to 95.5 per cent in 1929. In the same year, the floating debt was practically extinguished. The Belgian railroads, which had been state-owned, were converted into a state-controlled corporation.

Although the small middle classes suffered in the process, the active population profited greatly from the resumption of trade and from the general industrial progress. The country benefited considerably, of course, from the prevailing optimistic tendency of world trade. The second half of the 'twenties, therefore, was a period of high vitality in every respect in Belgium, especially in Flanders. The Kempen region, which, until then, had been a wasteland of poor soil, was gradually transformed into an industrial center. The coal mines of Limburg developed rapidly and proved to be richer and less dangerous to work than the mines of the Borinage. Industries which had been traditionally Walloon in their location sprang up in the northern part of the country; there were glass factories, radium extraction plants, and others. It was as though the center of gravity of the country actually had moved northward.

Under the dynamic leadership of its mayor, Frans van Cauwelaert, the port and the city of Antwerp developed with rapid strides; port installations grew to tremendous proportions, and port traffic, which was 14,146,000 Moorsomtons in 1913, climbed to 23,465,000 in 1930. The booming spirit of the epoch expressed itself nowhere better than in the construction at Antwerp of the Boerentoren, the first skyscraper in Europe.

Under the influence of constant economic progress, the late 'twenties witnessed an ever-increasing interest in scientific and artistic achievements. The Palace of Fine Arts in Brussels, a remarkable building which included concert halls and enormous facilities for expositions, and which was directed with an enterprising spirit, became an artistic center unique in Europe. In 1927, at the initiative of King Albert, a National Fund for Scientific Research was created, and the state universities, as well as the two private institutions for higher learning, improved their installations and even their standing. Parallel to the Royal Flemish Academy of Literature, an Academy for French Language and Literature was created in 1928. Besides the University of Ghent, where teaching was now given entirely in Netherlandish, the University of Louvain developed a bilingual system and Brussels University followed, although slowly, this example. The great scientist, Jules Bordet, received the Nobel prize for medicine and physiology. In 1931 a professor of Brussels University, A. Piccard, was the first man to ascend to the stratosphere.

French literature in that period, already deprived of E. Verhaeren (1917), suffered the loss of its most outstanding novelists and poets—Eekhoud (1927), Giraud (1929), Elskamp (1931). Flemish-Dutch literature knew a new blossoming, the younger generation of novelists proved eager to achieve true universality, and revolted against cozy provincialism. Flemish publishers engaged in many daring and interesting projects. In the plastic arts strong personalities either forcibly continued the impressionist tradition (Opsomer), or deliberately engaged in the expressionist technique (Permeke). Even the applied arts underwent happy changes, and attempts were made to revive tapestry weaving on a wide scale. Tourism flourished, thanks to the excellent roads, the easy communication by rail, and the tremendous development of the hotel industry along the coast, as well as in the Ardennes.

At the moment the international depression hit western Europe, Belgium was ready to celebrate its first century of existence as an independent power. It did so with all necessary pomp and ostentation and was able to show the world that twelve years after the war it had again become a prosperous, high-powered country, technically well organized, socially harmonious, and that even its most burning question—ethnic opposition between the two linguistic groups—could be solved legally, without violence. The World Fairs of Antwerp and Liége (1930), were very successful demonstrations of the technical, artistic, and intellectual achievements of both parts of the country.

Throughout this period, the influence of King Albert made itself felt in a most fortunate manner. His popularity among all parties gave him real prestige and made his intervention in times of crisis very effective. In 1918 the socialist leader, Edward Anseele, had greeted the King with the familiar but heartfelt words: "Everything is fine. We are satisfied with you!" Socialism, which, at the start, had been frankly republican, dropped the issue altogether and appeared reconciled with a constitutional monarchy which lived strictly up to the rules and was, at the same time, fairly democratic and unostentatious in its outward manifestations.

After his marriage to Astrid of Sweden, young Prince Leopold made extensive trips in the colonial territories to prepare for his task and showed a great interest in the welfare of Congo natives and in other colonial problems. Both father and son were instrumental in the creation of a natural reservation in the most typical Congo landscape, the Parc National Albert, and in the organization of the School for Tropical Medicine at Antwerp, named after Prince Leopold. In several critical moments King Albert intervened to stress the fact that the rules of parliamentarianism, like any other rules, should not be carried to absurdity, and that governments should not be overthrown on the pretext of some minor issue. These interventions of the King were extremely valuable in a period when parliamentarianism had a tendency to discredit itself by too numerous changes of cabinet. The King's tragic death in 1934 was a loss to the country. In difficult times he had always happily reminded the Belgians of their reputation for "good sense, moderation, wisdom, and energy." The people were going to need many of these national qualities in the decade from 1930 to 1940.

From 1930 on, the international crisis made itself strongly felt in Belgium. Foreign trade had declined in value by 50 per cent from the 1929 level, and for the first time since 1926 the budget showed a deficit. The country's financial and industrial structure was furthermore endangered by the fact that the banks had participated heavily in industry, which precipitated the crisis of 1935. The most vulnerable organizations were those which, besides their economic functions, also had a social and political significance; the Catholic farmers' corporation, the *Boerenbond,* had evolved from a coöperative into a powerful financial concern that invested in the stock market. When the collapse threatened, the *Boeren-bond,* because of its heterogeneous nature as a coöperative and banking enterprise, was unable to take advantage of the resources of the National Credit Institution for Industry which could help only banks. A panic developed and the ensuing collapse of the bank was responsible for considerable discontent among the rural middle classes. The socialist Banque du Travail, because of failing investments, also had gone bankrupt.

The crisis was fought by a second Theunis Cabinet which engaged energetically in a deflationary policy. State expenses were reduced by 46 per cent, in some sectors by 71 per cent. Salaries in administrative jobs dropped 22 per cent. Small savings were protected by the creation of a government control office in 1934. Unemployment had risen from 42,000 in 1930 to 355,000 in 1935. Soon the Cabinet realized that "the period of deflation was over in Belgium." The Government's efforts at deflation were attacked very sharply by the Socialist party and the credit of the country was undermined by some augurs who, by publicly proclaiming the inevitability of devaluation, destroyed public confidence, and, by precipitating the crisis, created a state of panic.

Thus, in 1935, the country entrusted its fate with enthusiasm and great expectations to the relatively unknown vice-governor of the National Bank, another nonpolitician, Paul van Zeeland. While the Rightist elements—at least most of them—gave Van Zeeland their support in the conviction that something entirely new should be done in the economic field, the Socialists had been prepared for "the Van Zeeland experiment" by the unusually violent propaganda for the Hendrik de Man plan which had been proposed to the masses as a panacea for all financial and social evils. The Van Zeeland Cabinet, in 1935, united all parties in a government of national restoration. It lasted two years and, by its daring methods, presented a contrast with the traditional techniques employed since the end of the war. It was launched after Belgium had proved to be the weakest member of the gold bloc, after commercial banks had collapsed, and her foreign trade had been considerably reduced. At the head of a coalition cabinet, Van Zeeland was, at least in the beginning, spared violent opposition; neither did he suffer the odium of having to apply a deflation policy.

The franc was devaluated 28 per cent more, but the new Cabinet was accepted almost generally in the same spirit as was the New Deal in the United States in 1932, and the ills of devaluation were soon forgotten. Funds were repatriated, money became cheap again, and the stock market boomed.

Drawing lessons from the immediate past, the Government provided for a separation of the deposit and investment functions of banks and for the creation of the Banking Commission that was to supervise the general policy of the banks. In January, 1935, the Rediscount and Guarantee Office for aiding banks, industrial, commercial, and agricultural enterprises, "with a view to the mobilization of their security assets," was created. The National Bank was reorganized, and for some time the belga was considered "the safest currency" in Europe. In an atmosphere of economic optimism, unemployment was reduced from 206,000 to 162,000. Fiscal burdens were also lessened. The only measure taken by the Van Zeeland Cabinet which provoked strong moral criticism, although it greatly improved the country's position, was the *de facto* compulsory conversion of the outstanding national public debt.

In 1935, Brussels' successful exhibition once more drew the attention of the world to Belgium's economic and artistic vitality. It furnished a strong impetus in the field of decorative art, the development of which was even more pronounced in the country's impressive participation in the specialized fairs of Paris (1937), and New York (1939–1940). The Brussels Annual Commercial Fair, attracting general European interest, became the equal of the great fairs at Leipzig, Lyons, Utrecht, and Paris.

Although by about 1937, a series of laws had ensured the Flemish people of equal rights in the schools, in administration, in the judiciary, and in the army, the nationalist movement made progress in Flanders. It had undergone a rather astonishing revolution. Antimilitaristic in its origin and made up, for the most part, of people who could be considered strongly individualistic intellectuals, it evolved more and more in close parallelism to Nazi nationalistic mysticism, while publicly disclaiming any connection with it. The Flemish nationalists successfully exploited certain minor issues, which were bound to occur, since the social evolution of the population and its mentality had not caught up with the legal system of equality. The Flemish question, which originally was a linguistic problem and had become a social problem in the last few decades, was used by the nationalists purely as a political weapon for opposition and agitation. After having abandoned the idea of a federalist Belgium, they went adrift on a vague program of sentimental *rapprochement* to a rather reluctant Holland, and more and more officially proclaimed their sympathy for the New Germany. They joined hands with the Rexists, who had clearly avowed fascist leanings and who recruited their sympathizers chiefly among the middle classes who had suffered three devaluations of their savings in fifteen years. Together they fought the Van Zeeland Cabinet with means which had never been used before in Belgian politics and which are characteristic of totalitarian amorality. These reactionary forces suffered a crushing defeat.[1] It was a great personal victory for Van Zeeland, as well as an affirmation of Belgium's stern belief in the democratic system. When Van Zeeland left office in 1937, the national problems of Belgium were being pushed more and more into the background by the international crisis. The country devoted itself entirely to the organization of its defenses, 20 per cent of the budget was spent on the army, and Belgium lived as an armed camp until the fatal date of May 10, 1940.

In 1938, satisfaction had been given to one of the major claims of the Flemings by the creation of the Flemish Scientific Academy. The last measure which tended to bring about the harmonious development of both language groups in Belgium was the creation of two cultural councils, one for French affairs, another for the Flemish-speaking population. They were supposed to foster cultural advancement, and their significance was so well recognized that they were among the first institutions to be entirely modified by the Germans after the invasion. In 1938, the Flemish University of Ghent was honored by the award of the Nobel prize for physiology to one of its professors, C. Heymans, and in the same year a French-writing Belgian, Charles Plisnier, was the first foreigner to receive the *Prix Goncourt* for one of his novels.

The last great public work—the greatest ever achieved in Belgium—to be completed before the invasion of 1940 was the Albert Canal. It shortened considerably the waterway between Antwerp

---

[1] See Chapter VIII, "Political Parties," by René Hislaire.

and Liége, which until then had been hampered by the existence of twenty-four locks. Formerly, barges traveling that way could not exceed 600 tons; they could now reach 2,000 tons. The canal, which constituted an excellent connection between Antwerp and its hinterland, the Kempen, where, in 1939, 7,000,000 tons of coal were produced, was a great technical achievement because of the difficulty of the terrain. It also was supposed to set up a strategic barrier against an invasion from the east. It was, as a matter of fact, on the Albert Canal that the Belgians withstood the first attack of the Germans on May 10, 1940.

Part Three

POLITICAL AND CONSTITUTIONAL DEVELOPMENT

CHAPTER VII

Constitution and Political Structure of Belgium

BY HENRI E. A. M. ROLIN

CERTAIN ELEMENTS of the political structure of Belgium antedate the Belgian Constitution of February, 1831. The significance of this fact becomes clear when it is remembered that the territory of present-day Belgium had been conquered by the armies of the First French Republic and annexed to France in 1795, to be detached from it only by the Treaty of Paris, May 30, 1814. During the fifteen years which followed (1815–1830), Belgium was merged with Holland into the Kingdom of the Netherlands, from which she was separated in September, 1830, by the insurrection of the Belgian Provinces. Belgium has been independent since that date.

The political structure of Belgium is strictly unitary, as opposed to federal; none of its subdivisions is a state in itself. If a cross section of the country's internal institutions were made, their stratified structure would be revealed: at the base the institutions (or free towns) of the communes; at the next level, those of the provinces; and on top, those concerning Belgium as a whole.

The Belgian Constitution devotes only 2 of its 139 articles to communal and provincial institutions, confining itself to the enunciation of a few general principles. Thus relegated to the background and left more or less shadowy, they do not show up in their true importance.

To begin with, these institutions are older than the institutions of Belgium as a whole. The Belgian communes, numbering 2,670 (according to the Annual Statistics of 1937) form the fundamental basis, the bedrock of the political organization. Antedating the Belgian State by several centuries, evolving in most instances from the parishes of the Roman Catholic Church, they go back to the Middle Ages. They existed and functioned long before the dukes of Burgundy, in the fifteenth century, succeeded in establishing a unified rule over the diverse feudal principalities of the Low Countries.

The provinces, nine in number, correspond geographically to the "departments" organized in Belgium by the French Republic at the time of the annexation in 1795. At the end of French domination, they were renamed after the various principalities of the *ancien régime*.

The Belgian communes and provinces are in no sense mere branches or agencies of the central government. Although their number, their boundaries, and, in the matter of the communes, their very existence, are at the mercy of the lawmakers, they are quite distinct from, and much more important than, local services of the national administration. Each province and each commune is a legal entity and constitutes a distinct governmental power emanating directly from the local electors. This power comprises the legislative (the making of local regulations) and the administrative, but lacks the judiciary. In Belgium, justice is rendered, in all its forms, by the courts and tribunals of the State.

The Constitution delegates to local authorities all matters concerning either the interest of the commune or of the province. However, local authorities are subjected to a certain control by the central authority, which is provided by law with the means of preventing them from overstepping their powers or interfering with the public welfare.

The system is complicated by the fact that, in many respects, the local machinery also serves as an instrument of the central administration, combining this role with its own autonomous activity. This is notably true of the provincial Councils, voted for by the same electors as the legislative Chambers, and of the permanent representatives of the Councils, whose salaries are paid by the State.

The Constitution does not define what is of provincial concern and what of communal concern; it is the business of the law to distinguish between them. It does so on the basis of traditions that are especially strong in the domain of the communes, where autonomy is more complete than in provincial matters.

This municipal autonomy is, and always has been, particularly dear to the Belgian, and foreign invaders have always come into direct conflict with it. They find themselves confronted, not with a mere governmental mechanism, artificially fabricated by lawmakers, but with a piece of *social* structure. Urban centers of population are numerous. From a Belgian city or town, the towers and steeples of neighboring towns are often visible. The more important centers during the Middle Ages often were small states, with a partial sovereignty of their own. Each has its individual history, often a glorious one.

By force of tradition, the communes today still exist as small local democracies, very much alive, where the inhabitants take an active part in the government through their elected representatives. It is through such civil experience that the politically minded get their training for parliamentary careers.

It is clear, then, that the institutions of Belgium, as a whole, go back little farther than one century (1831–1944). The prominence given them by the Constitution reverses the order of seniority, since it is the communes which represent the heritage of the past.

One of the first concerns of the provisional government, as early as October, 1830, was to have a project drawn up for a constitution. Its principal authors were Paul Devaux and J. B. Nothomb. As soon as the National Congress, elected November 3, 1830, had assembled, the national section of the assembly established a general outline which, after some detailed modifications, was adopted as follows: Section One, The Territory and Its Subdivisions; Section Two, Belgians and Their Rights; Section Three, Governmental Powers—(1) Legislative chambers, (2) The king, (3) The judiciary, (4) Institutions of the provinces and communes; Section Four, Finances; Section Five, The Police Force; Section Six, General Provisions; Section Seven, Amendment of the Constitution; and Section Eight, Provisions of a Transitory Nature.

It is significant that the first point studied, and subsequently discussed, was Section Two, Belgians and Their Rights. Above all was the thought that liberty must be guaranteed.

These provisions are different in character from all the others.

They do not *create* for Belgians the rights enumerated in Articles 4 to 24. These are considered as natural rights, in existence before the adoption of the Constitution, and recognized as belonging to the people of Belgium. These rights, being inherent and not granted, could not be taken away from them by any law whatsoever. Such a conception implies adherence to a religious or metaphysical philosophy according to which man is endowed with certain rights by the simple fact of his existence, prior to the formation of any political society.

But the Belgian Constituent Assembly applied this doctrine only to the citizens of their own country. They did not feel called upon to proclaim the "rights of man" in general, as the French Constituent Assembly had done in 1789. The Belgian point of view in this respect is closer to that of the Congress of the United States when it voted the first ten Amendments to the Federal Constitution known as the "Bill of Rights."

It follows logically from this Belgian principle that the provisions in Section Two of the Constitution of 1831 are, by their nature, not subject to amendment or abrogation. Another consequence of the same principle appears in Article 128 of the Constitution— foreigners in Belgium enjoy the protection accorded to persons and property, with certain exceptions which could be stipulated by law.

In theory, these constitutional rights are civil rights dating from time immemorial. The individual of Belgian nationality in possession of such rights is thus proclaimed, in his modest sphere, a small sovereign. Section Two of the Constitution, which enumerates these rights, indicates the limits of each with reference to public authority.

This harvest of inherited freedom is divided into two magnificent series. The first comprises: (1) Individual liberty, which may correctly be called physical liberty, the right of any Belgian citizen to come and go at will, and not be subject to arrest without a warrant; (2) Inviolability of domicile; and (3) Respect for private property. These three freedoms are primarily concerned with material well-being.

The second series concerns what may be called spiritual freedoms, rights of the thinking human being. (1) Freedom of expression in all matters, except for the repression of offenses committed in the exercise of such freedom. The chief application of this is in connection with expressions of religious opinion. The Belgian Constitution, without naming any particular faith or cult, devotes several articles to this subject (14, 15, 16, and 117). The result of these provisions may be summed up as follows: The Belgian State is not legally qualified to dictate in matters of religion. These questions belong to the individual conscience, and, hence, to the churches and associations of the faithful. The State intervenes only for the protection of interested parties. Since it must remunerate the ministers of the different cults, this obligation has led the State to recognize the Roman Catholic Church (most important of all, in fact, because of its numerous adherents in Belgium), the Jewish cult, and the various Protestant sects, united in a Synod. This system of complete freedom and absolute tolerance has had excellent results for more than a century. No church has offered any complaint.

The other spiritual freedoms are corollaries of this fundamental freedom of opinion, confirmed in every instance in the particular field involved: (2) Freedom in education; (3) Freedom of the press; (4) Right of assembly; (5) Right to form associations; (6) Right to petition; (7) Inviolability of the mails; (8) Right to employ (any of) the languages current in Belgium.

Numerous laws define in detail the exercise of these precious individual prerogatives, either singly or in combination. Since the war of 1914–1918, this supplementary legislation has been most evident in the fields of group organization and language.

Around these constitutional liberties, the drafters of the Constitution built, for the Belgians who enjoy them, a system of defenses or entrenchments guarded by the public authorities, or organs of the State. These authorities are grouped in three divisions known as "powers."

The prerogatives exercised by each division are also called "powers;" they are supposed to be of a single nature in each division, but, as a matter of fact, the classification of the powers exercised (of functions) coincides only *grosso modo* with the tripartite classification of the organs of government.

The role and functioning of these authorities, or powers, are carefully regulated by numerous legal texts. In an article of metaphysical aspect (the only one of this character in the Belgian Constitution) it is stated (Article 25) that "all powers emanate from the people," to which is immediately added, "They are to be exercised in the manner established by the Constitution."

In numerous articles, the Constitution specifies that all powers must be exercised in conformance with the law. Article 6 adds that "all Belgians are equal in the eyes of the law."

To interpret these texts literally and out of their factual context—that is, without considering the events which had taken place in America and in Europe during the half-century preceding 1831—would lead to completely erroneous conclusions. However, the Constitution was born in the atmosphere of a Christian civilization which had existed in Belgium for almost fifteen centuries, and its inspiration came from the traditions of the country. The drafters of the Constitution were hostile to the personal power of the kings, but they did not consider the people as omnipotent, and they did not delegate to the assemblies elected by the people unlimited power to govern.

The statement of Article 25 on the origin of governmental powers was merely a refutation of the doctrine, official in France under the *ancien régime,* of the divine right of the Bourbons. To this the people reply firmly: *"We* are the State." The Belgians were simply expressing themselves in a manner similar to that used by the authors of the Federal Constitution of the United States.

Equality in the eyes of the law is a phrase which constitutes a prohibition against making the application of legal provisions dependent upon arbitrary conditions which, in the last analysis, means conditions that violate the spirit of the law itself, and of reason in general. Judges, administrators, even legislators, in the exercise of their respective duties, must not be actuated by prejudices of race, class, religion, or the like—they must not create or observe thus, between citizens, distinctions which favor some and discriminate against others. (As examples of this, see Articles 6, 7, 8, 9, 75, and 94 of the Constitution.)

No article of the Belgian Constitution sets forth explicitly the principle of separation of powers. This famous doctrine, in itself, is not a specific rule of law. It is simply a recommendation addressed by one of the great masters of political science (Montesquieu) to

he makers of constitutions. See to it, he told them, that the differ-
nt powers (legislative, executive, judiciary), that is to say the
rgans of the state, to which are entrusted the corresponding func-
ions, be kept distinct and be sure that the same men are not in-
ested with heterogeneous prerogatives—that is, belonging to two
r three different powers. This recommendation may be followed
n whole or in part.

In Belgium the only power which is completely detached from
he others is the judiciary. The judges, by the very nature of their
unction, look toward the past. They note, as in all countries, in-
ringements of legal order, and prescribe various measures to right
hese wrongs. These tasks they perform in complete independence,
xempt from all interference on the part of those exercising defi-
itely "political" powers (legislation and administration). Even
he Public Prosecutors have very little contact with the Ministers.

It is true that the tribunals are entrusted, in addition, with cer-
ain secondary functions of a more or less administrative nature, as,
or example, a part in the administration of guardianship, or other
ransactions which come under the heading of what is known as
"voluntary jurisdiction." But this constitutes only a slight modi-
ication of the principle that, in Belgium, the judges do nothing
ut judge.

On the contrary, the separation of legislative and executive
ower, as laid down in the Constitution of the United States, is
ot found in the Belgian Constitution. The legislative power is
xercised collectively by the King and the two houses known as
he Chamber of Representatives and the Senate. The King pos-
esses, in addition, the sole executive power. This initial departure
rom Montesquieu's system is increased by the delegation to the
King of the power to make regulations and decrees necessary for
he execution of the laws (Article 67). The making of regulations
which serve as supplements to laws has always been, and has become more and more, a legislative activity.

Although it is stated (Article 65) that the King appoints and
dismisses his Ministers, this must be understood to mean—as it does
in the British parliamentary system—that a Minister in Belgium
keeps his post only as long as he enjoys the confidence and the
support of a majority in the two Houses.

The Representatives and the Senators, thus in a position to ex
ercise a control over most of the acts of the government, participat
in the governing process through an influence which the Minister
are scarcely able to combat. This situation is reinforced by the fac
that the two Houses vote the annual budget (Article 115 of th
Constitution).

Each Minister, it is true, in principle heads a department,
branch of the administration whose personnel owes obedience t
him. The independence of the administration, with reference t
the legislative branch, is thus reduced to the independence of tha
body which the Minister wishes to, or can, preserve for himself
Such being true, one may say that Belgium in reality is governe
by a mixed power, resulting from a close association of the legis
lative and executive branches.

The Constitution (Articles 25 to 30) enumerates the three Power
as: (1) Legislative; (2) Executive; and (3) Judiciary. It is not sur
prising that, since the Constitution was the work of a constituen
and law-making assembly, in the minds of its makers the two
Houses served as the main pillars of the State, the laws made by
them exercising the sovereign control. This was all the more natu
ral since, at the time the Constitution went into effect, Belgium
did not yet have a King.

When Leopold I was elected and then inaugurated, it is likely
that in the minds of many members of the Parliament, the King
as chief of the Executive Power, was destined to become simply
the second essential wheel of the political machine. In a monarchy
with a cabinet government, the use of the royal veto is, perforce
very rare.

As for the courts of justice, the men of politics have always
treated them with respect, without seeming to fear them. In fact,
they appoint the judges. The judiciary corps themselves limited
their own role by deciding, after some hesitation, that it did not be
long to the Judiciary Power to pass on the constitutionality of laws.

For a century past, events have contributed to an interpretation
of the Constitution tending toward an increase in the importance
of the role played by the King and his Ministers.

There may be cited as causes for the origin and accentuation
of this trend, the individual talents of the successive representatives

of the dynasty; the appearance of a new mechanism, the Ministerial Council, barely suggested in the Constitution; the difficulty and growing complication of the lawmaking process. The Houses themselves have recognized this and have consented to have more and more frequent recourse, even in peace time, to legislation in the form of decrees. The war of 1914–1918, the economic crises which ensued, and the invasion of 1940 must also be mentioned as factors in this development.

The Belgian constitution-makers of 1830–1831 deliberately chose the monarchical form of government in preference to a republican form, and experience has shown that they chose well. The crown passes to the descendants of Leopold I, in the male line, by order of primogeniture, and with the perpetual exclusion of women and their descendants (Article 60 of the Belgian Constitution).

The Belgian Constitution devotes only six articles (86 to 91) to the Cabinet Ministers. No special prerequisites in education, not even age limits are fixed. Legally, the only requirements for an appointment as Minister are to be native born (or to have become Belgian by the process of "grand" naturalization) making the subject eligible to high office; and not to be a member of the royal family. The appointment is made by royal decree. The King decides the number of Cabinet Ministers; from five at the outset, the number has gradually risen to twelve. The Legislative Houses can control this number at will, since they are called upon to vote the budget.

Here, more than ever, the facts must be known in order to grasp the realities of the situation. The King's choice falls almost invariably upon members of one House or the other. This is because there is an unwritten condition of capital importance to be met before any appointment to ministerial functions can become effective; if the appointee is to have any chance of remaining in his position, he must have a sufficient amount of support from the two Houses.

In back of this procedure is the fact that the principal function of the Ministers, in a constitutional sense, is to assume responsibility for the acts of the King. In fact, "no act of the King can be put into effect unless it is countersigned by a Minister, who thus renders himself responsible" (Article 64). The King cannot be held to account for his acts; his person is inviolable.

These rules have a double effect. First, the Ministers are really in the position of agents for the legislative branch, in relationship to the King. Second, the people can benefit from the King's initiatives, where such are required, in the domain where personal action is open to him; but such initiatives cannot go against the people if the majority condemns them (rightly or wrongly); in such event the Ministers must refuse to countersign, or must resign from their posts.

The purely military decisions of the King, made in his capacity as Commander in Chief of the Belgian forces on land or sea, become effective without the ministerial countersignature. This is the only exception to the rule established by Article 64. Any inability of the King to reign (for example, where he is taken prisoner by the enemy) invests the ministerial Council with all the royal powers.

The whole system of government established by the Belgian Constitution is founded on the principle that in all political debate, the public will is the supreme arbiter, and its decision is final. This is implicit in the text of Article 25: All powers emanate from the people.

The concrete functioning of this conception involves: (1) The institution of the two Houses, called the Chamber of Representatives and the Senate, which are supposed to be a faithful reflection of the public will; (2) The election of members to these two assemblies, in conformance with the rules laid down by the Constitution itself; (3) The existence of political parties, more or less stable and organized, as the framework in which the electors are grouped.

This last element, although it plays an essential role in the functioning of the political machine, is provided for by no specific text, probably because it is difficult, if not impossible, to define in a legal text exactly what is to be understood by "parties," and because it would be even more complicated to subject their formation, their activity, and eventually their dissolution, to legal rules. Experience has shown that the existence of two or three parties (at the most), provided they are strongly organized, has a beneficial effect on the recruiting of parliamentary personnel, and permits a clear-cut mandate from the electorate. A more profound examination of the fairly troublesome problems of political philosophy does not belong within the scope of this chapter.

The method of election for members of the legislature has been the principal question involved in the two amendments to the Belgian Constitution which have been undertaken since its inception (in 1893 and in 1920–1921). The latter amendment had the effect of enlarging the electorate by extending suffrage to practically all men twenty-one years of age, and to certain limited classes of women. In addition to those Senators voted for directly by the electors, the Senate includes Senators elected by the provincial Councils and others (called coöptative) elected by the Senate itself. Elections are held every four years, and voting is obligatory and secret. The system is one of proportional representation. There are 202 members in the Chamber of Representatives and 167 in the Senate.

The regime indicated above, in harmony with the age-old democratic traditions of Belgium, produces results which, in general, are satisfactory. One can scarcely say that the masses are sufficiently educated or clear-sighted to dictate spontaneously, and in all respects, measures which meet the real needs of the people. As in every country, it is the real statesmen who foresee what the general interests of the country demand, and even they are not always permitted by circumstances to carry out their conceptions. But, since the day of its independence, Belgium has not been ill-served in this respect. The country has not been torn by overviolent factions, nor has it fallen a prey to unscrupulous demagogues. Belgium possesses a general spirit of moderation which has contributed much to the success of its parliamentary institutions.

The elective system for judges, applied in Belgium during the first years of the French domination of the country, had not produced satisfactory results. It was abolished under the Consulate of Bonaparte. The organization of the judiciary, as it emerged from these reforms, was still in effect in Belgium in 1830. The makers of the Constitution maintained this organization, confining themselves to the establishment of certain guarantees, and the reëstablishment of certain institutions which had been suppressed under the Dutch regime (a Supreme Court of Appeals, for example, as well as trial by jury in criminal cases and in offenses connected with politics and the press). Various modifications, also, were made by a number of Belgian laws between 1831 and 1940. These changes have not destroyed the general resemblance which persists between the Napoleonic judiciary institutions and those of Belgium.

Since 1831, all judges in Belgium—with the exception of members of the commercial tribunals—are appointed by the King, under the responsibility of the minister who countersigns the decree of appointment. The free choice of the King, which is, in fact, that of the Minister, is limited only by legal rules governing the age and qualifications of the candidates for office in the lower courts (justices of the peace and judges of courts of the first instance).

The promotion of judges, however, depends on a system of nomination of candidates, and only by this system can the King make an appointment. The nominations being made, as the case may be, by the Court of Appeals or by the Supreme Court of Appeals and by certain political assemblies (who, in fact, usually base their nominations on those of the judiciary), the system works out in practice, for the higher positions, as one of coöptation. The Courts choose for the vacancies which occur the judges whom they consider the best qualified.

Functioning with most Belgian courts is a Public Prosecutors' Department (equivalent to the Attorney General and his Adjoints, the District Attorney and his Deputies, as well as other officials). All are appointed by the King and subject to dismissal. But in actual fact they are completely independent.

The Belgian courts have always judged civil and criminal cases brought before them with an absolute independence not only imposed by law but based on time-honored traditions. In the matter of administering justice in Belgium there are practically no examples of corruption, or even of partiality.

CHAPTER VIII

Political Parties

BY RENÉ HISLAIRE

THE HISTORY OF political parties in Belgium dates no farther back than the period of Belgium's reunion with Holland (1815–1830). From the beginning of this period, as soon as the Belgians were merged with the Dutch by the decision of the Congress of Vienna, two parties are distinguishable in Belgium—the Catholics and the Liberals.

The Catholics, direct descendants of those who led the struggle a quarter of a century earlier against Joseph II of Austria were, during the early years of the Dutch regime, what may be called ultramontanists. They felt in duty bound to demand for the Church that preëminence which it had enjoyed under the old regime.

The Liberals, on the contrary, great readers of the eighteenth-century philosophers, proclaimed themselves partisans of the revolutionary principles of 1789, and considered as their charter the "Declaration of the Rights of Man and of Citizens." Stating that they wished to put the Church in its place, they openly displayed an anticlericalism in doctrine which, among some of them, reached the point of anti-Catholicism. One of their number, one of the most fiery and the most popular, Louis de Potter, wrote several volumes in which he denounced the "crimes of the Popes."

Between these two trends of Belgian opinion any accord seemed difficult, if not impossible. For several years, King William skillfully made the most of this hostility. But in 1828 the faults of the Dutch regime made it clear to the most intelligent of the Catholic and Liberal leaders that they would get nowhere unless they succeeded in forming a common front.

This movement was facilitated by the attitude of the young Catholics who were under the influence of the "liberal" French Catholics Lamennais, Montalembert, Lacordaire. These young Catholic soon came to consider as belonging definitely to the past the privi leges of the clergy, the tithes, and the ecclesiastical courts. Ove the heads of their bishops, they sympathized with modern concep tions of liberty. On their side, the young Liberals broke, more o less openly, with the anti-Catholicism of their elders. They realizec that, in a country where nine-tenths of the inhabitants attendec mass, they could not hope to enlist the body of the people in : policy of war against the Church.

Thus in 1828 unionism was born. In the *Courrier des Pays-Bas* Louis de Potter extended the hand of reconciliation to the Catho lics, and the latter responded enthusiastically. In complete accord the Catholics and Liberals decided to fight for the freedom of the press, freedom of association, freedom of education, freedom o religion—the "Four Freedoms."

This accord was at the basis of the Belgian Revolution which, ir 1830, destroyed the work of the Congress of Vienna and, by the separation of the Northern Provinces and the Southern Provinces, forged the independence of Belgium. It remained the basis of the charter of the provisional government which was composed of Liberals and Catholics, youthful, ardent enthusiasts: Baron E. van der Linden d'Hooghvorst, F. de Mérode, A. Jolly, Sylvain van de Weyer, A. Gendebien, Charles Rogier, Louis de Potter, J. Vander linden, Baron de Coppin, and J. Nicolay. It dominated the elec tions for the Constituent Assembly; in many places Catholics and Liberals presented themselves to the voters on the same list. It inspired the drafters of the Constitution themselves who, faithful to the principles on which they had been elected, voted a constitu tion of which the greatest of the Belgian historians, Henri Pirenne, said: "It is the most complete and purest type imaginable of a par liamentary and liberal constitution. For a half-century it has stood as a model of its kind, a masterpiece of political wisdom. It has exercised a direct and often profound influence on all the States which, in the course of the nineteenth century, have revised or elaborated their institutions along parliamentary lines. Not one of them, however, has gone so far in accepting the consequence of these parliamentary principles, accorded such a large measure of freedom, and left the government of the people so entirely to the people themselves."

The unionism of 1828, which had survived the Revolution, was maintained in spite of some friction until 1847. It had almost gone down in 1832 when Pope Gregory XVI, after condemning Lamennais, launched his well-known encyclical against the modern freedoms. Some Catholics believed that this encyclical condemned the very principles on which the Belgian Constitution was constructed, particularly freedom of religion and freedom of the press. But several of the most esteemed Catholic leaders among the drafters of the Constitution, notably De Mérode and Canon de Haerne, defended the famous theory of "thesis and antithesis." They publicly proclaimed: "The encyclical is not binding upon us in political matters." As the Belgian bishops took good care not to repudiate them, their theory carried without difficulty.

Independent Belgium, at the beginning of its existence, thus escaped a grave danger. Conservative Europe, inheriting its ideas from the Congress of Vienna, eyed the new country with suspicion. King William of Holland had not yet recognized the decisions of the Congress of London. The King of Prussia and the Tsar of Russia, attached to the King of Holland through family ties, awaited an opportunity to intervene and bring the Southern Provinces of the Low Countries back under the House of Orange. If the Belgian Catholics had interpreted Gregory XVI's encyclical in the narrow sense and had broken the constitutional covenant, the England of Palmerston and the France of Talleyrand could not have saved the young kingdom which the Austria of Metternich regarded as a dangerous nest of revolutionaries.

The accord between Catholics and Liberals was easy to maintain since, on most of the questions of the day, the two groups were of the same opinion. The electorate, composed of less than 100,000 out of nearly 4,000,000 inhabitants, represented only the well-to-do classes, nobles, upper bourgeois, property owners, industrialists, and landed farmers who paid a certain amount of taxes, known as the *cens*. The theory was that those who had nothing and paid no taxes should have no part in the government of the State, since the essential task of Parliament was to control public finances. The theory sounds fantastic today, but then it was not even questioned.

As representatives of the same class, the Catholic and Liberal parliamentarians were in complete agreement on social questions. Or rather, the social question simply did not exist for them. The salary of the worker was governed entirely by the law of supply and demand, and nobody thought of a minimum wage, limited working hours, nor, obviously, of such things as family allowances, pensions, or social security. The unemployed had no rights, except to appeal to public charity, to official welfare bureaus, or to the societies of St. Vincent de Paul.

Because of freedom of education, the bishops had reopened the already celebrated Catholic University of Louvain, whereas the Liberals, on the appeal of Théodore Verhaegen, one of the leaders in Free Masonry in 1834, founded the University of Brussels on the principle of freedom of thought. In addition, two state universities were soon installed, one at Ghent and the other at Liége, where Catholic and liberal professors officiated side by side, though the latter constituted the large majority.

With the fall of the B. T. de Theux unionist Cabinet in April, 1840, an entirely liberal Cabinet under J. L. J. Lebeau and Charles Rogier was formed. There was little change, however, in general policy, this cabinet associating itself with a unionist program. In a few months, however, it was forced to yield place to a unionist Cabinet presided over by Jean-Baptiste Nothomb.

Nothomb succeeded in getting the Parliament to vote almost unanimously the last law of a unionist character—the law of March 24, 1842, on primary instruction. Up to that time, most of the rural communities had only private Catholic schools, whereas the larger cities had organized public schools. The law of 1842 required every community to support a primary public school. Still, the clergy were given the right to supervise religious teaching in these schools, and furthermore the communities, instead of creating new schools, could adopt the existing private schools, even though the teachers were men or women of the religious orders.

The majority of the Liberals had voted for this law through a desire to see each community endowed with a school. But, since in more than 80 per cent of the communities the public school was simply the Catholic school with a change of name, the Liberals soon felt they had been deceived.

Thus the Congress of Liberals meeting in Brussels in 1846 was to bring unionism to an end. Belgium as a nation was on firmer ground. Its existence was no longer questioned by the chancelleries of Europe, and, since 1839, even the King of Holland had accepted, with more or less good grace, the decisions of the Congress of London. Belgium could therefore, with some impunity, allow itself the luxury of party disputes. Furthermore, the normal functioning of a parliamentary regime demanded a majority to support the government of its choice, and a minority to check and criticize.

The Liberal Congress of 1846, in which Defacqz and Frère-Orban played the leading roles, established a program with the following as its principal points: (1) Complete and real independence of the civil power in all domains; (2) Organization of education in all its degrees under secular authority; (3) Free trade; (4) Improved conditions of life for the workers and the poor.

This last point appeared for the first time on the program of a Belgian party. For a long time it was to remain a dead letter. Belgian industry was progressing rapidly. But this progress for many years was to benefit only the bourgeois class, blindly obedient to the egotistical order of Guizot: "Get rich!" The working class was to wait almost half a century for the foundation of the Socialist party and the encyclical, *Rerum Novarum,* before obtaining its share of the profits—reasonably decent living conditions.

On August 12, 1847, Charles Rogier formed a Liberal Cabinet. When he appeared before the Houses of Parliament, he announced his intention of breaking with the past and governing according to the program of his party. From that time until August 4, 1914, the date of the German invasion, Belgium was to have party governments that were either purely Catholic or purely Liberal.

The voters on June 13, 1848, endorsed the program of Rogier. Their approval was manifested by the election of 85 Liberal and only 23 Catholic representatives. Rogier thought the moment had come to apply the program of his party in the matter of education. Too cautious to introduce again the law of 1842 on elementary schooling, he had passed in 1850 a law on secondary instruction which created 10 "Athenées" and 50 secondary schools supported by the State. This law provided that religion should be taught in the newly created schools. But the bishops, fearing that the competition of the Athenées would reduce the enrollment in the flourishing Catholic seminaries, forbade the clergy to teach religion in the official secondary establishments.

The elections of 1854 gave a slight majority to the Catholics. The Rogier Cabinet gave way to that of P. Dedecker. When the latter brought up a bill for charitable foundations, his adversaries launched a lively campaign throughout the country, accusing the Catholic government of trying, through the interpretation of this law, to reëstablish for the benefit of the religious communities the mortmain abolished by the French Revolution, which had left most distasteful memories in the provinces. Rereading the fairly harmless bill of Dedecker today, it is hard to conceive of its being given such a construction. However that may be, the campaign waged against what was dubbed the "convent law" swept out the first purely Catholic Cabinet, and on December 10, 1857, the electors sent to the House a solid liberal majority (70 Liberals as against 38 Catholics). The Cabinet of Charles Rogier—H. J. W. Frère-Orban—which came into power at that time, was to exist for thirteen years.

The new Liberal Cabinet featured in its program what it called "the protection of liberty against the attacks of the Church." It put through a series of laws designed to diminish the influence of the clergy. Among them were the law on charitable foundations (1859), the law repressing vicious attacks made in the pulpit against the State or individuals (1862), the law creating scholarships (1860), and finally, the law on religious revenues (1870).

In 1863, the first grand Catholic Congress, meeting at Mechlin, reorganized the Catholic party and gave ear to the great voice of Montalembert. About the same time two trends began to be manifest in the heart of the Liberal party which eventually came into violent opposition: the doctrinarians, attached to economic liberalism, to the Manchester theory of *laissez faire, laissez passer;* and the progressives who sought a betterment of conditions for the poor and the working classes, and their right to the franchise.

In 1870, the Cabinet of Rogier—Frère-Orban—in power since 1857, seemed to have outlived its usefulness. The electors having returned only 61 Liberals as against 59 Catholics and 4 antiministerial dissidents, the young King, Leopold II, entrusted the power to the Catholic, J. d'Anethan, succeeded a few weeks later by the

Cabinet of B. T. de Theux and J. Malou. In spite of its lack of a real majority, this Cabinet managed to govern without much trouble. Indeed, internal quarrels had passed into the background of the preoccupations felt by the Belgian people. The Franco-Prussian War broke out, and the chief concern of the Government was to protect Belgium's frontiers in an effort to keep out of the conflict. The Government was successful. Belgium confined its activities to taking in, caring for, and feeding the wounded of the two camps, as well as the French refugees, both civil and military, fleeing before the disaster at Sedan.

The pendulum swung back again in 1878. The Liberals had a majority both in the House and the Senate, and Frère-Orban, who had been Charles Rogier's second from 1857 to 1870, and head of the Liberal opposition, was asked by the King to form a government. He did not follow the wise course of his former chief. Urged on by his friends, for whom anticlericalism had become the dominating passion—especially after the encyclical, *Quanta Cura,* and the proclamation of the *Syllabus,* formal condemnation of modern ideas—Frère-Orban authorized his Minister of Education, Pierre van Humbeeck, to introduce on January 21, 1879, a bill revising the law of March 24, 1842, on elementary teaching. This bill made it obligatory that each community have at least one public school. The communities could not entrust this school to religious instructors. Nor could they adopt the private schools. Not wishing to incur too violent friction with Catholic opinion, however, the bill authorized optional religious instruction in the school buildings outside of class hours.

This precaution was useless. Against what was soon called the "law of ill omen," the Catholics rose as a man. The bill was passed, nonetheless, by a majority of one vote in the Senate. The bishops led the opposition. They even went so far as to decree that the sacraments be refused to the official teachers and to the parents who sent their children to the public schools. At the same time, because of millions of francs collected throughout the country, the Catholics erected schools everywhere, directly opposite the official school. The struggle went on fiercely for more than four years. Though the Liberal majority was sustained in the elections of 1882, this was no longer true in 1884, when the Catholics obtained a majority of 36.

To put this school program into effect, the Frère-Orban Cabinet had had to impose a considerable increase in taxes, a move perhaps more displeasing than the law itself to an electorate which was based on property assessments. This explains why the Brussels bourgeois, in large part Liberals, nevertheless elected the whole list of Catholic candidates, who had had the astuteness to camouflage themselves with an "independent" label.

Frère-Orban resigned. Neither he nor his Liberal friends were ever again to regain power. The Catholics were to keep it during the period of thirty years up to the First World War.

While the Catholic and Liberal parties were thus alternating in power, a new party was evolving, a party to acquire more and more importance. On January 12, 1879, a hundred or more intellectuals and workers, meeting in Brussels, founded the Belgian Socialist party. This step remained totally unknown to the public, since no newspaper even mentioned it.

In the following year, Edward Anseele and a few of his friends founded at Ghent, citadel of the great textile "barons," the coöperative *Vooruit* (Forward). It formed the point of departure for the Belgian coöperative movement, and, in a way, for Belgian workers' unions which were to be the most constructive and realistic aspects of Belgian socialism.

Similar groups sprang up in other cities of the country. They combined in August, 1885, at Antwerp, when the delegates of the entire country laid the foundations of the Belgian Labor party, and worked out a detailed program. The working class, this program declared, demanded the abolition of a property qualification for voters and the establishment of universal suffrage; it also demanded protective legislation regulating labor for women and children, determination of the length of the working day, workers' insurance for accident, illness, and old age, and a tax on incomes. Finally, the party came out for the republican system of government.

With the exception of the last point, all the articles of the party program were singularly moderate and had long been sanctioned by Belgian legislation. But sixty years ago they seemed very revolutionary. It must be recalled that, at that time, the workers had the right only to accept the jobs offered them or appeal to public charity. The liberal individualism of the nineteenth century refused them the right to unionize. Any concerted strike among them exposed the workers to trial and condemnation for conspiracy, even though the strike remained entirely nonviolent.

In 1886, however, violent strikes, accompanied by rioting, did break out in the mines, and among the metal and glass workers of the Liége and Hainaut provinces—strikes provoked by low wages, excessive length of the working day, and the desire of the workers to obtain recognition of their right to unionize. The new Labor party energetically supported the strikers, who also received the sympathetic support of a large number of young intellectuals from both the Right and the Left. For the first time the Parliament, elected by a suffrage based on property qualification, came to understand that such a thing as a social question actually existed. The head of the Catholic government of the period, Auguste Beernaert (he had replaced Malou when King Leopold II dismissed the two most outstanding Catholic Ministers, the leaders of bourgeois anti-militarism, Charles Woeste and Victor Jacobs), was a man of clear vision, not intimidated by the decision for bold action. He instituted a vast inquiry into the conditions of the workers, an inquiry which revealed a situation not to be tolerated. He introduced and persuaded Parliament to pass a series of bills, notably the following: (1) A bill forbidding women and children to work in the depths of the mines; (2) A bill regulating the work to be performed by women; and (3) A bill forbidding child labor under the age of twelve. Moderate as these reforms were, they did not pass without opposition. Most of the Catholic Senators and Representatives voted for them, in response to the appeal of their leader, as did the progressive Liberals. But this came about only after lively debate in which certain Catholics, grouped around Charles Woeste and Victor Jacobs, and the doctrinary Liberals, grouped around Frère-Orban, maintained in particular that, by forbidding women and children to work in the mines, the Parliament would attack the right to work—the right of the worker to work where he pleased and as long as he pleased!

While the Labor party was being consolidated, meanwhile covering the entire country with "People's Houses," coöperatives, and unions, a strong democratic movement developed in the heart of the Catholic party, and the progressives defended the advanced theories in the heart of the Liberal party. To the young Catholics, eager for more social justice in the relations between employers and employees, the encyclical, *Rerum Novarum,* of Pope Leo XIII, on the condition of the workers (1891), brought valuable encouragement and substantial support. Jules Renkin, Henri Carton de Wiart, Léon de Lantsheere in Brussels, the Abbé Daens at Aalst, Godefroid Kurth, Abbé Pottier and Charles de Ponthière at Liége united—as did the Laborites and the Progressives—in demanding, along with a series of social reforms, the institution of universal suffrage as the only means of giving the laboring classes a voice in the conduct of the State.

Gradually the evolution took place; the maintenance of a property qualification for suffrage appeared less and less desirable, especially in view of the fact that the dogged determination of the privileged classes to maintain it risked the provocation of more and more general political strikes which, in the end, would have developed into an open revolutionary movement. Auguste Beernaert understood this all the more clearly in view of the insistence of the young Christian Democrats, which was an organization as strong as its leader. Beernaert therefore had a Constituent Assembly elected (in the House: 92 Catholics and 60 Liberals; in the Senate: 46 Catholics and 30 Liberals) and entrusted with revising the Constitution. After lengthy debate and the rejection of a series of drafts, a majority finally agreed on the following formula: (1) Every male Belgian citizen, enjoying civil and political rights, obtained the right to vote for members of the Legislature; (2) A second, and even third, vote was accorded to property-holding citizens, to those who met certain requirements of the property qualification, or who possessed a diploma of higher learning.

This was not universal suffrage, pure and simple. But, as it was, this plural suffrage constituted an immense advance over the suffrage based entirely on property assessment. The right to vote was no longer restricted to the bourgeois class.

The results of the first elections (October 14, 1894) conducted according to the new formula, were encouraging to the Catholics and disappointing to the Liberals. The former were returned to Parliament, 104 strong, whereas the latter had only 14 left. As for the Laborites, they obtained a sizable representation, winning on their first round 34 seats in the House.

This Catholic majority was to persist, although gradually diminishing, to the First World War. Its existence was brought about by the moderate policy pursued by the majority of the governments which succeeded each other in power: the cabinets of J. de Burlet, P. de Smet de Naeyer, A. Vandenpeereboom, J. de Trooz, F. Schollaert, and Charles de Broqueville. It was distinguished, on the whole, by the cultivation of the middle ground, the "happy medium" so well calculated to appeal to the Belgian electorate. In 1899 P. de Smet de Naeyer succeeded in getting proportional representation adopted, and this reinforced the Liberal group. Numerous social laws were passed. In 1909, Schollaert put through the law for individual military service by a majority made up of only part of the Catholics and the entire block of Liberals and Laborites. It may be noted in passing that at the International Socialist Congress at Amsterdam, the Belgian Labor party in no uncertain terms declared itself against revolutionary action. Finally in 1912, when the storm was approaching, De Broqueville was fortunate enough to win the support of all his political adherents and a part of the opposition for a bill to increase considerably the Belgian army. It was because of De Broqueville's foresightedness that the Belgian troops in 1914 were able to hold up the German invasion long enough for France to complete her mobilization.

On the very day that Belgian neutrality was violated by Germany, the head of the Government, Charles de Broqueville, informed the House that, on his proposal, King Albert had decided to associate with the Government the Liberal leader, Paul Hymans, and the Labor leader, Emile Vandervelde. From that day to this, all Belgian governments have been coalition governments, usually including representatives of the three parties (Catholic, Liberal, and Labor), more rarely representatives of the Catholic and Liberal parties, and, on one occasion (Poullet Cabinet), representatives of the Catholic and Labor parties. The Prime Ministers succeeding each other during this period all belonged, with two exceptions (the Liberal, Paul-Emile Janson, and the Laborite, Paul-Henri Spaak) to the Catholic party. They were De Broqueville, Cooreman, Léon Delacroix, Georges Theunis, Henri Carton de Wiart, A. van de Vyvere, P. Poullet, Jules Renkin, Henri Jaspar, Paul van Zee land, and Hubert Pierlot. These coalition governments succeeded in settling the quarrels about religion and education by adopting conciliatory formulas which satisfied more or less the moderate elements of all three parties. These governments made it possible for a Belgium devastated and ruined by the invasion to bind up her wounds and reconstruct her destroyed cities in an atmosphere of national harmony.

On the morrow of the 1918 victory, the Delacroix Cabinet, in accord with King Albert, replaced plural suffrage by universal suffrage—one man, one vote. The elections which followed changed the character of Parliament considerably. The Catholics, with 73 of their number elected, remained the most numerous. But many conservative members had been replaced by Christian Democrats and by Flemish Nationalists. Laborites numbered 70, almost as many as the Catholics; the Liberals, 34. New parties appeared for the first time on the political horizon: the War Veterans had 2 representatives; the National Renaissance, 1; the Small Trades men, 1; and the Frontists, or Flemish Nationalists, at the outset, won 5 seats.

During the years immediately preceding the war of 1914, the Flemish question had taken on an actively dangerous character. Belgium in 1830 had recognized the complete theoretical equality of the languages. But in practice, although Flemish was the language of more than half the population, French, as the language of the ruling classes and of the property-qualified electors, had become the language of administration, of justice, and of secondary and higher education. This policy finally was intolerable in the eyes of most of the Flemings. A reaction had set in, and before the first invasion, the Franck-Segers Law had organized secondary schooling in Flemish. It was only a first step, and certainly did not go far enough. During the period between the two wars, the Belgian Parliament, often after bitter debate, was to satisfy most of the legitimate demands of the Flemings.

But in the meantime, during the war of 1914–1918, the Germans did their utmost to sow discord in Belgium. They found a few misguided Flemish intellectuals and with them formed a Council of Flanders entrusted with the government of Flemish Belgium, which they separated from Walloon Belgium. They replaced the French University of Ghent with a Flemish University, which was immediately called the "Von Bissing University."

At the time of the Armistice, most of the Activists of the Council of Flanders followed the troops of occupation in their retreat across the Rhine or fled to Holland. But they left descendants and followers of their cause who formed the Frontist or National Flemish party. Too astute to proclaim themselves inheritors of the Activists, the Flemish Nationalists emphasized only the Flemish claims, and declared themselves alone capable of getting redress for Flemish wrongs. Each time Parliament adopted laws designed to reëstablish in all fields equality between the French-speaking and Flemish-speaking parts of the country, they "raised the ante," thus winning the support of a portion of the electors. They had 5 representatives in 1919, 4 in 1921, 6 in 1925, 10 in 1929, 8 in 1932, 16 in 1936, and 17 finally in 1939. From the beginning of the German occupation in 1940, many of them threw off their masks, thereby acknowledging the fact that they were agents of Germany, as they had been called. Thus they lost all credit with their electors of the day before, who turned from them, condemning them as traitors.

The cohesion of the Labor party, the strength of its coöperatives and its unions, prevented the Communists from becoming more than an insignificant minority in Belgium. They had 2 members in the House in 1925, 1 in 1929, 3 in 1932, 9 in 1936, and 9 in 1939. During the occupation the Communists were indistinguishable from the rest of the Belgian population and showed themselves as patriotic and as strong in resistance as anybody else. Most of their representatives have been arrested by the Germans. Several have been shot, or have died in concentration camps.

It was only at the end of 1935 that the Rexist party was created. Its founder, Léon Degrelle, a journalist with a gift in the use of invective, made his political debut by a bold stroke. On November 2d he got into the hall of the little town of Courtrai, where the Congress of Catholic Associations and Clubs was in session, and, addressing the Catholic leaders in language of unprecedented violence, screamed: "We of the younger generation are here to take your places, to empty your decanters, and sound the clarion. Your regime is rotten. You have made money out of the souls of our children. We will purge the entire country, and throw you out."

The next day, Léon Degrelle was famous. He launched a campaign of meetings throughout the country, he flooded the tiniest village with copies of his paper, *Le Pays Réel,* and in the election of May 24, 1936, the Rexist party won 21 seats in the House.

This success was the outcome of several factors. First of all, just like Mussolini or Hitler, Léon Degrelle had an astounding dynamism as a "tribune of the people." Furthermore, he exhibited an exaggerated patriotism. He had founded his party at the moment when the economic depression of recent years was beginning to weigh heavily on the middle classes. While proclaiming himself the adversary of "international high finance," he was being subsidized (as was later proved) by big businessmen who were disturbed by the bold policy of the Van Zeeland government in both economic and social matters. To some he represented himself as more Catholic than the Pope, to others more royalist than the King. Among his warmest partisans were representatives of the Belgian nobility who had not yet come to understand that their role as a ruling class had ended and who dreamed of royal dictatorship, with themselves as the agents of its execution. These partisans included army officers, more or less tainted with Fascism; conservative Catholics, tired of the national union which left to the Laborites too much influence in the direction of the affairs of the country to suit them; petty bourgeois, people with small incomes, small businessmen, petty employees—a sort of white-collar class which had been the first victims of the successive devaluations of the currency. In a word, Degrelle grouped around him the many malcontents, good solid people for the most part, and good patriots too, but people who completely lacked political, or even critical, sense.

In Parliament the action of the Rexist group was purely negative, insult replacing argument. By their very extremes, the Rexist representatives did their utmost to discredit the parliamentarian regime. Léon Degrelle believed, however, that he had public opinion on his side. To force himself into power, he attempted to get the support of a plebiscite. He persuaded one of the Rexist representatives of Brussels to resign, and thus forced a partial election in which he was a candidate. But the Prime Minister, Paul van

Zeeland, took up the challenge. Van Zeeland went before the electors as a candidate himself, as the opponent of Degrelle, and was elected on April 11, 1937, by 275,840 votes as against only 69,242 cast for his Rexist competitor.

The decline of Degrelle was rapid. No man, and certainly not Degrelle, could successfully play the role of apprentice dictator in a country so attached to its constitutional liberties as Belgium. Not being authorized to speak on the Belgian state radio, he obtained permission from Mussolini to use the station at Milan. This intrusion of Fascist Italy into the internal politics of Belgium aroused the indignation of the population. Meanwhile, the rumor was spreading that the coffers of the Rexist party were fed by subsidies from Mussolini and Hitler. A trip which Degrelle made to Berlin appeared extremely suspicious. Thus, at the elections of April 2, 1939, the Rexist party lost 17 of the 21 seats it had won in 1936.

With the invasion, the Belgians as a whole united with the Government in refusing free passage to the German armies. The Rexist party was no longer anything but a general staff without troops, a group of a few dozen adventurers. With Degrelle at their head, they flung themselves at the knees of the occupying forces, begging, this one a position as provincial governor, that one as mayor. When the Russo-German war began, Degrelle formed an Anti-Bolshevist Walloon Legion, in German uniform, to fight on the Russian front. It recruited barely a few hundred mercenaries.

Thus ended the Rexist adventure which, at one moment, had awakened the curiosity of the world.

CHAPTER IX

The Flemish Movement

BY SHEPARD B. CLOUGH

IN 1930 THE LINGUISTIC CENSUS of Belgium indi‑
cated that 3,473,291 Belgians more than tw‑
years old spoke Flemish (which is the sam‑
language as Netherlandish), 3,093,315 spok‑
French, and 1,045,601 spoke both languages.[1] Roughly speaking, th‑
line of demarcation between the two linguistic areas runs from
Dunkirk in France southward to below Hazebrouck, then west‑
ward passing to the south of Courtrai and Enghien, arriving at th‑
frontier of the Netherlands north of Liége. To the south of thi‑
line French predominates; to the north of it, Flemish. Neverthe‑
less, there are important islands of French-speaking people in th‑
Flemish area, especially in Ghent, Ostend (Oostende), Antwerp
Mechlin, Louvain (Leuven), and, above all, in Brussels, where th‑
population is nearly equally divided. This linguistic situation ha‑
existed for centuries with no appreciable alteration.

Although the people of Belgium have been divided into nearl‑
equal linguistic groups, French early became the predominant lan‑
guage for governmental affairs. With the beginning of the Spanis‑
period (sixteenth century), French was used to supplant Flemis‑
in the oaths which new princes swore upon their *Joyous Entrie‑*
and also for correspondence between the provincial states an‑
the central government; during the Austrian period (1714–1792)
the use of French was greatly extended. French was fashionable
It was employed extensively by the court in Vienna for Austria‑
affairs as well as for official business with the Flemish cities. Flem‑
ish bourgeois admired things French, endeavored to have thei‑

---

[1] There were also 69,033 persons who spoke German, 67,140 who used German
and French, 9,332, Flemish and German, 54,089, all three languages, and 334,20‑
none of the three.

children educated in French, and tried to pattern their social life after Parisian styles. Concomitantly, a disdain for Flemish and Flemish culture developed, although Flemish was employed for local affairs by the provincial estates and by the cities of the Flemish provinces.

When, from 1792 to 1815, France became mistress in a land where her language and culture enjoyed great prestige, she immediately embarked upon a policy of Gallicization. Frenchmen were appointed to the more important official posts and French became the official language throughout Flanders. Consequently, since the young generation of lawyers had to use French, a new impetus was given to it in the schools, many of which were established by the French. By 1815 the predominance of French in the Flemish sections of the Belgian Provinces was supreme in intellectual and higher governmental circles.

Upon the creation of the United Kingdom of the Netherlands, a reversal of the trend was attempted. King William adopted a definite policy of making Flemish supreme in Flanders and French supreme in Wallonia. He decreed that Netherlandish should be employed in the primary and secondary schools of the Flemish-speaking districts of his realm. Furthermore, he insisted that Flemish be used in official business in Flanders and before the courts. Officials of the Flemish sections were inclined to accept this law and to use Netherlandish, but the lawyers would not. The generation then practising at the bar had been trained in French and they were not qualified, so they claimed, to follow the royal edict. Hostility of the lawyers and also of French-speaking Flemish bourgeois to the linguistic policy of the King fanned the flares of discontent among influential groups in Flanders and accounted for some of the Flemish support to the Revolution of 1830.

But the revolution was the result of other factors. The Belgians had been accustomed to a large degree of autonomy and, therefore, resented the inroads which the new state made upon what they considered their rights. The Revolution of 1830, which resulted in the creation of the modern state of Belgium, was initiated and conducted by French-speaking leaders, none of whom came from Flanders. Their logical reaction was to reëstablish French as the official language for the entire Kingdom. This they did, and, by limiting the electorate by property or by professional qualifications to 46,000, they placed authority in the bourgeois groups which were sympathetic to the use of French, even in Flanders. Consequently, French became the language of the army, the universities, the secondary schools, and to a large degree, of the primary schools as it was of the Government and of large business.

In the meantime, Flemish was not without its supporters and gradually a movement, later to become the Flemish Movement, got under way, to laud the virtues and review the glories of the Flemish language and Flemish culture. It began during the Netherlandish period, 1815–1830, when the political affiliations of the Belgians and the Dutch led to closer intellectual ties. Its leader was Jan Frans Willems (1793–1846), who is frequently referred to as the father of the Flemish movement. As a poet, Willems sang of the Low Countries freed from the yoke of France, of the greatness of the Netherlandish tongue, and of the wise policies of King William. As a philologist, in correspondence with the great Jacob Grimm, he prepared a system of Netherlandish orthography which was widely used in Flanders and he edited old Flemish manuscripts, the most famous of which was *Reynard the Fox*. As a champion of Flemish culture, he conducted a steady campaign through lectures, literary organizations, and articles.

Willems achieved notable success and inspired a small but ardent group of followers. Most famous of them was Jan David (1801–1865), a priest and teacher, who became Professor of History and of Flemish Literature in the Catholic University of Louvain. Here he prepared a Flemish grammar, founded a Flemish literary review, organized a pro-Flemish students' society (*Met Tijd en Vlijt*), and published his most elaborate work, *Vaderlandsche Historie*, in eleven volumes.

The work of men like Willems and David, which was characteristic of the early period of romanticism, was accomplished by popular literary romanticists. The fiery Flemish lion with his outstretched claws, his red tongue, and his crouching body, was taken from the coat-of-arms of the Counts of Flanders and made the symbol of the Flemish government. The Battle of the Golden Spurs was revived as a great triumph of the Flemings over the foreign French. Bruges was rediscovered as a cradle of architectural beauty.

Flemish heroes of the past were made to live again. And Flanders was given a new patriotic song—the hymn of the Flemish movement, "The Lion of Flanders."

Although many of these popular writers are famous in Flemish traditions—K. Ledeganck, author of *The Three Sister Cities* (Bruges, Ghent, Antwerp), J. van Rijswijck, the poet of the Flemish movement, and August Snieders, editor of the newspaper *Het Handelsblad* of Antwerp—the best known and the most widely read was Hendrik Conscience (1812–1883). The son of a French shipwright of Napoleon's fleet and of a Flemish mother, Conscience early turned to letters. Inspired directly by the style of Sir Walter Scott, he began turning out historical novels in profusion. In 1839 he published his most famous book, the *Lion of Flanders,* a glowing account of the struggles of the Flemings against the French in the fourteenth century. In the preface of the first edition he made his position on the Flemish question clear: "There are twice as many Flemings as there are Walloons. We pay twice as much in taxes as they do. And they want to make Walloons out of us, to sacrifice us, our old race, our language, our splendid history, and all that we have inherited from our forefathers."

The agitation of the Flemish romanticists led, in 1856, to the appointment of an official commission which was to report on Flemish grievances. The findings of the commission became the manifesto of the Flamingants—a name given those who sympathized with the Flemish cause. The list of grievances began with the charge that the Belgian State had committed *lèse-langue*—a crime as terrible in modern times as *lèse-majesté* in times gone by. It recalled how French had been adopted for use in the army, in the constitutional convention, in general and local administrations, in the communal councils, in the courts, by the police, and in the universities. It contended that the unity of Belgium did not depend upon the unity of language. It insisted that Flemish be used in the primary and secondary schools of Flanders, in the normal school at Lier, in the trade schools, and at the University of Ghent. It suggested the creation of a Flemish Academy to lend prestige to Flemish culture, the use of Flemish in all relations between the central government and the Flemish provinces, the translation of all the legal codes of Belgium into Flemish, the use of Flemish in the courts when that language was requested by the defendant, the division of the army into Flemish-speaking and French-speaking regiments, and the use of both Flemish and French by all members of the Belgian foreign service. The report of the Grievance Commission ended with this statement of faith:

> The Flemish movement is not an isolated and narrow effort without roots in the past, without fruition in the future. It is the continuation of all that which is noble and great in our annals. Its mission is holy and it is its duty to realize it without fear for or discouragement by the obstacles to be overcome. The Flemish movement is the expression of the general need for independence whose spirit is manifested every day by new events.
>
> In Belgium partisan spirit and personal interest are more or less completely separated from the linguistic question. They work outside the national principle and the national principle outside of them. Which will be the victor? Language is more than personal interest. It is identified with that which the people hold most dear. It is more than political consciousness, which is subject to many modifications due to exterior circumstances. It is dearer to a people than religion, because it is older and more individual. What intelligent government would violate the individual, political, and religious conscience of a people in order to impose its own opinion? The question of language is a question of conscience in which nobody other than the possessor of the language has the right to interfere. It is therefore a question which will not suffer discussion.

The "grievances of 1856" became the platform of the Flamingants and remained their guide until well after the First World War. Little was done before 1870 to grant concessions to the Flemings, for the Liberal party, hostile to their position, was in power during most of this period. Nevertheless, more and more Flemings were coming to appreciate their language and their culture. A poet in this period, Guido Gezelle, set standards of which the Flemings were justly proud, and another poet, Albrecht Rodenbach, stirred the enthusiasm and fired the imagination of the youth with his emotional patriotic verse. A review, *Today and Tomorrow (Van Nu en Straks)*, became a medium of literary expression of the highest order and one of its editors, August Vermeylen, who was an ardent Flamingant, enjoyed wide renown. Flemish composers, like Peter Benoit, began to capture the Flemish "spirit" and at least a few Flemish painters revived the style of the great Flemish masters.

Flemish culture also became more widely disseminated during the fifty years prior to the First World War. Cheap newspapers multiplied in number, some with large circulations, such as the

Socialist *Vooruit,* the Catholic *Het Nieuws van den Dag,* and the Liberal *Het Laatste Nieuws.* The Flemish cause was propagandized by the *Willemsfonds* and the *Davidsfonds,* not to mention a vast variety of lesser societies of a literary character. And July 11th, the day of the Battle of the Golden Spurs, began to be recognized as the Flemish holiday.

The reawakening among the Flemings of pride in their language and culture had repercussions in politics—repercussions which became much more forceful after the extension of the suffrage in 1893 and during the periods when the Catholic party, which was sympathetic to Flemish demands, was in power, from 1871 to 1879 and from 1884 to 1914. This new phase was ushered in by a determined campaign to have the use of Flemish permitted in the courts. This issue came to a head after two innocent Flemings had been condemned to death and guillotined following a trial conducted in French—a language which neither understood. In 1873 a bill was passed which provided that in the provinces of East Flanders, West Flanders, Antwerp, and Limburg, and in the *arrondissement* of Louvain, procedure in criminal cases was to be in Flemish, that in criminal cases the defendant could indicate the language in which he wished to be tried, that both languages should be employed in the Court of Correction in Brussels, and that the criminal code be translated into Flemish.[2]

Gradually Flemish became recognized as having a place in governmental affairs. The law of 1878 provided that in the provinces of Antwerp, East and West Flanders, and Limburg, as well as in the *arrondissement* of Louvain, state officials should address communications to the people in Flemish, or in Flemish and French, and that the governmental correspondence with Flemish communes and individuals should be in Flemish unless otherwise requested. Flemish was used from time to time in the Chamber of Deputies, although more as a gesture than anything else. The *Moniteur,* the organ in which Belgian laws and decrees are published, began to appear in the two languages in the 1880's; stamps,

---

[2] This law was amended in 1889 to require the use of Flemish in the courts of Flemish towns and to make the state employ the same language as that chosen by the defendant.

In 1891 the bilingual regime was extended to the Courts of Appeal. Not until 1925 was a commission appointed to translate all the codes into Flemish.

money, and public buildings began to bear bilingual inscriptions; and in 1898 the Flemish text of laws was declared to be official along with the French.

In the field of education, the Flemish minimum platform demanded the thorough instruction of Flemish and the use of that tongue in teaching Germanic languages, while the maximum program called for the exclusive use in Flemish districts of Flemish in the lower grades and the gradual introduction of French in the upper ones. The first step forward in the realization of these goals was the law of 1883 which stipulated that Flemish be used in the preparatory sections of public secondary schools, that Flemish, English, and German be taught in Flemish, and that after 1886 two other courses be given in Flemish. This law did not work well because qualified teachers of Flemish were few and the administration was unenthusiastic about enforcing it. Nor did the law have any effect upon private schools in which the largest proportion of Flemish students were enrolled. Finally, with the introduction of obligatory education in 1914—a step which was important in reducing illiteracy in Flanders and thus making the people more susceptible to printed Flemish propaganda—the language problem in elementary schools was handled by allowing a parent to determine, subject to approval by the head of a school, in what language his children should be taught.

In addition to agitating for use of Flemish in the elementary and secondary schools of Flemish-speaking districts, Flamingants endeavored to stimulate the higher intellectual activity of their people. To this end they made a strong stand for a Flemish Academy and for the transformation of the State University of Ghent into a Flemish institution. They obtained the former desideratum in 1886, but were less successful in achieving the latter reform. Nevertheless, a Flemish normal section was established at the University of Ghent in 1883, doctoral dissertations in Flemish were permitted in the Faculty of Philosophy and Letters in 1890, and several courses in Flemish were established prior to the First World War.

In other phases of Belgian public life the use of Flemish made little headway. In the army slight progress was realized even though the instruction of Flemish was required in officers' schools after 1892. The fact that most officers were Walloons, or French-speaking

Flemings, was of especial importance after 1913, when compulsory military service meant the incorporation in the army of a great many Flemish youths who did not know French. In business affairs, too, French continued to be predominant, although the growing industrial and commercial importance of Flanders indicated the possibility of some change. In the Congo, Flemish made no headway, although nearly all the trade with the colony was with Antwerp and many of the colonial administrators came from Flanders.

On the eve of the First World War, therefore, the Flemish language had regained considerable prestige among the people of Flanders, although the upper bourgeois of this section of Belgium were inclined to be *Fransquillons,* that is, upholders of the French language and of French culture. A revival had also taken place in Flemish letters and in art. Flemish linguistic grievances had been listed and some redress had been made. In governmental affairs and in education concessions had been greatest. Yet in Flanders an important element of the population was discontented because of the inferior position which Flemish held. This discontent was to appear boldly under the stress of the First World War.

Up to 1914 the leaders of the Flemish movement had demanded relatively mild reforms of a linguistic character and had operated within the framework of the existing political parties in an effort to secure remedial legislation. Political Flamingants like A. van de Perre and F. van Cauwelaert (Catholics), Louis Franck (Liberal), and E. Anseele and C. Huysmans (Socialists) had no thought of disturbing the political unity of Belgium, and rare was the person who even dreamed of such action. During the First World War, however, a more radical element appeared among the Flamingants—a group that stood for greater political autonomy for Flanders, if not complete separation from Wallonia. Hence, the First World War marked a turning point in the Flemish movement.

The ultimate German designs on Belgium were not entirely clear. General von Bissing, the Governor-General of Belgium from the conquest of the country in 1914 to April, 1917, seems to have favored annexation. German domination, he believed, would give Germany a stronger strategic position and would enable her the better to control her colonies and the Belgian Congo. Yet he stated that he did not "nourish the thoughtless hope of seeing the Flemings make the domination of Belgium easy." His successor, Von Falkenhausen, and Chancellor Bethmann-Hollweg and his followers took a somewhat different attitude. Although they said little about the final disposition of Belgium, they believed, as Bethmann-Hollweg stated, that "a Belgium . . . , in which a Flemish majority is free from the domination of the Walloon minority, will be more easily made useful to German interests than a Belgian state under its present form . . ."

In pursuance of this attitude, the Germans endeavored to make capital of the Flemish movement by granting some of its demands. They enforced rigorously the law which provided that children should be taught in the language indicated by parents; they required the strict use of Flemish in administrative affairs in Flanders; they divided the Ministry of Arts and Sciences into two sections—one Flemish and one French; and they made the University of Ghent a Flemish institution, although nearly all the professors in that institution resigned in a body as a protest.

Such acts placed Flemish leaders in an embarrassing position. If they accepted these reforms at the hands of the invaders, they would be branded traitors; yet if they refused them, they would appear to be repudiating a course for which they had fought long and hard. Some Flamingants decided to collaborate actively with the Germans in the realization of the Flemish program and, hence, became known as "Activists," whereas others refused to have anything to do with the conquerors, deciding upon a course of passive resistance, hence earning the name "Passivists."

Among the Activists were to be found none of the older and more distinguished Flemish leaders. The new group comprised, for the most part, humble intellectuals—school teachers, young university professors, a few priests, a poet, lawyers, and doctors. Characteristic of them, perhaps, was August Borms, a former secondary-school teacher, who had no great strength of leadership, no great experience in public affairs, and only a small following.

The Activists believed that Germany would win the war and that they should begin at once to get the best settlement possible for the Flemings. One step upon which they agreed was to secure the administrative partition of Belgium based on linguistic lines and, when the Germans made their first peace proposals (December 12, 1916), they concluded that the time to act had come. Consequently in February, 1917, they formed a Council of Flanders.

The Germans decided to cajole the Council. The new body was allowed to form regular departments of government, to hold mock elections for the second Council of Flanders (January and February, 1918), and to draft, in collaboration with German political scientists, a constitution for Flanders. Furthermore, the occupying Power decreed the administrative division of the country along linguistic lines, with the administration of Flanders centered at Brussels and that of Wallonia at Namur. It even permitted the Council to evolve to a point where a declaration for the independence of Flanders was prepared—a declaration which ended as follows: "The oppression under which the Flemish people has lived since 1830 has ceased. The state of Flanders is born. Flanders follows the current of world politics—the independence of nationalities. The Flemish people have finally been saved."

Yet, in spite of such apparent leniency, the Germans kept close control over the Council. They never regarded Flanders as independent—they always treated it as a dependency. Even in the Council's "declaration of independence," they insisted upon the substitution of the word "autonomy" for "independence." Yet they went far enough to encourage the extreme Activists and to bring upon themselves the damnation of the Passivists.

Eventually the Activist agitation within Belgium began to have repercussions within the army. Some ground for complaint existed within the Belgian fighting force, for, although about 80 per cent of the men were Flemings, French was used almost exclusively for orders, for signs in the trenches, and for officers' examinations. Several unpleasant incidents occurred as a result of the language situation, and groups of Flemish soldiers organized to consider abuses. Gradually, as word of events in Belgium came to them, they became bolder. They formulated a slogan, "A Free Flanders in a Free Belgium" (*Een Vrij Vlaanderen in een Vrij België*), and used the sea gull as a symbol of the awakening of Flemish youth to a sense of nationality. Finally, they founded the Front party (1917), which adopted a defeatist attitude. It actually advocated (June, 1918) surrender in event of a Belgian retreat or a strong German attack.

Before Flemish frontism had caused any serious damage, the débâcle of German arms began. As the victory of the Allies became more certain, the Activists strove to convince the Passivists that what gains had been made in realizing the redressing of Flemish grievances should be guaranteed for the future. But their efforts in this direction were of no avail. Nor did their attempts to bring the Flemish question before the Peace Conference prove successful. Belgium was restored with all its linguistic laws of 1914 intact.

One of the first important episodes of the Flemish movement after the establishment of peace was the trial of the Activists. Many of the leaders fled to the Netherlands to escape the hard lot which they expected would be theirs, but they were tried *absente reo*. One of the few prominent Activists who remained behind to face the music was August Borms.

Passions ran high during the Trials. Belgian patriots considered the Activist chiefs as traitors and hated them as only traitors can be hated, whereas Activist sympathizers considered the defendants at the bar as martyrs. Forty-five Activists were condemned to death, 11 to life imprisonment, 20 to twenty years of jail, 16 to fifteen years, and 65 to shorter terms. Actually no one was put to death, for Borms, the only person within the grasp of the Belgian authorities who had been given the extreme penalty, had his punishment according to Belgian tradition, commuted to life imprisonment. He became, however, the "great martyr," until pleas for amnesty resulted in his release (1929).

As the excitement of the Trials subsided, the political aspects of the Flemish movement began to be more clearly delineated. In a general way, the Flamingants were divided between those who believed that the Flemish question could be solved only by changing the political structure of Belgium and those who insisted that a satisfactory linguistic settlement could be arrived at within the existing political state. Those who took the former position, which was similar to that of the Activists, became known as the "Maximalists," while those who took the latter stand, similar to that of the Passivists, became known as "Minimalists." The Minimalists operated within the framework of the established parties and were fortunate in having such distinguished leaders as F. van Cauwelaert (Catholic), E. Anseele and C. Huysmans (Socialists), and Julius

Hoste, Jr. (Liberal). The Maximalists, on the other hand, endeavored to establish separate political parties—the most important of which for several years was the Front party. In the elections of 1919 its candidates for the Chamber of Deputies secured 5 out of approximately 200 seats—an inauspicious result. The great majority of Flemings retained their allegiance to the traditional parties and sought through them the much-desired linguistic reforms.

In the years between the two world wars, the broad cultural and economic base upon which the Flemish movement was built became more solid. Flemish painting, music, and literature showed renewed vigor and displayed an increase of Flemish consciousness.

Flemish cultural societies assumed their tasks with new energy. Youth societies and students' unions became stronger and more vocal, the latter being involved in numerous demonstrations. The Catholic-Flemish *Landsbond* was founded to instill a Flemish spirit into Catholic organizations. A Flemish Touring Club was organized to impress upon Flemings the touristic virtues of their countryside and of their cities. Flemish houses were opened in many places as centers of Flemish public life. And an annual pilgrimage to Dixmude was established to honor Flemish victims of the First World War—a pilgrimage that was highly emotional and patriotic.

The economic development after the First World War stressed greater industrialization, at least until the depression. Flamingants began to play a larger role in the management of some of the newly developed industries and in banking, insurance, and commercial enterprises. In agriculture, too, Flemish initiative gave a new importance to the great coöperative of Flanders—the *Boerenbond*. Yet, for the most part, the wealthier classes of Flanders continued to use French and to favor French culture. As a result the Flemish movement remained, in part, a social movement—a movement supported by the lower classes. This fact was greatly stressed by Socialist writers as the impact of the depression of the early 'thirties began to be felt keenly. In spite of their contentions, however, the economic position of Flanders was improving relative to that of Wallonia, thus giving the Flemish movement a firmer material foundation.

The cultural, economic, and political aspects of the Flemish movement gradually made their weight felt in realizing the greatly delayed linguistic reforms. Upon the conclusion of the First World War, it was clear that much had to be done in this regard. King Albert, in a famous address to the legislative chambers of November 22, 1918, had said, "In the domain of languages the strictest equality and the most absolute justice will characterize bills which the Government will submit to the national representatives."

The first linguistic law, after the establishment of peace, had to do with the use of Flemish in administrative affairs. This law, published in the *Moniteur* of August 12, 1921, divided Belgium into two linguistic sections, the Flemish part consisting of the provinces of Antwerp, East Flanders, West Flanders, Limburg, and the *arrondissements* of Louvain and Brussels in the province of Brabant; the French part including the provinces of Liége, Luxemburg, Namur, Hainaut, and the *arrondissement* of Nivelles in the province of Brabant. The law went on to prescribe that state, provincial, communal, and all subordinate administrative services must use Flemish in the Flemish section of Belgium and French in the French section, but that provincial or communal councils could use the second language to supplement the first and that in Brussels a bilingual regime would be created. Furthermore, the law stipulated that all central state administrations in their relations with local persons, either public or private, should use the language of that section of the country where these persons resided unless requested to do otherwise; that official employees who came in contact with the public should use the language of those whom they served; that state and provincial local services should publish notices in the language of the area involved or in both languages; and that notices addressed to the citizenry of all Belgium should be in the two national languages.

Although this law of 1921 marked a real step forward, it did not meet the demands of the more critical Flamingants. They pointed out that the law had no teeth—no penalties for infractions—and that it did not give promise of bringing Flemings into the higher governmental services. Hence, they fought for additional legislation pertaining to the use of languages in administrative affairs and finally won in 1932. This new law provided that in the central bureaus of the state, "where it was necessary," a unilingual official should be assisted by a bilingual officer of equal or next lower grade, and that candidates for central administrative posts must pass examinations in the language or languages of the areas with which they were to deal. Furthermore, rules governing the languages used by officials in their communications were tightened and a commission was created to oversee the enforcement of the law.

Legislation also was enacted to improve the linguistic situation before the courts. As has been seen already, considerable progress had been made in the use of Flemish for criminal cases before the war. But little had been done for civil, commercial, and military cases and Flamingants demanded that linguistic equality be established for them. This the law of June 15, 1935, attempted to do. In principle, Flemish was to be used for civil and commercial cases in the Flemish section of Belgium (as defined in the law of 1921) and French in the French section, except that in the *arrondissement* of Brussels both languages were to be employed, and the litigants before high courts could indicate the language that they preferred. In the army both Flemish and French courts were provided and a person being tried could select either the one or the other. Finally, magistrates were required to pass examinations in order to meet the linguistic requirements of the bench where they expected to officiate.

In the army, also, an important reform was enacted. The linguistic difficulties encountered by the Belgian army during the First World War have been alluded to above and now an earnest effort was made to avoid them in the future. Accordingly, a bill was passed in 1928 and went into effect in 1930, stipulating that the Belgian army be divided into Flemish and French regiments. Men were allocated to them according to the district from which they came or the language which they habitually employed. Furthermore, the two languages were put on an equal footing at the Miliary School at Brussels and commissioned officers were required to know the language of the men under them. This law gave rise to dire forebodings concerning the division of Belgium, but it apparently operated satisfactorily and did not result in any disloyal acts during the brief Belgian campaign of the Second World War.

One of the most bitter political struggles connected with linguistic reform after the First World War concerned the transformation

of the University of Ghent into a Flemish institution. The Fleming
had agitated for this change early in the history of the Flemis
movement and the Germans had encouraged them by establishin
such an institution in 1917. After the restoration of Belgium i
1918, however, the University of Ghent was returned to its forme
linguistic status and the campaign for its alteration went on. I
1923, the Chamber voted a compromise measure (the Nolf law
which provided that in the faculties of philosophy and letter
law, science, and medicine, students might take two-thirds of thei
courses in Flemish and one-third in French (the Flemish program
or two-thirds in French and one-third in Flemish (the French pr
gram). This arrangement suited only a few. Gallicized Fleming
immediately established, in the city of Ghent, *L'Ecole des Haute*
Etudes where students might study in French under university pr
fessors the same subjects which they were required to study i
Flemish at the university. On the other hand, Maximalists co
tinued and increased their agitation for a complete Flemish Un
versity of Ghent. Ultimately in 1930 this goal was reached. Th
law stipulated that, beginning with the scholastic year 1930–193
instruction in the University of Ghent should be in Netherlandis
but that the technical schools should be permitted to continu
instruction in French until 1935 when they would be moved t
Liége. Thus another landmark in the Flemish "list of grievances
had been reached.

The transformation of the University of Ghent into a Flemis
institution and the laws pertaining to the use of Flemish in admi
istrative branches of the Government had an important bearin
upon the linguistic situation in the elementary and secondar
schools. The principle which had been adopted before the Fir
World War was that instruction in the public schools should be i
the mother tongue of the child. In the law of July 15, 1932, th
principle was overthrown and in its place was substituted the do
trine that instruction should be given in the language most wide
used in the district in which the child lived. With elementar
schools, however, certain exceptions to the new rule were allowe
Classes in the second national language might be organized in di
tricts where 25 students per grade requested them, and in are
where at least 20 per cent of the population spoke a language n

hat of the majority, "transmutation classes" could be organized to
prepare pupils, after the third year, for instruction in the predominating language.

In public secondary schools, the same general pattern was followed, with French classes being provided in those parts of Flanders
where at least eight students per class qualified for them. A special
regime was permitted in Brussels, however, for both elementary
and secondary schools—a regime based on the older policy of
"mother tongue, school tongue." This breach in the new principle
irked the more radical Flemings, as did also the fact that private
schools could still use the language of their choice. But in spite of
criticism on such issues, the school language law of 1932 was favorable to Flemish. Indeed, it began to elicit from the Walloons cries
that French was being discriminated against.

By the middle of the 1930's the Flemings had realized their major
linguistic demands. Henceforth the Flemish movement was to consist of efforts to improve the economic and cultural life of Flanders,
and of agitation to alter the political organization of Belgium. In
other words, the movement was to be divided upon essentially
Minimalist and Maximalist lines.

Concerning the Minimalist program, little can be added to what
has already been said until sufficient time has passed for far-
reaching achievements. Concerning the Maximalist or nationalist
platforms, certain developments have taken place which are worthy
of note. In the first place, the Flemish Nationalists increased in
strength prior to the Second World War. Their representation in
the Chamber of Deputies rose from 5 in 1919 to 9 in 1929, and
to 17 in 1939. These men nearly always used Flemish in debates
and vigorously pushed Flemish demands. Among other things, they
worked for the amnesty of the Activists who had been condemned
after the First World War and finally obtained it, or at least clem-
ency, in 1929. The Activists were freed from the sentences against
them, although neither their property, which had been confiscated,
nor their civil rights were restored.

Of a much more significant nature was the platform upon which
the Flemish nationalists stood. In general, they wanted a revision
of the Belgian Constitution along federalist lines in order to give
Flanders greater autonomy. Some of them advocated the creation

of a great Netherlandish state, including the Netherlands and the
Flemish part of Belgium, although they secured little encouragement for this proposition from Holland. Moreover, in the 'thirties
fascist ideas began to be adopted by many of the Flemish nationalists. In West Flanders Joris van Severen, with Wies Moens, the
poet, as his lieutenant, founded the now famous *Dinaso* group
(*Dietsch-Nationaal Solidaristisch Verbond*). It was antidemocratic
and antiparliamentarian and in favor of a corporative, dictatorial
regime. It preached the formation of a Great Netherlandish corporative state, although Van Severen proposed a "Burgundian
state" or a "greater Belgium" comprising Flanders, Wallonia,
Luxemburg, and French Flanders. The relationship of this group
with the Rexists was very close.

The other important Flemish fascist organization was the
Vlaamsch Nationaal Verbond, more commonly known as the V. N. V.
It was led by Gustaaf de Clercq, formerly prominent in the Front
party. It followed closely the ideology of German national socialism, advocated corporation of the German variety, and preached
the virtues of the Great Netherlandish idea. It received most of its
support in the Brussels area, in Aalst, and to some extent in Antwerp. It took over the Frontist newspaper, *De Schelde*, published
in Antwerp, and definitely destroyed the Front party.[3]

Although these Flemish national and fascist groups were not
particularly strong, they were to play an important role after the
German conquest of Belgium in 1940. From them came some of the
most famous, or infamous, Belgian collaborators of the Second
World War. The general character of their collaboration differed,
however, from the policies pursued by the Activists in the previous war. During the earlier conflict the extreme Flamingants
had sought to realize, with German aid, linguistic reforms which
large groups of Flemings considered legitimate. During the Second
World War, however, collaborators have more closely played the
German game—they have worked actively, not for linguistic reforms which had been obtained but for the success of the German
cause. There is another difference between the role of the Activists
of the First World War and the collaborationists of the Second. In

---

[3] A third fascist group was the pro-German *Dietsch-Vlaamsche Arbeidgemeen-
schap* known as *De Vlag.* It was organized in the middle 'thirties by Jef van
de Wiele.

the present conflict there is a sizable group of collaborators from Wallonia—from the Rexist party of Léon Degrelle—so that all the onus of disloyalty to Belgium is not being placed on the Flemings.

The form of collaboration among the extreme Flemish groups has been chiefly the acceptance of responsible governmental posts which allowed them to be used as German tools. The filling of such posts with collaborators was somewhat facilitated by the fact that the leading career officials of the various governmental departments, particularly the secretaries general, retained their places and carried on as best they could. Thus the Germans were able simply to change personnel in order to accomplish their purpose. For example, they placed Gerard Romsée, a Flemish nationalist deputy, in the important position of Secretary-General of the Ministry of the Interior, a position that allowed him to change personnel in almost all ranks of the administration, and Victor Leemans, in the post of Secretary-General for Economic Affairs. They reorganized the administration of the five largest cities of the country—Brussels, Antwerp, Liége, Ghent, and Charleroi—placing them directly under a Commissioner of State for Great Agglomerations and named as the first commissioner a well-known Flemish nationalist, H. Borginon. In Brussels, they had the hostile Burgomaster, Van de Menlebroeck, discharged, replacing him with Jan Grauls, and in Ghent ousted A. van der Stegen, appointing Dr. H. J. Elias, who became the "leader" of V. N. V. after the death of De Clercq (1943).

The planting of Flemish fascist nationalists in key positions, which was more extensive than the few illustrations given here might indicate, covers by no means all forms of collaboration, even though it has been the most important. The Germans, for their part, have attempted to curry favor by such acts as appointing a commission, headed ironically enough by the ex-Activist, Dr. Borms, to indemnify the Activists for the material losses suffered after the First World War. The Flemish fascists, on their side, have endeavored to rally their followers to support German policies, even to the drafting of Flemish workers for labor in Germany and to the punishing of Belgian underground patriots. The V. N. V., indeed, has organized with the Rexists a private guard to protect factories from sabotage and has had a hand in the newly established police training schools.

The Belgian Government in Exile has, of course, taken a strong position against collaboration in every form. On December 17, 1942, it declared that any Belgian would be considered a traitor who willingly helped the Germans in any way, and this declaration has the force of law. There was no especial vindictiveness toward Flemings in this act, nor could such be expected of a government that had among its counselors such prominent Flemish Minimalists as Camille Huysmans, Frans van Cauwelaert, and Julius Hoste, Jr. All collaborationists, both Flemish and Walloon, will thus run the risk of severe penalties.

What the future of the Flemish movement will be is difficult to foresee because of the myriad of influences at work. Nevertheless, certain possible lines of development, postulated upon the political restoration of Belgium after victory, much as it was in 1939, may be suggested. The fascist forms of Flamingantism will surely be condemned, both by Walloons and by the mass of the Flemings. More sober Flemish counsels will then undoubtedly prevail. The dominant ones may be socialist or communist, for their parties are likely to be increased in strength. The danger will be that even the more moderate Flemings may, through linguistic requirements, place Walloons in a position of inferiority before the law and thus give rise to a Walloon movement aimed at profound constitutional change. Among the Flemings, the Great Netherlandish Idea will probably grow, but for a time, at least, it will take the form of closer cultural relations and political understanding with the Netherlanders rather than actual political union of the Netherlands and Flanders.

Part Four

ECONOMIC
AND SOCIAL
DEVELOPMENT

CHAPTER X

Foreign Policy, 1918 to 1940

BY FRANS VAN CAUWELAERT

THE FIRST WORLD WAR wrought profound changes in the foreign policy of Belgium. Compulsory neutrality had failed. It had interfered with the military preparations of Belgium; it had not protected the country from invasion. By the violation of her pledge, Germany had martyrized Belgium. Everything in her occupation policy, as well as in her official and unofficial declarations—at least, until the threat of imminent defeat caused her to adopt a more circumspect tone—had shown clearly that German designs involved the very existence of Belgium.

Belgium, then, felt a natural and legitimate revulsion at the idea of a return to her former neutrality. She could not renew a trust which had been so odiously betrayed by one of its guarantors. She was obliged to fortify herself. Moreover, Belgium felt that the heroism with which she had fought for her independence and for the defense of right had placed her above a status which she considered contrary both to her dignity and to her interests.

The legitimacy of her attitude was recognized by the Allies. Article 31 of the Treaty of Versailles states: "Germany, recognizing that the Treaties of April 19, 1839, which established the status of Belgium before the war, no longer conform to the requirements of the situation, consents to the abrogation of the said treaties." Henceforth, Belgium was to be free to adapt her foreign policy either to the dictates of friendship or to the considerations of her own interest. At the same time, Belgium realized the necessity of providing for her defense. Foreign policy and military considerations assumed a prominent place in her public life, and thus, inevitably, events outside the country were to exercise a more direct influence upon her attitude. The international policy of Belgium, static before 1914, now became dynamic.

In the period separating the two wars, four distinct phases may be noted: The first, ending with the signing of the Pact of Locarno in 1925; the second, with the address by King Leopold III on October 14, 1936, inaugurating the "policy of independence"; the third, terminating in the outbreak of hostilities between Germany and Poland, at the beginning of September, 1939; and the fourth, the few months of voluntary neutrality, interrupted on May 10, 1940, by Germany's second aggression and invasion of the country.

The first period may be characterized as that of the reëstablishment and organization of the peace. Belgium played a particularly active role in the international negotiations leading up to it, and the nations which were her friends and allies made a gesture of special homage to her by entrusting her, in 1920, with the presidency of the first Assembly of the League of Nations. Several times Belgian prime ministers were called on to preside over important international conferences.

In the formation of her foreign policy during this first phase, Belgium was preoccupied with three problems: reparations for damages suffered in the war, the consolidation of peace through the League of Nations, and the safety of her frontiers. For the sake of completeness, a fourth should be mentioned—the revision of the 1839 Treaty between Belgium and the Netherlands.

The vicissitudes of reparations and war indemnities are too well known to require much discussion here. Germany was to pay them all. Eventually, by skillful maneuvering, she managed to absorb more cash in loans made by the Allies and the neutrals than she ever paid out to her war creditors. Like the other countries, Belgium was a victim of German guile. This situation was not without influence in the monetary difficulties in which Belgium became involved. The latter succeeded, however, in securing a priority right to 2,500,000,000 gold francs of the reparations which were to be paid by the Germans. The British and the French recognized the unusual sacrifices Belgium had made and, according to the Treaty of Versailles, annulled the war debts she had contracted. The priority right which Belgium claimed was based on her neutrality, recognized and confirmed several times in official declarations and documents during the war. At the time of the Versailles negotiations, however, this right was respected—and then very incompletely—only because of the personal intervention of King Albert, who attended a meeting in Paris with the "Big Three" on April 3, 1919.

Because of her particular interests, Belgium participated in the occupation of the Rhine provinces. By virtue of the arrangements concluded at Versailles, June 28, 1919, she was also represented in the High Interallied Commission, which was to govern these provinces.

In her position as a small nation, and as the victim of brutal aggression, Belgium could not fail to make a heartfelt contribution to any movement for reinforcing the legal rights and the security of the different peoples. She welcomed with joy the declarations to this effect made by President Wilson in his message of January 18, 1918. Belgium contributed enthusiastically to the constitution of the League of Nations and of the International Labor Organization, and her delegates and representatives took an important part in the work connected with international law, disarmament, and social legislation. The country participated in the organization of the International Court of Justice and later subscribed without hesitation to the Briand-Kellogg Pact for outlawing war in international relations. To the end, Belgium remained faithful to the League of Nations. In spite of the risks and disadvantages which might fall upon her as a small nation, she never hesitated either in the scrupulous observance of her duties or in the application of the measures which the League prescribed for its members. At the time of the Corfu incident in 1922, Belgium demanded the rigorous application of the rules of the Covenant, and in 1935 she was one of the first to declare herself in favor of economic sanctions against Italy, in spite of the dynastic ties which bound her to that country.

Notwithstanding her highest hopes, Belgium could not fail to recognize that the League of Nations by itself could offer only an insufficient protection to her security. The tragic experience through which she had just passed counseled her to surround herself with more immediate and more efficacious guarantees. Belgium turned naturally to those with whom she had been associated in long-standing friendship and who, through a glorious fraternity in arms, had been her natural allies. She had hoped for great things from America, so dear to her because of the relief work, and had welcomed President Wilson with wild enthusiasm in 1919. The failure of the Senate to ratify the President's achievement was a sore disappointment to the Belgians as a whole; but the fidelity and identity of views of England and France were not to be doubted. Here too, Belgian hopes were to be blighted. Neither England nor France ever failed Belgium in loyalty or friendship, but disagreements which soon became manifest between them on the subject of the treatment to be accorded Germany and the way in which the peace of Europe was to be assured, had a most unfortunate repercussion on Belgian foreign policy.

France had insisted upon a separate military alliance with Belgium. But Belgium could not undertake such an engagement without gravely compromising her political independence as well as her internal peace. In 1917 she had wisely refused, for the same reasons, an economic union which the French Minister, Clémentel, had more or less pressed upon her. Belgium went only so far as to conclude, in 1920, a so-called "General Staff Agreement," which established a technical background for military coöperation in the event of a new German aggression. The document registering this agreement was filed with the Secretariat of the League of Nations on November 2, 1920, but it never received the ratification of the Belgian Parliament, which alone could have made it an instrument of international policy.

The Belgian Government, well aware of the insecurity to which the country thus remained exposed, strove to conclude with England a treaty which would assure Belgium of immediate and complete support from the British army and navy, should Germany again attack her without provocation. A text to this effect was submitted to the Foreign Office in 1922. It was expected that a similar guarantee would be obtained later from France. At first it seemed that these efforts might meet with success, but the breakdown of the talks at Cannes in 1922 widened the breach between France and England and put an end, as well, to Belgian hopes for a tripartite agreement.

For some years, Belgium's international position remained precarious. She participated with France in the occupation of the

Ruhr; but this decision did not increase her security on the eastern frontier, nor the closeness of her association with England, nor, moreover, her internal unity, already menaced by the disagreement of the Flemings and the Walloons on the advisability of a military accord with France alone. This unrest was aggravated by the continued inability of the League of Nations to solve the problems of disarmament and collective security. The Baldwin Cabinet's rejection of the Protocol concluded by the Herriot and MacDonald governments had brought disturbing proof of the League's weakness.

The Locarno Pact, signed in London, December 1, 1925, was hailed with general satisfaction. It confirmed the frontiers of France and Belgium as recognized by the Treaty of Versailles, and seemed to assure tranquillity along the banks of the Rhine for a long period to come. For the first time, Germany took free action on a basis of equality with the other parties to the contract. England and Italy, guarantors of the Pact, had, on an essential point, reestablished the solidarity of the former Allies. Conciliation and arbitration, as methods of international procedure, had received outstanding confirmation. The League of Nations could now open its doors without reservations to a pacific Germany. Apparently the treaties of Locarno were to be a magnificent contribution to peace. The policy of Gustav Stresemann, inspirer of the Pact, commanded all the more confidence since it was furiously attacked by the die-hard nationalists, of whom General Ludendorff was one of the violent spokesmen.

It was only logical that Belgium should take part in this chorus of optimism and peace. More than any other country, she was concerned with the maintenance of peace in the Rhineland. She hoped to reëstablish a good-neighbor relationship with Germany, obviously of economic importance to her. Belgium rejoiced to find France and England at her side, since their common protection had always seemed to her an indispensable part of her defensive armor. Furthermore, by freely confirming the stipulations of the Treaty of Versailles referring to the abrogation of Belgian neutrality and the rectification of frontiers, under which the cantons of Eupen-et-Malmédy, and St. Vith were returned to Belgium, Germany had definitely renounced all claims against her small neighbor on the west. The Chamber of Representatives ratified the Locarno Pact—

also called the Rhineland Pact—with 124 members voting yes, voting no, and 4 abstaining. The Senate approved it unanimously

Public opinion was so much in favor of the Pact that even the Flemish extremists, who had violently attacked the Franco-Belgian accord, and who, on general principles, opposed any governmental policy, rallied to the parliamentary majority. No one felt called upon to dwell on the notable extension which the Pact created in the military and international obligations of Belgium, since, according to the duties of reciprocity set forth in the treaty, she would henceforth be inevitably involved in any armed conflict which might ensue between Germany and France. The Franco-Belgian military accord of 1920 was, by identical declarations of the two signatories, subordinated and limited to the eventualities provided for in the Pact. The international position of Belgium had been clarified. Her security seemed assured, as did the stability of the situations created in western Europe by the Treaty of Versailles.

The years immediately following the First World War were the only really happy ones for Belgium. Of course, Germany was far from meeting the full measure of her obligations in the matter of reparations. The Dawes Plan was followed by the Young Plan, the Young Plan by the Moratorium, and the Moratorium by complete default. But Belgium had reasons to believe in a better future. Since the monetary stabilization of 1926, she seemed to have definitely recovered her former industrial and commercial activity. Belgian money markets soared in euphoric flights, as in America and elsewhere. The Rhineland Pact had put her mind at ease about the security of her frontiers and she could confidently set about preparing for the celebration of her first Centenary of Independence, in 1930. But she was soon to encounter bitter disillusionment—first in the economic, and then in the international field.

Belgium's international difficulties were the direct and immediate consequence of Hitler's rise to power. Germany at once adopted a belligerent attitude. Hitler became Chancellor of the Reich on January 30, 1933. On October 14th, in the same year, Germany, after much blustering, withdrew from the Disarmament Conference and from the League of Nations. On March 7, 1936, Hitler invaded the left side of the Rhine, tore up the Locarno Pact defying the contracting powers and the guarantors by encroaching, without their assent and without previous negotiation, upon the provinces which definitely had been demilitarized, first by the Treaty of Versailles and subsequently by the Pact itself.

There was a strong emotional reaction in London, as there was in Paris, but no practical steps were taken. Belgium, obviously, was too weak and in too exposed a position to take an initiative at which both France and England hesitated. Nonetheless, on March 10th, Belgium joined France in an appeal to the Council of the League of Nations. As early as March 14th, this body met, and on March 19th, adopted a resolution declaring that the German Government, by its military action, had violated the treaties. On the same day, the representatives of the Locarno Powers, with the exception of Germany, met in London and agreed upon a provisional arrangement.

The main import of this arrangement was that the signatories maintained the validity of their mutual engagements. Their general staffs would immediately confer upon the preparations for eventual coöperation, should any of them be the object of unprovoked aggression. In addition to this, it was planned to make contact with the Reich, with a view to any indispensable revisions concerning the status of the Rhineland, and to submit the German claims to the judgment of the Permanent International Court of Justice. The conclusions of the London Conference were communicated to the League of Nations Council, and the latter decided to suspend deliberation on the matter while the proposed conversations were taking place.

These conversations never got beyond a preparatory stage. On April 1st, the London Government informed the Belgian Embassy, as well as the diplomatic representatives of the other Locarno Powers, that it was disposed to allow its General Staff to make contact with their respective military authorities, but on condition that these conversations remain technical and nonpolitical. An exchange of notes resulted, but no accord was reached, even within military limits. The Locarno Pact, and the system of joint guarantees for the peace of western Europe had seen their day.

Belgium cannot be blamed for this failure. She had shown that she was ready to fulfill her duty in collective action. She had even accepted, in the provisional arrangements, a certain extension o her obligations in mutual assistance. But Belgium could not close her eyes to the precarious nature of her alliances, nor to the danger menacing the peace from all sides. Japan had launched the series of defiant acts by seizing Manchuria. On October 3, 1935, Italy attacked Abyssinia. On March 7, 1936, Germany occupied the Rhineland. The Axis was being built. Its future partners were laying the foundation. And at each bold stroke, the weakness of the League became more evident. The entrance of Soviet Russia into the League failed to compensate for the withdrawal of Germany and Japan, the more so because the economic crisis, especially felt by the democracies, inspired an additional fear of Russian propaganda. The Soviets were accused of contributing to the social and political troubles in France; their intervention was more than evident in the Spanish Civil War.

The small European nations, determined not to be drawn into conflicts which might be quite foreign to them, tried to limit the danger by insisting upon the restricted scope of Article 16 of the Geneva Covenant. Each nation was making an effort to take shelter from the rising tide of danger. Belgium, the most exposed of all, could not withdraw into an attitude of perpetual expectancy. The Locarno Pact had lost its value as an instrument of peace. What was left of it constituted no more than a defensive formula, of doubtful efficacy against a very obvious peril. Belgium felt she could better her position by freeing herself from all reciprocal military obligations and by adopting, after the example of Holland, a policy known as that of independence.

This policy was inaugurated by an address of the King to a meeting of his Cabinet on October 14, 1936. Therein the Sovereign, in carefully weighed words, defined the motives which inspired the policy and the duties it imposed on the country. This address constitutes a historical document of high importance.

Judging the speech by events of the war, certain critics have thought they discerned in it a tendency to ignore the German menace, or even to come to terms with it. Nothing could be farther from the truth. One has only to read the document in its entirety to realize that, although the King was concerned with depriving Belgium's eventual aggressors of all legitimate excuse for hostility, his primary object was the union of all Belgians for the defense of their country and the acceptance of those sacrifices in men and money which the country had to make in order to perfect its powers of resistance.

"A number of reasons," the King pointed out, "force us to sharpen our vigilance and to develop our military resources to the maximum: (1) The rearmament of Germany, following the total remilitarization of Italy and Russia; (2) The transformation effected in the methods of warfare by technical progress, notably in aviation and motorization, making it possible henceforth to give to the initial operations of an armed conflict a power, rapidity, and amplitude particularly alarming to countries of restricted territory like Belgium; (3) The surprise reoccupation of the Rhineland; (4) The generally unsettled state of international security; and lastly, (5) The internal dissensions of certain States, which may lead to entanglement in the political and social rivalries of other States and the touching off of a general conflagration more desperate and more devastating than that of the First World War."

Events have since proved the farsightedness of this warning, but the King did not make it the basis for defeatist conclusions. On the contrary, he urged the country to measure up to the danger. "Our geographical situation," he said, "demands that we maintain a military equipment sufficient to dissuade any one of our neighbors from making use of our territory to attack another State.... An alliance, even if purely defensive, will not accomplish this end; for however prompt the aid given by an ally, it can come only after the overwhelming shock of invasion. The force of that first shock we must meet ourselves, in any case."

Belgium, heeding this appeal, agreed to extend military service for all able-bodied youths, from what had been a maximum of ten months to a minimum of seventeen months. The fortification of the eastern frontier, provisionally terminated in 1935, was resumed and amplified. But such a considerable effort could not be accepted nor carried out unless it was supported with equal confidence by the Flemish and the Walloon populations. "Any unilateral policy," said the King, "would weaken our external position and would, rightly or wrongly, stir up internal dissension.... Hence, we must pursue a policy that is exclusively and integrally Belgian.

... This policy must place us outside the conflicts of our neigh-bors." And to those who might be tempted to question the dignity and the feasibility of such a policy, the King cited the "decisive and proud example of Holland and Switzerland."

The royal address was received with great favor throughout the country. Its conclusions were ratified by a parliamentary majority recruited from all the traditional parties and from all the prov-inces; and this majority increased as the threat of war became more and more definite. In adopting a stand of complete independence, Belgium felt that she had recovered her equilibrium. She had re-covered her self-confidence.

In detaching herself from any unilateral alliance, Belgium had no intention of modifying her relations with the League of Na-tions. P. H. Spaak, Minister of Foreign Affairs, made this clear in a remarkable address before the Chamber of Representatives on April 29, 1937. In any event, it would be unjust to pretend that in giving up the principle of mutual assistance, as envisaged by the Treaty of Locarno, Belgium weakened the position of France. France declared war on Germany, and not inversely; hence, the principle of mutual assistance would not have been invoked, no matter what occurred. Furthermore, in event of attack, Belgium could not be expected to leave her own territory to fight on other fronts unless forced to do so by invasion. Her frontiers, totally with-out natural means of defense, are so long on the east and the south that her entire army would not be able, unaided, to give them adequate protection. Therefore, in deciding to concentrate hence-forth on her own defense and in reinforcing it, Belgium in no way weakened the aid that France could expect of her in event of Ger-man aggression; on the contrary, her action could only strengthen that aid, both materially and morally. Consequently, Belgium might justly hope that the guarantees of assistance promised her in virtue of the Locarno Pact would be maintained. And, in his address, the King made a discreet allusion to the point. "In accom-plishing this mission," he said, "Belgium makes an eminent con-tribution to the peace of western Europe; she creates for herself *ipso facto,* a right to the respect and the eventual aid of all the States which have an interest in this peace."

England and France were not slow to recognize the soundness of this conclusion. On April 24, 1937, their ambassadors in Brussels made a joint declaration to the Belgian Government, by which their respective governments, taking cognizance of the determination of Belgium to defend her frontiers with all her forces against aggression or against any attempt at passage by armed forces, stated that they considered Belgium as relieved of all obligations to them resulting either from the Locarno Treaty or from the arrangements agreed upon at London on March 19, 1936, and at the same time they "maintained toward Belgium the promises of assistance made her by the same acts."

On October 13th, the German Government handed the Belgian Ambassador in Berlin a declaration that was equally explicit. After having acknowledged in terms almost identical with those employed by England and France, the decision by which Belgium meant to assure the inviolability of her territory, the German Government added, with calculated hypocrisy: "The Government of the Reich recognizes that the inviolability and the integrity of Belgium are of common interest to the Western Powers. It confirms its determination in no circumstances to infringe upon that inviolability or that integrity, and at all times to respect Belgian territory; except, as goes without saying, in case Belgium, in an armed conflict in which Germany might be engaged, should coöperate in a military action against her.

"The Government of the Reich is ready, like the Royal British Government and the French Government, to accord its assistance to Belgium, in case she should be attacked or invaded."

This declaration had been preceded, as early as January 30th, by a speech of the Führer to the Reichstag, in which he said he was ready to recognize and to guarantee, at any time, the inviolability of both Holland and Belgium. And in the official commentary with which the Wilhelmstrasse accompanied its promises, the German Government boasted of having given Belgium an "assurance without reserves" and of having by its "magnanimous and disinterested gesture, made a new and important contribution to the safeguarding of peace in Europe." These declarations of Germany are typical of her diplomatic procedures.

As for Belgium, she conformed scrupulously to the rules of her new status. She officially renounced the General Staff Agreement which she concluded with France in 1920. On September 16, 1938, through the agency of her First Delegate, Count Henri Carton de Wiart, Belgium informed the League of Nations that she agreed with the already generally accepted restrictive interpretation of Article 16 of the Covenant, concerning the obligations of mutual assistance in event of aggression. But, at the same time, she consistently pursued the execution of the enlarged military program recommended as necessary by the King.

Faithful to the line of conduct which she had adopted since the end of 1936, Belgium declared her neutrality as early as September 3, 1939, the very day that hostilities broke out among the guarantors of her inviolability. In the concluding chapter Belgium's conduct during the few months which followed will be examined.[1] But the picture of Belgium's international policy during the twenty years of precarious peace would not be complete without a few words on her relationships with the Netherlands and on her foreign commercial policy.

If history has ever known twin nations, it would be hard to find a more obvious example than Belgium and Holland—similar population, similar size, similar traditions, and, in a large measure, similar civilization and culture. Between the two nations is a frontier marked by no natural obstacles. Without the religious conflicts of the sixteenth century, the two countries would have constituted a single nation. Only fidelity to their dynasties and their flags, rendered dear by the associations of a long past, separates them today.

But in spite of their close affinity, in spite of their sincere mutual friendship, Belgium and Holland were not able to arrive at the revision of the Treaty of 1839 provided for by the Treaty of Versailles and so desirable for the common interest. This treaty, like every accord reached after a violent conflict, bore the mark of its origin. It seemed as though the time had come to make it an instrument of close friendly relationship.

The object of the revision was a better definition of the legal control of the Scheldt in the part which crosses Dutch territory; the solution of long-standing questions of river drainage, of railway and maritime transportation across common frontiers; and, especially, an assurance to the port of Antwerp of more direct and

---

[1] See Chapter XXX, "Belgium in the Postwar World," by Paul van Zeeland.

feasible communications with the Rhine. In the failure of the efforts toward this revision, the responsibility is divided. In any event, the *rapprochement* which might have led to closer coöperation in both economic and military matters was retarded.

Nonetheless, the need for such collaboration became more and more pressing as the economic crisis deepened and the danger of a new war became increasingly evident. This gave rise, first, to the Agreement of Ouchy; it also stimulated new initiatives in favor of economic union and was reflected in more regular and more mutually trustful contacts between the governments. It found moving expression in the popular enthusiasm with which the Belgian King was received in the Dutch capital in 1938, and Queen Wilhelmina in Brussels during the summer of 1939. The sufferings and sacrifices which the two countries have since endured for the common defense of their liberties and their independent existence cannot fail to intensify the feeling of solidarity.

Among the important acts characterizing Belgium's policy directly after the last war, should be mentioned, also, the convention with the Grand Duchy of Luxemburg, signed on July 25, 1921, by which an economic union was concluded for fifty years.

As early as December 19, 1918, the Grand Duchy of Luxemburg had broken off the customs agreement which tied her to Germany. By Article 40 of the Treaty of Versailles, Germany recognized the validity of this renunciation and abandoned all claims to the railroads in Luxemburg.

In her union with Belgium, the Grand Duchy kept her political independence and Belgium carefully abstained from any meddling in that country's domestic affairs; but the two countries were one in the application of customs and excise taxes, negotiations concerning which were left to Belgium after due consultation with the Luxemburg Government. A permanent Supreme Council, composed of five members—three representing Belgium and two representing the Grand Duchy—was set up to supervise and facilitate the working of this treaty. Economic collaboration was completed in later years by a mixed Administrative Council, charged with regulating the impartial application of measures concerning the apportioning of imports, which the intensity of the economic crisis and the action taken by other countries had made inevitable.

Within extremely narrow territorial limits, the Grand Duchy possesses many economic resources; but for Belgium, the economic union had, unquestionably, a moral as well as a market value. The separation imposed by the Treaty of 1939 had been painful to her, and the economic union, although it respected the sovereignty of the Grand Duchy, created between the two countries a new community of interests which could not but have an increasing influence on their intellectual and moral relations. It was in this expectation that the two governments concluded, on September 2, 1923, an accord relative to their scientific, literary, and academic relations, which aimed to facilitate the exchange of students and professors, and the assimilation of courses of study. During the present war, the two countries cannot but become more than ever conscious of the solidarity of their interests and of their destinies.

In her foreign policy, Belgium has always had to give an important place to economic problems. To feed the exceptionally dense population concentrated on her restricted and naturally barren soil, it was necessary to pay particular attention to the development of her foreign trade. Before the First World War, Belgium's efforts had met with remarkable success. At that time, the importance of her seaports and the facilities of her rail and river transportation, her many markets, and her powerful industries had brought about an economic expansion which gave her fifth place on the roster of international trade.

Belgium never completely recovered from the disaster of the First World War. For four years, she was cut off from her principal markets. Her most important factories were stripped of their machines. Her transportation facilities were demolished, or damaged beyond use. When, after a magnificent effort at reconstruction, Belgium was ready to resume her former activity, she found herself face to face with a world economically unstable and full of disorder.

In the face of these difficulties, Belgium did the utmost to maintain her ancient traditions of liberty and commercial fair play. She took part in all the international conferences and efforts envisaging financial stabilization and the establishment of healthy commercial relations. The first international financial conference called by the League of Nations was held in Brussels in the Committee Room of the House of Representatives. The international economic conference of Geneva, in 1927, was presided over by M. Georges Theunis, former Prime Minister. Belgium has always been ready to espouse any measure which, on a basis of perfect equality, could favor the development of exchange and the fostering of commercial confidence between the peoples.

It was in this spirit that Belgium signed, in December, 1930, in the name of the Belgium-Luxemburg Union, the Oslo Agreement, by which she, Holland, and the Scandinavian countries, undertook not to raise their tariffs nor introduce any new protective measures except by mutual consent. In July, 1932, there was concluded with Holland the Ouchy Agreement by which the two countries agreed, according to a scale, to reduce their customs tariff in five years to one-half, the advantages of the agreement to be extended to any other nation which would accept the same obligations. This accord was inspired by a letter which King Albert wrote to Prime Minister Renkin, in which the sovereign underlined the disastrous consequences of an increasing nationalistic protectionism, and showed that only a concerted action of the nations toward international solidarity could cure the evils from which the world was suffering. "But," he added, "it is time that this solidarity assert itself otherwise than by speeches." Nevertheless, the wise and generous intentions of Belgium and Holland were not realized because England opposed the Ouchy Agreement as contrary to the most-favored-nation clause.

Belgium was also the first European power to sign a treaty of commerce with the United States, based on the principle of reciprocity, by which President Franklin D. Roosevelt wanted to expand foreign trade progressively. This treaty, concluded in 1935, was of real benefit to Belgium.

But Europe had already begun the descent which was inevitably to lead to the present catastrophe. The failure of the London Economic Conference had ruined the last hopes of an economic recovery, sustained by a spirit of international solidarity and directed toward the progressive freedom of trade. Already, Germany had resolutely adopted an economy of war, carefully camouflaged by doctrines of economic autarchy and controlled trade. By her example, as much as by the threats concealed in the Nazi policy,

Germany daily drew the peoples of Europe farther into the morass of "quotas," financial control, unfair competition, and feverish rearmament. Through the fog of economic trouble, loomed larger and larger the specter of war.

Up to the last minute, Belgium strove to avert the catastrophe. In the month of July, 1938, she participated at Copenhagen in a conference of the foreign ministers of the Oslo Group, at the conclusion of which the governments declared themselves ready to participate in any international action which, in a spirit of complete impartiality, would attempt to find a formula of conciliation among the different groups of powers. They repeated their effort, in more impressive form, on the eve of the conflict. On the initiative of King Leopold III, the foreign ministers of the Oslo nations met again in Brussels, August 23, 1939, and King Leopold, in the name of all the sovereigns represented, uttered a moving appeal to the people of the entire world, over the radio, urging them to unite before the final rupture and to unite for the triumph of peace, based on mutual respect and right, over the ever more threatening psychosis of war. The Pope and numerous governments joined in this appeal. England and France indicated their agreement. Italy remained silent. Germany replied, on September 1st, by the invasion of Poland. Faithful to their engagements, England and France joined with Poland.

Belgium's course was clear. The policy which she had inaugurated in the month of October, 1936, and which had been confirmed by the declarations and guarantees of her three great neighbors in 1937, demanded that she remain neutral. The Belgian Government published an official declaration of neutrality in the September 3d issue of the *Moniteur Belge,* together with a detailed list of the regulations and restrictive measures which were to govern the territory and the population of Belgium in order that her neutrality might be preserved and respected. In the radio message which, at the invitation of *Forum,* he addressed to the American people on October 27, 1939, King Leopold said: "We are conscious of our rights and of our duties; we contemplate the future with calm confidence and a clear conscience; we are ready to make our independence respected with all our might. Our good faith can be relied upon; following the example of my beloved father, and as the sovereign of a proud and free people, I shall always keep that good faith."

That faith was such that when Germany, betraying her own pledges, attacked Belgium, she could discover in Belgian conduct no pretext to cloak her infamy. In the economic field, the Belgian Government, pursuing the course of independence, had preserved a perfect balance among the belligerent powers; in the military field, it had exercised equal vigilance against any misuse of Belgian land, sea, or air by one or another of those powers.

Although, for reasons of national security, the Government had been constrained to great caution in public comment on events taking place and had required this prudence, in a lesser degree, of the principal organs of public opinion—the Parliament and the press—Belgium did not recognize or bow to the pretension of the Nazi leaders who sought to impose upon the neutral countries a further obligation of moral neutrality. Belgium did not allow herself to be silenced on the crimes of the German armies in Poland, nor upon the injustice of the aggression against Finland and, later, Norway. The Minister of Foreign Affairs himself openly expressed in Parliament the indignation felt by the Belgian people at these injustices which had been committed against peaceful and innocent nations.

By the end of August, 1939, the Belgian Government, conscious of the danger, had begun mobilization of the Belgian army. On August 26th, the German Ambassador in Brussels, at an audience he himself requested, had renewed, in the presence of the King and the Prime Minister, his Government's assurances that it would respect the engagements made October 13, 1937. On the following day, the Ambassadors of Great Britain and France made a similar declaration. But, determined to assure the inviolability of the territory primarily by the forces of Belgium herself, the Belgian Government pursued, without interruption and to the extreme limit of its means, preparations for the country's defense. By the middle of September, 1939, Belgium had under the colors an army of 640,000 men, almost 50 per cent of the masculine population between the ages of twenty and forty.

As early as October, it became evident that an attack could come only from the east, and it was in that direction that Belgium con-

centrated the greatest part of her military forces. A preliminary
alarm soon confirmed the wisdom of these precautions. Information of identical nature received by the governments of Brussels
and The Hague, in the early days of November, gave reason to fear
that Germany was planning an immediate aggression on the Dutch
frontier. Mr. E. van Kleffens, the Foreign Minister, took the cue
to advise Queen Wilhelmina to renew, without delay, the offer
of mediation which she and the King of Belgium had already made
on August 28th. King Leopold, at the invitation of the Netherlands' sovereign, went to The Hague on the evening of November
6th, accompanied by the Minister of Foreign Affairs and a military
adviser. The offer of their good offices was drawn up the next
morning and sent the same day to the heads of the German, British,
and French governments.

Inspired by a legitimate and a generous solicitude and a desire
to limit the horrors of the war, the cruelty of which had become
only too evident on the battlefields and in the devastated cities
of Poland, this intervention remained without effect. The threat
which had caused it disappeared temporarily from the foreground;
but there rose the question as to what Belgium's attitude would
be in event of an attack limited to the Dutch frontier. Upon her
conduct in such a case might depend the possibility of immediate
aid from France.

It is curious that some of the Flemish nationalists, who had
always pretended to have much more attachment to Holland than
to Belgium, maintained that, even in the event of an attack on
Holland, Belgium could not voluntarily abandon her neutrality.
Doubtless they were already in moral complicity with the Nazis.
Public opinion, however, was overwhelmingly convinced that, in
spite of the inevitable consequences, Belgium, in the interests of
her own defense, should not hesitate to consider an unjustifiable
attack on Holland as a direct threat to her own security. The Government could scarcely speak out so clearly, but, in an important
address before the Senate on December 19, 1939, the Minister of
Foreign Affairs alluded to the possibility of an aggression against
Holland, in terms which indicated that the Government shared
the feeling of the immense majority of the country and of the
Parliament.

There was another alarm at the beginning of January. This time it concerned Belgium herself. On January 10th, a German scouting plane came down on Belgian territory, near Mechlin-on-the-Meuse. The two officers on board pretended to have lost their way in the fog. One of them was the bearer of confidential papers, which, in the course of questioning, he suddenly threw into the fire. Most of the documents were destroyed but what remained seemed to establish beyond question the existence of a plan for the immediate invasion of Belgium. Apparently the documents contained instructions to that effect for the Commander of the German air forces. History will, perhaps, clear up the exact meaning of the incident. The emotion it stirred died down after a few days, but the Belgian army continued, with heightened ardor, to fortify its positions and to improve its defense preparations.

Suddenly, at dawn on the tenth of May, without a declaration of war, without previous warning, without the slightest justification, the German armies threw themselves upon Belgium with unprecedented savagery. When, three hours later, the German Ambassador came to inform the Belgian Foreign Minister of the decision by which Hitler, eclipsing the Kaiser, cast to the winds all his solemn vows and brought war and oppression to an innocent people, devastation had already been visited upon several open cities and upon the heart of the capital itself. Once again, Belgium became a martyr to the cause of right and justice.

CHAPTER XI

The Agriculture of Belgium

BY E. G. MISNER

ELGIUM IS A COUNTRY of small farms. Approximately 58 per cent of her area is used for agriculture, 4.2 per cent for horticulture, 17.7 per cent for forests, 3.0 per cent is agricultural land not used, and 17.1 per cent is used for villages, roads, rivers, canals, lakes, or for industrial and other miscellaneous purposes.

According to the Census of 1930, there were 1,131,146 farms in the country with 4,936,015 acres (1,997,578 hectares), an average size of 4.4 acres per farm. The median size of a farm was less than 2.47 acres (1 hectare); that is, there were as many farms of this small size as of all other sizes. Of the total number, 1,033,797, or 91 per cent, were less than 12.35 acres (5 hectares) in size, while only 464 comprised more than 247 acres (100 hectares). In 1930, farms of from 2.47 to 24.7 acres (1 to 10 hectares) comprised 22 per cent of the total number of farms and occupied 47 per cent of the total agricultural area in Belgium.

In 1930, owners operated 41 per cent of the land, and comprised 48 per cent of the total number of farm operators. The other 59 per cent of the land was operated by tenants who comprised 52 per cent of the total number of farm operators in the country. After the First World War, the sale value of land increased decidedly but the world-wide agricultural depression of the early 'thirties caused a sharp decline in land values. Agriculture in Belgium, as in other parts of the world, was recovering from the serious effects of depression when the Second World War crashed disastrously upon it.

Some 2,500,000 people were said to be on the farms of Belgium in 1930. A total number of 596,193 permanent workers—44 per cent women and 56 per cent men—who were members of the operators' families, and 66,189 hired laborers—25 per cent women, 75 per cent men—were reported for the 1,131,146 agricultural holdings in 1930. Of these workers, 72.5 per cent were on farms of less than 24.7 acres

TABLE 1

PER CENT OF TOTAL DISTRIBUTION OF CROPS AND OTHER FACTORS IN BELGIUM BY PROVINCES, 1929

	Ant-werp	Bra-bant	West Flan-ders	East Flan-ders	Hai-naut	Liége	Lim-burg	Luxem-burg	Namur
Population..........	15	20	11	14	16	12	5	3	4
Total area...........	8	11	11	10	12	13	8	15	12
Woods..............	7	5	1	2	8	17	6	34	20
Uncultivated land....	27	3	6	2	3	16	25	11	7
Total crop area......	8	12	14	12	14	12	7	10	11
Cereals...........	7	16	15	13	14	8	8	8	11
Legumes..........	6	6	46	11	9	5	1	3	13
Industrial plants...	0	12	32	9	17	14	7	0	9
Roots and tuber plants..........	12	15	18	19	11	6	6	6	7
Forage and pasture.	7	9	11	8	16	15	6	15	13
Gardens..........	13	27	9	10	18	9	4	3	7
Flowers..........	9	18	5	46	8	8	2	1	3
Fruit..............	2	14	6	15	11	27	14	3	8
Nurseries........ .	15	11	12	22	15	7	4	3	11
Osiers............	20	10	8	39	4	5	11	1	2
Miscellaneous......	20	16	10	5	12	5	5	10	17
Double-cropped area............	23	13	16	37	2	1	8	0	0
Glass houses, number.	8	52	7	17	8	3	1	1	3
Glass houses, square feet..............	8	65	5	16	3	2	0	0	1

(10 hectares) in size. The number of workers per unit of area on small farms of from 1 to 5 hectares in size was more than five times the number on farms of 50 to 100 hectares. It is not so much the lack of man power as the lack of land on which to produce food and feed that forces Belgium to import heavily of food supplies. The inefficient use of man power on the small farm units of the country is a disadvantage. When wars occur and imports stop, the population suffers.

TABLE 2
AREA OF CROPS AND OTHER FACTORS IN BELGIUM BY SELECTED YEARS, 1880–1939

	1880	1895	1910	1919	1929*	1939
			thousands of acres			
Cereals						
Wheat.................	681.8	445.7	399.0	342.6	380.7	305.3
Spelt..................	129.8	83.7	42.4	44.1	16.8	18.1
Meslin................	63.6	45.6	28.5	20.1	6.9	4.3
Rye...................	686.0	700.2	664.4	523.4	458.8	334.9
Winter barley.........	{ 99.3	{ 99.4	62.0	70.2	40.0	{ 47.9
Spring barley..........			23.6	8.2	21.8	
Oats..................	616.5	614.5	641.7	561.0	571.3	640.0
Buckwheat.............	32.6	11.6	9.0	8.6	2.6	1.2
Total.................	2,309.6	2,000.7	1,870.6	1,578.2	1,498.9	1,351.7
Legumes						
Horsebeans...........	47.2	39.4	20.8	44.5	18.5	20.2
Peas and vetch........	34.6	25.6	11.5	16.5	11.3	18.8
Total.................	81.8	65.0	32.3	61.0	29.8	39.0
Industrial crops						
Hemp.................	2.0	1.5	0.7	....	0.2	0.0
Flax..................	99.1	75.6	45.2	53.9	61.4	110.5
Colza.................	15.9	4.5	1.5	3.7	0.2	0.0
Tobacco...............	3.9	5.3	11.2	17.1	5.7	5.7
Hops.................	10.3	9.2	5.1	3.2	2.6	2.0
Chicory...............	27.3	31.5	23.9	17.3	15.8	12.0
Sugar beets...........	80.6	133.7	148.9	106.0	130.8	134.2
Total.................	239.1	261.3	236.5	201.2	216.7	264.4
Roots and tubers						
Mangels..............	64.7	100.2	172.1	165.5	201.6	214.0
Carrots and parsnips....	6.9	9.4	5.4	5.9	4.6	3.3
Turnips and rutabagas...	17.7	23.3	16.8	20.9	12.8	10.4
Cabbage..............	....	....	6.6	....	1.5	....
Potatoes..............	492.6	456.4	424.1	388.1	376.9	364.6
Total.................	581.9	589.3	625.0	580.4	597.4	592.3
Forage						
Red clover............	278.0	243.9	227.9	212.7	{	122.3
Crimson clover........	....	37.3	34.1	34.6		15.4
Hybrid clover.........	....	39.0	21.4		{ 192.9	
White clover..........	81.9	52.9	29.9	60.1		{ 34.3
Yellow clover..........	37.6	16.4	13.6			
Alfalfa...............	33.2	39.8	32.9	24.3	18.7	22.6
Hay..................	14.6	18.1	12.8	10.8	5.3	6.2
Serradella............	4.0	4.1	1.2	....	....	....
Mustard..............	....	....	1.5	....	....	....
Meadows						
Mown-grass........	527.0	573.6	660.7	573.0	616.8	621.2
Grazings...........	340.7	408.4	619.1	576.5	1,148.8	1,149.1
Rye grass..........	9.8	21.8	33.4	23.9	....	{ 32.5
Timothy...........	....	....	27.5	....	....	
Corn fodder........	....	3.4	6.8	....	....	....
Peas and vetch	....	....	5.2	....	....	....
Forage mixtures....	....	....	....	12.8	64.2	45.9
Total.............	1,326.8	1,458.7	1,728.0	1,528.7	2,046.7	2,049.5
Orchards................	93.8	117.6	156.5	151.6	173.7	182.0
Miscellaneous............	19.7	8.4	8.9	....	....	....
Total...................	113.5	126.0	165.4	151.6	173.7	182.0
Total, all crops..........	4,652.7	4,501.0	4,657.8	4,101.1	4,563.2	4,478.9

* In addition to the crops listed, the following acreages of horticultural crops were reported for 1929. Medicinal plants 442; kitchen gardens 87,011; nurseries 5,945; osiers 12,817; parks, etc., 34,752; total horticultural crops not included in the table 140,967 acres; total acres all kinds of crops, 4,704,200.

Source: Original data before conversion found in:

1880 1895 1910	J. L. Frateur, *Aperçu sur la Situation de l'Elevage Bovin en Belgique avant la Guerre.* Institut de Zootechnie de Louvain, Belgium, Bulletin No. 15, p. 12.
1919	*Répartition et Rendement des Cultures, Animaux des Fermes,* Brussels, Belgium, Ministère de l'Agriculture et des Travaux Publics, Phamphlet No. 9, pp. 2–11, 1922.
1929	M. J. Van der Vaeren, *Le Livre d'Or de l'Agriculture Belge.* p. 14.
1939	*International Yearbook of Agricultural Statistics, 1939–1940.* Rome, International Institute of Agriculture, p. 42.

The proportion of the total area in different crops in 1929, in each of the nine provinces, is given in Table 1. The relative importance of the different kinds of agricultural enterprises in the different provinces may be evaluated from this table.

Some of the outstanding facts shown by Table 1 are: (1) More than 70 per cent of the area in forest is in the three provinces of Liége, Luxemburg, and Namur; (2) about 60 per cent of the cereal area is in the four provinces of Brabant, West Flanders, East Flanders, and Hainaut; (3) half of the area of industrial plants is in the provinces of West Flanders and Hainaut; (4) more than half of the area in root and tuber crops is grown in the three provinces of Brabant, East Flanders, and West Flanders; (5) about two-thirds of the area in flowers is found in the two provinces of Brabant and East Flanders; (6) about 40 per cent of the fruit area is found in the two provinces of Liége and Limburg; (7) more than half of the area used for double crops is found in the two provinces of East and West Flanders, more than one-third in East Flanders alone.

In 1929, for Belgium as a whole, of the total acres of all kinds of crops, including horticultural crops (4,704,188), 8.6 per cent was in wheat, spelt, and a mixture of rye and wheat, 12.2 per cent in oats, 9.8 per cent in rye, 1.3 per cent in barley—a total of 31.9 per cent in cereals—also 0.6 per cent was in legumes, 4.6 per cent in sugar beets, flax, and other industrial plants, 12.7 per cent in root crops and potatoes, 43.5 per cent in forage crops, and 6.7 per cent in horticultural enterprises. Of the total crop, pasture, and forest area, 63.8 per cent was in crops and pasture and 36.2 per cent was in forests. The acres in the important crops in 1929, and in other census years, are given in Table 2.

In general, the change in the system of farming had been to less cereal production, more cattle, more poultry and hogs, the use of more land for pasture and meadows producing hay and grass for livestock, and greater dependence than formerly on imported concentrates.

In 1930, Belgium had 269,792 horses used in agriculture, 6,212 mules and hinnies, and 6,405 asses. Of the horses, 23,883 were less than one year old and 51,550 from one to three years old. There were 1,671,178 head of cattle, 184,867 sheep, 155,416 goats, 990,220 swine, 17,863,353 chickens, 37,048 geese, 172,755 ducks, 20,392 tur-

keys, 2,748,524 pigeons, 1,473,307 rabbits and 56,717 hives of bees
The data for 1939 indicated that the numbers of all kinds of ani
mals were less than in 1929. The total number of animal units o
livestock amounted to about 0.48 per acre of farm land.

Reduced by the First World War, in 1920 the number of farn
horses on hand was 205,200; this increased to about 270,000 in 1930

TABLE 3

PERCENTAGE OF TOTAL DISTRIBUTION BY PROVINCES OF LIVESTOCK
IN BELGIUM, 1930

	Ant-werp	Bra-bant	West Flan-ders	East Flan-ders	Hai-naut	Liége	Lim-burg	Luxem-burg	Namur
Population..........	15	20	11	14	16	12	5	3	4
Total area...........	8	11	11	10	12	13	8	15	12
Total crop area......	8	12	14	12	14	12	7	10	11
Horses..............	8	16	13	12	18	10	6	7	10
Colts, born..........	2	15	13	11	23	10	6	6	14
Cattle..............	9	11	14	14	13	15	7	9	8
Calves, born........	10	12	12	14	13	17	8	7	7
Hogs...............	8	12	18	19	5	16	10	7	5
Pigs, born	1	9	27	19	2	16	15	8	3
Sheep..............	5	13	13	16	22	10	6	6	9
Chickens...........	6	11	21	21	14	9	8	4	6
Rabbits.............	5	9	35	20	17	5	3	3	3

and was less in 1939. Many mares raise a colt and work too. There
were 37,029 colts born in 1930, and there were about 24,000 colts
less than a year old on hand. Because of the small size of many of
the farms, and, therefore, of the impracticability of the use of tractors for field work, horse raising may be expected to continue to
be an enterprise of some importance, for domestic replacements
if not for export.

From 1880 to 1910, the number of cattle in Belgium increased.
In 1920, at the end of the First World War, the number of cattle
was apparently about the same as in 1880. Since then the number
has been increasing, but in 1939 was still less than in 1910. A few
more young heifers were on hand in 1939 than in 1930 or in 1920,
but the number of milch cows was less in 1939 than in 1930 or in
1910. In 1930, the number of fat stock, steers, and young bulls not
for service was less than at any time since 1910, and the number of
work oxen was about 40 per cent of the number in 1910.

TABLE 4
Distribution of Livestock in Belgium by Last Four Decennial Periods, 1910–1939

	1910	1920	1930	1939
	thousands of head			
Horses				
Colts born..........................	(43.8)*	....	(37.0)†	....
Colts under one year old..............	....	....	23.9	....
Under three years old				
Stallions..........................	14.5	15.4	4.2‡	14.7
Mares............................	61.3	45.9	27.8‡	43.3
Geldings..........................	36.3	24.6	19.6‡	21.7
Three years old and over				
Stallions..........................	6.9	2.5	3.5	2.7
Mares............................	121.2	75.5	125.9	113.5
Geldings..........................	76.9	41.3	64.9	49.6
Total horses....................	317.1	205.2	269.8	245.5
Mules and hinnies......................	2.7	....	6.2	....
Asses................................	7.8	....	6.4	....
Cattle				
Calves born..........................	(789.2)	....	(730.9)	....
Less than one year old				
Males.............................	132.5	....	83.6	....
Females...........................	261.9	....	187.1	....
Under two years old				
Young bulls for service..............	10.9	11.4	9.4§	9.9
Young bulls not for service..........	28.8	121.8	19.8§	90.1
Heifers...........................	284.3	426.0	211.6§	474.8
Steers............................	65.6	91.5	45.7§	61.4
Two years old and over				
Bulls.............................	12.4	7.8	9.8	8.9
Heifers...........................	....	....	123.6	....
Milch cows........................	964.9	735.2	915.3	885.8
Draft oxen........................	32.9	30.5	13.8	11.8
Fat stock.........................	85.5	63.2	51.5	57.1
Total cattle....................	1,879.7	1,487.4	1,671.2	1,599.8
Sheep................................	185.4	....	184.9	....
Goats................................	217.8	....	155.4	....
Pigs				
Pigs born..........................	(1,769.5)	....	(1,147.8)	....
Under six months old..............	762.3	554.2	448.5	409.6
Six months old or over				
Boars.............................	4.5	3.3	3.9	3.5
Sows..............................	164.9	104.8	124.7	112.5
Pigs for fattening.................	562.6	306.3	413.1	330.3
Total swine....................	1,494.3	968.6	990.2	855.9
Chickens.............................	12,144.4	....	17,863.4	11,000.0
Ducks and geese......................	172.7	....	209.8	....
Turkeys and guineas..................	21.2	....	20.4	....
Pigeons..............................	2,992.6	....	2,748.5	....
Rabbits..............................	2,032.4	....	1,473.3	....
Hives of bees........................	62.0	....	56.7	....

* Colts born during the year included in other horses.
† Colts born are included in colts under one year old in 1930.
‡ Over one year but under three years old.
§ Over one year but under two years old.

    Source: Same as for Table 2.

The percentage of the total number of cattle in Belgium in each province in 1900, in 1910, and in 1930 was as follows:

	Ant-werp	Bra-bant	West Flan-ders	East Flan-ders	Hai-naut	Liége	Lim-burg	Luxem-burg	Namur
1900...............	9	13	15	16	13	10	7	9	8
1910...............	9	12	15	16	13	11	7	9	8
1930...............	9	11	14	14	13	15	7	9	8

The number of swine in Belgium increased to 1910, but has decreased steadily since then. Just under 500,000 pigs, six months of age, were inventoried by each of the last two census enumerations. Sheep are not important in Belgium. The number has decreased steadily from about 600,000 one hundred years ago to less than one-third that number. Goats are about as scarce as sheep; there is less than one of the two together for every three farms in the country. Information on the changes in the number of poultry, rabbits, and pigeons is meager. The number of chickens has increased decidedly. How much the animals of all kinds have been reduced by the present war is not exactly known. Presumably such reduction has been greater than in the First World War. In 1920, only 65 per cent as many hogs were enumerated in the country as in 1910.

Feedstuffs used by animals.—In 1910, a total of 2,520,000 animal units used an average of 1.08 tons of concentrated feedstuff per animal unit and in 1930, 2,260,000 animal units used an average of 1.06 tons per animal unit.

Fertilizers.—According to the Census of 1930, about 41 per cent of the total quantity of chemical fertilizers used was classified as phosphatic fertilizers, 28 per cent nitrogen fertilizers, 17 per cent potassium fertilizers, and 14 per cent other special fertilizers. An average application of about 534 pounds of all chemical fertilizer per acre of crops and pasture was made for the nearly 5,000,000 acres of cropped and pastured area in the country. Also some 174 pounds of calcareous amendments were applied per acre of crops and pasture.

Farm machinery used.—In 1930, there were 144,398 single plows enumerated. The number of harrows was 356,563 and the number of pulverizers 6,168.

During the twenty-year period from 1910 to 1930, the numbers of tractors, automobiles, double plows, weeding cultivators, mechanical distributors of fertilizer, potato planters, and threshing machines increased. The use of horse rakes, mowers, tedders, and reapers also increased greatly during that twenty-year period. Because of the small size of many of the holdings, a large amount of the labor on farms is still done by hand.

TABLE 5

FEEDSTUFFS USED FOR LIVESTOCK

	1910		1930	
	Thousands of tons	Per cent of total	Thousands of tons	Per cent of total
Cake and cake meals..........................	328.2	12.0	269.1	11.2
Corn and corn products........................	153.4	5.6	322.0	13.4
Beet pulp.....................................	1,287.1	47.2	1,070.9	44.7
Fresh malt grains..............................	421.0	15.4	208.7	8.7
Dry malt grains and barley sprouts..............	31.0	1.2	27.5	1.2
Bran and mill grindings........................	361.0	13.2	331.8	13.9
All other feeds................................	146.1	5.4	165.1	6.9
Total feed................................	2,727.8	100.0	2,395.1	100.0

Factors that determine the type of farming.—Agriculturally, the country may be divided into three parts—lower Belgium, middle Belgium, and upper Belgium. As one proceeds east, the country rises from below sea level to 2,275 feet in elevation.

Soil is one of the most important factors determining the type of farming in different parts of Belgium. In the northern part, the soil is sandy and low in fertility, adapted to rye, potatoes, and vegetables. In the central part, it is a loam or a sandy loam of high fertility, adapted to sugar beets and wheat. In the mountainous, southeastern part of the country, it is moderately productive, containing more lime than in the other districts.

Topography is the second important factor that determines the type of farming. In the west, because the elevation is below or near sea level, a drainage problem exists not found in central and southeastern Belgium. Central Belgium is gently rolling in topography, comparatively free from drainage ditches that interfere with cultivation, with an elevation of from 150 to 600 feet. The favorable topography, together with the high natural productivity of the soil, makes it a rich wheat and sugar-beet section. In the southeast, along the right bank of the Sambre and Meuse rivers, and extending to the Luxemburg border in the provinces of Luxemburg, Namur, Hainaut, and Liége, the elevation is more than 600 feet. The topography is rough and the area largely devoted to livestock raising, particularly horses and cattle.

Climate is the third important factor. Differences in climate such as precipitation, temperature, and length of the growing season are important. The average rainfall is 34 inches annually; about 60 per cent of the days are rainy or cloudy. The southeast has a shorter growing season and more rain than the northwest. The precipitation is lightest along the coast and increases as one proceeds to the eastern and to the higher parts of the country.

Nearness to the market also is a factor that determines the vegetable areas and the location of poultry production. Proximity to large city markets is an important factor in vegetable farming.[1]

The agricultural regions of Belgium have been described by Professor Van der Vaeren as: (1) The region of the dunes; (2) the polders; (3) the sandy region of Flanders; (4) the Kempen; (5) the sandy loam area; (6) the loam region; (7) the region of Herve and Eupen; (8) the limestone region of Condroz; (9) the Ardennes; and (10) the Marne region. The detailed descriptions of these regions in Van der Vaeren's book, and in other publications, furnish the basis of the descriptions that follow. The sum of the acreages given by districts is 95 per cent of the area of Belgium.

The dunes country.—The region of the dunes comprises a narrow strip of about 8,900 acres along the coast to the banks of the Scheldt in the province of West Flanders. The region is not important in agricultural production, being not more than 1 to 2 miles in width. The altitude of the sand hills is from 30 to 60 feet above sea level. There is a market-gardening area between Ostend and Nieuwpoort. Poultry, some hogs, some cattle, and some horses are kept in this district. The products are consumed in the neighborhood. The farming is mostly small units of a self-sufficient type.

---

[1] An excellent series of monographic maps showing the distribution of the different types of agricultural production in Belgium, based on the data from the Census of 1895, was published more than forty years ago.

The region of the polders.—This region comprises a fertile plain from 6 to 12 miles wide from the French frontier, inside the dunes, through the north of the two Flanders provinces to Zeeland Province in Holland, transected by many ditches. The polders are of two origins, reclaimed land from the alluvial deposits along the two banks of the Scheldt River and from the sea. The polders near

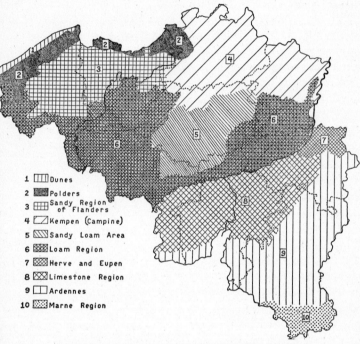

1 ☐☐☐ Dunes
2 ▨ Polders
3 ⊞ Sandy Region of Flanders
4 ◪ Kempen (Campine)
5 ◫ Sandy Loam Area
6 ▨ Loam Region
7 ▨ Herve and Eupen
8 ▨ Limestone Region
9 ☐ Ardennes
10 ▨ Marne Region

AGRICULTURAL REGIONS OF BELGIUM

the sea are protected by the sand dunes, but those along the river are protected from the overflow of water by dikes. The area of the polders is about 240,000 acres. The climate is essentially the same as in the region of the dunes, tempered both in summer and winter by the warm air from the sea.

The soils in the region of the polders—some of the best of the agricultural soils of Belgium—are heavier than in the dunes country, in some places compact clay, difficult to work and retentive of water in winter and after rains. The size of the farms is generally

not less than 25 hectares. Pastures here are of good quality. Because
of the heavy soil and generally moist climate, forage crops yield
much better than in regions of lighter soil, and livestock farming
predominates, with cattle and hogs of primary importance. Butter
and fat cattle are important in the Dixmude area. North of Bruge
and toward the frontier of Holland, especially along the Scheldt
horse raising is of some importance.

The sandy district of Flanders.—Southeast of the polder region
and comprising an area mostly northwest of the Scheldt River, i
the sandy region of the north central part of the province of East
Flanders and of the east central part of West Flanders. It is a plain
covering approximately 900,000 acres, the elevation of which grad
uates from about sea level to approximately 150 feet. An average
of 66 freezing days occur during the year. The sandy soil, originally
poor and dry, has been improved appreciably by liberal applica
tions of farm manure, vegetable refuse, and chemical fertilizer, and
by careful cultivation and intensive handling for many years.

The farms in this district are generally small, many of them from
two to five acres in size. Potatoes, oats, forage and sugar beets
coffee chicory, serradella, and market garden vegetables are com
monly grown. On the heavier, or richer soils some wheat is grown
Chicory raising has been expanded here. More than one-third of
the double cropping of land in Belgium is found in the province
of East Flanders. Because of the intensive cultivation of the land
there is a large agricultural population per acre, especially in the
eastern part. Many large cities in this area are excellent markets
for vegetables. One of the two hop sections of Belgium is in the
neighborhood of Aalst in this region. Here the cultivation of hops
is in small parcels, many not more than ten square feet in contrast
to more extensive production in the Poperinghe section. Flax de
creased from 1880 to 1910 but has increased since then. The most
intensive flax areas in Belgium are in this district. The production
of both nursery plants and of flowering plants is important.

The dry, sandy soils of the area resist the establishment of perma
nent pastures. Farmers pasture their cattle along the ditches and
streamlets. Some goats and sheep are kept and either goat's milk
or ewe's milk is used by the poorer farmers. More than half of the
rabbits in Belgium are in the Flanders provinces.

The Kempen.—The so-called Kempen (Campine) region of Belgium comprises practically all of the province of Antwerp, excepting the river polders along the Scheldt, a small part of the northern section of Brabant Province, and the northern two-thirds of the province of Limburg. The elevation ranges practically from sea level, near the river Scheldt, progressively upward to 300 feet in the east of the province of Limburg.

The Kempen comprises about 1,111,950 acres and has a sandy surface soil, with a subsoil quite impermeable to water. The climate is more continental than maritime, cold in winter and warm in summer, with a relatively clear sky. The average number of days of frost is from 80 to 85. Large areas of the region, perhaps one-fifth or more of the total, are uncultivated—neither roads nor railroads cross it. The population, formerly principally agricultural, in part has become industrial. Agriculture consists almost exclusively of farms of from 2 to 12 acres. The crops grown are rye, potatoes, forage beets, oats, serradella, buckwheat, and forage. Wheat is grown on the heavier, well-drained soils. Along the canals of the Kempen are found some 5,000 acres of irrigated meadows which give good yields. The provinces of Antwerp and Limburg in the Kempen have 16 per cent of the total area of the kingdom, but 52 per cent of the uncultivated area. Much of the area is too wet for woodland.

The sandy loam region.—North of the Meuse and Sambre rivers, largely in the southeastern half of Brabant Province, but extending slightly into Hainaut and Namur provinces, including the cities of Brussels, Louvain (Leuven), and Tirlemont, is the sandy loam region of Belgium comprising approximately 586,000 acres. The elevation ranges from about 115 feet in the north to 245 feet in the south. The number of frosts in this region is from 60 to 70 annually.

The soil is essentially sandy in the north and grades into loam as one proceeds south. The subsoil usually is sandy and well-drained. It is one of the best agricultural regions of Belgium. Reference to Table 1 will show the exceedingly high percentage, relative to the total area, of practically all types of crop production for Brabant Province. Because of the proximity to Brussels and the favorable soil, a large amount of market gardening is done. The witloof chicory industry is extensively developed in this region. There are many producers of open-air and of forced plants in the area. Strawberries, gooseberries, cherries, and some apples, pears, and prunes are also produced. Some tomatoes, melons, and cucumbers are produced under glass. The production of grapes and peaches under glass has become a highly developed industry, at and near Hoeylaert, some 10 miles southeast of Brussels. Some 30,000 glass houses have been built for this purpose. In 1929 the total number of glass houses reported in the country was 57,676, occupying an area of 65,640,721 square feet. Because of the disappearance of foreign markets and the development of similar businesses in other countries, especially in Holland, this industry suddenly found itself overdeveloped, with consequent financial hardship among the producers.

The numbers of cattle and horses in relation to area are also fairly high, relative to the total area in this region. Milk production for the fluid market has been developed around Brussels. Many of the cows in this region are purchased and fattened for the butcher after their usefulness is past. On small farms that produce milk, milch cows furnish draft power, but on most farms the larger horses are used. Horse raising is also found in the area. The number of horses and colts, per square mile, is higher in Brabant than in any other province except Hainaut.

As one proceeds away from Brussels, the usual cropping system is wheat, rye, oats, sugar beets, potatoes, and forage crops. The yields, although high, are not so good as those obtained in the loamy region of Belgium.

The loam region.—This is the largest agricultural region of Belgium and covers in the neighborhood of 1,750,000 acres, extending throughout the center of the country from the south of West Flanders to the east of Limburg Province, north of the Meuse River. It comprises the largest part of middle Belgium, with an elevation in the north of from 130 to 165 feet and in the south of around 650 feet. The climate is the same as in the sandy loam region. The soil is a deep and productive mixture of clay, sand, and calcareous material. According to the proportion of these three ingredients, the soil is more or less compact and difficult to work. In general, the heaviest loam is found in the south and in the east of the area. In the vicinity of Mons, in the southern part of Hainaut Province and in the northern part of the province of Liége, the soil contains natural phosphates and calcium.

The largest farms in the country are in the loam region. Most of the 2,490 farms of 120 acres or more in Belgium are found in this region. There are also small farms, the occupants of which are either industrial workers or are in the regular service of the larger farmers.

Judged by the quality of the soil and by the variety and abundance of its products, the loam region is the most productive agricultural part of Belgium. A loam soil permits the production of all of the crops of a temperate climate. Wheat, oats, barley, sugar beets, beans, potatoes, forage beets, all the vegetables, clover and alfalfa are grown, and high yields obtained. Production of chicory for coffee is localized in the vicinity of Tournai. Market gardening is carried on near the villages and industrial centers.

This region of middle Belgium, especially in the province of Hainaut, is the most important area in the country for the breeding and raising of Belgian horses. They are on most of the important farms. Exported to many countries before the depression, they were easily sold because of their strength, unusual action, and quiet disposition. When times were best, more than 30,000 head were exported annually. Cattle are raised, especially on average and small farms where the necessary labor can be obtained easily. Some hogs and sheep are kept.

The region of Herve and Eupen.—This region of about 90,000 acres comprises the northeastern part of the province of Liége, north of the Vesdre River, and east of the Meuse to the border, an area of undulating plateaus and depressions. The elevation is from 800 to 1,060 feet. The soil, a loam, in many parts calcareous, suitable largely for grass farming, has been kept in grass for many years. The size of the farms is from 7 to 25 acres.

Most farms keep only one horse, for transportation, and one head of cattle per acre. The cattle run on the meadows a large part of the year and, in winter, are fed hay supplemented with concentrates. The fat-test for the year is generally low. Milk is sold as fluid milk in Liége or made into butter, cottage cheese, or clotted cream. Cheese of the Herve is of excellent quality. Butter factories and milk plants have been established in the region. Pigs are bought in markets near by and fattened on by-products of butter and cheese manufacturing supplemented by barley meal. Most of the farms have small flocks of hens.

The equipment on farms of this region is limited to that necessary for transportation, for harvesting the hay and for the milk business. Land values here have always been high as compared with values in other agricultural regions of Belgium.

The limestone region.—This region comprises around 1,250,000 acres in the provinces of Hainaut, Namur, Liége, and a very little of northern Luxemburg, south of the Meuse. About half of it is in the area between the Sambre and the Meuse rivers. The elevation is from about 650 feet in the north to 1,150 feet in the south. The region is a plateau, intersected by valleys formed by the dissolving of carboniferous limestone and the erosion of schists. The soils, although often close to rock, are naturally good. In some places they overlie fissure subsoils containing considerable limestone. They warm up, cool off, and dry off readily.

The climate in this area is much like that of the Ardennes at the south. The number of days of frost is about 90. The region, sometimes called the Condroz, has a number of large farms of more than 250 acres and farms of about 120 acres. The best lands are cropped with wheat, oats, rye, spelt, sugar beets, potatoes, pasture, and forage. Alfalfa and red clover are grown here because of the high lime content of the soil. Nursery products are important also.

In the area between the Sambre and Meuse rivers, strawberries, apples, cherries, pears, plums, and currants are found. Strawberries have been grown for fifty years. Industrial communities in the vicinity of Charleroi and the other large cities of Belgium provide good markets for more than 400 acres of strawberries. Strawberries are sold under the trade name of *Wépion*.

Less horse raising is carried on than in other regions. To some extent, horses are used as power but are less important than in many regions of Belgium. Cattle raising to sell for fattening in other areas is the most important animal enterprise of the region. A few pigs are kept for home use.

The Ardennes.—The Ardennes area includes the southern tips of the provinces of Hainaut and Namur, the southeastern third of the province of Liége and almost all of the province of Luxemburg, an area of around 1,000,000 acres. The elevation is from 1,300 to 2,275 feet. The region is colder, especially in winter, than the rest of Belgium and has more rain, but in summer it is only a little cooler than low Belgium. The rainfall is from 39 inches to 49 inches. The days of frost number from 100 to 120. The region is less densely populated than the other regions. It is covered with large state-owned and private forests and is not important in agricultural production. Oats, potatoes, forage crops, and pasture are the more important crops grown.

The old race of horses raised in the region, called the Ardennes, enjoys a world-wide reputation. They are of smaller stature than the heavier Belgian horse and make excellent general-purpose horses.

Raising of cattle is the most important enterprise in this region. Cattle are of varying breeds, but are either blue-gray or black and white and are mostly of large frames. Compared with other regions, the proportion of young animals to older animals is relatively high. They are sold rather young, and respond favorably when transferred to better regions of the country for fattening. Pigs occupy second rank among the animal industries of the region. Heavy breeds of fowls have been replacing the light breeds here.

The Marne region.—This region comprises about 235,000 acres in the extreme southeastern section of the province of Luxemburg, next to the French-Luxemburg frontier, called the Belgian Lorraine, or low Luxemburg. It takes its name from a similar region in Lorraine and in the Marne in France.

The soils are calcareous sand, clay, marl and sand, heavy and wet and frequently found in meadows in the bottom of the valleys, especially where the rivers overflow. Flooding by the rivers has permeated the soils with fine clay particles that make them difficult to cultivate.

The elevation, in the neighborhood of 1,000 feet, is not quite so high as in the Ardennes. The climate is less rigorous than in the Ardennes, improves from north to south, the growing season being two or three weeks longer than in the Ardennes. There are from 90 to 100 days of frost. The rainfall is less frequent and less heavy than in the Ardennes.

The farms are from small to average in size, usually comprising not more than 50 acres. The farm family does most of the work. The countryside is traversed by valleys and most of the cropland is on the flanks of such valleys. Rye and potatoes are grown mostly on the lighter soils, beets and wheat on the heavier soils. Forage crops are important.

Horses are limited to the needs of the farms. The cattle of the region are a cross between local breeds and Durham bulls, and are kept for milk production, which is relatively low, and for fattening. Pork is raised largely for the production of smoked hams which are noted for their excellence. Along the river lands there are other agricultural specialties, particularly ducks and gray geese. Table fruits of excellent quality are grown along the French frontier.

Price levels.—Index numbers of wholesale prices of groups of commodities in Belgium have been prepared by Dr. F. A. Pearson, Professor of Prices and Statistics at Cornell University. In 1939 price levels in Belgium were slightly more than six times the pre-First-World-War averages. In the 1927–1928 period, prices were at levels about eight times prewar, then precipitously declined to lows in 1933 and 1934 in sympathy with the general decline in prices throughout the world.

Wholesale prices of basic commodities, when prewar (1910–1914) prices were taken as 100, increased from an index of 358 in 1922 to 897 in 1927, then declined to 461 in 1934, stood at 840 per cent of pre-First-World-War (1910–1914) prices in April, 1940.

Livestock and livestock product prices at wholesale rose to an index of 883 per cent of prewar, as an average for 1929, then declined to 478 in 1934, but stood at 742 per cent of prewar (1910–1914), in April, 1940.

Wholesale prices of grain rose to an index of 958 per cent of prewar as an average for 1928, declined to 342 in 1934 and in April, 1940, stood at 767 per cent of prewar (1910–1914) prices.

Food prices at wholesale, including grains, livestock, livestock products, and vegetable fats, rose to an index of 858 per cent of prewar for the year 1928, declined to 418 per cent for 1934, and were 750 per cent of prewar in April, 1940. On other foods, such as coffee, cocoa, tea, and sugar, prices at wholesale rose to an index of 822 in 1927, declined to 457 in 1934, and stood at 727 per cent of prewar (1910–1914) prices in April, 1940.

Each of the two devaluations of the currency was accompanied by an increase in the wholesale price level, in the first instance of some 300 points in the index, and in the second instance of about 200 points, or two-thirds as much as the first. The position of the farmer and of the manufacturer improved each time devaluation of the currency occurred.

TABLE 6

INDEX NUMBERS OF WHOLESALE PRICES IN BELGIUM IN CURRENCY*

	Forty basic commodities	Livestock and livestock products	Grains	Foods	Other foods†
1910.................	98	97	95	96	96
1911.................	98	97	99	99	104
1912.................	103	103	108	105	105
1913.................	102	104	102	101	97
1914‡................	99	100	98	98	95
1921.................	355	364	335	347	338
1922.................	358	344	340	330	280
1923.................	510	447	445	438	408
1924.................	573	488	554	517	495
1925.................	577	536	602	554	484
1926.................	776	647	804	722	690
1927.................	897	758	930	842	822
1928.................	890	782	958	858	794
1929.................	886	883	878	853	734
1930.................	749	820	612	694	614
1931.................	591	634	465	545	535
1932.................	494	521	419	470	478
1933.................	483	527	355	450	499
1934.................	461	478	342	418	457
1935.................	522	536	410	477	500
1936.................	583	578	511	544	549
1937.................	707	627	661	641	626
1938.................	646	672	615	629	569
1939.................	644	628	565	697	600

* 1910–1914=100.
† Coffee, cocoa, tea and sugar.
‡ Prices 1915–1920 not available.

Research institutes and laboratories for agriculture.—Scientific research in agriculture is carried on by the State at Gembloux, Ghent, Libramont, and by the Catholic University of Louvain at Lovenjoul and Heverlee. Sugar-beet research is done at Thienen also. State-operated, chemical-analysis laboratories are located at Antwerp, Ghent, Liége, and Gembloux, and state seed-analysis laboratories at Gembloux and Ghent. An approved seed-control station is located at Louvain, and chemical-analysis laboratories, approved by the State, are located at various places.

Agricultural and horticultural associations and coöperatives.— The largest coöperative organization in Belgium is the *Belgische Boerenbond* (League of Farmers), a social and economic institution. This has grown from 49 guilds, with 2,280 members in 1891, to 1,245 guilds, with 110,271 members in 1938. The *Unions Professionelles Agricoles de Belgique,* the *Alliance Agricole Belge,* the *Eigenaars en Landbouwersbond* at Bruges, the *Société coöpérative des Cultivateurs luxembourgeois* at Virton, and *Redt u Zelve,* a purchasing coöperative at Aalst, are other important farm coöperative organizations. Many mutual societies for the insurance of livestock against death, coöperatives for the sale of milk, of butter and of cheese, and local firms and societies engaged in the purchase of seeds, commercial fertilizer, livestock, feed, and farm machinery function throughout the country.

Schools of agriculture.—Instruction in agriculture is given at the University of Louvain and at agricultural and horticultural schools at Ghent, Gembloux, Vilvorde, and Huy. Domestic science is taught separately in girls' schools.

Three schools, one each at Ghent, Gembloux, and Louvain, give a higher degree, after four years of study, with a diploma in agronomy or in agricultural-chemistry engineering. After a fifth year of study a degree in forestry, rural engineering, horticulture, industrial agriculture, or colonial agricultural engineering may be earned. A middle degree is given at 16 schools of agriculture at the end of two or three years of study. A lower middle degree is given for two years and a lower degree is given for winter study.

CHAPTER XII

Economic Development of Belgium

BY B.-S. CHLEPNER

AT THE BEGINNING of her historical period, in the time of Julius Caesar, Belgian soil was inhabited by scattered tribes whose economic activity was of a primitive order. During the Roman occupation roads were built and a few towns appeared. Deforestation and conquest of the soil went on, the population grew. Cultivation of land, the raising of pigs and geese made progress; wool weaving and rudimentary iron work expanded. Roman villas were built, and Romanization of the country was far advanced.

The infiltrations of Germanic tribes, from about the end of the third century, disrupted the economic development. Weakness of the central power, the neglect of roads, and general insecurity brought about a slowing up of trade and economic recession. Decentralization resulted. Large domains were established either by nobles or by the church, with a pronounced tendency toward economic self-sufficiency. The large abbeys—economic organizations as well as religious foundations—were particularly characteristic of this epoch.

In the eighth, and particularly in the ninth, century, Norse invasions, in addition to vast inundations of the low coastal lands by the sea, wrought complete havoc. The central power disappeared completely; instability and insecurity were everywhere; the abbeys were ruined; the country bristled with fortified castles.

When the Norse invasions ceased, economic activity again began to make progress; it was accelerated in the eleventh and still more so in the twelfth century. The conquest of the soil, deforestation, drainage, and dam-building were renewed. The population increased rapidly. Because there was land still to be reclaimed from the sea, or conquered from the forests—a sort of frontier-expansion —the feudal regime in the Low Countries was not as complete and did not last as long as in the rest of western or central Europe Serfdom completely disappeared and feudal taxes were considerably reduced around the thirteenth century in Flanders, a little later in Hainaut.

The rapid increase in the population seems to be the principal reason for the large peasant emigration during the twelfth and thirteenth centuries, the only one of this kind ascertained in Belgium. The skill of the Flemish and Brabant people in the building of dikes and in the improvement of land was so renowned that lords, bishops, and abbots in different parts of northern and central Europe recruited groups of Flemish farmers, to whom they granted large stretches of land and certain privileges. Veritable Flemish colonies (which included Walloons, too), grew up in Pomerania, Saxony, Silesia, and Hungary, where many regions owe their agricultural progress to these immigrants.

Along with some sections of Italy, the Low Countries were the first regions in Europe to rise out of the economic torpor of the Middle Ages. From the eleventh and twelfth centuries on, new forms of economic activity and of social organization developed and spread over the rest of western and central Europe. These forms consisted principally in the growth of a monetary economy, the development of industry, the rise of towns, the movement of urban emancipation, and trade with foreign lands.

The expansion of industrial activity would not have been possible without the accumulation of population in the towns and without foreign markets; on the other hand, the formation, or at least the expansion, of towns resulted from the development of trade and of relations with countries abroad. Of course, such terms as "industry" or "towns" should not be understood in the contemporary sense. The industry was carried on by artisans, the towns were small agglomerations. In the fourteenth century the population of Bruges and Ghent certainly did not exceed 50,000, and these were relative metropolises. But for that time, the development of craftsmanship as well as such urban expansion were revolutionary.

From the twelfth to approximately the middle of the sixteenth century, the Low Countries witnessed an economic expansion without parallel at that period. Prosperity was interrupted several times by wars or by political and social struggles; also, pauperism developed in the large towns. However, in general this period witnessed the expansion of a prosperous economy, known as the "urban" economy, although already possessing some features of the contemporary "capitalist" and international economy.

The importance of the development of towns in economic expansion since the eleventh century can hardly be overemphasized. They prospered and expanded where their location was economically favorable in regard to communications. Bruges was on a river in the interior of the country, at a point reached by seagoing vessels—Ghent, at the confluence of the Lys (Leie) and the Scheldt, while Brussels, Louvain, and Liége developed at points where the great road from Bruges to Cologne crossed navigable rivers.

Prosperous Bruges during the thirteenth and fourteenth centuries was, above all, a center of international trade, whereas Ghent, Ypres, and other towns were chiefly producing centers. Such was the density of population that, from the thirteenth century on, the inhabitants of Flanders were obliged to import a part of their food. In the middle of the sixteenth century the country appeared as one continuous town to the Italian author, L. Guicciardini.

The development of towns brought about a great movement of urban emancipation. The population, with its inclination toward trade and production, could no longer endure the narrow and strict regulations of the feudal lords, the multiple and arbitrary taxes, the absence of regular justice. Through long struggle, and partly by financial means, the towns obtained charters, of which the oldest seems to have been granted in 1066. The towns obtained an autonomous administration and local courts, they became political and juridical units; their town halls, their belfries, their town walls, showed their power; the town seal appeared on documents, as evidence of their immunities and privileges. They became the centers not only of economic activity but also of political and cultural expansion.

The most important economic event in the Low Countries, from the twelfth to the fourteenth centuries, was the development of cloth production, which was an urban and largely an exporting industry. Flemish cloth was exported not only into neighboring countries but even into Russia and the Near East. In a short time, the native wool was no longer sufficient. Wool had to be imported, mostly from England. A similar phenomenon occurred in the Liége country, where coppersmelting and the production of the famous "dinanderies" (table and kitchen utensils) expanded to a point where the metal had to be imported, whereas the product was exported even to far-off lands. As a result, from the fourteenth century on, the Belgian Provinces possessed certain "transforming" industries (importing raw materials and exporting finished products), which heralded, in a small way, what the Belgium of the nineteenth century was to become.

During the thirteenth and fourteenth centuries, many Flemish weavers went to England, attracted by the intelligent policy of its sovereigns. They contributed greatly to the formation of the cloth industry there. Although recent historians no longer consider the Flemings as the actual founders of the English woolen industry, they, nevertheless, admit their preponderant role. The well-known English historian, J. H. Clapham, wrote about Belgium: "Once she was England's schoolmistress in industry."

On the other hand, the Flemish cloth industry was undergoing a complete transformation. Artisanship is a form of production perfectly suited to the local market. But the artisan is not in a position to buy raw materials abroad or to export his products. He must have recourse to the services of the merchant. In the end, the merchants controlled the entire organization of production and distribution. During the thirteenth and fourteenth centuries, a large section of workers who were engaged in the woolen industry at Ghent or at Ypres were not independent producers; they were salaried people. In the language of the nineteenth century, they formed an urban proletariat. Strikes were not unknown.

The fifteenth century, characterized by the centralizing action of the dukes of Burgundy and the decline of Bruges with the concurrent growth of Antwerp, marked the transition from the economy of the Middle Ages to the economy of modern times. Although the "old" urban cloth industry was on the wane, new textile industries, producing lighter cloth, were growing up; the tapestry,

THE PORT OF ANTWERP

COAL MINES AND INDUSTRY, CHARLEROI

linen, and lace industry also was expanding. New industries developed, such as diamond cutting and printing, particularly in Antwerp. However, Antwerp became primarily a trading and a financial center.

Because of a liberal policy which rejected the guild regulations, Antwerp attained such prominence that, at the beginning of the sixteenth century, it was probably the most important trading center of the world, the "town common to all nations," as Guicciardini wrote. In many respects, Antwerp may be considered as the first "capitalist" center in the modern sense of the word. Many foreigners settled here; the first exchange was established, where not only commodities but also foreign currencies and public bonds were negotiated. Speculation on merchandise, on land, on foreign currencies developed.

During the wars of religion, in the second half of the sixteenth century, the prolonged struggle between the Spanish troops and the insurgents, the plunder committed by the soldiery, and quarrels between some sections of the population ravaged, on an unprecedented scale, the provinces which had been among the most prosperous in Europe. The country was laid waste, the death rate was high, and a mass emigration bled the country of its most energetic, talented, and wealthy people. Some historians state that the wars of the sixteenth century reduced the population of the Low Countries by half.

There is positive evidence of a large-scale emigration. Veritable colonies from the Low Countries settled in England where they introduced important innovations in the cloth industry, especially in the technique of dyeing, to such a point that some contemporaries called it "new drapery." Other colonies from the Low Countries settled in Germany and in France, where they established new industries—such as the making of cloth, laces, and carpets. Still other colonies settled in the United Provinces (present-day Holland), just across the border from the Southern Provinces, and coöperated, to a great extent, in the commercial and maritime expansion of that state. It is known that Walloons from Hainaut, who had gone to Holland at this time, went on to participate actively in the foundation of what was known first as Nova Belgica or New Amsterdam, and later as New York.

During the seventeenth century, large sections of the country were frequently in the hands of foreign troops. Foreign commerce was practically at a standstill, even before the closing of the Scheldt by the Treaty of Westphalia (1648). Economic policy, particularly the tariff, was controlled by neighboring states.

In the eighteenth century, under the domination of the Austrian Habsburgs, the so-called Austrian Low Countries enjoyed a relative peace, a period when military operations on Belgian soil were short and infrequent. However, the Scheldt remained closed. The Austrians, like the Spanish, considered the Belgian Provinces mainly as a pawn in the diplomatic game. They never hesitated to injure Belgian interests for the benefit of their dynastic policy. A notorious example was provided when, in 1723, some Belgian merchants established the famous Compagnie d'Ostende, for oversea trade. When Holland, England, and France raised objections, the Emperor of Austria first answered that "the sea is open for all"; however, he agreed to suspend the company, ostensibly for "the good of Europe," but actually because he wanted to gain the good will of foreign courts.

Cut off from the sea, without any national economic policy, the country retired within itself. Foreign trade was reduced to very small proportions, the economic activities of the towns remained on a very low level. But because of the period of relative peace and political stability, the population increased, roads and canals improved; important agricultural progress was made. Fallow land disappeared, rotation of crops was general, the use of manure increased, breeding expanded. At the end of the eighteenth century, at the time of the French Revolution, the agriculture of Belgium was the most prosperous on the Continent. Moreover, some home industries[1] (linen, cloth, lace, etc.), were also carried on extensively in the villages, particularly in Flanders.

On the contrary, the Walloon sections of the Low Countries—particularly Hainaut—although still preëminently devoted to agriculture and forest cultivation, witnessed some expansion of what were to become the heavy industries. Coal mines, probably the oldest on the Continent, began to be worked regularly in the seven-

---

[1] Industries performed at the worker's home (*industries à domicile*), usually done for a town merchant.

teenth century; iron mining, based on the use of charcoal, increased. Some coal was exported to France and to Holland.

Present-day Belgium also includes the former principality of Liége, whose political evolution was quite different. Since the sixteenth century this "ecclesiastic principality," headed by a Prince-Bishop, maintained a relatively independent existence. Its economic development was not hindered, and its industrial character was already quite pronounced at the end of the eighteenth century. At that time, the Liége coal industry was the most advanced on the Continent, and its mines probably the deepest in the world.

The Liége armament industry was universally known. The manufacture of nails, cutlery, bolts, paper, leather, and crystal steadily prospered; the woolen industry had been set up at Verviers. That these were small enterprises—even often "home industries"—does not alter the fact that the valley of the Meuse was the first on the Continent to present, even if on a small scale, a picture of what industrial regions were going to be during the nineteenth century.

The turn of the century witnessed a decisive change in the political and economic destinies of Belgium. At this time, the Belgian Provinces did not constitute a unified "national" economy. Each province (rather each state), had its traditional laws, its currency, its fiscal system, its customs, its corporative organization. Even within each state there were tolls, transit taxes, and monopolies of all kinds.

The dominant features of the French period (1794–1814) were political and economic unification and the beginning of the Industrial Revolution. All restrictions, all monopolies—corporative or otherwise—were abolished. Freedom of industry and commerce was proclaimed. Uniform civil legislation was introduced. Civil affairs and public relief were secularized; fiscal exemptions were abolished, and the tax system simplified.

The first period of the French occupation (until around the end of the century) was a very troubled time. The population, in great majority ardently Catholic, was opposed to the trend of ideas of the invaders, particularly in rural districts. Insurrections broke out. In the towns was a latent opposition among the ruling classes and in the local administration. Large requisitions, drafting of young men, heavy levies, introduction of French paper money (the "assignats"), whose value was dwindling, all these factors aggravated the already disturbed situation and aroused the discontent of the people.

However, when political and administrative stability was at last achieved, and the former excesses liquidated, when the opposition from the ruling classes and the local administration disappeared, or at least largely subsided, the economic situation improved considerably. The Belgian Provinces, with their old economic traditions, already had a class of experienced manufacturers and merchants. They benefited from the large market, the whole French Empire, of which they were the most industrialized section.

At this time, Belgian manufacturers began to introduce the mechanical inventions and improvements which radically had changed the English industry. The "schoolmistress" was taking lessons from her former pupil; the Industrial Revolution was entering the Continent via Belgium. At Ghent, Bauwens created the first factory for the mechanical spinning and weaving of cotton, having imported from England machine parts and designs at the risk of his life. At Verviers, and later at Liége, a wandering English engineer, W. Cockerill, manufactured the first mechanical looms for the wool industry. Production expanded to a point where soon he was able to export *mécaniques* into various European countries. The zinc industry began at the same time. Coal mining progressed under the requirements of large works undertaken by the French administration, especially at Antwerp. Agriculture progressed also; the culture of sugar beets developed. All industries benefited from having a market of 40,000,000 consumers at their disposal.

In 1815 Belgium was united to Holland and became the southern part of the Kingdom of the Low Countries. She lost a large continental market; she found, however, an important colonial market, particularly for the cotton industry. But a radical readaptation was necessary. Moreover, Belgium left the strongly protected French economy to enter a relatively free-trade kingdom. The commercial policy was to be one of the main reasons of disputes between the Northern Provinces—essentially agricultural and commercial, and therefore favoring free trade—and the Southern Provinces, where budding industries demanded a protective tariff.

Nevertheless, the Southern, or Belgian, Provinces continued to make industrial progress. In Liége and in the Hainaut regions the old charcoal-burning furnaces began to be replaced by furnaces using coke. The Cockerill firm built the first steam engines on the Continent, and soon J. Cockerill established at Seraing, near Liége, the iron works which, around 1840, were the most important on the Continent. Engineering industries also developed; the gas industry was born. On the whole, the Dutch period (1815–1830) was a period of industrial progress and of relative prosperity.

At the moment of the proclamation of her national independence, in 1830, Belgium was the most highly industrialized country on the Continent. Modern coal mining, iron working, and engineering were already firmly rooted in the country; mechanized textile industries employed a large number of workers. However, these were only the beginnings of a profound economic transformation.

In industry proper, corporate enterprise was almost unknown; most workshops were small. Enterprises with more than 100 workers were few, except in coal mining, where some works had several hundred employees, an enormous figure for that time. Also, the use of steam was in its infancy. The most powerful steam engine had a strength of only 80 h.p., less than some modern automobiles. Manufacturing industries commanded no more than two hundred steam engines with a total power of 2,000 h.p. The coal mines were better equipped. Their total motor force was as high as 10,000 h.p. In the aggregate, Belgium then possessed a steam force of 12,000 h.p., which is two or three times less than the power used at present by any of her large metallurgical works. And yet, Belgium then was industrialized to a greater degree than any other country on the Continent.

From 1830 on, Belgium knew a century of economic progress without precedent. Until about 1860–1870 she was, in fact, the only country to keep pace with the industrial expansion of England. She was favored by her deeply rooted economic tradition, by her geographical position, and also by her possession of certain raw materials, particularly coal, iron, and zinc. She also extracted from her soil such secondary materials as clay, sand, and slate.

The building of railways was the outstanding event of the first decade which followed the national revolution. Belgium built the first railway network on the Continent. After some hesitancy and discussion it was decided, in 1834, that the main lines would be built by the Government. In 1835 the first section (Brussels-Mechlin) was finished. The construction of railways not only was a decisive factor in linking Belgian economy with the neighboring countries; it also gave impetus to the modernization and expansion of coal mining, or ironwork operation, and of engineering. The first three or four locomotives used in Belgium were imported from England, but soon the Cockerill plants manufactured the first national locomotive (proudly called *La Belge*), which was followed by many others.

Expansion of these industries, and, to a minor degree, of some others, was fostered by the development of what was then called "the spirit of association," now called, more prosaically, "the corporate movement." Whereas the business corporation (*société anonyme*) was almost unknown before 1830, it spread largely from 1834–1835 on, and was the prime factor in the development of large industrial enterprises. Modern banking also began practically in the same decade. The oldest Belgian banking corporation, the *Société Générale,* was established in 1822 by William I, King of the Low Countries. For about a decade its main business was the development of landed properties (handed over by the King), the issuance of public loans and transactions in foreign exchanges. In the 1830's the *Société* engaged largely in commercial banking, and even more so in investment banking. It established tight connections with industrial enterprises and became the first organization to practice what later was known as "mixed banking," a type of organization followed subsequently by German and by most of the other continental banks. Other banking and financial organizations were established in the 1830's, although the movement developed largely only in the second half of the century, when these organizations—with the *Société Générale* at the head—played a prominent role in the industrial development of the country as well as in its expansion abroad.

In the first decades of national existence, economic expansion took place mainly in the Walloon section of the country. Flanders, on the contrary, was going through a difficult period. The cotton industry complained about the loss of the colonial market, the old home industry of linen, based on hand work, was undergoing a severe crisis as a result of competition in the mechanical production of English cloth. The crisis was aggravated by a few bad crops, and, above all, by a terrible potato blight. As a result, Flanders went through a period of great misery between 1845 and 1850.

It was the misery of Flanders which led the Government to decree the free entry of grain. Gradually, other breaches were made in the protective edifice which was to go to pieces around 1860–1870 when, for one thing, industry asserted its interest in exports, and, in addition, agriculture itself was restored, principally because of the use of artificial fertilizers that brought about a veritable agricultural revolution.

From about 1870 on, Belgium was practicing a policy virtually of free trade. The import of food and raw materials was completely free. Only finished and some semifinished products were subject to very small duties. Belgium was one of the most earnest protagonists of lower tariffs and of the "most favored nation" clause.

The destiny of Belgium as an industrial country thus emerged more and more clearly from the middle of the century on. Toward 1870–1880, her own reserves of iron and zinc were exhausted—even coal production became insufficient. But because she possessed technical personnel, machinery, experienced and enterprising management, easy communications, Belgium imported raw materials and semifinished goods and became, essentially, a manufacturing and exporting country.

During the second half of the century, the main steps forward were the expansion of coal mining, metallurgy (which underwent a remarkable change through the introduction of steel), glass making, mechanical construction (particularly steam engines and railroad material), and, of course, textile manufacture. From the end of the century there had been a large expansion of the chemical industry (the Solvay process of soda making spread the world over), and of the electrical industry.

From about the 1860's on, Belgium became a large exporter of equipment (machines, rails, locomotives and similar heavy equipment). As such, she was obliged either to grant long-term loans abroad or to take a direct interest in foreign corporations. In other words, she was obliged to invest abroad. In the 1860's Belgian capital largely participated in the construction of railways in southern Europe (Spain, Italy, and the Balkans). Later, Belgian technicians and capitalists built railways and streetcar lines in central Europe and in South America. At about the end of the century, railways, electrical plants, hypothecary banks, and similar institutions were established in Argentina, in Egypt, in China, and elsewhere. Around the turn of the century there was an exodus of Belgian capital and technicians toward Russia, where coal mines, metallurgical plants, chemical works, glass works, and streetcar lines were being built. In 1900, 130 Belgian industrial corporations had plants in Russia, with large capital investments in Russian corporations. Belgian skill and capital were concentrated in the Donets Basin, sometimes called "the Russian Belgium."

Although the industrialization of the country was steadily progressing, agriculture was not neglected. Even while, proportionately, the farming population was slowly decreasing, its role in economic activities remained important. About 1880 agriculture in Belgium, as everywhere else in Europe, suffered from the famous agricultural crisis created by the importation of American grain. But, unlike most other continental countries, Belgium did not adopt a protective policy. Her agriculture underwent a remarkable transformation; the cultivation of cereals was discarded and replaced by that of plants (the sugar beet in particular), and of vegetables. Above all, cattle raising and dairy production expanded.

Chiefly because of the intensive use of fertilizers, the soil was made increasingly productive; the production of most crops, per acre, was among the highest, if not the highest, in the world. However, because of the density of the population (which doubled in the hundred years between 1830 and 1930), and because of the rising standard of living, Belgium at last had to import a large proportion of her food (particularly wheat, followed by butter, meat, and other products), and of cattle feed. On the contrary, she was an exporter of such products as sugar, grapes, vegetables, and poultry. In the final analysis, however, she was a large importer of food, one of the main reasons why her total imports were higher than her total exports. This trade deficit was largely offset, however, by other elements of her international balance (chiefly by the income from foreign investments and from transit trade).

SCHOOL, LÉOPOLDVILLE, BELGIAN CONGO

WILD LIFE, CONGO JUNGLE

The evolution before the First World War was not as steady and regular as it appears from a short sketch. There were boom periods and depressions. As the country became more and more industrialized, and as its dependence on foreign trade increased, it felt in an ever-increasing degree the ups and downs of international business cycles. Belgian business cycles coincide closely with the British, or, for that matter, with the international cycles. Profound changes

APPORTIONMENT OF ACTIVE POPULATION AMONG DIFFERENT OCCUPATIONS
(in thousands)

	Inde-pendent	Helpers	Employed	Total	Per cent
Agriculture (including fishing and forestry)....................	267	239	131	637	17.0
Industry.......................	197	43	1,553	1,793	47.8
Transportation.................	20	7	229	256	6.8
Commerce and finance..........	269	190	84	543	14.5
Liberal professions (including churches)...................	...	...	...	140	3.7
Employees of public administrations (including teaching, army).	...	...	...	169	4.5
Personal services...............	...	...	...	184	5.0
Miscellaneous..................	...	...	...	28	0.7
				3,750	100.0*

* In Belgian statistics the term used for the first column is "patrons." But it does not seem advisable to interpret this term by the use of the corresponding English term, "bosses." "Heads of enterprises," or "entrepreneurs," could do, but as the majority are very small farmers, tradesmen or artisans, without any hired help, the term "enterprise" might be misunderstood. The term "helpers" is used in Belgian statistics for members of the family who regularly assist the head of a business in the exercise of his job. They are found mostly on the farms and in the small shops. The third column includes laborers and employees, the first category being, of course, the overwhelming majority.

were brought about in the economic and social structure of the country by the industrial expansion of the nineteenth century. The first change to stress is the radical modification of the activities performed by the population.

The total Belgian population in 1930 was 8,092,000 (710 inhabitants per square mile, as compared to 280 in the state of New York and 41 in the United States as a whole). Almost half of them— 3,750,000—were gainfully employed. The apportionment of this active population among different occupations is shown in the accompanying table.

Whereas, at the beginning of the nineteenth century and even in 1830, the majority of the population earned a living from tilling the soil, in 1930 the agricultural population amounted to only 17 per cent. On the other hand, almost half the population was engaged in industrial activities, which included first and foremost manufacturing industries. The extractive industries (coal mines and quarries) included only slightly more than 10 per cent of the industrial population. These figures are a striking illustration of the "transforming" character of the Belgian industries. The other illustration is provided by the statistics of foreign trade, showing the role of food and raw materials in imports and the role of semi-finished and finished goods in exports.

Not only was the entire life of the country changed by the expansion of industry, to which should be added the development of transportation, of commerce, and of financial activities, but the social status of the majority of the population also was modified. A hundred years before, most people had independent jobs, as small farmers, artisans, traders, or other workmen, and the number of wage earners was relatively small. A completely changed situation is illustrated by the table above. In agriculture only did the social structure of the population remain about the same. By American standards, the overwhelming majority of Belgian farms would be considered tiny. They are worked mostly by the farmer and his family. Only a small number of larger farms use hired help. Consequently, wage earners form, roughly, only 20 per cent of the total agricultural population. The situation is quite different in industry, where the percentage of wage earners amounts to 87.

It means that a large proportion of the population are no longer independent producers but work for a wage under the direction of entrepreneurs. The entire economic trend of the nineteenth century favored the expansion of large enterprises. As a result, not only is a large section of the industrial population composed of wage earners, but they are employed in a relatively small number of large plants.

Of the total number of 206,000 industrial enterprises existing in 1930, 136,000 enterprises did not employ any hired labor; in other words, they were small artisan shops. The remaining 70,000 enterprises employed around 1,200,000 workers. Of these workers, 355,000 were employed in 67,000 small and medium-sized enterprises (with less than 50 workers each); 485,000 were employed in

3,500 large enterprises (employing each from 50 to 500 workers); 350,000 were employed by 280 very large enterprises (with more than 500 workers each). In other words, less than 4,000 enterprises (almost exclusively corporate businesses), or less than 6 per cent of the enterprises employing labor, had on their pay rolls approximately 70 per cent of the total number of workers.

This actually means that Belgium witnessed a movement of industrial concentration and the development of a wage-earning class, a proletariat. Trade unionism began to spread, although rather slowly; in 1914 not more than 20 per cent of the workers were unionized.

During the nineteenth century, the standard of living of factory workers, although slowly rising, remained fairly low. Partly because of the necessity of competing on foreign markets and of keeping costs as low as possible, and partly because of the lack of unionization, the tendency of Belgian manufacturers was to keep the level of wages very low. Moreover, during the "long depression" of the 1870's and 1880's, there were pronounced periods of unemployment. The discontent of workers exploded sometimes in violent, if short, outbreaks. In 1886—"the black year"—troops were sent into the industrial district of Liége and Charleroi.

Summing up the evolution which preceded the First World War, one could say that Belgium was a prosperous country with a hard-working population. However, the lack of raw materials, the density of the population, the obligation to compete in foreign markets, to some degree, also, the weakness of the labor movement and of social legislation, resulted in a standard of living, for a large section of the population, lower than in England or in France for instance, limiting the comparison to western Europe.

Although less brutal than the present one, the 1914–1918 occupation inflicted much suffering and hardship on the population. Large quantities of materials, of machinery, of factory implements were requisitioned. Entire plants were dismantled and shipped to Germany. In the second half of 1918, the occupying power proceeded with a systematic destruction of industrial plants; steel furnaces and rolling mills suffered particularly from such demolition. The complete destruction of coal mines was in preparation for the moment of retreat and was prevented only by the threat of reprisals from the Allied Military Headquarters. Belgium emerged from the war impoverished, disorganized, with its stock of machinery greatly reduced. Moreover, the political and economic changes in the international situation inflicted large losses on Belgium's foreign holdings; investments in eastern Europe, particularly in Russia, became practically worthless.

Because of outstanding efforts of management, of technicians, and of workers, and despite the shortening of the working day, around 1925–1926 Belgium saw her plants restored and her productive capacity increased. Moreover, the movement of industrial expansion continued in the decade following the Armistice and did not appreciably diminish until the depression of the 'thirties.

Old industries were modernized and developed. The coal industry was entirely mechanized and the production of the new basin (in the Kempen) was added to the production of the old basin (in the south). Coal production, which was 22,800,000 metric tons in 1913, amounted to from 28,000,000 to 29,000,000 in 1937–1938. It remained nevertheless insufficient, and large quantities had to be imported.

Steel production, which was 2,400,000 tons in 1913, exceeded 4,000,000 in 1929. It fell considerably during the depression of the 'thirties. However, in 1937 it reached the figure of 3,900,000. The zinc industry, using ore which came from overseas exclusively, proved more difficult to restore. However, in 1937 the production reached 226,000 tons compared with 204,000 in 1913. The production of other nonferrous metals (copper, tin, cobalt, and radium), almost unknown in 1913, also made great progress because of ore provided by the Congo.

Textile industries, glass making, chemical production, and the manufacture of mechanical equipment expanded remarkably. Steam engines aggregated 3,100,000 h.p. in 1913 and 5,400,000 in 1929 (6,000,000 in 1936). The electrification of the country was greatly advanced; the capacity of the electrical industry amounted in 1938 to 2,500,000 kw. compared with 500,000 in 1913. New industries were developed in the realm of textiles, of synthetic chemistry, and of related fields. At the same time, considerable progress was made in the agricultural field. The output of most crops per unit of land increased considerably.

During the two decades following the war, the Flemish section of the country made particularly important economic progress. Flemish agriculture benefited from the electrification of the country and from progress in the production of fertilizers; her produce was sold under most favorable conditions by the extension of transport facilities. Furthermore, Flemish agriculture and the small towns (particularly along the coast) largely benefited from the tourist trade resulting from the increase in the number of automobiles. On the other hand, the industrialization of Flemish regions made remarkable headway through the development of the coal fields of the Kempen and through the establishment of many industrial plants near the coal mines and near the port of Antwerp (through which raw materials, particularly ore from the Congo, were imported).

Unlike the pre-1914 era, less attention was paid to foreign investments, partly because capital was attracted to the restoration and the expansion of domestic industry and partly because too many losses had been sustained in former foreign investments. However, expansion abroad was not neglected, particularly in eastern and in southeastern Europe (in such industries as electric plants, oil fields, and sugar plants). But the largest effort outside the country itself was made in the Congo, where economic equipment made exceptional progress.

However, in spite of the expansion of the productive capacities of the country, economic and social development, during the period between the two world wars, was extremely disturbed and agitated. The experience of that period shows that material destruction does not necessarily entail the most lasting or the most harmful effects. Material reconstruction has proved, after all, to be easier than the restoration of economic equilibrium in national and in international relations. The brutal disturbance in social relationships (of which the depreciation of currency was one of the principal factors), and the profound dislocation of international economy have been the strongest factors in the evolution of Belgian economy since 1919.

Until 1926, the depreciation and instability of currency was the most disturbing factor not only in the economic evolution proper, but in the entire life of the country. Then in October, 1926, the franc was stabilized at one-seventh of its prewar gold value. In the following years, the repatriation of Belgian capital from abroad and the influx of foreign capital brought about an abundance of liquid funds and contributed largely to the expansion of investments, as well as to the increase of speculation in the stock market.

But the World Depression of the early 'thirties and the fall in the gold value of sterling since September, 1931, was a blow to Belgian exports and provoked widespread unemployment. However, it was not deemed advisable to follow the English example. The depreciation of the franc in the 'twenties had remained in everyone's memory. Maintenance of the gold value of the currency became a leading principle of governmental policy. The strategy of "economic deflation" was aimed at reducing wages and costs in order to maintain the competitive position in foreign markets. However, the policy was doomed by the persistence of the fall of sterling. In 1935 a reduction in the gold value of the currency became inevitable and the franc was devalued to one-tenth of its pre-1914 gold value. But the currency was again immediately linked to gold and since October, 1936, when France, Switzerland, and Holland went off gold, Belgium has remained the only European country with a currency based on the gold standard.

The problem of public finances was another almost new problem rising out of the war. Before 1914, Belgium was among the European countries with the lowest taxation, one of the factors which accounted for the low cost of living. After 1918, taxes were increased to meet such burdens as military expenditure and social legislation. The whole fiscal system was overhauled; an income tax was introduced and the rates were increased several times. Estate duties were increased. The changes affected the interests of various groups of the population diversely and were not accomplished without friction.

The instability of international markets and the world-wide encouragement of protectionist policies finally brought important changes in Belgian commercial policy. The revision of tariff legislation in 1924 increased somewhat the "protection" for a few manufacturing industries. However, the main purpose of the revision was to give the Government a weapon for bargaining with foreign countries. The purpose was not so much to preserve the home market for the national industries as to obtain reductions in the tariffs applied by other countries to Belgian exports. On the whole, the tariff remained moderate and there was no attempt at agricultural protection. The "most favored nation" clause remained the basis of Belgian policy.

However, such factors as the accentuation of protectionism in the early 'thirties, the spread of quota systems and of foreign-exchange regulations closed many markets for Belgian manufacturers, whereas the Belgian market became one of the favorite dumping spots for foreign goods, particularly for agricultural products. From 1931 on, Belgium engaged in agricultural protection by putting import duties on sugar, butter, meat, and on other food products. Gradually, protection was extended to such industrial products as coal, leather, and other products. Moreover, under the pressure of circumstances, Belgium also became involved in the policy of contingents, licenses, and clearing agreements. However, Belgium was one of the last countries to engage in restrictive policies and remained constantly a champion of lower tariffs and freer trade. She was one of the most ardent promoters of concerted action for liberating world trade, as witness her role in international conferences and in such agreements as those of Ouchy and of Oslo.

The development of "social" legislation, both under conservative and democratic cabinets, was one of the most significant factors of the postwar political and economic evolution.[3] The trend toward concentration of business also attracted much attention. It was particularly manifest in the financial field where the typical independent "unit" bank of prewar times was finally superseded by branches of large banking corporations. Because of the "mixed" character of Belgian banking and its close connections with industry, a small number of large banks came to play a leading role in the entire business life of the country. This concentration of business control and, more important, the financial crisis of the first half of the 'thirties were the decisive reasons leading to the law of 1935 which provided for the regulation and supervision of banking and of the issuance of securities.

Furthermore, there was a large extension of the so-called "public sector of the economy" manifested particularly in the expansion of

---

[3] See Chapter VIII, "Political Parties," by René Hislaire.

official or semiofficial credit institutions (The National Company
for Industrial Loans, credit institutions for small business and for
agriculture, and the outstanding government guaranty for export
credits are examples).

The professional and political organization of most social groups
developed considerably. There was an extraordinary expansion of
labor unions and of organizations formed by farmers, by members
of the middle classes, by public employees, and by members of other
groups. Each sought the protection of its particular interests.

But the expansion of group organizations did not result merely
in pressure policies. There was also a marked tendency to use these
groups for the solution of many economic problems such as the
formation of "mixed" committees (management and labor) for the
solution of labor questions, or the use of professional[4] groups for
the implementation of some regulations concerning foreign trade
and of some fiscal laws. It resulted, also, in many projects concerning so-called "professional organization," projects intended to give
to professional groups a precise place in the economic system and
in legislative action. The question undoubtedly will rise again
after the liberation of the country.

As a result of economic and political difficulties, the position of
the Government became less stable than before. Just at a time when
the role of Parliament and of the administration in economic life
was growing, their prestige was lessening and their action was weakened by instability and by internal struggles.

In 1939, the productive capacity of Belgium and the standard of
life of the people were much higher than in 1900 or even in 1914.
But the economic position was much more precarious and the political situation less settled because of the international political
unrest, the disorganization of world economy, and the growing rest-
lessness of social groups.

---

[4] In French, "profession" is used in a larger sense than in English. It means
occupation or "job."

CHAPTER XIII

Social Legislation

BY MAX GOTTSCHALK

JUST BEFORE THE PRESENT WAR, Belgium was among those countries which prided themselves upon having a most progressive social legislation. This had not always been true of Belgium. Although participating, from the beginning, in the Industrial Revolution of the nineteenth century, Belgium was slow to introduce measures on social security for her working population—measures which, in our day, are considered the corollary of modern economy. As late as the year 1910, Seeboom Rowntree, the great English industrialist, who had just finished a study of working conditions in Belgium, wrote: "The factory legislation should give to the workers much more protection from the worst abuses of competition than they now have, especially in the matter of the length of the working day, and the authorities must see that it is enforced."

Today, by contrast, Belgium is among the most progressive nations as far as her social legislation is concerned. She is even in the forefront of industrial countries. The number of international labor conventions ratified by the different countries may be taken as a criterion. Belgium ratified 34, whereas the number of these ratifications by the great industrial countries is respectively: for France and England, 31; Holland, 24; Italy, 21; Poland, 20; Germany, 17; Czechoslovakia, 15; and Japan, 14. An agreement, made internationally, to ratify certain conventions, must, of course, be followed by corresponding measures introduced into national law. The agreement to do this, as well as the strict application of national law, was vigilantly watched by interested parties who had eventual recourse to the international courts, and, as a last resort,

to the Permanent International Court of Justice at The Hague.
The 34 conventions ratified by Belgium cover the most varied
phases of working life. The most important are: the convention
tending to limit to eight hours a day, and to forty-eight hours a
week, the number of working hours in industry; the convention
providing for the establishment of public employment bureaus;
conventions establishing a minimum age of fourteen for children
in industrial and nonindustrial, farm, and maritime work; the convention prohibiting night work for children under eighteen years
of age; conventions on workmen's compensation in industry and
agriculture, and on compensation in case of occupational diseases;
conventions concerning the establishment of methods for fixing
minimum wages, particularly for home work; the convention concerning the annual paid vacations for seamen; and the convention
concerning the elimination of forced or obligatory labor in dependent territories.

The development of social legislation in Belgium took place
principally during the period between the two world wars, and
was spurred on mainly by the progressive development of labor
organizations.

Because of the existence of numerous coal deposits in the subsoil
of the central part of the country, linking the valleys of northern
France and Pas de Calais to those of the Roer and the Ruhr, Belgium experienced, from the beginning of the nineteenth century
on, the development of a number of industries. The population of
the country was attracted to the industrial centers. The resulting
changes in composition of the population can be measured by a
few over-all figures:

	1846	*1928*
Agriculture	1,000,000	500,000
Industry	750,000	1,500,000
Commerce	100,000	550,000

The 1940 census indicates that out of a population of 8,361,220
inhabitants, Belgium numbers, 1,484,780 male and 325,268 female
manual workers, 224,553 male and 67,814 female salaried workers,
or a total of 2,102,415 employees. These working masses, with identical interests, were, however, for a long time unable to take united
action in defense of their interests. As a matter of fact, the Le

Chapelier Law of June 14–17, 1791, which was supposed to put an end to the tyranny of the guilds, prohibited employers from banding together; but the measure also covered employees, and stipulated in Article II that: "Workers and journeymen of no matter what craft shall not, when gathered together, elect a president or secretary or syndics, keep books of account, enact laws or resolutions, establish regulations of their so-called common interests." In a word, workers were prohibited from organizing. By this fact, the worker, theoretically free otherwise, was, in reality, disarmed before an increasingly powerful master who completely controlled employment.

The Belgian Penal Code of 1810 confirmed the principles of the Le Chapelier Law. It remained in effect up to 1867. The revised penal code no longer prohibited workers from organizing, but punished with fines and prison sentences any person who sought to enforce an increase or decrease in wages, or who, in an attempt to obstruct the free exercise of industry and labor, tried to impose fines, prohibitions, injunctions, or any limitations whatsoever, either against those who worked or against those who provided work. This injunction covered employers, workers, and union organizations. From 1898 to 1920, the courts imposed no less than 4,706 sentences in the application of this provision, 1,865 of which were prison sentences. This situation lasted until 1921.

The law of May 24, 1921, on the freedom of association, finally permitted the free development of trade union organizations. As can be understood readily, the number of members under the preceding systems was not very high.

Just previous to the war of 1914, the Trade Union Commission of Belgium (*La Commission Syndicale de Belgique*), made up of trade unions with socialist leanings and affiliated with the Belgian Workers' party (*Parti Ouvrier Belge*), numbered 250,000 members. The Confederation of Christian Trade Unions (*Confédération des Syndicats Chrétiens*), comprised 100,000 members. In 1939, these two organizations had respectively 581,951 and 344,618 members. The Trade Union Commission, a short time before the war, had assumed the name of General Confederation of Belgian Labor (*Confédération Générale du Travail de Belgique*). There was a third union organization, the General Center of Liberal Trade

Unions of Belgium (*La Centrale Générale des Syndicats Libéraux de Belgique*), which numbered 56,999 members in 1939.

The Confederation of Labor adhered to the concept of class struggle, whereas the other two groups were based on the peaceful collaboration of employer and employee, the Christians uniting with the Liberals on all points except those of philosophical concepts. As stated, the increase in number of trade unionists is explained primarily by the possibilities for propaganda and action thereafter allowed to the unions by the law on freedom of association, and also by the increasingly numerous advantages granted members of workers' organizations because of governmental subsidies from which their members benefited in instances of unemployment, sickness, and disability. In addition, the growing strength of the trade unions and the representation of their interests in Parliament by Socialist, Catholic-Democratic, and Liberal-Progressive delegates, contributed largely toward assuring the passage of new laws for protection of the workers. A majority of Parliament, composed of these elements, was a prerequisite for social progress.

Attention should be drawn to the unusual structure of Belgian labor organizations. These organizations covered three fields of activity: (1) The assured defense of the workers' interests, beyond their indirect political action, by the trade unions themselves. By means of assessments of the members, resistance funds were established which assured relief to workers in case of strikes or lockout. (2) Unemployment funds and the fraternal orders, organically independent, but having strong ties with the trade unions. By means of additional assessments, they were able to pay out benefits to their members in cases of unemployment, sickness, or disability. (3) Producers' and consumers' coöperatives, created principally for the members of trade unions and which procured substantial benefits. In fact, the workers remitted to their trade unions an over-all dues payment which assured them all of the above-mentioned benefits, the trade unions distributing the sums thus collected.

A brief word should be given on the efforts made by the unions to develop their leadership. The Socialists conducted, for example, a workers' education center and an advanced workers' school. The Catholics had a number of social-service schools for men and women, and organizations for workers' education, the most important being the J.O.C., Young Christian Workers (*Jeunesse Ouvrière Chrétienne*).

In contrast to the individual worker who, at the beginning of the last century, had only himself to depend upon for the defense of his interests, the solidly organized Belgian working class, during the last decades, became a political, economic, and social force of the first order.

In examining the status of the working class just before the present war, the first question is that of the living standard of the worker. Nominal wages were relatively low in Belgium. Why, under the present political and economic regime, this should of necessity be so demands a brief discussion. Belgium has 710 inhabitants per square mile, as against 41 in the United States. To feed this relatively large population, Belgium must import 70 per cent of her foodstuffs, if the necessary feed for cattle is included. To pay for these imports, Belgium has to export. Since the only raw material contained in her soil is coal, and that in relatively unimportant quantities, her principal export product is labor. To be in a position to compete on the international market with the great industrial countries, rich in raw materials of all kinds, favored, besides, by a large domestic market and the saving which is realized on the transportation of raw materials from the point of extraction to the processing plant, Belgium must, under the present economic system, maintain relatively low wages. In the past, employers, taking advantage of the situation, were guilty of abuses. Since 1919, progressive adjustments in wages have been made by a redistribution of the national revenue, with more widespread benefits for the working class. Following the disturbances resulting from the economic crisis, which began in 1929, and from the devaluation of the Belgian franc in 1935, which was one of the consequences, a new wage adjustment was necessary. Just before the war, at the intervention of the Government, a committee, on which the various interests were represented, fixed the minimum wage of the adult, unskilled worker at 32 francs a day, for eight hours of work, in a large number of industries. At the rate of exchange of the period, that represents $1.06 for eight hours, or 13½ cents an hour. After a study made in 1938, the wages in industry varied between 5.50 and 7 francs; only a few highly skilled workers earned more than 7 francs, which equals 15 to 21 cents an hour. These wages applied to skilled workers, or to those who were considered as skilled.

Although a great many workers earned a wage above the 32-francs-a-day minimum, an important fraction of the working class had to be satisfied with the minimum or with an amount just above it. Nevertheless, the important thing to consider is not the nominal wage, but the real wage. The worker spent between 15 and 18 per cent of his wages on rent. The majority of Belgian workers were decently lodged at this price, but, very generally speaking, commodities such as running water, outside of the kitchen or the servants' hall, and baths or showers, were, so to speak, unknown in low-rental houses. Ice boxes were found only in a few apartments with high rentals, naturally inaccessible to workers. The automobile was a luxury item, which only the well-to-do bourgeois possessed. The wages indicated permitted a healthful diet, varied and substantial. It should also be taken into account that a great many workers lived in the country, and that more than 100,000 urban workers cultivated small plots of ground near the towns which furnished them with fruits and vegetables. Wages were high enough, then, to assure the essential needs of the worker and his family. Certain risks, inherent in the life of the worker and his family were, nevertheless, not sufficiently covered without the aid of the State, but a number of legislative provisions assured the worker of numerous benefits in addition to his wages.

At the instigation of certain groups of employers, anxious to alleviate the hardships suffered by married workers, fathers of varying numbers of children, the Benefit Funds for Family Allotments (*Caisses de Compensation pour Allocations Familiales*), was organized, into which the owners of certain industries or groups of industries paid an assessment for each gainfully employed wage or salaried employee. The benefit fund, in its turn, allotted to the worker's wife a sum, not based on his wages, but in accordance with the number of his children. A law of August 3, 1930, made employer contribution to such benefit fund obligatory. A royal decree of December 19, 1939, coördinated the law of 1930 and several subsequent laws relating to the same subject. Thereafter, the law applied to all industrial, commercial, or agricultural enterprises.

The State contributed to a National Benefit Fund. Its contribution for the year 1939 amounted to 8,750,000 francs. The employer's contribution is fixed by royal decree, according to the cost-of-living index. It rose from 213,000,000 francs in 1931 to 435,000,000 francs in 1938. Its beneficiaries are the mothers or persons in charge of children under fourteen years of age (eighteen years of age if they are attending a trade school). The amount of the allotment is in accordance with the cost-of-living index, but there is a monthly minimum of 20.60 francs for one child, 55.60 francs for two children, 113.60 francs for three, 202.60 francs for four. The law which, in the beginning, covered only wage earners, was broadened in 1937 (law of June 10th), and in 1938 (royal decree of December 28th), to include free-lance workers and management personnel.

The benefit funds, furthermore, provided their beneficiaries with auxiliary services, such as visiting nurse's care and similar services. On December 31, 1938, there were 545,315 families of wage earners, with a total of 999,560 children, receiving allotments. As for family allotments to nonwage earners, the decree which covered them computed at 1,256,000 persons the number of beneficiaries.

Belgium has no actual law covering the insurance of wage earners against sickness. However, there are numerous fraternal organizations, called *Mutualités,* which furnish various medical services to their members. These fraternal orders were organized by the Socialist, Christian, and Liberal trade unions, or by independent organizations. Their origin dates back to the time of the guilds, and some of them managed to exist even after the appearance of the Le Chapelier Law. The modern fraternal organizations granted benefits to their members during the period of their disability, as well as medical and pharmaceutical services. For an additional payment, the families of those insured could also receive the same medical and pharmaceutical services. In 1935, these fraternal orders aided 1,233,807 members; the family medical service covered 3,136,143 persons. The majority of members were also insured against disability; approximately 1,500,000 had subscribed, in addition, to maternity insurance, and approximately 3,500,000 to insurance against tuberculosis.

The fraternal organizations had polyclinics, hospitals and sanatoria, some of which might be considered as models of their kind.

The State granted subsidies to the fraternal organizations which, in turn, offered their members the minimum benefits fixed by the State and agreed to abide by the State's contract. The subsidies paid by the State to fraternal organizations in 1939 amounted to 112,000,000 francs.

Belgium has, since 1897, encouraged the worker to insure himself against unemployment by granting subsidies furnished by the cities, the provinces, and the State. The Varlez system, or Ghent system, was established throughout Belgium before the First World War. The gravity of the crisis, which began in 1929, necessitated a reform which resulted in the establishment, in 1935, of the National Office of Placement and Unemployment, charged with the administration of this branch of social insurance. Labor's unemployment fund is still the major factor. The state intervenes as underwriter, in case the fund becomes depleted or in order to provide relief during the period not covered by the fund. There were about 1,000,000 workers insured in 1940, of which 600,000 contributed to the Socialist fund, 350,000 to the Christian fund, and 50,000 to the Liberal fund. The unemployed received the benefits due him, either from his fund or from the State, after a short waiting period, from the beginning of unemployment to the time of his reëmployment. The benefit could not amount to more than two-thirds of his wages (three-quarters for large families). It was estimated according to the size of the family. During 1939, it amounted to an average of about 18 francs a day. The insurance did not cover agricultural or domestic workers.

Obligatory unemployment insurance for all workers was being prepared. The National Office of Placement and Unemployment assured the creation of a network of public placement bureaus and controlled the administration of placement bureaus created by private, nonprofit organizations subsidized by the State. The public placement system was considerably broadened during recent years; it used the most modern methods—special offices for each trade, regional and national benefits, use of the radio for publicity on available jobs, and similar methods.

For a long time there was a law on old-age pensions which granted a ridiculously small sum to all needy persons of sixty-five years of age. A law of December 10, 1925, establishing old-age insurance on a general scale and giving it a serious basis may be considered the point of departure of the present-day system, as is shown by the coördinated decrees of December 15, 1937. This law is obligatory for all Belgian wage earners or foreigners working or domiciled in Belgium. There are special laws for miners, seamen, and salaried workers in private industry. A different system covers public employees. Employer and wage earner pay a monthly contribution. The contributions vary between 2.50 and 12.50 francs a month, according to the amount of wages. Contributions range from 4 francs to 18 francs in those industries which present health hazards. The sums paid in are administered by a State Pension Fund. This contributes up to 50 per cent of the capitalized amount of payments. The contribution made by the State in 1939 amounted to 596,416,000 francs.

The pension is payable at sixty-five years of age, but this limitation is reduced to fifty-five years for men and fifty for women in industries hazardous to health. The pension may be collected at sixty years of age for men and fifty-five for women, at a reduced amount. The pension is 3,200 francs for married men. During the period in which the insured is establishing his right to the pension through his payments and those of his employer, the State makes up the deficiency. The law also provides various benefits for the widow of the insured and for any of his children who may be under age. Disability, old-age and death laws covering miners, seamen, and white-collar workers are based on the same principles, but the amount of assessments, the age, and the benefits granted the insured vary to a certain degree. The number of insured workers in 1933 was 1,772,769, that of white-collar employees 235,000, that of miners 180,645, and that of seamen, 2,953.

The sum paid the wage earner for his vacation may also be considered as a part of his wages. A law of July 8, 1936, later amended, required employers in industry and commerce, in public services and maritime shipping, to grant their employees paid vacations. The employee was entitled to six days a year, this period being doubled for workers under eighteen years of age. The sum to be paid to those entitled to vacations came from a fund made up of employer contributions amounting to 2 per cent of the wages paid.

This, in brief, concludes the review of the various elements which must be considered as entering into the wages of the Belgian worker. Besides the sum paid the worker as remuneration for his labor, the employer contributes 2 per cent of these wages toward vacations for his workers and salaried employees. The employer and the State contribute to the Family Allotment Fund. And, finally, the State contributes generously toward the payment of unemployment benefits and subsidizes sickness insurance, as well as disability, old-age, and life insurance. The wage earner is thus spared deducting money from his wages which he needs as a guarantee against a series of risks to which human beings in general and workers in particular are exposed. The Belgian worker and white-collar employee are the concern of a whole series of other measures which protect them in the exercise of their trades and which will now be discussed.

A basic law of December 24, 1903, established workmen's compensation, based on the assumption that the fault lay with the employer who was required to pay a lump sum to the injured worker. Numerous modifications have been made in this law. Today, it covers every worker or white-collar employee under a work contract whose earnings are not higher than 24,000 francs. In the event of temporary incapacity, the injured worker may draw, for a period of thirty days, benefits equaling 50 per cent of his wages and, after thirty days, two-thirds of his wages. In a partial permanent disability, the benefits are equal to two-thirds of the loss in wages, and in case of permanent disability, the pension equals two-thirds of the annual wage, the maximum wage to which this applies being not over 20,000 francs. Special rates apply to those requiring the aid of a third person. The injured worker has a right to medical care and to the costs of prosthesis. Pensions are provided for the survivors in case of death. A law of July 24, 1927, treats victims of occupational diseases in somewhat the same way as it treats injured workers. The list of these diseases is periodically revised. Benefits are calculated in the same way as for injuries, but take into consideration the cost of therapeutic treatments.

The basic law limiting the length of work to eight hours a day and forty-eight hours a week was passed on June 14, 1921. Numerous amendments have been added since then. In a general way, the eight-hour day is applicable in Belgium to all employees—manual and white-collar workers—in all Belgian enterprise with the exception of agriculture. The provisions relating to supplementary hours, and to cases where the law may be suspended, conform to the international labor convention of 1919. A law of July 9, 1936, reduced the work week to forty hours in unhealthy, fatiguing, or hazardous industries. A law of July 17, 1905, has made general a day of rest for all wage earners.

A whole series of measures protecting working women and children also should be mentioned. These measures completely prohibit, or permit women only above a certain age to be employed at night or in certain unhealthy, fatiguing, or hazardous industries, or in work underground. A rest period is provided for pregnant women. It should suffice to say also that, in this regard, Belgium has, in general, adopted the norms established in the international labor conventions.

Mention should be made here of the steps taken in the matter of conciliation of disputes. From the law of 1887, which created labor-management committees, up to the royal decrees of 1926 and 1929 on conciliation committees, constant efforts have been made by the successive cabinets to settle disputes peacefully. These institutions have been instrumental in diminishing greatly the number of strikes and it is accepted procedure, as much on the employer's part as on the worker's, to attempt to level out differences through negotiations. In times of tension, the Government has interceded at different points as mediator between national groups of employers and workers.

This brief review of social legislation does not give the reader a very precise picture of the functioning of the various institutions created for the benefit of workers nor an exact measure of the advantages which they accord them. It will have indicated, however, as was stated at the beginning, that Belgium, after vigorous efforts to advance on the road of social progress, found itself just before the war among those nations which could consider themselves really progressive.

Enemy occupation, with all its brutalities, its miseries, and its horrors, suspended the functioning of all these laws. Liberation has seen their reëstablishment. Projects, already drawn up in detail, will open the door to new progress.

~~~~~~

CHAPTER XIV

Communications and Transportation

BY JAN FRANS HOSTIE

BELGIUM, LUXEMBURG, and the Netherlands, in the eyes of international law, as well as in the textbooks, are three sovereign states, each independent of the other. For both the historian and the economist, however, the fundamental unity of the Low Countries is a dominant fact. The student of government also cannot fail to perceive striking analogies in the political systems of the three States, and to realize that, although the south and the north have alternately been the torchbearer, it is to the Low Countries as a whole that western culture is indebted for their contribution to the federal form of government, constitutional rule, and human freedom. That fundamental unity of the Low Countries is nowhere more apparent than in the field of communications, paradoxically the very field where, less than twenty years ago, Belgium and the Netherlands failed to reach an agreement.

The five most important ports of the world are, unquestionably, Rotterdam, New York, London, Antwerp, and Hamburg. To the layman, it may seem a simple job to determine their relative importance. Those familiar with traffic statistics know that there is no single criterion which does justice to the complexity of the problem; several sets of figures are needed, all of which are strictly comparable; moreover, each figure and each set of figures needs interpretation.

In recent years, before the war, Rotterdam was the seaport of the world which handled both the largest bulk of tonnage and the greatest weight of goods. It is the most favored port for transshipment between the seagoing vessel and the Rhine barge, the largest maritime outlet of what is, after the Great Lakes of North America, the world's most important system of inland waterways. If one divides Rotterdam's maritime traffic, however, in long and short voyages (i.e. taking 2,000 miles as the limit between the two), one will find that it is primarily a port visited by ships engaged in trade between ports which are not very far apart, the traffic with the United States and that with the Netherlands territories overseas, however, excepted. As a final touch, it might be mentioned that the relative importance of Rotterdam has been steadily growing in the last four decades.

Antwerp is, unquestionably, the Continent's largest port for the export of finished or semifinished industrial products. By rail it is nearest of all ports to every place in the great industrial triangle, Calais-Strasbourg-Hamm in Westphalia, with the exception of the Ruhr, which is equidistant to Antwerp and Rotterdam. If one divides Antwerp's maritime traffic in the same way as that of Rotterdam, one finds that, in the instance of Antwerp, the accent is on long-distance traffic; hence, the goods handled here have a higher value per ton. Antwerp's reliance on the railway is not exclusive; the Franco-Belgian waterways system, the Albert Canal, and the Rhine together contribute no less than half of its traffic.

Comparable with Antwerp and Rotterdam in its relation to the industrial hinterland is Hamburg, main maritime port of the Elbe-Havel-Spree-Oder system. From the point of view of maritime traffic, however, Hamburg's hinterland has much less to offer than that of Antwerp and Rotterdam. Distant Upper Silesia is the only steel-producing region in it. The Berlin area, Czechoslovakia, Saxony yield little of those heavy products that are basic for shipping, and the little there is (Stassfurt potash, for example), does not generally travel very far. Hamburg, however, had been sponsored, under William II, by the youthful energy and the nationalism of German shipping and commerce; under the Republic, by the centralizing forces of Berlin; under Hitler, by autarchy. Long the Continent's most important market for overseas products, Hamburg, in later years, as compensation for what it had lost, was given the bulk of the trade—which she shared with her lesser sister, Bremen—of the Reich's state-controlled maritime trade, such as it

was. Antwerp and Rotterdam received what was left. Though no
longer one of the world's main ports, Amsterdam, the capital of the
Netherlands, still holds a leading position in the European trade
with the Isles of Spice and the Caribbean Sea.

In the companion volume to this book, *The Netherlands,* Dr.
Hendrik Riemens has ably shown how, during the Middle Ages
and the sixteenth century, first Bruges, later Antwerp, was the
emporium of northwestern Europe. With the discovery of America and of the sea route of the East Indies, Antwerp became the
world's greatest market and financial center. It is worthy of notice
that, even then, Southern Netherlands took little part in seafaring,
an activity which was steadily growing in the Northern Provinces.

The Low Countries, or Netherlands, in the historical sense of
the word—also called, at the time, the Seventeen Belgic Provinces—reached the height of their prosperity under their great
national sovereign, Emperor Charles V. The partial failure of their
revolution against Philip II brought Antwerp's prosperity abruptly
to an end.

Strategic reasons alone account for the success in Holland and
Zeeland of the common struggle for liberation and for its ultimate
failure in Flanders and Brabant. The great national leader, William
of Orange, stood for mutual tolerance between Catholics and Protestants and the maintenance of the Union of the Seventeen Provinces. It was in Antwerp, the leading city of the Low Countries, that
these ideas were most popular. Shortly after William's assassination, Antwerp was recaptured by the enemy (1585). This brought
about the closure of the Scheldt by national forces, a measure
which was, moreover, maintained in peacetime in virtue of the
treaty of 1648. Thus began for the Southern Netherlands a long
period of foreign domination and decay which lasted, almost un-
interruptedly, until 1814. Dunkirk, the only good port on the Flemish coast, was lost to France in 1662. Efforts made after the Peace of
Utrecht (1713), for using Ostend as a port of access to world trade
were thwarted by Northern Netherlands and by England.

During the short-lived amalgamation of Northern and Southern
Netherlands in a unified kingdom (1815–1830), the Industrial Revolution spread from Great Britain to Belgium; the beginnings of
this revival, fostered by King William I, brought, after 230 years,

a renewal of activity to Antwerp. The king's antiliberal policy concerning navigation on the Rhine was as unpopular in Antwerp, however, as it was in Cologne. In 1815, this river had been placed under the control of the first international organization created in Europe, the Central Commission for Navigation on the Rhine, a board of plenipotentiaries of the riparian states, assisted by a staff of international officials.

King William contended that the jurisdiction of this Commission which, according to the Final Act of the Congress of Vienna, was to go *jusqu'à la mer,* as far as the sea, did not extend to the two main branches of the Rhine in the Low Countries, the Waal and the Lek, below the points where, supposedly, the effect of the tide ceased—Gorinchem, on the Waal, and Krimpen, on the Lek. With characteristic obstinacy, the sovereign stuck to this untenable thesis for fifteen years, when a restrictive solution was reached which still affects adversely Belgian interests on the Rhine.

The dissolution of the Union, in 1830, held a grave menace to that freedom of access to the sea which Antwerp had enjoyed for fifteen years. Of the great ports of the world, Antwerp was, henceforth, the only one separated from the sea by waters held to be part of another state's territory, a handicap which treaty provisions could alleviate, but never eliminate. More precarious still was Antwerp's new position concerning the Rhine. Although the Rhine, Meuse, and Scheldt have a common estuary, Belgium ceased to be represented on the Central Commission for ninety years.

The treaties and agreements of 1839–1843, which determined the conditions of the separation of north and south, stayed below the level of what, even at that state in the development of engineering, trade competition, and international coöperation, could be considered as fair and reasonable for the safeguard of a country with such unfavorable boundaries as those of Belgium.

After a sharp, but relatively short, setback, Belgium's industrial progress, after 1830, was resumed at such a pace that Great Britain's level of industrialization was soon reached, all other continental states being left far behind. This was the era of *laissez faire,* when the tolls on the Scheldt—which the Belgian Government had been paying to the Netherlands in lieu of the shipowners—were bought off, as they had been on the Sound, by a pro rata payment of all seafaring nations (1863), and people in Antwerp believed that, henceforth, the Scheldt was "free." This was also the time when statesmen thought that railways would soon eliminate waterways altogether, and the Belgian Government which, in virtue of the treaties of separation, had an option between a canal and a railway through Dutch Limburg—a territory which extends across any route from Antwerp to Cologne and the Ruhr—unwisely chose the railway.

Antwerp benefited from the industrial progress of its national hinterland and from the rapid development of railways in and around it. Belgium became at that time, as it still is, the country with the densest network of railways in the world.

When the curve of Great Britain's industrial development flattened out and that of Germany—mainly because of the Ruhr and, later, because of German Lorraine and the Grand Duchy of Luxemburg (in the Zollverein since 1842)—began to rise, Belgium's industry kept pace with the new competitor. Antwerp rose to the first rank among the ports of the European Continent, German shipping, German goods, and German commerce playing, particularly in its long-distance traffic, a very important, though never predominant part.

At the height of its prosperity, however, in the years that immediately preceded the First World War, Antwerp failed, somehow, to reach its full development and to consolidate its position. Parochialism, tardiness in the construction of new quays and in the acquisition of sufficient grain elevators and other similar equipment, and the persistent weakness of the national merchant marine were some of the causes. In addition, Rhine traffic was undeniably gaining on the railroad and, although every city on the left bank of the Rhine from Cologne to Crefeld was advertising plans for an Antwerp-Rhine canal, nothing could be done about it without the consent of Berlin, which favored Emden in Prussian East Frisia, and the consent of the Netherlands, which was not forthcoming. In the meantime, Rhine traffic had to wind its way through the devious channels and byways of the Scheldt-Meuse-Rhine delta.

As time went on, the old treaty provisions, applied in a conservative spirit, proved more and more inadequate to meet the growing technical requirements of Antwerp and Belgium. New problems and difficulties arose when Ghent also became a seaport of some importance, for this port was doubly dependent on the Netherlands, both as regards the Scheldt itself, and the Ghent-Terneuzen Canal. Rotterdam, endowed with a magnificent new waterway to the sea, was diverting some of the water-borne traffic of Liége, and certain people said this was caused by the bottleneck of Maastricht, a Netherlands enclave on the left bank of the Meuse.

Antwerp's vast hinterland extends as far as Creil-sur-Oise, in the direction of Paris, and Dôle on the Doubs, in Franche-Comté, thus including the whole north and east of France. In the last few years before the First World War, French Lorraine, in its turn, had become yet another great industrial basin in that hinterland. Thus France's share in the traffic of Antwerp was becoming more significant. An antiquated system of supertaxes on import of goods into France via any but French ports unbalanced this traffic, however, to the common prejudice of Antwerp and Ghent and of those regions of France which could best be reached from the sea through these ports.

Three changes of major importance for Antwerp were brought about by the First World War: Belgium secured, with the agreement of the Netherlands, its representation on the Central Commission; the Grand Duchy of Luxemburg ceased to be part of the Zollverein and, soon afterward, formed an economic union with Belgium; both industrial basins of Lorraine, together with Alsace, were now French. Alsace had recently become important from the point of view of maritime trade. New potash mines were ready to be operated there on a large scale and the regularization of the Rhine, whereby the river was made navigable almost the year round, had now reached Strasbourg.

To extend the French system of supertaxes to this resurrected Rhine port was unthinkable; almost equally unthinkable was that the passage of Alsace-Lorraine from German into French hands, as a result of a victory to which Belgium had vitally contributed, should mean that Antwerp's traffic with that region would be curtailed. Belgians hoped that the whole superannuated system of supertaxes, of which they were the main victims, would now be abandoned by France. This hope was not fulfilled; the price to pay proved too high; but the traffic from Belgian ports, by rail, to

Alsace-Lorraine and, by water, to Strasbourg, was exempted from
those duties. The latter provision created an invidious distinction
between Belgian and Netherlands ports.

Not many years after the end of the war, the extension of Antwerp's harbor was at last completed, and offered adequate traffic
facilities. But Antwerp and Belgium failed to recover their prewar
prosperity. Belgium's industry had been rebuilt, its equipment
better than before, and its sturdy, hard-working and thrifty population had recovered from the hardships and the losses of four
years of war and foreign occupation; but many overseas markets
were irretrievably lost; large investments abroad had to be written
off as a result of confiscatory policies; overt or hidden restrictions
and discriminations hampered export more and more; devaluation
became a recurrent evil.

The Congo acquired a growing importance in the nation's economy as a secure outlet for its manufactures. Here, at least, the open
door really remained open, and where Belgian industry can compete on equal terms it need never fear being driven out of a market
by foreign competition.

The new seaport of Bruges, with its outer harbor, Zeebrugge,
had not fulfilled unduly sanguine expectations, but Brussels' new
waterway proved a great success, more as an inland port, though,
than as a maritime one.

Antwerp's traffic, measured in goods, and still more, in tonnage
of ships, rose to higher and yet higher levels, but, with all that, its
prewar prosperity did not return. The time had passed when world
commerce remained vested in maritime ports unless these had
grown into world centers of population, such as London and New
York. From Havre and Antwerp, Bremen and even Hamburg, it
moved to Paris and Berlin, even to Brussels. Besides, free commerce
itself was on the downgrade. In the early days after the First World
War, German businessmen were not welcome guests in Antwerp
and they themselves, as far as possible, preferred to deal with Rotterdam and to settle there. Efforts at expanding Belgium's merchant marine suffered a sharp setback shortly after the war; in
1939 Belgium's flag—in sharp contrast with those of the Netherlands and the Scandinavian States—was still among the "also-ran,"
taking fifteenth rank among those of the maritime nations of the

world. On the Rhine, however, it had a fairly important share in the traffic (about 15 per cent at the Dutch-German frontier, only slightly less than that of Germany), and on the French waterways—although freedom of navigation was hemmed in and curtailed by protectionist rules, even on the international Lys (Leie), Scheldt, Sambre, and Meuse—the Flemish barge was still a salient feature, not only in the Nord and in Lorraine, but also in Paris.

In the vast economic basin of the Rhine, traffic tended, even more than in the past, to favor the waterway as against the railway, and the waterways system expanded with the regularization of the Rhine itself as far as Strasbourg (1913), and later as far as Basle (by 1937, Basle port had a traffic of 3,000,000 tons). It was extended farther with the canalization of the Neckar and the Main. All this tended to benefit both Antwerp and Rotterdam—the former, though, to a lesser degree—and to render their competition more severe.

Although the prize was a larger one than before 1914, particularly as far as water-borne traffic was concerned, the position of the ports of the Low Countries as against their German rivals, Bremen and Hamburg, underwent a profound change. The freight-rate policy of the Prussian-Hessian Railways, aided by differential taxes and towage charges on the Rhine-Herne and Dortmund-Ems canals, in the past had caused some diversion toward Emden and the Hansa cities. For a series of articles, there were, even then, special railway rates for the maritime export of goods via German ports. In 1912, the Chamber of Commerce of Antwerp drew attention to an extension of the list of these goods, urging common action by the seaports of the Low Countries and the German Rhine ports; it is true that Belgium has similar tariffs, but no place in Belgium is nearer to a foreign seaport than to a Belgian one. Further, there were through rates combining the railway rate with the maritime freight in a lump sum; these were available for German East Africa and for the Near East via Bremen and Hamburg.

It would serve no useful purpose today to go into all the issues which divided Belgium and the Netherlands and which they endeavored to solve by treaty in 1920 and again in 1926, when the treaty signed between them failed to be approved by the Netherlands First Chamber. It is enough to say that the main issues were:

a question of sovereignty, or jurisdiction, over certain waters (Wielingen Pass), lying between the Belgian port of Zeebrugge and the high sea; the statute of the Scheldt below Antwerp, primarily regarding hydro-technical improvements required, from time to time, by progress in the techniques of the shipbuilder and of the waterways engineer; an up-to-date canal direct from Antwerp to the Rhine in the vicinity of the mouth of the Ruhr; and another such canal, avoiding all the obstacles and detours of the present route from the Waal to Antwerp. In 1920, the first of these four problems proved to be the stumbling block; in 1926, both countries wisely agreed to avoid it; this time, however, the fourth problem was the one over which the treaty fell. Subsequent negotiations proved unavailing.

Controversies between Belgium and the Netherlands had wide repercussions. The General Convention and the Statute of Barcelona (1921), for Freedom of Navigation on Waterways of International Concern, concluded under the auspices of the League of Nations, was signed by numerous states of all parts of the world, Belgium and the Netherlands among them, after the Conference had successfully reconciled the divergent views of the Belgian and Dutch delegations. The Netherlands Government, however, was not willing to submit this instrument to parliamentary approval. This was one of the reasons why the convention did not secure ratification by any large number of states. In Strasbourg, the revision of the Statute of the Rhine was held up until 1936, when a *modus vivendi* was initialed by the Member States, with the exception of the Netherlands; it was to be signed within six months; the day before that term expired, Germany withdrew from the Commission.

Disharmony in the Low Countries produced regrettable consequences of a technical, as well as of a diplomatic nature. The Netherlands built an all-Netherlands canal (Juliana Canal) to link the new coal mines in southern Limburg with the rest of the country and Belgium, an all-Belgian canal to link up Liége and the new Belgian coal mines in Limburg with the port of Antwerp (Albert Canal). A claim by the Netherlands as to the feeding of these canals, and a counterclaim by Belgium, were dismissed by the Permanent Court of International Justice. Today, communications by water between Liége and the Netherlands remain as inadequate as those between the Waal and Antwerp.

The lack of harmony also had financial consequences which became increasingly burdensome for both countries, particularly in the years which followed the impact on Europe of the great economic depression. As communications between Antwerp and the Rhine were not as good as between Rotterdam and the Rhine, the equalization of Antwerp to a French port as to the exemption of supertaxes was made conditional by France upon Belgium's undertaking to bear the cost of towage from Antwerp to Dordrecht, where the waterways from Antwerp and Rotterdam meet; too, Belgium, in an effort to offset that handicap for its Rhine traffic as a whole, resorted to a system of bounties to Rhine navigation intended to equalize Rhine freights between Rotterdam and Antwerp. Pilotage dues and port dues also were reduced on both sides, either directly or as a result of currency devaluations.

In the fall of 1936, Germany, as is known, withdrew from the Central Commission, repudiating her international obligations concerning the Rhine under the Treaty of Versailles, the Convention of Mannheim of 1868 and, implicitly, the Final Act of the Congress of Vienna of 1815. In an effort at appeasement, Belgium, France, and Great Britain made to Germany, as against previously adopted solutions, all manner of concessions which fairness and intrinsic merit did not justify; for example, the substitution, for justiciable disputes, of arbitration for adjudication by the Permanent Court of International Justice; the suppression of the Vienna system of international judicial organization for the Rhine, in matters of penal and private law, which should, on the contrary, have been revitalized, brought up to date and expanded; the weakening of the position of the Secretariat, and other concessions. In the spring of 1936, at a festive meeting of the Association of German Rhine Shipowners held at Duisburg, which the Secretary-General of the Central Commission was attending, the Minister of Communications of the Reich expressed the Führer's great satisfaction that a complete agreement had been reached, adding that the Führer saw, in the success of this important negotiation, a good omen for coöperation between Germany and her great western neighbor, France. A few months later, without warning, without even an attempt at further negotiation, through the mouthpiece not of her accredited plenipotentiaries, who failed to meet their colleagues at the appointed time, but of a junior member of the staff of the Paris Embassy whose role was limited to the reading of a declaration, Germany ruthlessly and insolently brought 120 years of coöperation on the Rhine to an abrupt end. The pretext was the continued presence in the Central Commission of plenipotentiaries of nonriparian states (Great Britain and Italy). Simultaneously, Germany adopted a similar attitude concerning the Elbe (where Belgium had been represented since 1920 as a result of a request made at the Paris Conference by Czechoslovakia), the Oder, and the Danube.

After the secession of Germany, the delegations of the countries that remained faithful to law and order continued to meet in the Central Commission as before. These were all the other countries represented on that Commission, with the exception of Italy. For some time, the Italian delegation had ceased to play the honorable part it had previously fulfilled; it now abstained from taking further part in the work of the Commission. At these meetings of the plenipotentiaries of Belgium, France, Great Britain, the Netherlands, and Switzerland, the rift between Belgium and France, on the one side, and the Netherlands, on the other, was acutely felt. It seemed more desirable than ever that the Rhine problems which divided these countries be solved at last.

On a broader stage, the slow but steady economic *rapprochement* between the Belgium-Luxemburg Union and the Netherlands, illustrated by the formation of the Oslo Group and the conclusion of the Ouchy Agreement, and the political community of views which now existed between the Netherlands and Belgium, also favored an understanding in matters pertaining to the competition between Dutch and Belgian maritime ports. This was brought about through friendly conversations for which the Rhine problems afforded an occasion and a starting point.

Thus, at long last, on April 3, 1939, an agreement was reached at Brussels among Belgium, France, and the Netherlands. France, with the agreement of Belgium, undertook gradually to extend to the Dutch ports of Amsterdam, Dordrecht, and Rotterdam the advantages of traffic with Strasbourg hitherto held by Antwerp and Ghent (exemption from the French supertax and analogous advantages concerning the preferential treatment by the French customs authorities at Strasbourg of goods coming from a French port overseas, and vice versa). Beyond that, as to Rhine traffic, there was to be a "truce" of ten years between Belgium and the Netherlands; in particular, during that period, the sums devoted by Belgium to bounties for the Rhine traffic were not to be increased; a sliding scale in these bounties aimed at keeping the share of the Belgian ports in the upstream traffic passing the Dutch-German frontier at approximately 21 per cent of the total. Furthermore, as far as the three contracting states were concerned, decisions of lasting importance were reached regarding the future status of the Rhine: Antwerp and Ghent would be dealt with as Rhine ports, on an equal footing with Amsterdam, Dordrecht, and Rotterdam; the Rhine regime, so far as it was applicable to the waterways connecting these Dutch ports with the Waal and the Lek, would apply equally to the waterways connecting Antwerp and Ghent with the Waal. A provisional regime, along similar lines, was adopted between Belgium and the Netherlands, pending the revision of the Convention of Mannheim. Finally, the three countries pledged themselves to work for "the reëstablishment of the Rhine community in full equality of rights."

Important as these provisions are, another part of the agreement is of still greater interest: the formation by Belgium and the Netherlands of a mixed commission to consider the possibility of fixing, by common agreement, the taxes and dues chargeable in the ports of Antwerp, Ghent, Rotterdam, and Amsterdam; this goes beyond the sphere of Rhine interests and involves the vaster issue of coöperation among the major seaports of the Low Countries.

Thus, on the eve of the present world tragedy, for the first time in their history since the sixteenth century, the Low Countries took an important step toward ending the feud between their seaports, an issue which was not a cause of the separation of 1830, but was a fatal source of weakness and disunion in past centuries and again in recent times, particularly after 1918. It was a significant step. Both sides made important concessions; although Belgium is the main victim of the French system of supertaxes, that country agreed to share the water-borne traffic to Strasbourg with the Netherlands;

except for the traffic by rail to Alsace-Lorraine (of no practical interest to the Dutch ports), the Belgian ports were thus crushed between the netherstone of Dunkirk and Havre, artificially protected for the whole of France except its easternmost part, and the upperstone of Rotterdam, with its shorter and better Rhine route. The Netherlands, however, also made important concessions to Belgium. It is no mean advantage to have the final agreement of the Netherlands on the unity of the Rhine-Meuse-Scheldt system, including the ports of Antwerp and Ghent and the waters of hitherto ill-defined character connecting these ports with the Waal, and, thereby, to see Belgium's status as a riparian state in the Rhine community finally established on a permanent and incontrovertible basis.

The unity referred to, however, is still an imperfect one. In particular, the fundamental rule of the Rhine regime that each riparian state will see to it that, within its territory, the waterway is put in good condition is not declared applicable by the agreement of 1939 to the waters connecting Antwerp and Ghent with the Waal; the application of that explicit rule of the Convention of Mannheim is still confined to the waters above Gorinchem and Krimpen—to the Waal and the Lek. There is no promise to let a canal be built as a substitute for the present roundabout and obsolete route through Zeeland. Even less is there a promise that, one day, a direct canal will be allowed across Dutch Limburg along the old line laid out by Napoleon I, a modern version of that Canal du Nord which still ends where work was abandoned in 1812, a *cul-de-sac* on the moors a few miles southwest of Venloo.

It should be noted that the first of these two canals would not serve exclusively as a better link between Antwerp, western Germany, eastern France, and Switzerland; it also would improve vastly communications between Belgium and the Netherlands. It is no mere accident that the name of a more direct route, which was practicable in the past, but now is diked off at both ends, the waterway between the Island of Tholen and the mainland, is called *Eendracht,* the Union. In the Low Countries, the waterway will always be more important than the railway or the highway; an up-to-date waterway connecting Brussels and Antwerp with Rotterdam and Amsterdam would be worthy of that old and glorious name.

Both on the sea and in the air, the Belgian flag plays a more modest part than that of the Netherlands; Belgian ships, however, have a share in the trade of Central Africa which is far from negligible. Taken as a whole, the merchant marines of the Low Countries would have occupied fifth place in 1938, after the British Commonwealth of Nations, the United States, Japan, Norway, and Germany. Taking age and quality into account, they would have ranked even higher. Belgium's share in this was small—less than one-eighth—and was diminishing.

In the field of aerial navigation, Belgium's position is very strong. Before the war, she held the seventh place among the nations of the world. While the Dutch KLM and KNILM were primarily concerned in the Far East, the Belgian SABENA was first in the world to operate regular air services over uncivilized countries. These airlines have been in scheduled operations since 1919 and connected with the Belgian European network in 1935 when the Brussels-Paris-Marseilles-Algiers-Léopoldville-Elisabethville line was inaugurated in coöperation with the French Régie Air-Afrique whose services had their terminal in Madagascar.

Although many Sabena planes were lost in North Africa, as a result of the French armistice, the company today, either independently or in agreement with British companies, operates more lines in the vast interior of the Congo than it did before the outbreak of the war and, in addition, lines to Cairo, South Africa, and the Gold Coast.

Conditions for Belgo-Dutch coöperation are assuredly favorable on the sea and in the air, where a spontaneous repartition by regions is already in existence. Coöperation of the two Rhine fleets is a more delicate matter; more delicate still, and also more important, is that of the seaports.

Coöperation always implies give and take; because of Belgium's unfavorable frontiers, however, give and take is not enough; there has often been a temptation in the past for the Netherlands to use its dominant territorial position, on the Scheldt and in Limburg, as a brake on Belgium's development in competitive ventures. Treating the Low Countries as a whole in all matters of communications will best serve, in this writer's opinion, the durable interest of the Netherlands as well as that of Belgium.

Only a common policy can effectively curb the diversion by France and Germany of the traffic that would naturally flow through the ports of the Low Countries. This is a common interest of Belgium and the Netherlands; it is also a European interest. Europe will recover its prosperity sooner if every ton of food and raw material and every finished product is allowed, in the future, to follow the most advantageous route.

The common interest of Belgium and the Netherlands in matters of communications is merely one aspect of a broader community of social, economic, and political interests. Coöperation will lighten the burden of reconstruction; it will help the Netherlands and Belgium to recover the resources and the vitality required by that task, as well as by the continued material and educational development of their respective territories overseas. Coöperation also will secure to Belgium, Luxemburg, and the Netherlands the maintenance of an adequate participation in international councils.

The location of the Low Countries is such that their interests are affected by technical, economic, or social change anywhere within western and central Europe. Brussels-Liége-Cologne and Brussels-Luxemburg-Basle are two hands of a signpost where the main routes from London to the Near East, that via Vienna and that via Italy, diverge. The great European highway, which will extend to Istanbul, begins at Ostend. The route from London to Berlin, Warsaw, and Moscow passes through Rotterdam; that from Paris to Berlin through Namur and Liége. The highway from Paris to Amsterdam has special historical as well as actual importance; it is, so to speak, the spinal column of the Low Countries; it is a tie within France; it is also a link in the chain between Scandinavia and the Iberian peninsula.

The future extension of the Rhine waterway from Basle to Lake Constance, that of the Neckar above Stuttgart, that of the Main to Bamberg and the construction of a modern canal between that town and the Danube, the possible extension of inland navigation up the Aar and ultimately, perhaps, to Geneva, are as important to Antwerp and Rotterdam as they are to Germany, Austria, and Switzerland. The tariff policies of the Reichsbahn and of the French National Railways affect these seaports as directly as though they were French or German cities.

No countries are more cosmopolitan than the Low Countries. Situated as they are at the crossroads of the world, none has a greater interest in world organization. This applies particularly to the field of communications, where Belgians and Dutchmen play so important a part. It would be regrettable, and perhaps not exclusively for these nations, if their governments were not called upon from the beginning to participate in international reorganization in this field.

Part Five

CULTURAL
ASPECTS

CHAPTER XV

The History of Christianity
in Belgium

BY FELIX MORLION

THE HISTORY OF CHRISTIANITY in Belgium goes back to a time before there were any written records in western Europe, when the only writing practiced was by travelers from the south or the east. Two documents referring to the beginnings of Christianity in the Low Countries survive, but even these refer to oral traditions that cannot be checked. One document states that St. Servaes was installed in the City of Tongeren in 344. The other confirms the existence of a church at Tongeren and quotes St. Irenaeus as stating that Christianity had spread to the two Roman provinces, Germania Superior and Germania Inferior, in the third century, and that there was a church in Trier under St. Eucharius. There are numerous stories which are doubtless tinged by popular fancy but which, nevertheless, have some basis in fact. These stories tell of the untiring efforts of Irish monks and other missionaries to convert the descendants of the tribes inhabiting the territory now known as Belgium.

Belgium is dotted with churches dedicated to the saints who, in the early centuries of Christianity, underwent great hardships in order to preach the Gospel to this vigorous people. When, in 496, the King of the Franks, Clovis, was baptized, legend has it that St. Remigius commanded: "Bow thy head, proud Sicamber; adore what thou hast destroyed and destroy what thou hast adored." This was probably an eloquent exaggeration, for the chronicles of the time agree that the Sicambers, who were akin to the Salian Franks, had as a general rule preserved the churches they found

in Maastricht, Tongeren, and Trier when they settled in the territory between the Scheldt and the Meuse, in the latter half of the
fifth century.

The conversion of Clovis did not result in the forced conversion
of the Franks. St. Elooi, who traveled extensively in the Lowlands
from 590 to 606, reported that Flanders was still predominantly
heathen. It required the labor of scores of saints, among them St.
Amandus, St. Willebrord, St. Rombout, St. Lambert, and St. Ar-
nout to implant the Christian religion in the hearts of those warring
tribes. Most of these saints died as martyrs. When, in 772, Charlemagne unified these territories, the Christian faith was already
solidly rooted in Belgium. He not only introduced numerous judicial and governmental measures but, through persevering care, he
organized Christian education in the schools he set up all over the
country.

When Christianity had to prove its worth at the call of the Crusades from the eleventh century on, the leaders of the Belgian
people responded to the Pope's summons. The Walloon Duke
Godfrey of Bouillon, became, in 1099, the first king of Jerusalem.
A Belgian noble, Thierry of Alsace, was prominent in the Third
Crusade, and Baldwin, the first Latin emperor of Constantinople,
also was of Belgian origin. Certainly the number of more obscure
though no less heroic Crusaders from Belgian territories, was proportionately great. From the very beginning, the Flemish people
showed a remarkable sense of independence which developed parallel with a deep sense of Christian life. The school of Flemish
mystics, which has profoundly influenced the life of the Church,
developed simultaneously with the traditions of the Flemish free
cities which started a democratic movement in the Middle Ages.
There is a link between these two phenomena; the slow but deep-
rooted growth of Christian convictions in the Flemish people
brought a sense of the dignity of the human person and a sense of
the importance of giving the common man the economic and political rights necessary to attain his full stature. In 1127, Charles
the Good, who has been canonized, was killed by political enemies
while praying in the Church of St. Donat at Bruges. He had defended the common people to such an extent that he was considered a menace to the privileges of the few.

The steady development of civil liberties in Belgium cannot be understood without an insight into the marvelous intellectual and spiritual flowering which made the Flemish Middle Ages famous. As early as the eleventh and twelfth centuries, Flemish chroniclers forged the Flemish language in their records of the life in the growing free cities. Famous theologians such as Henry of Ghent drew flocks of students from all over Europe. Two of the most profound poets and masters of spiritual life, the nun Hadewych and Jan van Ruysbroeck, were among the first to produce spiritual literature in the vernacular. Mystery and morality plays like *Elkerlyck* (*Everyman*), had their origins in Flanders. Masterworks of Gothic architecture—in belfries, town-halls and churches—studded the country. The first great Christian school of painting, the school of the Flemish Mystics, gained world renown. A great school of religious music, headed by Willaert and De Monte, introduced polyphonic music into the Church.

The territory around Liége first belonged to the Flemish diocese of Tongeren and later to the German diocese of Cologne. In 705, St. Lambert completed the Christianization of this province. Later, Bishop Notger organized the Bishopric of Liége into a political state which was headed by a bishop from its earliest beginnings. Liége soon became an international center of education which could boast of famous professors like Durandus and Reginald. The city had the rare honor of seeing two of its citizens elected pope, Urban IV and Gregory X. The universal feast of Corpus Christi, for which St. Thomas wrote the text, was established through the persistent efforts of Blessed Juliana, a nun of Liége. Although in the cultural field there were many relations between the principality of Liége and the counties of Flanders, Liége, unlike the other Walloon principalities, remained independent for nearly a thousand years. The deep-rooted Catholic spirit, however, produced the same results as in Flanders. While the rest of Europe was still unaware that there could be an end to despotism, in 1378 the artisans of Liége founded the Democratic Popular party which, for all practical purposes, was the first democratic party in the world.

Antwerp became identified with the printing of the first polyglot Bible (1569–1573). The printing establishment of Christopher Plantin published this Bible, thereby launching a long and distinguished service in publishing in Antwerp, which was carried on later by Moretus. Antwerp thereafter became one of the greatest international printing centers in Europe. Indeed, the rise of Antwerp on the Scheldt marked the opening of the new world of the Renaissance, while the decline of Bruges marked the end of the Middle Ages.

The background of the cultural achievements of the country continued to be religious. The University of Louvain, the center of Catholic faith in the Lowlands, was created in 1425 by a Papal Bull of Martin V at the request of the Duke of Brabant, John IV. In 1431, Louvain was recognized as the *Studium Generale* with permission to confer doctor's degrees bestowing the right to teach anywhere. The constitution of the University of Louvain is an outstanding example of an elective constitution. The *Rector Magnificus* was appointed by delegates of the various faculties and the whole organization of the University is a model of the checks and balances of democracy. Louvain became famous for its humanistic spirit and its studies and was the refuge of many famous men, among them Thomas More. This was the period when Louvain was famous for its jurists, its doctors, and its philosophers. One of its professors was later to become Pope Adrian IV. Names such as Vesalius, Van Helmont, Justus Lipsius, are internationally famous. Louvain was foremost in the defense of human liberty, when, under Protestant domination—"Whose is the kingdom, his is the religion," *Cujus regio, ejus religio*—the theory of the divine right of kings broke with the democratic traditions founded on scholastic doctrines.

There followed a period, during the struggle against Spain, when the Lowlands were torn by religious strife. Faithful to the Catholic Church, Belgium at length broke away from the Netherlands in the north. But this loyalty to the Church did not mean acquiescence in reactionary doctrines. Louvain became the center of the fight against absolutism, against the myth of the divine right of kings, and it was here that the theory of a limited monarchy which is one of the oldest forms of democracy, was elaborated. Here too, the great Bellarminus, a professor at the University, penned his democratic doctrines (based on Cajetan, commentator of St Thomas), combating the theory of the divine right of kings by defining the principles of the equality of all men based on their inalienable rights and on government by consent of all the people, which principles were taken over by Thomas Jefferson in the opening sentence of the Declaration of Independence.

From the fifteenth to the seventeenth century, Belgium was the battleground of Europe and subjected to continual invasion by France. The Austrian regime in the eighteenth century brought no hope of betterment to the impoverished and intellectually neglected population. The final act of Austrian domination was the clerical oppression known as "Josephinism," when the Emperor, Joseph II, attempted to rule from Vienna not only the religious life, but also the secular life of the Belgian people. Climaxing these centuries of trials and sufferings, in 1794 Belgium was subjected to a systematic religious persecution organized by the French revolutionists who occupied the country. Religious houses were closed, communes forbidden to contribute to the expenses of public worship. Every external symbol of religion, including religious garb, was forbidden. But the people resisted to a man and soon the measures were partly repealed by Camille Jordan, a more moderate member of the French "Directoire." After the *coup d'état* of the Fifth of Fructidor, which overthrew the first revolutionary regime, the persecution of the Church was even more severe. Churches, religious institutions, and even the University of Louvain were closed.

The Belgians seemed already to have developed a technique of resistance. Under the pressure of the people, many officials ignored the orders and the priests, with very few exceptions, refused to take the oath exacted by the French atheists. Of the 7,500 priests who, though condemned to be deported, remained in Belgium, only 400 were caught, and the Belgian bishops took refuge in England and continued directing their flock from there. When the French tried to enforce their measures, the Flemish peasants resisted in the famous Peasant War, waged much like guerrilla warfare today. By 1802 Napoleon realized this religious persecution could not succeed, and therefore made a Concordat which restored the liberty of religious worship in the Low Countries. When Napoleon was overthrown, Belgium's allies joined Belgium to Holland. The Dutch King, William, made the grave error of imposing on the liberty-loving Belgians many despotic measures, some of which interfered with their freedom of religion. Resistance was organized and, in 1829, the King had to capitulate, withdrawing his most hated measure, the compulsory education of future priests by a government "Seminary." But in the meantime, the revolutionary impetus had gathered strength and, with the help of the French Republicans, Belgium obtained her independence in 1830, inaugurating what has been considered the most liberal democratic constitution in Europe.

The Belgian Government has been scrupulously correct about living up to the clauses of the Constitution guaranteeing full freedom of public worship, of expression of opinion, of private instruction, and of freedom of the press. In 1828 Belgian unity was born of the joint efforts of Catholics and Liberals. This Unionism endured for some years after the establishment of independence. In 1842, however, the Liberal party obtained the majority vote and passed a measure known as the *Loi de Malheur* (Law of Misfortune) excluding religion from secular schools and barring the graduates of the free religious normal schools from teaching in state schools. Immediately the Church accepted this challenge, and in one year 3,000 schools were founded under its supervision. Thus each village had a religious school which gave parents an alternative to the nonreligious schools of the State. The consequence was that 61 per cent of the children went to Catholic schools whereas only 39 per cent preferred the material advantages offered by the state schools. Gradually these laws fell into disuse and a more reasonable solution was adopted. It was decided that whether religious instruction should be given in the state schools was a matter to be determined by the wish of the parents and the disposition of the municipality.

The second great religious battle was waged within the Catholic ranks. New Catholic liberal ideas had been circulated by the generation of Montalembert, Lacordaire, Demun, calling on Catholics to throw over the last vestiges of conservatism and to abandon the desire to regain the clerical privileges of the old regime. In 1863 these ideas were publicly defended at the Catholic Congress of Mechlin which brought together great leaders of all classes. The opposition diminished gradually and the desire for equal rights for all prevailed over the desire to gain easy advantages. In 1879 a new party, the Socialists, in the beginning affirmed Marxian materialism as openly as the Liberals had upheld rationalistic thinking. After the First World War, with the advent of universal suffrage, this party obtained a strength nearly equal to that of the Catholic party. The organization of the Catholic peasants, the *Boerenbond,* became the strongest coöperative in the country. With great capital at its disposal, it systematized its work through a series of scientifically managed branches. In 1938, the Christian trade unions and affiliated organizations had more than 800,000 members, and membership of the Socialist trade union remained around 700,000. This remarkable growth of social-mindedness in Catholic circles was quite naturally accompanied by the gradual domination of the Catholic party by the progressive elements. As early as 1860 there had been strong movements toward social justice among the Catholic conservatives. But only when, at the beginning of the twentieth century, progressive ideas found clearer expression as a result of the social encyclical of Pope Leo XIII, *Rerum Novarum,* did these movements take the lead. A group of Catholics, who, though differing from the Socialists on philosoph-ical and theological principles, advocated approximately the same measures in the social field on behalf of the proletariat, became known as the Christian Democrats. This group became more or less a party within the party. Although some of the cabinets of this period were constituted on a basis of coöperation between the Socialists and the Christian Democrats, this did not break the unity of the Catholic party, because in the various crises the unity of religious principles proved a still stronger bond.

But, after the First World War, extreme nationalism and, in its wake, fascism, became a dividing factor among Catholics. The Flemish movement was closely linked with religious motives and based on the religious tradition of Flanders. However, various circumstances infected a section of the Catholic youth and intel-lectuals with the nationalistic virus based on the oversimplified conception "one people, one state." The strongest influence was the demagogic and sentimental appeal of racial propaganda, dis-seminated by a group of extreme nationalists, some of whom had been quislings in the First World War.

A fascist movement, brought about by the Rexist party, spread through Wallonia and even numbered adherents among the Flemish counties. Both Flemish nationalism and Rexism made a great display of "Catholic" arguments against the "decadent democrats." It is to the honor of Cardinal Van Roey, the successor of Cardinal Mercier, and of the Belgian bishops, that they dared to hit hard at Flemish nationalism and fascist Rexism before practically anyone was aware of the deeper danger that was taking shape. They braved hypocritical accusations of "political clericalism" when they condemned the Flemish nationalists in 1930 and the Rexists in 1936 before these movements had a chance to take root in the Catholic masses. There was no real danger from either of them until the Nazi invasion puffed them up into representatives of the "New Order."

Besides its progressive religious achievements in the social and political field, Belgium became the testing ground for the great modern movement of the Church, Catholic Action. The theories of the lay apostolate were formulated in Rome, but it was to Belgium that young priests and laymen came from all over the world to study the practice of Catholic Action. Belgium became an international influence, not only through the famous congresses and conferences at Mechlin, given impetus by Cardinal Mercier, but also through its social schools, centers of Jocism, organizations for Catholic men and Catholic women, and its film, radio, and press organizations. In the cultural field as well, Belgium has regained its international influence. The University of Louvain again ranks among the outstanding institutions of Catholic learning where the fruits of a great tradition are preserved and transmitted. The American College in Louvain has known many famous bishops, professors, and lecturers who were sent from America to complete their training. Among the daring Expressionist painters who have once more made Flemish names world famous, there are men of great religious inspiration. In the field of music Belgium has enriched the world by such composers as Benoit, Gilson, Tinel, and César Franck; many of the best works of these men have a religious atmosphere. Among the modern-theater movements, the Flemish school has matched and even surpassed the stage productions of other countries in the application of new techniques in staging religious plays.

In the period between the two wars there have been few countries where the progress of religion has been so evident in all fields as in Belgium. And yet, although Belgium has been a country with a Catholic tradition for a thousand years, other denominations were not hampered in their development. According to the last census (1935), there were 30,000 Protestants with 43 ministers and sextons listed among the state-subsidized personnel. The same census listed 12,000 Hebrews with an officially recognized and subsidized personnel of 17. More than 100,000 Jewish refugees fled to Belgium to escape Nazi persecution and found there an atmosphere both congenial and friendly. It has been true throughout the history of Belgium that anti-Semitism and interdenominational struggles have been remarkably rare. The Flemish Nationalist party and the fascist Rexist party tried to breed intolerance but without any lasting success.

A stubborn religious spirit has proved to be one of the driving forces in Belgian culture and growth.

CHAPTER XVI

Education in Belgium

BY HENRI GRÉGOIRE

ELGIUM IS THE classic country of humanism and liberty. Therefore it is only natural that its educational system from the elementary or primary school up to the university should be conspicuous for freedom of teaching and for a marked faithfulness to the humanistic legacy of the Middle Ages and of the Renaissance handed down to modern generations by the Jesuits—those very Jesuits to whom Belgium probably owes her national name: for it was the appearance of the words *provincia belgica* on the countless textbooks used in the schools of the order, during the seventeenth and eighteenth centuries, which helped make generally popular the revived name of the "bravest of the Gauls."

But in Belgium freedom of teaching does not mean, as one would expect, a motley variety of all possible kinds of schools and educational methods. Although the constitution and laws permit and guarantee complete liberty to the founders, managers, and teachers of all institutions dedicated to public or private education, there are, nevertheless, two controlling elements which contribute toward keeping a certain standard—even a rather rigid one—in all teaching establishments. The first element is the right to confer degrees, diplomas, and certificates. This right can be granted only by law, and those who apply for it have to prove that their schools, colleges, or universities are operated in full compliance with certain requirements of a very strict nature. In other words, even the freest schools founded by individuals, religious denominations, or other corporations, by the municipalities or by the provinces, are in a sense state schools, because their curriculum has to be a state curriculum fixed by law. Of course, this provision is compulsory only for those schools which wish to confer diplomas and degrees, recognized by the State, but it suffices to nip in the bud many extravagant or whimsical educational initiatives. The second element which contributes to the same result is the Belgian principle basically due to the action of the dominant Catholic church, the system called subsidized liberty. Every school, college, or university which complies with the general regulations on education, which gives the State certain guarantees, for instance teachers who have the required qualification and a curriculum conforming to the minimum curriculum set by the State, is not only empowered to deliver degrees and diplomas but is also entitled to financial support.

The idea naturally is that public education is one of the primary responsibilities of the State and that every school run according to the official standard saves the State a part of the money which the same State would otherwise have to devote to the education of a section of the population. This characteristically Belgian principle was not adopted at once, nor was it generally recognized as binding until a recent date. Its triumph was the result of long and bitter strife between the so-called "liberals" who claimed for State schools alone the privilege of state support, and the Catholic masses who wanted establishments capable of satisfying their religious aspirations. The result was an agreement, now generalized, as to what is called *le droit au subside*.

This agreement was a compromise. The Catholics were traditional opponents of State education because it was neutral in religious matters, and for many generations it could even be said of Catholic cabinets that they were hostile to their own public education. A Catholic statesman even proclaimed that in the field of education the State's duty was to pave the way for its own resignation (*Le devoir de l'Etat en matière d'enseignement est de préparer sa propre démission*). But the natural sense of proportion—one might even say of humor—of the Belgian people led to the agreement that this paradoxical and challenging formula was not right. On the other hand, the fierce opponents of church education finally bowed to the self-evident truth that, after all, the religious section of the people was entitled to schools whose spirit should be in accordance with their deepest religious feelings.

The final and lasting result was peace and harmony in the field of education. It was a successful synthesis of liberty, state support, and state control. And note that state control is making itself felt in the mildest way. It limits itself to the setting up of a minimum curriculum. Even state universities, as far as their right to confer degrees is concerned, are not treated in a more favorable or privileged way than so-called "free universities." Diplomas and degrees granted by the state universities of Liége and Ghent, for example, are recognized by the State only after a formal checking by a joint committee, called the *Commission d'entérinement*, just like diplomas and degrees from the Catholic university at Louvain or from the liberal university at Brussels. The present system, of course, although it is deeply rooted in Belgium's liberal tradition, is the product of a century-long evolution, and one of its most striking and satisfactory aspects is certainly traceable to a recent and dire necessity and emergency.

The magnanimous state support lent by the Government to the two free universities dates back only to 1919. In this instance, as in many others, the First World War had brought about decisive changes in the partisan trend of mind of the Belgian people, created a strong sense of unity, did away with picayunish quibbles and legalistic controversies, put an end to ideological and religious disputes between Catholics, Liberals, and Socialists, and convinced the nation at large of the necessity of maintaining at any cost the two universities which symbolized, so to speak, the two souls of the national body: the Roman Catholic belief and spirit, and the fighting zeal of the freethinkers. The two types of Belgians had equally deserved the survival of their intellectual strongholds: Brussels University had reared Burgomaster Max, and Louvain had become associated forever in world history with Cardinal Mercier. Now the financial basis of these two shrines of higher learning, already shaken before the First World War, had been impaired to such an extent by the catastrophe of 1914–1918 that both would have perished but for the intervention of the State. American readers will certainly be reminded of similar circumstances which may present themselves in the near future in this hemisphere or are even at hand. It will interest them to know that a state may give material support to a university without enslaving it in the least.

But America has to be mentioned in this context for other reasons. The generous decision of the Belgian Parliament to uphold the free universities was certainly accelerated, if not prompted, by the admirable influence of the celebrated Commission for Relief in Belgium, founded by Herbert Hoover, and of the Educational Foundation into which the Commission transformed itself immediately after the armistice. A large part of the generous funds which had been collected in America for the benefit of Belgium's starving population was, by a splendid and enlightened gesture, dedicated to the support of higher education, learning and research, in the liberated country. Large gifts in money were donated by American benefactors to the four Belgian universities without discrimination, and this policy undoubtedly reinforced the new tendency toward a fair and impartial treatment by the State of the universities, so often and so long separated by lively political and intellectual feuds. It is by no means an exaggeration to say that in 1918–1919, after having saved the Belgian people from starvation, America brought Belgium liberty, peace, goodwill, tolerance, and coöperation. But these are not the only American watchwords and familiar expressions which Belgium borrowed from her benefactors. While Belgians remained faithful to their educational system and improved it along their own lines, the brisk intercourse between universities, American and Belgian, ushered in by the Educational Foundation, through scholarships, exchange of professors and similar means, introduced into Belgium's academic habits and customs the best traits of American university life. If Belgians have not yet adopted the sabbatical year, at least they talked of full-time professors; assistants and associates of all kinds became the fashion, even in a rather inflationist way. But America's most precious lesson was manifested when rich industrialists and other wealthy people, realizing the importance of education, began to vie with the State in enriching the universities, museums, and libraries.

Finally, the great King Albert, in 1927, with much insight and foresight in the period of greatest prosperity, reminded the magnates of heavy industry of their duty toward Belgian scientific institutions. His memorable speech or manifesto delivered at Seraing, near Liége, and widely publicized by the press, opened a drive in the American manner which struck and moved the Belgian public by its very novelty. Its success was really royal. More than 100,000,000 francs were raised in a short and dramatic campaign of a few months. A new foundation came into existence and began at once to work along with the Fondation Universitaire. It received its charter in 1928 and was called Le Fonds National de la Recherche Scientifique (in Flemish, Nationaal Fonds voor Wetenschappelijk Onderzoek).[1]

Few people, even in America, realize the tremendous impetus given by these two foundations to Belgium's scientific and scholarly life and production. Within a short space of twenty years, little Belgium developed a truly gigantic activity in most sectors of the front of research. In another chapter this scientific effort has been beautifully summarized and illustrated.[2] This account is limited to the fields of history and philology, two Belgian specialties existing at least since the Renaissance. It would be unfair to deny that the exceedingly flourishing state of these studies during the last quarter of the century had been prepared by a whole school of really great men who started their work and teaching in the 'eighties or 'nineties of the last century. Among them it suffices to cite Belgium's greatest historian, Henri Pirenne; the famous historian of oriental cults in the Roman Empire, Franz Cumont; the classical philologist and biographer of Julian the Apostate, Joseph Bidez; the linguist, Emile Boisacq; the world-famous student of Buddhism, Louis de la Vallée-Poussin; the Egyptologist, Jean Capart, a frequent traveler to America and highly esteemed adviser to American museums; the Arabist, Victor Chauvin; and many others,

---

[1] The Fondation Universitaire (Universitaire Stichting) whose capital is or was, in all, 55,000,000 francs, is, according to a very true definition, "an unofficial center for the promotion of higher education in all its branches in Belgium. It provides aid to technical and scientific publications, makes grants to scientific and university associations, carries on regular exchanges of students and professors between Belgium and Great Britain, promotes similar exchanges between Belgium and the United States, and so on; last, but not least, it provides in its building at 11, rue d'Egmont, Brussels, a meeting place for professors and laymen interested in higher education. The Fonds National fosters scientific research by aiding already existing Belgian institutions. It provides research fellowships, assists qualified research workers, aids eminent Belgian savants, grants traveling fellowships, supplies scientific instruments to laboratories and so on. Twenty-four scientific commissions were set up by it in the various fields."

[2] See Chapter XVII, "Science in Independent Belgium," by Jean Timmermans.

such as the Liége masters, Charles Michel, Léon Parmentier, Jean Pierre Waltzing, Henri Francotte, and Godefroid Kurth.

Special mention should be made, of course, of the modern Bollandists, whose record, since their huge collection was started in 1643, was never so brilliant and productive as during the last sixty years. All these great men were of course in full production when the First World War broke out, and some of their disciples had begun their own careers. But how dark were, too often, the prospects of the latter! Political strifes and political bias were then at their height. One party had been in control of state education for thirty years (1884–1914). Young scholars, even talented and promising ones, who did not belong to that party had no chance whatever of obtaining fellowships (with the sole exception of a very limited number of *bourses de voyage*), and still less of being allowed, even without a salary, to teach their favorite subject at state universities. To these independent *apprentis savants* only Brussels remained open. But its professors got only minimum salaries and were obliged, in order to eke out a living, to become teachers in secondary schools or in private institutions. Many an outstanding scholar was hampered in his productivity by unfavorable material conditions. Many others left the country or simply gave up. It is not strange that in 1918–1919 American aid in the field of Belgian education brought liberty and enthusiasm, activity and production, to the scholarly little army whose numbers, instead of diminishing, suddenly increased by leaps and bounds.

The example of America wrought miracles in the sector of feminine education too. In this respect Belgium was incredibly backward. In 1914 there was not a single state secondary school for girls in the whole kingdom. Now there are in Belgium more than 40 *lycées de jeunes filles* whose curriculum, by the way, is exactly that of the Athénée (the Belgian name corresponding to the French Lycée and the German Gymnasium).[3] When one speaks of American impetus he means that Belgian education was stirred and speeded up by America, morally, so to speak, compelled to hasten its pace, but always along the path of national tradition. The

---

[3] In Belgium the word "Lycée" is used to connote a secondary school open to girls alone. An Athénée is open to boys and, in many instances, especially in places where there is no Lycée, equally to girls.

Lycée became an exact counterpart of the Athénée, humanistic in essence, that is to say, faithfully preserving the model of the Graeco-Latin school of old.

There is certainly in every Lycée or Athénée a parallel section without the two classical languages, which are replaced by more compulsory teaching in mathematics, natural science, and modern languages. The name for that section is beautifully noble—*humanités modernes*.[4] But it does not seem to attract Belgian youth for the simple reason that holders of that certificate are not allowed to enter, without a special examination, the university courses leading to most of the liberal professions. In other words, not only Latin, but also Greek, are still entrance requirements for all branches and subjects in Belgian universities. Latin and Greek are compulsory for all boys and girls who want to become educators, physicians, chemists, or lawyers. Only future engineers of all types therefore choose the modern section. Statistics compiled shortly before the war in order to make the French public acquainted with the school system, exceedingly progressive and amazingly conservative like all things Belgian, showed that a plurality of 62 per cent of all young people attending both the Lycée and Athénée were supposed to learn Greek and Latin. These old language requirements are by no means sham requirements. The result is that, with the possible exception of Holland, there is no country in the world which has preserved to such an extent (and even developed) the traditional scheme of classical education. This may sound paradoxical, for Belgium was and is noted for her realistic spirit of enterprise, mostly in the industrial field. To the outer world it appears as *la terre classique des ingénieurs* who founded for instance, in a great many capital cities of both hemispheres, the streetcar companies and other public utilities. But a dense population like Belgium's is full of surprises. It has been said that Belgium's soil rears more poets per square mile than any other country. Similarly, the country has by far the biggest crop of Hellenists.

This then being the background, it is now possible to try to sketch against it the marvelous development of Belgium's historical

---

[4] There is also an intermediate section with Latin only, but it leads to no advanced studies and has practically no enrollment.

and philological sciences during the interval between the two
World Wars. Here a few paragraphs may be quoted from an
American:

"In the two decades which followed the first Allied victories,
historians the world over had cause to stand astounded at the productive genius of the tiny nation which had borne the war's greatest sufferings. Concentrated in a minute corner of Europe, a group
of men raised themselves to leadership in one area of study after
another—until an outsider, unfamiliar with their genius, would
have sworn that they stood on the shoulders of a mighty nation's
academic armies. It wasn't so. They stood out in the world's crowd
of learned men because of their own stature.

"It is hard to account for things like that. We in their profession
spend our lives in an effort to explain why at one moment or another superiority rests with this or that people or group. Perhaps
a partial measure of our success in that attempt is our own inability
to prescribe the exact formulae for application to other groups in
other times and circumstances in hope of reviving or creating such
leadership. But in the present lull we can weigh Belgium's magnificent two decades, to appraise the forces which made her great and,
now repeated, can make her great again."

These magnificent words are literally true, but the Belgian problem in itself is clear. The great leaders to whom Reynolds[5] is allud-
ing were there, and their stature had been enhanced, in many
instances, by the firm stand they took under foreign occupation.
It was fortunate for the prestige of Belgium's scholars that one of
them, the historian, Henri Pirenne, through his captivity in Germany became, like Cardinal Mercier and Burgomaster Max, the
shining symbol of national resistance and won for his manly attitude, as a champion of freedom, the admiration of the liberal
world. He came back to his University of Ghent with an authority
which he used to the full for the loftiest of purposes. While carrying
on his teaching, attracting brilliant students, among whom were
many Americans, while completing his monumental *Histoire de
Belgique,* he devoted a considerable part of his time to fertile

---

[5] Robert Reynolds: "Henri Laurent, a Belgian Scholar" (*Annuaire de l'Institut
de Philologie et d'Histoire Orientales et Slaves,* Tome VII, 1939–1944, pp. 495–
497).

discussions in manifold committees, attempting to improve the
educational system. He did not win all his battles. He failed to
obtain, for instance, a state entrance examination which, in his
opinion, was "a sorely needed barrier, a fence capable of keeping
the barbarians away from the holy shrine of learning (*l'examen
antibarbare*)," but he fully succeeded in bringing about the important law on higher education, passed by the Parliament in 1929.
Since that year, the requirements for even the lowest grade of
university teachers have been rather severe and the results were
certainly excellent. At one time in Germany it could be said that
a Belgian doctor's degree was cheap. Conditions have changed since
then, and the numerous international congresses which met in
Belgium, often summoned by Pirenne himself, like the famous
Brussels *Congrès International d'Histoire* in the year 1923 and the
sixth Congress of the History of Religions, 1936, or, on the eve of
the war, the congresses of Orientalists, 1937, and of Linguists, 1938,
established the leading position of Belgium in all these learned
fields. The progress was amazingly rapid. In some instances, the
process of organization of a new branch of instruction took only
a few months. The meeting of the committee which, in 1922, was
planning the Congress of Historians is still remembered. Pirenne,
sketching the outline of that international parliament of historians, warned his listeners not to forget the Byzantine field. Father
Delehaye, the great Bollandist who was a Byzantinist *sans le savoir
et sans le vouloir,* expressed his doubts about the possibility of
organizing even a small Byzantine section. The new department,
he said, called into existence by the Bavarian, Krumbacher, would
not survive the death of its founder and of the international catastrophe of the First World War. But Pirenne protested, saying that
a country so full of young Hellenists should take the lead and
immediately occupy the deserted field. The Byzantine section was
so successful that Nicholas Iorga, who attended it, conceived in
Brussels the bold idea of summoning for the next year the first
Byzantine Congress (Bucharest, 1924), and in 1925 the first volume
of *Byzantion* appeared through a generous subsidy of the Fondation Universitaire. A few years later a German scholar said that
the Belgians had literally created overnight a great center of Near
Eastern studies (*aus dem Boden gestampft*).

The same enthusiasm was noticeable throughout the period in many other fields and brought the same results. In all instances the material support of the Educational Foundation was decisive. The great neighbor nations which did not possess the equivalent of the Fondation were clearly lagging. In a few years new and authoritative organs of different branches of instruction were launched and all of them, so far as is known, have been so successful that, in general, they were practically self-supporting when the Second World War broke out. There was certainly an unrivaled series of scholarly journals of the type of the *Revue Belge de Philologie et d'Histoire,* founded in 1922; *L'Antiquité Classique,* founded in 1931; *La Chronique d'Egypte,* edited by Jean Capart, probably the most readable, instructive, and entertaining of all scholarly journals; *Latomus, Revue des Etudes Latines,* founded by the lamented Kugener and Léon Herrmann; *Les Etudes Classiques,* published by the flourishing College of the Namur Jesuits; while periodicals of old standing like the *Analecta Bollandiana* of the Brussels Bollandists, the *Revue d'Histoire Ecclésiastique* of Louvain, the *Revue Bénédictine,* edited by the Abbaye de Maredsous, *Le Muséon,* organ of the Orientalist School of Louvain, are upholding their fame and that of Belgium. There is no exaggeration in saying that in all the fields covered by these journals, because of the mass of original research digested in them and the fullness of their bibliography, Belgian scholars are already fulfilling the task which, a few years ago, was considered to be the natural, and some thought, the eternal mission of German scholarship. Of course, the parallel decadence of German erudition which became so striking after 1933 rather stirred the energies and nourished the warrantable pride of men who felt that again the honorable duty of preserving a part at least of a glorious European tradition rested upon their shoulders.

It will suffice to consult the periodicals mentioned above, in order to appraise the truly amazing quantity of this scholarly production. It can be said that, because of the series of publications issued by the four universities, by the different academies, or to the ever-ready help of the Fondation and the Fonds National, no book really worth publishing remained in manuscript form, just as no important paper is ever doomed to the discouraging delays which are the plague and scourge of young scholars in America. But here again, American generosity has often helped directly or indirectly. The Bollandists, for example, owe much to the support and sympathy of Catholics in the United States.

One of the most delicate and interesting aspects of Belgian intellectual life should be mentioned. Belgium has, there is no gainsaying it, a linguistic problem. The Flemish question gave rise, in the interval between the two wars, to a protracted and often fierce and embittered strife. The struggle was especially hot around the key position which the Flemings wanted to conquer and which they have fully occupied at last: the French University of Ghent in Flanders. It was gradually transformed into a completely Flemish institution, after a short period during which a complicated linguistic compromise prevailed. Foreign pessimists, well- or ill-wishers, used to speak, in those times, of a menacing disruption of Belgian unity, and the French-speaking Belgians were not without fears about the future of an institution where Pirenne, Cumont, and Bidez had taught, which they had hallowed and from which their language was to be banished forever. They failed to recognize three points: that the Flemish people were really entitled to a university of their own, that Ghent was the natural intellectual center of the Flemish section of the country, and that a staff of numerous and competent teachers was ready to take over and eager to prove to their Walloon fellow countrymen and to the world that a Flemish university would maintain and even raise, if possible, the high level of the glorious French one. Although only a few years have elapsed since the *vervlaamsching* of what is now the *hoogeschool*, the quantity of bulky publications issued in the Flemish language by the different faculties, and their outstanding quality, are truly reassuring and prove that if the transformation was really a national necessity, it has not involved the cultural regression which was feared. In this connection, praise should be given to the excellent, respectful, and friendly relations between the retired French masters of Ghent University and their Flemish successors. A Flemish thesis which appeared a few months before the war carries a commendatory preface by Joseph Bidez. The present writer, having been a fervent and constant fighter for *Gand-français* throughout many years, feels that it is his duty, writing now in America and for an American public, to bear testimony to the spirit of reconciliation which shortly after the decision spread over a doggedly contested battlefield which he would like, for the sake of domestic peace, to address in the Byronian style: Thou first and last of fields! Needless to say, because of the discipline and authority of the Catholic church, the linguistic evolution of Louvain had proceeded more smoothly, and the system gradually adopted by the bishops was an almost mathematical duplication of all professorships and courses, with an almost equal number of French- and Flemish-speaking students attending both sections. Technical details do not belong in this general picture, but it was undoubtedly a blessing for the country that, on the eve of the invasion, this grave issue had been peacefully settled.

One cannot fail to add that Belgian liberty in the field of education asserted itself again by the foundation in Ghent of a free Institut des Hautes Etudes where courses are conducted exclusively in French and which is already conspicuous for some important publications. In the midst of the dangerous linguistic struggle, the Educational Foundation and the Fonds National de la Recherche Scientifique behaved in the most conciliatory and impartial way, bringing about in their different committees constant and friendly contacts between the contending parties and upholding, above the partisan strife, the loftiest scholarly ideas. A new foundation, the Francqui Foundation, established in 1932, also acted as a powerful factor of unity. A Francqui prize is awarded to a Belgian who has made an important contribution to science thereby increasing the prestige of Belgium. The prize is given regardless of language and of specialty, science proper being treated on an equal footing with scholarship. Awards have been made to the late Professor Henri Pirenne (History), to the Abbé Georges Lemaître (Physics), to Franz Cumont (History), to Jacques Errera (Chemistry), to Pierre Nolf (Medicine), and professorships were established so that eminent foreign scholars might be invited to Belgian universities for a year of academic teaching and research.

It is hoped that this will lead to the foundation of a super-university, both national and international, Belgian and universal, on the lines of an internationalized Collège de France. At Anderlecht, somewhere in the neighborhood of the House of Erasmus, of the statue of Justus Lipsius—at Overijssche,—of the Museum Bollandianum, and of Capart's Musée du Cinquantenaire, where are to be found the Syrian splendors of Apameia, excavated under the auspices of the Fonds National, a Collegium Belgicum would thrive and flourish. Belgium's olympic soil awaits this last benefaction from the American-Belgian "belle alliance."

CHAPTER XVII

Science in Independent Belgium

BY JEAN TIMMERMANS

THE INFLUENCE OF environment as a condition of scientific progress is particularly striking in the history of Belgium. At the end of the Middle Ages and during the Renaissance, the Low Countries constituted one of the richest regions of Europe. The manufacturing industries, foreign trade, and banking had been instrumental in building great patrician fortunes, while in the urban communities the struggle for democracy was developing. In this atmosphere, so alive, so complex, there was a general flowering of arts, letters, and sciences. The University of Louvain, which was founded in the year 1425, experienced a new period of splendor when, in 1517, the College of Three Languages (Latin, Greek, and Hebrew), was opened there—this course to serve as a model for Francis I in creating the Collège de France. Erasmus (1467–1536), though born in Rotterdam, had chosen as his favorite residence an estate near Brussels—in Anderlecht, where the house is preserved as a small museum. It was only a little later that the press of Christopher Plantin (1514–1589) was founded in Antwerp, a printing establishment whose workshops were active until the middle of the nineteenth century. They are still intact, evidence of a time when the actual printing of books, as well as their wise editing and publishing, could be carried out by the same men.

From that amazing period date the works of a group of scientists of exceptionally high caliber: Andreas Vesalius (1514–1564), the renovator of topographical anatomy; Rembert Dodoens (1517–1583), whose treatises on botany have long been considered authoritative; the iatro-chemist, J. B. van Helmont (1577–1647), who coined the word "gas" and also proved that there are different kinds of gases; the geographer, Gerard Kremer (1517–1594), known as Mercator, whose cartographical projection is still the foundation of navigation. Lastly, there is Simon Stevin (1548–1620), the creator of computation by decimal fractions, who was as eclectic as Leonardo da Vinci, being at the same time physicist and military engineer; his works also foreshadowed the creation of a decimal system of money, weights, and measures.

So, in a brief period of about a century and a half, there appeared many illustrious figures in the country. But the picture changes when the Low Countries became the possession of foreign princes, the kings of Spain who, after Philip II, no longer had their residence in Belgian provinces.

The religious persecutions drove out of Belgium the most energetic men, who, by taking refuge in the principalities to the north, contributed to the greatness of the United Provinces. It was then that a native of Belgium, Pieter Minuit, led the first colonists of New Belgium (1623), which later became New York, while in China the Belgian Jesuit, Ferdinand Verbiest (1623–1688) created the Imperial Observatory of Peking.

Civil war and struggle against the invader ravaged the country; the port of Antwerp, blockaded, fell into disuse; the bankruptcy of the country brought about a corresponding weakening of spirit, so that, in the middle of the eighteenth century—a period of intellectual brilliance in France and in England—travelers complained of finding a distressing intellectual mediocrity in Belgium.

The first moves toward revival came through the efforts of the benevolent despotism of Austria. In 1772 Empress Maria Theresa established the Imperial and Royal Academy at Brussels; it was found that enough members could be secured only by appealing to foreign scholars. At the same time, the former library of the dukes of Burgundy was opened to the public. This library later was to constitute, with its illuminated manuscripts, one of the treasures of the Royal Library of Brussels.

At this time, the University of Louvain had fallen into an almost irretrievable decline, and people who wanted good higher education were obliged to become expatriates, by preference in Paris which was a renowned intellectual center. Unhappily, these first efforts of renascence were ruined by the conquests of the French Revolution (1794). Under the regimes of the Directory, the Consulate, and the Empire, Belgium was smothered in the French organization of western Europe and no longer had a real university, but only schools for training officers of the regime like the schools of medicine in Brussels, Antwerp, and Ghent; the schools of law in Liége and Brussels.

The Dutch rule from 1815 to 1830 improved this condition; the three universities created by the State at Ghent, Louvain and Liége trained a few good scholars and, at the same time, by creating a national elite, paved the way for the downfall of Dutch domination. During the revolution of 1830, these three universities once more were closed. It was not until 1834 that a Catholic University was founded, under the auspices of the Bishops at Mechlin, which was transferred to Louvain the following year, while the Freemasons established a "Free" University at Brussels. Finally, in 1835, the Belgian Government decided to establish two state universities, one at Ghent, the other at Liége.

Nevertheless, the influence of Belgian higher education made itself felt only slowly. Until about 1850 the majority of eminent Belgian scientists were self-trained men who continued their training through contact with Paris. In 1841 the Royal Academy of Medicine took its place beside the Royal Academy of Science, Letters, and Fine Arts, which had been revived in 1816 by the Dutch Government and later by the Belgian Government. After the middle of the nineteenth century the development of science in Belgium was extremely rapid and impressive.

During the course of these three periods—the greatness of the Renaissance, the deep depression around 1700, and finally, the revival at the end of the eighteenth century—the development of science in Belgium paralleled the vicissitudes of the national economy. Though the origin of the Belgian people goes back farther than does the white population of North America, still, from the point of view of intellectual development, particularly in scientific realms, the Belgium of today is no older than the United States. Therefore, to judge fairly the results which have been achieved, it is necessary to remember in each instance from what point the two countries started a little more than 150 years ago.

Mathematical sciences, pure and applied.—This chapter will
trace the progress of science in Belgium since the beginning of the
nineteenth century. The considerable amount of material, however, permits treatment only of the most important men who are
of interest in scientific circles abroad, exclusive of scientists of
secondary importance with whom they had intellectual ties. Representatives of such subjects as pure mathematics, astronomy, geod-
esy, theoretical physics, and statistics are presented. This selective
treatment is justified because, in most instances, the scientists pursued their work concurrently in the realm of mathematical speculation and its applications.

Adolphe Quetelet (1796–1874) is one of the great world figures
in international science. A geometrist and analyst, he worked in
astronomy and in meteorology. As early as 1826 he suggested that
the Academy found an observatory in Brussels. This plan was
realized in 1832. Quetelet was able thus to begin quite early his
observations in the field of terrestrial magnetism, in climatology,
in atmospheric electricity, and in the periodic phenomena of the
growth of plants. After 1847, he measured the difference of longi-
tudes of the observatories in Greenwich and in Brussels and began
a study of the stars of absolute motion. Permanent Secretary of the
Academy for forty years, Quetelet rendered great service to the
development of science in Belgium in various fields; but the works
which made him best known abroad were those which he published, from 1825 to 1848, on population movements, on the development of man's faculties, works which created—out of nothing,
so to speak—a kind of social physics, which won for him the well-
deserved title of "creator of scientific statistics."

The career of one of his successors at the Observatory, Jean
Charles Houzeau de Lehaye (1820–1888), demonstrates very well
the difficulties which Belgian scientists faced at this time. Houzeau,
who was independent by nature, could not adapt himself to the
regular university courses, and went to Mons, Brussels, and Paris
to follow courses which interested him. In 1842, he was appointed
to the Observatory in Brussels; but, after being involved in the
republican movement of 1848, he was dismissed and began to travel
extensively. In 1854 he published a distinguished essay on the
physical geography of Belgium, and in 1857 a natural history of

European soil. Then followed geodetical surveys necessitated by the making of a new general map of Belgium. After 1860 the surveys necessary for a map of the whole country, on a scale of 1:5000 were carried out by the personnel of the Military Cartographic Institute, whose efforts furnished Belgium with a map comparable to the finest foreign ones.

Houzeau soon after left for America, where he was to spend nineteen years. He went to Texas, then to New Orleans, became active in the ranks of the abolitionist party, and in 1868 had to flee to Jamaica. The fact that he never gave up his astronomical observations, however, permitted him to publish in 1874 a *General Uranometry* containing a catalogue of 6,000 stars visible to the naked eye, on the whole surface of the celestial sphere, with their positions and their size, and a description of the Milky Way which has remained a classic. Houzeau was called back to Belgium to succeed Quetelet at the Observatory. During his last years Houzeau published, with the collaboration of A. Lancaster, another general bibliography of astronomy, a masterly work relating to the whole body of astronomical publications.

In 1898 the Astronomical Observatory and the Meteorological Institute were made separate institutions. Under the direction of Paul Stroobant the Observatory was entirely reëquipped. One of the most active departments is that on the study and research of small planets; Eugène Delporte, the present Director of the Observatory, for example, is well known for his discoveries in this field.

A brilliant group of geometrists and analysts continued to emerge in Belgium. One of these was Louis Philippe Gilbert (1832–1892), professor at the University of Louvain, who was engaged in work on mechanical physics, especially in research on gyroscopes and "mechanical proof of the rotation of the earth" (1833). There was also Joseph Marie de Tilly (1837–1906), professor at the Military Academy, who cast new light on the very principles of non-Euclidian geometries and the foundations of mechanics; also General Henri Alexis Brialmont (1821–1908), a military engineer who invented the system of entrenched camps in use until 1914.

Finally, of the most recent generations first of all should be cited Paul Mansion (1844–1919), professor at the University of Ghent, a great geometrician and the founder of the Belgian review *Mathesis,* which brings together the works of all Belgian mathematicians; Charles de la Vallée Poussin, professor at the University of Louvain, honorary President of the International Union of Mathematicians; Alphonse Demoulin, Clément Servais, Adolphe Mineur, Jacques Deruyts, Modest Stuyvaert, E. A. Théophile de Donder, professor at the University of Brussels, a specialist in the theory of relativity; Giuseppe Cesaro, Professor of Crystallography at the University of Liége, a scholar of Italian origin. Further, Abbé Lemaître, a professor at the University of Louvain, is a physical-mathematician well known for his theory of the expanding universe.

There were also a large number of Belgian mathematicians and astronomers who were interested in the history of their science; notable among these were the Jesuit, P. Bosmans (1852–1928), author of the best biography of Simon Stevin, and George Sarton, born in Ghent and now a naturalized American, who has acquired a world reputation as the editor of the review of the history of sciences, *Isis,* published in Brussels until 1940 and since then in New York.

Physics, chemistry, engineering.—In this domain, as well, the eighteenth century was sterile in Belgium, but in the nineteenth century discoveries were many. The first name to be mentioned is Jean Servais Stas (1813–1891), the greatest chemist Belgium has produced. He began, at the University of Louvain, the only really well-organized course of scientific study of the period, that of medicine; he did his first original research in that field, the discovery of phlorizine in the roots of the apple tree.

Stas's teacher, J. B. van Mons (1765–1842), sent him to study in Paris under the direction of the great French chemist, J. B. Dumas, who entrusted Stas with the making of a new gravimetric synthesis of carbon-dioxide gas; in a work published in 1840, Stas showed that the atomic weight of carbon, contrary to the findings of his predecessors, is exactly 12 if the atomic weight of oxygen is set at 16. He was thus led to investigate whether the fractional atomic weights of other elements was not also the result of experimental error. In studying other elements he succeeded in determining, with a precision which has been surpassed only by the twentieth-century works of the American scientists, Richards and Baxter, the atomic weights of about 15 other elements. In 1867, Stas represented Belgium at the conference which created the International Bureau of Weights and Measures, and, in collaboration with Sainte-Claire Deville, made ingots from an alloy of platinum and iridium which served in the manufacture of the standard meter which is the foundation of all contemporary metrology.

In an admirable biography of Stas, written by his friend and disciple, W. Spring, his work is described as characteristic of a critical rather than a creative mind. This tendency is common to many other Belgian chemists who preferred to test the hypotheses and theories of others by very thorough experiments rather than to state new ones themselves. Such a turn of mind was in harmony with the realistic and persevering character of the Belgians in general.

Joseph Plateau (1801–1883), a contemporary of Stas, was his emulator in the field of experimental physics. In his first investigations he demonstrated the persistence of the impression of luminous images on the retina, discovering in this way the physiological effect which was later to help the development of the cinematographic industry. After 1843 Plateau undertook a series of ingenious experiments on the surface tension of shallow sheets of water, the geometrical description of which led his friend G. P. Dandelin (1794–1847) to new works on theoretical geometry.

Stas had the greatest possible influence on the development of chemistry in Belgium. He had called to Ghent, as professor, the German scientist, F. A. Kekulé, already famous for his theories on the structure of organic compounds, whose successor was a Belgian, Théodore Swarts, also an organic chemist, whose son Fréderic Swarts (1868–1940), acquired an international reputation. Almost alone, the latter assembled the whole chapter of organic chemistry devoted to fluorine compounds, of which he prepared several hundred by original methods and which he studied from such points of view as reactivity, heat of combustion, and refractive index. These experiments of Swarts gave the idea to a young Belgian, A. L. Henne, a student at the University of Brussels and now professor at Ohio State University, of preparing a series of mixed halogenated derivatives of methane and its homologues, of which one, dichlorodifluoromethane, has already proven itself an important refrigeration agent in American industry.

Mention should be made, too, of L. Baekeland (1863–1944), the inventor of bakelite, the prototype of artificial plastic substances, who was born in Ghent but who went to the United States to make his career. Another well-known scientist of Belgian origin was Julius A. Nieuwland (1878–1939), professor at the University of Notre Dame. The Nichols medal was given to him in 1935 by the American Chemical Society, for having discovered the reaction for the synthesis of neoprene (artificial rubber).

At the time when Kekulé was teaching in Belgium, German science was enjoying a well-earned reputation and many young Belgians went to Germany to start their research. Notable among them were Louis Henry and Walthère Spring. Louis Henry (1834–1913), professor at the University of Louvain, devoted fifty years to the study and teaching of organic chemistry. He is known especially for his ingenious syntheses on dipropargyle, on isomere of benzene, and on acetonitrile. He was very much interested in the relations between physical constants and chemical composition, a subject which is still a preoccupation of the Louvain school today. Also working at Louvain at this time was Professor Alexandre de Hemptinne, who became famous for his research concerning the action of electrical discharges on chemical reactions.

Walthère Spring (1848–1912), was a physical chemist of great originality. Before entering the University of Liége, where his father was a professor, he spent a year as a workman in the shop of an armsmaker in his native town. In this way he acquired a technical skill which permitted him to carry out particularly delicate experiments, one of which was to produce a fusion of metals under extreme pressure, but at ordinary temperatures. That is, a block of copper was placed in perfect contact with a block of zinc, pressure was applied, and an intermediate layer of brass was formed by the fusion of the two. He also produced coal and artificial shale by the compression of powder.

In another series of remarkable experiments, Spring analyzed, day by day, the composition of the water of the Meuse and in this way came to study the color of pure water. Spring also constructed the first ultramicroscope.

The greatest name in Belgian chemical industry is Solvay, creator of the Solvay process soda industry. Ernest Solvay (1838–1922), a

self-educated man, through extraordinary ingenuity and perseverance, developed industrially the double decomposition and reaction of ammonium carbonate and sodium chloride which results
in the formation of sodium carbonate. At the end of the last century
this process had practically a world monopoly. During the First
World War, Solvay endowed the Comité National de Secours et
d'Alimentation which, in collaboration with the Committee for Relief, saved the Belgian people from famine. Later, in 1927, his son,
Armand Solvay, answered King Albert's appeal to create a national
fund for scientific research by endowing it with 25,000,000 francs.

It has been said that after 1870, Belgian chemists often went to
German laboratories for training, but after the beginning of the
twentieth century, the opposite tendency was felt. German impe-
rialism which was beginning to take form aroused general distrust,
and the Belgian universities once again called for the collaboration
of French scholars. So it happened that at the time of the German
invasion in 1940, the chair of general chemistry in Brussels was
occupied by Georges Chavanne (1875–1941), whose works on organic chemistry have a very decided physico-chemical leaning. Two
of the chairs of physics there were occupied by the Frenchman,
Emile Henriot, and the Swiss, August Piccard. In the laboratory of
the former the first electron microscope was perfected, and the
latter had acquired a world reputation for being the first to construct a stratosphere balloon in which he succeeded in ascending
to an altitude of 18,000 meters. At the University of Liége was
another Frenchman, Victor Henry (d. 1940), a well-known physical chemist.

Belgium, however, does not lack native scholars of value in the
field of exact sciences. It is a fact worth noting that the school at
Brussels created by Chavanne, just as those of Swarts at Ghent and
of Bruylants at Louvain, is distinguished by great attention given
to the study of the purification of organic compounds. This fact
shows the influence of Léon Crismer, at whose instigation the
International Bureau of Physico-Chemical Standards was created
in Brussels in 1921 and placed under the auspices of the International Chemical Union. He died in 1944, having performed a
remarkable role in the field of physico-chemical analysis.

In the field of pure science the Belgian chemists are superior to the physicists, in number at least. But it is not so in the field of applied sciences, for the art of the engineer, which is but applied physics, has long played a very important role in the Belgian universities.

It is not always easy to give credit to each of the different collaborators who succeed in starting a new industry, but it was in Belgium, between Brussels and Mechlin, in 1835, that the first railroad on the European Continent was constructed. It was also an engineer of the Belgian railroads, Belpaire, who inaugurated the use of thermodynamic diagrams in the study of the efficiency of steam engines. It was a Belgian technician, Zénobe Gramme (1826–1901), of Liége, who constructed the first dynamo which could be used. In Liége, also, Professor Erich Gérard founded the Montefiore Electrotechnical Institute, the students of which have spread the reputation of Belgian industry throughout the world. It is interesting, too, to remember that at the beginning of this century Belgian engineers had such pronounced skill in the construction of electric streetcar lines that Belgian companies operated them not only in their own country, but also in cities in France, Holland, Germany, Spain, Portugal, Norway, Rumania, Serbia, Greece, Argentina, Brazil, and China. In the coal-mining industry Belgian engineers perfected the method of sinking shafts by freezing, which permits passage through the regions of loose sand.

Natural history—biology.—In Belgium, too, as has been true generally in the evolution of science, the natural sciences were seriously studied before the physical sciences, since the study of natural phenomena is of great interest and does not necessitate any considerable amount of equipment. The intensive cultivation of Belgian land and the working of the coal mines which has been going on for centuries have been reasons for the study of geology since the beginning of the nineteenth century.

Jean Baptiste d'Omalius d'Halloy (1783–1875), the undisputed master of regional geology, is the first brilliant name among the geologists. After traversing a great part of western Europe on foot, hammer in hand, in paths radiating from his native chateau, d'Omalius was able to lay the foundations of stratigraphic geology in his famous essay on the geology of the north of France (1808), in which he worked out the classification, still in use, of quaternary, tertiary, secondary, and primary regions. In 1828 he published a paper on the geologic description of the Low Countries, France, and certain neighboring territories in which he refers to his geological map of the same countries published in 1822.

The more detailed classification of the layers of coal-bearing regions was soon to be made by André Dumont (1809–1857), professor at the University of Louvain, who presented a paper on the geological description of the province of Liége at the Academy in 1830. Among the other scientific contributions of André Dumont, the most important is the publication in 1849, after thirteen years of stubborn work, of a geological map of Belgium on a scale of 1:160,000 which is almost without defects.

Interpretation of the aspect of the coal-bearing regions of Hainaut, through the phenomenon of overthrust, was accomplished by A. Briart and F. L. Cornet (1876). The study of this coal basin resulted also in the finding of the iguanodons at Bernissart (1878), a detailed survey which enriched the Museum of Natural History in Brussels with the only collection of skeletons of these saurians in the world. On the other hand, the theories and the borings made by A. Dumont, Jr., also a professor at the University of Louvain, led to the discovery of the new coal-bearing basin of the Kempen, now being thoroughly worked.

Since then, the progress of geology in Belgium has been achieved through the collaboration of a considerable number of research workers, many of high caliber, whose names cannot be included in this short resume. They drew up a detailed map, on a scale of 1:20,000, in the preparation of which they used the most recent results of paleontological and stratigraphical research.

The study of eruptive terrains was not well advanced in Belgium, where this kind of terrain was rare, a fact which explains also the small number of Belgian mineralogists, of whom the best known was Alphonse Renart (1842–1903), collaborator in the study of petrographic specimens collected by the "Challenger."

In botany, the work of the nineteenth century consisted notably in the making of a complete survey of the flora of the country by a multitude of specialists. This survey resulted in the publication of several books on phanerogamia, especially the one by F. Crepin (1830–1903), of a book on cryptogamia by J. J. Kickx, and of a

general list of Belgian flora compiled by Th. Durand and E. de
Wildeman in 1907.

Besides being conducted at the university botanical laboratories
and at the laboratories of the Agricultural Institute in Gembloux,
much of this research was carried on at the State Botanical Gardens
in Brussels. Plant and ethologic geography were developed particularly at the University of Brussels, in the experiments and research
of Jean Massart (1865–1925).

Belgian professors of botany have in general devoted a great part
of their activity to the study of plant cytology and physiology. In
a like manner, zoölogy started with the examination of the fauna
of the country. Baron de Selys Longchamps (1813–1900) was particularly noted for the development of systematic ornithology and
entomology. Soon, with the inspiration and stimulus of the illustrious Pierre Joseph van Beneden (1809–1894), professor at the
University of Louvain, zoölogy came into its own.

Among the principal works of Van Beneden, perhaps the most
important is a systematic study of the coastal fauna made in a laboratory installed in 1843, near Ostend. In 1849 Van Beneden discovered the migration of intestinal worms, with the change from
one animal species to another, when the bladder worm becomes a
tapeworm. Before 1870, when interesting fossils were discovered
in excavating the fortifications of Antwerp, Van Beneden devoted
part of his energy to works on anatomy and paleontology.

In the field of comparative anatomy of mollusks, the name of
Paul Pelseneer, Permanent Secretary of the Royal Academy of
Medicine, is particularly brilliant.

The observations of a great number of scholars permitted Auguste Lameere (1861–1942), professor at the University of Brussels,
to set up his classification of the fauna of Belgium (1895–1905) and
his masterly treatise on zoölogy.

Paleontological excavations naturally predisposed Belgian naturalists to become interested in anthropology. A Dutchman, P. C.
Schmerling (1791–1836), professor at the University of Liége, discovered the prehistoric man of the quaternary period in the grottos
in the region of Liége. The research was carried out by E. Dupont,
Director of the Museum of Natural History in Brussels, who made
many discoveries in the caverns of the Meuse and the Lesse, so that

today, because of E. van den Broeck (1851–1932), speleology has become a very popular science in Belgium.

In geography, the most important explorations have been made in the Congo. The American, H. M. Stanley, who had discovered the immense expanse of the upper Congo in 1876, at the request of Leopold II started out once more and succeeded in putting a great part of the Congo Basin under the patronage of the International African Association; thus was founded the Belgian Congo colony in 1879.

In 1881 Jules Cornet discovered the rich deposits of copper in upper Katanga. The working of these deposits gave Belgium a virtual monopoly of the production of radium until the discovery of radium in Canada.

The most experienced specialist in Congolese flora is De Wildeman, the former director of the Botanical Gardens in Brussels. The establishment at Tervueren of the Congo Museum, which contains an important zoölogical department, has aided its present Director, Henri Schouteden, in developing the investigation of this new chapter of natural history.

The detailed study of flora and fauna led to a more thorough examination of the structure and the functioning of the organs which constitute the principal subject of biology. Théodore Schwann, a German, professor at the University of Liége, developed in 1839 the cellular theory in zoölogy; and since then the study of the cell (cytology) has consistently claimed the attention of Belgian scientists, several of whom have founded veritable schools in the universities. First in this group was Edouard van Beneden (1846–1910), professor at the University of Liége, son of the eminent zoölogist, Pierre Joseph van Beneden, who discovered the phenomenon of caryogamic reduction. A pupil of Van Beneden, Hans de Winiwarter, now a professor at the University of Liége, has continued detailed research in this field.

Canon J. B. Carnoy (1836–1899) was the founder of the Louvain School of Cytology, and founder also of the review, *La Cellule,* which acquired international renown; it was at Louvain also that his pupil, A. van Gehuchten (1861–1904), conducted experiments on the anatomy of the nervous system. In Brussels, a disciple of Edouard van Beneden, Albert Brachet (1869–1930), ventured on a new branch of work—experimental embryology, which permitted him to go deeper into the question of the existence of germinal spots, a study which also had interested Jules Duesberg, former President of the University of Liége. The school of E. van Bambeke (1829–1918) at Ghent, and the research of E. Marchal and his son at the Agricultural Institute of Gembloux, in part were devoted to problems of the same kind.

The development of physiology and physiological chemistry in Belgium dates from the period after 1870, during which research laboratories were installed in the medical schools.

In Brussels, the school of physiology goes back to Paul Héger (1847–1925) and to the botanist Léo Errera (1858–1905). Among the many scientists who worked in these laboratories Jules Bordet, who won the Nobel Prize in medicine for his research in the mechanism of immunity, should be named first. With O. Gengou, he described the serological reaction which bears their name.

At Ghent, the best-known scientist was C. Heymans, whose experiments with the nerve centers regulating respiration won for him the Nobel Prize in physiology. Finally, at Liége, Léon Fredericq devoted his long, rich career to the experimental examination of a great variety of physiological phenomena. His collaborator, Professor Pierre Nolf, put forth a new theory on blood coagulation which opposes that of Bordet.

Long before the development of research in pure biology, problems of pathological biology had held the attention of the medical world. As early as the eighteenth century, the Belgian school had gained renown by the invention of the forceps by the anatomist obstetrician, Jan Palfijn (1650–1730). At the beginning of the nineteenth century the Society of Medieval and Natural Sciences in Brussels gave evidence of great activity under the inspiration of its secretary, the surgeon, L. Seutin (1793–1862).

Since that time the activity of the medical schools has developed along both the line of pure science and that of applied science. The two have never been completely separated, and actually tend to be interdependent.

Among the great Belgian doctors are the following: Malvoz, one of the eminent hygienists, who organized the first antitubercular dispensaries and started the fight against miners' anemia caused by the hookworm (ancylostomiasis); E. van Ermengem (1851–1932) discovered the bacillus of botulism. René Sand has contributed to the development of public health and participated in numerous groups for the organization of international hygiene.

Evolution of higher education and research institutions.—The four Belgian universities have kept on developing ever since Belgium became independent. In each, the standard of teaching and research has ever been on the upward trend, and the number of professors has increased steadily. In the field of experimental and natural sciences it was only at the very end of the nineteenth century that the university centers of research acquired the personnel and material indispensable to permit work under relatively favorable conditions.

It was especially after 1920, however, and during the period of the reconstruction of the country that the laboratories of the four universities obtained the resources necessary to permit a really large expansion. At the time of the second invasion Belgium held a very honorable place in this respect.

Around each university there has grown up a series of annex institutions, often constituted with the aid of wealthy patrons, which have permitted the study of certain chapters of science. Such are the Solvay Institute of Physiology and the Provincial Institute of Bacteriology, directed by Jules Bordet in Brussels; and in Liége, the Montefiore Electrotechnical Institute and the new mechanical and thermodynamic laboratories of Heverlee.

There also have developed, little by little, a few other establishments of higher education independent of the universities. These institutions, created because of some practical or technical need, have not failed to benefit scientific research. For example, there is the Military Academy, created in 1834, which has had such men on its staff as Stas, General de Tilly, and Léon Crismer; the School of Mines and Metallurgy at Mons (Technical School of Hainaut), founded in 1836, where Jules Cornet, the great geologist, taught; the Jesuit College, Notre Dame de la Paix at Namur; the School of Veterinary Medicine in Brussels, where Professor Louis Melsens (1814–1886), who perfected the lightning rod, taught, basing his work on the principle of the experiment of the "Faraday cage"; the State Agricultural Institute in Gembloux, among whose professors was Emile Laurent (1861–1904), who discovered the assimilation of atmospheric nitrogen by the nodosities of leguminous plant roots; and the Colonial University in Antwerp, inaugurated in 1920.

Of the great state scientific institutions, the oldest is the Botanical Garden in Brussels (1826); the Royal Observatory (1827) is next in age. The Museum of Natural History (1846), is unique in the world for its collections of iguanodons. There is also the Geological Service of Belgium, which has resumed the publication of geological maps on a scale of 1:20,000, as well as the Museum of the Belgian Congo in Tervueren, started in 1897, which has some very fine collections.

The oldest of the large scholarly bodies is the Royal Academy of Sciences, Letters, and Fine Arts (1772). The class of sciences contains two sections: the first devoted to physical and mathematical sciences, the other to natural sciences. Its *Bulletin* and its *Mémoires* have brought together the scientific writings of Belgium, and are still publishing particularly interesting works.

The Royal Academy of Medicine, created in 1841, plays an equally important role and now has two Nobel Prize winners among its members. A Royal Colonial Institute, founded in 1928, brings together Belgian and foreign scholars who are engaged in colonial problems, and includes a section of natural and medical sciences and a section of technical sciences. Finally, in 1937, Flemish academies were created, one for medicine and one for sciences, letters, and arts.

Besides the academies there are a great many scientific societies covering all the special branches. The Society of Sciences of Brussels, dating from the beginning of the nineteenth century, later gave birth to the Royal Academy of Medicine. The Scientific Society, which is made up of groups of scientists from the University of Louvain, publishes annals and a bulletin which are highly esteemed. At Liége the Medico-Surgical Society also includes naturalists, chemists, and other scientists; and, lastly, the Flemish scientific congresses center around the University of Ghent.

At the present time, however, the most active societies include specialists of every branch of science—astronomy, chemistry, different medical specialties, and natural sciences—and, during the last twenty years, new associations have sprung up representing studies which had no society until then—physics, mathematics, history of sciences, and other fields.

Various efforts have endowed Belgium, in the course of these last twenty-five years, with a series of national foundations which have played an important role in the development of the sciences and from which one can again expect great results, once peace is re-established. The first of these is the University Foundation (Fondation Universitaire), created in 1920 with a capital of 55,000,000 francs given by the Commission for Relief in Belgium represented by its chairman, Herbert Hoover, and the Comité National de Secours et d'Alimentation, presided over by Emile Francqui. This institution makes loans for study to Belgian students, gives traveling fellowships to students who have excelled in government competitive examinations, and assumes the living expenses of American professors and students sent to Belgium by the Belgian-American Educational Foundation of New York, which, in exchange, gives scholarships to a great number of young Belgian scholars who spend one or two years in American universities.

The National Foundation for Scientific Research was founded in 1927 to foster original research. From a capital of 100,000,000 francs, 80 fellowships were created for associates and research assistants, grants were made for the laboratories of qualified researchers, and life pensions accorded to scholars who are awarded a decennial or a quinquennial government prize.

Finally, in 1932, this group of institutions was completed by the Francqui Foundation which gives a prize of 500,000 francs biennially to the Belgian who has made the most important contribution to science, thus augmenting Belgium's prestige in other countries. This same foundation endowed a professorship which passes yearly from one university to another and which invites a foreign scholar to teach a new branch of learning. This chair has been held successively, at Liége by the Dutch physicist, P. Debye, now in the United States; then at Louvain by the English physical chemist, Hugh S. Taylor, now at Princeton; at Ghent by the specialist in colloidal chemistry, Professor Kruyt of Utrecht, and, during the year preceding the war, at Brussels by Professor G. I. Finch of the Imperial College of Science in London, well known for his works on electron diffraction.

CHAPTER XVIII

Art in Belgium

BY CONSTANT VAN DE WALL

I**N THE EARLY PERIOD** of Belgian art, two great styles can be observed which are fundamentally opposed to each other, but both of which have served Christianity. They are the Byzantine and the Romanesque styles.

The Byzantine and Romanesque period.—The Byzantine style may be considered as the finest expression of Christian "dogma." Greek in origin, it sought to express the idea through form. Romanesque art, too, was Christian, but in a secondary Latin form. It had a far stronger imprint from Celtic and Teutonic elements and, as a result, was not intellectual, but emotional, lyrical, and ecstatic in its approach toward religious concepts. All through the history of Flemish art, up to the very present, this strong, mystical trend is found.

These styles can be studied best in the illuminated manuscripts and in the work of the ivory carvers and the goldsmiths. Early illumination is found in the scriptoria of some important abbeys. In the year 670, St. Gertrude of Nivelles had sent from Rome and from the British Isles a number of illuminated manuscripts, which combination meant infiltration of Byzantine and Celtic styles. A Latin Gospel from the Abbey of St. Laurent at Liége (Brussels Library, No. 18383), shows both styles.

Belgium's illuminated manuscripts show very well the migration of styles in the Middle Ages. During the eleventh century the Byzantine element was dominant. In the twelfth century the refining influence which radiated from Cluny can be felt distinctly in the illumination of the Southern Netherlands.

Ivory carving and goldsmith work were done mainly in the

Mosan Valley. Great individuality is shown in the baptismal font in the church of St. Barthélémy at Liége by Renier de Huy (1113). Godefroid de Claire (1100–1175), Nicolas Verdun, and Hugo d'Oignies were famous for their beautiful reliquary shrines.

Many bas-reliefs were sculptured in the second half of the twelfth century, among which should be mentioned the Madonna of Dom Rupert at Liége (1150–1175), the Porte Mantile of Tournai, and the Samson bas-relief at Nivelles. A special industry at Tournai was the sculpturing of baptismal fonts in the beautiful bluish stone taken from the local quarries. These fonts were exported to the coastal towns of England and France.

The Gothic period.—In the Gothic period the artists began to strive not only for realism, which included love for the particular, but also for the infinite and the universal. This infinite was something most readily realized in painting. There was a place in this art for the humblest forms of nature, which did not appear in Romanesque or Byzantine art. The Gothic artists, especially in Flanders, had the mystical ability to contemplate as an emanation from God both the divine and the material.

As to painting in the Gothic period, a most precious and unique manuscript is in the Royal Library at Brussels (No. 1175), known as "Le Vieil Rentier d'Oudenarde." It contains bookkeeping records of some lord who held properties in the southeast of Flanders and in northern Hainaut for the years 1275–1291. Between the written texts are numerous pen drawings, which are most refreshing as to subject matter and style. There is a strong realism in the fluent narrative of this artist who must have been an artistic forefather of Pieter Bruegel.

The fourteenth century shows not only more refinement of illumination but also qualities of eclecticism and internationalism. At this period Liége produced its finest works. Beautiful work was done in the west, too, as is illustrated by the missals of Master Laurent (1365), and the Bible of Jean de Bruges, painted in honor of the French King, Charles V.

The "Très Beau Livre d'Heures" (Brussels, No. 1106), has been attributed to Jacquemart de Hesdin, while the "Très Riches Heures" in the Condé Museum at Chantilly brought world fame to the Limburg brothers, Polequin and Hannequin, and to Herman Malouel. This was the highest peak of book illumination. Other important illuminators were Jan van Eyck; Marmion, the Girart Master; Tavernier; Vrelant, the Hortulus Master; and Simon Benning.

Illumination came to a rather sudden end with the appearance of the printed book. A few more times, however, an important illumination appears, as in the Breviary Grimani, which shows work by Gerard Horenbout, Lieven van Lathem, and probably by Alexander Benning.

In the latter part of the Middle Ages the Flemish artist, like artists all over western Europe, regarded the material world as a reflection of the spiritual world and it was his function to remind the people, through his art, of religious principles. Standardized systems of symbolic representation had developed slowly but steadily, so-called "iconographies," which differed only slightly in neighboring localities and, on the whole, were universal for vast regions. In such a system of representation there was scarcely a need for perspective and texture in painting; the main purpose was symbolic interpretation and not actual rendering.

However, in the beginning of the fifteenth century, spiritual changes can be observed readily in Flemish art. Truthful rendering of visual appearances began to fascinate the artists who gradually took some artistic liberties within the limitations and the decorum of the iconographic scheme. Man realized the significance of his own individual spiritual existence. The development of portrait painting was significant in this respect. It was an assertion of the individual. A landscape background began to appear in representations where previously there had been an abstract, golden background. The personages became more and more realistic; they became live actors and the drama took place in a real landscape.

The most important painting of the fifteenth century in Flanders is the great folding altarpiece of the brothers Van Eyck, Hubert (c. 1370–1426), and Jan (c. 1365–1440), at Ghent. The central panel represents the "Adoration of the Mystic Lamb," with the majestic figures of God, John the Baptist, the Virgin, Angel Musicians, Adam and Eve appearing above. On the wings the composition of the central panel is elaborated by the representation of the religious procession in which prophets, doctors, philosophers, holy women, and fathers of the Church take part. The main topics on the reverse of the wings are representations of St. John the Baptist and St. John the Evangelist, portraits of the donor, Judocus Veydt, and his wife, and a beautiful Annunciation.

The spiritual message of this altarpiece is a synthesis of scholastic thought. Its great artistic quality has impressed the world ever since its unveiling in 1432. For five centuries its brilliancy and depth of coloring have endured. Connoisseurs have credited the lasting quality of this masterpiece to the great artistic talent of the Van Eycks and to the still-unexplained innovations in their process of oil painting. The technique of the smaller altar paintings and portraits by Jan van Eyck is even more baffling.

The next important artist was Rogier van der Weyden, or De la Pasture (1399–1464), a more deeply religious artist than Van Eyck and one more limited in talent. His work was somewhat stereotyped as to composition and gesture of the figures. He emerged from the group around the Master of Flémalle (1375–1444), but he was more refined and showed a definitely aristocratic quality inherited from the Burgundian court. One of his greatest works is the "Descent from the Cross" in the Escorial.[1]

Petrus Christus (1415–1472/73) came closest to Jan van Eyck, whose pupil he was. But he lacked the great talent and science of his master. He also came under the influence of Rogier. The landscape settings for his figures are interesting.

Dirk Bouts (1420–1475) and Gerard David (1460–1528) democratized somewhat the aristocratic art referred to above. Their art was more northern in spirit—solemn in Bouts, while an appealing quality of sweetness is found in David's work.

Hugo van der Goes (1440–1482) is outstanding, especially for the psychological analysis of his models. His compositions show monumental quality.

Hans Memling (1430–1494) spent the greater part of his life in Bruges and reflected its spirit, its quietness and security, in his work. He is not as intense as Van der Goes, and is warmer in tone

---

[1] Some scholars believe the Master of Flémalle is identical with young Rogier van der Weyden. Others regard him as a senior artist to Jan van Eyck, and not identical with Rogier. There is much evidence but no absolute proof that the Master of Flémalle was actually Robert Campin, who had Rogier and Jacques Daret as pupils.

than Rogier van der Weyden, in whose studio he may have worked around 1460. There is a vague echo of Lochner in his work. He was the first Flemish artist to adopt Italian Renaissance decoration. His style was uniform throughout his life.

Quinten Massijs (1466–1530) preferred to follow older masters like Jan van Eyck, the Master of Flémalle, and Rogier. He also shows the influence of Leonardo. He was a splendid colorist, applying *sfumato* effects and rendering iridescent fabrics beautifully. He made magnificent portraits, for example the double portrait of Erasmus and Peter Aegidius. His composition is very advanced.

In close relation to painting was the art of tapestry weaving. The cities of Brussels and Audenarde were the chief centers of production, especially after the city of Arras had come to grief. In 1466 the Burgundian dukes were already buying tapestries in Brussels. Great artists were asked to make the cartoons—Rogier van der Weyden and later on Raphael, Bernard van Orley, Rubens, and Jordaens. Especially under the Habsburg-Spanish rule, Brussels made gorgeous tapestries. Famous weavers were the Leyniers, the Pannemakers, and the Raes.

The average artists in the fifteenth century in the Netherlands were influenced more by tradition and routine than by rationalization or individual theorizing on aesthetic principles. Although the subjects painted were somewhat monotonous, because of the long deathbed of iconography, the artists developed a craftsmanship almost inexplicable and processes that produced time- and climate-resisting canvases. An innate love for fine workmanship by the artists established very high standards, from the time of the illuminated mediaeval manuscript, through the period of the Van Eycks, and that of Rubens and Leys in the nineteenth century.

The fifteenth-century art of Flanders, as a whole, remained deeply religious. The lyrical, mystic contemplations of Jan van Ruysbroeck (1293–1381) and of Thomas à Kempis (1380–1471) were definitely reflected in the painting of this period. The painting of these Flemish Mystics was a continuant of the illuminated manuscripts, containing a quality of irresistible appeal for intimate contemplation similar to that found in the earlier works. Their canvases seem actually to speak to the observer. There was musical character in the color treatment, in the deep, warm chords, and between the soft and delicate lyrical legato transitions of light and shade.

No wonder that, in the fifteenth century, Flanders offered artistic examples to France, Germany, Italy, and Spain. The evolution within Flemish art was mainly toward a more integrated composition, a tendency which explains why Flemish artists in the sixteenth century were so receptive to the advanced training to be had in Italy. Memling and Van der Goes especially made such contributions.

In the field of sculpture during the Gothic period, very little was done in the thirteenth century. The fourteenth century was more productive; the "Apostles" of the portal of Tournai Cathedral, the tympanum of St. John's Hospital at Bruges, and the "Coronation of the Virgin" at St. Jacques at Liége should be mentioned. An increasing French influence is seen, but at this time Belgian sculpture, as a whole, was somewhat heavier than that of France.

Toward 1390 many artists from the Netherlands worked at the Chartreuse of Champmol near Dijon. Claus Sluter was the leading genius. He became world famous for his "Well of Moses" and his "Bust of Christ." Other sculptors around him were Jean de Marville and his nephew, Claus de Werve, as well as Pepin de Huy, André Beauneveu, Jean de Liége, Jacob de Baerzé, Jean Delmer, and Jacques de Gérines. They formed the School of Dijon which influenced the Tournai sculptors. Their works found an echo again in the paintings of artists like the Master of Flémalle and Rogier van der Weyden.

Sluter and Claus de Werve made the imposing tomb of Philip the Bold (1411). Claus designed an almost identical tomb for John the Fearless and his wife, Margaret of Bavaria. Sluter's work is unique for the realism of the heads and postures, and for the strong individualization. Closely related to the Dijon and Tournai sculpture of this period is some of the sculpture of the town halls of Brussels and Mechlin.

Sculptured altar retables date from as early as the twelfth century. The fourteenth century witnessed a climax in the retables of Jacob de Baerze, which he made for the Chartreuse of Champmol. Another beautiful retable is the one of Hakendover. During the fifteenth century the retable production increased still more,

especially in Brabant and Antwerp. The subject matter of this
sculpture was influenced by the mystery plays. The little statuettes
were very graceful and reflected an influence from contemporary
painting. Jan Borremans from Brussels should be mentioned here
for his retable representing the "Martyrdom of St. George" of 1493.

The sixteenth century.—The sixteenth century was a period of
doubt in many spiritual fields, a period in which a great amount
of artistic experimentation was done. The Netherlands saw an increase in the number of masters; but, even so, the individual weight
and personal influence of these men were not great. Artistic intercourse with Italy increased steadily. There was an increase also
in the number of workshops and their size. The rules of the guilds
were less strictly observed. The guilds themselves became more and
more political and less artistic in their objectives. The artists who
had been in Italy, the Romanists as they wanted to be called, came
home with a greater feeling of independence. Former rigid traditions were observed less. Curious changes in iconography appeared.
Art divorced itself from the church, slowly but steadily. It began
to court mythology and allegory. Art was no longer restricted to
the mere reflection of a spiritual beyond in which the Lord was
glorified with the Saints and the Blessed. Furthermore, medieval
art was not as venerable as it was supposed to be. There was a
tendency to depict the devil as humanly bad and as mean as possible, and to present some acquaintances among the damned, siz-
zling in hell. This was intended to remind the spectator that he
should prepare himself better for his salvation. However, since the
Flemish people have much good humor, their art had a comic and
realistic side as well. Bosch and Bruegel utilized their art for a
thoroughly humanistic, if not for a deeper religious purpose.

During the Renaissance, man no longer beheld himself in relation to a strictly theological concept. He gradually began to discover beauty in himself and in the humble things of earth. He
pondered the multiplicity of natural forms, which he wanted to
understand in a more logical way. Italy surpassed the Netherlands
in such studies. Anatomy and perspective developed as sciences
essential to the Italian artists, Alberti and Leonardo, and to the
German painter and engraver, Dürer, who had worked in the
Netherlands.

The period of humanistic evolution demanded secular art. Indicative of this humanism was the now rapidly growing portrait school. The life-size portrait developed gradually from a single head or bust type in the fifteenth century to the full-length figure. Generally speaking, the portrait in Southern Netherlands somewhat lost its intimate character but gained, instead, a public and a more monumental aspect. The sixteenth century produced some exceedingly fine portraits. There were among the "Fiamminghi," as the Flemish artists in Italy were called, some portrait painters who worked irritatingly close to Titian.

In the art of composition, strides were made by Hugo van der Goes and by Quinten Massijs. Because of the influence of these highly talented men, sixteenth-century Flemish artists were conditioned to realize the significance of Italian Renaissance art. The means of rendering the linear and plastic qualities of visual impression were explored. The Italian artists were less easily frustrated by the multiplicity of appearances. They sought the dominating principle, the highest law, the ideal, the norm. They were convinced that reality contained the perfect and that they had to project it in its beauty and clarity.

However, the "Fiamminghi" were not immediately ready to absorb such highly synthesized art as the Italians produced. Many of them did not possess the qualities essential to fresco painting or monumental decorating. However, they left sketchbooks which finally came into the possession of Italian museums and libraries. The books contain sketches, probably made on Sundays, in the artists' free time, on their strolls in the country, which are skillfully executed drawings of goats and donkeys, trees and bushes, and intimate little corners of landscape. All these subjects are strikingly alive compared with the lifeless, academic subjects they were forced to copy in the workshops.

Renaissance ideas did not enter into the art of the Netherlands only through the immediate contacts of the artists with the Italian masters and their works. Albrecht Dürer (1471–1528), who worked in the Netherlands from 1520 to 1521, also had his share in this evolution. His Italo-German art was understood in the Netherlands.

Italian artistic movements had their parallels in the Netherlands, but a style always changes when it travels. Among the Romanists, who reacted strongly to the classical masters, were Jan Gossart of Mabuse (1472–1533), Bernard van Orley (1491–1542), Pieter Coecke van Aalst (c. 1502–1550), Lambert Lombard (1506–1566). In speaking of Gossart, Carel van Mander wrote: "He was one of the first to bring back from Italy the true manner of arranging and composing 'histories,' full of nude figures and all manner of poetry, which was not practised in our lands before."

Bernard van Orley, court painter to the two regents of the Netherlands, Margaret of Austria and Mary of Hungary, made designs for world-famous tapestries, and for the stained-glass windows in St. Gudula at Brussels.

The Antwerp Mannerists form an interesting group not so much from an artistic point of view as from an art-historical one. The artists belonging to this movement had a definite style which was characterized by crowded composition, restless movement of the figures, exaggerated expression in the faces, long-necked women, men with streaming beards, exotic types and nervously fluttering draperies. Striking artists of this group were Jan de Beer and Jan de Cock.

A more important role in figure painting in Belgium was played by Frans Floris (1516–1560), who contributed much toward popularizing imitations of ancient sculpture and the adaptation of mythological and classical subject matter for large compositions. His portraits are excellent. Floris' studio was a forerunner of the Rubens workshop.

A more fluent style, the so-called "Second Mannerism," was developed by Sprangher (1546–1627), who played a most important role in Prague, to which city he was called by Rudolph II.

In Flanders itself, especially toward the close of the century, classicist tendencies became stronger and it is that spirit which can be found in the teachers of Rubens, Adam van Noort, and Otto van Veen, and in Ambrosius Francken.

The new outlook on nature, characteristic of the sixteenth century, brought about new categories of painting such as landscape, genre, and still life, which are typical of northern painting. Such work had been done before, but now these subjects asserted themselves, emancipated from their servitude as detail or background material in religious art.

Landscape painting followed a similar course. It became the art of the Netherlands par excellence. The use of landscape painting primarily as background for religious painting was excelled in by nearly all the great Flemish painters of the fifteenth, sixteenth, and seventeenth centuries. To list their names would be to recapitulate all those already mentioned, from the early illuminators of manuscripts on. Among the landscape artists were also some who, as refugees from Southern Netherlands, played an important role in other countries, especially in Holland and Italy.

Genre painting also had an early start in Flanders. The love for this type of work is already reflected in illuminated manuscripts, especially in calendar illustrations. The sixteenth century gave a special impulse to it. Its evolution can be traced in Quinten Massijs, Marinus van Roemerswael, Jan Sanders (van Hemessen), the Brunswick Monogrammist, and the Master of the Flémalle half-length figures. Important work in this field was done later by Pieter Aertsen (1507–1575) and Joachim de Beuckelaer (1530–1573). These artists began to depict the kitchen and its accouterments, from the buxom cook to the mouse trap.

Still-life painting flourished in Belgium, especially animal still life. Frans Snijders (1579–1657) and Paul de Vos (1590–1678), the great collaborators of Rubens, should be mentioned first, followed by Jan Fijt (1611–1661), the pupil of Snijders who surpassed the others in this genre.

There is one artist in the sixteenth century who stands artistically alone among his contemporaries—Hieronymus Bosch (c. 1450–1516). As far as the elements of his subject matter are concerned, he goes back to the Middle Ages, but his interpretation and his daring exploits in the world of fantasy are very modern. He painted cataclysms of the universe and carries the observer from heaven to hell. With great imagination Bosch projected the most grotesque and animated of nightmares. He painted with a great refinement, typical of the Burgundian period, and used thinly covering tints and pearl-like accents. He did not care about perspective, but put details in his landscape corners which are most convincing. Some of his fantastic creations recall Oriental work. Philip II, King of Spain, had quite a number of the works of Bosch in the Escorial.

The artist who immediately followed in the artistic footsteps of

Bosch was Pieter Bruegel (1525–1569). He was perhaps the most purely Flemish painter who ever lived; yet he should not be considered as entirely free from Italian influence. He reacted to the early baroque movement in which art began to express the disturbed emotions, either the tragic or the joyous. Pieter Bruegel and El Greco were expressions of early Baroque outside of Italy.

Bruegel looked on the world in general with an optimistic humor, and did not work with stark contrast of light and dark. His colors are moderate and subtle. He presented nature in its vast expansiveness, with little men struggling against odds and sometimes seriously pantomiming the proverbs. He let the children play a thousand games. He painted a serene "Adoration of the Magi." His was always a self-contained cosmos, a totality of coördinated forces which were projected for his spectator. Bruegel was the supreme stagemaster.

With all his universal characteristics, Bruegel painted in terms of his native land and of his time. The "Census of Bethlehem," the "Slaughter of the Innocents," and other religious subjects are painted in terms of the tyrannical forces of the Spanish operating in the Flemish scene. It is a Flemish village which represents Bethlehem, and Spanish soldiers who represent the Roman oppressors. Thus, his paintings had a burning actuality for their time. As for the deep wells of folklore he drew upon, scholars have not yet explained all the events and relationships depicted by the artist.

Sculpture in the sixteenth century strove to idealize form. It came more and more under the influence of painting, engraving, and tapestry. That influence can be noticed in the altar retables of Herenthals, Auderghem, and O. L. V. Lombeek, also in the choir stalls of Matthys de Wayere, in the tomb sculpture of Conrad Meit. Lancelot Blondeel designed his famous mantel in Bruges (1529). Other fine sculptors were Jean Mone and Jacques Dubroeucq of Mons (1505–1584).

An enthusiastic follower of the Italian Renaissance was Frans de Vriendt or Frans Floris (1518–1575), who made the Tabernacle of Zoutleeuw, the rood screen of Tournai Cathedral, and the tomb for King Christian of Denmark at Roeshilde. The Floris style was named for him; it was very rich in decorative accessories and easily understood. Jan Veldeneer and Pieter Coecke van Aalst must be mentioned too. Alexander Colyns (1529–1622) was called to Innsbruck by Emperor Ferdinand to work for the mausoleum of Maximilian I. Flanders may be equally proud of the sculptor, Giovanni da Bologna (1524–1608), in whom Michelangelo was deeply interested and who, by his facile and decisive work, gave a strong impulse to the Italian Baroque.

The seventeenth and eighteenth centuries.—The seventeenth century is the century of the Baroque. This style was of Italian origin, but it soon became an international style. The Baroque was an art of the Church, a highly emotional art; an art of movement of figures as well as of architectural forms. Painting was its expression par excellence and its greatest exponent in this medium was Rubens.

Pieter Paul Rubens (1577–1640) was born in Siegen in Westphalia where his parents were in exile. In Antwerp he became a pupil of Tobias Verhaecht, Adam van Noort, and Otto van Veen. In 1600 he went to Italy where he was interested especially in the works of Titian, Tintoretto, Correggio, and Caravaggio. Returning to Antwerp in 1608, he became the official court painter and confidential aid to the archdukes. From 1627 to 1630, he was at the courts of Madrid and London as ambassador.

Rubens possessed unflagging energy. He felt everything exuberantly. He started to paint with the same saturated colors as Titian used. The "Raising of the Cross," and "The Descent from the Cross," in the cathedral of Antwerp, strongly reflect the heavy tones and emotional energy of the late Bolognese School. Rubens organized assistants and pupils into a commercial but most artistic enterprise for the making of pictures. He knew how to coördinate the abilities of highly talented and powerful artists like Van Dyck and Jordaens. He made the sketches in color and his helpers worked them out. Most of these sketches are phenomenally fluent.

Rubens had a special gift for the representation of martyrdom and scenes of triumph. His mythological figures radiate vigor, grace, loveliness, and joy. His imagination was such that he could decorate a church as easily as a royal palace or a town for the reception of a monarch. His compositions are broad, frequently based on diagonal effects, and in them the figures are strongly built and move imposingly and with great vitality. The carnation of his nudes, and especially that of the children, reflects abundant good health. His color is iridescent. A very interesting phase of his development came toward the end of his life when he painted landscapes. His magical color control, the exceedingly dynamic quality of his brush stroke, his gift for arresting in color that which is fleeting, made the landscape the finest in Flemish art. Although Rubens had a great influence upon his pupils and collaborators, after his death a rapid decline in painting occurred which took the form of a definite decadence in the eighteenth century.

Anthony van Dyck and Jacob Jordaens have frequently been compared with Rubens. Rubens seems to have appreciated them both. Van Dyck (1599–1641) was not a pupil of Rubens. He came as a fully developed master, although not yet in his twenties, to work for Rubens. He specialized later as a portrait painter. He went to Italy for a period of five years and returned in 1626. He became court painter for Charles I of England. Some of his finest portraits are the ones he made of his fellow artists and their wives, upon his return from Italy, as well as the one of Charles I which is now in the Louvre. Van Dyck made a number of portrait etchings of his friends and of famous men. This collection was called the "Iconography," and especially beautiful in this series are the portraits of Pieter Bruegel the Younger, Erasmus, Snellinx, Sustermans, and Josse de Momper. Van Dyck had a far more limited program than Rubens. He is a virtuoso rather than a genius, but his influence on English portrait painting lasted long, even into early American portrait painting.

Jacob Jordaens (1593–1678), in contrast to Van Dyck, liked to show the obesity, avoirdupois, fecundity, and good health of the Antwerp burghers. His art is readily understood. His gods, his heroes, and his saints all are indigenous to Antwerp. His painting is thoroughly democratic; he meets the observer frankly and openly, with a radiant smile. His technique is based on a somewhat heavy impasto of color, but his color is not as iridescent as that of Rubens. However, he too had a special swing to his brush stroke which reflected intense joy in his work. Perhaps at times he felt too sure, which can never be said of Rubens. Compared with Van Dyck, he is far less refined, but he leaves a more healthy impression. He painted religious subjects, classic myths, and numerous compositions illustrating the festivals and merrymaking of the common people whom he loved.

There was only one artist great and individual enough to proceed on the road shown by Bruegel—Adriaan Brouwer (1606–1638). Brouwer went to Holland where, as a youth, he worked under Frans Hals, returning to Antwerp about 1631. He painted fights in taverns and other peasant genre subjects, rendering the atmosphere of inns and similar interiors in most refined and subtle coloring. He painted landscapes in which the moods are expressed in the most unexpected of color harmonies and his work is surprisingly close to that of the nineteenth century. It was understood better in Holland than in Flanders.

His pupil, Joos van Craesbeeck (1605–1661), was less famous in this same field. Even David Teniers the Younger (1610–1690), in spite of his great popularity, could not compete artistically with Brouwer. Teniers' work seemed too smooth and academic, too stereotyped. His rustic subjects were continued in the nineteenth century when there was demand for the picturesque in tapestries, copper and silver tea trays, and other tourist souvenirs.

One would like to pass the eighteenth century in silence because of its lethargy. A few anemic altar paintings were made, but these are hardly a credit to the nation. P. J. Heremans (1717–1776) painted sentimental domestic scenes. B. Beschey (1708–1776) and his pupil Cornelis Lens (d. 1751) showed some individuality and tried to introduce a French neoclassicism into Belgium. Pieter Verhaghen (1728–1811) and Jacob Herreyns (1643–1732) attempted a neo-Rubens style.

However, Belgian art began to restore itself toward the end of the century through the work of some "animal-in-landscape" painters. The most important was Balthazar Ommeganck (1755–1826). He painted landscapes, showing sheep and other animals, with great skill and a warm love, enveloping them in mellow light. He was followed by Jean Louis de Marne (1754–1821), who added a humorous touch to this type of painting.

A great number of the sculptors of the seventeenth century came readily under the influence of Rubens; Luc Fayd'herbe of Mechlin (1617–1697) shows that influence strongest because he worked immediately after drawings and pictures which Rubens made for this purpose. He created a relief for the Church of Our Lady of Mechlin which represented the Road to Calvary.

Closer to Bernini was the work of Jean Delcour (1627–1707). He made a very beautiful "Christ in Death" for the church of Hasselt. Francoys Duquesnoy (1594–1654) and his son, Jerome, were responsible for the beautiful tomb of the Bishop of Trieste in St. Bavo at Ghent. Artus Quellin the Elder and his nephew, Artus the Younger (1609–1668), produced that powerful sculpture of the pediment of the City Hall of Amsterdam with its splendid caryatids.

Pulpits were a very important feature in Belgian sculpture, especially in the eighteenth century. They were very elaborate. The pulpit in St. Gudula at Brussels was carved by H. A. Verbruggen (1655–1724), and the one in the St. John's Church at Mechlin by Théodore Verhaeren in 1741. Another famous pulpit is the one in Antwerp by Jan Frans van Geel and Jan van Hool for the Church of St. Andrew. There were many carved wooden confessionals which were no less sensational. A reaction against this type of sculpture set in and one of the first monuments of the neoclassical movement was the fountain of Jacob Berger in the Place du Grand Sablon in Brussels.

The modern movements.—Neoclassicism could not have been suggested more strongly to the Belgians than by Louis David, who came as a French refugee to Brussels after the fall of Napoleon. He remained until his death in 1825. His best pupil was F. Navez (1787–1869), whose self-portrait in the Brussels Museum will always be a stimulating painting to a young artist.

Romanticism broke through rather suddenly. The country was following French artistic movements somewhat closely. Gustave Wappers (1803–1874) and Nicaise de Keyser (1813–1887) produced large melodramatic canvases. Louis Gallait (1810–1887) was a better Romanticist, in that he expressed deeper feelings. Antoine Wiertz (1806–1865) was a painter with great ambitions. He tried to achieve a synthesis of Michelangelo and Rubens, and bewildered his spectators with enormous canvases of weird subject matter in which he included pathological aspects of life.

Hendrik Leys (1815–1869) towers high above the other Romanticist painters. He did not like their showiness and preferred quietness, as well as psychological and historical truth; he developed a very personal style. His fresco decorations of the Antwerp Town Hall are remarkable.

Romanticism also affected Belgian landscape painters. Théodore Fournois (1841–1871) painted in the Kempen, in the Ardennes, and later in France. Joseph Stevens (1816–1892), the unsurpassed painter of ordinary dogs, painted at the same time that his brother, Alfred, was the *enfant chéri* of Paris for his fine portraits of society ladies. Lieven de Winne was another very able portrait painter. Charles de Groux (1825–1870) showed analogy with Joseph Stevens. The most imposing bold work was done by H. Boulenger of Tournai (1837–1874). He did not follow the Barbizon masters, but obeyed his own inner voice and developed his own impressionism. Hendrik de Braekeleer (1840–1888) had a very rich palette; his paintings of Flemish interiors are perhaps the closest approach made by a Flemish artist to the seventeenth-century Dutch masters.

The two last decades of the nineteenth century witnessed much experimentation in techniques, and apparently subject matter had to make place for the rendering of light effects. The result was a gradual dematerialization of form.

Belgium's Impressionists grouped themselves in different localities. They show a great variety of talent and also of technique. These groups were the School of Tervueren (the Flemish Barbizon) with Boulenger, Coosemans, Verheyden, and Courtens; the School of Kalmthout with Meyers, Heymans, and Rosseels, and later Verstraten and Baron; the School of Dendermonde, which was established later by Rosseels; the School of the Ardennes fostered by Baron. Henri Evenepoel, who died very young, left some very fine portraits. Among the Impressionists should be mentioned also Oleffe, Shirren, I. Opsomer, A. Saverys, A. Baertsoen, and Théodore van Rysselberghe.

Another artist who died young was Rik Wouters (1882–1916). He was a very spontaneous painter and a sculptor of merit too. He came under the influence of Cézanne and Ensor, but threw this off. His colors sing exuberantly and naturally. He was strong in artistic conviction, dematerialized form for the sake of color, and maintained a sunny suggestion of his model. He was too young to have reached the magnitude of a modern Rubens, but he belonged to the same race.

Jacob Smits (1856–1928) was a solitary, wandering painter in the Kempen. The pious simplicity of his subject matter and the accentuated light effects give a mystical atmosphere to his works. Eugene Laermans (1864–) is an artist spiritually related to Jacob Smits, but has a stronger narrative element. He paints solidly and with firm conviction.

The mystical tendency which is noted in many painters comes out most clearly in the works of Valerius de Saedeleer, Albert Servaes, and Gustave van de Woestijne, who serve their churches with their art. Georges Minne's black-and-white work is a very impressive symbolism of his deep religious thoughts.

James Ensor (1860–) is probably the modern Belgian artist who is most widely known outside his country. His work does not belong in any specific category and yet one finds in his vast work the various tendencies described above in other artists. To a spectator not familiar with the history of Flemish art, many elements of folklore might be regarded as a product of his special whim. Nevertheless, he has a vivid imagination, almost as great as that of Bosch, and he, too, likes to paint nightmare visions and the tensions of a suspicious mind.

Ensor declares he has learned everything from the North Sea. One easily neglects Ensor's great technical ability because of his intriguing subject matter. He belongs to that race of painters which produced Bosch and Bruegel, also Fijt and Paul de Vos. His glorious still-life canvases of fishes and sea monsters betray that. But he could have gone a little farther, for his palette is enriched with new and weird color combinations of which the older masters did not even dare to dream.

The Flemish Expressionists, a very active group at St. Martins-Laethem on the River Leie, show a great variety of dynamic talent, although the movement started with a very modest, but most sincere week-end painter, Albijn van de Abeele. The sculptor, Georges Minne, was the central figure.

The great painter of Laethem is Constant Permeke, who was led into the movement by Servaes. There is an elementary power in Permeke, perhaps an uneven one, but it is recognized as a force of nature. In some respects he reminds one of Bruegel. Permeke's color is sometimes intensely hot and then again ash gray. In his finest work there is an infinite space and an absolute silence which weigh on the spectator.

Other artists of this group are Valerius de Saedeleer, Gustave van de Woestijne, Hippolyte Daeye, Fritz van den Berghe, Gustave de Smet, and Ramah. Not immediately linked with this group but still close is Edgard Tytgat, whose paintings and whose wood blocks win the heart of the humble by their kind humor.

In connection with woodcuts, Belgium may be proud of this rather recent art. Its great master is Frans Masereel, whose prints "La Ville" and "Souvenir de mon Pays" are splendid examples. These prints show most definitely a new concept of printmaking.

Very fine artists working in this medium are Joris Minne, Henri van Straten, Joseph Cantré, Jan Frans Cantré, Lempereur Haut, and Jean de Bosschère, also Karel Maes, Jef Brusselmans, and W. Paerels. It can be stated, without reserve, that these artists form a definite Belgian school.

Nineteenth-century sculpture in Belgium reflects the same tendencies as painting. G. Godecharle (1751–1835) was a very fine sculptor who, in spite of his great reverence for neoclassicism, still manifests in his work a certain liveliness and grace, especially in the portraits of women. Louis E. Simonis (1810–1882) was the next significant sculptor. His equestrian statue of Godfrey of Bouillon is a forceful work. During the second half of the century, naturalism expressed itself, first modestly in the work of Paul de Vigne, then stronger and more monumental in Charles van der Stappen, while Juliaan Dillens was somewhat more subtle and sought to express a Florentine grace. The work of Jef Lambeaux (1852–1908) reminds one immediately of Rubens and Jordaens.

Constantin Meunier (1851–1905) was the dominating figure, the most original and vigorous among the realistic sculptors. He glorified labor. He influenced many other sculptors, among whom were Thomas Vinçotte, Jules Lagae the animal sculptor, Josué Dupon, Egide Rombeaux, Victor Rousseau, Alois Beule, and Jacques de Lalaing. Oscar Jespers is an expressionistic sculptor whose work has a definite plastic character. The sculpture of Georges Minne (1860–1943) is as beautiful an expression of his mysticism as his graphic work. Ernest Wynants (1878–) grew to an expression of pure grace and sometimes great power.

CHAPTER XIX

Architecture

BY GEORGES PHILIPPART

FROM THE TIME when Belgium was a fragment of Caesar's empire only vestiges of architecture remain along the great Roman roads. Nothing built under the Merovingian kings has been preserved. Many monasteries and churches were constructed, but all these monuments of early Frankish Christianity were only too perishable, having been built of wood.

With the coming of Charlemagne everything changed. The future Low Countries became the pivotal point where two great currents of civilization converged. The Empire of the West extended from the Elbe to the Pyrenees and naturally took in the basin of the Meuse, attached to the Rhenish region not only geographically but by ecclesiastical and administrative ties as well.

The palatial Chapel of Aix-la-Chapelle (796–804) served as a model to Notger, Bishop of Liége, a great builder of churches, in the construction of the Chapel of St. Jean (982) in Liége. The Carolingian churches follow the basilical plan, laid out in the form of a Latin cross. To this they sometimes added important modifications.

Up to the decline of the imperial church, at the beginning of the thirteenth century, the valley of the Meuse was dotted with these sanctuaries, including many cloisters. Of those which have survived in great part to the present, two belong to the Meuse Valley, that of Tongeren, the best preserved, and that of Nivelles, of which little is left since May 10, 1940, when German shells destroyed it.

Anglo-Norman architecture penetrated as far as Champagne, by way of Tournai, on the Scheldt. Tournai, admirably situated, had the advantage of a certain religious independence. The "Grand

Procession" of September also made it an important place of pilgrimage. Moreover, materials were found there which could be hewn on the spot and exported. Thus the Scheldt style acquired homogeneity and originality. In the old Collegiate Church of St. Vincent of Soignies, the oldest parts of which date from the pre-Romanesque period, the rayonnant plan, which was applied also to the Cathedral of Tournai, was introduced in the eleventh century. The nave and the transept of this church are the definitive and grandiose manifestations of this style (1110–1171). This five-towered church, one of the most beautiful Romanesque cathedrals of Western Europe, exerted a considerable influence, even extending to the cathedrals of the north of France, and Champagne, Laon, Reims, Noyon, and others, although these already were Gothic. The Romanesque parts of Our Lady of the Chapel at Brussels, the crypts of St. Peter (Anderlecht), of St. Bavo (Ghent), of St. Hermès (Ronse), and the Chapel of the Holy Blood at Bruges also date from the beginning of the twelfth century.

The influence of Tournai as an architectural center can be further appreciated by studying what remains of the cloister of St. Bavo at Ghent, the "House of the Staple" in Ghent, the first to have a crow-stepped gable, and some houses of Lille and Tournai.

Through the influence of Tournai, Gothic art was introduced in the following century, manifest by the ogival arches of the Episcopal Palace and the Cathedral, built by Bishop Etienne about 1200. There was a felicitous exchange between France and Tournai, which transmitted to the east and to the north as far as the Flemish Zeeland, the great western trend. Everything conspired in this effervescent period to favor contacts and to spur onward religious and civil construction: commerce found its natural outlets in the famous fairs of Provins and Troyes, where all Europe and the East commingled; roads were developed, and lands were reclaimed in the coastal and forest regions. This resulted in the growth of new population centers and in the construction of churches to fill the needs of a growing population. The art of the Ile de France had a fair share in this. Flanders, Hainaut, Brabant, and even the Meuse country blossomed with Gothic edifices.

To be sure, these churches differed appreciably from one another, even though this difference consisted only in the materials used—

bricks from the Veurne-Ambacht at Veurne, brick and fieldstone at Bruges, brownstone from along the river Meuse, sandstone in which Brabant is so rich and which lends itself so well to the ogival arch. There were other local characteristics. At Damme, the church, of the type prevailing in the flat country, is a "hallekerk" with a triple choir, a variation of the German "Hallekirche" found on the eastern frontier where the evolution of the economic activity and artistic form was not so far advanced. In Brabant, because of the geological peculiarity mentioned above, the secondary Gothic and especially the flamboyant, which gave full play to artistic invention, developed intensively. But the churches which sprang up on all sides had a common tendency to accentuate breadth rather than verticality, according to the French model.

One of the most beautiful examples of this epoch, even though bearing signs of the transition period, is Our Lady of Pamele at Audenarde (1234–1238), the only church of which the architect's name, Arnoul de Binche, is known. The choir of St. Brice, at Tournai (1225) determined the style of the churches of Damme and Audenarde. At Ghent, St. Nicolas (1231) might be considered the magnificent Gothic counterpart of the Cathedral of Tournai. In the reconstruction of Our Saviour of Bruges, brick was used for the first time (beginning of the thirteenth century). Tongeren, and Huy, where the rose window, the famous "Rondia," is unique in Belgium, show great purity of style. The choir, transept, and tower (early thirteenth century) of Our Lady of the Chapel at Brussels, because of similar characteristics, may be logically attributed to the architect of the chevet of St. Gudula at Brussels. Our Lady of the Chapel is decorated with realistic sculpture. G. des Marez believes that foreign "ymaigiers," belonging rather to the Rhenish school than the French, were the first builders and decorators of this church. In its soberness, it is one of the most beautiful and moving examples of this period when Romanesque art blended with Gothic.

The choir of the Cathedral of Tournai (1234–1255), of an unsurpassed elegance and vigor, is incontestably the masterpiece of an architecture, which, in this instance, rises above local standards. It may be favorably compared with the finest French specimens which preceded it (Soissons, 1212; Amiens, 1220). The man responsible for its construction, the successor of Bishop Etienne, is Walter de Marvis, whom the Franciscans and Dominicans found a powerful support in their struggle against the regular and secular clergy. If indebtedness is due to the Cistercians for the abbeys of Villers, Orval, and Aulnes, and to the Norbertines for the Park abbey at Louvain, then it is to the Mendicant Orders that indebtedness is due for the churches of Maastricht and Louvain. In spite of their internal strife, both contributed to the expansion of the Burgundian style. The Preaching Friars and the Minorites exercised a salutary influence on the society of merchants and artisans who were thus induced to assume their responsibilities in the community and to take pride in their duties of citizenship.

During the whole course of this century, which ended in the Battle of Groeninghe (1302), a triumph of Flemish arms over the French, the economic and social development of the Belgian provinces brought about the construction of admirable market halls, belfries, and town halls. The towers which rise above Belgium belong not only to the churches but also to the public buildings.

In the course of the fourteenth and fifteenth centuries, the splendor of the cities was enhanced by civil monuments. The cloth merchants built their warehouses among their bourgeois dwellings. The first of these "halles" were those of Ypres, destroyed during the First World War then partially restored. The construction was started at the beginning of the thirteenth century and finished in 1304. With the two upper stories extending for a length of more than twenty pointed equilateral arches, to the right and left of the base of the massive tower, this imposing building is a forceful and impressive testimony of the commercial prosperity of the country. Cloth halls were also erected at Bruges, at Mechlin, at Kortrijk, at Dendermonde, and at Brussels, where the cloth hall was so well set up that it attracted admirers from Cologne and other cities.

Sometimes these trade halls were crowned with a belfry, as at Bruges and Ypres; sometimes the belfry was erected independently, as in Tournai, Ghent, Lier, and Aalst. These towers rang out the tocsin and glorified the independence of the burghers. Within them, or within the church towers were hung the carillons, the first of which dates from 1370. For these chimes Belgium became world renowned.

The town halls contributed to the glory of the cities. The trade halls and the manor houses of the Middle Ages were the most magnificent expression of Flemish Gothic architecture. Two of the finest examples are the town halls of Louvain (1445–1463) and of Audenarde, completed in three years by Van der Pede (1527–1530). That of Mons, in the general lines which it assumed during the third quarter of the fifteenth century, may be considered with the town hall of Louvain.

The ground of the market place in Brussels was so damp that the Bakers' Guild Hall had to be constructed on a foundation of piles. Doubtless the Brussels belfry had already been built when a decision was made to construct the left wing of the town hall (1402); this wing was probably executed by Jacques van Thienen. The right wing was added in the middle of the fifteenth century. The ensemble is dominated by a tower designed by Jan van Ruysbroeck, in a style elegant and bold, topped by a pyramidal spire ornamented with crockets. This tower is of an unsurpassed elegance and beauty.

One of the last manifestations of the patrician grandeur of Bruges is the town house of the Gruuthuuse family (1420). The prosperity of Bruges ended a half-century later. With the decline of Bruges, Antwerp began to rise. It was in this city that the first International Exchange was built. Its fairs supplanted those of Champagne; its port was enlarged; from the New World via Spain spices and treasures of gold and silver were brought back by the conquistadores from Mexico. The center of gravity of the provinces changed. Mechlin, Mons, and Brussels began to share with the "Genoa of the North" the benefit of its rich trade.

This gave more impetus than ever to architecture. It was expressed in the churches, in the dwellings of the aristocracy and the bourgeoisie, and also in the "Greffes," the offices of the clerks of the court. At Brussels, the towers of St. Gudula gave the church a French character. Our Lady of the Sablon is a graceful monument in which all the technical possibilities of the late Gothic were brought out. At Mechlin, the tower of St. Rombaut gives an impression of power more similar to the communal belfries than to the church steeples. The tower of St. Rombaut has a tutelary significance, intended to inspire confidence in the faithful whom it protects and in whose eyes it is the imperious token of the power it represents. The tower of Our Lady of Antwerp, infinitely more French, is as majestic as St. Rombaut although its architecture is one of lightness and grace. The second tower of this church has remained unfinished.

The Brabantine architecture, which introduced the flamboyant style into Flanders, branched out widely as far as Bourg-en-Bresse, where the Regent Margaret intended to retire. There the Brussels architect, Louis van Bodeghem, constructed for Margaret, in 1504, the Church of Our Lady of Brou, which contains her mausoleum and that of her husband, Philibert the Fair. Van Bodeghem collaborated with Michel Colombe and Conrad Meit. To the north, at 'sHertogenbosch, today in Dutch territory, was begun in 1419 the construction of the choir of the Church of St. Jan, which is probably the masterpiece of the Brabantine school.

A late Gothic, foreshadowing the Renaissance, persisted here and there. This is true of the Antwerp Exchange, built in 1521 by Domien de Waghemakere, who, with his father, directed the construction work of the cathedral. Sir Thomas Gresham considered this exchange such a splendid building that he patterned after it the Stock Exchange of London, which was destroyed by the Great Fire of 1666.

Fidelity to traditions is still more marked at Ghent, as is seen in the House of the Free Boatmen (1537). Likewise, in the Palace of Margaret of Austria, at Mechlin, now the Law Courts, only timid signs of the Renaissance were introduced—the earliest signs, along with those of the Cloth Merchants' House at Antwerp.

The Waghemakeres and the Keldermans, architectural dynasties, were prolific exponents of the declining Gothic. The Keldermans obstinately refused to give it up. The struggle against the influence from Italy is evident also in the ancient Bakers' Guildhall at Brussels, incorrectly called the King's House.

The Gothic style was continued in the Cathedral of St. Waudru of Mons up to the end of the sixteenth century, even though the noble families of Mérode and Lalaing succumbed to the capricious fancies from the south in the decoration of their manor houses at Antwerp in Brabant. In spite of his predilection for the Renaissance, Evrard de la Marck, Prince-Bishop of Liége, and petty

king in his principality, did not prevent the famous Palace of the
Prince-Bishops of Liége (today the Law Courts) from giving the
lion's share to Gothic architecture.

It was with evident reluctance that this beautiful domestic Flemish architecture was abandoned. The first signs appear at the beginning of the fourteenth century (the Biloke, Ghent). The house
in which the printer, Christopher Plantin, lived in 1579 at Antwerp
is a complete, though fairly rare, realization of the Renaissance in
the Low Countries. The purest and most grandiose Renaissance
building is the town hall of Antwerp, built by Cornelis de Vriendt,
called Floris, after the plans of an Italian architect. Here the monumental style borrows the basic elegance of the Florentine palaces;
it nevertheless succeeded in uniting harmoniously certain characteristics of native inspiration with the arcades in the Bramante
manner and the pilasters superimposed according to Leo Battista
Alberti. This happy combination, moreover, gives the building
an interesting and original attractiveness which is the identifying
mark of this Nordic art.

The Greffe at Bruges (1534–1535), designed by Jean Mone, an
artist from Lorraine, the guildhalls clustered around the Antwerp
town hall, the houses of Mechlin, Ghent, Brussels, and Liége are
sporadic traces of the new art.

Also to be borne in mind are the achievements of Jacques Dubroeucq in Hainaut—the château of Mariemont for Marie of Hungary, the château of Binche and that of Boussu, destroyed when
they were barely finished by the wars which brought an end to
the prosperity of Mons.

In sum, classic architecture has left hardly any traces in Belgium.
Architecture, more than any other art, is intimately linked to political, economic, religious, and social happenings. Circumstances
were not propitious, in the course of the sixteenth century, to the
development of new tendencies. The struggles of the Reformation,
the bloody repressions by Philip II, the fratricidal antagonisms
which they provoked, created extremely deep-reaching disorders
which resulted in the ruin of the country.

It was necessary for a period of calm to supervene before the
architects could go back to work. The Low Countries came out of
the frightful tragedy of the Wars of Religion dismembered and

divided. Rubens was twenty-three years old when the seventeenth century began. The curtain was about to rise on the full flowering of the second Flemish Renaissance.

It is noteworthy that the Baroque did not develop expansively in the Calvinistic states of Holland. However, it did grow side by side with the increasing influence of the Jesuits, although it was not instigated nor encouraged by them. As proof of this, there is the fact that when the Jesuit fathers, Henri Hoeymaker and Jean Du Blocq, built churches for the Order in the first twenty-five years of the seventeenth century—and the same is true in Switzerland and in Germany—it is the *Gothic* which inspired them. Later on they intelligently embraced the new vogue, which seemed to coincide logically with the spirit of the Order, where "there was no longer any place for the monastic mortifications which belonged to another age of religious life." Indeed, the advice of one of its theorists, Father Balthazar Gracian, was "to do oneself what will assure favor."

However, if Bernini was the greatest advocate of the Jesuits, it is not proved that the Jesuits wanted to be the protagonists of the Baroque. To call the Baroque "Jesuit" style is as erroneous as to call it "Rubens" style. As a matter of fact, the formidable personality of Rubens was a powerful influence in the spreading of the Baroque style. But one cannot go farther than this statement. The fact that he designed the plans for his own house—the only architectural plans which can be attributed to him—or that he is supposed to have decorated the Church of St. Charles Borromaeus at Antwerp is not sufficient evidence for calling this luxuriant style of the Baroque "Rubens."

This latter church (1614–1621) is the masterpiece of the Jesuit, Pieter Huyssens, the great architect of Brabantine Baroque. The unusual proportions of the nave of this church, the ostentatious luxury of its decoration, the prodigal and massive combination of many Italianate architectural formulas, make St. Charles Borromaeus less a house of prayer than a palace.

The architects of the Baroque churches were not always happily inspired, particularly in the use of the Italian cupola. Our Lady of Hanswyck at Mechlin, by Luc Fayd'herbe, is a better example than Our Lady of Scherpenheuvel, by Wenceslas Coebergher. They

did not succeed, however, in obtaining as pleasing a result with
the cupola as they did with the tower.

Additions in the Italian Flemish style were made to churches,
notably those executed at Brussels for the De Tour and Taxis family in Our Lady of Victory of the Sablon—the Chapel of St. Marcou,
and especially the one dedicated to St. Ursula, the work of Luc
Fayd'herbe. New churches also were erected at Lier, Ghent, Bruges,
Liége, Namur, Louvain; in the Norbertine abbeys of Grimber-
ghen, of Park, and of Averbode. The series of Baroque churches
in Brussels gave this city an irresistible charm. The old quarters
of the city are alluring even today, notably those surrounding
Our Lady of the Riches-Claires, Our Lady of Perpetual Help, and
especially St. John the Baptist. It is unfortunate that judgment
can no longer be passed on the Church of the Augustines, doubtless
the masterpiece of Jacques Franquart.

The most beautiful expression of Flemish Baroque is certainly
the Market Place of Brussels. The guildhalls which encircle the
town hall on a vast square form a unique ensemble. Reduced to a
rubble of ruins in 1695 by the bombardment of Marshal Villeroy
who had taken aim at the spire of the town hall, it was rebuilt
four years later. A city ordinance laid down strict rules that the
unity of style and harmonious proportions of this historic site
should be kept. On these façades with three orders, one upon the
other, with their imbedded columns, are accumulated the most
varied adornments of gadroons, trophies, vases, garlands of flowers,
and fruit. The architects indulged in this pagan lavishness without
vulgarity. Such painters as Jordaens and Snyders have had a great
part in the message of this second Renaissance in architecture.

The Spanish and the Austrian regimes considered the Belgian
provinces only as a distant territory and were not inclined to encourage the arts. Under the reign of Maria Theresa (1740–1780),
however, the situation was improved. Already, in 1756, on the
site of the magnificent town house of the Nassau family dating
from the "quattrocento" period, Duke Charles of Lorraine, Governor of the Low Countries, had a residence built. In building
this palace the architect, Faulte, had the collaboration of a great
number of artists, as well as that of Laurent Dewez, the promoter
of the neoclassic style. Dewez executed, in 1779, the château of

Seneffe, for which he drew upon the plan of the Roman villas, the spacious courtyards of which were encircled with long galleries of colonnades. Dewez also was architect of the town hall of Tournai, and certain abbeys, among which were those of Gembloux, Orval, and Floreffe.

The aristocratic life directed in Liége by the prince bishops of Bavaria, in addition to the vogue for Louis XV furniture, led to the creation of beautiful interiors, of which the house of the Ansembourgs is one of the most successful types. During this period, at Antwerp the elegant Royal Palace, the old town house of the Van Susterens (1745), built in Louis XV style by Van Baurscheidt, and many other patrician dwellings, such as the Osterrieth town house, were constructed. In Brussels, Fisco designed the Place des Martyrs in 1775, a structure of melancholic charm well suited to become a national site; here are buried the heroes who fell during the war for independence in 1830.

Charles of Lorraine, remembering the splendor of Vienna, was ambitious to increase the attractiveness of his own capital. At his initiative, it was decided to transform completely the quarter of the Park which had held the ancient ducal garden, renowned all over Europe for its natural beauty. In order to accomplish this plan, it was necessary to demolish a delightful construction of the seventeenth century, the "Domus Isabellae." In 1774, the French architect, Barnabée Guimard, was commissioned with the laying out of the Place Royale, which was planned as a replica of the Place Stanislas at Nancy. Immediately after accomplishing his assignment, Guimard urbanized the outskirts of the Park, for which the court gardener, Joachim Zinner, laid out new plans. Today the royal palace and the Belgian Parliament building face each other across this vast expanse, lined with streets which exhibit the aristocratic houses of a former period.

During the entire nineteenth century, Belgium, like the rest of Europe, suffered from the deficiencies of architects who did no more than make a modern style out of the old. However, F. T. Suys and P. F. Gineste are noteworthy, if only for the part they took in building the greenhouses of the Botanical Garden; François Beyaert, the architect of the National Bank building; and Alphonse Balat, designer of the imposing façade of the Museum of Ancient

Art, who was responsible for the dignity with which some of the architects restored the old monuments. Finally, Joseph Poelaert will be remembered as long as the Law Courts of Brussels is standing. One of the remarkable characteristics of the Courts is the area of 286,300 square feet which they cover. This engineering feat, accomplished with stone, is as exceptional as the erection six years later (1889) of the Eiffel Tower. The Law Courts has been the subject of many ironical comments; however, in its majesty, it is a fitting temple of the law.

From 1893 on, as a result of the agitation of the English group "Arts and Crafts," the modern movement spread over the Continent. Paul Hankar (1859–1901) was the precursor of the great masters of architectural modernism, Victor Horta (born in 1861) and Henry van de Velde (born in 1863). Horta may take pride in being the originator of such outstanding works as the Palace of Fine Arts in Brussels (1923–1930), and that of Tournai (1928). Set back from the Park, the Palace of Fine Arts is a prodigious achievement.

Comparable perhaps with Frank Lloyd Wright and several Austrian architects, Henry van de Velde has contributed more than anyone else to the triumph of the esthetic revolution in modern architecture. As a theorist, he instigated in Germany, where he had been called at the beginning of his career to the court of Saxe-Weimar, a renovation which produced the movement of the Werkbund and the Bauhaus of Dessau. His book, *Formulas for a New Aesthetic* (*Formules d'une esthétique nouvelle*), appearing in 1923, became a classic of modernism. He created the theater at the Exposition of the Werkbund at Cologne (1914), and the Kröller-Müller Museum of Hoenderlo (Holland, 1925). Today the most brilliant Belgian modernists consider him as their master.

Directly after the First World War, the modernistic architects, faced with the task of rebuilding devastated regions, instituted a campaign, given impetus by F. van der Swaelmen, to promote healthy comprehension of urbanism. Thus sprang up a whole series of "garden cities" providing inexpensive dwellings for people with modest incomes.

Religious architecture did not remain inactive. The pseudo-Gothic churches began to yield to beautiful buildings which reflected the spirit of modern times.

There were also numerous cinema theaters, some of which were of real distinction, like the Métropole in Brussels, decorated by the sculptor, Ossip Zadkine. Antwerp acquired the only skyscraper in Europe, the Torengebouw.

On the eve of the Second World War, the city of Brussels commissioned the architect, Joseph van Neck, and the engineer, J. Celis, to construct a series of large buildings near the royal palace of Laeken. These buildings were intended to relieve the congestion of the city and were destined to play an important part in the economic, artistic, and worldly life of the capital.

CHAPTER XX

Belgian Literature in the Dutch Language

BY JAN GRESHOFF

THE HISTORY OF intellectual life, and particularly of literature in the Low Countries, is one of subtle and deep psychological kinship, primarily as a result of the contrast between south and north and as a result of the interplay of accents which resulted therefrom. This contrast, at times very sharp and at other times hardly noticeable, overlies a profound inner union of the two regions.

The cleavage between the Southern and the Northern Low Countries, which took place after the transition from the sixteenth to the seventeenth century, has never been complete. In this alternation of attraction and repulsion two factors asserted their influence—the first, naturally, the Reformation with all its consequences, the second, the hidden power of Latinity.

During the Middle Ages, and for many years thereafter, the culture of the Low Countries was borne and characterized by the south. The term "south" connotes a strange fusion of two hostile elements inseparably connected, namely Catholicism and the indestructible aftereffect of Graeco-Roman antiquity. The belief that the Renaissance was a period exclusively of rediscovery of classical culture has long since been abandoned. The Renaissance represents a period in which a different interpretation was given to classical culture, a period in which knowledge of that culture was disseminated among a broader stratum of population; but the great scholars of the Middle Ages, it is now agreed, were duly familiar with the ancient writers and philosophers.

Not only in the Low Countries, but wherever any form of culture developed, a fusion of Christian and classical influences took place. Like the Mediterranean Sea, the fusion formed a source of warmth, the benefit of which distributed itself in waves in all directions, including the north.

The semibarbarous tribes which inhabited the marshy regions along the lower course of the Rhine, the Meuse, and the Scheldt received their first revelation of a higher life from the south. And they gradually developed into civilized human beings under the immediate influence of Christianity and Latinity.

At a somewhat later stage it is hardly possible to overestimate the influence of the Crusades on the subsequent development. The East with which the Crusaders became acquainted, no matter how completely it was Mohammedanized, nevertheless had not remained entirely free from a former Christian influence. As a result of the expeditions to the East and to the Levant, European Christianity received a colorfulness and a luxuriance which came to full flower much later in the Baroque. After the Gothic, which is the apotheosis of the South, there followed the Netherlands Baroque which reached its climax in painting, in the south (Rubens), and in literature, in the north (Vondel). If the relation of the southern and northern countries through the three main periods of the literature in the common language are examined, then a Gothic influence is found which is almost exclusively southern, a Baroque which is exclusively northern, and a Romanticism which leads to a synthetic fusing of north and south. This process has not yet been entirely completed. But during the past few years the intellectual connections between the Southern and Northern Low Countries have become so intimate that, aside from slight differences, linguistic and literary unity becomes more and more clearly marked. This phenomenon was ushered in by the emancipation of the Catholics in the Northern Low Countries (1845). This permitted a natural interplay which rose of itself between the Roman south and the heterogeneous north.

The urge for poetical expression and enjoyment of beauty is greatest in youth. This is as true for the youth of a nation as for the youth of an individual. Primitive man and the young are not spoiled yet by the most terrible danger of all—practical existence.

They live, consciously and unconsciously, in an atmosphere conditioned by sentiment and not by intelligence, and they are not ashamed to express their inner feelings candidly in words, gestures, and acts.

Something akin to this quality of candidness characterizes the whole art of the Middle Ages. Especially does the art of the Netherlands during this period reflect the characteristic of candidness of the people. Candidness, impartiality, and freedom from worldly prejudice can go very well with extreme refinement of manners and form. The poetry of the Middle Ages is naïve but never rude, natural but extremely subtle. The language, of limited and simple vocabulary, befits these characteristics. The numerous, and for the most part anonymous, authors know how to do extraordinary things with language. Their artistic ideal is to reach a maximum of effect through a minimum of means.

This ideal has been achieved in several periods of history, and most effectively in the Middle Ages. Many famous songs, in their simplicity, are models of technique. Their language, which consists of words used only in daily life, contains a wealth of remarkable and enchanting nuances. The poem of the Middle Ages shows what can be achieved in the realm of poetry with frugal wording. This kind of lyric poetry unites simplicity and clarity with richness, direct expression with inexplicable mystery.

There existed at this period a poetry of the knights, a spiritual poetry, and a poetry of the third order. The first exalts earthly love, combat, and play; the second, the Trinity, the saints, contemplative life, and renunciation; the third, everyday life with its joys and pains, the pleasures of matter. The poetry of the third order which is satirical—that is, critical—has produced the greatest masterpiece of Dutch literature, *Reynard the Fox,* an allegorical animal epic, abundant in amusing allusions to social relations and rich in psychological interpretation. In many parts the epic has a direct and purely poetical quality. Among the abundant devotional writings of the period the legend of Beatrijs, the vergeress, is a masterpiece of pure, poetical feeling and of deep psychological insight into human nature.

The great, endlessly variegated richness of the literature of the Middle Ages provides songs, purely lyrical in style—May songs, the simple spiritual, and the intentional or, one might say, the sophisticated, spiritual song. Next come the tales of the knights, half-lyrical, half-narrative, classified according to their sources, or originals, as Frankish, Breton, classical, or oriental tales. To these may be added the epic and didactic poems, the moral and mystical meditations and allegories, the lay plays, the mystery plays, the farces, and the folk legends.

The most beautiful and the most important of the folksongs are "Halewijn" and "Van Heer Daneelken"; the social song reached its highest peak in the unforgettable "Kerelslied," the amorous song in *Ic stond op hoghen berghe*. Among the spiritual songs the best are "Des Soudaens Dochterken," "De Nagtegael" and "Egidius."

The tales of the knights are known to everyone who studies the Middle Ages—*Ferguit, Halewijn, Alexander's Yeesten, Floris ende Blanchefloer*. The dramas of later date are also international in theme—*Elkerlyck, Karel ende Elegast, Lancelot van Denemarken, The Seven Joys of Mary* (of which only the first and the seventh plays are extant), and *Marieke of Nymwege*.

Very few authors of this period are known. Jacob van Maerlant, born at Damme near Bruges, should be mentioned. In his best moments he possessed a poetical power of conviction that made him a great poet.

The Middle Ages, seen as a very mobile and changing whole, with all its flights and descents, constituted the greatest period of Southern Netherlands, which, at that time in every aspect, spiritually, economically, and politically, was at the height of its force, *élan*, and tension.

A remarkable figure in the transition from the Middle Ages to the Renaissance is that very aggressive enemy of the Lutherans, Anna Bijns (1494–1575), who published three collections of violent poems; another is the not less violent enemy of Papacy, Count Marnix van Sint Aldegonde (1540–1598), to whom is attributed, without certainty, however, the Dutch national anthem, the acrostychon, "William of Nassau."

In Anna Bijns and Marnix van Sint Aldegonde the medieval accent is still strongest; in Jonker van der Noot (1539–1595) and in Carel van Mander (1548–1606) the spirit of the Renaissance and of the Baroque dominates.

Although Dutch literature in Southern Netherlands was not totally unimportant after the separation from Holland, as some literary historians have claimed, still the south did not produce any great men during the Spanish, Austrian, and French dominations. To be just, one should cite the names of Justus van Harduyn (1590–1640), Adriaan Poorters (1605–1674), and, above all, Michiel de Swaen, a shoemaker of Dunkirk, who wrote a number of plays in which the human appeal is great enough to warrant their being performed today.

Joost van den Vondel (1587–1679), the greatest poet of the Baroque and the most impressive literary figure of the Netherlands, is claimed by the Dutch. He was born in Cologne, in which city his parents had stopped on their flight to Amsterdam from Antwerp for religious reasons. Vondel's character and work are strongly South Netherlandish. His conversion to Catholicism (1641) was consistent with this natural affinity.

In the nineteenth century the Flemish movement, which revived letters as well as national feeling, like any other movement of national resurrection, was romantic. The Flemings, who, in the first part of the nineteenth century, started to fight the systematic "Francization" initiated by the independent Kingdom of Belgium, were conscious of the fact that they had to find their arguments in two sources: the history of Flemish power in the Middle Ages, and the primitive, national force expressed in folklore. The exaltation of the past was used in order to create examples for the present; the exaltation of the joy of life in a very depressed rural population, expressed in folklore, was used to give hope of a new existence.

From the very beginning these two tendencies are completely realized in two great authors who dominate Flanders in the nineteenth century: Hendrik Conscience (1812–1883) and Guido Gezelle (1830–1899). Notwithstanding his poor language, his lack of psychological insight and plasticity, Conscience succeeded remarkably well in reviving the past and making it acceptable. Gezelle did so through the magic of his marvelous poetical gifts. Those who judge Conscience by purely literary standards arrive at an unfavorable judgment of his work, but they commit an injustice against him and against the beginning of Flemish literature. One should not judge works produced in a period of transition from a purely artistic standpoint. Conscience's language is, at the same time, both trivial and emphatic. His personages lack inner truth and the vitality to make them human. His horizon is as limited as his spiritual background, but in spite of all these shortcomings, Conscience remains an important writer not only of his period but from a general standpoint. The present writer read his masterpiece, *The Lion of Flanders*, as a boy; he reread it, after forty years, and still was fascinated and, notwithstanding a critical inclination, was conquered again by it. In Conscience, with all his bombast and his conventionalism, there lives an inner faith that is still alive and active. He was a born raconteur, and he could keep alive the interest of his readers, who were in fact listeners. Moreover, his love for Flanders and the Flemish past, and his hope to revive Flanders through this love were so sincere and so great that one forgets his rhetoric.

The case of Gezelle is entirely different. Like Conscience, he possessed the faculty of holding the reader's interest. He too loved Flanders with an almost superhuman devotion. He hoped to endow Flanders with a magnificent new life reflecting the richness and the glory of the Middle Ages. But he also was one of the greatest lyric poets who ever lived in Northern or Southern Netherlands. With heart and soul he lived the life of the simple people and exalted it to an hitherto unknown beauty. Earthly and divine love in him were not distinct. He knew but one imperative: to love God, nature, his country, the people, man.... In his vision of childlike profundity, God, the people, and Flanders formed one indivisible unity. He loved God, Who created man so weak and pitiful, Who made Flanders so brilliant with beauty and joy of life; and he loved man and Flanders while he recognized God's greatness and goodness and purity in them.

Guido Gezelle consecrated Flemish letters and brought them to a height they scarcely attained in the flowering of the Middle Ages. While in Northern Netherlands authors were still ensconced in the bourgeois banality of the literary period which preceded 1880, Gezelle in Southern Netherlands wrote a number of poems which were a revelation in their novelty and their conviction.

No revolutionary movement in literature comes suddenly or unannounced. In Holland the renewal of literary life, known as the

"Movement of the 'Eighties," or *De Nieuwe Gids* movement (after their review *De Nieuwe Gids*), was heralded by Multatuli (Eduard Douwes Dekker). The corresponding movement in Flanders, the *Van Nu en Straks* movement (after their magazine, *Van Nu en Straks*), was announced and made possible by the poetical work which Gezelle had accomplished.

The authors who made *Van Nu en Straks* an important review and even more so, a decisive event in Flanders, were, to cite only the most important, Stijn Streuvels, August Vermeylen, Herman Teirlinck, Fernand Toussaint van Boelaere and the youngest, but as an artist the most fascinating, Karel van de Woestijne. There were a great many more, younger and older, predecessors and followers, who contributed to the spiritual renaissance awakened by *Van Nu en Straks*.

The men around *Van Nu en Straks* undoubtedly had undergone the influence of the principles prevalent among the young Dutch authors. Of course, they were thoroughly familiar with French symbolism. They also knew English and German letters. But all these influences, although unmistakably present, were absorbed and transformed. This was made possible by three factors: the strong personality of the writers of the movement, their pronounced Flemish character and, finally, the exceptional position of the Flemish authors in the upsurge of the forceful vitality of Flanders and its language. Through all this, *Van Nu en Straks* acquired a character of its own, with a real aim, and a definite color.

Those who fought for a young and free art, in the strictly political sense of the word also had to fight for a free and rejuvenated Flanders. In this double fight, August Vermeylen was in the front line. More clearly than any of his contemporaries he perceived the great truth he formulated which, for many years, remained a guiding tenet: "We must be good Flemings to become good Europeans." This sentence shows the complete difference between *De Nieuwe Gids* and *Van Nu en Straks*. In the north the question of national intellectual revival did not arise.

Every spiritual movement is sustained by a few personalities whose importance for their movement derives from their personality more than from their artistic gifts. This is true of August Vermeylen. If, in the evolution of his time, he had written only

The Wandering Jew (*De Wandelende Jood*), he scarcely would have a right to be mentioned here. This novel, which contains some beautiful passages, has the twofold defect of being too intellectual and too "beautifully" written. The influence of Flaubert's *Tentation* seems present. But in Vermeylen's rich and vigorous life *De Wandelende Jood* was not much more than an incident. The inestimable and imperishable importance he has for his people and its literature is based on his combative essays and on his personal action. The essays of Vermeylen are a monument in the letters of Southern Netherlands. They have a strong dialectic basis, are nobly written, severe and still colorful in writing, rich in factual content. If polemic writings and comments on events of a day fifty years past can still be read with pleasure and profit, then their right to existence, it seems, is proved. Furthermore, as a Senator and as a professor of Ghent University, Vermeylen has rendered great service to the Flemish cause.

August Vermeylen belongs to the forerunners who have had the joy of seeing their ideals, in great part, accomplished. Around him and after him a generation of artists developed that makes it possible and justified to speak about a Flemish Renaissance—prose writers, poets, critics, and also painters, composers, and architects. To compare *De Nieuwe Gids* with the *Van Nu en Straks* movement one must realize that, in some aspects, the period preceding *De Nieuwe Gids* in Holland was richer than the years preceding *Van Nu en Straks* in Flanders, in other aspects it was poorer. From a general cultural standpoint it was richer; it was poorer if one bases an estimation on the value of a few individual artists. In other words, in the north, before the renewal, there existed a diversified spiritual life, although no individual poet was so exalted, so pure, so majectic, or so original as Guido Gezelle. It would seem that this purity, together with genius, gave to the *Van Nu en Straks* movement a better opportunity. This proved true in practice. *De Nieuwe Gids* movement did not have novelists of such natural creative power as Stijn Streuvels and Cyriel Buysse. One of the poets, however, Karel van de Woestijne, belongs among the supreme authors of both south and north.

Stijn Streuvels (1872–) (writing under the pen name of Frank Lateur) has created his own world of laws and myths, a world without complications or nuances. Such systematic simplicity usually suggests greatness in literature. In Streuvels' world nature, as well as man, seems to be above normal in every movement; every gesture is supernormal, every character seems to have a different reason for existence than does mundane man. Personages of such unusual tendencies, and deeds of such unusual dimensions are beyond the idea of time. In Streuvels' work, therefore, the past and the future have no role.

Stijn Streuvels' greatness lies in the fact that, notwithstanding his tendency to simplify life and to slow it down, he always succeeds in keeping nature natural and people human. Although one may expect penetrating psychological analysis in novels of this kind, Streuvels does not indulge in it to the point of rhetorical schematism, a practice which constitutes a great danger for writers of his type. Streuvels' schematism is genuine. His childlike surrender to the fundamental facts of life in his writing derives from a deep and sincere desire to present nature honestly. Because of this undeniable and essential fidelity, Stijn Streuvels is one of the few writers who can combine elementary psychology with primitive nature in an atmosphere of folklore without sacrificing reality.

Compared with Streuvels, who created a legend out of nature and man in their relation and their contrast, Cyriel Buysse (1859–1932), is the authentic realist. He has little interest in mystical thought and he sees nature only as the natural setting for men. Buysse's men have the proportions of those seen in everyday life. His realism is based on a formula that became famous in Dutch letters, the love of copying everyday life. Buysse sees men and their doings clearly and mercilessly. His books abound in interesting psychological details. He paints the milieu with extreme skill and with the completeness of French naturalism. He is a born raconteur. He knows the human value of the anecdote, he knows how sometimes to dramatize his anecdote in a touching way, but he lacks Streuvels' cosmic force and love of life. Even when he tells rural stories, Buysse remains the man of the world, knowing and skeptical, who is well aware of what his public demands, and knows how to fascinate it.

In his later books one discovers a tenderness that gives them a quiet radiance, which the works of his youth lacked completely. A book like *Tantes* (about 1930) is richer and more noble than *Het Ezelken* (1914), which is almost too fine a piece of workmanship.

The most remarkable thing about *Van Nu en Straks* remains the diversity of the talents the review had to offer. There were the great imagination of Streuvels, the sharp critical realism of Buysse, with little or no connection between them, and there was also Herman Teirlinck (1879–), a witty writer, versatile, overrefined, lyrical, elegant, whose writing was in constant motion and change. He wrote much and his productions are of unequal value. Such a novel as *Het Ivoren Aapje* is a mixture of surprising beauty and painful banality; it has elements of a modern metropolitan epic and, at the same time, elements of old-fashioned sentimentality. His collection of tales, *Mr. Serjanszoon*, grouped around the figure of a timid eighteenth-century Epicurean, is a masterpiece, enchanting from beginning to end, extremely rich in charming, witty, playful notes, written in a language full of arabesques which suits the characters and the time, making the whole novel natural and irresistible.

But notwithstanding this complete success in the realm of prose, the real significance of Teirlinck lies in the drama. Through his theories he rejuvenated the drama in Flanders. He was also a decisive influence in the theater of the Netherlands, where his plays were produced many times, especially *De vertraagde Film*. His plays have the virtue that, in spite of frequent deliberate effects, they remain enthralling and convincing. His force of conviction is so great that his faults are as acceptable as his virtues. In his dramas his whimsically original personality finally comes completely to the fore. His best-known plays are *De vertraagde Film, Ik Dien, Het AZ Spel, De Man zonder Lijf, Ave,* and *De Ekster op de Galg.*

Mention should also be made of Toussaint van Boelaere, a writer of brief but tense and pure stories. He is one of the few authors who can write haughtily, yet move his readers. He wrote rural novels in a style of highly refined symbolism, and the product was new and surprising. His style is limited, but within its limitations it is perfect. His best books are *Landelijk Minnespel, Petruske's Einde, Lente, De Doode die zich niet verhing,* and *Turren.*

The word genius is insufficiently defined as to extent and applicability, yet it is the only term with which to describe a man who unmistakably was moved by a surpassing spirit. Gezelle was a genius and so was Karel van de Woestijne. But there was a great distance between these two. In its endless richness, life for Gezelle was really very simple, since all phenomena are referred to their origin and their final destination—God. Nature, men, animals, and things—everything derives from God and goes back to Him. And God is supreme simplicity. So believed Gezelle.

Karel van de Woestijne, on the contrary, a pious man but with his entire being attached to the earth, fought the angel his whole life. In his work earthly and heavenly love are so fantastically interwoven that, next to the Gothic Gezelle, he may be considered the epitome of the modern Baroque poet.

Gezelle's world, although not as simple as one may initially and superficially think, is a quiet, pure world compared with Karel van de Woestijne's universe, where lust and bitterness, joy and remorse, excess and asceticism follow each other often with astonishing speed. A designation for Van de Woestijne's poetry would be "ornamented self-torture." Everything is torture to this poet, everything ends in self-reproach. A constant, silent terror gives his poems, especially his love lyrics, a quality that the present writer has never found anywhere else in any language. He is a great artist of language. His expression usually is heavy, somber, and plaintive, but at times it becomes clear, elevated, and pure. Karel van de Woestijne is first, last, and always a poet, even in his rich prose and in his critical essays.

A spiritual movement derives its value and significance not from its size but from its richness and intensity. The movement that found its expression in the review, *Van Nu en Straks,* was indeed highly diversified, and the young Flemish writers themselves certainly did not lack intensity. The years 1900 to 1914 were incomparably rich in Flemish letters.

Such a movement is never a closed entity. One cannot determine exactly when it begins and when it ends, nor is it possible to say, with certainty, who belongs to it and who does not. To simplify matters one groups Willem Elsschot, Felix Timmermans, and Jan van Nijlen together; they constitute a transition between *Van Nu en Straks* and the so-called moderns. Timmermans, who, more than Streuvels but with less right, represents Flemish literature abroad, continues the tradition of the rural novel. His book,

Pallieter, which created a sensation, became a great success. One feels that this book has been overestimated, and to consider it the most characteristic of Flemish books is to do an injustice to the Flemish spirit. At its best, *Pallieter* represents only one side of Flanders—the easy-going attitude, the joy in earthly things, and the enthusiasm for nature in its simplest aspects. But even this expression of one phase of Flemish life is too greatly exaggerated and too "arty" to give a real impression.

Nevertheless, Timmermans wrote one masterpiece, *Boerenpsalm.* The success of this novel lies in its restraint. Where Timmermans formerly overextended his limited possibilities, here he concentrates and creates a balanced whole. For the first time his personages attain the greatness and timelessness essential to a rural novel.

One cannot imagine a greater contrast than between Felix Timmermans and Willem Elsschot (Alfons de Ridder). By nature Timmermans is inclined to be loud, jovial, and exaggerative. Elsschot, on the contrary, is sobriety itself. His bitterness, his soberness, his tendency to understatement, are remarkable. He entered upon the literary scene, before the First World War, with a novel about a French pension, *Villa des Roses.* The great success of this book in the Netherlands was only among the literati; the general public was not attracted by its cynical wit. In Flanders people felt instinctively that this new author possessed a number of characteristics which did not fit into the traditional pattern of art and society. Elsschot also wrote *Een Ontgoocheling, De Verlossing* and, during the First World War, *Lijmen.* The indifference of the public discouraged him to such an extent that he stopped writing. Much later, in 1930, an appreciation of his work developed first in Holland and later in Belgium. He started writing again and published in quick succession *Kaas, Tsjip en de Leeuwentemmer, Pensioen,* and *Het Been.*

It became more and more apparent in these later books that cynicism and hardness were used by Elsschot unconsciously to hide a sensitivity that was almost childlike. This bitter cynic is, in fact, a defenseless man who suffers from a split personality.

Jan van Nijlen, who published two extensive, critical studies on Charles Péguy and Francis Jammes, by nature is a lyric poet—a lyric poet with a limited universe, but in this universe a master.

In Flanders, where reality is of such tremendous importance, he is the "absent one," the man who, wherever he is, has but one desire, to be elsewhere. This desire in Jan van Nijlen is not, however, an impulse strong enough to express itself; it is, rather, a state of silent protest, usually ironical, sometimes a little bitter, but always contained.

During the First World War, and immediately after, a two-fold influence made itself felt in Flemish literature, especially in poetry. German Expressionism was felt principally through Paul van Ostayen; French influence came through the poets who belong to the school of the Fantasists, of whom P. J. Toulet is by far the most important. Still other poets of influence, who, from the name of the review they founded, are called the poets of *Het Fonteintje,* were Richard Minne, Raymond Herreman, Maurice Roelants, and Karel Leroux.

Paul van Ostayen (1896–1928) was an exceptional writer. Although he did not found a school, he left his imprint on a number of contemporaries and followers. Despite his gifts, he lacked spontaneity. His works, which consisted of poems, stories, and essays, are intelligent—probably a little too intelligent—different, and with many striking verbal pyrotechnics. But one is always prevented from completely appreciating his works by the "intellectual" attitude of the author. Theory in Paul van Ostayen's work is always present as theory, it is not absorbed by the flesh and blood of the achieved poem or prose piece. Furthermore, Van Ostayen lacks the quality of naturalness. One feels how insistently he tries to be modern. He is counted as one of the writers whose focus was a review called *Ruimte;* this group attacked what they called "the aestheticism of *Van Nu en Straks.*" They wanted to achieve an ethico-social art—a requirement which could hardly be reconciled with "poésie pure"—a poetry of exclamations, exhortations and invocations as used by Van Ostayen and his friends. In spite of the great talent of several of its members, the whole movement leaves an impression of uncertainty and lack of artistic purity.

The poets of *Het Fonteintje,* who had a more limited aim, succeeded in expressing themselves far more purely. In their work, playfulness of mind and feeling expresses itself in the most charming manner, and one is impressed by the fact that although they ridiculed all solemn words and weighty slogans, in their writings they were far more genuine, warmer, and more purely human than the neohumanitarian poets who announced a new society.

It was a time of hesitation, enquiry, and struggle, when a great poet might synthesize these experiences. The first really poetical figure of significance after Van de Woestijne is Marnix Gijsen (pen name of Jan-Albert Goris) who humanized the modernism of *Ruimte* and modernized the humanism of *Het Fonteintje.*

The work of Marnix Gijsen is the fulfillment of the promises made by both groups, *Ruimte* and *Het Fonteintje,* a synthesis of the poetry of revelation and that of confession. One can hardly underestimate the importance of Marnix Gijsen's book of poetry, *Het Huis.* In itself it is a collection of poems practically without flaw, but more than that, it is a milestone in the evolution of Flemish letters. Seldom does one encounter poetry in which all elements and qualities are so happily united. It has the quality of mystery found in good poetry and yet it is understandable; it is abundant in nuances, full of diversity and modulations, and yet gives the impression of simplicity. It is unearthly and, at the same time, intelligent, sane, and impassioned. Paradoxically, it is both free and restrained.

After *Het Huis,* Marnix Gijsen published only a few poems in reviews. These poems show a change, in that their tone has become much warmer and much more dramatic. With Van de Woestijne, Marnix Gijsen is Flander's most outstanding critic of poetry. His critical writing derives its value from its penetration of the external and anecdotal elements and its complete lack of bias concerning any theory. Gijsen appreciates poetry as poetry, and from the standpoint of poetry.

Gijsen's most important contemporaries, Maurice Roelants and Gerard Walschap, dedicated themselves essentially to the novel. Of these two, writers of the same age who present only slight relationship, Roelants stands far from Walschap; his method of writing is closest to *Van Nu en Straks.* But he is distinct from this group through his subtle psychology and, above all, through his sense of the aesthetic values of moral differences. Roelants developed his own narrative style; he presents his problems with clarity and simplicity. His people are clear and simple. Events happen in a quiet, transparent atmosphere and—this is Roelants' strength and predominating characteristic—there is a constant impression, in this clarity, of living through a miracle, of participating in a mystery—a mystery in full daylight. Roelants wrote three novels, *Komen en Gaan, Het Leven dat wij droomden, Alles komt terecht,* and an excellent short story, *De Jazzspeler.*

In sharp contrast to the purity and reserve of Roelants stands the somber intensity of Gerard Walschap, the irresistible forcefulness, the tendency to extremes. The element of good taste, which is supreme in Roelants, is lacking in Walschap. Instead, he achieves a penetrating force of conviction that never fails to impress. In Roelants' books, the standards constantly are high; in Walschap's work are found the very best, a burning truthfulness, and the very worst, an impetuosity which becomes maniacal. With Roelants, however, Walschap has in common a very important and unique quality—a disdain for the outside world, for local color, in short, for all that which diverts from psychological interpretation and action, from the story in its essential significance.

Walschap's great novel, *De Familie Roothoofd,* a trilogy comprising the novels, *Adelaide, Carla,* and *Eric,* is a masterpiece. *Trouwen, Sybille,* and *Houtekiet* are excellent novels, each with its own character and with its own autonomous existence. Walschap, a deeply tormented spirit with a marvelously rough and eager temperament, is one of the great figures of Flemish prose. He belongs to those few writers whose less successful works and even whose failures are interesting and important, if only for the fact that they disclose something about the fascinating and important personalities of the authors.

Up to the time of the invasion and since, a number of young talents have emerged and begun to develop, but there is insufficient evidence to decide on their significance or to give them a place in relation to their predecessors.

CHAPTER XXI

French Literature in Belgium

BY BENJAMIN MATHER WOODBRIDGE

ELGIUM'S ASPIRATION to a strictly national literature is hardly a century old, yet it should not
be forgotten that certain universally known
authors and works of the past belong to her.
A glance at her literary history reveals that the gem of medieval
tales, *Aucassin and Nicolette*, was probably composed on what was
a part of her territory. All literary genres known to the Middle Ages
were cultivated in Belgium. The persistent cult of historiography,
even during periods of relative barrenness, is a reminder that
Chastelain, Froissart, and Commines were born on Belgian soil
and that all enjoyed the favor of noble patrons. The fiery Protestant soldier and statesman, Marnix de Sainte-Aldegonde, wielded
both French and Flemish as vigorously as the sword. Jean Lemaire
de Belges, recognized as a forerunner of the Renaissance, was not
without influence on the French Pléiade. In the eighteenth century
the Prince von Ligne, cosmopolitan soldier, diplomat and moralist,
enjoyed a European reputation. But, although he loved his estate
at Beloeil in the province of Hainaut, he felt no more national
consciousness than did Froissart.

The spirit engendered by the French Revolution unquestionably favored the growth of patriotic sentiment in literature and
novelists, too, began to seek inspiration in national history. With
independence in 1830 this interest became paramount and there
appears a growing desire for literary expression worthy of a prosperous young nation. In 1839 *La Revue Nationale* remarked: "Belgium will have a literature as soon as we can see in the work of her
authors a faithful representation of the good and bad traits which
distinguish her from other nations." The Duke of Brabant prom-

ised his aid, declaring: "Literary glory is the crown of every national edifice." And the rising generation set to work eagerly, inspired like Rubens of old, "by the thought of the beloved fatherland."

One of the marked characteristics of Belgian literature is its close alliance with plastic art, of which there exists a long and glorious tradition. In the decade 1874–1884, some twenty-five literary and artistic reviews were founded. They were preceded by substantial periodicals dealing primarily with *beaux-arts*. Many modern Belgian novelists, like Lemonnier and Demolder, have made permanent contributions to artistic criticism and nearly all reveal by their style influence of masters of the brush. Charles De Coster, whose *Ulenspiegel* (1867) remains one of the masterpieces of world fiction, proves his claim to have studied deeply both old books and painters. *Ulenspiegel* is the culmination of a long series of efforts in the historical chronicle; the scene is the struggle of the Low Countries against Spanish oppression in the sixteenth century. The author aims at a vast panorama, in which an invocation of the past is joined to the present and seeks to forge the future. Reservations may be made as to the historical accuracy of the ensemble, but the separate scenes engrave themselves unforgettably in the mind of the reader. De Coster uses an archaic language which he regarded as essential both to the period he was portraying and to the presentation in French and Flemish manners—hence, a cult of style which, alone, would suffice to set him apart from his contemporary novelists. Beside closing gloriously the period of historical fiction, *Ulenspiegel* anticipates the novel of manners which followed.

One trait distinctive of the national temperament untouched by De Coster is the mystic. For it one must turn to his contemporary, Octave Pirmez, who spent his life in meditation. His attitude is well summarized in *Heures de Philosophie* (1873): "I dedicate this book to religious minds—thinkers, poets, artists—to all who cherish nature through love of the ideal and are deeply concerned with the mysterious destiny of man." Montaigne, Rousseau, and Chateaubriand were among his favorite authors; he drew from them not only a philosophical bent but also an appreciation of the value of style. In the hecatomb decreed by *La Jeune Belgique* in the following generation, De Coster and Pirmez were spared. Criticism of the present day has accepted the verdict.

The majority of Belgian authors since 1880 are essentially poets, whatever their mode of expression. The two literary genres most successfully cultivated are fiction—especially the short story—and lyric poetry. A glance at representative masters in these fields will serve as initiation into Belgian literary life.

Camille Lemonnier was a younger contemporary of De Coster whose genius he admired even while following a distinctly different road. He sought his matter primarily in the life about him, but, like most of his successors, he remembered De Coster's advice: "Study the people, the bourgeois are all tarred with the same monotony." An innate love of the picturesque doubtless favors this democratic trend in the majority of Belgian novelists, of whom Lemonnier is among the most prolific; he took the entire country for his province, and his masterpiece is perhaps *La Belgique* (1888). "Mine is the passion for all life, mental and physical," he declared, but above all he is a worshiper of nature. His enthusiasm was contagious and his role in the creation of a truly national literature in Belgium can hardly be overestimated. Lemonnier believed society was in need of rejuvenation by close contact with unconscious nature. In him the final result is an idyllic pantheism.

With Georges Eekhoud, somber novelist of Antwerp and the surrounding countryside, a similar conviction leads to violent revolt against all conventions. He is at once fascinated and horrified by the intense industrial life of Antwerp (*La Nouvelle Carthage,* def. ed. 1893). His sympathy is with the downtrodden who become outlaws. Having spent his mature life in Brussels, his peasants seem often ideological creations of nostalgia rather than realistic portraits: reality wounded his sensibility and he sought refuge in imagination. He is essentially a *conteur* and the power of his novels is more in separate scenes than in the ensemble, *Kees Doorik* (1883). He distrusts subtle psychology and presents no complex characters, yet his intense love of his native region makes him one of the most original of Belgian novelists.

Georges Virrès chose as his province Limburg and, while influenced by both Lemonnier and Eekhoud, he leaves a distinctive mark. He supplies the mystic sentiment which he feels to be lacking in Eekhoud's peasants; he possesses a delightful humor tinged with gentle irony, and finally his style is more restrained than that of his Flemish colleagues. *La Bruyère Ardente* (1900) reveals full comprehension of the truculent side of the rustic temperament while *Les Gens de Tiest* (1903) offers a gallery of subtly drawn characters in the simplest of plots. Virrès has spent his life in the region he describes, and drew inspiration directly from it rather than from painters. Eugène Demolder on the contrary is steeped in traditions of masters of the brush. He usually deals with scenes of the past. His masterpiece, *La Route d'Emeraude* (1899), evokes Rembrandt and seventeenth-century Holland. Like Gautier, Demolder was a man for whom the visible world exists almost exclusively; his style is a transposition of painting. He married the daughter of the painter and etcher, Félicien Rops, and the whimsicalities of that artist fascinated him. Yet the humanitarian note is strongly marked in him and the milk of human kindness tempers his aestheticism. Doubtless the lack of human sympathy in Georges Rodenbach, whose once-famous *Bruges la Morte* (1892) attempts to fuse completely characters into the atmosphere of a city, contributes to the sense of artificiality inescapable today in his work.

The typical Walloon novelists of the same period show certain marked traits. They are less influenced than their Flemish colleagues by painters, and hence less given to description for its own sake; landscape is reflected in men rather than men in landscape. As character more than colorful environment holds their attention, they are keener psychologists; exuberance in either joy or melancholy is most often replaced by an austerely tragic view of life; finally, their humor is more subtle. Exceptions prove the rule: at times Virrès seems to belong among the Walloons, whereas no Fleming has outdone Maurice des Ombiaux in sheer joy of physical expansion. Regionalistic inspiration and sympathy with humility mark both groups, but the Walloons seek especially the *quod semper quod ubique* in close observation of familiar scenes and folk; they would be universal realists.

Hubert Krains, whose mature work promises to stand the test of time, is a typical Walloon. "The instincts which guide humanity are identical," he declares. "Degrees of latitude do not change the heart." His is the pessimism of the Stoic *Le Pain Noir* (1904); there is no sentimentality in him nor does he ever subordinate his art to any plea for social reform; discreet humor, especially rich in *Mes*

Amis (1920), relieves the somber tone of his stories. He possesses always the power of vivid characterization of both protagonists and accessory figures. He wrote relatively little, but critics are agreed in placing him among the classic stylists of his country. Edmond Glesener shares many of the qualities mentioned in Krains, although his range of theme is wider. *Le Cœur de François Remy* (1904) is often hailed as his masterpiece. Sympathy with erring humanity is paramount in this work. *Chronique d'un Petit Pays* (1913) offers virulent satire of social climbers and corrupt politicians. The tales of *L'Ombre des Sapins* (1935) are poignant tragedies of peasants, so broadly universalized as to symbolize humanity in all its range. An *obiter dictum* in *Une Jeunesse* (1927) reveals clearly the author's own ideal: "Even more than the studied literary technique, readers admired the implacable sincerity of this work. Here is an anatomical slide of which the cruel precision marks the havoc wrought by nihilism in minds led astray from traditional conceptions of honor and personal dignity. Behind the psychologist appears the moralist." Thus he replies to the charge of cynicism which his objectivity has occasionally brought.

The characteristic trait of Hubert Stiernet is his use of forces realistic yet mysterious, never fantastic and never separated from everyday life. These forces spring from the soil, from violation of tradition or from some incident in the past; they are literally *revenants*. The title of one of his collections, *Histoires Hantées* (1906), might serve for the majority of his works. Occult powers appear as prolongations of some word or act which escapes from unreflecting passion or from the subconscious; once released these powers guide the destiny of an individual. Stiernet's masterpiece is *Le Roman du Tonnelier* (1922), which contains realistic pictures of rustic manners, sympathy for the straying, ardent passions, poetry, and a brooding contemplation of the enigma of human destiny, all made concrete by the use of a village in Hesbaye as a microcosm. His manner of introducing the supernatural recalls that of Hawthorne, but he adds a whimsical humor rare in the austere American novelist.

Louis Delattre, primarily a *conteur*, found himself irresistibly urged to literary composition by the passion to communicate his own joy in the bounteousness of existence. In one of his last works,

Les Grains d'Anis (1936), he declares that all his life he had sought the art of happiness by the complete grasp of intelligence, the art of living by extracting from the humblest fruits of the earth the last drop of satisfaction. And again: "The *conte* is the search for emotion through sympathy." There is the essence of his books. He had amassed a store of memories from his boyhood on a farm and these, recollected in the tranquillity of later years, gave him an inexhaustible fund. A doctor by profession, and for a time medical advisor to state prisons, Delattre widened his experience and deepened his psychological acumen; he was fascinated by every experience. "There is nothing more beautiful, more noble nor more holy than life and its suffering," declares an aged nun who envies a sorely tried companion of her childhood. This restrained exuberance strikes a new note in Belgian fiction.

Lustiness is the word which first comes to mind when thinking of Maurice des Ombiaux. "The smallest pleasure in life makes me forget all its goals," he writes. He delights in legends and folklore and draws more inspiration than his Walloon colleagues from pictorial artists. His Rabelaisian joy in action recalls De Coster, as he writes now of the past of the region between the Sambre-et-Meuse, *Le Joyau de la Mitre* (1901), now of the present, *Mihien d'Avène* (1904). Dealing habitually with elemental folk, he has created a gallery of unforgettable "irregulars."

Among the younger Walloon novelists Jean Tousseul stands preeminent. Idealism stamps his life no less than his work; scorning every compromise, he has devoted himself uniquely to letters. A self-taught man, sprung from manual workers, he speaks with intimate knowledge of the humble. "In my books," he says, "I have usually kept company with tragic characters." Yes, but what poetry he distills from their sufferings! He has become a master novelist through love of his village, whose epic he has written in *Jean Clarambaux* (1927–1936). "While his books pass beyond the limits of our tiny country by virtue of their intensity and perfection, they retain all the aroma of the Walloon countryside," wrote Krains.

The novelists mentioned, whether of the Flemish or Walloon traditions, are primarily regionalists. But although regionalism has been a rich inspiration for Belgian fiction, it is not the only one. Three of the younger writers may serve as illustrations. Franz

Hellens, fellow townsman of Maeterlinck, offers a synthesis of the trends of contemporary fiction outside Belgium, and his intentions are usually clearer than those of most of his foreign peers. His first work, *En Ville Morte* (1906), is a vision of Ghent by a surrealist in embryo. Convinced that the realm of the rational has been fully explored, he would invoke a sixth sense to sharpen the perceptions of the normal five. The title of one of his collections of stories, *Réalités Fantastiques* (1923), serves as a thumbnail characterization of his work; he is a veritable explorer of uncharted realms of mystery. His manner recalls Poe, although he found Poe's hallucinations too mechanical and preferred to investigate subtler psychic sources. His eyes are turned inward: the overtones of music and line more than color in the plastic arts have attracted his attention.

Maurice Gauchez, leader of the vivacious group, *La Renaissance d'Occident,* has inherited from Edmond Picard the title of *animateur.* His extensive voyages into literary criticism have inspired him to essay again the themes of many of his predecessors; De Coster's *Ulenspiegel* has especially fascinated him. The spirit of the man is in one of his early poems:

> *Et la vie est l'écho d'un rire prolongé*
> *Dont je puis à mon gré répandre ou propager*
> *L'eurythmique splendeur où tout se perpétue.*[1]

Max Deauville has written a number of plays, narratives of war experience, and fiction. "Irony is the richest source of consolation; aid it to gnaw away the slumbering pain in your heart," he advises. He is fundamentally an idealist; hence, the contrast between the life man leads and what should be his, has embittered him as he contemplates the victims of destiny, *L'Amour dans les Ruines* (1910). Deauville faced the war with stoic resignation; reconstruction, *Jonas* (1923), left him all but a cynic. He uses a trenchant, often epigrammatic style, aiming at ideas rather than colorful language. Maurice Gauchez would place him in the spiritual family of La Rochefoucauld.

Women have made an essential contribution to Belgian literature. Seventy women writers, using French as their medium, were represented at an exposition in 1936. In fiction they reveal a deli-

---

[1] And life is the echo of prolonged laughter whose eurythmic splendor where all becomes eternal, can, at my will, be spread or sown.

cacy when dealing with feminine psychology rare among their masculine colleagues. Julia Frezin, with the vigor and poise which she combines with her intuition, is among the most incisive. Her vision of life often recalls Ibsen; by their conciseness her novels suggest that she has studied the technique of the stage. She excels in the portrayal of stoic idealists placed against a realistic background, *Le Nid Ravagé* (1937). Her interest is always in her characters; their environment is largely shaped by animate beings. She possesses the art of intensifying the deepest and most tragic passions by reserve and directness of style as she guides one through the maze of human hearts caught in anguished crises, *Marèse* (1935).

Periodicals have been prominent in Belgian letters: 166 were shown in an exposition held in 1930. The champions of the movement of the 1880's were the Parnassian *La Jeune Belgique* (1881–1897), *L'Art Moderne* (1887–1914), whose fiery director, Edmond Picard, sought to unite social reform with a strictly national literature, and *La Wallonie* (1886–1893), guided by A. Mockel in the interests of symbolism. *Le Thyrse,* founded by L. Rosy in 1899, Gauchez's *La Renaissance d'Occident* (1919), and Maurice Quoilin's *Avant-Poste* (1930) have aided valiantly in carrying on the tradition in our day.

Mention of *La Jeune Belgique* leads directly to the poets, for its directors count among the most gifted of Belgian masters of verse. Only a few can be mentioned here, but it is recalled that seventy-eight, beginning with Rodenbach, are discussed and translated in F.-D. Najara's *Un Siglo de Poesia Belgá* (1931). *La Jeune Belgique* championed the doctrine of art for art and perfection of traditional form. Max Waller, whose effort to arouse his countrymen from their literary lethargy won him the nickname, *Son Impertinence le Page Siebel,* died too young to give the full measure of his genius, but Albert Giraud's *Hors du Siècle* (def. ed. 1897) represents the pervading philosophy of the group:

> *Je m'exile à jamais dans ces vers nostalgiques*
> *Et mon cœur n'attend rien des hommes d'aujourd'hui.*
> *La multitude abjecte est par moi détestée,*
> *Pas un cri de ce temps ne franchira mon seuil;*
> *Et pour m'ensevelir loin de la foule athée*
> *Je saurai me construire un monument d'orgueil.*[2]

[2] Forever I withdraw in these nostalgic verses:
My heart expects nothing from men of today.

Giraud remained the most uncompromising champion of Parnassian doctrines. His colleague, Iwan Gilkin, who at first shared his views, evolved into a poet of cosmic inspiration. The magnificent pantheism of Gilkin's dramatic poem *Prométhée* (1899) seems to symbolize his hope of reconciliation among the warring groups of Belgian poets. In these lines Zeus is speaking, after Prometheus is chained to the cliff:

> *Je suis tout ce qui est, qui fut et qui sera,*
> *Et seul par-dessus tout, je suis l'Unité même.*
>
> * * * * *
>
> *Quand l'un se fit plusieurs, il déchira son être*
> *Et l'unité sous mille aspects dut disparaître.*
> *Mais ce n'est là qu'un rêve; et la réalité*
> *Unique, c'est toujours l'éternelle unité.*
> *Le mal n'est que le choc entre mes apparences;*
> *La douleur, l'aiguillon secret de l'existence*
> *Sur le chemin caché qui remonte vers moi.*
>
> * * * * *
>
> *Je t'aime, ô fier Titan, car moi-même je m'aime;*
> *Je suis ton être et ton néant; va, maudis-moi,*
> *Tu me retrouveras un jour au fond de toi.*[3]

Albert Mockel, leader of the Belgian symbolists, has been profoundly influenced by music: "Our soul is like a musical theme developing in a symphony," he writes. He relies on intuition, and his

---

The abject multitude is abhorred by me,
Not a cry of this time shall pass my threshold;
And to enshroud myself far from this atheist crowd
I will build round me a stronghold of pride.

[3] I am everything that is, was and will be
Alone over the world, I am Unity incarnate.

When oneness changed itself into plurality, its being was torn down
And Unity under a thousand aspects was forced to disappear.
But it is only a dream, and the unique reality
Is forever the eternal Unity.
Evil is but the conflict between my appearances;
Sorrow, the secret spur of existence
On the hidden path leading upward towards me.

I love thee, proud Titan, since I love myself;
I am thy being and thy nothingness; go, curse me,
Thou wilt find me again one day in thy inner self.

aerial imagination links him to his friend Charles van Lerberghe.
Both were fascinated by the Pre-Raphaelites:

> Ne m'attends point. Je suis rebelle
> Au cœur que je n'ai pas surpris.
> Ne me nomme pas en tes cris:
> Je ne viens point, quand on
> m'appelle.

> J'apparais, je brille et m'efface.
> Goûte mon amour décevant,
> Mais ne cherche pas: ma trace
> Est pareille à du sable au vent.
> —La Flamme Immortelle (1925)[4]

Some form of pantheism, reached by various means, is a marked
trait of Belgian letters. It appears in Lemonnier, Verhaeren, Maeterlinck, and in Van Lerberghe's *Chanson d'Eve* (1904), "that divine
childhood of the first woman, the eternal legend of the maiden who
wakes from innocence to love, to the intoxication of understanding
and the sadness of knowing" (A. Mockel). Yet the diaphanous Eve
has only slightly infringed the command of the Lord; she is too
much a pantheist to feel any sense of sin, and at the end:

> L'âme chantante d'Eve expire,
> Elle s'éteint dans la clarté;
> Elle retourne en un sourire
> A l'univers qu'elle a chanté.[5]

Maeterlinck and Verhaeren are the only Belgian writers well
known in America, yet they are not isolated figures and some ac-
quaintance with the work of their countrymen contributes to a full
understanding of them. *"Toute la vie est dans l'essor"* (In aspiration is the whole life), sang Verhaeren. The line might stand as
epigraph for the whole effort of modern Belgian literature, but
each author gives his own interpretation. Some seek the ideal
through action, others in contemplation. Maeterlinck is a spiritual
descendant of Pirmez and a close relative of Van Lerberghe, whose

---

[4] Await me not, I am rebel
To the heart not taken by surprise.
Invoke me not in thy clamor:
I come not when called.

I appear, I shine and vanish.
Taste my fleeting love,
But do not seek: my trace
Is like sand in the wind.

[5] Eve's singing soul is expiring,
In the brightness she closes her eyes;
In a smile she returns
To the universe she has hymned.

play *Les Flaireurs* (1889) preceded *L'Intruse* and may well have aided Maeterlinck in shaping his conception of static drama. *"Les Flaireurs* presents the whole retinue of death: agony, terror, destruction," wrote Van Lerberghe. When *L'Intruse* appeared shortly after, charges of plagiarism were raised. Van Lerberghe replied: "What is more natural than that we should have influenced one another? We were born neighbors, were friends from childhood, attended the same school and read the same books until we came of age." Verhaeren's spiritual ancestry includes De Coster, Lemonnier, and Eekhoud. There can be no more question of impugning his originality than that of Maeterlinck; both have played a large part in the symphony of Belgian letters. Verhaeren's line: *Le rêve ancien est mort et le nouveau se forge* (The ancient dream is dead and the new is on the forge) holds for both, but they should be seen in their true perspective.

Verhaeren's cult of paroxysm, the studied aloofness of the Parnassians, and the vague creations of the symbolists may fascinate for a time, but still they leave something unsatisfied within one. Then one turns to Fernand Severin who inherited from Pirmez the love of reverie before the calmer aspects of nature. His cunningly wrought verse hides its art, producing the effect of complete spontaneity:

> *O penseur! La beauté du printemps dans les bois*
> *T'a saisi, ce matin, pour la première fois,*
> *Et malgré toi, l'odeur de la terre t'enivre ...*
>
> *Tes jours se sont passés à méditer en vain*
> *L'énigme que propose à l'homme son destin,*
> *Et ton front studieux a pâli sur maint livre.*
>
> *A quoi bon? Laisse aux dieux leur sublime secret,*
> *Et, pendant que tu vis, savoure sans regret,*
> *Ce qu'il tient de douceur dans ce simple mot: vivre.*[6]
>
> —*La Solitude Heureuse* (def. ed. 1930)

---

[6] O thinker! The glamor of Spring in the woods
This morning, for the first time, has caught thee,
And despite thyself, the aroma of earth intoxicates thee ...

Thy days passed away in vain meditations
On the enigma proposed to man by his destiny,
And many a book has turned pale thy studious face.

To what end? Leave to the Gods their sublime secret,
And while thou livest, savor without regret
All the sweetness enclosed in the simple word: life.

The statement is often made that the Belgian temperament, primarily lyric and descriptive, is unfitted for the theater. It is true that few Belgian authors have devoted their effort exclusively to the stage and that there is no national tradition in this field. But lively interest is proved by the large number of poets and novelists who have composed dramatic compositions, often not intended to see the footlights, and the lack of tradition may foster pioneering. Maeterlinck made one of the most original contributions of the last half-century; more recently Michel De Ghelderode in *Don Juan, drame-farce pour le music-hall* (1928), Fernand Crommelynck in *Le Cocu Magnifique* (1921), Hermann Closson in *Godefroid de Bouillon en 15 jeux de scène* (1935), and *William* (based on the life of Shakespeare), and Max Deauville in *Ecce Homo* (1931), are experimenting audaciously. *Le Mariage de Mlle Beulemans* (1910), in which the clever authors, F. Wicheler and J. F. Fonson, portray the picturesque speech and manners of Brussels, met with international success. Two gifted dramatists who remain closer to tradition in their handling of the theater of ideas are Gustave van Zype in *Les Etapes* (1907) and Marguerite Duterme in *Vae Victis* (1905). It seems certain that the prestige of the Parisian playwrights, who largely preëmpt the Belgian stage, is primarily responsible for the relative underdevelopment of the national theater.

Literary criticism in Belgium is shared with professional scholars, like Professors M. Wilmotte, G. Charlier, and A. Doutrepont, by novelists and poets. The leaders of *La Jeune Belgique* rendered yeoman service in this branch: Francis Nautet, whose *Histoire des Lettres Belges d' Expression Française* (1892) is still of value, belonged to the group; Maeterlinck has written essays which display a profound insight into philosophical problems; H. Krains' *Portraits d'Ecrivains Belges* (1930) presents definitive judgments of six; Mockel, Gauchez, and G. Rency divide their effort between criticism and creative effort. Among the most brilliant of professional critics is L. Dumont-Wilden, well known for his grasp of general ideas. Younger men like J. Culot, L. Sosset, and G. Vanwelkenhuyzen are making their mark. Belgian historiography glories in Henri Pirenne's magisterial *Histoire de Belgique* (1899–1931).

There is every evidence that the seed sown by *La Jeune Belgique* has not fallen on barren ground, yet the question still arises: is there a national literature in Belgium? Perhaps the foregoing notes may bring some evidence for an affirmative answer. The conclusions of the writer are supported by the French historian, Camille Jullian, who wrote: "What makes the originality of a nation is the way it works with the various elements brought to it by races and language. It is its own Prometheus.... And there is not, at the present time, in Europe, a nation which, to the same extent as Belgium, works with both its soul and its soil."

Note on Walloon Literature

BY JAN-ALBERT GORIS

THE WALLOON DIALECT, or language as its revivers proudly call it, is "a language that has known better days." It is a Romance dialect, belonging to the same group as the Picard, the Lorrain, and the Francian, out of which evolved the French language. It was probably spoken by the Franks who settled in Belgium and who, at the time of the Germanic invasions, retired to their woods and caves, thus safeguarding their Romanized tongue. Later on, however, under the constant pressure of Netherlandish and of German, a great number of Germanic elements infiltrated the Walloon language, which is considered by M. Wilmotte as "the most Germanic as to accent and tonality of the northern French dialects."

There are four Walloon dialects, the *liégeois*, the *namurois*, the *chestrolais* (Neufchâteau) and the West-Walloon variety. To this group are related the *hennuyer*, a Picard dialect, and the *gaumais*, which belongs to the orbit of the Lorrain. They are spoken in the provinces of Liége, Namur, Luxemburg, Hainaut, in part of Brabant and Limburg, and they spread also a little over the French border.

This dialect of the *langue d'oïl* became distinct from the Roman language about the twelfth century. For some time, historians and philologists have tried to make a case for an early Walloon literature, which would comprise the oldest written traces of the French language. According to Marius Valkhoff, however, it seems that although traces of Walloon appear in the celebrated *Cantilène d'Eulalie,* in the *Homélie de Jonas,* and in the *Vie de St. Léger,* these writings, which are more interesting from the historical than from the literary standpoint, may not be considered as pure Walloon texts, the Francian and Picard elements being predominant in them. The same criticism applies to the medieval masterpiece *Aucassin et Nicolette* which, definitely Belgian (produced probably in the province of Hainaut where the Picard dialect prevailed), is not a Walloon work.

Walloon literature, however, begins at about the same date and can boast in the twelfth and thirteenth centuries a number of hagiographies and other pious writings of certain merit, the most famous being *Li Ver del Juïse, Le Poème Moral, Li Dialoge Gregoire lo Pape,* a number of sermons, and the *Gloses sur Caton.*

In the fourteenth and fifteenth centuries, Jacques de Hemricourt, Johan des Preis d'Outremeuse, Jehan de Stavelot, and the anonymous author of the *Chronique de Floreffe* used it to write their chronicles of the local rulers. The *Mystère de la Nativité* is a refreshing exception among their rather dusty compilations. To these works should be added a number of writings of Walloon authors who tried to write French, and of Frenchmen who tried to write Walloon, the result in both instances being a mixture of Walloon and the predominant French language.

In the modern period, the Walloon dialects survived partly because of the political isolation of Liége, which was their stronghold. Although combated by the authorities, the language asserted itself. In the seventeenth century, Walloon literature really came into existence. Its first modest manifestations were an *Ode* (1620), a *Sonnet* (1622), and a *Moralité* (1623), which was the first modern Walloon play extant. The seventeenth and eighteenth centuries produced some fifty lyrical pieces of popular flavor and inspiration; most of these pieces express the feelings of the farmers plundered by soldiers, proffer satirical remarks on women's fashions, or concern political or religious events of the day. Their literary value is not very high, but they all have in common a humorous verve which well reflects the philosophy of the Walloon population.

Religious life is reflected by the *Noëls* of the eighteenth century, which were meant to be sung. The *cramignons* are meant to be danced and sung; they are the vocal motive of popular farandoles without great meaning or literary value. Most abundant were the *paskèye,* or pasquilles, which were meant to be read and not sung; they comment on events of the day in a satirical manner. Outstanding in this period is *Les Ewes di Tongue* (The Waters of Tongeren), 1700, by L. de Rickmann, which ridicules an attempt made by the city of Tongeren to attract customers for its spa. This is colorful writing which follows the tradition and the spirit of the *fabliaux* of the Middle Ages.

The Walloon language gained great impetus and popular prestige in the middle of the eighteenth century through a small number of burlesque comedies of real significance: *Li Voyèdje di Tchaufontaine*, 1757; *Li Lîdjwè égadjî*, 1757; *Li Fièsse di Hoûtes'i-ploût*, 1757; and *Lès-Hypocondes*, 1758. A musician of charming facility, Jean Noël Hamal, wrote the music for these burlesque operas. They depict with ironic sympathy the bourgeois milieu of Liége and the Walloon countryside. During the many political changes Belgium underwent in the second half of the eighteenth century and in the first half of the nineteenth, the sense of humor of the Walloon popular authors found abundant inspiration.

The Société Liégeoise de Littérature Wallonne was founded in 1856; it was the expression of a movement parallel to that of the *Félibrige provençal*. The society has been extremely successful; not only did it restore dignity to a language which was looked upon askance by the upper classes and was quarantined by the intelligentsia, but it succeeded so well that at present there is scarcely a town in the Walloon country that has not its weekly paper in dialect, and its Walloon dramatic society.

The nineteenth century produced many lyric poets of value: C. N. Simonon, Joseph Lamaye, F. Bailleux, C. Wasseige, Nicolas Defecheux (author of a delightful blues song *Léyiz-m'plorer*), Emile Gerard, Jean Bury, Joseph Vrinds, and A. Delchef, the author of *Li Galant dil Servante*, 1857, which was a successful farce. The Walloon authors have remained faithful to the caustic vein. The most typical expression of their art still is the drama and the lyric song. The best-known, talented writers of short stories are M. Lejeune, the Abbé Pietkin, H. Bragard, L. Loiseau, G. Willame, and C. Bernus.

Although the material for the study of Walloon philology or literature is comparatively poor (there is no real scientific dictionary available), its defenders and students have proved, according to M. Wilmotte, that "the Walloon language too has a long literary tradition. It is also the vehicle of a remarkable regional literature; like the Provençal, and, perhaps to a higher degree, it is interesting from the linguistic and folklore standpoint." M. Valkhoff feels that "there exists in Walloonia a regional literary movement that, in certain regards, is much more lively than the French Provençal."

The Walloon language has, for a number of years, been encouraged by the Belgian Government so far as its literary expression is concerned. It has not, however, been recognized as a national language, and no attempt has been made in this direction.

CHAPTER XXII

Belgian Music

BY CHARLES LEIRENS

THE GREAT PERIOD of music in the Belgian provinces corresponds to an epoch in which the musical language has little in common with that of the so-called classical era. This musical language of the fifteenth and sixteenth centuries was, in some aspects, much more complicated and even richer than the one familiar today. The musician then sought, above all, to express a religious ideal. He made no effort to please the public, to bring the listeners under his spell. He was offering up to God the homage of a work in which the particular resources of his art were made to yield all that was in them. In classical music—especially the romantic—the composer looks for a means of self-expression, a channel for confession. Some of Beethoven's adagios, for example, certain Chopin nocturnes or Wagnerian preludes, in spite of their intrinsic beauty, virtually are diagrams of the emotions, temperature charts of the composer himself. The contemporary musician speaks *to* the people, the fifteenth-century musician spoke *for* them.

Logically, such an aspiration, such an ideal, required an adequate language. Musical historians have sometimes wondered why the art of sound passed first through a stage purely polyphonic to arrive at a style almost entirely harmonic, compromising meanwhile, for almost a century, on the admirable combination of polyphony and harmony formulated by Johann Sebastian Bach. The phenomenon at least is partially explained by the fact that the purely polyphonic style corresponded more exactly than any other to the aesthetic ideal of the fifteenth and sixteenth centuries in music. It was a form, sometimes incorrectly called "primitive," which was admirably fitted to express the contemplative attitude, and which adapted itself to the quality of immutable sentiments. Its mechanism was established. It offered no temptation to the artist for those sudden shifts which, in the romantic style, often by a single chord mark a change in mood, a revolt, an ecstasy that is purely of this world.

The early period.—The style of the fifteenth and sixteenth centuries—that of a Guillaume Dufay, a Johannes Okeghem, a Josquin des Prés—is ideological, symbolical, not adapted to the expression of the passing or the changing in life, almost incapable of modulation (this last is essentially a harmonic property). It is a style devoid of those tensions which the composer tightens or relaxes as he communicates to his audience the tumult of his passions. The polyphony of an Okeghem or an Adriaan Willaert, elaborated with the same skill as that of Bach, is pure in that it is innocent of all reference to tonal or harmonic functions. The counterpoint of Bach or Handel, on the contrary, achieves its relief and its volume through the harmonic structure which sustains it. One is like a painting executed in flat colors, and the other like a stained-glass window whose design is only visible when lighted from without. More important still is the fact that the music of Belgian fifteenth- and sixteenth-century artists was based on the ancient liturgical modes which have fallen into disuse with the almost tyrannical adoption of the C Major and the corresponding A Minor scale. In the formulation of harmony as a musical language, Johann Sebastian Bach, and the predecessors who laid the foundations of his task, had to work out a simplification which involved the sacrifice of nearly all the scales which had been developed in the Greek system and in the Gregorian plain song. Consequently, music which antedates the seventeenth century gives an impression of strangeness and instability, which certain arrangers of the beginning of that century tried to remedy by adding an organ accompaniment to the Gregorian chants and by "embellishing" the masses of Palestrina or the motets of Orlando de Lassus with instrumental parts! The music of the past is coming back into the light of today. Excellent records have already familiarized the public with the early polyphony of the thirteenth and fourteenth centuries; and the period dominated by the genius of Binchois, Dufay, Okeghem, Jacob Obrecht, Des Prés, and De Lassus will inevitably profit by the great Renaissance movement which is on the way. The genius of these musicians, who are the most outstanding of the Belgian school, did, in fact, dominate for a century and a half the whole of Europe from Belgium to Prussia, Italy, and Spain.

Binchois, born either at Binches or at Mons around 1400, became Choirmaster for Philip of Burgundy at the age of twenty-five. Seven years later he was appointed canon at St. Waudru in Mons, receiving at the same time the benefices of Cassel, Bruges, and Soignies. In 1452 he was permanently installed in the service of the Duke of Burgundy, and died at Lille in 1460. His work is mostly secular, and seldom goes beyond the composition for three voices most popular in his day. He enjoyed a high reputation during his lifetime, but history does not seem to have confirmed the unreserved recognition granted him by the musicians of his own time.

Present-day musicologists attach much greater importance to Binchois' contemporary, Guillaume Dufay (born in Hainaut before 1400, died at Cambrai in 1474), considered, with Binchois, the founder of the first Belgian school. In contrast to Binchois, Dufay was liberal in his acceptance of Italian influences, while remaining true to the Gothic traditions, and the reconciliation of the two trends was largely his accomplishment. This eclecticism explains the special quality of his inspiration, since his work is characterized by a skillful compromise between the rather rigid style of the Gothic constructions and the more polished and elegant manners of the Florentines. From a purely technical viewpoint, Dufay's work is of great importance in the freer use of the canon, which he rejected as a set piece, to employ it as a means of giving unity to a composition. Dufay was a vocalist at the Cathedral of Cambrai and then at the Papal Chapel in 1428; he later became canon at Cambrai and at Mons, posts which he kept until his death. Philip the Good entrusted him with the musical education of his son, Charles.

Jacob Obrecht (Utrecht, *circa* 1430–Ferrara, 1505) and Johannes Okeghem (probably born at Dendermonde [Termonde] early fifteenth century, died around 1495) are of the second polyphonic school of the Belgian Provinces. Although Obrecht, because of his Dutch origin, does not belong exactly within the limits of this study, his name may be included, since his most important activities were centered in Belgium. From 1489 to 1500 he practiced his art at the St. Donat Church in Bruges. To this post he added that of Choirmaster in the Cathedral of Antwerp which, because of his presence, became one of the principal musical centers in Europe. The name of Obrecht is forever linked to one of the greatest forms of religious music, the Motet of the Passion, of which he offered the first example in a work dedicated to the Duke of Ferrara.

The figure of Johannes Okeghem is outstanding for a different reason. His work marks a definite turning point in the evolution of the art of sound. It was Okeghem, and in a lesser measure Obrecht, who discovered a musical rhetoric which, for centuries, was to establish the continuity of musical discourse. Already Dufay had made use of the canon, whose contours he had rendered more flexible in order to fit it into the musical structure. But its resources were limited, and the danger of sterile repetitions lay in the path of the composer at every turn. It was at this point that Okeghem and Obrecht discovered the almost unlimited resources of the principle of "imitation." Henceforth, a given melody or song repeated itself, but not in identical form; the voices built up a series of imitations with liberty and audacity. Subsequently this process was abused by others and by Okeghem himself, in augmentation, diminution, inversion, and reversion. These various artifices were to provide Josquin, Orlando de Lassus, Palestrina, and Vittoria with one of their richest means of expression, and to culminate two centuries and a half later in the superb syntheses of "The Art of the Fugue" and the "Musical Offering" by Bach. But in the general search for unity and coherence, these devices, in spite of their richness, were not enough. In this musical discourse, which streamed into wide horizontal perspectives, a vertical element was indispensable. Harmony, the art of logically and agreeably linking together blocks of simultaneous sound, was about to be born. All that was now required was a composer of genius to exploit this fresh domain and to combine the contrapuntal resources of the former period with a coherent and logical system of simultaneous sounds.

The musician to fulfill this need was Josquin des Prés (*circa* 1445–Condé, 1521). Historians usually place him in French Flanders, most often in Condé. That being true, he does not strictly

belong to the group of composers considered here. But he is unquestionably a member of the same line, and also the most famous
pupil of Okeghem, hence to be noted briefly. His work actually is
too rich and too vast to be given adequate treatment without the
aid of musical examples. His innumerable motets, hymns, psalms,
songs, his masses demonstrate the diversity and abundance of his
inspiration. This word "inspiration," which one scarcely would
be tempted to employ for his predecessors, comes instinctively to
critics writing of his work, for Josquin des Prés is the first musician
in the modern sense of the word.

With Adriaan Willaert (born in Roeselaere [Roulers], probably
in 1480, died in Venice, 1562), the sixteenth century is reached. The
Flemish Willaert is the most famous among the Nordic musicians
of his day who exercised so general an influence throughout Europe
that certain historians of the art describe this influence as "colonization." Paris, Madrid, Florence, Venice, Ferrara, Rome, Vienna,
Munich, and Prague all welcomed Belgian musicians, entrusted
them with the direction of schools, academies, and cathedral classes;
gave assiduous attention to their teachings before taking stock of
their own genius. Nowhere was this influence more profound than
in Venice. When, in 1527, Willaert was appointed Choirmaster at
St. Mark's, after having served the King of Bohemia as Cantor, he
was certainly struck by the elaborateness of the setting, as well as
by the sumptuous impressiveness of a liturgy which the Nordic
countries were never to know. Music was becoming more and more
divorced from the liturgy and from its most perfect ornament, the
four-voiced choir without accompaniment. The two great reigning
forms, the motet and madrigal, were being rapidly transformed.
Polyphony was ceasing to be purely vocal; from then on it accepted
instrumental principles. The madrigal, in particular, was to attack
the problem of expressing all the subtleties and all the bold qualities of secular poetry. Like the sonata form of the nineteenth century, the madrigal was destined to become the vehicle for new
ideas, the chosen medium for all musicians desirous of escaping
from the forms worn thin by time and routine. It is hard to estimate
Willaert's exact part in this process of crystallization and formulation. However, Willaert is without question the foremost madrigal-
ist of his time, and the founder of the Venetian school which was

to reign for a century and a half, with his pupils Zarlino, one of the greatest theorists of the sixteenth century, and Cypriaan de Rore (a Fleming, whose boldness profoundly influenced his contemporaries), Andrea and Giovanni Gabrielli, Donato Croce, and Francesco Cavalli, as its most illustrious representatives.

It has seemed necessary here to emphasize the outstanding role played by Belgian musicians in the rapid transformation of the language of musical sounds, at the risk of somewhat overshadowing the intrinsic value of the works they have left to us. The historical importance of the Nordic composers has been explained sufficiently for the reader to realize that the schools referred to exercised, for almost a century and a half, a veritable supremacy on the European Continent; yet this supremacy never took the form of conquests which swept away the past, stifled national genius, or imposed sterile disciplines. The death of Willaert marks with fair exactitude the moment when the teaching of the masters was to bear fruit, and their influence to be absorbed in the rise of the first national schools.

For Italy the names are Philippe de Monte and Orlando de Lassus (Mons, 1530—Munich, 1594), both of Belgian origin, destined to leave their mark on the final synthesis of the polyphonic style which rose from the movement of Catholic Reform and the counter-reformation. Their glory has been somewhat eclipsed, and wrongly so, by that of their great contemporary, Palestrina. From a purely musical viewpoint, De Monte and De Lassus are perhaps more representative of the spirit of the century than is Palestrina. That spirit was one of innovation, of the search for formulas based on tradition but constantly renewed in the effort to find unused modes of expression and fresh sources of inspiration. Their contribution to the solution of that problem which the genius of Bach was finally to solve—a balancing of the contrapuntal style with harmonic writing—is equalled in importance only by that of a Josquin des Prés. Although the innumerable madrigals of De Monte may, in some ways, be identified with the Italian models in that genre, the writing of the Belgian composer preserves a more polyphonic character, his structure is more closely knit, his craftsmanship more meticulous. In this respect he remains Nordic, more so than his contemporary, De Lassus.

The work of Philippe de Monte, though of considerable extent

(35 masses, more than 1,000 madrigals, more than 300 motets are known), was neglected for three centuries. This injustice occurred, partially at least, because an inventory of his work demanded laborious research, and musicologists hesitated before the task. But in 1927, through the influence of Canon Van Nuffel, Director of the Choir School at St. Rombaut in Mechlin, and to a maecenas from Antwerp, Henri Fester, the Queen Elizabeth Foundation and the Belgian University Foundation granted the necessary funds for the publication of his entire work.

History has been more generous, and more just with Orlando de Lassus. De Lassus and Palestrina are, without question, the two greatest composers of their century. De Lassus' "Magnum Opus," published in 1604 after his death, bears witness to a production as vast as it was eclectic: it includes no less than 500 motets for two, three, four, five, six, seven, eight, nine, ten, and twelve voices. His "Seven Penitential Psalms," composed between 1563 and 1570, at the request of Duke Albert, are sufficient to place the Mons musician among the most eminent masters of religious music, and it is no exaggeration to say that rarely in the course of the ages has so grandiose and austere a theme been transposed into the language of music with such imposing breadth of style.

At the dawn of the eighteenth century the flowering of talent blossomed first in Italy, then in Germany. Belgium had other musicians in the periods to follow, but these artists were solitary figures. But it must not be forgotten that, with the exception of France, whose presence on the musical stage is almost uninterrupted from the thirteenth century down to the present, few countries have exercised such a decisive and prolonged influence on the destiny of art.

The modern period.—The great variety of material to be treated from now on will not permit of the chronological system adopted in the previous pages. The personalities to be dealt with exercised their activities in fields that were scarcely heard of during the preceding periods. Along with composers, there were eminent virtuosos, historians, musicologists, and pedagogues. Certain among them have accomplished their missions in the service of institutions whose existence is so closely associated with the activity of Belgium that an explanation should be made of the influence of these institutions and the determining role which they have played in the development of artists and the education of the public. This statement applies particularly to the nineteenth century, for the preceding century is dominated by two great figures who, in themselves, represent Belgium's great contribution to the "Concert of Europe."

François-Joseph Gossec (Vergnies, 1734—Passy, 1829) and André-Ernest Grétry (Liége, 1741—Montmorency, 1813) were composers in two very different fields.

Gossec above all is a "symphonist"; Grétry a man of the theater. The work of the former is mainly historical in its importance, whereas the latter had qualities whose charm persists for the listener of today. The official career of Gossec began in 1751, when he entered the service of the Farmer-General, La Pouplinière. Curiously enough, the composer who was to have such an important role in the revolutionary scene owed his first success to the patronage of personalities of outstanding importance in the *ancien régime*. At the death of the Farmer-General, who had engaged Gossec on the recommendation of Rameau, he moved to the House of the Prince of Conti and the Prince of Condé. Not only did he have sufficient leisure to allow free rein to his inspiration, but he was provided with that much rarer resource for the composer—a ready means of performance for everything he wrote. It was for the musicians of the Farmer-General that he wrote his quartets and symphonies, the first of which (1754) preceded by five years the first symphony of Haydn. In his position as comptroller for the Prince of Condé he enjoyed an enormous prestige which he used to good purpose in extending his field of activity. His "Mass for the Dead" (1760) created a sensation, through a procedure which doubtless stems from Willaert and the Venetian school. He wrote the "Tuba Mirum" for two orchestras—one of wind instruments placed outside the church, and a corresponding string orchestra set up in the choir. The success of this staging was such that the composer used it again in his "Oratorio of the Nativity," in which a choir of "invisible" angels produced an effect of distance which may have been the model Wagner had in mind for certain scenes of *Parsifal*. Posterity has not ratified the judgment of his contemporaries with regard to Gossec, but it is undeniable that his influence on the development of instrumental music in France was enormous. During the period of the Revolution, the composer followed the example of his colleagues Lesueur, Méhul, and Cherubini, in transferring with facility to the service of new masters. He contributed largely to the festivals and ceremonies of the new cult in a series of grandiloquent works in the spirit of the time, like his "Fourteenth of July Hymn," "Tribute to Liberty," "Hymn to the Supreme Being," "Music for the Funeral of Mirabeau" (in which there is a striking effect achieved with gongs). "When one thinks," writes Landormy, "of the pomp and circumstance of those ceremonies, where military symphonies were played in the public square by huge orchestras, where patriotic hymns were chanted by thousands of choristers and repeated by all the gathered multitude, one cannot help thinking that Berlioz, the pupil of Lesueur, and the composer of 'La Symphonie Funèbre et Triomphale' and the 'Requiem' for five orchestras, inherits directly from those musicians of the revolutionary period."

In contrast to this composer of highly colored grandstand effects, the personification of delicacy, poise, measure, and discretion was André-Ernest Grétry. Grétry is much more representative of an epoch—the close of the eighteenth century—than he is of either his native country or his adopted ones, France and Italy. Mozart and Beethoven borrowed themes from him. The Théâtre Favart and the Académie de Musique (which became the Opéra Comique and the Opera of Paris) ordered pieces from him. Then came official recognition: Napoleon granted him a pension; the Institute, in its year of foundation, conferred upon him one of the three chairs designated in the by-laws for composers. This was a distinction which he shared with his colleague, Gossec.

He composed tirelessly, writing 50 operas, 6 symphonies, quartets, sonatas. And above that groundwork there are numerous pieces of a light and graceful charm, like the "Tableau Parlant," "Céphale et Procris" (the ballet of this piece, in a version by Felix Mottl, still figures on the program of all concert societies), "Richard Cœur de Lion," in which his muse successfully deals with a subject of greater scope. From the point of view of pure aesthetics, he took his stand once and for all: he belongs with the Encyclopedists; he was part of all the fads of his period, and it is hard to tell which he fell in with, and which he started himself. For him, music in dramatic form was more important than in any other form. He extolled the "back to nature" theory, which, for the theater meant a declamation following as closely as possible the inflection of the speaking voice.

Before any consideration of the nineteenth century and of contemporary musicians, at least a passing glance must be given to three great virtuosos of the bow.

Charles August de Bériot (Louvain, 1802–1870), and Henri Vieuxtemps (Verviers, 1820–Mustapha-lez-Algers, 1881), both exercised an influence at once profound and lasting on the technique of their instruments. Both belonged to that group of virtuosos who, like Paganini, Thalberg, Joachim, Rubenstein, and Liszt, toured the world (Vieuxtemps even made three tours in the United States), arousing enthusiasm everywhere, and, more important still, inspiring a vogue of virtuosity which eventually was of great benefit to music itself. Bériot, whose career was cut short by blindness, visited England, France, and Italy, in the company of his wife, the famous singer, La Malibran. Appointed professor at the Brussels Conservatory, Bériot continued his musical apostleship over a period of nine years. He shares, with his colleague, Vieuxtemps, the glory of having founded that Franco-Belgian school of the violin of which Eugène Ysaye, at the close of the century, was the most illustrious representative.

Of more robust constitution, his pupil, Vieuxtemps, was able to give a more complete accounting of his ability. He was widely associated with the most eminent personalities of his epoch—Paganini, Schumann (who wrote enthusiastically about him), Richard Wagner, Czerny, Spohr, Thalberg (with whom he made his second tour in America), the great cellist, Servais (1807–1866), a Belgian like himself, who accompanied him on his second tour of Russia. He was one of the greatest violinists of modern times. His compositions are perhaps the best evidence of his prodigious technique. In spite of a certain turgidity and a constant striving after effects, they display a virtuosity which is transcendent, and are high above the general level of virtuoso compositions. A number of them still figure in the repertoire of the most noted violinists. Vieuxtemps contributed largely to the reputation of the Royal Conservatory of Brussels, where he headed the violin classes from 1871 to 1873.

The name of Eugène Ysaye (Liége, 1858—Brussels, 1931), is so closely associated with the contemporary musical movement, and there are still so many to bear witness to his extraordinary career, that long commentaries could add nothing to his prestige. He possessed one of those rare personalities which stirs the heart of each listener. He toured extensively in Germany, Russia, England, and America, appearing as soloist, conductor, and as member of a quartet. In 1918, he was appointed Director of the Cincinnati Orchestra.

From a more strictly Belgian point of view, it is important to remember the profound influence Ysaye exercised for twelve years (from 1886 to 1898) as professor at the Royal Conservatory of Brussels, as well as the distinguished services he rendered the cause of modern music by the foundation of the Société des Concerts Ysaye (1898). The "revolutionary" programs given at these concerts introduced the public to the notable works of Franck, Lekeu, Vincent d'Indy, Chausson, Dukas, Debussy, and Fauré.

The two dominant figures of the nineteenth century are, without question, César Franck (Liége, 1822—Paris, 1890), and Guillaume Lekeu (Heusy, 1870—Angers, 1894), whose creative activity was interrupted in its prime by his premature death. Everything, perhaps even too much, has been said concerning the work of Franck. The exaggerated enthusiasm of certain disciples has tended to weaken rather than strengthen his fame. They have made the mistake, in analyzing his work, of putting too much emphasis on the systematic character of his technique. Franck was a born composer, and history will remember him more because of the spontaneity and abundance of his inspiration than because of certain aesthetic theories which tended to overweigh his work. In spite of a rather poor orchestral craftsmanship, the "D-Minor Symphony," "The Accursed Huntsman" (notwithstanding certain overly Wagnerian echoes), the "Symphonic Variations," "Psyche," and the "Béatitudes" (in part), remain masterworks whose glory neither time nor fashion can dim. And yet, it is not here that Franck is at his best. His "String Quartet," his "Quintet with Piano," the "Choral Prelude and Fugue," "Prelude," "Aria and Finale," the "Sonata for Violin and Piano" (which certain exegetes of the works of Proust identify as the sonata of Vinteuil), all reveal other enduring qualities. Here all is to be admired—almost without reservation; the solidity of the construction, too greatly stressed perhaps in the symphony and the quartet, the refinement of the harmonic language, a polyphony more natural than elaborate (the canon in the finale of the sonata is remarkable in this respect), a firm melodic structure, such are the most characteristic qualities of these works. But Franck was an organist above all, and it was when seated at the organ keyboard that he really felt at ease. The three "Chorales"— his last work—are equalled only in organ literature by the works of Bach. This opinion, which may seem hyperbolic, was held by Liszt.

Guillaume Lekeu, who died at the age of twenty-four, left only four works, but the originality of these compositions and their depth of inspiration is such as to assure for all time the fame of their composer. They are the "Sonata for Violin and Piano," the "Quartet with Piano," the "Fantasy on Two Angevin Folk Tunes," and the "Adagio for Strings," which undoubtedly is his masterpiece. The dominant note in these compositions is a sort of nostalgia, a fierce despair. A presentiment of early death perhaps explains this special atmosphere, so marked that three measures chosen at random in these celebrated works will serve at once to identify their author.

The influence exercised by Franck and Lekeu upon their successors has been overwhelming. In some instances the influence was indirect. Men like Joseph Jongen (Liége, 1873), Victor Vreuls (Verviers, 1876), Théo Ysaye, brother of the famous violinist (Verviers, 1875–Nice 1918), either consciously or unconsciously follow the lead of Franck's great disciple, the French composer, Vincent d'Indy.

Nevertheless, Joseph Jongen composed some music of very real merit; his pieces are skillfully written and the best of them are related to Walloon folklore: the "Fantasy on Two Noels," the "Trio for Piano, Violin, and Viola," the second "Quartet," the "Impressions of Ardennes," the "Symphony with Organ" show an irreproachable craftsmanship and a freshness of inspiration which should assure their permanence. Jongen is clearly the most artistic representative of the Franco-Walloon school.

Something more virile and resolute breathes through the work of Vreuls, composer of an opera *Olivier le Simple* (libretto by Jules

Delacre), which has not, perhaps, been sufficiently appreciated by either public or critics. He also composed a "Sonata for Violin and Piano," but his youthful promise has not been completely fulfilled in later works.

A group of Flemish composers, the great Pieter Benoit (Harlebeke, 1834—Antwerp, 1901), Jan Blockx (Antwerp, 1851–1912), and August de Boeck, participated, perhaps unconsciously, in the movement of regionalism which has had great manifestations in Norway, with Grieg, and in Russia, with the "Five." Also important were Adolphe Samuel (Liége, 1824—Ghent, 1898), Edgard Tinel (Sinay, 1854—Brussels, 1912), and Paul Gilson (Brussels, 1865–).

The generation of contemporaries shows perhaps greater originality than this early group, but by its very eclecticism forms less of a national school. Musicians like Jean Absil, Fernand Quinet, Chevreuil, De Bourguignon, Paul de Maleingrau, Marcel Poot, Shoemaker, René Bernier, and André Souris are worthy contributors to a movement of which men like Bartok, Stravinsky, and Hindemith are the most eminent representatives; these musicians are not so much innovators as adapters of their own inspiration to the new language invented by their great predecessors. The two most interesting personalities of the group are unquestionably Jean Absil and Fernand Quinet. Absil (Peruwelz, 1893) excels particularly in chamber music; his second quartet and his trio especially, are of the first rank. But he is such a sure craftsman that no type of writing is outside his range of possibility. His choral work is done with spontaneity and skill; his orchestral compositions have body and boldness of effect; his piano concerto, which won the prize at the contest organized by the Queen Elizabeth Foundation in 1938, held the attention of the jury and the public in spite of twenty successive performances—a test which few works could successfully withstand. Robust in its inspiration, sometimes rhapsodical in character, Absil's work is of definite originality, and if certain harsh qualities, certain jarring rhythms may be derived from Bartok, this influence is sufficiently assimilated to offer no violation to the unity of style or to the fundamental adjustment between the inspiration and the means of expression employed.

The musical output of Fernand Quinet (Charleroi, 1898) is unfortunately very small, the artist's career having been interrupted

by a long and serious illness. His special gift is in short compositions of "tabloid" form in which humor and sarcasm mingle with
brief effusions interrupted by an abrupt reticence. It is a music full
of allusions, in which everything is measured, calculated, gauged
to produce exactly the effect desired.

The work of André Souris (Marchienne, 1890) belongs to the
same aesthetic order, but in his case the humor is more direct, the
allusion less veiled. Souris, however, seems to be the victim of an
exaggerated self-criticism. When he no longer fears to express himself freely he will produce works worthy of his true personality.

There is not enough space to dwell upon the qualities of verve
that mark the music of Marcel Poot, the craftsmanship of that excellent "symphonist," Chevreuil, the mysticism of Maleingrau, the
shy charm of Bernier, the truculence of Shoemaker, the picturesque-
ness of Bourguignon. All these musicians, who have not yet said
their last word, are characterized by a profound faith, an absolute
disinterestedness, and an artistic honesty which approaches the
overscrupulous.

Parallel to the manifestations of the national genius in the realm
of pure creation, a group of savants were exploring the past, opening new perspectives in musicology. François Joseph Fétis (Mons,
1784–Brussels, 1871), François Auguste Gevaert (Huysse, 1828–
Brussels, 1908), and Charles van den Borren (Ixelles, 1874–), are
merely the heads of a long line including (to cite only the principal names), Van der Straeten (1826–1895), whose chief work is: *La
Musique aux Pays-Bas;* de Burbure (1812–1889); Van Maldeghem
(1810–1893), author of the *Trésor Musical*, 29 volumes of sixteenth-
century vocal works; Van Doorslaer, *La Vie et les Œuvres de
Philippe de Monte;* Paul Bergmans, *La Typographie Musicale en
Belgique au XVI siècle;* Ernest Closson, *Grétry* and *Chansons Populaires des Provinces Belges.*

The importance of the great musical organizations so vital in
Belgian cultural life should not be neglected here. In Brussels four
share in a fairly logical distribution of the musical material.

The Concerts Populaires de Musique Classique, founded in 1865
by Adolphe Samuel, have played an outstanding role over a period
of sixty years. Directed first by their founder, and thereafter by
Vieuxtemps, Joseph Dupont, Sylvain Dupuis, Edouard Brahy, and

Franz Ruhlman, the Concerts Populaires initiated the general public of Brussels into the whole classical repertoire. The Populaires merged in 1930 with the Société Philharmonique, which had been founded by Henri Le Bœuf. From this time on, modern and contemporary composers have occupied a large place on the programs: the masterpieces of Stravinsky, Honneger, Darius Milhaud, Prokofieff, and Markevitch are performed, sometimes in first audition, in conditions of unrivaled perfection.

The Société des Concerts du Conservatoire, directed by Desiré Defauw naturally reflect the personal preferences of their director. They specialize in the rendition of the classical, romantic, and impressionist compositions, and have played a capital role in familiarizing the public with the great works of Franck, Lekeu, Fauré, d'Indy, Debussy, Ravel, and Florent Schmitt.

The Maison d'Art was founded in 1930 by the author of this chapter. Its field is strictly limited to chamber music (from the sonata to works for small orchestra). Its programs are designed to be eclectic and to initiate the public into a knowledge of the least known works in the preclassical, classical, and contemporary repertoires. Each performance offers music lovers first hearings of certain compositions, and the repertoire ranges from Pérotin, Léonin, the composers of the French Renaissance, through such composers as Gabrielli, Teleman, Dowland, and Purcell to moderns like Hindemith, Stravinsky, Bartok, Alban Berg, and Schoenberg.

The Orchestre de la Chapelle de la Reine Elisabeth, recently formed, emanates from the Foundation through the personal initiative of the Queen. It has attained a rare perfection, due, at least in part, to its coöperative organization. The Foundation itself, it is felt, is destined to play an important role in the artistic progress of the country. Not content with offering scholarships for foreign study, the Foundation houses annually, in a pavilion constructed on the border of the forest of Soignies, eight students in residence whose general and musical education is rounded out according to a broad and wisely conceived course of study.

All these concerts are given in the concert hall of the Royal Conservatory or in the great auditorium (seating 2,200) of the Palais des Beaux-Arts, a building (construction finished in 1929) which has transformed the artistic life of the capital. All artistic activity since has been centered here. With its forty exhibition rooms, its vast sculpture hall, its two concert chambers, its movie auditorium, the Palais des Beaux-Arts lends itself to artistic displays of a highly varied nature. The organization remains its own free agent, in spite of a theoretical control exercised by the State. The plan which enabled the founders, the late Henri Le Bœuf and Mayor Adolphe Max, to realize their bold schemes is extremely ingenious and might well serve as an example abroad. The funds necessary for the erection of the building were subscribed by the great financial organizations of the country. The interest and the amortization of the capital, as well as the operating expenses, were the responsibility of the organization, but they were "guaranteed" by the State, which was to intervene, however, only if the organization found itself unable to meet its obligations. Following the amortization of the debt, the building belonged entirely and without question to the organization.

It would be unjust to omit here the work accomplished at Antwerp and Mechlin, respectively, by Lode de Vocht and Canon van Nuffel, the first as the head of the choral society, La Caecilia, which he founded, and the latter as Choirmaster of the Collegiate Church of St. Rombaut. The Caecilia society has specialized in the execution of great contemporary compositions and has frequently been invited to other countries to take part in the performance of works of Stravinsky, Milhaud, and Honneger. Van Nuffel has devoted his life to the revival of polyphonic works of the fifteenth and sixteenth centuries, and, under the imposing arches of one of Belgium's finest churches, he gives regular performances, at once meticulous and impassioned, of the masses and motets of Philippe de Monte, Obrecht, and Okeghem.

Among the numerous groups devoted to chamber music, mention may be made only of the Quatuor pro Arte, so closely connected with the name of Mrs. Elizabeth Sprague Coolidge and the Library of Congress as to be well known to American readers; and the Trio de la Cour de Belgique, founded by one of Belgium's most eminent musicians, the pianist Emile Bosquet (violin, Alfred Dubois; cello, Maurice Dambois). These ensembles, together with a number of eminent virtuosos such as the pianists, Jean du Chastain, Marcel Maes, and Gazelle; the singers, Maurice Wynants, Frédéric Anspach, and Maurice de Groote; the violinists, Wagemans, Chaumont, and Raskin; the cellists, Pitch and Soiron; the harpsichordist, Aimée van de Wiele, pupil of Landowska, have contributed largely to the maintenance of the foreign renown which Belgium enjoys in the field of instrumental technique.

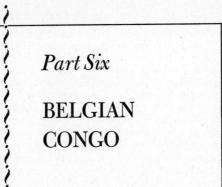

Part Six

BELGIAN CONGO

CHAPTER XXIII

Geography

BY JAMES P. CHAPIN

THOUGH BELGIUM is one of the smaller countries of western Europe, the colony with which it was endowed by King Leopold II bulks large on the map of Africa, for it covers about 902,000 square miles in the well-watered equatorial region and extends from the west coast two-thirds of the distance across the Continent. To it are attached on the east the mandated territories of Ruanda-Urundi, occupying 20,535 square miles, so that the area administered by Belgium in Africa is more than 78 times larger than the homeland.

This vast, rich colony which lies mainly in the basin of the Congo River, second stream of the entire world when measured by the volume of water it carries, covers nearly two-thirds of the area of the entire basin. Africa differs from the other continents in having the form of a great plateau, the top of which is occupied by about ten large interior depressions, most of them drained by an important river except when the rainfall is so deficient that this river cannot reach the sea. Lying as it does directly across the equator, the Congo Basin is one of the most favored parts of the African Continent. The Belgian Colony includes most of the central, eastern, and southern sections, and extends beyond the basin only on the west, in the Mayombe district, and in the northeast, near Lake Albert and Lake Edward. The territories of Ruanda-Urundi are largely drained by rivers that are headwaters of the Nile. Other European nations which administer lesser sections of the Congo Basin are France, on the northwest, Portugal, on the south, and Great Britain, to the southeast.

The boundaries of the basin, for the most part, are not high chains of mountains, but rolling country rising gradually to levels of 3,000 to 5,000 feet, there to form the divides separating the Congo River system from the basins of the Ogowé, Shari, Nile, Zambesi, and Cuanza. The lowest divide is that which separates the greater part of the Congo Basin from the Atlantic coastal plain. Through this divide the mighty Congo makes its way in a series of cataracts and falls between Stanley Pool and Matadi, descending some 900 feet in about 250 miles. This area is hilly country, long known as the Crystal Mountains, because of white blocks of quartz scattered here and there; but its highest elevations are around only 3,000 feet. For nearly four centuries the combination of rough, sparsely populated country, with a river that forbade navigation, prevented Europeans from gaining access to the vast central basin.

The northern boundary of the Congo Basin, lying from 5 to 8 degrees north of the equator, is somewhat higher, though its general level is scarcely over 3,000 feet; and the southern margin, between the Benguela province of Angola and the Upper Katanga, 11 to 13 degrees south of the equator, is a plateau region of 4,000 to 5,000 feet, with few higher peaks rising from it.

On the east, however, conditions are different; and here the edges of the basin in many places rise to really high plateaus and chains of mountains. Relatively recent movements and fractures of the earth's crust have brought this about.

The eastern half of tropical Africa is traversed from north to south by two rift valleys. These mark long lines where the crust rose, then broke, and subsided for thousands of feet in the middle, leaving elevated scarps, in most instances, on both sides of the long depression. The Great Rift Valley, the more easterly, runs from Palestine and the Red Sea through Ethiopia and Kenya Colony south to central Tanganyika territory. The more westerly one, the Albertine Rift, is shorter, but extends from the upper Nile, near Wadelai, for 860 miles to the southern extremity of Lake Tanganyika. Farther south there is again a single rift, enclosing Lake Nyasa and the valley of the Shiré River.

Along the Albertine Rift are the most striking of all the highlands associated with the Congo Basin. Each principal depression contains a lake, and each lake has some exceptionally high land on its western side. Thus Lake Albert has the Lendu Plateau, bor-

dered by a chain of peaks reaching to more than 7,000 feet. Lake
Edward has a still higher region, culminating in Mount Tshabi-
rimu, 10,214 feet. The highland west of Lake Kivu culminates in
a peak of 9,840 feet; and Lake Tanganyika, on its northwest and

BELGIAN CONGO

southwest sides, is bordered by notable elevations. The escarpments
on the eastern side of the Albertine Rift are often not so prominent. But the Ruwenzori Range, rising in a slight fork north of
Lake Edward, is the greatest of all, reaching 16,794 feet. Its western
slopes lie largely within the boundaries of the Belgian Congo,
although its waters all drain into the Nile River system. About a
hundred miles farther south, a great group of eight volcanoes rises
from the floor of the rift just north of Lake Kivu. The tallest of

them is Karisimbi, 14,783 feet high, which marks the boundary between the Congo and Ruanda.

Lake Albert and Lake Edward, with Congo territory on their western shores, drain into the Nile; but the chain of volcanoes diverts the water of Lake Kivu to the southward into Lake Tanganyika, and there the overflow is carried by the Lukuga River into the Lualaba, the upper section of the mighty Congo. Thus the highlands along the northern part of the Albertine Rift separate it from the Congo Basin; but south of the Kivu volcanoes the rift becomes an extension of the basin, drawing water from a part of Ruanda-Urundi and considerable areas of Tanganyika Territory. Lake Bangweulu, too, is mainly filled by water from the northeastern corner of Northern Rhodesia.

Although the rift valleys are of relatively recent development, and their very beginning may not date back forty million years, the Congo Basin is plainly an ancient feature of a continent that has long resisted any serious encroachment of the oceans. In late Triassic times, perhaps one hundred and sixty to one hundred and eighty million years ago, it was well developed and filled with a great brackish lake or inland sea, in which were deposited the beds of soft sandstones now forming the floor of all its central part, and extending far into the French Congo and Angola. All around them is a raised rim of older, harder rocks. On both the eastern and western sides, there are Permo-Carboniferous beds of the Kundelungu System and still older Paleozoic rocks, partially metamorphic. Beyond these come the crystalline rocks, including granites, which represent the old foundations of the Continent. They form most of the divides separating the Congo from the other important basins, and show also at the inner edge of the Atlantic coastal plain, where other rocks reveal submergence during the late Mesozoic and early Tertiary periods.

Just where the basin found its outlet during its early ages would be difficult to say. It probably did not remain flooded after the Jurassic, and its rocks are lamentably poor in fossils. But during the Pleistocene, it was again dammed, and eventually the waters found their way out by the present channel. The narrow gorge it occupies between Stanley Pool and Matadi is an indication that the river has not been long at work carving it down. In the central parts of the basin, Lake Leopold II, Lake Tumba, and the marshes of the Ngiri River are the last remnants of this latest flooding, to which extensive alluvial deposits also bear witness.

Along the encircling watersheds, the older, harder rocks often rise above the general level as hills and mountains. In these regions there has been considerable folding and metamorphosis of the rocks, which now enclose exceptionally valuable mineral deposits of copper, tin, and other metallic ores, injected through fissures from below. The alluvial gold in the stream beds of the northeastern Congo can be traced back to quartz veins and perhaps other rocks in the mountains near the Albertine Rift. The diamonds of the Kasai, now contained in alluvial formations, are believed to have been formed in diabase at a higher level in Angola. The volcanic pipes known from the Katanga have revealed few diamonds.

Volcanic activity in the Albertine Rift has been decidedly local. Just north of Lake Kivu, it built up eight great cones and many more small ones, so that nearly the entire width of the Rift is there occupied by lava fields. Elsewhere there are small areas of volcanic rock only near the eastern base of the Ruwenzori Range. The raising of Ruwenzori itself was the result of a great folding or upthrust, and the rocks one sees on its slopes are mainly mica schist, gabbro, and gneiss, with granite and other crystalline rocks protruding above 12,000 feet to form the higher snow-crowned summits.

The Ruwenzori Range has six distinct mountains exceeding 15,000 feet, all snow-clad, and each named for a geographer or explorer: Emin, Gessi, Speke, Stanley, Baker, and Louis of Savoy. Mt. Stanley is the highest, reaching 16,794 feet at the summit of Margherita, one of its twin peaks. A number of glaciers extend down its slopes to about 14,500 feet.

The principal volcanoes of the Kivu are eight in number, forming three groups. The central group, with Visoke, Mikeno, and Karisimbi, is highest, reaching 14,783 feet. The eastern group consists of Muhavura, Gahinga, and Sabinyo, all relatively old and eroded. The western group contains only Nyiragongo and Nyamulagira, both young enough to have retained their craters. Nyamulagira is still active, its lava glows in the crater, and from its southern slope there was an outbreak of lava in 1938 that flowed down to the shore of Lake Kivu.

The soils of the volcanic area in the Kivu are naturally very fertile. Elsewhere in the Congo the value of the ground for agriculture varies greatly. The nature of the soil is determined by the climate and vegetation of the region as well as by the kind of rocks beneath it. In districts with heavy rains throughout a large part of the year deep red soils, lateritic loams, are conspicuously widespread. In some central areas, however, the soil is sandier, because of the soft sandstones beneath. Districts with a prolonged dry season and torrential rains during a few months have, in general, poor soil, except in broad river bottoms where humus and moisture can be retained. Elsewhere there is usually a conspicuous lack of visible humus, perhaps because of the activity of termites. The burning of the grass by natives in savanna areas during each dry season is an old custom, not likely to improve the soil.

An equatorial country, like the Congo, is certain to receive an abundance of rain, indispensable for many kinds of tropical agriculture. Because of its extended area and its rather level floor, the Congo Basin holds many great rivers which gradually merge before finding their outlet to the sea. The main stream is always regarded as that of the Congo-Lualaba, and its names are many among the natives living on its banks.

The Lualaba, as it was called by natives in the Lower Katanga, rises on the border of Northern Rhodesia, in latitude 11° 50′ south, flows northward through the great marshy areas around Lake Upemba and Lake Kisale, and then on over rapids and low falls above Stanleyville, half a degree north of the equator. There its official name becomes the Congo, though the natives along its middle course speak of it as Ebalé, and those near its mouth call it Nzari. Europeans thus knew the river first as the Zaire, and later borrowed the name Congo from that of a tribe, the Bakongo, living near by.

After leaving Stanley Falls, the Congo turns westward and southwestward in a great arc, recrossing the equator close to Coquilhatville, and finally reaches the Atlantic Ocean at 6° south latitude. The total length of the Congo-Lualaba is about 2,200 miles. This figure, however, does not represent the greatest extent of the system, and indicates nothing as to the many great tributaries received from all sides. As seen by the air traveler near Lisala, the Congo

River is awe-inspiring, several miles wide, and dotted with heavily forested islands. A little lower down, where it contains the large islands of Ukaturakea and Sumba, it is almost 9 miles across, though still 800 miles from its mouth.

On the easterly side of Lake Tanganyika is found the Malagarazi River draining water from near the center of Tanganyika territory, within 350 miles of the Indian Ocean, and carrying it into the Congo system. In northeast Rhodesia, the Chambezi flows southwestward into marshy Lake Bangweulu, which empties into the winding Luapula. This in turn enters Lake Mweru, and its water finds its way by the Luvua into the Lualaba. One may say that the extreme length of the Congo, including its most distant headwaters, is somewhat over 2,650 miles, without counting any minor meanderings.

It need scarcely be said that no part of the Congo has anything resembling a desert climate. The average annual rainfall over the whole colony is around 50 inches. Districts farthest from the equator have a pronounced dry season, sometimes of five months, when rivers are low and many lesser streams quite dry. Then come abundant rains to flood them once more. In the equatorial belt the drier periods are of little consequence.

The principal affluents from the right-hand side to the Congo-Lualaba are the Luapula-Luvua, the Lukuga, Lowa, Lindi, Aruwimi, Itimbiri, Mongala, Ubangi, and Sanga. From the left-hand side the Congo receives the Lovoi, Lomami, Lulonga, and Kwa, not to mention a host of lesser tributaries. The Kwa itself is formed by the union of the Fimi with the Kasai, and the latter drains a great southern area with the aid of the Lulua, Sankuru, Kwilu, and Kwango. There are two large lakes in the central Congo depression; Lake Tumba empties directly into the Congo at Irebu, and Lake Leopold II joins with the Lukenye River to form the Fimi.

The Kasai system lies to the south of the equator, and is therefore in flood during the months of March and April. The Ubangi system, with its headwaters in the Mbomu and Uelé, lies north of the equator, and is in full flood toward October and November. Moreover, a good part of the upper Congo River itself is north of the equator, the Lualaba to the south of it, so it can readily be seen how water supplies from the north and the south tend to balance each other and keep the main stream of the Congo open for navigation. Its middle course has two periods of high water, from April to June and from October to December. At the two intervening periods of low water, around February and August, many sandbars emerge, but navigation by large stern-wheel steamers is never interrupted.

Although the Congo, unlike the Amazon, can accommodate ocean steamers for only 90 miles of its lower course, up to Matadi, it has a vast network of navigable rivers in its upper basin. The focus of the system, at Léopoldville, now the capital of the colony, is a very modern town on the southwest shore of Stanley Pool, an expansion of the river just before it plunges into the cataracts. A well-run railway now brings passengers and goods from the port of Matadi in a single day, over the hilly region where the pioneers toiled on foot or sweltered in a machilla for eighteen days.

From Léopoldville, comfortable steamers sail on regular schedules for Stanleyville, 994 miles upstream, and for Port Francqui on the Kasai, 450 miles away. From Brazzaville others leave for Bangui on the Ubangi River. These are the main routes. By changing at appropriate points to smaller steamers, one can travel up many of the tributaries, and by using railways that alternate with navigable stretches of the Lualaba, one may continue on from Stanleyville to Bukama, the gateway of the Katanga. Another route to the same region is the railway from Port Francqui.

Steamers ply also on many of the larger lakes. Civilian air travel was well developed in the Congo long before the present war, and from Léopoldville one can fly to all the other important centers. A great network of automobile roads covers all but the central portion of the basin where rivers are so numerous. The Katanga is also connected by rail with Lobito Bay on the coast of Angola, with Beira in Portuguese East Africa, and with Cape Town.

From Kongolo and Kabalo on the Lualaba there is a railway to Lake Tanganyika, where steamers connect with another railway to Dar-es-Salaam on the Indian Ocean. Lesser rail lines lead from the Itimbiri River to the Uelé, and from Boma on the lower Congo into the Mayombe district.

All this reflects the great activity in the Belgian Congo, where the total white population is only about 30,000. There are many more Africans than that in the single city of Léopoldville, and the total native population of the Belgian Congo numbers around 10,000,000, with another 3,750,000 in Ruanda-Urundi. There is not space here to mention more than a few of the important towns in the Congo. Each of the six provinces is now named for its administrative center. Léopoldville is the capital of the colony, and in its province are Boma, the former capital, and Matadi, the head of ocean navigation. Coquilhatville on the Congo, 380 miles above Stanley Pool, is the center for the western forest area. Lusambo, near the head of navigation on the Sankuru River, is the headquarters of the Kasai region. Stanleyville, terminus for steamers on the upper Congo, is the gateway to the whole northeastern area. Costermansville, at the south end of Lake Kivu, is the beautiful, healthful center for the eastern highlands. The metropolis of the important mining area of the Katanga is Elisabethville. Ruanda-Urundi is governed at present from Usumbura at the north end of Lake Tanganyika.

Despite the equatorial situation of the Congo, it must not be concluded that its climate is in the main oppressive or unhealthful. The greater part of the colony is more than 1,000 feet above sea level, and all the peripheral areas above 1,600 feet. So only the Lower Congo, near Matadi and Boma, has the really hot climate of coastal West Africa. On the other hand, it may be contended that the most agreeable climate on earth is to be found near the equator at elevations between 5,000 and 6,000 feet, because there the days are not too warm, the nights are always cool, and the changes of season are slight. Such are the conditions obtaining in the region around Lake Kivu.

Much of the Congo, of course, is warm the year round, and only in regions at least 5 degrees from the equator does one feel that there is any cool season during the dry months of the year. The mean annual temperature at Coquilhatville, near the center of the upper basin, is 76.8° F., and at Luluabourg in the Kasai district 76.5° F. The variation in monthly means at these two localities is only 2.5° and 1.26°. But the daily range of temperature would be about 15° at Coquilhatville and 24° at Luluabourg, with the thermometer lowest between 5 and 6 A.M. Relative humidity is usually high, from 62 to 84 per cent.

Coquilhatville is virtually on the equator, a good starting point
for a brief discussion of Congo climate. Somewhere near this latitude, throughout the year, there is a broad atmospheric zone, the
doldrum belt, lying between the two zones of trade winds blowing
in from the southeast and the northeast. The doldrum belt, several
hundred miles wide, is an area of calms, of rising air currents, and
of violent thunderstorms, all resulting from the heating of the belt
by the vertical rays of the sun. The air can rise and flow out only
poleward at the upper levels.

This rainy doldrum belt moves north and south seasonally, following the vertical position of the sun. Thus it is that the rainy
months on the northern border of the Belgian Congo are those
from March to November. In the period corresponding to the
northern winter, very little rain falls. The doldrum belt then lies
mostly south of the equator. The annual precipitation in the northern Uelé district is from 50 to 55 inches.

To the southward the Congo extends much farther from the
equator, and there it has a more prolonged season of drought. At
Elisabethville in the Katanga, for example, the annual rainfall is
47 inches, occurring mostly from November to April, so that the
dry season occupies nearly one-half of the year. The altitude of
Elisabethville is 4,059 feet, its mean annual temperature is 69.1° F.
The climate there is reasonably healthful; in the hot season, toward
October, the thermometer may rise to 96° F. at noon, but it will go
down to around 51° F. at night. In the first half of the dry season,
the corresponding diurnal variation is from 84° F. to 39° F.

There is of course an intervening zone, entirely across the Congo,
where some part of the belt of rains is nearly always overhead. At
Coquilhatville, for example, there are about 130 days with rain in
the year, and no period that could be called a dry season. The wet-
test weather comes in February or March and again in August and
September, the total rainfall for the year being around 70 inches.
As the land rises in the equatorial region of the eastern Congo the
mean temperature falls, but even so there is no long dry season.
On the shores of Lake Kivu the annual rainfall is between 50 and
60 inches, with very little in the months of June, July, and August.
On the highland west of Lake Albert, conditions are similar, save
that the period of least rainfall is from December to February.

Except on the slopes of the higher mountains, the rains are not troublesome, the temperatures ideal, and their variation less than at Elisabethville.

These conditions are plainly indicated by the vegetation that covers the landscape. An annual rainfall of 60 inches, distributed over almost every month of the year, is the prime requisite for a rain forest, and this is just what is found stretching across the whole Upper Congo, from about 3.5 degrees north of the equator to about 4 degrees south of it. This block of forest, continuous with that of the French Congo and Cameroon, extends about 750 miles from west to east in Belgian territory, with a width of 530 miles from north to south. There are of course minor irregularities in its outline, some due perhaps to activities of men, and some to local climatic peculiarities. In ascending the Congo River, for example, one might expect to enter the forest belt at Kwamouth, especially as there are some tangled woods along the river bank much lower down. But it is really only at Yumbi, 77 miles higher up, that one finally reaches the solid forest. The savannas of this region extend across the river and invade the French Congo to a point very near the equator. Then, farther west in the Gaboon, the forest bends southward again and pushes a long tongue, the Mayombe forest, parallel to the coast almost to the lower Congo River at Boma.

In the eastern Congo, on the other hand, it is a surprise to find that after the equatorial forest reaches the highlands near the Albertine Rift, it comes to an abrupt end. Only here and there in the rift, and on its eastern side, are there small areas with sufficient rains to support a true forest growth.

The higher mountains in the equatorial zone, it is true, gather clouds about them; and they commonly have rings of cool mountain forest growing on their slopes above 5,000 or 6,000 feet. Still higher up there may be bamboos, stately groves of cusso trees, or tree heaths. On peaks rising above 12,000 feet one expects groundsel trees, giant lobelias, and the other strange alpine plants that grace the cold, misty heights of Ruwenzori and the Kivu volcanoes.

The forest areas of the Congo are of great interest and value, not alone as a refuge for their fauna. They hold a vast store of useful timber with qualities peculiar to tropical woods, and of fuel for local consumption, as in the furnaces of river steamers. These are also the only regions in which certain plantations can be developed, as of cocoa, rubber, and bananas. Coffee thrives in forest regions of moderate altitude and on the better-watered plateaus. Oil palms grow well only in or near the forest belt.

The forest needs wise management. In many districts, native agriculture has already made serious inroads; and once the primary forest has been destroyed, its place is invariably taken by a tangled second growth which has next to no economic value. A real rain forest in Africa would require a century to reëstablish itself completely, if left severely alone. But with the active human population of the Congo, it is rarely left undisturbed.

Considerably less than half of the Belgian Congo is covered with rain forest. Little of the remainder is treeless, but the trees are more widely spaced in the grasslands that are called "savannas." In regions just north and south of the forest belt the rains still are copious and spread over eight or nine months of the year. Here are often found long arms of true forest vegetation extending out along the stream beds, forming what are known as gallery forests. Away from the valleys, the country is covered with a growth of high grasses, interspersed with trees and bushes that are able to survive a few months of drought, when the grasses dry up and are often burned off by the natives. Such are the conditions in a large part of the districts of the Ubangi, Uélé, eastern Ituri, Kivu, Manyema, Kasai, and Kwango, as well as the Lower Congo.

Continuing farther south, as the dry season becomes more prolonged, the grasses are likely to become shorter and finer, the trees crowding closer together until their crowns begin to touch. The gallery forests have largely dwindled away, but the higher ground may be covered with an open woodland, carpeted with grasses, which is called a "savanna wood." The trees are largely of species not found at all in the equatorial forest. Conditions are entirely different, yet in the upper Katanga and in Rhodesia these woods have often been spoken of as forest. In the lower land along streams, the woods often give way to open wet meadows, "dambos," so that in a way the conditions are opposite to those in the rainier districts.

On the higher plateaus of the Katanga, the Marungu, and Ruanda-Urundi trees become scarce, and grasses, mingled with other low plants, predominate. These are the best cattle countries, with good pasture and no tsetse flies. But cattle also are being raised in the Lomami and in the Lower Congo, under European supervision.

It would be impossible here to discuss the botanical features of the Congo in any detail. One characteristic of the lowland forest is the diversity of its larger trees. Their height is often exaggerated, 150 feet is close to the maximum. Among the many kinds of woody creepers are some that yield rubber; wild rubber trees are not abundant. Orchids are numerous, but they do not flower very frequently. Although oil palms and borassus palms are often abundant, the variety of palms is not great in the Congo. Bamboos are usually scarce except on mountains.

The fauna of the Congo is rich and diversified, and space will not allow any adequate description of it. The outstanding mammal is the African elephant, and for many years its ivory was one of the important exports. As late as 1925 it was estimated that although 25,000 elephants died annually in the Belgian Congo, their number was not being rapidly depleted. The ivory trade has long been strictly regulated, but in populous districts there is scarcely room for creatures so destructive to agriculture. They inhabit both forest and savanna countries, lowlands and highlands. Buffaloes, hippopotami, leopards, and some other well-known African mammals are found both in and out of the equatorial forest; but in general the lowland forest fauna is very distinctive, and much the same from the Ubangi to the Semliki.

Among the wide-ranging forest species are chimpanzees, monkeys of many kinds, a few lemurs, duiker antelopes and the larger situtunga and bongo. Patient hunting is required to see many of the animals that really are common in the forest. The red river hog is one of these, but the larger black forest hog is rarer. Of small carnivores, especially genets, civets, and mongooses there are many; of rodents there are legions, including rats, porcupines, squirrels, and flying squirrels. The bats are well represented, and some of the large fruit bats are very noisy at night.

The okapi, forest-dwelling member of the giraffe family, is restricted to a fairly large area in the eastern Congo forest. Gorillas, in the Belgian Congo, are found mainly in the highland forests of the Kivu district and in adjacent areas.

Among the conspicuous birds of the Congo forest are the gray parrot, a number of hornbills, and plantain eaters. The crowned eagle, less often seen, feeds largely on monkeys. There are blue-spotted and black guinea fowl, a few forest-dwelling francolins, and a few ducks. More than a thousand distinct species of birds are known within the limits of the Belgian Congo, so it can be seen readily that the forest is well supplied with small birds, some of which sing well, despite legends to the contrary. One remarkable bird, found nowhere except in the eastern Congo forest, is the Congo peacock, the only true pheasant known from the African Continent.

Reptiles are well represented, and though there are many venomous snakes, including the truly beautiful rhinoceros viper, the danger of being bitten is slight. Crocodiles in the rivers are far more dangerous, and often more numerous than one might suspect.

In the savanna districts many of the large mammals and the birds are more readily seen; but only in a few favored areas does game seem as abundant as in the plains of eastern Africa. The next largest mammal after the elephant is the white rhinoceros, found in the border regions of the northeast Congo, while the black rhinoceros occurs in the Upper Katanga. The giraffe reaches only the northeastern frontier of the Congo; zebras are seen only in the southeast. Eland occur in some of the marginal areas, but other antelopes such as waterbuck, cob, and bushbuck, are generally distributed in the grasslands. Lions may be found where the larger game is abundant; hyenas and jackals are more generally distributed in the grasslands. The wart hog replaces the forest species of pigs. Baboons are much more characteristic of savannas than of the forest. With the smaller monkeys the reverse is true. Among the lemurs only bush babies venture out into the trees of the grassy districts. Rodents, bats, and other small mammals of course are abundant, the species distinct from those of the forest.

Among game birds the francolins, horned guinea fowls, bustards, ducks, and geese are characteristic of the savanna country. Birds of prey are more in evidence, and here the kites and vultures find it easier to locate their food. There are hornbills, but few of any size except the ground hornbill. Small songbirds are abundant, and a famous savanna bird is the honey guide, which regularly leads men to the hives of wild bees. For the naturalist the highland areas above 5,000 feet have a special attraction, because the fauna there is certain to contain many species differing from those of the lowlands, and often more localized on isolated mountains or plateaus.

The diet and ways of life of the natives must be adapted to the conditions of climate and vegetation. Only in the relatively small areas where cattle are kept can the natives have milk; the hunger for meat is all but universal. In the equatorial forests there are few domestic animals save dogs and, occasionally, goats. The basic starchy food in the western and central regions is manioc, in the east plantains and rice are preferred. Many other vegetables are grown, fish are caught in every river, and whatever game may be available is eagerly hunted. Palms often provide oil; winged termites, caterpillars, and large beetle larvae are esteemed as food; but few edible fruits or nuts grow wild in the forest.

The Pygmies are primarily hunters, and with poisoned arrows, spears, traps, and nets they kill monkeys, duikers, wild hogs, and even an occasional elephant. They do little or no planting, and often trade meat for plantains and other vegetables.

Around the edges of the forest, in the high-grass savannas, manioc and plantains can usually be grown, maize too, and a few kinds of millet. Beans, peanuts, and other vegetables vary the fare, and here oil palms are often abundant. Fish, and the flesh of antelopes, wild pigs, and many smaller animals are highly regarded, often being smoked for preservation and trade. Grasshoppers and termites of certain kinds are eaten.

In the districts which have a prolonged dry season the consumption of millet and guinea corn is greater. Sesame and gourd seeds provide oily nourishment; wild meat is likely to be more plentiful. Sheep and goats are kept in many areas where cattle do not thrive. When one considers the various kinds of squashes, beans, and other vegetables in use, the diet is found to be reasonably varied.

Despite the many ills that always afflict a primitive population in the tropics, the natives of the Congo usually impress the visitor today as a sturdy and active people who have learned, through centuries, to be contented and gay in a land that is favored in many ways by climate, and yet requires real effort and planning in farming, hunting, and the providing of shelter.

Such, then, is the Belgian Congo—a narrow strip of coast, a great river, and a vast interior basin, traversed by the equator. A railway over the hilly cataract region gives access to the interior and its many navigable rivers. The Belgian colony is heavily forested over a large part of its northern half, with a fringe of grassland near its northern border. The southern half is mainly a savanna country, with forest fringing many of the rivers. Far to the southeast, the land rises to a healthful plateau country with great mineral wealth.

The eastern edge of the colony is marked by a chain of large lakes, near which are plateaus and mountain ridges, partly forested and scenically so attractive that many an experienced traveler is tempted to settle there. It seems a long way from the mangrove swamps of the Congo estuary to the thrilling heights of the Kivu and Ruwenzori, and within those 1,200 miles are to be seen a succession of climates from the humid equatorial lowland to that of perennial snow and ice. But the glaciers of Ruwenzori are not arctic. Extreme cold is never felt, nor is there any summer.

Travel today is easy and safe, because of the efficient development of the whole region under King Leopold II and Belgium during the past half-century. The Congo is making most valuable contributions to the cause of the United Nations today, and is clearly destined to render similar service to the civilized world of the future.

CHAPTER XXIV

Peoples and Cultures

BY MELVILLE J. HERSKOVITS

THE NATIVE POPULATION of the Belgian Congo, in 1942, numbered more than 10,000,000 persons,[1] divided into many tribal units of unequal size. In its racial affiliation this population is Negroid; its languages are principally Bantu; despite its diversity of tribal groupings, its cultures represent a high degree of homogeneity. Except the Pygmies, who, in any discussion, constitute an exception, the area can thus be treated as a unit. Even the heterogeneity of the Congo folk in physical type is merely that of all central African Bantu-speaking Negroids, who, as a group, can be differentiated from the Nilotic peoples of East Africa, or from the true Negroes of the Guinea coast, or from the Khoisan (Bushman-Hottentot) tribes of the Union of South Africa.

The unity shown by this population, however, does not stop at the boundaries of the political entity known by that name. Rather the resemblances represent but a part of a wider homogeneity; for ethnic, linguistic, and cultural boundaries are no respecters of political alignments which, in this instance, resulted from the partition of Africa among the Powers of Europe. Its inhabitants, then, are to be regarded as only a part of the larger population which inhabits the basin of the entire Congo River system. They thus share their characteristics with many tribes of Angola, of French Equatorial Africa, and of the westerly and northwesterly fringes of the British Colonies lying to the east and southeast. An exception to this from the Belgian possessions must be noted, however, since the cultural ties of the tribes living in the Ruanda-Urundi enclave are with East Africa rather than with the Congo Basin.

[1] Exclusive of the mandate territories of Ruanda-Urundi.

Until recently, no one knew how many tribes could be distinguished within the Belgian Congo nor, in many instances, was there any consensus of opinion regarding the names of many of these groups. The problem was like that elsewhere in Africa, as in most of the world inhabited by nonliterate folk, where primary affiliations of the individual and the group are local; so that where larger political entities exist, the boundaries between them are not strictly drawn, nor does the name of the total unit take on any great importance. In 1930, however, Dr. J. Maes and Miss O. Boone of the Belgian Congo Museum (Tervueren) prepared an analysis which should stabilize, if not solve, the status of this perplexing matter. Their procedure was to scrutinize all the literature, noting every version of a tribal name, and the area within which any group mentioned might be said to live. Then, by comparing various reports, they reached a designation they considered proper for each group, and a delimitation of the area inhabited by it. The total is striking—144 Bantu tribes, in addition to 5 major and "a large group of other" Pygmy aggregates. These figures make possible some calculations that throw light on the size of these tribes, which are thus seen to average about 70,000 persons. In view of the inequality of the areas inhabited by the various groups, this means that some tribes are larger than 100,000, and in some instances more than 250,000. Since the total number of Pygmies is small, the Pygmy tribes need not be taken into account in estimating average tribal size.

How long the Congo has been inhabited, who were its first inhabitants, and what later migrations and crossbreeding produced its present peoples form one of the unsolved problems of African research. There has been no dearth of speculation over the question, however. The principal difficulty is the lack of studies based on systematic archaeological research. In the Belgian Congo Museum are great cases of stone implements from the Congo area, but, except for a few papers, there is no analysis of these data. In any event, the almost complete absence of collections of skeletal remains would handicap seriously any attempt to reach a solution. The finds of early man from East Africa and South Africa do help to the degree that they demonstrate the antiquity of human habitation of the African Continent. Yet, no remains, comparable in antiquity to these others, have been uncovered in the Congo proper. What can be learned of the past history of the Congo folk when turning to the evidence afforded by comparative study of distributions of physical types, languages, and cultures? The Congo Pygmy poses many difficult questions. Does he represent the aboriginal type of African, now forced back into the unoccupied nooks and crannies of the forest by his larger neighbors? What is his relationship to the pigmoid Bushmen of South Africa, and to the wider range of Pygmy stocks, all of Negroid affiliation, found in India, the Andaman Islands, Ceylon, Indo-China, the Philippines? Haddon says of the Congo Pygmies:[2] "We may safely regard them as relics of a primitive type of Negro which at one period inhabited tropical Africa from the southern borders of the Sahara to the Zambezi-Congo watershed and from the east coast to the Atlantic. ... They and the Bushmen may be regarded as divergent branches of a small variety of Negro, to which main stock they undoubtedly belong." Sir Harry Johnson, however, comes to the conclusion that, "The Congo Pygmy seems to be little else than a primitive and dwarfed form of the Forest Negro, perhaps representing one of the earliest types of Negro that invaded Africa." He therefore differentiates this type from the South African Bushmen. Thus, on the basis of present knowledge, the only reasonable assumption would seem to be that the Pygmies represent an early substratum of the Congo population.

The past of the larger-sized Bantu-speaking inhabitants is almost as obscure. Their heterogeneity of physical form argues that they are the result of mixture between the various types of Negroids that swept across the northern part of the sub-Saharan continent from east to west, across the central portion from northeast to southwest, and along the eastern part from north to south. The great range in their stature, variation in head-form, pigmentation, and other physical traits bespeak such mixture, and betoken such migrations. Compared on a purely statistical basis with samplings of the true Negroes who inhabit the Guinea coast, or of certain Nilotic folk of Kenya and Tanganyika, the relatively greater degree of homogeneity of these latter makes the point and confirms uncontrolled observation.

[2] Alfred Cort Haddon, *The Races of Man and Their Distribution*, p. 47.

The Negroid character of the Congo folk indicates that these immigrant peoples must have been of the type now found in the Guinea coast area. On the other hand, the fact that the Congo population deviates from this type can be regarded as the result of mixture with the pigmoid folk they perhaps found in the region; and, with the Semito-Hamitic and Nilotic types to the east with whom, for many years, they have had contact. It is worthy of note that though the Negroid race generally is long-headed, most African folk who are brachycephalic inhabit the Congo Basin. Complicating the entire problem, however, are the northward countermigrations of recent times, which are attested by native tradition and the findings of comparative ethnography.

Except for certain tribes in the northern and northeastern parts of the Congo Basin, and the Pygmies, all Congo languages belong to the Bantu family. Those in the north and northeast, such as Zande (spoken by the Azande, or Nyamnyam), are classified as Sudanic, their affiliation being with the languages of this stock which stretch in a broad band across the Continent from the Guinea coast to the Great Lakes. Of Pygmy speech little is known, since no systematic studies of it have been made. Thus Sir Harry Johnston, through stating that, "If the original speech of the Pygmies lingers anywhere at the present day, it is in the very center of Congoland," can only conclude his summary by saying, "So far, however, no traveler has recorded any words from the mouths of Pygmies which do not belong definitely to one group or other of African speech identified as that of the big Negroes living alongside each Pygmy tribe."[3]

This was in 1910; today, there is little more by way of documentation. Father Paul Schebesta, who studied the Pygmies during two field trips, speaks of a "trading language," which each group uses in its contacts with its larger neighbors, and a "camp language," which the members speak among themselves. "If a genuine primitive Pigmy language does exist," he states, "it must be one of the many 'camp languages'." Because the Efé of the northeastern Congo are monolingual, whereas most of the Pygmies are multilingual, and in view of other factors, Father Schebesta concludes: "Not only is it probable that Efé is an aboriginal Pigmy language,

---

[3] Sir Harry Johnston, *George Grenfell and the Congo*, vol. 2, pp. 834–835.

but it seems a very reasonable inference, if we sum up all the available evidence on the point, that it was the language spoken formerly by all the Ituri Pigmies before the negro tribes made incursions into the Congo forest."[4]

Bantu has been well studied, and its outstanding traits are worthy of some review. Best known is its classificatory system, which is based on the use of prefixes that indicate the class to which a word belongs. The word *bantu* itself illustrates the principle; *-ntu* means "a living thing," *mu-ntu,* "a man," *ba-ntu* "people," and the like. This principle gives rise to the phenomenon of the concordance, by means of which the relationship of the words in a sentence is shown. An early grammar of the Bantu languages in the Congo[5] gives the following example: *Ma-kemba ma-na ma-tanu ma-lau ma-kwe,* Plantain those five fine fell "Those five fine plantains fell down."

Various numbers of prefixes have been recorded for various Bantu tongues, but it is safe to put the number for any given dialect at between fifteen and twenty. Their utility is increased, and their use made easier, by the fact that the normal Bantu word-stem is of two syllables, to which prefixes, suffixes, and, on occasion, infixes can be added to give subject-pronoun, tense, and object-pronoun. How much flexibility the use of suffixes gives can be seen from the following forms, which are derived from the verb, *kang-a,* "to tie": *kangema,* "to be tied"; *kangela,* "to tie for, by," etc.; *kangana,* "to tie each other"; *kangia,* "to cause to tie"; *kangola,* "to untie"; *kangomela,* "to be tied for"; *kangenela,* "to tie each other with"; *kangolela,* "to untie for" or "with," etc. Bantu languages have three demonstratives, indicating nearness to the speaker, nearness to the person spoken to, and distance from both. The language is given much "flavor" by the large use of onomatopoetic words, interjections, vocal images, ejaculatory phrases, and the like.

Bantu phonetics are not as complicated as those in other African tongues, but significant or semantic tone introduces an element which at once makes the language difficult for the European to learn and yet agreeable to his ear. The principle involved can be illustrated by reference to Shona, a Bantu language of Rhodesia,

---

[4] Father Schebesta, *Among Congo Pigmies,* pp. 232–233.
[5] W. H. Stapleton, *Comparative Handbook of Congo Languages.*

which has been thoroughly analyzed from this point of view by
C. M. Doke. Thus the word *rudzí,* where tone rises on the last syllable (as indicated by the accent) means "bark rope," while *rudzi,*
the same phonetic combination with a falling tone on the last
syllable, signifies "tribe." In like manner *edzá* means "try," *edza,*
"fish"; *rambá,* "to be sterile," *rambà,* "refuse"; *tshúro,* "orphan,"
tshurò, "hare." Some Bantu tongues have more than a three-register
system, which, even in this form, is complicated by the glides from
one tone to another. Zulu, according to Doke, has nine such tones,
and Laman's analysis of tone in Kongo shows that here, also, nine
registers are employed.

The basic unity of the Bantu tongues has permitted the rise of
"trade languages"—common auxiliary modes of speech used over
large areas. The best-known of these, Swahili, is spoken in all the
eastern part of the Belgian Congo; in the west are Chikongo and
Chituba. It is easy also to see how the similarities between the
many Bantu dialects has facilitated communication even where
there has been no *lingua franca.* As any comparative study of the
vocabularies, phonetics, and grammar of Bantu languages demonstrates, to know one of them makes learning another a simple
matter. These speech resemblances, together with the essential
homogeneity of the natural environment in the Congo Basin, go
far toward accounting for the widespread resemblances between
the cultures of these folk. For with similar problems of meeting the
demands of nature, and an effective medium of communication at
hand, the diffusion of cultural traits through the entire region
could be achieved without difficulty.

Before discussing the culture of these Bantu-speaking folk, however, it will be well to sketch the mode of life of the Pygmies. In the
fields of material culture and economics Pygmy cultures are strikingly simpler than those of the Bantu peoples. Unable to resist
superior power, deficient in numbers, technical equipment, and
organization for war, they have been forced to live by their cunning, constantly alert for attack. Like the Bushmen, who were
driven into the inhospitable Kalahari desert, or the Vedda in the
rocky hills of Ceylon, or the Negritos in the depths of the Philip-
pine forest, the Congo Pygmies eke out a bare existence.

They are nomadic, hunting folk, living in crude shelters, obtaining their livelihood by trapping and shooting the game they are able to bring within range of their arrows. In the use of traps they show extraordinary cleverness, while they tip their arrows with poison to aid in resolving the handicaps under which they labor. Each group has its own hunting territory, and trespassing is resented. Because the Pygmies are so difficult to reach in their forest fastnesses, and because of fear of their poisoned arrows, their neighbors respect their hunting grounds.

In earlier days, suspicions were too strong to permit first-hand trading, and out of this situation rose the "silent trade." Here, barter was conducted by the larger partners coming to where the little people left their skins, or bark, or other trade materials, and under the watchful but unseen eye of the owners of the goods, took it away, leaving in place an equivalent in other goods. The poisoned arrow was the guarantee of honesty, whereas, if the articles left were not what was desired, the Bantu trader would either find them when he next returned, or would discover the Pygmy had left nothing for him to take away.

The social structures of these people, so far as they are known, seem also to be simple—the immediate family, based on monogamy conditioned by the difficulties of the economic life, without larger relationship groupings such as clans. Political institutions are, as might be expected among such folk, a headman, exerting influence rather than wielding power, and without other formal manifestations. Little is known of the Pygmy's world view, but it is apparent from the rites that have attracted most attention from visitors, and from Schebesta's account, that the Pygmies do have a well-formed system of belief. The African pattern of music and dance, as manifested in their ceremonies, is operative in their lives. The drum accompanies their singing, and their dancing, as far as photographs indicate, is of the same basic type found elsewhere on the Continent. Graphic and plastic arts are almost nonexistent, but there is a considerable body of folk tales and, presumably, myths.

In contrast, the Bantu cultures are distinguished by their complexity. They represent a degree of technical development, a level of economic and political integration, and a measure of religious and artistic sophistication that have been achieved by but few peoples who, not having devised a system of writing, are thus technically termed "primitive." The basis of the productive system of the Bantu tribes is agriculture, whether they live in the densely forested central and eastern parts of the Congo Basin, or in the more open prairie-like setting of the southwest. Unlike the peoples outside the colony to the east and south, and in the Ruanda-Urundi district of the Belgian Congo itself, they do no herding, having only such small domesticated animals as sheep or goats; but they keep many fowl. Those tribes living along the rivers fish, and hunting is carried on everywhere, but these are supplementary means of providing food except in a few instances among fisherfolk. The chief crops, which vary throughout the area as to relative emphasis, are maize, manioc, millet, and peanuts.

The Congo is famous for its crafts—ironworking, basketry and mat-making, weaving and dying of raffia cloth, pottery making, and wood carving. Traps of an amazing variety, whether to be used on land to catch animals or in the rivers for fish, are everywhere; leatherworking is done in some parts of the area; calabashes are worked to serve as containers for palm oil; and in the heavily forested regions, bark cloth is made. Yet, with all this variety, there is but relatively little individual specialization, for, except in metalworking, the knowledge of how to make these various articles is had by all, and it is only individual preference and ability that causes a person to make one object rather than another. Ironworkers, who are held in great esteem, keep their techniques not only secret but sacred, to be passed down in the family and taught to the forger's sons or nephews in accordance with the rules of descent and inheritance.

Tribal specialization gave rise to intertribal trade. Thus, the Bantu imported raw copper from the Basongo Meno and exported this commodity to the Akela, from whom they received a form of worked copper which was used as money. They also exported salt to the same people, receiving iron in return. Markets are held at periodic intervals, especially among the tribes of the southwesterly part, where the people of several villages gather to exchange their goods. Women are usually charged with the selling of foodstuffs; otherwise, commerce is in the hands of the men.

At the present time it cannot be said to what degree these exchanges are carried on by the use of native money. Available reports indicate that Belgian currency has almost entirely supplanted these earlier forms. Yet these forms comprised one of the most interesting aspects of the aboriginal economic system. Consisting of iron knives, hoes, copper forms of various sorts, bars of salt, cowry shells—to name but a few of these found among the various tribes—their value, both in terms of each other and of the available commodities, were well understood and have been given in tabular form by various authors, notably Torday and Joyce. They were a symbol of prestige as well as commodity currency; they could be used as bride wealth, or to purchase animals, or slaves, or other goods.

The basic unit in the social structure is the village. In the main, the outer appearance of these villages is similar in all the Congo—rectangular houses, placed evenly on both sides of a street, each with its series of outhouses. The farms are at a distance, often a considerable distance. The village is ruled by its chief and his council of elders, and practically all those who live in a community are related, except those women who have married into it and who retain their own family affiliations. As everywhere in Africa, these affiliations are very strong. Clan organizations are known to exist, and totemic clans are found in the northern part of the Congo Basin and in the east. Elsewhere the case is not clear, though descent, in the main, is counted either on the father's or the mother's side. Yet, just because descent is not counted as insistently on one side or the other, as is true elsewhere in Africa, the relationships between children and the families of both parents is closer than would otherwise be the case.

Selection in marriage is, of course, controlled by these considerations, which thus regulate incest lines. Polygamy is everywhere found, but, in the main, only the chiefs possess the resources needed to acquire plural wives, and among some groups only chiefs are authorized to have them. The family head is the father, and succession runs from father to eldest son. As elsewhere in Africa, much respect is shown the old. While the spiritual power of the ancestors is held to be great, the extent to which the social structure is integrated through the functioning of an ancestral cult, as in the case among the South African Bantu or the Guinea coast natives, is a problem for future study. But evidence in hand indicates that, as among the Akela, the reverence demanded by ancestral spirits is not left to individual whim.

The political aptitude of the Congo native has long been recognized. At the first contact with Europeans, in the fifteenth century, the kingdom of Congo was a success, and the early voyagers and missionaries have left many accounts of it. Similarly, first contacts between Europeans and Congo natives in the southern section of the Congo Basin was through the Balunda empire, which flourished in the eighteenth and latter part of the nineteenth centuries, and which gave rise to a number of subsidiary kingdoms. Another famous political entity was the Bushongo state, whose political history has been given full treatment by Torday and Joyce. These larger groupings generally resulted from conquests which incorporated neighboring tribes into the original unit. Whether large or small, each showed a closely knit, stable organization, with a hierarchical series of offices, usually hereditary, involving duties and rights that were clearly defined and well recognized.

Outstanding in this area was the administration of law. The rules governing conduct are well understood, and before European occupation disputes were carried to the local chief for settlement, when arguments were presented on both sides to him and his elders, who rendered their verdict. Where the chiefs were not strong, the local "assembly," functioning democratically, decided the issue at stake. In the larger political entities, appeals were permitted, and went to higher courts until they were argued before the king. Murder, theft, adultery, the practice of black magic, and other offenses were brought to book and punished; where fines were invoked, a considerable proportion of the amount paid over went to the chief who judged the case. In these courts, appeal was often made to the ordeal. There were many forms of these ordeals, but the one most often mentioned in the literature involves swallowing a poison that had been ritually treated. Death was proof of guilt, whereas if the poison was vomited, the accused was deemed innocent and his accuser had to pay him heavy damages. Many disputes involving property rights, or questions following on divorce, were brought before these courts, and in the old days there were many matters of indebtedness raised which might lead to the enslavement of the debtor.

The many accounts of the religion of the Congo natives are usually fragmentary, and often contradictory. But even from the materials in hand, it is apparent that the world view of these folk is anything but simple. Most observers state that the tribes of the Congo recognize a supreme deity who is removed from the earth and who, therefore, is rendered little worship. Zambi is the best-known name of this being, though many others have been recorded for him. Among some tribes he is regarded as the sun. There is some reason to believe that this Great God is not as far removed from mankind as has been thought—as, for instance, in those cases where oaths are sworn on his name, on pain of death if violated. Reports only rarely speak of subsidiary deities, but powers, often of a nonanthropomorphic nature, which punish evil-doing and the violation of taboos of various sorts, have been widely recorded.

The many secret societies of the Congo tribes derived their sanctions from the magical force of the charms which bound the members together, and in terms of native belief gave them the power to carry out their objectives. These societies were one of the less pleasant aspects of Congo life. Guardians of morality, the punishments they exacted were cruel, and ritual cannibalism often marked their gatherings. The power of magic, however, goes far beyond whatever sanctions it may have given secret societies, for magic, both good and bad, invades all aspects of life and is ever-present. Practitioners of magic are important members of society. As elsewhere in Africa, to perform "black," or evil magic is regarded as antisocial, but it goes on nonetheless, and is subject only to the superior power of a skilled worker of magic to control it by overcoming the power behind it, often sending it back to wreak vengeance on the one who commissioned it, or at whose behest it was dispatched.

The artistic achievements of the Congo remain to be mentioned. The plastic arts are highly developed, and so are music, dance, tale, and myth. As among most non-European folk, they are an integral part of everyday life, not set aside as something special and somewhat remote, as among ourselves. Woodcarvings and worked ivory are especially famous. Masks from the area are among the most prized possessions of art collectors. The famous portrait statuettes of Bushongo kings, now deposited in the Belgian Congo Museum and the British Museum, which date from the eighteenth century, are recognized as among the finest known examples of the wood carver's craft. Incised decorations on drums, on pigment boxes, on cups, on headrests, and the like, and small figurines are among some of the other better-known forms. The small stylized representations of human faces done in ivory, which come from the southeastern part of the Congo, have been accorded first rank for their sophisticated, sensitive treatment. The subtle arrangements of form shown in the asymmetrical throwing knives have often received comment, while the motifs used to ornament baskets and woven cloths are major achievements in design and execution. Of particular note is the pile cloth of the Kasai River tribes, where form and color are combined to make them remarkable examples of the art of weaving.

Music is heard everywhere, and the instruments, often employed in orchestras of twenty pieces or more, include drums of various kinds and range, xylophones, sanzas ("African pianos"), and other instruments. These are used, individually or together, to accompany singing; and both song and orchestra provide a setting for the dance. Dances are both ritual and social; in particular, the funerary dances have been remarked by most of those who have written of Congo peoples. Today, only the few phonograph records available for general distribution can be called on to give the layman a conception of the musical resources of these folk. It is a field well worth further exploration. As for "literary" forms, which are likewise numerous, most of the animal tales of the Uncle Remus type, widely spread throughout Africa, are told. In addition, a more serious form consisting of a large body of myth is found. To date, however, little is known of Congo mythology.

How the cultures outlined in the preceding pages have fared in recent war years is not known. At the turn of the present century, before the Congo Free State came under the official control of Belgium, policies of native administration had the effect in some parts of the area of demoralizing and undermining the aboriginal ways of life. Later, as Belgian colonials, the people fared better, but the processes of war and industrialization have, and will continue to call for new adjustments. Yet, experience has taught that the cultures of Africa possess a high degree of tenaciousness. It is not likely, therefore, that native cultures in the Congo will be too seriously affected so far as their underlying sanctions are concerned, except perhaps in the largest centers where contacts with Europeans and Americans are most intensive, and tribal controls over the individual are set aside. In most of the vast area, among the native folk who live far from these centers, it can be assumed that, in general, the patterns of living continue much as they have been sketched here, and will so continue for many years to come.

CHAPTER XXV

Historical Development

BY R. STANLEY THOMSON

IN SEPTEMBER, 1876, there assembled at the Royal Palace in Brussels, at the invitation of Leopold II, an illustrious company of geographers, explorers, and philanthropists. They had been called together to outline a program for opening the "Dark Continent" of Africa to civilization. Leopold opened their deliberations with an appeal that rang like the call to a crusade. The members of the Geographical Conference, as the gathering has since been called, responded by founding the International African Association with the twofold mission of opening central Africa to civilization and abolishing the slave trade. They chose the King to be President of its executive committee, and charged this committee with the task of planning and directing the expeditions which should establish the stations for its civilizing mission. They agreed to form national committees in each country to arouse interest in the humanitarian program of the Association and to collect the funds necessary for its work.

From the outset the Association became an essentially Belgian organization. The national committees, with the exception of the Belgian committee, acted perfunctorily and without enthusiasm. The Great Powers were unwilling to pursue their imperialistic designs under the banner of internationalism. Besides, they were jealous of one another. However, Leopold went ahead with his plans. In 1877 the executive committee, meeting for the first and last time, decided to send an expedition to East Africa to establish stations in the vicinity of the Great Lakes. At this time no one dreamed of piercing the vast unknown expanse of central Africa, except by way of the territories of the Sultan of Zanzibar.

The spot chosen for the first station was on the border of Lake Tanganyika. At Karema the flag of the Association, a gold star on a field of blue, floated over African soil for the first time, a symbol of civilization and international humanitarianism, a challenge to barbarism. But Karema was the result of Belgian initiative. It was a Belgian enterprise. Other stations were later founded in this same general area. But they were all as truly Belgian as the posts which flew the Union Jack or the Tricolor were British or French.

From 1878 on, Leopold's heart and soul were preoccupied with an enterprise operating in West Africa, which had no connection whatever with the International African Association except for the flag of the latter, which it appropriated. This enterprise came into existence because Leopold II was one of the few men in Europe to catch the future significance of the arrival of Stanley, the explorer, at the mouth of the Congo in October, 1877. For three years Stanley had been lost to the world. During those years, with untold hardships, he had made his way through the jungle of equatorial Africa from the shores of Lake Tanganyika to the Atlantic, compelling the mighty Congo to yield up the secret of its course. Stanley's exploration was sufficient to challenge a man of vision and imagination. A vast new area beckoned whosoever would have the hardihood to enter and civilize, truly a labor of Hercules. Leopold resolved to be that man. Belgium was too small to contain his energy or occupy entirely his restless intellect. He asked Stanley to help him in opening the Congo Basin to civilization. Stanley demurred at first because he wanted England to get this rich region he had revealed to the world. But England was indifferent. Stanley accepted Leopold's offer. Leopold had won his most valuable collaborator, for without Stanley there would have been no Congo State. Leopold, persistent, farsighted, astute and imaginative, could direct. Stanley, able, experienced in African ways, ruthless and realistic, could execute. The talents of these two were complementary. The instrument which Leopold forged for Stanley's hand was the *Comité d'Etudes du Haut Congo*. This association of Belgians and others, all friends of Leopold, subscribed a million francs for an expedition to study the commercial possibilities of the region and the feasibility of constructing a railway to facilitate communication between the upper and lower Congo.

Stanley arrived on the Congo at the end of August, 1879. Founding stations and clearing a road as he proceeded, he reached Stanley
Pool at the end of 1881 where, to his consternation, he found flying
the French Tricolor. Savorgnan de Brazza, a French explorer, had
made his way thither by the Ogowe River in a swift thrust. De
Brazza returned to France claiming both banks of the pool for his
country. Leopold was alert to the danger that France might appropriate the upper Congo and strangle his nascent enterprise. He
entertained no illusions that the commercial and scientific stations
of a private company would be respected by a great power if they
stood in the way of its territorial ambitions. If he wished to protect
himself against possible attack, then he must acquire sovereign
rights over the territories on the Congo through treaties signed
with the native chieftains. But the *Comité d'Etudes,* which he had
founded, had renounced any political aims. Therefore, he utilized
the first opportunity to rid himself of his collaborators by reimburs-
ing them for their subscriptions. There should be no one to ask
inconvenient questions if he embarked upon a political program.
Then, imperceptibly, the name International Association of the
Congo came to be used by him in referring to his Congo enterprise.
The use of the word "international" was calculated. Many people
associated it with the International African Association. In fact,
there was no connection whatever between the two organizations.
The International Association of the Congo was always political,
although its political program was not openly publicized until
Leopold was ready to seek the recognition of the Powers.

When Stanley paid a brief visit to Europe in 1882 he found himself in accord with Leopold concerning the necessity of a political
program. He returned to the Congo with instructions to conclude
as many treaties as possible, conveying rights of sovereignty to the
Association. Meanwhile Portugal presented another threat. That
country had appealed to England to recognize her long-standing
claims to the lower Congo. If the stations of the Association along
the river were to be cut off from the sea, their continued existence
would become doubtful. While Stanley signed treaties with the
chieftains all the way to Stanley Falls, his lieutenants acquired
sovereign rights over the Niari-Kwilu Valley all the way down to
the sea. This was Leopold's strategy, partly to provide an alterna-

tive outlet to the coast, and partly also to have territory with which to bargain for the left bank of Stanley Pool, if France insisted that her claim was good.

But even treaties ceding sovereignty to the Association were no guarantee that it would survive. Portugal and France denied that a private association could acquire sovereignty like a state. This line of attack proved so embarrassing that one of Leopold's collaborators appealed to the Belgian Government to solve the legal problem by taking over the stations on the Congo. But the Government would have nothing to do with the suggestion. Leopold's fertile brain found another way out of the dilemma; he would create in the Congo Basin a confederation of native tribes which would display the flag of the International Association and accept its direction. The Association would seek recognition by the Powers as the agent of these native tribes. Naturally, the native confederation would disappear in favor of the Association when it had served its purpose. Leopold gave the mission of organizing the confederation to an Englishman, General Goldsmid.

Early in 1884 came the unpleasant news that the British Government, fearful that France might seize the Congo, had signed a treaty with Portugal recognizing the latter's long-standing claims to the Congo mouth. This might well be the end. However, two diplomatic triumphs in April encouraged Leopold to fight on. On the one hand, he persuaded the United States to recognize the Association by cleverly appealing to the humanitarian impulses of the American people while at the same time he offered them freedom of commerce in the Congo Basin. On the other hand, he gained the friendly neutrality of France by offering her a "right of preference," in event he should ever choose to dispose of his possessions. This gesture accomplished another result which was perhaps unforeseen; the other Great Powers, Great Britain and Germany were, in effect, warned to do everything henceforth to insure the survival of the Association so that its territories would never fall to France. The news of the Anglo-Portuguese treaty was no surprise. It was known all during 1883 that the two Powers were negotiating, and Leopold had not waited for the announcement of the successful conclusion of their talks. Before, as well as after the signature, he was busily at work among his influential friends and in the press, cleverly contrasting the protectionist policy in Portuguese colonies with the freedom of commerce which would prevail in the Congo Basin if it were in the hands of the Association. This line of attack met with great success among the chambers of commerce in England. It also won the support of Bismarck. As Germany had no colonies at this time, Bismarck was very eager to safeguard the interests of German houses trading with central Africa. The Anglo-Portuguese treaty was also made the object of Bismarck's attack, because, at this moment, he was quarreling violently with Great Britain over other colonial issues. Opposition to the treaty became so pronounced throughout both England and the Continent that the British Government finally notified the Portuguese that there would be no justification for proceeding to ratification.

In November, 1884, Leopold gained the recognition of the Association by Germany, and with it the powerful support of Bismarck. In November, also, Germany and France jointly convoked a conference in Berlin to establish rules for the development of the African Continent. The fundamental idea of the program, Bismarck told the delegates, was to facilitate access to the interior of Africa for all nations engaged in commerce. The Association was not invited to the Conference, but it was in the minds of the delegates throughout their deliberations. They decreed freedom of commerce in a "conventional" basin, including all of the territory claimed by the Association. They knew that their decisions would depend for execution upon the state which had jurisdiction over this region. So outside the Conference, but during its sessions, the agents of the Association, assisted by the Belgian delegates and by Bismarck, labored unceasingly to secure recognition from all the states represented. Their efforts were successful, but they paid a high, though under the circumstances not too high, price for recognition by France and Portugal. They ceded the Niari-Kwilu Valley to France and abandoned the enclave of Cabinda on the coast north of the Congo to Portugal. The Association emerged in possession of the right bank of the Congo from Manyanga to the sea and the entire left bank down to a point in deep water in the vicinity of Noki.

At the final session of the Conference, Bismarck read the document by which the Association announced its adhesion to the General Act. Adding his personal word to the tributes already paid to Leopold by the delegates, Bismarck praised "the noble efforts of the King of the Belgians, the founder of a work which will confer most important benefits on mankind" and expressed the hope that the noble aspirations of the illustrious founder of "the new Congo State" might be fulfilled. The eulogies were deserved. Never before in history had one man, by his vision, by his genius, and by his indomitable perseverance created a state, member of the family of nations. And never before had any state been the property of its ruler as the new state was the patrimony of Leopold. Louis XIV's reputed dictum, "I am the State" was literally true in the case of the founder of the International Association of the Congo.

The time had arrived for Leopold to slough off the cloak of an organization which many people still thought of as international. Some even confounded it with the International African Association. The Belgian Chambers granted his request to become the head of the new state with the understanding that the union was to be purely personal. His next step was to avail himself of the permission granted by the General Act of the Berlin Conference to proclaim the new state perpetually neutral. The proclamation, addressed to Bismarck, was accompanied by a map. Now, Germany had recognized the International Association in November, 1884, with boundaries as indicated on a map attached to the Convention of recognition. The map which Leopold annexed to the proclamation of neutrality added very considerably to the territory previously claimed. But Bismarck offered no objections. Perhaps Leopold's territorial appetite was whetted by this easy paper annexation. At all events, he continued to push an aggressively expansionist policy down to the day when his creation became a Belgian colony.

Between 1892 and 1906 Leopold was engaged in a campaign to annex the basin of the upper Nile to his domain. The Egyptian Government had recently abandoned the region to the Mahdists. Leopold planned to reoccupy it and then to negotiate for a recognition of his claim with the argument that possession means title. Even the lower Nile tempted him. The majesty and the grandeur of the Valley of the Kings haunted his imagination. Might he not conceivably duplicate, on the Nile, the function of a neutral guardian, acceptable to all the Great Powers, which he was performing on the Congo? A neutral regime in Egypt, he hinted in *Belgique Coloniale,* would be preferable to exclusive control by Great Britain.

So, by armed intervention and by diplomatic finesse, he sought to win the prize of Equatoria and the Bahr-el-Ghazal in the Egyptian Soudan. As always, he balanced the Great Powers against each other, tempting their ambitions, feeding their mutual distrust. Alternately he turned to Great Britain and to France for support. The story is dramatic both for the daring and hardihood of the military expeditions and for the skill with which Leopold used the resources of his adroit diplomacy. In this case, however, the prize he sought was not virgin territory like the Congo. Great Britain tolerated Leopold's pharaonic empire only as long as it served her purpose. When she had reached an understanding with France about North Africa, the *entente cordiale,* Great Britain was ready to reassert the claims of Egypt to the upper Nile. In 1906 Leopold bowed before the inevitable. In place of his dream empire he accepted a clear title to the port of Mahagi on Lake Albert, and the right to construct a railway from the Congo to a point on the Nile accessible to navigation. (He was confirmed in the lease of the enclave of Lado, the lease to lapse and the enclave to revert to the Anglo-Egyptian Soudan six months after his death.)

Leopold's first official act, as ruler of the Congo, was to organize an administration. It consisted of three departments—foreign affairs, finance, and the interior. The departmental heads constituted the cabinet of the sovereign and were directly responsible to him. On August 1st, he notified the Powers that "His Majesty, in accord with the International Association, has taken the title of Sovereign of the Independent State of the Congo." As the butterfly emerges from its cocoon, so, in this sybilline phrase, did the founder of the new state cast aside the useless garment of the Association. The new state was proclaimed on the Congo in a letter addressed by the Governor-General to the resident Europeans. He stated as the aims of the Congo State the preservation of law and order, the promotion of industry and commerce, and the protection and welfare of the native population. He enclosed in the letter the text of an ordinance effecting title to the soil; no contract with the natives relative to land was to be valid unless it had been made with the approval of the authorities; the State guaranteed to the natives possession of the land then in their occupation; all vacant lands were to be considered as belonging to the State.

The first years were difficult. Administrative and all other activities were supported by the personal fortune of the sovereign. Here there was no mother country to come to the aid of its colony with an allocation of funds provided by taxation. Too, the vast area of the State, more than seventy-eight times the size of Belgium, was largely unexplored. Natural resources were scarcely touched, even their existence in some instances unknown. Leopold distrusted the Great Powers and feared that they might encroach upon his territory before he could occupy it effectively. The railway, which Stanley had insisted was a prerequisite to the commercial penetration of the upper Congo, remained to be built. Private capital was raised for this purpose. It was 1898, however, before the line was open to traffic between Matadi, on the lower Congo, and Stanley Pool.

By 1890 Leopold was near the end of his resources. He turned naturally to his own country for help, for he always had intended that Belgium should eventually inherit his Congo. Belgium did not fail him. From this occasion down to the date of annexation she came repeatedly to his aid. At the same time that the Prime Minister submitted the loan convention to the Chamber for approval he made known two remarkable documents; one was the testament of the King-sovereign bequeathing the Congo State to Belgium *after his death;* the other was the covering letter addressed to the Prime Minister. The testament had been drafted only a short time before its publication, but it was predated August 2, 1889, in order that the public would not conclude that there was any connection between the solicitation of a loan and the royal bequest. In the letter, Leopold envisaged the possibility of an earlier transference of the Congo. He wrote: "If . . . it seemed wise to the country to form closer ties with my possessions on the Congo, I should be happy to see my country in the enjoyment thereof during my lifetime."

The Brussels Conference of 1889–1890, summoned by Leopold to discuss measures for the suppression of the African slave trade, also came to his assistance. He reminded the delegates that their decisions would have the effect of imposing new duties on the states in the "conventional basin" of the Congo, and requested that these states should be allowed to levy a tariff on imports to support the increased financial burden entailed by this program. The plenipotentiaries recognized the validity of this argument and voted to modify the provisions of the Berlin Act to permit the levy of import duties up to ten per cent *ad valorem*. Loyally and efficiently in the years following, the Congo State discharged its responsibility toward its cosignatories. Between 1892 and 1894 its forces met and completely crushed the power of the Arab chieftains whose *razzias* had blighted the whole vast region between Stanley Falls and Lake Tanganyika. No page of the civilizing and humanitarian mission of the Congo State shines more brightly than this.

After 1890 the financial position of the Congo State steadily improved. Primarily, the more favorable outlook was produced by the economic policy adopted in 1891 and adhered to steadily thereafter. This policy, limited in its initial application to certain areas, was applied eventually to the greater part of the territory. All vacant land was to be exploited by the State as state domain. Ivory, and especially rubber, became "domanial fruits." The native population were to pay their taxes in the form of labor expended upon the collection of these products. Inherent in this regime was the temptation to exploit native labor in the interest of a maximum return.

Naturally, when the new policy was inaugurated there was a torrent of protest from the companies which had already risked their capital to establish trading factories in the Congo State under the regime of freedom of commerce. The State was compelled to arrange a temporary compromise. It divided the entire territory into three zones; the first reserved to the State for exploitation by the State; the second set aside in the interest of public security; and the third open to exploitation by private capital under the regime of freedom of commerce. But this regime was to cease in 1901 when Belgium might exercise its right to annex the Congo by virtue of the loan agreement of 1890. After 1901, exclusive of the state domain and the private domain of the sovereign *in stricto sensu*, the entire territory was exploited by large companies, each of which had a monopoly over a region and in each of which the Congo State was a shareholder.

Out of the lands set aside for private exploitation, Leopold created a curious organism, a sort of *imperium in imperio,* which he called the *Domaine de la Couronne.* By a "sovereign resolution" he assigned to this *Domaine* roughly one-sixth of the total area of the State. In 1901 he transformed it into a foundation. The conception of a corporation endowed with legal personality he borrowed from the public law of England. He believed that he had fashioned an instrument which, functioning autonomously and in perpetuity, would perfectly serve certain philanthropic purposes of its creator in Africa and provide revenues for the embellishment of Belgium "in order . . . to augment its prestige in the world."

Belgium had the right to annex the Congo State in 1901. But the question of annexation came up in 1895. It came up then because an arrangement, which Leopold was considering and by which he would grant a vast concession of territory in return for financial help, suggested the disquieting possibility of unending future alienations. The Cabinet determined to propose immediate annexation as a means to liquidate the past and avoid future embarrassment. The Foreign Minister was obligated to negotiate with France for her consent, because she had been accorded a "right of preference" if Leopold disposed of his territory. France accepted the argument that the right was not intended to exclude the eventual transfer of the Congo to Belgium. The only international obstacle had thus been removed. Then, at this point, the Cabinet dropped the project entirely. Leopold had made it clear that he was opposed to annexation, and the Cabinet was unwilling to press the issue against their King. In 1901 the question came up again. This time there was a sharp but brief conflict between the King-sovereign and annexationists in Parliament. The Cabinet maintained an aloof attitude. Again the ruler was victorious. He now sought to take the initiative away from Parliament for the future by a *Note Verbale,* in which he promised to notify Belgium, as a patriotic duty, when the moment for annexation should come.

Criticism of the administration of the Congo State was increasing. It centered in England. The "Aborigines Protection Society" and the "Congo Reform Association" organized meetings of protest and appealed to the British Government to take diplomatic action. There were repercussions of the campaign in Belgium. In 1900 the

Belgian Cabinet declined to intervene on the ground that they had no right to mix in the domestic affairs of another state. Three years later the debate over an interpellation on the Congo ended in a vote of confidence in "normal and progressive development under the protection of the King-sovereign of the Congo State." Leopold finally accepted the suggestion of the British Cabinet that he undertake an impartial investigation of conditions. He appointed a Commission of Inquiry made up of a Belgian, a Swiss and an Italian, all men of unimpeachable integrity and excellent reputation to whom he gave complete freedom of investigation. Their report, exposing the existing evils of the "rubber system," was published in November, 1905. Leopold thereupon designated a second commission to examine the report and formulate recommendations giving effect to its conclusions. These recommendations were embodied in the reform decrees of 1906 which met certain specific criticisms of the inquiry report, but maintained the basic theory of vacant land on which the whole "rubber system" was organized.

The report of the Commission of Inquiry was the inciting cause of an interpellation of the Belgian Government in February, 1906. That a notable change in sentiment had occurred within the past five years was shown by the fact that the Chamber agreed to take up the study of a colonial charter without delay. Even the Cabinet, in this instance, announced its agreement with the Chamber. It was an act of open defiance against the King-sovereign, and Leopold recognized it as such. But how should he meet the challenge? He chose to explain his disapproval and regain the initiative by means of a letter addressed to the heads of his three administrative departments. Haughtily he declared that his rights on the Congo were indivisible, the creation of his fortune and his endeavor; the claims of Belgium were due solely to his patriotic interest. The letter concluded: "If you are questioned as to my intentions, you are to answer that I consider myself morally bound to inform the country when, without formulating any opinion in advance, I judge that the moment to examine the question of annexation is at hand and appears favorable. I have nothing to say at present." This language might become the absolute Sovereign of the Congo. But it was really addressed to the subjects of a constitutional King upon whom it reacted unfavorably. In another letter, testamentary in form and written the same day, Leopold altered the testament of 1889 by requiring Belgium to assume the obligation to respect his engagement toward third parties, his philanthropies and religious endowments, and his foundations. When, soon after, he conceded to three newly organized companies all the rights to the subsoil of the Congo State not previously alienated, he found himself engaged in a final decisive duel with the Belgian Parliament. This time he apparently suffered defeat. King and Cabinet were obliged to concede that the codicil to the testament of 1889 should be regarded as containing "solemn recommendations" rather than binding conditions. Leopold had sought to protect his cherished Fondation de la Couronne. Belgium announced in effect that the state she proposed to annex must be master in its own house. Study of a colonial charter was begun.

But the amazing fact is that Leopold, even at this late hour, refused to acknowledge defeat. The treaty of cession, which the Cabinet presented to the Chamber for approval, preserved "the foundations existing in the Congo." The imperious will of the King-sovereign had exerted a stronger fascination over the ministers than the obvious determination of the people's representatives. The triumph was only momentary, however. A second time Leopold yielded, but he exacted a price: An *Acte Additionnel* stipulated that Belgium should take over and complete the great public works financed by his Foundation and should donate 50,000,000 francs to him "as a mark of national gratitude." This sum he would expend on different enterprises related to the Congo. There was considerable dissatisfaction with this way of disposing of the "solemn recommendations" of 1906, but the Belgian chamber finally voted for annexation on this basis. At the same time, they accepted as the constitution of the new colony a colonial charter whose point of departure was the principle of trusteeship.

On November 15, 1908, Belgium assumed the role of a colonial power, and on the day following the Belgian Congo was proclaimed at Boma. Royal decrees had already instituted a minister of colonies and a central administration. The law for the government of the colony created a colonial council to advise concerning all proposed colonial legislation. Far-reaching reforms were enacted without delay: freedom of commerce was restored; natives were free to gather and sell the products of the soil to the highest bidder; they were to pay their taxes in money; their health, their education, and their general welfare were to receive more attention.

Since 1909 the development of the colony has been phenomenal. King Albert's faith in Belgium was justified when he declared in his accession speech: "Belgium has always fulfilled her promises and when she undertakes to apply to the Congo a program worthy of herself, no one has the right to doubt her word." Progress has been moral no less than material. Albert and his son, Leopold III, have steadfastly championed the dual objective of colonial statesmanship—to raise the status of the native population by means of a broadly humanitarian program and to establish a sound economy that will fertilize the civilizing mission. The peaceful development of the Belgian Congo, like that of the mother country, has been interrupted by the First World War and by the Second World War. In both conflicts the colony has aided the fight for freedom with all its resources. It was a colonial force which waged a victorious campaign in German East Africa in the former conflict and occupied the important center of Tabora. As a just recompense for her contribution to allied victory in Africa, Belgium was given a mandate over the ancient native kingdoms of Ruanda and Urundi which had formed a part of the former German colony. It was a colonial force which, in the present war, received the surrender of nine Italian generals and some 15,000 troops in Ethiopia. But the Belgian Congo's greatest contribution to the cause of the United Nations is economic.

In January, 1943, the Belgian Government formally joined the group of nations having lend-lease agreements with the United States; by an exchange of notes between the Belgian Ambassador at Washington, and the Secretary of State, Belgium, in return for American aid under the lend-lease formula, agreed to supply the United States with essential war materials produced by the Belgian Congo. The British Empire and the United States take the maximum output of such strategic war materials as copper, cobalt, tin, and, to fill industrial demands, palm oil, fibers, gum copal and rubber. The Belgian Congo proudly financed, out of its expanded exports, not only its own war effort, but also, by way of loans, the treasury of the Belgian Government in Exile.

The Congo State began as a dream. That dream became a reality through the ability and unceasing energy of Leopold II. No one can belittle the grandeur of his achievement. He destined the Congo for Belgium, to open to his people new horizons and new opportunities. For a time they were indifferent, even blind; then they caught the vision. Today the Belgian people are proud of their Congo. They are finding satisfaction in the civilizing task which they have assumed. They are showing their conviction that the words of Albert are true: "Nothing great and lasting can be achieved without reconciling the interest of the two races who are engaged in fruitful collaboration."

CHAPTER XXVI

Administrative Structure

BY ALBERT DE VLEESCHAUWER

ELGIUM IS A constitutional democracy. Article I of the Constitution proclaims that "all powers arise from the nation." In another paragraph, it is stated that the overseas possessions and protectorates are governed by special laws. Within the framework of Belgian democratic institutions, the principle of separation of powers, with a certain interdependence between them, is observed in the Congo as well as in the mother country.

The constitution of the Belgian Congo is the Colonial Charter enacted in 1908 by the Belgian legislature, which, alone, has the power to amend it. The Charter is the basic law by which the colony is governed. Custom forms, however, a source of unwritten law, especially with respect to the native population. The legislative power is vested in the Colonial Charter, in the Belgian Parliament, in the King, and in the Governor-General.

The Belgian legislature is empowered to pass laws relating to the Congo. In practice, it votes the colonial budgets, has the sole right to modify the Colonial Charter, and is called upon to intervene in matters specified by the Charter. For example, laws are enacted by the Belgian legislature to establish the colony's budget receipts and expenditures, approve accounts, authorize borrowings, determine the responsibilities of the Minister of Colonies, or ratify treaties regarding the Congo. Enactments granting railroad concessions, mineral rights, or land rights must be submitted to both Houses of Parliament for examination during a period of thirty days of session before they come into force.

In practice, the legislative powers in regard to the Congo are currently exercised by royal decrees. Such decrees issued by the

King must be countersigned by the Minister of Colonies and have been previously considered by the Colonial Council. This council is a consultative body of which eight members are appointed by the Crown and six by the Belgian Parliament, three by the Chamber of Representatives, and three by the Senate. The Minister of Colonies presides at the meetings. Although the advice of the Colonial Council is not binding, it is generally followed. In two or three cases the views of the majority have been overruled by the Minister of Colonies who has submitted a contrary decision for the royal signature. Legislation by decrees has proved highly flexible and well suited to the requirements of a country in the course of rapid development.

The legislative power is also vested in the Governor-General: in instances of emergency he can issue "legislative ordinances," valid for a period not exceeding six months. Such ordinances may not conflict with a law enacted by the Belgian legislature, but they may suspend the application of decrees. On the other hand, a decree can always repeal a legislative ordinance.

The legislative system is temporarily modified because of the war. A legislative order issued at Bordeaux on June 18, 1940, vested in the Minister of Colonies, or in his stead, the Governor-General, all powers of the King or Cabinet in matters pertaining to the Colony. The Cabinet in London amended this order on April 29, 1942, reserving to the Council of Ministers the paramount authority of issuing legislative orders, attributing to the Minister of Colonies the power of making decrees, and confirming a legislative ordinance of the Governor-General issued under the Bordeaux order, whereby his ordinances are rendered valid until repeal.

Finally, native custom, which constituted the legal system of the aborigines, continues to govern their relations wherever it has remained in force among them; it is respected if it conflicts neither with Christian ethics nor with the written law.

The executive power is vested in the King assisted by the Minister of Colonies. In the Congo the executive authority is represented by the Governor-General. Thus, the executive power originates in the metropolitan government and is continued in the Colony in a manner which differs from the system applied to other colonial areas.

The Department of Colonies, under the direction of the Minister of Colonies, is concerned with all aspects of the colonial administration. It comprises the various services of government: general affairs, finance, native affairs, public health, justice, education, economic affairs, trade, mines, public works, agriculture, defense.

The Minister of Foreign Affairs, who, in the name of Belgium, acts for the Colony in its relations with foreign powers, is the only other member of the Belgian Cabinet who participates in the executive functions of the Minister of Colonies.

Under the authority of the Minister of Colonies, responsibility for the local administration of the Congo rests with the Governor-General. He is assisted by a central staff, whose services cover the various fields of administrative action. His immediate aides, responsible to him, are the Vice-Governor-General and the State Inspector. He also has supreme command of the army, over and above the orders of its generals—just as the President of the United States is the commander in chief of American military forces.

The Governor-General meets with his aides at least once a week in a standing committee for the discussion of current affairs. He is thereby kept in close touch with all administrative problems. Every three months the Permanent Committee is enlarged by the admission of five members not belonging to the Administration but who represent various groups of interests. Once a year, if not more frequently, the Governor-General convenes a Government Council which the heads of the provincial governments and a number of private residents, including qualified spokesmen for the native interests, are called to attend. He submits to this Council for their views and advice the principal projects of policy, budget estimates, fiscal measures and welfare legislation.

The provincial governments, assisted by similar Councils, administer the six large provinces of the Colony, each having at its head a Governor assisted, for the ordering of provincial affairs, by a Provincial Commissioner and with officials corresponding to those of the Governor-General.

The province is divided into several districts, headed by District Commissioners subordinate to the Governor. Their duties consist of the supervision and coördination of the activities of the Territorial Administrators.

The District likewise is divided into several territories. Each territory is administered by a Territorial Administrator assisted by several Territorial Agents. Within his territory the administrator holds very wide powers in matters of finance, economic development, and native policy. His agents, who are en route at least half of their time, maintain personal contact and a constant liaison between the administration and the native population.

Because of this administrative system, the vast area of the Colony is under continuous supervision in every section, and its advancement is promoted more rapidly and more intensively than is true in most new countries. This remark implies no lack of appreciation of the great contribution brought to the material and spiritual development of the Colony by private initiative and native leadership. Within the framework of governmental authority thus outlined, the native population has its own organizations with which the Territorial Administrators and Agents act in constant cooperation.

In primitive communities all powers—legislative, executive, and judicial—are exercised by the Chief or Sub-Chief, usually assisted by a Council of Elders. For fear of disrupting tribal life, the Belgian colonizer upholds, and if need be revives, this organization, and allows the native communities to develop along their traditional lines.

Custom is a recognized source of unwritten law so far as it is consistent with the principles of humanity and progressive betterment, which the laws and regulations of the country seek to carry into effect. In regard to the administrative organization of the native communities the traditional conceptions of the Congo aborigines have been adopted or adapted.

There are three types of native communities: chiefdoms (*Chefferies*) sectors (*secteurs*) and extra-traditional townships (*centres extra-coutumiers*). The chiefdoms are communities which have retained, more or less, their tribal structure. Each chiefdom has its Chief, recognized as such according to local custom and invested in his office by the Government. Assisted by a Council of Elders, again instituted according to custom, he represents the chiefdom in its dealings with the administration. The sectors group together smaller communities of common tribal tradition between whom

political ties have loosened. These communities are reunited in
the spirit of local custom on the same lines as the chiefdoms. The
extra-traditional townships are creations of the Government. They
afford administrative units for those natives who have definitely
ceased to participate in the political life of their tribe and have
settled permanently in the vicinity of a missionary center, a large
industrial and planting undertaking, or a white man's township.
These "uprooted natives" are organized in order to form communities administered by a chief and council appointed by the
Government from among the local educated natives. The administration is carried on according to customary principles under the
guidance of a white official specially entrusted with this task. It has
proved an unqualified success. The townships are developing into
communities closely akin to the Belgian municipalities. Those of
Léopoldville and Elisabethville count some 80,000 and 50,000 inhabitants respectively and are administered in a truly exemplary
fashion.

The administrative organization thus given to the native population is a remarkable achievement. It may compare with the best
existing in other areas where similar conditions obtain. It is a form
of government by the people, for the people, upholding and improving native rule and traditional institutions. The same spirit
inspires the organizations of the native judiciary.

It may be mentioned that as soon as a white settlement reaches
a sufficient permanency and size it is given, through a Royal Ordinance, the status of an "urban center." With an "Urban Committee" (town council) and a special district commissioner acting as
a full time mayor, these communities administer themselves in the
manner of Belgian municipalities.

Civil and criminal courts are established in the Congo on the
same lines as the judiciary in Belgium. In civil cases decisions of
the lower tribunals are open to revision by an appellate court whenever the money value in dispute exceeds a given sum; the supreme
court in Brussels, Belgium, is the highest authority before which
a Congo case can be brought, but its decisions bear only on the
observance or breach of the law or rules of procedure. All sentences
of criminal courts are subject to appeal.

Besides this judicial system there is that of the native communities. To the native mind judicial power is the very expression of authority. Jurisdiction by the natives for the natives is established in the three types of communities. Each chiefdom has its tribunal (*Tribunal de Chefferie*) instituted according to custom. The Government does not create, but rather recognizes it. Some chiefdoms have a hierarchy of tribunals. Sector tribunals are established by the Government similarly to the administrative agencies. The same principle is extended to the extra-traditional centers.

These native courts apply the customary unwritten law and may be empowered to apply the written law. They deal both with civil and with criminal cases. A civil action can in practice lead to a penal sentence, and a criminal action on the other hand can be settled through a payment of damages. Save where native custom provides for an appellate court, the decisions of those tribunals are final with certain following reservations. A verdict of the native judge is always subject to revision by the Territorial Tribunal, on which the territorial administrator sits, assisted by native judges from a tribunal other than that against whose decision the appeal is lodged. When a native community is without a tribunal—an exceptional situation—the territorial tribunal acts in lieu thereof.

The public prosecutor's tribunals, formed of officers of the governmental judiciary, have power to nullify the findings of native tribunals, leaving it to the parties to carry the case before the same or another court. The native plaintiff and defendant are thus assured the fullest protection afforded by custom or law and the rules of legal procedure.

This native judiciary forms a complement to the powers of self-government bestowed on the native communities. Both the native judiciary and self-government are developing among the peoples of the Congo a sense of political responsibility and individual freedom.

CHAPTER XXVII

Economic Development

BY MAX HORN

THE BASIN of the Congo River was, in a not far remote geological time, a great inland lake about 1,000 feet above sea level. The waters of this lake pierced the Crystal Mountains and made a vast system of waterways, more than 7,500 navigable miles, which pour into the Atlantic Ocean through a channel 250 miles long, intersected with cataracts. The wide edge of the basin is rich in mineral wealth. Gravel has rolled down next to the rim, and is in places heavy with diamonds and gold. Sandy soil covers the bottom of the cup; dense forests have sprung up in some parts, prairie grass in others. Generally, it is poor soil, deficient notably in lime. However, thanks to abundant heat and moisture, a luxuriant vegetation readily proliferates, leaving a layer of mold, which becomes quickly exhausted under cultivation unless it is methodically fertilized.

The physical geography of the Belgian Congo explains the Colony's sparse native population: 10,500,000 scattered over an area of 900,000 square miles. In contrast, the high and fertile plateau of the adjoining Ruanda-Urundi Territories—which Belgium governs under a mandate from the League of Nations—affords an adequate living space to four million people in an area of only 20,500 square miles. A poor soil is conducive to nomadic shifts of the inhabitants and discourages the formation of permanent settlements. The inhabitants are likely to be underfed and to offer little resistance to disease. (Cannibalism may be regarded as a primitive means of remedying an inadequate supply of meat.) In fact, the health of the Congo aborigines was in dire need of improvement, except perhaps in the communities of fishermen. Early explorers, finding the banks of the main river and of its larger tributaries relatively well populated, were tempted to overestimate the total population of the Congo. Furthermore, the poor quality of the soil promoted intertribal antagonism, for each tribe or clan would resist alien settlement within its area, strive to enlarge its "lebensraum," and strenuously uphold its exclusive hunting and fishing rights. But, apart from this tendency to tribal isolationism, another and weightier circumstance caused the Congolese aborigines to rank among the most backward communities until the great task of opening up their country was begun seventy years ago. Despite Arabic and Sudanic infiltrations, the Congo was practically shut off from the outside world. In wide reaches, even such simple appliances as the wedge, the lever, and the wheel were unknown. The Crystal Mountains formed an almost impassable barrier until the completion of the Matadi-Léopoldville railroad in 1898 established a gateway to the heart of Africa. These facts must be remembered in appraising the work that was accomplished in less than half a century.

The successful fight waged against endemic diseases, the improvements brought to the natives' standard of living, and the dissemination of learning and technical skill are subjects discussed in other chapters of this book. The first obstacle which the pioneers of development encountered in the Congo was insecurity. They devoted their initial efforts to occupying and pacifying the country, freeing it from the incursions of Arab slave raiders and putting an end to intertribal warfare. In this connection a peculiar feature in the history of the Congo, from 1885 onward, deserves to be stressed. Although, ordinarily, new areas have been opened up through gradual penetration commencing from the seaboard, the interior being developed long after settlements were established along the coast line, occupation and survey of all parts of the Congo proceeded almost simultaneously. (When Belgium took over the administration of the Ruanda-Urundi Territories they were practically unexplored, although they had come under German rule at the time that the Congo Free State was founded.) Yet, economic progress and trade expansion are necessarily dependent on means of communication and transportation. As soon as pacification was accomplished the Congo Government concentrated its efforts on providing an adequate system of communication and transportation.

The magnificent system of waterways with which nature has endowed the Congo shows serious imperfections. The main river and its tributaries above the Stanley Pool are shallow, so that vessels with a draft of more than three feet are excluded. Moreover, navigation is made difficult by shifting banks, and is interrupted on some stretches by rapids. However, methodical charting, and buoying of the most favorable channels, has made more than 1,500 miles of the 7,500 miles of navigable waterways accessible to craft of 800 to 1,200 tons, and the remainder accessible to 200- to 250-ton craft. The bulk of the water-borne freight is carried by tugs and lighters, the passenger traffic mainly by paddle steamers or tunnel-screw vessels. The river system is supplemented by a number of lakes: the Great Lakes on the eastern boundary of the colony, and Lakes Tumba and Leopold II in the central area.

There are a dozen well-equipped ports on these lakes, some ten others on the main river and the Kasai, whereas the ocean ports of Banana, Boma, and especially Matadi are numbered among the most modern of West Africa. Matadi's outer harbor, Ango-Ango, is the source of a pipe-line carrying oil to Léopoldville.

The necessity of linking the navigable waterways was realized from the outset by the Congo Government. A railway connecting Matadi and Léopoldville and thus negotiating the Lower Congo cataracts, was completed in 1898, at great expense in lives and money, with the aid of a grant from the Belgian Treasury. It has since been rebuilt on a wider gauge. As early as 1906 King Leopold II planned, with remarkable vision, the layout of a complete system of railway connections. This plan has been steadily carried out and is now practically completed in twenty-three sections totaling 3,100 miles. Only one of the rail links contemplated by the founder of the Free State—a connection between the Uele River and the Upper Nile—has not come into being, although its construction is covered by an agreement in which the Government of the Anglo-Egyptian Sudan entered in recognition of the Congo's aid in the defeat of the Mahdists. This connection is established by a motor highway which has rendered conspicuous service during the present war. A plan for a railroad from Port Franqui to Léopoldville is under consideration with a view to saving a transshipment in the transportation of goods between southeastern Congo and Matadi. The Katanga railway is linked with the Rhodesian and South African railway system on the one hand, and the Benguela railway on the other. A line between Kabalo and Albertville gives access, through Lake Tanganyika, to British East Africa.

"Sabena," the Belgian airlines company, operates regular services within the Congo over an area of 4,400 miles, and in conjunction with British Airways carries passengers and merchandise between Léopoldville and Cairo, Takoradi, and Johannesburg. During 1943, its planes flew 2,800,000 miles in Africa as compared with about 150,000 miles a year before the present war. The fortnightly service between Brussels and Léopoldville has, of course, been suspended. An agreement made in 1941 with Pan-American Airways provides for a similar service between Miami and Léopoldville. Interrupted since Pearl Harbor, this service was reëstablished in October, 1944.

Telephone lines, outside the principal centers of population, are of small extent; Elisabethville is connected by wire with Rhodesia and the South African Union. Telegraph lines follow the railroad tracks. A propensity on the part of the natives for collecting copper wire for bracelets and leg bangles discouraged extensions of this system.

As early as 1910 the Congo Government decided to establish radio telegraph stations; by 1914 thirteen of these were erected. A service between Belgium and the Congo was opened in 1925. At present 30 telegraph and telephone public stations are in operation in the Colony, and many of the larger mines and plantations have their own installations for conveying service communications. A broadcasting transmitter at Léopoldville has sent out news to occupied Belgium since May, 1940, and relayed American broadcasts since 1941. A new and powerful short-wave station (50,000 kw.), completed in 1942 is issuing programs throughout the world in close coöperation with the U. S. Office of War Information, fourteen hours a day, in eight languages. For the white population and for a number of native listeners, receiving sets constitute a most valuable source of information and relaxation. Radio has strengthened the morale of the population during the present crisis.

Five local dailies and some twenty periodicals contribute to the dissemination of news. Grievances against the administration are aired without restriction.

The Berlin Conference of 1885 instituted a regime of absolute free trade in the Congo Basin. No preferential treatment was to be granted to the nationals of any country in the matter of trade or navigation. The necessity of providing the Congo Free State with revenue caused the Brussels Conference of 1890 to authorize import duties at rates not exceeding ten per cent. This limitation was waived in 1925 by the Treaty of St. Germain-en-Laye, but the non-discrimination clause remains in force concerning all members of the League of Nations, and the United States.

This policy has been followed unwaveringly. At no time was Belgium favored in the Congo by any trading priority or privilege. It a recent address before the Royal African Society, London, the Belgian Minister of Colonies, M. Albert de Vleeschauwer, described it as "the most liberal and the most generous policy, and the one that can most quickly bring about a harmonious development of a colonial country."

In many African possessions the liquor trade has afforded a substantial source of revenue; in the Congo, however, the sale of spirits was severely restricted from the outset. The Congo Treasury derives more than half its annual income from import and export duties. Capital goods enter free; consumer goods other than food-stuffs pay a moderate duty, which may reach 25 per cent on luxury goods. Export duties have been greatly increased for the duration of the present war. They comprise a tax equal to 40 per cent of the difference between actual and prewar sales prices. Considering the rise in prices as principally owing to the currency depreciation, this additional export duty is equivalent to a high war tax on profits. Further limitations are placed on earnings through a rigorous system of price control, which at the same time tends to stabilize so far as possible costs of production and the cost of living. Direct taxation is on a moderate scale, as behooves a young country anxious to attract capital and stimulate enterprise. However, a decree of June 15, 1944, has instituted a drastic "special and temporary" levy on exceptional war profits. Corporate reserves applied to capital expenditure in the Colony within five years are exonerated with a view to promoting investments. Such adult male natives as are not liable to income tax pay a head tax which varies according to areas, being equivalent to about a fortnight's earnings. In order to discourage polygamy among the natives, a progressive tax is assessed on the possession of wives in excess of one. About 8 per cent of the Treasury's annual receipts consists of dividends accruing from shareholdings in mining concerns which have issued stock to the Government in lieu of royalties. The Government owns and operates the Lower Congo railways, as well as a fleet of river craft, and holds deferred shares in railway companies. Hitherto these assets have not proved remunerative, cheap transportation being considered essential to the economy of the Colony; in fact, the Treasury is called upon to provide part of the interest owing on railway bonds. Some local taxes are levied in the principal townships. The native communities administer their own budgets, to which the Government allocates a portion of its direct taxes. The receipts go to administrative and judicial expenditures of the communities and to public works carried out by them in their own interest, such as the maintenance of roads within their area.

Although the country affords a checkered pattern of contiguous chiefdoms and townships, a distinction is made, according to Belgian juridical ideas, between authority over and possession of the land. In principle, the ownership of unoccupied land, that is, land which is neither individual nor communal property, is vested in the State. This view tallies with that of the Congo natives according to which an exclusive right to a given tract of land exists only as it is improved—cleared, under cultivation, or built upon—and so long as the improvements last. Communal hunting and fishing privileges, and exclusive community rights to the wild products of the forest, prairie, or swamp may cover a much wider field.

In the 'nineties of the last century, the Government embarked on a policy of ceding to private corporations its claims to the natural products of unoccupied land. This was done to hasten development at a time when large-scale investment in the Congo seemed an extremely hazardous venture. In carrying out this scheme the Government laid itself open to criticism on three counts: the areas covered by such "concessions" were, in several instances, abnormally extensive; the definition of occupied and, consequently, of unoccupied land set excessive limitations to native rights; and since native taxes were levied in kind, their collection was included in the claim to natural products granted to the concession-holding corporations. The practice of farming out taxes was currently accepted in many countries at that time; but the confusion of governmental prerogatives and commercial interests is fraught with dangers which have since caused it to be condemned and abolished, in the Congo as elsewhere.

The yearly quantity of produce which an individual taxpayer was expected to deliver was originally calculated to involve one month's, or at most two months', labor; but when he was obliged to go farther and farther into the forest in order to supply that quantity, the impost frequently grew to be exorbitant. The defects and abuses of the system met with criticism in Belgium as early as 1898, and later were the subject of unfavorable comment in British and American consular reports. The London Anti-Slavery and Aborigines Protection Society protested and lent its authority to a Congo Reform Association, which was sponsored by sincere philanthropists while, in all probability, receiving support from German secret funds. The Association aroused a world-wide outcry against the "red-rubber" exactions, which it claimed were obtaining in the Free State. In evidence of the maltreatment, which the native taxpayers were suffering, it adduced photographs of mutilated negroes. As a matter of fact, no white man has been shown to have ordered such mutilations, and many of the photographs either were faked or depicted persons in no way engaged in rubber (or ivory) collection; mutilations were, however, penalties inflicted for theft, according to native customs, and since the ownership of the produce was deemed to be vested in the Crown or its concession holders, native chiefs may in some instances have inflicted that barbarous punishment on subjects guilty of "embezzlement." In 1905 King Leopold instituted an international inquiry commission which reported that the alleged excesses were grossly exaggerated but recommended substantial amendments to the juridical system in which they were inherent. A more liberal definition of native rights was enacted in 1906, and as soon as the Belgian Government took over the administration it afforded the natives a much wider access to the natural products of their tribal areas and set out to negotiate with the large concession-holding companies drastic reductions of their concessions. At the same time native taxes in cash were substituted for taxes in kind. Under the Colonial Charter of October 18, 1908, which formulated the Constitution of the Colony, mineral rights and grants of land exceeding 10,000 hectares are subject to previous consideration by the Belgian Parliament. Moreover, increasingly stringent regulations insure effective development; land and mineral rights not duly utilized within a given time revert to the State. Abundant room is provided for native settlement and development, and for competitive enterprise.

Where large capital equipment is needed for economic production the undertaking must be assured of adequate supplies of raw materials. The high cost of transportation from the seaboard to the interior of the Congo obliges factories to look exclusively to local supplies. In view of these circumstances, a system of "protected zones" has been experimented with for the past few years. For example, a cotton ginning or oil milling undertaking is granted an exclusive right to purchase the products it requires within a specified area. Minimum prices, fixed from crop to crop by the Government, insure a fair remuneration to the suppliers. This system has greatly encouraged native farming and established close coöperation between farmers and manufacturers. All cotton plantations in the Congo are owned by the natives. A "cotton growers' fund," to which part of the export duties is allocated, enables the Government to pay a bonus to the farmers when a severe decline in world prices would otherwise preclude a satisfactory remuneration.

A transition from communal to individual tenure is progressing among the natives. The fourteen experimental stations of the Government Agricultural Service, besides distributing selected seeds to negro and white farmers, send out specialists to instruct them in better methods of cultivation, cattle breeding, and poultry raising. The principal municipalities grant loans to native residents for the building and acquisition of homesteads.

The Colonial Charter provides that "none shall be compelled to work in behalf of or for the benefit of private persons or corporations." Recruiting and employment of native labor are strictly regulated. Undertakings employing four hundred native workers or more are subject to special obligations in the matter of housing, medical attendance, and even education. On the other hand, employees of the Government as well as of corporations are free to form unions.

The Congo administration has persistently adhered to the principle that no white man shall carry on an occupation which a native could perform as well or better. This explains the relatively small number of white men in the Congo, and the total absence of "poor whites." Gradually the natives are being trained to fill any kind of post; many today are clerks, teachers, medical assistants, radio operators, mechanics or craftsmen, to say nothing of farmers and traders; soon the ablest will rise to positions of greater responsibility.

Saving is encouraged among the natives, a number of whom are "capitalists" operating not only stores, but substantial plantations and minor industrial enterprises, such as brickworks and furniture factories.

In speaking of capital, mention may be made of the aid which three banking institutions, with branches in every center of importance, are giving to trade while furthering the distribution of currency. A postal-check service also facilitates remittances throughout the country. Barter is prohibited between registered traders and natives. The Central Bank—Banque du Congo Belge—has issued notes since 1909 and, under a unique clause of its amended charter of 1905, equally all coins (except gold coins) which are treated in all respects as "metallic banknotes." From 1885 to the time of the second German invasion of Belgium, the Congo franc was on a gold basis, at par with the Belgian franc. In May, 1940, at the urgent request of the French Government which wished to see the Congo franc at par with that of French Equatorial Africa, it was devalued from about 120 to 176.625 francs to the pound sterling. This parity has since been maintained by an agreement with the British Government. Currency devaluation momentarily facilitated exports at a time when the Congo was obliged to seek new outlets for its products; it also brought about an increase of 40 per cent in the price of imported commodities and greatly increased the cost of living, which in turn necessitated a general rise in wages. Adjustments still are continuing.

The Congo's external trade has shown an almost continuous expansion. From about $2,000,000 in 1891, it rose to $25,000,000 in 1913, and to $108,000,000 in 1938. Prior to 1913, and again from 1926 to 1930 imports considerably exceeded exports; the country was in course of equipment. Before the present war the Congo shipped more than four-fifths (in value) of its produce to Belgium, where it entered free of duty, and derived from Belgium nearly one-half of its imports, although granting no preferential treatment to Belgian supplies; at present, practically the whole of the Congo's exports go either to the United States or to the British Empire under directions of the Combined Raw Materials Board and Combined Food Board, Washington, D. C.; the United States has become the largest source of supply. In 1943 exports passed the $105,000,000 mark, with imports valued at only $51,000.000. (Exports from and imports to the Ruanda-Urundi Territories were about $5,000,000, and $3,500,000 respectively, as compared with $2,500,000 in each direction in 1938.) These figures indicate the expansion of production under the strain of the Congo's war effort, and the restrictions placed on the exportation of goods by the governments of the supplying countries.

Production in the Congo steadily increased in quantity, quality, and variety as the development of the country increased. In their original state the Congo natives grew only a small number of foodstuffs and manufactured only a few rudimentary implements, although some weaving of cloth, making of pottery, of ornamental weapons, and musical instruments was done; wood carving of truly artistic designs was also done. Stanley drew up a fairly long list of products potentially suitable for export, but actually, up to 1906, the only noteworthy exports were ivory, native manufactured palm oil, palm kernels, cocoa, and rubber. The last-named item looms large in the memory of those who are remotely acquainted with the history of the Congo; in fact, the wild-rubber output barely exceeded 5,000 tons in any year, and by 1938 it had dropped to 71 tons. However, prospecting for mines, and agricultural research work were proceeding. Copper, gold, and diamond production was beginning when Belgium took over the administration of the Congo from King Leopold II in 1908.

In the brief period that elapsed between that moment and the outbreak of the First World War, native institutions and economic

activities received further encouragement; mineral resources continued to be developed in addition to the promotion of tin and
radium ores. At the same time cotton cultivation was introduced
with the help of American experts recommended by the British
Cotton Growing Association, and in 1912 the Congo could claim
the distinction of being the first country in which the mechanical
production of palm oil was developing successfully. The first large
cattle ranches date from the same period. During the First World
War the raw materials and gold supplied by the Congo contributed
to the common resources of the Allies; but, although appreciable,
this was a modest contribution compared with the fruits of the
present war effort.

A few figures will illustrate both the stage reached on the eve of
the present war, and the development since achieved in the output
of strategic matériel. Quantities produced in 1939 and 1943 respectively, were: copper, 135,000 and 170,000 tons; cobalt concentrates,
0 and 2,300 tons; manganese concentrates, 2,800 tons and 33,000
tons; zinc concentrates, 35,000 and 54,000 tons; tin, 9,900 and 20,000
tons; palm oil, 99,100 and 132,000 tons; gum copal, 13,000 and
18,700 tons; rubber, 1,250 and 13,200 tons; fibers akin to jute, 6,000
and 11,000 tons; timber, 1,460,000 cubic feet and 5,950,000 cubic
feet. The output of diamonds (mainly industrial), attaining the record figure of 8,360,000 carats in 1939, or about 82 per cent of world
production, rose to 10,237,000 carats in 1943. On the other hand,
the gold output dropped from 550,000 ounces to 470,000 ounces
because equipment and labor were diverted to other products,
notably tin, regarded as an urgent need of the United Nations.
Production of palm kernels declined from 96,000 to 88,000 tons,
largely because of the better grade of palm fruit milled (a higher
palm oil content spelling smaller kernels). The cotton output remained at approximately 47,000 tons in both 1939 and 1943, and
27,500 tons of coffee were produced in 1943 as compared with
24,000 tons in 1939. War necessities stimulated the production of
some rare metals and ores, such as uranium, wolframite, and tan-
talite. Among new ventures of strategic interest is the growing of
pyrethrum, at the request of the United States Government, and
the production of silkworm guts, of which over 2,000,000 were supplied in 1943 to the Allied Medical Services. Rubber plantations

have been greatly extended, particularly under an agreement with the United States Rubber Reserve.

Thanks to the increased efficiency of native farmers, not only have the food needs of the larger number of wage earners been met, but the standard of living of the entire population has been raised. The Congo's resources sufficed to relieve the scarcity caused by a severe drought in 1943 in some of the eastern districts, and in addition to make substantial shipments of maize, rice, manioc, and peanuts to neighboring British areas suffering from a shortage owing to drought.

The equipment of some of the principal mines and smelters equals the best to be found in any country. However, the most characteristic evidence of economic progress in the Congo may be seen in the steadily increasing growth, in number, variety, and size, of manufacturing undertakings. Shipyards, cotton spinning and weaving mills, sugar factories, sawmills, cement works; factories producing hand tools, copper wire, explosives, sulfuric acid, cement or clay tiles, footwear, clothing; foundries utilizing scrap; repair shops, garages, retreading plants; oil mills (in addition to the palm-oil factories) crushing cotton seed, palm kernels, peanuts, and so on; apart from a number of waterworks and electric power stations, of which the largest produce almost 1,000,000 kw-hr a day.

Here, as in any other country, economic expansion is evidenced by the activities of the building trades. In lieu of the early settlements with their log and mud houses, and corrugated iron roofing, modern cities are springing up, with attractive dwellings, stately cathedrals, impressive hotels, bank buildings and stores, swimming pools, sports arenas, golf links, and so on. Léopoldville, with about 100,000 inhabitants, including some 6,000 white residents, is a charming garden city on the banks of the beautiful Stanley Pool. Elisabethville has the aspect of a prosperous European community, Stanleyville the lure of an Arabic township. On the larger mines and plantations the managerial personnel or the owners are housed in substantial villas. In native villages throughout the country brick cottages are gradually superseding the traditional grass huts.

The Belgian Congo is yet a very young country. Large areas are but little developed; in almost all there is room for a more intensive utilization of the soil and subsoil. As yet no oil fields have been discovered, save for some low-grade deposits of shale oil, and only one minor coal mine is in operation. Rich iron ore is abundant, but unexploited for lack of coal. Gigantic reserves of cellulose, such as exist in the jungle and in the papyrus-clogged reaches of the Lualaba River, remain untapped. This reserve affords great possibilities for the manufacture of cellulose and plastics.

Only 6,000 tons of phosphates are being imported annually, green manures being used as fertilizers, and although the Government imposes reforestation, soil erosion is still a menace in many regions. However, the natives are being educated gradually to improved methods of cultivation, whereby their standard of living is raised and their purchasing capacity increased in proportion to the larger volume of marketable goods they are producing. Thus, one of the main obstacles to the country's advancement—its poor soil—is being remedied.

Of the two other hindrances which were cited—the difficulty of access, and the scanty and backward population—the network of communications, already very extensive, should go far to assist in surmounting. Some day a navigable waterway will no doubt connect Matadi and Léopoldville; this would be a feasible project, provided there is a sufficient volume of traffic to warrant duplication of the existing railroad facilities, and one which incidentally might make available a portion of the huge reserves of hydraulic power pouring through the Cataracts, if suitable uses can be found for electrical energy. The problem of man power is being solved on the one hand through mechanization, on the other through the successful fight waged against tropical diseases as well as with improved food and better infant care, bringing about a steady decline in the death rate, and a rapid increase in the birth rate. The Negro population is growing in number and strength. It is growing in knowledge, also. Technical skill is increasing among the natives, and their spirit of enterprise is stimulated by a new feeling of freedom and responsibility, and the acquisition of new habits and wants.

The country stands, however, in need of more white leaders and teachers, and of more capital, which only the older communities can provide. The Belgian Congo remains open to the coöperation and private initiative of men of good will, regardless of their nationality. Although the country still contains an abundance of untapped wealth, it is not an Eldorado; the average yield of investments has hitherto proved very modest; but a generous outlay of money and work may expect a fair return. The tourist seeking picturesque and novel surroundings will find ample enjoyment in the wide vistas of the Congo, the snowcapped volcanoes of the eastern reaches, the beautiful national parks, and the simple life of the outlying native communities. The Congo Tourist Office caters to visitors, and the expansion of tourist traffic, no less than industrial progress, will provide occupations for white craftsmen and traders.

CHAPTER XXVIII

Health, Education, and Social Welfare

BY GEORGE W. CARPENTER

O N RETURNING FROM his first visit to the Congo, King Albert remarked: "The chief wealth of the colony is its people." Time has vindicated his judgment. Obviously material wealth can be exploited only so far as laborers and craftsmen are there to do the work. Labor shortage often limits the rate of progress. Destructive exploitation of African man power has been recognized as stupid and self-defeating—it lowers the country's potential productive capacity. Hence, both Government and industry are today greatly concerned for the physical and social welfare of African peoples.

But beyond this immediate concern one must clearly look forward to a growing participation by African peoples in their own development and leadership, to growing social and political autonomy, and to expanding intercourse between them and the world at large. This implies a vast field of change and growth. The African who, a generation ago, knew no world beyond walking or paddling distance from his village now finds himself thrust into active relations with peoples half a world away. His cultural world, limited then to the crafts and traditions of his ancestors, now expands in a bewildering succession of new experiences and fresh ideas as modern world culture sweeps across Africa. The old shell of isolation is broken.

It is fortunate that this process of change, now so rapid, had a more gradual onset. In an age of air transportation and radio communication it was bound to come; but it is well that a half-century of slower growth in mutual understanding came first. During that time effective contact has been made with all the peoples of the colony, basic knowledge of many kinds has been acquired, schools, hospitals, and other agencies set up, problems and resources surveyed, and personnel, both African and non-African, trained and brought into service on a vast and growing scale.

The pioneer work of Christian missions.—In Belgian Congo, as elsewhere in Africa, the pioneers in movements for the advancement of the people have generally been missionaries. Early in 1878, before any formal European government had been set up in the Congo Basin, the first missionaries began work there. Formidable difficulties confronted them. Hardly anything was known about the language spoken by the people. Mysterious diseases struck them down. Access to the interior by water was blocked by cataracts; by land the hostility of the people stood in their way, for the coastal people feared the loss of their monopoly of trade with the inland tribes.

Gradually these difficulties were overcome. A chain of stations was set up along the ancient caravan trail—the road over which slaves had for generations been marched to the coast. Each new group of missionaries was helped forward from station to station to fill the gaps made by sickness and death, or to establish new bases still farther inland. When navigable water was reached at Stanley Pool, steamboats were brought out and transported over 250 miles of caravan road in thousands of head-loads, reassembled at the Pool, and used to advance the process of exploration and settlement still farther. It was in one of those first tiny steamboats that George Grenfell, the British missionary, surveyed the river and drew the basic navigation charts which are still in use.

Meanwhile, language study was progressing, together with constant inquiry into the customs, traditions, and beliefs of the people. Dispensaries and hospitals were built, and medical workers began to assemble the clinical data from which have come great advances in tropical medicine. At first the people feared to trust themselves to the foreign doctor, but they soon came to depend on him; so that in the long run nothing has done more to establish mutual confidence and coöperation between the races than has Christian medical service.

Schools also began to take form. Casual instruction in crafts came first, as the white man trained helpers in all the kinds of work he had to do. Then followed classes for Africans who wished to know more of the white man's ways, skills, and ideas. From those classes went forth the first African teachers, young men who wanted to share with their own people all that they had learned.

Naturally, the heart of this teaching was religious. The missionary constantly seeks to share this highest good with any more tangible benefits he may be able to render. Some of the missionaries regard schools, hospitals, and other public institutions chiefly as a means by which to arouse interest and gain a hearing for the Christian message. A more profound and more general view recognizes the inherent value of these services and welcomes them as practical expressions of Christian brotherhood and as contributory means toward securing the "more abundant life" which Christ promised. All would agree, however, that the Christian "way of life" itself is the central and basic contribution which they have to offer, and that it is the essential factor in the remaking of man and of society in Africa—and elsewhere. Hence, one of the primary preoccupations of the missionary is the development of an indigenous African church, a church fully integrated into the newly emerging African culture, with its roots deep in the people's inherited religious awareness and its influence reaching into all their attitudes and relationships. Such a church is taking shape; its constructive and stabilizing influence must henceforth be taken into account.

This process of entering into the life of an African people through service has been repeated time after time across the Continent. Even today one may visit outposts deep in the equatorial forest where the people's confidence is still to be won, where language barriers still limit intercourse, where all disease is still attributed to witchcraft and the white doctor is regarded as a practitioner of magic. From this primitive beginning one may find every stage of growth, up to the established central station, complete with hospital, nurses' training school, maternity center, grade school, teachers' institute, and other services, ringed about with hundreds of villages where school, church, and medical services are gradually transforming African life.

Throughout the years, a certain measure of uniformity in programs and methods has developed. All the Roman Catholic missionary orders at work in the colony (some forty-six in number) are subject to the authority of the Apostolic Delegate at Léopoldville. Their policies and lines of development are thus effectively correlated. More than four-fifths of the Protestant missionaries (belonging in all to some forty-five missions) are related to the Congo Protestant Council, which, through its annual meetings and permanent secretariat, also encourages joint planning and unified policies. Both groups are strongly committed to collaboration with the Government in every type of project for the promotion of African welfare.

The development of government services.—Prior to the annexation of the Congo by Belgium in 1908, the colonial government was too preoccupied in establishing its own authority to devote much attention to African welfare. The most noteworthy event of that period was the Concordat with the Vatican, signed in 1906, whereby education in the colony was entrusted to Roman Catholic missions. This agreement underlies the practical monopoly of official recognition and financial aid for educational work which Roman Catholic missions still enjoy.

The First World War supervened before the new government had time to develop long-range plans. Current policies therefore date largely from the decade 1920–1930, a time of strong public concern for the welfare of subject peoples. By that time many basic questions in tropical medicine were in process of solution; therefore, constructive public-health work could be begun. Many important applications of this new knowledge were made first in Congo.

Public health services.—It was foreseen early that many specially trained workers would be needed to deal effectively with the health problems of the Congo. A School of Tropical Medicine was therefore established at Brussels in 1923. (It was later moved to Antwerp.) Advanced courses were offered for doctors already qualified in general medicine, and an elementary course for laymen. Both were made available to all interested prospective residents in the Colony. Through the work of this school a large and able corps of medical workers has been built up in the colony. Nearly all the missionaries who have had the courses are associated with the Government in public-health work. The Brussels course, or its equivalent, is a prerequisite to the practice of medicine in the Congo.

The primary objectives of the government health services are to accelerate the rate of increase of the population and to improve the health and physical efficiency of the people. There are two lines of approach: control of the major endemic diseases, and reduction of infant mortality.

The disease-control program centers in the campaign against African sleeping sickness (trypanosomiasis). This disease, transmitted by the tsetse fly, was invariably fatal until a treatment was worked out (in collaboration with the Rockefeller Institute) using a synthetic compound of arsenic. Injections of this drug destroy the trypanosomes in the blood stream and make the patient noninfective, but in advanced cases trypanosomes may remain active in the nervous system and prevent a complete cure. Rapid examination and diagnosis is made possible by a typical swelling and hardening of certain glands in the neck.

The characteristics of the disease suggested a method of control which has been highly successful. An area of heavy infection is selected, a staff of numerous doctors, sanitary agents, and African medical assistants is organized and distributed, and a complete census of the population recorded, with the result of a medical examination of each individual. All cases of sleeping sickness are placed under compulsory treatment. At intervals of six months each village is revisited and reëxamined. All new or recurrent cases are again brought under treatment. This procedure is repeated until new cases become very rare. The special staff is then transferred to another district, the regular local staff making periodic reëxaminations thereafter at intervals of one year or longer.

At the same time, other widely prevalent diseases which can be treated effectively with the staff and resources available are also diagnosed and treated, thus reducing the rate of infection and improving the general level of health in the area. Among the diseases thus dealt with are malaria, the dysenteries, smallpox, yaws, syphilis, typhoid, hookworm, and other parasitic infections.

By this systematic program trypanosomiasis has been brought under effective control in the Bas Congo and Kwango areas where it threatened wholesale depopulation, and the campaign is being extended to other areas as rapidly as the staff permits. Reduction in the incidence of some of the other diseases is also noteworthy, and the people's readiness to coöperate in public-health measures is enhanced by the success of the campaign.

A large share of the burden of this campaign has been carried by FOREAMI (*Fondation Reine Elisabeth pour l'Assistance Médicale aux Indigènes*), a body established under the patronage of Queen Elizabeth of Belgium for the promotion of public health in the Congo. FOREAMI, Government, and missions have worked amicably together in the campaign, and results amply demonstrate the value of such collaboration.

Leprosy presents another major problem. The treatment is prolonged and severe, though recent researches have greatly reduced the discomfort involved. Complete cure is not often obtainable, but the disease can often be arrested and the danger of infection greatly reduced. Formerly, lepers were segregated to avoid infection by contact, but patients' families are now permitted to remain with them; the improvement in morale far outweighs the slight danger of infection. The leprosaria which are associated with many mission hospitals in the Congo therefore resemble African villages, each centering around a dispensary and notable for cleanliness, orderliness, and cheerfulness. Garden lands are provided to give occupation and subsistence to the able-bodied. Government financial aid helps to meet the cost of subsistence and medicine. The American Mission to Lepers contributes largely both to the first cost of leprosaria and to the annual cost of operation. Residence at a leprosarium is purely voluntary, but a large proportion of the patients remain until discharged.

Despite the fact that thousands of patients are being cared for, existing facilities cannot cope with the total task of bringing the disease under control, nor is there much prospect that this can be done until the etiology of leprosy is better understood. Further research is necessary.

General hospital and dispensary services are provided chiefly at the initiative of the Government in the large urban centers, of companies at mines, factories and large plantations, and of missions in smaller centers and in rural districts. Government aid to the missions takes the form of specific grants such as allowances for medicines and for child-welfare work, compensation for time devoted to sleeping-sickness control, and grants (to "national" missions) for buildings and staff. A large part of the cost of providing general medical service to the people is borne by the missions themselves, since the people are too poor to contribute very much.

The second major aspect of public-health service aims at increasing the birth rate and reducing infant mortality. In support of this aim the administration promotes monogamous marriages among the young and healthy, and discourages polygamy which tends to bind many of the potential mothers to senile old men while virile youths remain unmated. Polygamous marriages are therefore taxed, while a man having four or more living children by monogamous marriage is exempt from head tax. An effort is made to control the withdrawal of young men from their villages for labor at a distance, and to develop communities having a normal family life at industrial centers. Tribal customs involving promiscuity or impairment of the sexual function are frowned upon and Christian teaching and practice encouraged.

More directly, the medical authorities collaborate with the missions in providing prenatal clinics and instruction courses, baby clinics, and feeding centers for undernourished infants. Through these means much valuable instruction is brought home to the women who are often conservative and inaccessible to more formal teaching. FOREAMI is particularly active in developing and supporting this program.

Government and missions also share the task of training African medical assistants. From early days mission doctors have been training their own helpers. Several missions have regular courses where village dispensers as well as hospital staff are trained. During the past two decades the Government has worked out standard courses, which these schools now follow; it has also created its own medical training schools, located at the provincial capitals with a more advanced school at Léopoldville. After three years of resident study students are assigned to approved hospitals for practical experience, following which they return for final qualifying examinations.

All students in these courses are graduates of mission-conducted elementary schools, but high schools do not yet exist in any number, so the medical students have rather poor preparation in general knowledge. Many graduates are already sharing the labors of white doctors and nurses in hospitals, dispensaries, leprosaria, and village medical centers. Several served with the Congo medical unit in the military campaigns of northeast Africa. The medical courses of the newly established University of Elisabethville are accessible to qualified native medical assistants, who thus will be enabled to graduate as doctors.

Medical research centers in the magnificently equipped laboratory operated by the Government at Léopoldville. This unit has a very able staff and the most complete and modern equipment obtainable. It works in intimate collaboration with the whole medical personnel of the colony. In addition to many research activities the laboratory manufactures vaccines, serums, and cultures for use throughout the Congo. The University of Louvain also maintains a medical research unit at Kisantu in the Bas Congo.

Education.—Although the Concordat of 1906 led to the establishment in the Congo of several Roman Catholic teaching orders, a general plan for African education was not worked out until about 1922. Programs and curricula were first issued about 1927. The missions, both Catholic and Protestant, had already gone far in the development of elementary schools and the training of teachers. The Congo Government sought rather to build upon these foundations than to lay new ones. However, it limited its subventions to schools conducted by "national" missionaries, thereby practically withholding financial aid from Protestant schools. Provisions for a revision of this situation are under consideration.

The government program provided for three classes of schools: "official" schools, operated at government expense, and generally located in urban centers though administered by a religious body such as the *Frères des Ecoles Chrétiennes;* "aided" schools, maintained by a "national" mission with the aid of government grants; and "unaided" schools which receive neither help nor supervision from the Government. The prescribed courses for "official" and "aided" schools are quite similar, both being modeled closely on the primary-school curricula of Belgium. "Aided" schools are assigned a five-year course in two stages, two years in the "first degree" and three years in the "second degree." "Official"—urban—schools cover slightly more ground in an undivided six-year course.

The instructions to teachers state that many details may need change to adapt them to Congo conditions, but few specific suggestions are offered. The importance of agriculture and handicrafts is stressed.

This highly formal program has been undergoing revision for several years, but no new plan has been promulgated. It is quite widely held that the present program does not afford a satisfactory "education for life" for African children, whose background is completely unlike that of Belgian children, and whose needs and interests are correspondingly different. But there is little agreement as to what is required, so the old program continues to be followed.

Beyond the elementary level the official plan provides for several types of professional training (as teachers, clerks, agricultural assistants and artisans), and also for a "middle-school" program without technical content, which is roughly equivalent to an American junior high-school course. The technical courses include much practical training. The three-year senior high-school course which, in Belgium, follows the middle school is not envisaged generally for the Congo, though at least one such school is in operation.

The division of the elementary course into two levels was apparently intended to separate the program of the very numerous village schools from that of the relatively few schools at mission stations. Actually, the division may occur at a higher or lower level, depending on the ability of the village school teachers and the general tone of the community. The whole program is necessarily much more fluid than the printed instructions would indicate.

As in other parts of Africa, a very large number of village schools are still below the lowest recognized standard. Many teachers have had hardly any formal training; they are merely doing what little they can to share the meager knowledge they have. As long as the economic status of the African community remains low, as long as many villages remain small, isolated and remote, and as long as village education adheres largely to European academic patterns, the educational opportunities of many African village children will remain poor. Yet a large share of all African education goes on in these scattered schools, and, despite their limitations, they afford to thousands of boys and girls the first and often the only schooling available.

Educational advance in a country like Belgian Congo thus depends first on better-trained teachers, and second on more favorable conditions for their work. Teacher-training schools hold an important place in the activities of both Catholic and Protestant missions. At least thirty-five of them are in operation. The official scheme, followed generally by the Catholic missions, assumes that these schools will be frequented by adolescent youths, recently out of elementary school. The course reviews the whole elementary curriculum from the teacher's standpoint, but contains little fresh material to stimulate the student's own mental growth. This type of teacher training is not readily conducive to the reconstruction of primary education which is needed.

Protestant missions are free to develop their own educational patterns, though they follow the general framework of the official scheme and many of its details. They usually prefer a somewhat more thorough program of teacher training, although of necessity many partially trained teachers are in service. Normal school students are usually young married men, with some practical experience in teaching. The course includes as much fresh and stimulating material as possible, with emphasis on the social orientation of the student and his people amid current change. The wives of married students are trained to help their husbands exemplify better patterns of living, particularly regarding home sanitation, infant care, child training, food preparation, and other family responsibility. The aim is to provide community leadership in a program of which the primary school is an integral part, but only a part. At least six teacher-training schools are working on courses of this type. Many more are needed, but the lack of resources has retarded their formation.

To afford larger scope for capable teachers where villages are small and scattered, "regional schools" are being developed. A regional school is usually a distinct, self-contained community near, but not in, a centrally located village. All the villages within reach unite to provide the buildings and share in supporting the teachers. Children come from the whole area, spending week ends at home but living at the school throughout the week under the supervision of the teachers. School gardens and communal kitchens provide much of the food, and the chores of the community are shared by staff and pupils. Their corporate life together thus contributes to the educational process.

The village schools, and regional schools where they exist, feed into the higher primary schools at mission stations, numbering over 500 in the colony. Very few of the pupils in village and regional schools can find places in these higher schools, and very few of their graduates can hope to enter the professional courses at middle-school level.

The schools at mission stations are supervised and partly taught by missionaries. French is taught everywhere and used in part as a language of instruction; though apart from the polyglot communities of the large cities the local African tongues still have a large place in the schools.

The existence of several hundred languages in the colony presents a major problem. Primary teaching can be effective only when the child understands the language used; but this means that textbooks must be produced in scores of languages. Some compromise is inevitable, for many language groups are too small to support literatures. In practice, related dialects have to be grouped together and one leading language chosen for literary use. These choices are often hampered by ignorance of the structural relations between languages and by local prejudices, but they are gradually being made.

Many new fields of colonial education await development after the war, such as adult literacy movements, mass education in nutrition, sanitation, and public hygiene, improved methods in agriculture and the crafts, the use of radio, and visual education. Full progress in these fields will require the wholehearted collaboration of all agencies whose work brings them into close touch with the people, and the pooling of knowledge and experience between bodies in many parts of Africa and in other lands. It is to be hoped that official policies will foster this broad collaboration and promote this advance.

Political development and general social welfare.—The political and social development of the peoples of Belgian Congo is a major preoccupation of the administration. Current policies stem largely from recommendations of the *Commission pour la Protection des Indigènes* which was reëstablished in 1912 by King Albert after a lapse of several years. The commission includes government representatives, missionaries, and other leading colonials. It meets annually, and although it has no legislative power its recommendations carry great weight with the Government.

Belgian colonial authorities recognize, as do the British, that African institutions must undergo a gradual development, with increasing experience in local self-government under modern conditions, before effective self-government on a colony-wide scale will be possible. The Congo administration always seeks to associate with itself the chiefs and notables in each area, assigning to each that measure of authority and responsibility which his status in tribal society should enable him to exercise. Innovations are made gradually, as far as possible in the direction of strengthening and systematizing the administrative and judicial powers of the local authorities. A somewhat similar program is being worked out among the less homogeneous populations of the cities.

Labor recruiting and conditions of work are under government control. In some areas the establishment of new agricultural or industrial enterprises has been forbidden because their labor needs would have taken too many young men from their villages, thereby impairing social stability and threatening gradual depopulation. Minimum standards as regards wages, hours, food, housing, and clothing are enforced to assure the health and protect the reasonable interests of the workers. (Many enterprises, notably the *Union Minière,* voluntarily go far beyond these minimum provisions to assure the welfare of their employees.)

The Government is also interested in the betterment of village life through improved agriculture, cash crops, and assured markets. To this end agricultural experimentation is being carried on, notably by INEAC (*Institut national pour l'Etude agronomique du Congo Belge*). African agricultural demonstrators are being trained by certain of the "national" missions. Selected crops are introduced, by compulsion if necessary, and by agreement with commercial processing agencies the Government assures the sale of the total crop produced at standard prices. Cotton, palm oil, and hemp fiber are typical crops. Each adult male is required to clear and plant a certain area each year. Compulsion is used only until the community sees the value of the practice so that its continuance on a voluntary basis becomes assured. In some cases crop failures have led to difficulties. In other instances success has been notable, with corresponding financial advantage to the African planters.

The total task of an African colonial government, in relation to the people it governs, is extremely complex. The welfare of the people and the development of the country depend on many inter-related and sometimes conflicting factors, among which the Government must keep a due balance and proportion. Even the goal to be sought has not always been clear—nor is it entirely so yet—though world opinion tends increasingly to regard full participation of all peoples in a common world culture and life on an autonomous basis as a practicable and perhaps a necessary aim. That the African peoples possess inherent capacity for such participation is now certain. How and when they will reach it, or in what relation they will then stand to the European Powers that now guide their progress, are matters which only the future can unfold. For the present, it can be said only that, despite the limitations which have been noted, the Belgian administration is earnestly endeavoring to advance the welfare of the peoples of the Congo, with a due sense of its responsibility as trustee of their interests.

Part Seven

SECOND WORLD
WAR AND AFTER

CHAPTER XXIX

Belgium under the Occupation

BY ARTHUR WAUTERS

FOREIGN OCCUPATION is no novelty in Belgian history. Belgium, invaded six times in five centuries, has lived under the domination of other Powers for more or less extended periods of time. Belgium owes this dubious privilege to her geographic position. Her valleys constitute natural paths of invasion. She also affords battlefields where belligerents may settle their accounts. One could name at least twenty places in Belgium which, in past centuries, were the theaters of great, historical battles. This is true of Fleurus, Neerwinden, Hondschooten, Veurne, and even the French town of Sedan, near the Belgian border.

The strategy of the armies which meet on Belgian territory is not a mysterious one. There is nothing unusual about it. It contains no element of surprise. It is the logical development of the classical military concepts of the ages.

Today, once again, it is over Belgian territory that some of the greatest air battles of the Second World War are taking place. Technics have changed, but this inevitable meeting ground of armies remains the same.

Belgium has always lived in a permanent state of international insecurity. The curse of war has never ceased to overshadow the land. For some time before this war, 20 per cent of the budget was devoted to assuring national defense. This percentage, in peacetime, was one of the highest in the world. The general mobilization brought under arms 10.5 per cent of the population. Up to the eve of the second German invasion, May 10, 1940, the Belgian High Command had been building fortifications which were believed to be strong. Aside from the air force which, in so small a country, could not be developed to the same degree as the other arms of the service, the national army was prepared for the unhappy events which obviously were coming.

To everyone's suprise, the army did not resist as long as had been expected. Those who passed too hasty a judgment, when it was crushed under the sheer weight of superior numbers and matériel, were even harsher when they recalled the heroic and prolonged resistance of the Belgian Army during the First World War. Then, when the regrettable confusion of those days in May, 1940, had passed, a clearer perspective emerged. The unbelievable strength of the enemy attacking the democracies was revealed by one setback after another of the democracies. Not a single ally was spared the revelation.

Educated by long and repeated experiences, the Belgians knew exactly what foreign occupation held in store for them. It loosed upon them plunder, destruction, hunger, and persecution. But because of this very experience, they understood the effective and hidden arms which had to be used to conquer the oppressor from within.

The Nazis did not conceal their intentions. They had organized a special corps of men, responsible for the systematic and scientific plunder of occupied territories. Special units, which advanced with the troops, were led by officer-economists (*Wirtschafts-Offizieren*). One of their writers, H. Baumgarten, in an article entitled "Die Neue Waffe" in *Der Deutsche Volkswirt* of October 18, 1940, scarcely five months after the German penetration of Belgium, described the technic of plundering. "Everywhere," he wrote, "where stocks of raw materials or finished products were found, signs were put up reading *Beschlagnahmt von Armee Oberkommando* (requisitioned by the Army High Command). The speed of this plundering could be measured by what took place at Antwerp. An American writer, L. Moën, who lived in Belgium under the German occupation, says, in his book *Under the Iron Heel,* that German troops seized the town of Antwerp on May 18, 1940, at eight o'clock in the morning. By three in the afternoon, military trucks were already leaving for the Reich, loaded with part of the loot stolen from the docks and warehouses of the port.

The economic seizure of Belgium, like that of other occupied countries, had a triple objective: to steal raw materials and finished products; to use the economic framework of the conquered regions to produce for the German war machine; to disarm the occupied countries and take away from them any material basis of resistance.

This brigandage was carried out in a country which possesses one of the best-equipped ports in continental Europe, the densest railroad network on the European Continent, abundant and highly skilled labor, and which exported, before the war, more than 50 per cent of its production. This economic raid was made on a nation which possessed no raw materials at all, outside of coal, and which, in normal times, imported 70 per cent of its wheat. The results, of course, were disastrous. They were beyond all expectations.

First, the entire economic regime of Belgium was *gleichgeschaltet* (brought into line). It was changed to meet the more rigorous demands of totalitarian economy, inspired by the harshest of Nazi "corporate" concepts. Requisitioning of goods and control of all economic activity were submitted to an implacable discipline. Industrial production and commerce, agriculture, transportation and communications, foreign trade, and financial institutions were imprisoned in a belt of steel which left no room for the slightest individual initiative.

The country was crushed under the enormous costs of the occupation. These reached a sum greater than the ordinary budget of prewar Belgium. The national revenue dropped and, in spite of the decrease, the expenses of occupation absorbed almost a third of it. It was estimated that the support of one soldier of the army of occupation cost five or six times more than the support of a Belgian soldier. At one time, this occupation army numbered almost 1,000,000 men. The public debt and circulation of money spiraled upward. The manipulation of stocks was one of the favorite technics of the Germans for facilitating their plunder. By buying up industrial and financial stocks at ridiculously low prices, they acquired more and more influence in these national organizations, thus assuring themselves of their control.

The chapter of destruction in Belgium is, alas, not yet concluded. But in seventeen days of fighting, Belgium saw more destruction

than did England during the first seventeen months of the war.
Then the English unfortunately experienced serial bombardments.
But the Belgians were not spared this either, although they bravely
endured it as one of the inexorable necessities of war. Even the
underground movement was bent upon the destruction of key
positions in order to paralyze enemy action.

The destructive activity of the Nazis not only affected the material side of the country; the Nazis were also determined to wipe
out the free institutions, whose time-honored benefits the Belgian
people have long enjoyed. The occupier, aided by a very few
traitors, ousted government officials, city magistrates, professors,
judges. At the end of a year, the Germans had already issued enough
decrees, all unconstitutional, illegal, or violating The Hague Convention, to cover 8,000 pages of what they brazenly called "The
Official Gazette." The most outstanding example was the German
creation of courts of last appeal.

In March, 1941, less than a year after the invasion, 64,000 of the
140,000 freight cars of the Belgian railroads had disappeared. Without any doubt the situation has considerably deteriorated since
then. There is no record of the number of valuable locomotives
carried off to central Europe, nor of the number of coaches used
by the German Army as improvised winter quarters on the Russian
front during the disastrous campaign which ended in so many
defeats for Hitler.

Another fact gave an accurate measurement of the extent of Nazi
greed. Prewar Belgium exported coal. But under the occupation
the schools were closed in the winter because of lack of fuel. This
fact exposed the persistent perfidy of the Germans who blamed the
English blockade for the dire want which caused so much suffering
among the population.

The food shortage in Belgium was one of the most acute in all
of occupied Europe. No outside aid was forthcoming. The consequences were disastrous for the population. They were aggravated
further by the fact that the Belgians were still suffering from the
physiological effects of the privations inflicted upon them twenty-
five years ago. So rapid was the physical deterioration of the people
that several generations will feel the effect. This result was revealed,
for example, when the youth of Belgium submitted to medical

examinations for conscription. What the famine of the occupation has done to the most populated country of the world cannot yet be told.

The normal prewar food ration in Belgium was about 2,800 calories. During the occupation the food, theoretically issued by the Germans, amounted to about a third of the prewar figure. In addition, the distribution was, more often than not, merely a pretense, since the consumer could not obtain the food allowed by his ration cards. The black market, with the coöperation of the Germans, grew to proportions unheard of elsewhere. There have been long weeks without potatoes, and there have been days even without bread. As for the basic foods, there has never been a sufficient quantity. The serious results of this shortage may be observed in children from six to fourteen years old and the most affected are the adolescents. Hunger has stunted their growth and reduced their weight. Although attempts were made to institute an official and special rationing for pregnant women and nursing mothers, there was a serious shortage of fats and proteins. The fate of the old people was tragic. Often their disabilities prevented them from standing in line in front of the food stores. The situation was complicated by a shortage of soap and a scarcity of clothes and shoes.

The consequences for the nation are most frightening. Premature births, anemia, and rickets have increased. Tuberculosis, which had been successfully brought under control before the war, is making inroads, the only remedy for which is more food. Careful and scientific research reveals that the birth rate of the nation is in grave danger. A large part of the adolescent section of the population shows suspended development in puberty, an unbalancing factor to the vitality of the population.

Besides the aid which might have come from outside and which remained unorganized, one could hardly count on the inside resources of Belgium. The country produces much less agriculturally than Holland or France. On the other hand, a shortage of feed for cattle and poultry has resulted in a considerable reduction in their numbers. Some ten years will be needed to restore this situation to normal, even supposing that the elaborate postwar plans for the economic rehabilitation of Belgium meet with no unforeseen obstacles.

From the moment of their entry into Belgium, the Germans abolished all traditional liberties such as freedom of association, of assembly, of demonstration, of the press, etc. They introduced anti-Semitism which hitherto was completely unknown. In spite of being the most densely populated country in the world, Belgium had always welcomed foreigners. Three or four hundred thousand workers, of some forty different nationalities, lived side by side with their Belgian comrades. The Poles and the Italians even had their own schools, with their own textbooks and their own teachers. The Belgian State, that is, the taxpaying public, supported these institutions.

The Nazis prohibited Jews from holding government jobs; they drove them from the newspapers, the Stock Exchange, and the professions. They took away their radios, confiscated their bank deposits, and forced them to declare their property. They then took measures humiliating in their vulgarity. They prohibited Jewish children from attending school and all Jews from frequenting public parks or swimming pools; Jews were required to wear the Star of David. Thousands were deported en masse; women were separated from their husbands; children were kidnaped and their persecution recalled the blackest days in the history of the Jews.

Freemasonry was not spared. Offices were seized, files were stolen, and its emblems held up to derision. The high dignitaries of Belgian Freemasonry were beaten under circumstances reminiscent of the most vicious of crimes. The Nazis were especially harsh in their treatment of the labor movement, a powerful factor in this highly industrialized country. Out of 8,300,000 people, about 1,000,000 were members of unions. These were dissolved, their funds confiscated, their offices seized, their militant leaders hunted down and imprisoned or executed. Strikes were outlawed. With a very few Quisling workers, the Nazis tried in vain to establish a totalitarian labor organization. The attempt was a resounding failure.

Members of the teaching profession, who openly demonstrated their love of country, were ousted. Standard textbooks were rewritten in the light of Nazi "culture."

Soon the rhythm of persecutions began to step up. Unemployment relief was abolished for any worker refusing to go to Germany. In certain cases, food cards were withdrawn, and when all these restrictive measures produced only the feeblest results, the Nazis had recourse to a method with which they had already experimented a quarter of a century earlier. Over 500,000 Belgian workers, of both sexes, were deported to German war factories. They were arrested in movies, in churches, at factory gates, on trains, in streetcars, on the streets. Reports received from Germany by Christian workers' organizations revealed revolting physical and moral conditions in the camps for deported workers.

After the capitulation of the Belgian Army, there reigned in Belgium, as elsewhere, great mental confusion. But at the end of a few weeks, the Belgians recovered. They had become convinced that their liberation would not come from the outside only, and that they must actively coöperate with the Allies.

Memories of the occupation during the First World War, still vivid in their minds, helped them to pick up again all the old technics which they had successfully used in the past. They perfected them. One of the first examples of inside resistance was the reappearance of the underground press. During the last war, newspapers like *La Libre Belgique* had acquired universal fame and had justified the admiration which the entire world felt for the heroism, the skill, and the cunning of those who thus maintained—in spite of the secret police, in spite of the army of occupation—one of Belgium's traditional liberties, that of the press.

The Belgian press from 1940 to 1944 did not fail the previous reputation for loyalty which it had acquired a quarter of a century earlier. Not a single Belgian newspaper reappeared with the voluntary agreement of its owner or of its editor in chief. The Nazis exercised unheard-of pressures to obtain certain concessions. Failing this, they arrested the most outstanding men in the profession and deported them to Germany. Many of them died in Gestapo camps. Others, on street corners, were attacked and beaten.

But by now Belgian patriots, anticipating the legal and judicial punishment of war crimes, meted out punishment in their turn, with revolvers, to some of those few newspapermen who had turned traitor. Reprisals for this were of unexampled cruelty. An eighteen-year-old student was hung after having undergone third-degree torture at the hands of the German police. But, in spite of all this violence, the underground press grew. There came into existence more than 200 newspapers, published in one or the other national language. Some newspapers, of course, have had an ephemeral existence; their editors and distributors promptly paid with their lives for their silent heroism. But others, issuing sometimes several regional editions, had a wide circulation. The remarkable thing is that these publications, in the midst of so many restrictions, maintained an admirable liberty of expression, discussing theories and doctrines of neighboring countries, thus upholding the strict tradition of a free press.

It is easy to imagine what it means to edit, print, and publish a newspaper in a country where paper and lead are scarce and where all workshops must function underground. Distribution, above all, was an extraordinary tour de force. Sometimes wily patriots even used envelopes of the German administration to send literature to the official who owned the stationery.

In the schools, teachers taught English, dictating to their pupils the speeches of Churchill and Roosevelt, which they had taken down in shorthand while listening to the radio; this had been done at the risk of their lives, since to listen to the enemy radio was forbidden under penalty of severe punishment. On the day when an attempt was made to force German professors into the University of Brussels, the more than 2,000 students went out on strike. Since then, the school has been closed and its principal professors have been arrested. Although the instructors were released, some of them were arrested again later on. The Brussels students were cordially welcomed by their comrades into the universities of Louvain, Liége and Ghent. At the University of Ghent, students had for some time ostentatiously refused to address each other except in English. The odious deportation decree struck also at the youth in the schools. As railroad sabotage increased, students were required to ride on trains as hostages, in an attempt to prevent further damage. There were underground student newspapers also.

Resistance against the occupation rose in all sections of the population and at all social levels. It picked up a totally unexpected speed among the farmers who generally have had the reputation of being timorous. The Nazis forced them to join the "Agricultural Corporation"—a German economic vehicle for the systematic plundering of the country. The farmers refused to hand over their crops for requisition. The effectiveness of their opposition was revealed by a newspaper in the pay of the Nazis, *Le Pays Réel,* which reported that 50 to 75 per cent of the milk, butter, and wheat went to the black market rather than to the commissariat of Hitler's army.

Then, suddenly, with a courage which revealed their sharp spirit of independence, the farmers refused to pay their dues to the Agricultural Corporation. They were forced into court. Here they pleaded violation of their constitutional right of free association. This mass trial provoked a widespread scandal. The accused found themselves on firm judicial ground. The Belgian judges, ruling according to Belgian law, decided in favor of the Belgians and against the Germans. The latter immediately issued a decree, henceforth prohibiting the judges from questioning the constitutionality of their edicts. The farmers' resistance took on the speed of a peasant uprising in certain sections of the country. To break the will of the rebels, it was necessary for German army forces to surround some of the small villages in Luxemburg Province.

Resistance among the clergy was no less willful. Obscure country priests refused to say mass at funeral services for Flemish Nationalist or Rexist traitors. The Rexists committed violence in sacred places. Curates and vicars refused communion to Quislings who wore the dishonorable insignia of their servitude. With the aid of the villagers, these curates and vicars gave shelter to British aviators, shot down over Belgian territory. Many were arrested and some were executed.

Cardinal van Roey denounced the heresy of the German racial theories. He showed that Christian ethics could not accept the new materialist interpretation of Naziism. He protested against the deportation of workers. "These measures of human requisition," said the Cardinal, "are absolutely unjustifiable. They violate natural law, international law, and Christian ethics.

"They take into account no considerations whatsoever—neither of the dignity and the essential liberty of the human being which is annihilated by coercion, threats and harsh sanctions; nor of the well-being or the honor of families, painfully wounded by the violent separation of their members; nor of the supreme interest of society which will fatally suffer later from the anger and dull hatred sown in thousands of oppressed hearts.

"Physical and mental coercion is a serious thing. More serious still is violence against a conscience. Belgian citizens are being forced to coöperate, directly or indirectly, in the military preparations of a foreign power, which unjustly subjects their country to an extremely harsh regime of occupation and which offers not the least assurance as to its future."

The Belgian bishops, who signed this statement with their archbishop, added this further warning:

"Human reason and Christian ethics condemn and brand these unworthy and barbarous procedures; any collaboration in the execution of these measures is seriously illicit in conscience. The civilized nations, if made aware of this state of affairs, cannot help but express their profound disapproval."

The resistance of the clergy particularly irritated the few collaborationists. One of their newspapers wrote:

"The British Broadcasting Corporation broadcasts are discussed in Catholic schools and the occupying authority is ridiculed from the pulpit. Our churches have been transformed into political meeting halls, and sermons, full of bitterness and hate, are preached. Certain priests have advised peasants not to deliver their produce to the distributing organizations. Others keep hidden stores of arms, and there is no doubt that the terrorists and wealthy folk, who want to escape forced labor, find safe refuge in the monasteries. In short, this is how the clergy responds to the consideration shown them by the occupying authorities."

For their part, the Belgian workers, inspired by a long past of obstinate and victorious struggles, showed an admirable persistence in adversity. They constituted a coveted prey to the Nazis, whose war machine ceaselessly exacted more and more war materials and munitions.

The workers scornfully refused to join the Nazi labor organization—that booby trap which could not fool men who had fought for fifty-five years in free trade unions. They secretly remained faithful to their old organizations. They went out on strike, in spite of its being prohibited. Some of these strikes involved 125,000 workers and lasted some eight days. In the Lower Sambre region, the strikers, hunted by the Gestapo, took refuge in the woods. At the great Cockerill steel mills, employing more than 10,000 workers, they successfully resisted deportation, forcing the Germans to back down before their menacing and stubborn attitude. The Christian workers fought side by side with their Socialist comrades in this implacable struggle.

The Belgian Workers' party reorganized underground. It even held a secret convention which lasted two days. Communist workers, forgetting old ideological differences, were drawn into illegal activity, and showed great ingenuity in the underground struggle.

Acts of sabotage increased. Soon the coördinated movement took on a strictly national character, with a merging of all parties and all opinions.

Real guerrillas and the maquis formed bands in rural areas. The partisans not only struck down traitors, but, calm and methodical, they systematically set about destroying the Nazi war machine. They organized raids on the Labor Exchange to destroy files on the requisition of skilled workers. They stole ration cards to feed their comrades living underground. The Belgian underground struck at factories, bridges, canal locks, railroad stations and food depots. Eight thousand acts of sabotage, according to German newspapers, were carried out in Belgium in 1943. This figure, in itself, is an indication of the size of this astonishing movement.

A number of these operations revealed a strictly military discipline. A large chemical factory was dynamited, resulting in several hundred victims. In one month, 110 trains were derailed. The effectiveness of this violent activity can be measured by the fact that to rebuild a damaged locomotive, 10,000 workdays are needed. In a single day, in a single district, 15 electrical distribution stations were destroyed in twenty minutes. Electric current to western Germany was cut off for a long period. Railroad stations were militarily occupied and held by partisans for several hours. Patriots raided prisons and hospitals to free their imprisoned or wounded comrades. The workers also employed the "slowdown" and resorted to sabotage by refined methods which killed motors, provoked short circuits, stopped the cylinders of rolling mills, and misdirected trains to the wrong destinations.

Since the beginning of the war, from 3,000 to 5,000 partisans have been executed by the occupying authorities. This figure in itself is a measure of the heroism of occupied Belgium and the effectiveness of the underground movement. This death list, which is not by any means complete, bears the names of citizens from every region of the country. Every profession is included—metallurgists, priests, bakers, notaries, lawyers, barkeepers, miners, farmers, etc.

The Belgian ministers who were able to escape from occupied France reorganized the legal government of their country in London. This legality has never been contested. The Pierlot government was recognized not only by all the United Nations, but by neutrals as well. It included among its members two men who came from occupied Belgium, where they had taken an active part in the underground resistance movement. Thus, besides the secret means of contact, the Government had as perfect as possible a liaison with inside opinion.

Among the governments in exile, the Belgian Government was distinguished by the fact that it took the wise precaution of placing the gold reserves of its National Bank in safekeeping in a free country. It could, therefore, with the powerful financial aid of the Belgian Congo, pay all its expenses. And they were many.

It was aided in this task by an advisory committee, composed of Belgian members of Parliament in exile in England, as well as of prominent persons from the business world, from social welfare fields, and from labor circles.

The first responsibility of the Government was to reorganize its army. It called to arms Belgian citizens from all over the world. The Belgian Air Force, in spite of the army's capitulation on May 27, 1940, never ceased to fight. Its pilots took part in the great air battle over England in the autumn of 1940. Only two of them survived this glorious ordeal. Since then, numerous young men, escaping from Belgium at the risk of their lives, joined these survivors. And each day they prepared, with their comrades in the Royal Air Force, for the liberation of their compatriots.

Belgian seamen sail not only on English boats, but also with the Belgian merchant fleet, which was successfully evacuated to British shores. A large number of the ships have been torpedoed. Belgian seamen have made a great contribution to the solution of Great Britain's food problem.

Almost all the Belgian fishermen succeeded in reaching the British Isles. Their fishing boats, with modern equipment, are equaled only by those of the Norwegians. Their first job was to aid in the evacuation of Dunkirk in the summer of 1940. Here a number of Belgian fishermen, braving gunfire, water, and flames, returned several times in their boats to rescue soldiers of the British Expeditionary Force in France.

Three-fourths of the diamond cutters of the world worked in Belgium before the war. The great majority of them succeeded in reaching England or America, where they were engaged in their trade. Eighty-five per cent of the industrial diamonds they work on come from the Belgian Congo. Twenty thousand Belgian citizens found refuge in the United Kingdom, and 85 per cent of them were employed in war factories, where their skill and zeal made a real contribution to the war effort.

Belgian refugees reorganized their national life on the hospitable shores of Great Britain. They opened schools for their children. Belgian youth was educated in the two national languages, by Belgian teachers, according to Belgian scholastic programs. A hundred or more students were warmly welcomed into English universities. Workers have reconstituted their Belgian unions, which function according to national methods. The Belgian Red Cross created a great number of clinics, rest homes, and retraining centers for the sick and wounded. Belgian judges in the Belgian War Councils and the Maritime Law Court held sessions and passed judgment, in accordance with Belgian law.

England, anxious to respect the liberty of others, not only gave these refugees food and lodging, when she herself had so many pressing problems to solve; she also gave them that most precious thing of all, freedom of expression. The Belgians had two radio stations at London, over which they spoke in their two national languages to their compatriots several times each day. They published a half dozen periodicals, which were subjected to no political censorship whatsoever.

Belgium was among the first nations to apply herself to postwar problems. To do this, she set up a commission which has devoted itself to an examination of all the aspects of the country's rehabilitation.

In her struggle for liberation, Belgium has had the unexpected good fortune of having at her command her colonial empire, whose size is more than seventy-eight times her own size. The Belgian Congo not only has furnished the Allies with raw materials indispensable to the war effort; it has given them an army made up exclusively of Negro volunteers, led by Negro noncommissioned and white commissioned officers. This army, outnumbered by the enemy one to five, participated in the Ethiopian campaign, where it captured 15,000 Italian prisoners, including 9 generals. But the Congo has given something else to the Allies. By perfecting, at its own expense, its rail, river, and road transportation, the Belgian Congo has given the Allies a strategic route to the theaters of military operations in the Middle East, saving them two-thirds of the time, two-thirds of the personnel and two-thirds of the tonnage required by the longer route around the Cape. It has also offered shelter to thousands of Greek refugees.

Belgium, bruised and wounded, fought on. And lives!

CHAPTER XXX

Belgium in the Postwar World

BY PAUL VAN ZEELAND

N O ONE WHO HAS read the chapters of this book, reviewing the trials and triumphs of Belgium through the centuries, can help but feel admiration for a past which was so rich in accomplishment in all those fields in which civilization has advanced the farthest. But, what will tomorrow bring?

Belgium once again is laid waste, crushed by the invader, bled white, stripped of her goods, isolated from her markets, despoiled of her works of art, her thoughts confused under a hail of lead, the finest of her sons reduced to slavery or killed. Will she rise again? What role will she play among the nations? Will she succeed in rejoining the links of her chain and in crowning her future labors with the brilliance of her past?

The first of these questions answers itself. Belgium will live again! For Belgians, the rebirth of their country is as certain as the fact that day follows night.

For history has taught the Belgians a very harsh lesson, a lesson so often repeated that it has penetrated by now to the very depths of their souls. How many times during the centuries have not they been, as today, invaded, despoiled, persecuted! How often have not the pessimists put up over their doors the sign *Finis Belgicae!* And each time, in spite of everything, with unswerving fortitude, with unfailing tenacity, and with a surprising success, the Belgians have rebuilt their ruins and set out toward new destinies. So will it be tomorrow—once again. The past is the guarantee of the future.

But this confidence, this certitude in the survival and perpetuity of the nation must not be confused with sanctimonious optimism. The job awaiting the Belgians, after the war, is a colossal one.

There are countless difficulties. When, through limited experience, some light is shed upon the future of the countries to be freed from the German yoke, the difficulties seem more serious and more numerous than had ever been expected. The Belgians must call upon all the resources of their ingenuity and courage to build for their children the kind of life which is worthy of their history.

When hostilities ceased, there was a tremendous outburst of joy. The Belgians needed to breathe deeply of the air of liberty, to open their windows, sweep out their houses, eliminate the worst traces of the occupation. Another outburst, ominous and almost inevitable, accompanied it—that of hatred; hatred for the oppressor; hatred perhaps even deeper and more implacable for those Belgians who became the oppressor's valets.

But the question of the necessities of life had to be faced at once; there must be found food to eat and clothes to wear; the most important damages must be repaired, transportation must be reëstablished; order must be restored and maintained, Belgium's own order, order in freedom.

All this will be done, with the coöperation of her Allies, in the full exercise of a definitively reëstablished Belgian sovereignty. But still this is only a transition, a bridge. Where does this bridge lead?

No one can answer this question. It is literally a secret of the future. No one even tries to guess at it. But what can be done is to present briefly a few resolutions, a few hopes, culled from among all of those which quicken the hearts of a large number of Belgians, inside as well as outside the country.

Belgium is one of the classical lands of civil and political liberty. Belgians have always cherished their liberties, all the more dearly since they have been threatened so often. Fortunately, they have known how to preserve them. The Belgian form of government has been one of the most liberal in existence. The 1830 constitution was a complete success. Its authors really succeeded in attaining a balance between the principles of liberty and the demands of an orderly government. This constitution was widely copied and imitated throughout the European Continent. For more than a century, it provided Belgium with institutions which were sound, peaceful, and adapted to the outstanding needs of her people.

But political formulas, of whatever kind, well-balanced and

timely as they may seem, wear out or become outmoded, or are one day by-passed by events. The parliamentary regime in Belgium was not a foreign importation. It was, in very large measure, the spontaneous fruit of the natural development of Belgium's local institutions, many centuries old. Her people had attained a high degree of political maturity, because of the time-honored observance of communal liberties and the responsibilities which accompany them. They made altogether good use of parliamentary institutions. However, for several decades now, the political system has "knocked," like an overworked motor; economic problems and social questions have assumed a greater and greater importance in the life of the community; and the nineteenth-century institutions, whose aims were mainly political in the restricted sense of the word, no longer were sufficiently adapted to the new needs.

But if this lack of balance was true in Belgium, it was still more so in other countries politically less stable.

The period between the two wars saw rise throughout the world a whole series of extremist revolutions, varying from Naziism to Communism. Belgium felt, in her turn, repercussions from these shocks. All in all, before the war, the need to adapt her institutions to new circumstances was clearly seen by a great number of people; the parliamentary system seemed to be faltering.

Then came the war, followed by military catastrophe and invasion. For a while some people let themselves be fooled by the outward appearances of totalitarian order. But the illusion was short-lived. At the touch of this abominable system, Belgium's old passion for liberty awoke. A curious movement in ideas took place. In the beginning, a series of projects had been advanced in anticipation of a revision of Belgian political institutions; at first, their trend was obvious; in varying degrees, under more or less fallacious forms, they tended toward reinforcing authority, to the detriment of liberty and the individual. As time passed and enlightenment came, these trends changed in deed as well as in thought. But soon the great desire of all Belgians was to return to "the good old days." The faintest odor of "totalitarianism" revolts them. There is no longer any doubt; Belgium has been, and will remain, the land of liberty. The fundamental institutions—that is, civil liberties which have marked Belgian political development for centuries and particularly her prosperity during the last century and a quarter of independence—will live. Belgium will remain a representative, constitutional parliamentary monarchy.

Does this mean that the constitution will not be modified? No, but it will be modified by regular, legal, constitutional procedure!

After the catastrophe, which has shaken Belgium to her very marrow, everyone will recognize the wisdom of a policy which made respect for the constitution and for legality its sheet anchor.

But it will be necessary to return to the essence of the system, to find in it the living tradition, eliminate what is excrescent or parasitic, or even transitory. Belgium must return to the various government bodies, to the executive as well as to the legislative, the sense of their respective roles; at the same time, she must place at the disposal of these bodies new media which will permit them to perform these new tasks which more and more clearly are their responsibility. It is necessary that the deep-rooted forces of the country, on the economic and social as well as on the purely political plane, find their expression in the institutions whose job it is to make the law and to apply it. Parliament must again be enabled to center its attention on the political aspects of problems submitted to it; in other words, the purely technical aspects must be sorted out and in some way digested before the projects are submitted to it. This can be attained by the creation of auxiliary councils, duly incorporated, in the functioning of representative institutions.

As for the Government, it is necessary that it have instruments appropriate for its new tasks on the economic and social planes. Profound administrative reform is necessary. It is to be hoped that it may be brought about by reviving and utilizing methods which have already undergone the test of national life and which correspond to the particular aspirations and peculiar temperament of the Belgian people.

Herein lies a great and beautiful experiment; the Belgians are preparing themselves for it; detailed studies have been made, both inside and outside the frontiers. Their aim is lofty; it is nothing less than to rebuild, in 1945, by adaptation to the needs of the times, what the fathers of the country built in 1830.

But if Belgium means to remain mistress of her destiny, she well knows that she cannot hope for this achievement except in an

orderly and peaceful world. There is no need for lengthy arguments
to show that a small country, exposed on all sides and situated near
the confines of the most turbulent and powerful nations in Europe,
cannot think of isolating herself. The policy of Belgium is necessarily an international policy; every Belgian problem has its ex-
terior side. The Belgian Provinces always have been an important
pawn on the chessboard of the great nations of Europe, and of the
world. Belgians accept, with pride, the dangerous life which geographic conditions impose upon them. For them, interest in peace,
in international order, in freedom of trade and of international
relations are synonymous with the interests of the country. It has
always been so, and it will be so again.

In her foreign policy, Belgium has never ceased to have a clear
and concise outlook; she has always done fully what devolved upon
her—no matter how minor a responsibility—to support and defend
the interests of peace, international harmony, world economic expansion, order in international liberty.

To serve this ideal she has, for more than a century, accepted the
engagements and limitations of neutrality. Freed from these fetters,
she supported the League of Nations with all her power, taking, on
certain occasions, bold stands which events, with the passage of
time, have proved just and courageous. To mention only a few,
there were the sanctions in the Ethiopian affair, the Oslo Convention, the Ouchy Agreement. In the span of a generation, she
has twice fought, without hesitation, against a force of crushing
superiority.

After this war, Belgium will continue the same basic policy; but
she will adapt this policy to circumstances. According to the declarations of Allied leaders, the nations are moving toward a peace
organization which corresponds to the governing ideas emerging
from the League of Nations; this organization surely will avoid
certain of the League's defects. It no doubt will have the means of
protecting right by might. In any event, Belgium will rally to its
support with the full measure of her energies.

But the history of the old League of Nations proved that it is
well to slip intermediate bodies in between the national state and
world organization; among these, some will have a "horizontal"
character—the regional groupings; others a "vertical" character—

the so-called functional institutions. There is no doubt but what Belgium will take her full part in these various organizations.

Among all the intermediate bodies, there is one which has a good chance of being born out of the chaos of the postwar period; that is the grouping of western Europe, or "Occidental Europe." Such a grouping must rest, as does all international organization, on respect for national sovereignty, on the fundamental equality of partners before the rights and obligations of the community; to such a community, Belgium will be happy to make her full contribution.

There has been much talk recently of the role of the small countries, of their future, of their place in the concert of nations. Occasionally they have been placed in opposition to the great states. It is a mistake to handle the problem in this way. There always have been great and small nations in the world. Both answer profound needs in the life of men in society. In international policy, as in everyday life, the old adage, "The mouse can often help the elephant," is always found to be true. The role of Belgium in the past repeatedly has been the role of an intermediary for the greatest good of those who have recourse to her services.

In the world of tomorrow, great and small nations will have an opportunity to use all their energies in the service of humanity.

An important distinction—the distance separating "hegemony" from "leadership"—too often is not made; it would, however, prevent confusion from the very beginning. Let a nation, or a group of nations, no matter how strong, desire to exercise hegemony, masked or open, throughout the world, and failure is certain. On the contrary, let the Great Powers, strong in their responsibilities, point out the road, guide their sisters toward the aims of common interest; such leadership will not only be accepted by the small nations, but it will be welcomed, because each recognizes that it is necessary.

The Belgian State will take her place among her equals in this concert of peoples. She will serve at the same time, her own interests and those of the great family of nations.

How many discussions rise over whether wars spring from misery or whether misery provokes wars—superfluous, vain discussions! War and misery are, indeed, closely associated, in the reciprocal bonds of cause and effect. This at least is certain: if the world, after this most devastating of wars, does not recover sufficient economic balance to better progressively the living conditions of the masses, the seeds of a new war, which inevitably will be sown, will bear fruit sooner or later.

For Belgium, economic questions have an exceptional importance. Eight million and a half inhabitants must live on a narrowly limited territory, devoid of almost all raw materials, whose survival depends largely on man's labor. Belgians cannot live, in the most literal sense of the word—that is, cannot find the means by which to nourish and shelter themselves—unless their labor lets them procure elsewhere, outside their frontiers, the greater part of their needs.

The country will emerge cruelly weakened from this war. Destruction provoked by the 1940 campaign and by following aerial bombardments in itself is already enormous. The working class will have lost, by the atrocious conditions under which a great number of their sons have been forced to work, a part of its manual skill. The portion of industrial machinery which has not been destroyed or carried off either will be worn out or outmoded. Belgian technic, which always has been of the first order, has found itself isolated during these long years of occupation from all contact with the astonishing progress which the war has brought to Belgium's great allies, the United States and England.

Finally, Belgium has been cut off radically from her markets; here, the consequences are particularly serious. War and the establishment of war economies throughout the entire world will have thrown all traditional economic currents into confusion. This disorder will be so profound that it would be better to consider the past as definitely abolished and think about re-creating an entirely new order in this field. Moreover, a transformation from an economic point of view has taken place in the world, profound and certainly, to a large extent, lasting. A series of markets which formerly were essentially agricultural and had to import industrial products of all kinds, from half-finished articles to the most completely finished, have changed the bases of their economy; a number of them, as a result of war conditions, have been industrialized with signal success. One might simply mention many

Latin-American countries and a list of dominions, like Canada, Australia, New Zealand, South Africa. Belgium's principal clients were the great neighboring countries which form her natural hinterland and with whom she was traditionally and intimately united. But the marginal importance of her relations with overseas countries was enormous, perhaps even decisive.

The production of half-finished articles or of those of simple manufacture held an important place in Belgian economy. It is better to face reality. A great number of her traditional markets are lost for good. She will have to replace these either with other markets in new countries, or by means of different products. This will not be easy. All industrial transformations are complex; ordinarily they evolve slowly; but Belgium has to make haste.

However, a dark cloud sometimes has a silver lining. Perhaps Belgium will find, in the preponderance of certain difficulties confronting her, a way by which to succeed. In many instances, she will be able again to create entirely new factories, with ultramodern machinery and with recourse to the most highly perfected technics. There will be times when she can jump the transition or groping period, and thus avoid the hardships or errors which beset certain of her eventual competitors. She will be able to throw herself into modern technics, into the production of plastics, for instance, without taking the early experimental steps.

On the other hand, the changes undergone by the overseas markets—to the extent that they are sound and lasting—must enrich them and raise the living standards of their populations; consequently new occasions must be found here to sell Belgian products.

Whatever it be, Belgian economy is going to find itself face to face with a tremendous problem; not only must it rise from ruins, but it must reëstablish itself on new bases and branch out into hitherto unknown directions.

Can this be done without a change in methods? Certainly not.

It is likely that fundamentally Belgium will remain faithful to the large directives which have always made up her economy. Expansion within and without; maximum liberty compatible with economic and social progress; tenacity; honesty; all that has so well served her in the past will continue to mark her efforts tomorrow.

But this economic organization also must suffer the repercussions

of new conditions which will influence political life. The intervention of the State in economic fields is a necessity; one can no
longer avoid directing economy along the lines of the general
interests of society.

Whatever principles are favored, no one can deny that after the
war, throughout the world and during the full transition period,
controls will be exercised at the key points of international economy—in the field of capital, monetary relations, basic raw materials, and so on. This being so, it is obvious that Belgium must
create and use instruments which will correspond to international
organizations.

But it will be necessary to take a further step. The Belgian State
must define more clearly the framework in which her economic
life is to be restored, in which will be reëstablished the bases of
national prosperity. Will this be detrimental to private enterprise,
to individual initiative? On the contrary! The "organized" or
"directed" political economy, as conceived, cannot and must not
establish more than a general framework, serving as a "bulwark"
or a "guide," within which private initiative will, to a greater
extent than ever, find free rein. The establishment of this framework must assure to sound and stable enterprise better opportunities to assert itself, to develop; the phrase "better opportunities" is
used because if the conditions of their activity are more clearly
defined, they will also be stabler and sounder than before.

Of course, the mere use of the term "directed economy" is, by
itself, meaningless; first, it must be known in what direction Belgium wants to go; and this choice of direction is neither without
difficulties nor risks. On the other hand, even if the chosen direction
is right, it still remains to be seen whether the measures of execution, from day to day, will be good or bad. But whatever it be, the
experiment will be tried, because it will be impossible to do otherwise. The responsibility of its success or failure will of necessity
fall upon those who will have their hands on the helm.

There is much room for confidence. If the general conditions of
the peace are fairly good, that is, if they assure the maintenance
of peace and a minimum of liberty and decency in international
economic relations, Belgium, by the combined efforts of her leaders
in government, her captains of industry, and her workers, will

surely find the means for rebuilding what has been destroyed, and reëstablishing Belgium's place in the sun. It would not be surprising if, under such general conditions, she needed less time than might be supposed to smooth over her war-torn land and resume her march toward a higher material prosperity.

Belgium cannot fail in her attempt at economic restoration because defeat would sound the death knell of her dearest ambition, namely, to create social conditions under which her people may again resume, with every quarter given, their eternal pursuit of happiness.

For Belgium, even more than for any other nation, the proverb of "sharing the cake" is clear and transparent. Her population cannot secure the standard of living to which it has the right unless the country succeeds in regulating and assuring economic prosperity. Fortunately, the Belgian asks only to be allowed to work; he likes his work; a job well done is one of the sources from which he draws a part of his satisfaction in living.

But granting an assured economic base, it remains no less necessary that a generous, comprehensive, intelligent, and active social policy utilize the goods produced to assure the maximum welfare to the greatest number of people. Already, before the war, a relatively advanced degree of social organization had been attained in Belgium. Social insurance had made great strides; social welfare was widely organized. What must be done by the Government upon the liberation of the country is to perfect this work.

There should be very little opposition to a policy which would tend to give to all those who work and to all those who suffer the security of the morrow. The Belgian worker will be insured against all risks beyond the individual's control—risks which society owes to itself to cover for the profit of its members.

But it will be necessary to go farther. Such a stage is passed. It has been realized that it was necessary not only to protect the worker against such risks as sickness, accidents on the job, old age, and death, but, if he himself made the effort which was his to make, to assure him also of the opportunity to gain his livelihood. The emphasis which, for some time, was placed on social insurance now is placed on job security—in other words, on the right to work.

But here the problem becomes extremely complicated; its character is no longer social alone, but is economic and political as well. No one will claim that such a problem is easy to solve; but that it must be solved, everyone will agree. Studies have been made toward this end. Here again, it is an experiment which will of necessity be tried. There is good reason to believe that it will succeed, if a minimum of good will is shown at all stages of progress.

No doubt such marked social improvement, which everyone desires, will not be achieved immediately after the war. During the transition period, many difficulties will rise, but by increasing, little by little, the volume of consumer goods placed at the disposal of the masses, and by gradually increasing rations, and arriving progressively at the point where rations will correspond to the need, rationing itself can be eliminated.

But what matters, from the first day after the war, is that the curve of social progress be upward and that the new regulations, backed by legal power, bring to the masses not only hope but the conviction that, by the common effort of all Belgians, the production of goods will multiply, and be placed equitably at the disposal of the community as a whole; in other words, that all classes of Belgians, beginning with the poorest, will know that all economic progress will serve to assure them better living conditions, nearer to their aspirations, and worthier of their efforts.

Perhaps the extent of moral damage caused, during the last fifteen or twenty years, by the development of totalitarian doctrines has not yet been exactly measured. Ideas which seemed elementary and unequivocal before the last war, such as respect for human life or subordination of might to right, or horror for needless suffering inflicted on other human beings—all these ideas and so many others which were the expression of long centuries of patient efforts, have suffered a profound blow. It will be necessary to fight, to fight hard and long, before these ideas again assume the character of intangibility which they had before.

In Belgium, also, the admirable struggle carried on by the entire population against the enemy will have inevitable repercussions. Some of these will be good, others dangerous. Human life will have lost some of its value. Respect for authority necessarily will have decreased by the very fact that during these long years it has been exercised too often, either by enemies or by traitors. On the other hand, during these long years of oppression, the country will have been separated from the living sources of human thought throughout the world, through lack of intellectual intercourse, of contact with free universities, of exchange of magazines and other publications; by the closing down of the University of Brussels, by public opinion's lack of guidance, by the absence of a great free press. Profound confusion is bound to result. All that regrettably is true; the burden of it must be borne after the war.

And still, there is no cause for excessive anxiety in a country which, considering the abominable conditions under which it has had to live during the hard years of occupation, has succeeded in keeping intact its homogeneity, its will to resist, its confidence in the future. Such a people are assured of triumph over all difficulties, moral as well as material. The inexpressible heroism of the resistance has developed, in a large section of Belgian opinion, a remarkable reaction to the worst ordeals of life. Certain heroes of underground resistance made the following statement, which revealed an almost unbelievable fortitude in the mass of the people: when an agent of Belgian resistance was cut off from his organization and, in order to continue his work, had to expose himself to a stranger, there were nine chances out of ten that he would obtain, by this hazardous proceeding, the assistance which he needed; and this in spite of the fact that the least contact with work of this kind meant death without reprieve, should the Gestapo be warned!

The sources upon which this extraordinary vitality of the Belgian spirit feeds are multiple. All Belgians, whatever their religious, philosophical, or political convictions, draw freely and widely upon these sources. Attention should be drawn to one of the sources from which a large part of the Belgian population has traditionally drawn strength—the Catholic faith. During this war, the attitude of those who represented the religious ideal, no matter what faith they professed, has been irreproachable in courage and foresight. The struggle has awakened in wide circles a rebirth of religious feeling. This is one more reason for hope in the future.

In conclusion, one must go back to the question at the beginning of this chapter: "What future is in store for Belgium?" The answer is that a long series of difficulties, dangers, trials, pain, and, finally, success await her.

Belgium has been and will remain a land of liberty; the marks of her destiny will be representative constitutional parliamentary monarchy; expansionist economy, based at once on a progressive industry looking toward the most difficult, the most scientific, the most perfect production; greatly diversified agriculture, employing the latest scientific teachings; and a firm and progressive social organization, protecting its citizens against all risks beyond their control and making their right to work a living reality. These achievements would create profound and gradually satisfied aspirations toward the fulfillment of human destiny, on a material as well as a spiritual plane.

What, then, will be Belgium's status in the world of tomorrow? What will be the role of this little state, so often trampled under foot and so often cited as an example, traveling thus through history, from pinnacle to pillory and from pillory to pinnacle? Belgium's role, like that of any other state, is a double one. She has obligations toward her citizens; she has obligations toward the rest of the world.

First of all, with respect to her citizens Belgium owes it to herself to organize their life in such a way as to assure them at least as satisfactory living conditions as those of citizens in the most advanced countries in the world. It was so in the past; it will be so in the future, in spite of grave difficulties.

But, to be satisfied with this would be to look upon Belgium's role from a narrow point of view unworthy of her past. No country in the world can egotistically isolate itself; each is an active member of and responsible for the society of nations.

A great country has particularly heavy responsibilities, and if it does not assume them, it is seriously shirking its duty and, sooner or later, men will pay in the form of wars, crises, and misery in different forms. But, in proportion, the international responsibility of the small countries is no less. Their life is more difficult, more dangerous; but when they succeed in surmounting these handicaps, the results bring worthwhile compensations.

Belgium has always been closely involved in the vicissitudes of Europe. Her lot has often served as an example, as it will again in the future. Her very existence, her successes, her accomplishments, can, and must, be a lesson for all.

As a classic land of experimentation, Belgium, after the war, will have the responsibility of demonstrating the soundness of those theories to which she will try to give life. If the Belgians succeed in regaining their balance quickly, in restoring the conditions for a prosperous national economy; if they find the necessary balance between the guiding action of the State in economic matters and the full utilization of the live forces of private initiative; if they succeed in distributing equitably among their population the products accruing from a soundly expanding economy, and in thus satisfying the legitimate aspirations of all classes of the population; if they succeed, finally, in raising upon the foundations of a temporarily threatened civilization a new edifice in which order, justice, liberty, prosperity, and security join harmoniously—what lesson will they not have offered to a troubled world! More even than a lesson in economic accomplishment will be the lesson in social accomplishment because Belgium's population is composed of diversified races and cultures. Indeed, they will have demonstrated, by their success, that racial discrimination is false as well as unjust, and that unity in variety can be a fertile source of material and moral enrichment.

Here is an ambitious program. But this hateful war has demonstrated that greater demands can be made upon humanity than humanity ordinarily was believed capable of fulfilling. This epoch will have seen profound upheavals, revolting crimes, destruction without end; but it will also have been illuminated by an extraordinary amount of courage, heroism, and sacrifice; in sum, with all its faults, it will have lived under the sign of grandeur, because in the end, having passed the periods of weakness and evasions, the forces of good will be affirmed and will bring victory!

It is the Belgian's right and duty to be ambitious for his country. This ambition is noble, since it serves Belgium's neighbors as well as her sons. If a like state of mind is substituted in international relations for the abominable totalitarian doctrine, according to which force is justified in itself and finally justifies everything, it can truly be hoped that the tragedy of this era will end for a long time the epoch of world wars, and that, in a peaceful world, again orderly and serene, Belgium will be able to reassume her traditional role in the service of her people and of mankind.

A SELECTED
BIBLIOGRAPHY

A Selected Bibliography

For readers who wish to continue their study of Belgium, the following works have been selected by the authors and arranged according to topics.

Further reading about the land and people of Belgium (chap. i) may be found in: (1) J. Verschueren, *Algemeene Atlas voor België*, Groningen, 1924; (2) M. Mourlon, *Géologie de la Belgique*, Brussels, 1880–1881; (3) F. Crépin, *Manuel de la flore de Belgique*, Liége, 1913; (4) A. Lameere, *Manuel de la faune de Belgique*, Brussels, 1895; (5) G. Jouret, *Le Géographie humaine de la Belgique*, Brussels, 1920; (6) A. Jacquemin, *La Belgique et le Congo belge: Géographie*, Brussels, 1925; (7) J. Fraipont, *La Belgique préhistorique et protohistorique*, Brussels, 1901; (8) E. Picard, *Essai d'une psychologie de la nation belge*, Brussels, 1907; and (9) Marnix Gijsen, *Ons Volkskarakter*, Mechlin, 1932.

Additional reading on the formation of the Belgian Kingdom (chap. ii) may be found in: (10) Henri Pirenne, *Histoire de Belgique*, Brussels, 1920, 7 vols.; and *Les Villes du moyen âge*, Brussels, 1927; (11) E. Poullet, *Histoire politique nationale*, Louvain, 1892; and (12) P. Poullet, *Les Institutions françaises de 1795 à 1814*, Brussels, 1907; (13) Godefroid Kurth, *Notre Nom national*, Brussels, 1910; and *La Frontière linguistique en Belgique*, Brussels, 1896; (14) Franz Cumont, *Comment la Belgique fut "romanisée,"* Brussels, 1914; (15) H. des Marez, *Le Problème de la colonisation franque et du régime agraire dans la Basse Belgique*, Brussels, 1926; (16) P. J. Blok, *History of the People of the Netherlands* (Translated from the Dutch), New York, 1907–1909; (17) E. de Borchgrave, *Histoire des rapports de droit public ... entre les provinces belges et l'Empire d'Allemagne*, Brussels, 1870; (18) Léon Vanderkindere, *Histoire de la formation des principautés belges au moyen âge*, Brussels, 1920; (19) E. de Marneffe, *La Principauté de Liége et les Pays-Bas*, Liége, 1887; (20) G. Bigwood, *Le Régime juridique et économique du commerce de l'argent dans la Belgique du moyen âge*, Brussels, 1921; (21) F. Funck-Brentano, *Philippe-le-Bel en Flandre*, Paris, 1896; (22) Joseph Billioud, *Les Etats de Bourgogne au XIVᵉ et au XVᵉ siècles*, Dijon, 1922; (23) Léon van der Essen, *Alexandre Farnèse, prince de Parme, gouverneur général des Pays-Bas au XVIᵉ siècle*, Brussels, 1933–1937, 5 vols.; (24) R. Putnam, *William the Silent*, New York, 1895; (25) Max Bruchet, *Marguerite d'Autriche*, Lille, 1927; (26) Ernest Gossart, *La Domination espagnole dans les Pays-Bas à la fin du règne de Philippe II*, Brussels, 1906; and *L'Etablissement du régime espagnol dans les Pays-Bas et l'insurrection*, Brussels, 1905; (27) Eugène Hubert, *Les Pays-Bas espagnols et la République des Provinces Unies*, Brussels, 1907; (28) H. Lonchay, *La Rivalité de la France et de l'Espagne aux Pays-Bas 1635–1700*, Brussels, 1896; (29) Charles Pergameni, *L'Esprit public bruxellois au début du régime français*, Brussels,

1914; (30) Suzanne Tassier, *Les Démocrates belges de 1789*, Brussels, 1930; and *Histoire de la Belgique sous l'occupation française en 1792 et 1793*, Brussels, 1934; (31) Paul Verhaegen, *La Belgique sous la domination française, 1792–1814*, Brussels, 1923–1926; (32) Léon Lanzac de Laborie, *La Domination française en Belgique: Directoire, Consulat, Empire*, 1895, 2 vols.; and (33) Frans van Kalken, *Le Belgique contemporaine 1780–1830, histoire d'une évolution politique*, Paris, 1930.

For the Dutch Regime and the Kingdom of Belgium (chap. iii) and consolidation and expansion between 1840 and 1914 (chap. iv) see: (34) J. J. Thonissen, *La Belgique sous le règne de Léopold Ier*, 1861, 3 vols.; (35) Louis Hymans, *Histoire parlementaire de la Belgique de 1830 à 1890*, Brussels, 1877–1901, 8 vols.; (36) H. T. Colenbrander, *Gedenkstukken der Algemeene Geschiedenis van Nederland van 1795 tot 1840*, The Hague, 1905; (37) P. J. Blok, *Geschiedenis van het Nederlandsche Volk*, Groningen, 1907, t. VII; (38) D. C. Boulger, *A History of Belgium*, London, 1909, 2 vols.; (39) Frans van Kalken, *Histoire du royaume des Pays-Bas et de la révolution belge*, Brussels, 1910; (40) J. de C. MacDonnell, *Belgium, Her Kings, Kingdom, and People*, London, 1914; (41) R. C. K. Ensor, *Belgium*, New York and London, 1915; (42) Léon van der Essen, *A Short History of Belgium*, Chicago, 1920; (43) A. de Ridder, *Histoire diplomatique du Traité de 1839*, Brussels, 1920; (44) T. H. Reed, *Government and Politics of Belgium*, New York, 1924; (45) Henri Pirenne, *Histoire de Belgique*, Brussels, 1900–1926, 6 vols.; and *Bibliographie de l'histoire de Belgique*, Brussels, 1928; (46) Comte E. Corti et Baron C. Buffin, *Léopold Ier, oracle politique de l'Europe*, Brussels, 1927; (47) E. Banning, *L'Origine et les phases de la neutralité belge*, Brussels, 1927; (48) Comte L. de Lichtervelde, *Léopold II*, Brussels, 1935, 4th ed. (English translation: *Leopold of the Belgians*, by T. H. Reed and H. Russel Reed, New York, 1929); and *Léopold I*, Brussels, 1928 (English translation: *Leopold First*, by T. H. Reed and H. Russel Reed, New York, 1930); (49) J. Deharveng, *Histoire de la Belgique contemporaine*, Brussels, 1928–1930, 3 vols.; (50) F. de Lannoy, *Histoire diplomatique de l'indépendance belge*, Brussels, 1930; (51) Emile Cammaerts, *Albert of Belgium*, New York, 1935; and *The Keystone of Europe*, London, 1939.

The following books offer additional information on Belgium in the First World War (chap. v); No. 42, above, and (52) Lt. Gen. Emile Joseph Galet, *Albert, King of the Belgians in the Great War*, Boston, 1931; (53) Lt. Col. Maurice Albert Tasnier and Major R. van Overstraeten, *L'Armée belge dans la guerre mondiale*, Brussels, 1923; (54) Emile Waxweiler, *La Belgique neutre et loyale*, Paris, 1915; (55) Godefroid Kurth, *Le Guet-apens prussien en Belgique*, Brussels, 1919; (56) General Victor Deguise, *La Défense de la position fortifiée d'Anvers en 1914*, Brussels, 1921; (57) Pierre Daye, *Avec les vainqueurs de Tabora*, Paris, 1918; (58) Pierre Nothomb, *Les Barbares en Belgique*, Paris, 1915; (59) M. Maeterlinck, C. Buysse, and L. Dumont-Wilden, *Le Belgique en guerre*, Le Havre, 1918; (60) P. Heuze, *L'Epopée belge dans la Grande Guerre*, Paris, 1923; (61) E. Beyens, *La Belgique pendant la guerre*, Paris, 1923; (62) Emile Vandervelde, *Dans la mêlée*, Paris, 1919; (63) L. Gilles, A. Ooms, and P. Delandsheere, *Cinquante mois d'occupation allemande*, Brussels, 1919; (64) Brand Whitlock, *Belgium under the*

German Occupation, London, 1919; (65) F. Mayence, *La Correspondance de S. Em. le Cardinal Mercier avec le Gouvernement général allemand pendant l'occupation*, Brussels, 1919; (66) A. Henry, *Le Ravitaillement de la Belgique pendant l'occupation allemande*, Paris, 1924; (67) F. Passelecq, *Les Déportations belges à la lumière des documents allemands*, Paris, 1917; and *La Magistrature belge contre le despotisme allemand*, Paris, 1918; (68) E. von Ludendorff, *Meine Kriegserinnerungen*, Berlin, 1919 (English translation: *My War Memories*, London, 1919); (69) *Der Weltkrieg 1914 bis 1918*, Deutsches Reichsarchiv, Berlin, 1924; and (70) H. van Staabs, *Aufmarsch nach zwei Fronten*, Berlin, 1925.

Additional data concerning the period between the two wars (chap. vi) may be found in the following works: Nos. 33 and 51, above, and: (71) Eva J. Ross, *Belgian Rural Coöperation*, Milwaukee, 1940; (72) Fernand Baudhuin, *La Structure économique de la Belgique*, Louvain, 1926; (73) Robert Sand, *La Belgique sociale*, Brussels, 1933; (74) Louis Piérard, *Belgian Problems since the War*, Harvard, 1929; (75) Camille Gutt, *Pourquoi le franc belge est tombé*, Brussels, 1935; (76) Anon., *The Van Zeeland Experiment*, New York, 1943; (77) Ernest Mahaim, *La Belgique restaurée*, Brussels, 1926; (78) H. L. Shepherd, *The Monetary Experience of Belgium 1914–1936*, New York, 1936; (79) Tilla Vulhopp, *Une Politique des familles nombreuses*, Louvain, 1928; (80) Hugo Kats, *Les Effets du nouveau régime monétaire en Belgique depuis la stabilisation*, Brussels, 1933; (81) *L'Encyclopédie Belge*, 1931; (82) Jan-Albert Goris, *Antwerp 1918–1928*, Antwerp, 1929; and (83) Sylvain François, *Le Port d'Anvers, sa fonction nationale et la politique commerciale belge après la guerre*, Louvain, 1935.

For the constitutional and political structure of Belgium (chap. vii) see. (84) Jean Servais, E. Mechelynck, Paul Servais et Louis Schnock, *Les Codes belges*, Brussels, 1929, 18th ed.; (85) J. Berta et Ernest Vandeveld, *Code des lois politiques et administratives*, Brussels, 1924, T. 1re; (86) Emile Huyttens, *Discussions du Congrès National de Belgique*, Brussels, 1844–1845; (87) E. Brunet, J. Servais et C. Resteau, *Le Répertoire pratique de droit belge*, Brussels, 1925; (88) Karel Brants, *De Staatsinrichting van België, beginselen van grondwettelÿk Recht en van administratief Recht*, Louvain, 1931; (89) Paul Errera, *Traité de droit public belge*, Brussels, 1919, 2d ed.; (90) J. J. Thonissen, *La Constitution belge annotée*, Brussels, 1879, 3d ed.; (91) Alfred Giron, *Dictionnaire de droit administratif et de droit public*, Brussels, 1895–1896; (92) M. Vauthier, *Das Staatsrecht des Königreichs Belgien*, Freiburg i. B., 1895; and (93) O. Orban, *Le Droit constitutionnel de la Belgique*, Liége-Paris, 1906–1911. An English translation of the Belgian Constitution has been published by J. M. Vincent of Johns Hopkins University, in the *Annals of the American Academy of Political and Social Science*, 1896, vol. 7.

Further references on political parties (chap. viii) are in the following: No. 48, above, and (94) Frans van Kalken, *Histoire du royaume des Pays-Bas et de la révolution belge de 1830*, Brussels, 1910; and *La Belgique contemporaine*, Paris, 1930; (95) Théodore Juste, *Le Congrès national de Belgique*, Brussels, 1880; and *Jean-Baptiste Nothomb*, Brussels, 1874; (96) J. J. Thonissen, *La Belgique sous le règne de Léopold Ier*, Liége, 1858; (97) Louis Hymans, *Histoire parlementaire de la Belgique*, Brussels, 1878; (98) T. H. Reed, *Government and*

Politics of Belgium, New York, 1924; (99) Charles Woeste, *Mémoires pour servir à l'histoire contemporaine de la Belgique*, Brussels, 1927; (100) Paul Hymans, *Frère Orban*, Brussels, 1905; (101) Louis Bertrand, *Histoire de la démocratie et du socialisme en Belgique depuis 1830*, Brussels, 1907; (102) Emile Vandervelde, *Le parti ouvrier belge*, Brussels, 1925; and (103) *Souvenirs d'un militant socialiste*, Paris, 1939; and (104) Henri Heyman, *La Belgique sociale*, Paris, 1916. Additional information may be found in such periodicals as *Revue de Belgique*, *Revue Générale*, *Le Flambeau*, *Revue Politique et Parlementaire*, and *Revue de l'Université de Bruxelles*.

Additional titles on the Flemish movement (chap. ix) are: No. 45, above, and (105) Shepard B. Clough, *A History of the Flemish Movement in Belgium*, New York, 1930; (106) Paul Fredericq, *Geschiedenis der Vlaamsche Beweging*, Ghent, 1906, 3 vols.; (107) A. van de Perre, *The Language Question in Belgium*, Brussels, 1919; (108) A. de Ridder, *La Littérature flamande contemporaine, 1890–1923*, Paris, 1923; (109) B.-S. Chlepner, *La Banque en Belgique*, Brussels, 1926; (110) L. de Raet, *Vlaanderen's economische Ontwikkeling*, Brussels (1920); (111) Henri Pirenne, *La Belgique et la guerre mondiale*, New Haven, 1928; (112) G. N. Clark, "The Great Netherlandish Idea," in *Edinburgh Review*, April, 1926; and (113) Herman Vos, *Het Vlaamsche Vraagstuk*, Brussels, 1936.

The foreign policy of Belgium from 1918 to 1940 (chap. x) is further developed in the following publications: (114) Belgian Ministry of Foreign Affairs, *Belgium. The Official Account of What Happened, 1939–1940*, London, 1940; (115) Emile Vandervelde, "Belgian Foreign Policy and the Nationalities Question," in *Foreign Affairs*, July, 1933; (116) F. van Langenhove, "La politique commerciale de la Belgique," in *Le Flambeau*, Brussels, 1926; (117) Henri A. Rolin, *La Politique de la Belgique dans la Société des Nations*, Geneva, 1931; (118) Eelco van Kleffens, *Juggernaut over Holland*, New York, 1941 (Published in London under the title: *The Rape of the Netherlands*); and (119) J. B. Condliffe, *The Reconstruction of World Trade: A Survey of International Economic Relations*, New York, 1940. Further information may be found in *Documents Parlementaires Belges*.

For additional references on agriculture (chap. xi) see: (120) J. L. Frateur, *Aperçu sur la situation de l'elevage bovin en Belgique avant la guerre*, Institut de Zootechnie de Louvain, 1915, Bul. 15; (121) *Nouvel Atlas de Belgique*, Brussels: Société Coöpérative, 1933; (122) J. van der Vaeren, *Le Livre d'or de l'agriculture belge*, Brussels, 1939; (123) *Statistique de la Belgique—Recensement Général de 1895* [Atlas], Brussels: Ministère de l'Agriculture, 1899; (124) *Annuaire statistique de la Belgique et du Congo, 1934*, Ghent: Ministère de l'Intérieur, Office Central de Statistique, 1934; (125) *Statistique de la Belgique—Agriculture—Recensement général de 1910*, Brussels: Ministère de l'Agriculture et des Travaux Publics, 1914; (126) *Annuaire statistique de la France, 1938*, Paris: Direction de la Statistique Générale et de la Documentation, 1938; and (127) *International Yearbook of Agricultural Statistics, 1939–1940*, Rome: International Institute of Agriculture, 1940.

For the chapter on economic development (chap. xii) see: Nos. 45 and 77, above, and (128) Henri Pirenne, *Les Anciennes démocraties des Pays-Bas*, Paris, 1910 (English translation: *Belgian Democracy: Its Early History*, Manchester, 1915);

Medieval Cities, Princeton, 1927; and "The Place of the Netherlands in the History of Medieval Europe," in *Economic History Review,* 1929; (129) G. des Marez, *L'Organization du travail à Bruxelles au XV° siècle,* Brussels, 1904; "Les Luttes sociales en Flandre au moyen âge," in *Revue de l'Université de Bruxelles,* Brussels, 1900; and *Etudes sur la propriété foncière dans les villes du moyen âge et spécialement en Flandre,* Ghent, 1898; (130) Victor Brants, *Histoire des classes rurales aux Pays-Bas jusqu'à la fin du XVIII° siècle,* Brussels, 1881; (131) L. Vanderkindere, *Le Siècle des Artevelde,* Brussels, 1879; (132) R. Haepke, *Brugge's Entwicklung zum mittelaelterlichen Weltmarkt,* Halle, 1908; (133) R. Ehrenberg, *Das Zeitalter des Fugger,* Berlin, 1896; (134) Jan-Albert Goris, *Etudes sur les colonies marchandes méridionales à Anvers de 1488 à 1567,* Louvain, 1925; (135) M. Huisman, *La Compagnie d'Ostende,* Brussels, 1904; (136) L. van Houtte, *Histoire économique de la Belgique à la fin de l'Ancien Régime,* Ghent, 1925; (137) L. Dechesne, *Histoire economique et sociale de la Belgique,* Brussels, 1932; (138) F. Donnet, *Coup d'œil sur l'histoire financière d'Anvers,* Antwerp, 1927; (139) V. E. Guffs, *The Story of the Walloons,* New York, 1923; (140) G. Jacquemyns, *Histoire de la crise économique en Flandre (1845–1900),* Ghent, 1928; (141) J. Derbru et E. Vandervelde, *Le Socialisme en Belgique,* Brussels, 1900; (142) B. S. Rowntree, *Land and People: Lessons from Belgium,* London, 1910; (143) A. Vermeersch and A. Muller, *Manuel social,* Brussels, 1910; (144) Ernest Mahaim, *La Belgique restaurée,* Brussels, 1926; (145) B.-S. Chlepner, *Le Marché financier Belge depuis cent ans,* Brussels, 1930; *L'Etranger dans l'histoire économique de la Belgique,* Brussels, 1932; and *Belgian Banking and Banking Theory,* 1944; (146) Fernand Baudhuin, *Le Capital de la Belgique et le rendement de son industrie, avant la guerre,* Brussels, 1924; (147) R. Ardenne, *German Exploitation of Belgium,* Washington, 1942; and (148) H. Laurent, *Un Grand Commerce au moyen âge. La Draperie des Pays-Bas en France et dans les Pays Méditerranéens. XII°–XV° siècle,* Brussels, 1935.

The social structure and development of Belgium (chap. xiii) is treated further in the following references: Nos. 71, 143, and 144, above, and (149) Arthur Jauniaux, *L'Evolution et les conquêtes de la mutualité,* Brussels, 1923; (150) Emile Vandervelde, *L'Enquête sur les associations professionelles d'artisans et d'ouvriers en Belgique,* Brussels, 1891; No. 143, above, and (151) A. Vermeersch and A. Muller, *Les Organismes sociaux officiels en Belgique,* Brussels, 1923; (152) L. de Brouckère, *La Coöpération,* Brussels, 1926, and *Le Contrôle ouvrier,* Brussels, 1924; (153) C. A. Kiehel, *Unemployment Insurance in Belgium,* New York, 1932; (154) C. Mertens, *Trade Union Movement in Belgium,* Amsterdam, 1925; and (155) Louis Bertrand, *Histoire de la coopération en Belgique,* Brussels, 1902.

Additional information on communications and transportation (chap. xiv) will be found in the bibliographies on chapters x and xiii.

The best reference material on religion in Belgium (chap. xv) may be found in: No. 10, above, and (156) *Catholic Encylopedia.*

Further readings on education in Belgium (chap. xvi) may be found in: (157) E. Greyson, *Histoire et origine de l'instruction publique in Patria Belgica,* Brussels, 1875; and *L'Enseignement public en Belgique,* Brussels, 1893–1896;

(158) Léon Beckers, *L'Enseignement supérieur en Belgique,* Brussels, 1904; (159) *La Patrie belge, 1830–1930* (Edition du Soir), Brussels, 1930; and (160) *Encyclopédie Belge,* Brussels, 1933. Reports of the Fondation Universitaire and the Fonds National de la Recherche Scientifique may be referred to.

For general works containing chapters on the evolution of science and research in Belgium (chap. xvii) see: No. 159, above, and (161) *Livre d'or du centenaire de l'indépendance belge, 1830–1930,* Brussels, 1931; (162) *Histoire de la Belgique contemporaine* (Edition DeWitte), Brussels, 1930, t. III; (163) J. Timmermans, *The Part Played by Belgium in the Development of Modern Chemistry,* London, 1941. See also the Bulletins, Memoirs, and Yearbooks of the Royal Academy of Belgium. The Academy published in 1872, on the one hundredth anniversary of its founding, a volume which traced the evolution of science, and again in 1922, on the one hundred and fiftieth anniversary, a volume containing articles on the biological sciences by J. Massary, and on the mineral sciences, by P. Fourmarier; the Bulletins and Memoirs of the Academy of Medicine and of the various Belgian scientific societies: Malacology, Zoölogy, Entomology, Biology, and Chemistry are useful; other scientific publications of value are: *Les Archives de Physiologie, La Revue des Questions Scientifiques,* the annual reports of the Fondation National de la Recherche Scientifique, and of the Fondation Universitaire.

On art in Belgium (chap. xviii) the following titles will give additional information: (164) H. Fierens-Gevaert, *Histoire de la peinture flamande des origines à la fin du XVe siècle,* Paris, Brussels, 1927; (165) M. J. Friedlander, *Die altniederländische Malerei,* Berlin, 1924; *Von Eyck bis Bruegel,* Berlin, 1916; and *Die niederländische Maler des XVII. Jahrhunderts,* Berlin, 1923; (166) Fr. Winkler, *Die altniederländische Malerei, Berlin,* 1924; and *Die flaemische Buchmalerei des XV. und XVI. Jahrhunderts,* Leipzig, 1925; (167) G. J. Hoogewerff, *Vlaamsche Kunst en Italiaansche Renaissance,* Mechlin, 1935; (168) E. Renders, *La Solution du problème Van der Weyden-Flémalle-Campin,* Bruges, 1931; (169) P. Rolland, *Les Primitifs tournaisiens, peintres et sculpteurs,* Brussels, 1932; (170) Ch. Tolnay, *Pierre Brueghel l'Ancien,* Brussels, 1935; (171) R. Hedicke, *Cornelis Floris,* Berlin, 1908; (172) C. van Mander, *Het Leven der Doorluchtighe Nederlandtsche en Hoogduytsche Schilders,* Haarlem, 1604, 1618 (American Edition: *Dutch and Flemish Painters,* New York, 1936); (173) A. J. J. Delen, *Histoire de la gravure dans les anciens Pays-Bas et dans les provinces belges,* Paris, 1924–1934; (174) Luc et Paul Haesaerts, *Flandre, Essai sur l'Art flamand depuis 1880, L'Impressionisme,* Paris, 1931; (175) Paul Clemen, *Belgische Kunstdenkmäler,* Munich, 1923, 2 vols.; (176) Stan Leurs, *Geschiedenis van de Vlaamsche Kunst,* Antwerp, 1935; (177) Jan Denucé, *Antwerpsche Tapijtkunst en Handel. Bronnen voor de Geschiedenis van de Vlaamsche Kunst.* IV, Antwerp, 1936; (178) G. L. Hunter, *The Practical Book of Tapestries,* Philadelphia, 1914; (179) H. C. Marillier, *Handbook to the Teniers Tapestries,* London, 1832; (180) Marcel Laurent, *L'Architecture et la sculpture en Belgique,* Brussels, 1928; (181) Marguerite Devigne, *La Sculpture mosane du XIIe au XVIe siècle,* Brussels, 1932; and (182) M. Konrad, *Meisterwerke der Skulptur in Flandern und Brabant,* Berlin, 1930–1935.

Architecture in Belgium (chap. xix) is discussed in the following works: Nos. 175 and 180, above, and (183) H. de Bruyn, *L'Art religieux en Belgique depuis la Renaissance jusqu'à nos jours*, Brussels, 1925; (184) P. Clemen and C. Gurlitt, *Die Klosterbauten der Cistercienser in Belgien*, Munich, 1916; (185) Paul Fierens, *L'Art en Belgique du moyen âge à nos jours*, Brussels, 1939; (186) H. Fierens-Gevaert, "L'Architecture et l'art décoratif modernes en Belgique," in *L'Amour de l'art*, Paris, April, 1923; (187) J. Helbig and J. Brassine, *L'Art mosan, depuis l'introduction du Christianisme jusqu'à la fin du XVIIIe siècle*, Brussels, 1906–1911; (188) Edouard Michel, *Hôtels de ville et beffrois de Belgique*, Brussels, 1920; and *Abbayes et monastères de Belgique*, Brussels, 1923; (189) André Michel, *Histoire de l'art*, Paris, 1905–1929; (190) Charles Muquardt, *Monuments d'architecture et de sculpture en Belgique*, Brussels, 1852–1854; (191) Paul Parent, *L'Architecture des Pays-Bas méridionaux aux XVIe et XVIIIe siècles*, Brussels, 1926; (192) Nikolaus Pevsner, *Pioneers of the Modern Movement from William Morris to Walter Gropius*, New York, 1936; (193) Max Rooses, *Art in Flanders*, New York, 1924; (194) A. G. B. Schayes, *Histoire de l'architecture en Belgique*, Brussels, 1849–1852; and *A Treatise on the Pointed Style of Architecture in Belgium*, London, 1844; (195) Marcel Schmitz, *L'Architecture moderne en Belgique*, Brussels, 1937; (196) J. J. van Ysendyck, *Documents classés de l'art dans les Pays-Bas du Xe au XVIIIe siècle*, Antwerp, 1880–1889; (197) F. A. Vermeulen, *Handboek tot de Geschiedenis der Nederlandsche Bouwkunst*, Amsterdam, 1928–1932; (198) Jan Denucé and Jan-Albert Goris, *Vlaanderen Door de Eeuwen Heen*, Amsterdam, 1932–1933; and (199) A. J. Wauters, *L'Architecture romane dans ses diverses transformations*, Brussels, 1889.

Additional references on Belgian literature in the Dutch language (chap. xx) may be found in: (200) J. Persijn, *A Glance at the Soul of the Low Countries*, London, 1916; (201) G. L. van Roosbroeck, *Guido Gezelle, the Mystic Poet of Flanders*, Vinton, Iowa, 1919; (202) P. Hamelius, *Introduction à la littérature française et flamande de Belgique*, Brussels, 1921; (203) A. de Ridder and W. Zimmerman, *Anthologie des écrivains flamands contemporains*, Brussels, 1926; (204) Marnix Gijsen, *De Literatuur in Zuid-Nederland sedert 1830*, Brussels, 1940; (205) J. Bithell, *Contemporary Belgian Literature*, London, 1915; (206) A. Vermeylen, *Van Gezelle tot Timmermans*, Amsterdam, 1923; (207) Frank Baur, *Geschiedenis der Vlaamsche Literatuur*, Brussels, 1938; (208) Gerrit Kalff, *Geschiedenis der Nederlandsche Letterkunde*, Groningen, 1906–1910, 6 vols.; (209) P. Arents, *Flemish Writers Translated*, Antwerp, 1931; and (210) F. de Backer, *Contemporary Flemish Literature*, Brussels, 1939.

Other references on French literature in Belgium (chap. xxi) are: (211) M. Wilmotte, *La Culture française en Belgique*, Paris, 1912; (212) G. Charlier, "Les Lettres Belges," in Bédier and Hazard's *Histoire de la littérature française illustrée*, Paris, 1924; (213) B. M. Woodbridge, *Le Roman belge contemporain*, New York, 1930; (214) G. Doutrepont, *Histoire illustrée de la littérature française en Belgique*, Brussels, 1939; and (215) *Contemporary Literature in Belgium*, New York, 1939.

Certain references on Walloon literature are: (216) *Bulletin du Dictionnaire Wallon*, 15 vols.; (217) *Bulletin de la Société de Littérature Wallonne*, 62 vols.;

(218) *Annuaire*, 32 vols.; (219) *La Vie Wallonne* (monthly), 1920–; (220) *Wallonia: Archives wallones de jadis, de naguère, et d'à présent*, 1893 ff.; (221) *Bibliothèque de philologie et de littérature wallonne*, Liége, 2 vols., 1909–1928; (222) Joseph Closset, *Littérature Wallonne*, Liége, 1910; (223) J. Haust, *Pages d'anthologie Wallonne*, Brussels, 1924; and also "The Walloon Literature," *Encyclopaedia Britannica;* (224) Marius Valkhoff, *Philologie et littérature wallonne*, Groningen, 1938; (225) Maurice Wilmotte, *Le Wallon*, Brussels, 1893; and also *La Littérature wallonne au XIXᵉ siècle. Marches de l'Est*, Paris, 1909.

Additional sources of information on music in Belgium (chap. xxii) may be found in: (226) Francois-Joseph Fétis, *Mémoire sur les musiciens néerlandais*, Amsterdam, 1829; (227) E. de Coussemaker, *Histoire de l'harmonie au moyen âge*, Paris, 1852; (228) E. van der Straeten, *La Musique aux Pays-Bas avant le XIXᵉ siècle*, Brussels, 1888; (229) A. Soubies, *Histoire de la musique*, Paris, 1900; (230) Edouard Fétis, *Les Musiciens belges*, Brussels, 1848; (231) J. P. O. Comettant, *Histoire d'un inventeur au dix-neuvième siècle, Adolph Saxe, ses ouvrages et ses luttes*, Paris, 1860; (232) Ch. van den Borren, *Orlando de Lassus*, Paris, 1920; (233) M. Brenet, *Grétry, sa vie et ses œuvres*, Paris, 1884; (234) V. d'Indy, *César Franck*, Paris, 1921; (235) E. Grégoir, *L'Art musical en Belgique sous les règnes de Léopold Iᵉʳ et de Léopold II*, Antwerp, 1879; and (236) E. Evenepoel, *Le Wagnérisme hors d'Allemagne: Bruxelles et la Belgique*, Brussels, 1891.

Following are references on the geographical aspect of Belgian Congo (chap. xxiii): (237) Maurice Robert, *Le Congo physique*, Brussels, 1923; (238) Louis Franck, *Le Congo belge*, Brussels, 1930, 2 vols.; (239) James Chapin, "Birds of the Belgian Congo," in *Bulletin of the American Museum of Natural History*, New York, 1932–1939, vols. 65–75; (240) Lord William Malcolm Hailey, *An African Survey*, London, 1938; (241) Harry Johnston, *George Grenfell and the Congo*, London, 1908 (New York, 1910); (242) X. de Grünne, *Le Ruwenzori*, Brussels, 1937; (243) H. M. Stanley, *In Darkest Africa*, London, 1890, New York, 1891, 2 vols., and (244) A. C. Veatch, "Evolution of the Congo Basin," in *Geological Society of America*, New York, 1935.

The cultural background of Belgian Congo (chap. xxiv) is discussed further in the following references: No. 241, above, and (245) Leo Bittremieux, *Mayombsche Namen*, Brussels, 1934; (246) British Museum, *Handbook to the Ethnographical Collections*, Oxford, 1910; (247) Etat Indépendant du Congo, *Notes analytiques sur les collections ethnographiques du Musée du Congo*, t. 1, "Les Arts—Religion," 1902–1906; t. 2, "Les Industries indigénes"; fasc. 1, "La Ceramique," Brussels, 1907; (248) Joseph Halkin and Ernest Viaene, *Les Ababua*, Brussels, 1911, vol. vii; (249) Melville J. Herskovits, "The Culture Areas of Africa," in *Africa*, vol. iii (1930); and "Physical Types of West African Negroes," in *Human Biology*, vol. ix (1937); (250) M. W. Hilton-Simpson, *Land and Peoples of the Kasai*, London, 1911; (251) Alexander Ihle, *Das alte Königreich Kongo*, Leipzig, 1929, vol. 1; (252) David Livingston, *Missionary Travels and Researches in South Africa*, New York, 1859; (253) Carl Meinhof and N. J. Warmilo, *Introduction to the Phonology of the Bantu Languages*, Berlin, 1932; (254) J. Maes and O. Boone, "Les Peuplades du Congo belge," in *Musée du Congo Belge*, ser. 2, vol. I (1935); (255) C. van Overbergh, *Les Basonge* (Collection des monographies ethnographiques III), Brussels, 1908; (256) C. van Overbergh and E. de Jonghe, *Les Bangala* (Collection des monographies ethnographiques, I), Brussels, 1907; *Les Mayombe* (Collection des monographies ethnographiques, II), Brussels, 1907; (257) Xavier Stainier, "L'Age de la pierre au Congo," in *Annales du Musée du Congo Belge*. Ethnographie, Anthropologie, ser. I, t. 1, fasc. 1 (January, 1899); (258) Walter H. Stapleton, *Comparative Handbook of Congo Languages*, Yakusu, Stanley Falls, Congo Independent State, 1903; (259) Frederick Starr, "Rude Stone Implements from the Congo Free State," in *Wisconsin Archaeologist*, vol. vii, no. 3 (June–September, 1908); and "Ethnographic Notes from the Congo Free State: An African Miscellany," in *Proceedings, Davenport Academy of Science*, vol. 12 (May, 1909); (260) Paul Schebesta, *Among Congo Pigmies*, London, 1933; and *Vollblutneger und Halbzwerge*, Salzburg-Leipzig, 1934 (also published as *My Pygmy and Negro Hosts*, London, 1936); (261) Emil Torday, "Der Tofoke," in *Mitteilungen der Anthropologischen Gesellschaft in Wien*, vol. 41 (1911); *Camp and Tramp in African Wilds*, London, 1913; *On the Trail of the Bushongo*, London, 1925; and "The Influence of the Kingdom of Kongo on Central Africa," in *Africa*, vol. 1 (1928); (262) Edmond Verhulpen, *Baluba et Balubaïsés du Katanga*, Antwerp, 1936; (263) John H. Weeks, *Among Congo Cannibals ... Thirty Years' Sojourn amongst the Boloki and Other Congo Tribes ...*, London, 1913; and *Among the Primitive Bakongo*, London, 1914; and (264) Alice Werner, *Structure and Relationship of African Languages*, London, 1930.

The historic development of the Congo (chap. xxv) is discussed further in: Nos. 48 and 51, above, and (265) Pierre Daye, *Léopold II*, Paris, 1934; (266) Louis de Lichtervelde, *Leopold of the Belgians*, New York, 1929; (267) Charles Liebrechts, *Léopold II, fondateur d'empire*, Brussels, 1932; (268) R. Stanley Thomson, *Fondation de l'etat indépendant du Congo*, Brussels, 1933; and (269) A. J. Wauters, *Histoire politique du Congo belge*, Brussels, 1911.

For a study of the administrative structure of the Belgian Congo (chap. xxvi) see: No. 269, above, and (270) A. Michiels and N. Laude, *Notre Colonie*, Brussels, 1925; (271) A. J. Wauters, *L'Etat indépendant du Congo*, Brussels, 1899; (272) Michel Halewyck, *La Charte coloniale*, Brussels, 1910; and (273) Octave Louwers and Iwan Grenade, *Codes et lois du Congo belge*, Brussels, 1923.

The economic development of the Belgian Congo (chap. xxvii) may be read further in: Nos. 124, 238, and 268, above, and (274) F. Goffart, *Le Congo*, Brussels, 1907; and *L'Outillage économique et la mise en valeur du Congo*, Antwerp, 1912; (275) E. Vandervelde, *La Belgique et le Congo*, Paris, 1911; (276) F. Cattier, *Etude sur la situation de l'etat indépendant du Congo*, Brussels, 1906; (277) *Traité d'annexion du Congo belge*, Brussels, 1908; Rapports sur le Gouvernement du Congo belge présentés aux Chambres, Brussels, 1909–1913, 1919–1938; Annales parlementaires, Brussels, 1907–1940; (278) *Bulletin agricole du Congo belge*, Brussels, 1910–1940; (279) A. J. Wauters, *Histoire politique du Congo belge*, Brussels, 1910; (280) the publication *Congo*, Brussels; and (281) *Annuaire statistique de la Belgique et du Congo*, Brussels, 1908–1940.

Literature on the subjects of health, education, and social welfare in the Belgian Congo (chap. xxviii) is contained in the publications of Catholic and

Protestant missions published in Belgium and in the United States. No general work covering the subject exists. The best source is the annual report on the Congo Government presented to the Belgian Chambers and mentioned above in the bibliography on the preceding chapter.

For outstanding sources on Belgium under the occupation (chap. xxix) see No. 114, above, and (282) Roger Motz, *Belgium Unvanquished*, London, 1942; (283) Robert Goffin, *Le Roi des Belges, a-t-il trahi?* New York, 1940; (284) Jan-Albert Goris, *Belgium in Bondage*, New York, 1944; and by the same, *Strangers Should Not Whisper*, New York, 1945; (285) Emile Cammaerts, *The Prisoner at Laeken*, London, 1941; and the reviews *Marine*, London; *Message*, London; *News from Belgium and the Belgian Congo*, New York; *Belgium*, New York; *La Belgique indépendante (Onafhankelijk België)*, London; and the underground press in Belgium, as well as official German publications.

The material on Belgium in the postwar world (chap. xxx) is based on the material gathered by the Commission for Postwar Problems in Belgium, presided over by Paul van Zeeland, and on its unpublished report. A volume on postwar reconstruction in Belgium, edited by Jan-Albert Goris, which is in preparation, will be published in 1945 by the University of North Carolina Press.

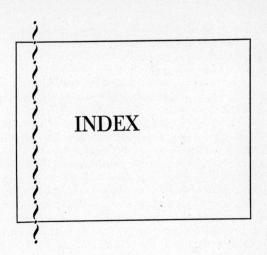

INDEX

Index

Aalst (town), 102, 124, 158
Aalst, Pieter Coecke van, 264, 266–267
Activists: descendants of, formed Frontist party, 105; name, 116; aim of, 116–117; repercussions in army from, 117; trial of, 118; freed, 123; compared with Collaborationists, 124. *See also* Council of Flanders
"Administrative Structure" (Congo), by Albert de Vleeschauwer, xxvi, 380–385
Aduatici, 6
African campaign in First World War, 62–63
Agriculture: chief industry, 8; estates along routes to Gaul, 15; Flemish coöperatives in, 119; small farms, 148, 155, 180; suffered from depression, 148; census, 148; population, 148–149; crop distribution in, 150–151; change in system of, 151, 178; livestock statistics, 151–154; factors determining type of, 155; influence on, of: soil, 155; topography, 155–156; climate, 156; agricultural regions: dunes country, 156; polders, 157–158; sandy district, 158; Kempen, 159; sandy loam, 159–160; loam, 160–161; Herve and Eupen, 161–162; limestone, 162; Ardennes, 162–163; Marne, 163–164; price levels in, 164–165; research institutes for, 165; associations, 166; schools of, 166; important progress in, in eighteenth century, 172; sugar beet culture in, 174, 178; crisis in, from grain importation, 178; destruction of, in war, 419; Agricultural Corporation, 422–423
"Agriculture of Belgium, The," by E. G. Misner, xi, 148–166

Air Force, 426
Aix-la-Chapelle, Treaty of, 20
Albert Canal, 76–77, 199, 206
Albert of Austria, Archduke, 20
Albert, Lake, 337, 338, 340
Albert of Belgium: succeeded Leopold II, 51; reign of, 51–52; reorganized army, 54; in command of army, 55 ff.; appeal of, 59; headquarters of, at De Panne, 64; entered Brussels, 66; quoted on public sentiment, 68; instituted Fund for Scientific Research, 72; influence of, 73; quoted on language, 120; intervened for reparations, 130–131; letter of, to Renkin cited, 143; Seraing speech of, for education, 229–230; quoted on Congo, 378, 400; reëstablished *Commission pour la Protection des Indigènes*, 410
Albertine Rift, 338–341 *passim*, 347
Alsace, 55; offensive toward, 58
Amiens, English reverses at, 61
Amsterdam, 200; coöperation with other seaports, 209
Anderlecht, 237, 239
Anethan, J. d', 98
Angola Province, 338, 340, 341
Anseele, Edward, 73, 100, 115, 118
Anspach, Frédéric, 333–334
Anti-Bolshevist Walloon Legion, 107
Antwerp (Antwerpen): capital of Flemish culture, 8; people of, 9; dockers, 10, 69; not freed by armistice, 31; French besieged, 36; fortifications of, 41, 57; base of Belgian army, 57, 58; siege of, 58–59; maritime installations at, 70; -Docks, 70; rapid development of, 71; World's Fair at, 72; School for Tropical Medicine, 73, 403; Albert Canal, 76–77; Germans reorganized administration of, 125;

Antwerp (*Continued*)
question of direct communication with Rhine for, 141, 209; growth of, in fifteenth century, 170; trading and financial center, 171, 200, 278; commission to fix port dues and taxes in, 209; important port, 198, 199, 202; revolution ended prosperity of, 200, 240; recaptured, 200; renewal of activity in, 201; peculiar position of port of, 201; failed to consolidate position, 202; plan for, -Rhine canal, 202; hinterland of, 203; supertaxes on French goods through, 203; three important changes in, by First World War, 203; extension of harbor of, 204; traffic increased, 204; competition with Rotterdam, 204, 205; publishing in, 219–220, 239; rise of, marked opening of Renaissance, 220; Mannerists, 264; a principal music center, 321; Germans seized, 416

"Architecture," by Georges Philippart, xix, 274–285

Architecture: no examples of early, 274, 280; basilical plan of Carolingian churches, 274; Scheldt style of, 274–275; rayonnant plan in, 275; Gothic, 275, 278, 279–280; materials for, 275–276; examples of church, 275, 276, 281, 282; Burgundian style in, 277; of "halles," 277–278; impetus of trade to, 278; Brabantine, 279; Renaissance, 279, 280; architectural dynasties, 279; beautiful domestic Flemish, abandoned, 280; Baroque, 281–282; beautiful interiors for, 283; for houses, 283; nineteenth-century, 283; modern movement in, 284; of "garden cities," 284; plans at Laeken, 285

Ardennes: woodlands on, plateau, 5, 12; summer playground, 5; School of the, 271

Arlon (Aarlen), 5, 67

Army: compulsory service in, 52, 115; concentrated behind Liége, 55–56; immobilized 150,000 German troops, 58; "race to the sea," 58–59; increased, 103; language situation in,

114–115, 117, 121; 80 per cent of, Flemings, 117; French and Flemish courts in, 121; extended military service, 137; mobilization, 145, 415; fortified positions, 147, 415; per cent of population in, 415; crushed, 416

Art: two great schools of painting, 7; lyrical quality of, 7; Palace of Fine Arts unique center, 71; Impressionist tradition continued in, 72; Expressionist technique, 72; applied, 72; Flemish painters revived style of masters, 112; school of Flemish Mystics, 219; two styles in early period, 256 ff.; Byzantine, 256–257; illuminated manuscripts, 256; bas-reliefs, 257; Gothic period, 257 ff.; book illumination, 258; spiritual changes in Flemish, 258, 260; tapestry weaving, 260; sculpture, 261–262, 266; sixteenth-century, 262 ff.; secular, 263; Italian Renaissance influence, 263–264; stained glass, 264; Mannerists, 264; seventeenth and eighteenth centuries, 267 ff.; Baroque, 267, 287; modern movement, 270; neoclassicism suggested by David, 270; Romanticism, 270–271; Impressionist schools, 271; Expressionists, 272; definite Belgian school of woodcuts, 273; of Netherlands reflects candidness, 288

"Art in Belgium," by Constant van de Wall, xviii, 256–273

Artois: religious strife in, 19; after treaties of Westphalia and Nijmegen, 20

Astrid of Sweden, 73

Aucassin and Nicolette, 301, 315

Audenarde: tapestry weaving at, 260; church at, 276

Bach, Johann Sebastian, 318, 319, 321, 323

Baekeland, L., 246

Balat, Alphonse, 283–284

Baldwin Cabinet, 133

Bambeke, E. van, 252

Bangweulu, Lake, 340, 343

Bantu: speech, 353, 355, 356, 357–358; cultures, 359–360

Index

Barcelona, Statute of, 206
Baroque. *See* Architecture, Art
Baumgarten, H., 416
Beernaert, Auguste, 101, 102
Belga, 71, 75
Belgian Congo Museum, 354, 363
"Belgian Literature in the Dutch Language," by Jan Greshoff, xx, 286–300
"Belgian Music," by Charles Leirens, xxii, 318–334
Belgian Provinces: listed, 17; linked to Spain, 18; under Charles V, 19; England looked upon, as cornerstone of European policy, 20; Spain lost 11 cities of, 20; robbed under Napoleonic Empire, 23; equality under Treaty of Eight Articles, 27; declared independent state, 31; "transforming" industries in, 170; corporative organization for each, 173
Belgian Workers' party (*Parti Ouvrier Belge*), 189
"Belgium between the Two World Wars," by Jan-Albert Goris, vi, 66–77
"Belgium in the Postwar World," by Paul van Zeeland, xxx, 429–442
Belgium-Luxemburg Union, 143, 208
"Belgium under the Occupation," by Arthur Wauters, xxix, 415–428
Bellarminus, 220
Beneden, Edouard van, 251
Beneden, Pierre Joseph van, 250, 251
Benedetti, Vincente, 43
Benefit Funds for Family Allotments, 192
Benguela Province, 338
Benoit, Peter, 112, 224, 330
Bernini, Giovanni, 270, 281
Bethmann-Hollweg, Theobold von, 54; quoted, 116
Bidez, Joseph, 230, 236
Binche (town), 11
Binche, Arnoul de, 276
Bismarck, 42, 50; supported Leopold, 370–371
Bissing, Moritz Ferdinand von, 64; favored annexation of Belgium, 115
Boelaere, Fernand Toussaint van, 292, 295
Boerenbond, 73–74, 119, 223; *Belgische* (League of Farmers), 166

Bollandists, 231; support of U. S. Catholics for, 236
Bordet, Jules, Nobel prize to, 72, 252
Borginon, H., 125
Borinage, coal mines of, 71
Borms, August, 116, 118, 125
Bosch, Hieronymus, 262, 265, 272
Boulogne, German objective, 59
Bouvines, Battle of, 17
Brabant, Duke of, quoted on literature, 301–302
Brabant: higher plateau of, 4; colors of, 29; memories of Revolution of, 33; Province, 159 *passim*
Brachet, Albert, 251–252
Brazza, Savorgnan de, 368
Bremen, 199
Briand-Kellog Pact, 131
Broqueville, Charles de: Prime Minister, 64, 103; bill by, to increase army, 103
Brouwer, Adriaan, 12, 269
Bruegel, Pieter, 257, 262, 266, 269, 272
Bruges (Brugge), 4; quaint, 9; thriving community, 17; Frenchmen massacred in, 17; architectural beauty of, 110; horse raising near, 158; center of international trade in thirteenth and fourteenth centuries, 169; decline of, in fifteenth, 170; new seaport of, 204; Church of St. Donat at, 218; decline of, marked end of Middle Ages, 220
Brussels: capital, 8, 19; charm of, 8; revolt of people of, 19, 24, 25, 29, 30; "keys to," 20; bombarded, 21; German entry into, 57; Royal Family reentered, 62, 66; Annual Commercial Fair at, 75; University of, founded, 96, 228, 241; population of, divided linguistically, 108, 120; Military School at, 121; new waterway of, 204; agreement at, 208–209; Congrès at, 234; Royal Academy and Royal Library at, 240; observatory at, 242; Botanical Gardens of, 250; tapestry weaving at, 259; Market Place of, 282; Royal Conservatory, 327, 328; Conference, 373–374; authorized import duties, 390; University closed, 422

Buysse, Cyriel, 293, 294–295
Byzantine Congress, 234

Caecilia, La, 333
Calais: German objective, 59; Straits of, saved, 66
Calais-Strasbourg-Hamm industrial triangle, 199
Calvinist(s), 19; tendencies of Netherlanders, 24
Campo-Formio, 22
Canal du Nord, 210
Cannes, talks at, 132
Capart, Jean, 230, 235; Musée du Cínquantenaire of, 238
Capetian dynasty, 17
Carillons, 277
Carpenter, George W., "Health, Education, and Social Welfare," (Congo), xxviii, 400–412
Carton di Wiart, Henri, 102, 103, 140
Castlereagh, Lord, quoted on Prussians, 23
Catholic Action, 224
Catholic party: in power, 47; policy of, 48; preponderance of, 48; in direction of Flemish peasants, 50; majority until 1914, 68, 103; unions, 69, 223; ultramontanists, 93; common front with Liberals, 93–96, 222; Cabinet, 98; Catholic Congress recognized, 98; opposed elementary education bill, 99; "independent" label of, 100; democratic movement in, 101–102, 223; moderate policy of, 103; sympathetic to Flemish demands, 113; social service schools, 190; domination of, by progressive elements, 223; Christian Democrats in, 223
Cauwelaert, Frans van, 71, 115, 118, 126; "Foreign Policy, 1918 to 1940," x, 129–147
Central Commission for Navigation on Rhine: first international organization in Europe, 201; Belgium not represented on, 201; represented, 203; Germany withdrew from, 207; other delegations met in, 208; Italy abstained from, 208
Chapelier Law, Le, 189, 193

Chapin, James P., "Geography" (Congo), xxiii, 337–352
Charlemagne, 16, 18; united territories, 218; organized Christian education, 218
Charleroi, 58, 125; troops sent into, 181
Charleroi-Brussels Canal, 70
Charles of Lorraine, 282, 283
Charles the Bald, 16
Charles the Bold, 18
Charles the Good, 218
Charles VI of Belgium. See Charles of Habsburg
Charles I of England, Van Dyck court painter for, 268
Charles V of France, 17
Charles of Habsburg: became Emperor as Charles V, 18, 22; England permitted Low Countries revert to, 21; became Charles VI of Belgium, 22; renounced sovereignty over Low Countries, 22; prosperity of Belgian Provinces under, 200
Charles II of Spain, 21
Chlepner, B.-S., "Economic Development of Belgium," xii, 167–186
Christian Democrats, 102, 222
Christus, Petrus, 259
Church: problem of, and State, 44–45; education and public welfare under, after sixteenth century, 44; subservience of, under rulers, 44; appointed ministers paid by State, 45; issues of quarrel, 45; Rogier Cabinet diminished influence of clergy, 98; first Catholic Cabinet, 98; first grand Catholic Congress, 98; polyphonic music in, 219; deep-rooted Catholic spirit in Liége, 219; clerical oppression under Joseph II, 221; religious persecution by French revolutionists, 221; Concordat of Naples, 221; 3000 church schools, 222; religious battle in Catholic ranks, 222; Catholic Action modern movement of, 224; Jocism, 224; le droit au subside, 227; religious persecutions drove energetic men out of Belgium, 240
"Circle of Burgundy," 19
Cistercians, 277
Clapham, J. H., quoted, 170

Clémentel, Etienne, 132

Clercq, Gustaaf de, 124, 125

Clough, Shepard B., "The Flemish Movement," ix, 108–126

Clovis, 16; baptized, 217, 218

Coal: only raw material, 10; in Limburg, 10, 71, 206; Kempen, fields, 182, 183, 249; production in post-war expansion, 182; industries because of, 188; method of sinking shafts, 248; classification of layers of, -bearing regions, 249; study of Hainaut, fields, 249

Coal Forest: a dividing line, 4; stopped Salian Franks, 6; Roman frontier zone, 6

Cockerill: W., 174; J., 175; firm, 175, 176; steel mills, 424–425

Collaborationists, 124–126

Comité d'Etudes du Haut Congo, 367, 368

Comité National de Secours et d'Alimentation, 247, 255

Commission of Safety, 29

Communes, history of, 81–82

"Communications and Transportation," by Jan Frans Hostie, xiv, 198–213

Communists, 105

Compagnie d'Ostende, 172

Compromise of the Nobles, 19

Concerts Populaires de Musique Classique, 331–332

Condroz, 4, 162

Confédération des Etats Belgiques Unis, 22

Confederation of Christian Trade Unions (*Confédération des Syndicats Chrétiens*), 189

Congo:

description: location, 337; agriculture, 342, 410; rainfall, 342, 343, 346–347; climate, 345–346; vegetation, 347–349, 386; fauna, 349–351

economic policy: not a settlement colony, 11; little Flemish spoken, 115; all trade with Antwerp, 115; progress in economic equipment, 183; metal discoveries, 251; value of ground for agriculture, 342, 398, 411–412; railway opened, 344, 373,

387, 388, 391; towns, 345; conference for development, 370–371; slave trade suppressed, 373–374; three zones for, 374–375; rapid development of, 378; supplies to Allies, 378, 428; insecurity of aborigines, 387; efforts for adequate communication and transportation, 387–388, 398; waterways, 388; airlines, 389; news dissemination, 389–390; trade, 390, 394–395; taxes, 390–391; unoccupied land vested in State, 391–392; "protected zones," 393; preference for native labor, 393–394, 411; banking aid, 394; production, 395–397

geography, 337–352; area, 337; rivers, 338, 343; lakes, 339, 340; volcanoes, 340, 341; mountains, 341; six provinces, 345

government: administration by three departments, 372 ff., 377; annexation, 375, 377–378; English criticism of administration, 375–376; separation of powers as in Belgium, 380; Colonial Charter as constitution, 380, 393; Belgian legislature passes laws relating to, 380; royal decrees, 380–381; Colonial Council, 381; Governor General, 381, 382; Minister of Colonies, 382; provincial, 382–383; unwritten law, 383; three types of native communities, 383–384, 385, 411; courts, 384–385

history: enterprise of single man, 46–47; incorporated into Kingdom, 47; expeditionary force organized, 62; German offensive against, 62–63; Stanley's explorations, 251, 367–368; Belgian-Congo colony, 251; Geographical Conference planned opening of "Dark Continent," 266–267; *Comité d'Etudes,* 367, 368; International Association, 368; political program for, 368–369; threat of Portugal, 368; Anglo-Portuguese treaty, 369; General Act, 370–371; Belgium aided Leopold, 373; annexation, 375

Congo (*Continued*)

people: population, 344–345, 353; native food, 351; Pygmies, 351; Negroid, 353; unity of population, 353; Bantu language, 353, 356–358, 410; homogeneous culture of, 353 ff.; self-government in native communities, 383–384, 385; aborigines, 354–355, 386–387; crafts, 360; trade, 360–361; social structure, 361–362; religion, 363; artistic achievements, 363–364; music, 364

welfare: Parc National Albert, 73; Museum, 354; work of Christian missions, 401–403; medical service, 401; education, 402, 403, 407–410; religious teaching, 402; government services, 403; public health service, 403–407; campaign against sleeping sickness, 404–405, and leprosy, 405; increasing birth rate, 406; polygamy taxed, 406

Congo Basin: favored, 337; nations administering, 337; boundaries of, 337–338; highlands associated with, 338–339; rift valleys, 338 ff.; geology of, 340–342, 386; outlet, 340

Congo River: size of, 337; system, 338; Lualaba becomes, 340, 342; course of, 342, 343–347; description of, 342; navigation of, 342–343

Congress, Liberal, 97

Congress of London, 95

Congress of Vienna, 23; Belgian Revolution destroyed work of, 94; conservative Europe inherited ideas from, 95

Conscience, Hendrik, 111, 290–291

"Consolidation and Expansion of the Kingdom (1840–1914)," by Baron de Gruben, iv, 37–52

Constitution, Belgian: 1831, ratified, 24; principle work of National Congress, 32; Title II of, recapitulates liberties, 32, 222; liberalism of, 32–34, 94; plus conservatism, 34; guaranteed freedom of press, 41, 222; principle of separation of Church and State in, 45; suffrage amended by, 48; general outline of, 83; Section Two of, on Belgians and Their Rights, 83 ff.; three freedoms in, 84; spiritual freedoms, 84–85; powers of, 85–92; Pirenne quoted on, 94; government lived up to, 222. *See also* Government

Constitution, Dutch: modified for extension of territory, 27; equality of right for Belgian Provinces, 27; rejected, 28; electoral college system of, replaced, 31

"Constitution and Political Structure of Belgium," by Henri E. A. M. Rolin, vii, 81–92

Convention of the Fortresses, 27

Coquilhatville, 342, 346

Corfu incident, mentioned, 131

Coster, Charles de, 302; quoted, 303; mentioned, 302, 306, 307, 311

Council of Flanders, 105, 117

Courtrai (Kortrijk): Golden Spurs at, 17; Degrelle's speech at, 105; linguistic area south of, 108

Crimean War, 42

Crismer, Léon, 247, 253

Crystal Mountains: description of, 338; waterways through, 386; barrier, 387

Crusades, 218; influence of, on culture of Low Countries, 287

Cumont, 230, 236; Francqui prize to, 237

Dar-es-Salam, 63

David, Jan, 110

Dawes Plan, 134

Defacqz. *See* Congress, Liberal

Degrelle, Léon, 105–107, 125

Dekker. *See* Multatuli

Delacroix, Léon, 68, 103; Cabinet replaced plural by universal suffrage, 104

Delattre, Louis, 305–306

Delchef, A., 316

Demolder, Eugène, 302, 304

Dendermonde, School of, 271

Deutsche Voksvirt, Der, quoted on plundering, 416

Devaux, Paul, 83

Dewez, Laurent, 282–283

Dinaso group (*Dietsch-Nationaal Solidaristisch Verbond*), 124

d'Indy, Vincent, 329, 332
d'Omalius d'Halloy, Jean Baptiste, 248–249
Dixmude (Diksmuide), 4; pilgrimage to, 119; cattle raising near, 158
Domaine de la Couronne, 375
Dordrecht, 207, 208, 209
Dossogne, Victor J., "From Caesar to 1814," ii, 15–24
Dubroeucq, Jacques, 266, 280
Dufay, Guillaume, 319, 320, 321
Dumouriez, Charles François, 22
Dunkirk: Spain lost, 20; lost to France, 200; Belgians aided at, 426–427
Dutch-Belgian union: Allies concluded, to maintain political order, 25–26; circumstances favored, 26; structure of, 27–28; Dutch Constitution adapted to, 27–28; William's despotism in, 28, 30; program for separation of, 29; French influence in, 30. *See also* Constitution, Dutch
"Dutch Regime (1814–1830) and the Kingdom of Belgium, The," by Baron de Gruben, iii, 25–36

Eburons, 6
Ecole des Hautes Etudes, L', 122
"Economic Development of Belgium," by B.-S. Chlepner, xii, 167–186
"Economic Development" (Congo), by Max Horn, xxvii, 386–399
Economic development: history of early, 8–10, 11, 18, 167; economic activity of tribes, 167; large domains characteristic of, 167; frontier expansion, 169; activity after eleventh and twelfth centuries, 168; importance of towns in, 169; cloth production, 169–170; transition from economy of Middle Ages to modern, 170–171; effect of wars of religion on, 171; foreign commerce at standstill in seventeenth century, 172; in French period, 173; Industrial Revolution, 174; colonial market, 174; free trade, 174–177; industrial progress in Dutch period, 175; banking, 176, 177–178, 185; importance of agriculture in, 178; trade deficit offset, 178; business cycles, 179

Economy after First World War: financial situation, 67, 69–70, 71, 182; debts, 69–70, 71, 130; free trade, 70; creation of belga, 71; return to gold standard, 71, 184; international crisis felt in, 73, 183, 191; stressed greater industrialization in Flanders, 119; commercial activity, 134; economic union with Luxemburg, 141; important in foreign policy, 142; failure of London Economic Conference, 143; deflationary policy of second Theunis Cabinet, 174; optimism under Van Zeeland, 175; manufacturing and exporting country, 177; taxes, 184; protectionism, 184–185; failed to recover prewar prosperity, 204; growing importance of Congo as outlet, 204; commission to fix taxes and port dues, 209; riparian state in Rhine community, 210; after Second World War: international insecurity, 415; economic seizure by Germany, 417–418; food shortage, 418–419; workers deported, 421
Education: illiteracy rare, 11, 114; law for primary, 44, 99; under clergy, 44; issue in quarrel of State and Church, 45, 227; policy of militant anticlericalism in, 47; "War of the Schools," 47; higher, under French domination, 49, 241; universities, 72, 253; primary schools compulsory, 96; clergy supervised religious, 96; Rogier's law, 97; Athenées, 97, 231, 232; Frère-Orban bill for elementary, 99, and Catholic opposition to, 99–100; secondary schooling in Flemish, 104; Flemish platform for, 114; obligatory in 1914, 114; linguistic situation in, 122–123, 232; 1932 law, 122; University of Louvain, 220; religion excluded from secular schools, 222; three thousand Church schools, 222; system of, faithful to humanistic legacy, 226; two controlling elements, 226; right to confer degrees, 226–227; system of subsidized liberty, 227; Church opposed State, 227; degrees checked by State Committee, 228; American aid to higher, 229,

Education (*Continued*)
230, 231; American traits introduced
into, 229; impetus to, by two foundations, 230, 235; history and philology Belgian specialties in, 230,
232–233; great teachers, 230–231;
Bollandists, 231; political strife in,
231; feminine, 231; Lycée, 231–232;
Hellenists in, 232; requirements for
university teachers, 234; Byzantine
history section in, 234; science in,
241 ff.
"Education in Belgium," by Henri
Grégoire, xvi, 226–238
Edward, Lake, 337, 339, 340
Edward I of England, 17
Eekhoud, Georges, 72, 303, 311
Eendracht (Union), 210
Eight Articles, Treaty of, Belgian
rights in, 27
Elbe-Havel-Spree-Oder system, 199
Elias, H. J., 125
Elizabeth, Queen, 405
Emden, traffic diversion toward, 205
Enghien, 108
"Enlightened Despots," 22
Ensor, James, 271, 272
Erasmus, House of, 237, 239
Ermengerm, E. van, 253
Ethiopia, 338
Etienne, Bishop, 275, 277
Eupen-et-Malmédy: to Prussia, 23;
Belgium regained, 68, 133
Expressionists, Flemish, 272
Eyck, Jan and Hubert van, 258–259

Falkenhausen, Ludwig von, 116
Famenne, woodlands in, 5
Fantasists, 298
Farnese, Alexander, 20
Fayd'herbe, Luc, 269–270, 281, 282
Fétis, François Joseph, 331
"Fiamminghi," 263
Fifth of Fructidor, 221
Fijt, Jan, 265, 272
Flamingants: list of grievances of, 111;
platform of, 112; agitated for Flem-
ish in schools, 114; stimulated intel-
lectual activity, 114; more radical
element among, 115; divided, 118;
in industry, 119

Flanders: in northern plain, 4; struggle against France, 17; emancipation
of, 17; a military base facing England, 17; Francis I renounced claims
to, 18; discontent in, 115; question
of political autonomy for, 115; leaders in, embarrassed by Germans, 116;
Germans treated, as dependency,
117; *Boerenbond,* 119; collaboration
among extreme groups in, 125; difficult period in, 176–177; economic
progress in, 183
Flanders, Council of: formed, 117; Germans cajoled, 117
Flaubert's *Tentation,* 293
Flémalle, Master of, 259, 260, 261, 265
Flemings: close contact with Walloons,
3–4; Germanic, 6; reputation of, 6;
physical aspect of, 6; in music, 7;
language only distinguishing mark,
16; equal rights for, 75; Scientific
Academy satisfied, 76; Parliament
satisfied demands of, between wars,
104; Germans sowed discord among,
104; claims of, 105
Flemish language: status of, restored,
49; originally the Flemish question,
75–76, 104; of half the population,
104; secondary schooling in, 104;
census for, 108; line of demarcation
between linguistic areas, 108; islands,
108; disdain for, 109; employed in
local affairs, 109; William made, official in Flanders, 109; orthography,
110; Flamingants' demands for, 111–
112; pride in, 113; in courts, 113; regained prestige, 115
Flemish Movement: purpose of, 110;
Willems leader of, 110; Conscience
quoted on, 111; report of Grievance
Commission on, 112; culture disseminated, 112–113; pride in culture,
113; Flemish Academy, 114; First
World War turning point in, 115;
Germans granted some demands of,
116; political aspects of, delineated,
118; cultural and economic base for,
119; remained a social movement,
119; efforts after 1930, 123; future
of, 126; in literature, 290. *See also*
Flamingants

"Flemish Movement, The," by Shepard B. Clough, ix, 108–126

Flemish Nationalists (Frontists): issues of, 75–76; in 1918 elections, 104; descendants of Activists, 105; emphasized Flemish claims, 105; collaborators, 105, 124, 146, 224, 423; defeatist attitude of, 117, 118; platform of, 123–124; insisted on neutrality, 146; bishops condemned, 224

Floris, Frans, 264, 266, 280; style, 266

Foch, Ferdinand, 59; ordered triple offensive, 62

Fondation Universitaire, 230 and n. 1; books printed through help of, 234, 235

Fonds National de la Recherche Scientifique, Le (Nationaal Fonds voor Wetenschappelijk Onderzoek), 230, 237

FOREAMI, 405, 406

"Foreign Policy, 1918 to 1940," by Frans van Cauwelaert, x, 129–147

Foreign relations: closer ties with England under William of Orange, 21; international status established, 36; Leopold I's domain, 37; devoted to principle of independence, 39–40, 47; practice of neutrality, 40, 42, 51; concern for general peace, 40; rejected economic absorption, 42; diplomatic, with Russia, 42; crisis from Italian War, 42; sought reaffirmation of 1839, 43; support in London, 43; question of methods in, 43; diplomatic status determined by 1839 Treaty, 53; compulsory neutrality failed, 129; Versailles Treaty left Belgium free to adapt, 129; four phases of, between wars, 130 ff.; three problems in reëstablishment of peace, 130; unfortunate repercussion on, of treatment of Germany, 132; France asked separate military alliance, 132; no tripartite agreement, 132; international position precarious, 132–133; difficulties in, due to Hitler's rise, 134 ff.; 1936 address of King, 136–138; relieved from obligations to defend own frontiers, 138–139; German declaration quoted, 139; with Netherlands, 140 ff.; convention with Luxemburg, 141–142; economic problems important in, 142

Forum, 144

"Four Freedoms," 94

Fournois, Théodore, 271

Francis I, 18

Franck, César, 9, 224, 328–329, 332

Franck, Louis, 115

Franck-Segers Law, 104

Franco-Belgian waterways system, 199

Franco-Prussian War, 43; produced crisis for Belgian independence, 50; Belgium's activities in, 99

Francqui, Emile, 71, 255

Francqui Foundation, 237, 255

Franks: in Isle of Batavia and the Kempen, 16; characteristics of, 16

Fransquillons, 115

Frederick, Prince, 29

Frederick III, Emperor, 18

Frederick William IV abdicated, 45

French, Marshal, 59

French language: influence in Flemish territory, 6; official tongue, 49, 108, 109; vehicle of higher education, 49; fashionable, 108; reversal of trend in United Kingdom, 109; reëstablished as official, 109–110; literature, 301 ff.

"French Literature in Belgium," by Benjamin Mather Woodbridge, xxi, 301–313

French Revolution, 22; aroused Belgians, 24; effect of, on Europe, 25

Frère-Orban, H. J. W., 97, 98; formed government, 99; resigned, 100; opposed child-labor laws, 101

Frezin, Julia, 308

Frisians, 15

"From Caesar to 1814," by Victor J. Dossogne, ii, 15–24

Frontists (Front party). *See* Flemish Nationalists

Fundamental Law (*Grondwet*), 27

Gauchez, Maurice, 307, 308, 312

Geerardsbergen, 12

Gembloux, 165, 166; Agricultural Institute in, 250, 252, 253

General Center of Liberal Trade Unions of Belgium (*La Centrale Générale des Syndicats Libéraux de Belgique*), 190

General Confederation of Belgian Labor (*Confédération Générale du Travail de Belgique*), 189

Geneva Covenant, 136

Geography: northern plateau, 4; central part, 4; southern, 4–5; physical, 5–6, 386; location, 7; nucleus of Charles V's empire, 19; southern border under Louis XIV, 20; eastern boundary, 26, 27; frontiers established, 35; Geographical Conference, 366

"Geography" (Congo), by James P. Chapin, xxiii, 337–352

German Confederation, 36

Germany: invaded Belgium, 52, 53; character of diplomacy of, 53–54; decision of General Staff of, to cross Belgium, 56; question of annexation of Belgium, 115–116; in League, 133; Hitler Chancellor of, 134; withdrew from League, 134; occupied Rhineland, 136; France declared war on, 138; declaration of, to Belgium quoted, 139; adopted economy of war, 143; invaded Poland, 144; attacked Belgium, 145, 147; planned aggression on Dutch frontier, 146; aggressions ended twenty years cooperation on Rhine, 208; decadence of erudition in, after 1933, 235; supported Leopold II in Congo, 371; occupation of Belgium, 416–421; Belgian resistance to, 421–425

Gezelle, Guido, 112, 290, 291, 293, 296

Ghent (Gent): a tormented city, 9; textile workers of, 10; wealth and power in, 17; most typical Flemish town, 70; French-speaking people in, 108; administration of, 125; producing center, 169; system of unemployment insurance, 194; a seaport, 203; a Rhine port, 209; commission to fix port dues, 209; natural intellectual center of Flemish section, 236; Institut des Hautes Etudes in, 237; Van Eyck altarpiece at, 258–259

Ghent, University of: made Flemish, 65, 76, 105, 114, 116, 122, 236; changed to Netherlandish, 70, 72; Catholic and liberal professors at, 96; "Von Bissing University," 105; bitter political struggle concerned with, 121–122, 236

Ghent-Terneuzen Canal, 203

Gijsen, Marnix, 299. *See also* Goris, Jan-Albert; *Het Huis*

Giraud, Albert, 72, 308–309

Goes, Hugo van der, 259, 261, 263

Golden Spurs, Battle of, 17, 110; day of, a Flemish holiday, 113

Gorinchem, 201, 210

Goris, Jan-Albert: "Land and People," i, 3–12; "Belgium between the Two World Wars," vi, 66–77; "Note on Walloon Literature," 314–317. *See also* Gijsen, Marnix

Gossec, François-Joseph, 325–326

Gottschalk, Max, "Social Legislation," xiii, 187–197

Government: Caesar organized, 15; political power to mayors of the palace and the Carolingian dynasty, 16; feudalism, 16; self, in Flemish towns, 17; under Charles V, 19; separate sovereignty, 20; principle of administrative centralization, 22; 173; satisfactory reign of Maria Theresa, 22; Confédération des Etats Belgiques Unis, 22; under Directory, 22; under Napoleonic Empire, 22–23; Dutch-Belgian union, 27–29, 81; Dutch Constitution adopted, 27–28; despotism under William I, 28, 30; Provisional, at Brussels, 31; limited monarchy, 33–34, 220; London Conference recognized independence, 32–34, 35; return to former dynasty, 32; constitutional monarchy, 33, 73, 89; property qualification for voting, 33, 45, 48, 95, 100, 102; political rivalry for choice of sovereign, 35; new State, 36; autonomy under Leopold I, 37–38; Monarchy, 38 ff.; interference of Powers, 40, 41; relation of Church and State, 44 ff.; period of internal organization of State, 44; reign of Leopold II, 46–47; Liberal party in power, 47; Catholic party in power, 47–48; three problems for, 48; factors contributing to decline of parliamentary regime, 49–50; crisis of Franco-Prussian War, 50; reign of Albert, 51 ff.; universal suffrage, 68, 69, 104; Albert checked parliamentarianism, 73; political structure unitary, 81; communes basis of, 81–82, 83; provinces, 82; local authorities, 82; municipal autonomy, 83; outline of National Congress, 83; Belgians and Rights, 83; constitutional liberties, 84–85, 219; judiciary power detached, 87; legislative power, 87, 91; executive power of King, 87, 90; Ministerial Council, 87, 89, 91–92; Ministers in, 87–88, 89–90; party, from 1848–1914, 97 ff.; coalition, from 1914, 103–104; in Exile, 126, 426; royal palace and Parliamentary buildings, 283; will continue with constitution modified, 431–432

Great Rift Valley, 338

Grégoire, Henri, "Education in Belgium," xvi, 226–238

Gregory XVI, encyclical of, against modern freedoms, 94

Grenfell, George, 401

Greshoff, Jan, "Belgian Literature in the Dutch Language," xx, 286–300

Grétry, André-Ernest, 9, 325, 326–327

Groeninghe, Battle of, 277

Gruben, Baron de, "The Dutch Regime (1814–1830) and the Kingdom of Belgium," iii, 25–36; "Consolidation and Expansion of the Kingdom 1840–1914)," iv, 37–52

Guicciardini, L., 169, 171

Hague, The: reintroduced Dutch language, 49; international conventions of, violated, 64

Hazebrouck, 108

Hainaut: part of, in northern plain, 4; higher plateau, 4; strikes among metal and glass workers in, 101; horse raising in, 161; coal mines of, 172–173

"Halles," 277–278

Hamburg: port of, 199; sponsored by rulers, 199

Han, grottoes of, 5

Handel, counterpoint of, 319

Havre, Belgian factories moved to, 60

"Health, Education, and Social Welfare" (Congo), xxviii, 400–412

Hellens, Franz, 306–307

Helmont, J.-B. van, 220, 239–240

Henry of Ghent, 219

Herriot, Edouard, 133

Herskovits, Melville, J., "Peoples and Cultures" (Congo), xxiv, 353–365

Hesbaye region, 4

Het Fonteintje, 298–299

Het Huis, 299

Het Laatste Nieuws, 113

Het Nieuws van den Dag, 113

Heymans, C., Nobel prize to, 76, 252

Hislaire, René, "Political Parties," viii, 93–107

History: intermittent pressure from without, 3; language frontier, 6; German influence on, 6; provincialism, 8; towns, 9–10; under four foreign powers, 11, 221; Caesar organized, 15; Frankish invasion last, 16; Belgian Provinces, 17; linked to Spain, 18; nucleus of Charles V's empire, 19; complete break between Catholic South and Protestant North, 19; war squeezed between Holland and France, 20, 221; recognized as separate sovereignty, 20; southern border under Louis XIV, 20; exposed to ambitions of France, 21, 221; setback to independence, 22; satisfactory reign of Maria Theresa, 22; under Directory, 22; under Napoleonic Empire, 22–23; fixed at Waterloo, 23; reunited with Holland, 26, 27 ff., 81, 174; revolution, 29–30, 34, 81; independence reconfirmed, 31, 32, 35, 81; frontiers established, 35; crisis of Franco-Prussian War, 50; Germany invaded, 52, 54–59, 145, 147; official declaration of neutrality; 53–54, 144; in First World War, 53 ff.; Treaty of 1839 ended Belgian-Dutch conflict, 53; nationalist movement, 75; happy years

History (*Continued*)

after war, 134; issues dividing Belgium and Netherlands, 205–206, 286, and agreement, 208–209; riparian state in Rhine community, 210; position in aerial navigation, 211; battlefields of Second World War, 415; foreign occupation, 416; Nazis wiped out free institutions, 418, 420; food shortage, 418–419; anti-Semitism in, 420; workers deported, 421; underground press, 421–422; resistance by farmers, 422–423, and by clergy, 423–424; strikes, 424–425; sabotage, 425

"History of Christianity in Belgium, The," by Felix Morlion, xv, 217–225

Hitler: Chancellor, 134; tore up Locarno Pact, 134–135; speech to Reichstag on inviolability of Belgium, 139; eclipsed Kaiser, 147; satisfaction of, in accord with France, 207–208

Holland: occupied eight cities of Southern Provinces, 21; reunited with Belgium, 23, 26; English plan for, 26; recompensed for colonial territories, 26; Fundamental Law for, 27; accepted Treaty of 1831, 36; position of language of, restored, 49

Hoover, Herbert, 229, 255

Horn, Max, "Economic Development" (Congo), xxvii, 386–399

Hoste, Julius, Jr., 118–119, 126

Hostie, Jan Frans, "Communications and Transportation," xiv, 198–213

Huysmans, C., 115, 118, 126

Hymans, Paul, first president of League, 64, 103

Iberian Peninsula, 18

Ick Hou (I hold), 18

Illuminated manuscripts, 256

Impressionists, 271–272

Industry: basic problem of, 7–8; agriculture chief, 8; textile, in Flanders, 10, 100, 176–177, 182; heavy, in Walloon from coal, 10, 175, 176; fishing traditional, on coast, 10; suffered in war, 66–67, 181–182; constant progress in, 71, 97; railroads state controlled, 71, 175–176, 202; in northern part, 71; 1935 crisis in, 72, 73; National Credit Institution for, 74; strikes in, 101; "transforming," 170; cloth production, 170–171; heavy, expanded in eighteenth century, 172–173; Industrial Revolution, 174, 187; most highly industrialized of European countries, 175; valuable raw materials for, 175; business corporation prime factor in development of, 176; manufacturing and exporting country, 177; proletariat, 181; trade unionism, 181, 186; industrial expansion, 182; progress in Flemish section, 183; as a riparian state in Rhine community, 210

INEAC (*Institut national pour l'Etude agronomique du Congo Belge*), 411

International African Association: a Belgian organization, 366; flag of, 367

International Association of the Congo: political, 368; treaties ceding sovereignty to, 368–369; as agent of native tribes, 369; Bismarck supported, 370; personal, 371

"In the First World War," by Georges Theunis, v, 53–65

Isis, 244

Italian War, 42

Italy attacked Abyssinia, 136

Janson, Paul-Emile, 103

Japan seized Manchuria, 136

Jaspar, H., 70, 104

Jesuits, 226

Jeune Belgique, La, 302, 308, 312

J.O.C., Young Christian Workers (*Jeunesse Ouvrière Chrétienne*), 191

Jocism, 224

Joffre, Joseph Jacques, 58

John I, Duke of Brabant, 17

John IV, Duke of Brabant, 220

Johnson, Sir Harry, quoted on Pygmies, 355, 356

Jordaens, Jacob, 260, 267, 268–269, 273, 282

Joseph II, 22, 93; clerical oppression by, 221

"Josephinism," 221

Jourdan, Jean Baptiste, 22

Juliana Canal, 206

Kalmthout, School of, 271
Karema, 367
Kasai, diamonds of, 341
Katanga, 341; Lower, 342
Kekulé, F. A., 245, 246
Keldermans, architectural dynasty of, 279
Kempen, the (Campine): in northern plain, 4; Franks into, 16; transformed into industrial center, 71; coal of, 182, 249; description of, 159; acreage of, 159; agriculture, 159
Kivu, Lake, 339, 341, 345, 346; volcanoes, 340
Kleffens, E. van, 146
Krains, Hubert, 304–305; quoted on Tousseul, 306; *Portraite d'Ecrivains Belges* by, 312
Kremer, Gerard (Mercator), 240
Krimpen, 201, 210
Kurth, Godefroid, 102, 231

Labor organization. *See* Unions
Labor party: campaign for suffrage, 48; mouthpiece of socialist doctrine, 49; foundations of, 100; supported strikers, 101; against revolutionary action, 103
Lacordaire, 94, 222
Lamennais, Felicite Robert de, liberal Catholicism of, 28, 94
"Land and People," by Jan-Albert Goris, i, 3–12
Landormy, quoted, 326
Landsbond, 119
Lassus, Orlando de, 319, 321, 324
Laurent, Emile, 254, 257
League of Nations, 130; offered insufficient protection, 131, 133; Germany withdrew from, 134, 136; Belgium and France appealed to Council of, 135; Japan withdrew from, 136; Belgium agreed with article 16, 140; financial conference called by, 142–143; Belgium supported, 433; nations moving toward organization like, 433
Lebeau, J. L. J., 96
Le Boeuf, Henri, 332, 333
Leirens, Charles, "Belgium Music," xxii, 318–334

Lek River, 201, 209, 210
Lekeu, Guillaume, 328, 329, 332
Lemonnier, Camille, 302, 303, 310, 311
Leo XIII, 102, 223
Leopold I: Prince of Saxe-Coburg-Gotha became, 35, 37; character of, 37–38; marriages, 37, 38; reign of, established Belgium's autonomy, 38; services to Belgium, 38; crown to descendants of, 89
Leopold II, brother of Joseph II, 22
Leopold II (of Belgium): succeeded father, 46; empire builder, 46–47; Congo enterprise of, 47, 318, 352, 366, 367–371, 379; suggested army reorganization, 54; President of International African Association, 366; collaborated with Stanley, 367; founded *Comite d'Etudes,* 367, 368; political program of, for Congo, 368–369; International Association of Congo of, 369, 371; opposed Anglo-Portuguese treaty, 370; won support of Bismarck, 371; head of new state, 371; expansionist policy of, 371; planned to annex Nile basin, 371–372; abandoned dream empire, 372; organized administration for Congo, 372; supported Congo, 373; documents bequeathing Congo to Belgium after death, 373.
Leopold III: interest of Prince, in colonial problems, 73; address by, inaugurating "policy of independence," 130, 136–138; appeal by, 144; address to Americans quoted, 144–145; to The Hague with offers of mediation, 146
Leopold II, Lake, 341
Lerberghe, Charles van, 310, 311
Leys, Hendrik, 260, 270–271
Liberals: majority in 1846 elections, 44; dominated political life, 44; government of, in power in 1878, 47; policy of, 47–48; almost eliminated, 48–49; petty bourgeoisie faithful to, 50; arbiters between Catholics and Socialists, 68; partisans of revolutionary principles of 1789, 93; anti-clericalism in doctrine of, 93; common front with Catholics, 93–96;

Liberals (*Continued*)
  program of Congress of, 97; two
  trends, 98; reinforced through proportional representation, 103; hostile to Flemings, 112
Libre Belgique, La, 65, 421
Liége (Luik): land of, 4; a fighting
  town, 9; location of, 9; industry in,
  9, 101, 170, 173; a Belgian Province,
  17, 219; Principalities of, to William
  I of Holland, 23, 219; fortifications
  at 51, 55; purpose of, position, 55;
  gateway to Belgium, 55; resistance
  of, 56; World Fair at, 72; University
  of, 96, 219; strikes in, 101; Germans
  reorganized administration of, 125;
  political evolution of, 173; coal
  mines of, 173; water communications from, 206, 207; Christianization
  of, 219; political Bishopric of, 219;
  center of education, 219; independent, 219; Democratic Popular party
  founded at, 219; stronghold of Walloon dialects, 315
Lier, normal school at, 111
Limburg: northern plain, 4; coal mines
  in, 10, 71, 206; a Belgian Province,
  17; Belgians evacuated, 36; in German Confederation, 36; railway
  across, 202; connecting canals, 206
Linguistic nationalism: a problem, 3;
  language frontier unchanged, 6;
  question ethnic opposition between
  two linguistic groups, 72; line of demarcation, 108, 120; William's policy, 109; bilingual inscriptions, 114;
  linguistic laws of 1914 intact after
  peace, 118; 1924 law, 120; 1932 law,
  120–121; 1935 law before courts, 121;
  Flemings realized major demands,
  123; struggle around University of
  Ghent, 236; evolution of Louvain
  proceeded smoothly, 237
Lion of Flanders, The: hymn of Flemish movement, 111; book by Conscience, 111, 291
Lipsius, Justus, 220, 238
Liszt, 327; cited, 329
Literature in French language: profited from world-wide use of French,
  7; lyrical quality of, 7; suffered losses,

72; fusion of Christian and classical
  influences in, 286–287; Romanticism
  in, 287; Flemish movement in nineteenth century, 290, 293; all literary
  genres of Middle Ages cultivated in,
  301; patriotic sentiment in, 301;
  close alliance of, with plastic art,
  302; mystic trait of, 302; fiction and
  poetry most successful in, 303; love
  of picturesque in, 303; traits of
  typical Walloon novelists, 304; inspiration of regionalism in, 306–307;
  women in, 307–308; periodicals in,
  308; poetry, 308 ff.; pantheism
  marked trait in, 310; no tradition in,
  for theater, 312; literary criticism,
  312
Literature in Dutch language: blossomed, 72; influence of Crusades in,
  287; synthetic fusing, 287; poetry of
  Middle Ages, 288, 289; three orders
  of poetry in, 288; variegated richness
  of, in Middle Ages, 288–289; "Movement of the 'Eighties,'" 292; German
  expressionism in, 298
Locarno Pact, 130; general satisfaction
  with, 133, 134; contributed to peace,
  133; Hitler tore up, 134; lost its
  value, 135, 136; principle of mutual
  assistance of, 138
Loi de Malheur (Law of Misfortune),
  222
London Conference: Belgium reunited
  with Holland at, of 1814, 23; of 1830
  recognized Belgian independence,
  35, and adjourned, 36; provisional
  arrangements of 1936, 135; failure
  of, Economic, 143
Lorraine: Belgian, 5, 55; offensive toward, 58; German, 202; French, 203
Lothair, 16; "middle kingdom" of, 18
Lotharingia (Francia Media), 16
Louis the German, 16
Louis Philippe: prudence of, 34; tried
  to impose customs union, 42; down-
  fall of, 42; fled, 45
Louis XI of France, 18
Louis XIV: imperialistic policy of, 20;
  claimed Low Countries, 21
Louise Marie, 38
Louvain (Leuven), University of:

Catholic scholastic center, 9, 220, 224; burned, 57; bilingual system at, 72; bishops reopened, 96, 110, 241; *Studium Generale*, 220; constitution of, 220; famous for men of, 220; closed, 221; rank of, 224; associated with Cardinal Mercier, 228; a free university, 228; linguistic evolution of, 237; College of Three Languages at, 239
Louvois, François, system of destruction of, 21
Lualaba River, 340, 342, 343. *See also* Congo River
Ludendorff, 56, 133
Luxemburg: picturesque, 5; a Belgian Province, 17; Grand Duchy of, to William I of Holland, 23, 27; Duchy member of German Confederation, 27, 36, 202; held by Prussians, 31; Belgians occupied, 35, and evacuated, 36; Bismarck bartered, 42–43; independent state of, 43, 198; economic union with Belgium, 141–142, 143, 203; economic resources, 142; no longer in Zollerverein, 203
Lyons, 9, 75
Lys. *See* Leie River

Maastricht, 31; bottleneck of, 203; early church at, 217
Madrid, Peace of, 18
Maeterlinck, Maurice, 9, 310–311, 312
Mahengé, Belgian successes at, 63
Main, canalization of, 205
Maison d'Art, 332
"Malcontents," 19
Malou, J., 99, 101
Malouel, Herman, 257–258
Malplaquet, Battle of, ended French domination, 21
Man, Hendrik de, plan, 74
Mander, Carel van: quoted on Gossart, 264; spirit of Renaissance and Baroque dominates, 289
Mannerists, 264
Mannheim, Convention of, 207, 209; rule of, 210
Maredsous, Abbaye de, 235
Margaret of Maele, Countess of Flanders, 18

Maria Theresa: satisfactory reign of, 22; established Royal Academy at Brussels, 240; arts under, 282
Marlborough, John Churchill, 21
Marne, Battle of, 58; second Battle of, 62
Mary of Burgundy, 18
Massijs, Quinten, 260, 263, 265
Maubeuge, 58
Max, Adolphe, 64, 228, 233
Maximalists: similar to Activists, 118; separate political parties for, 119; agitation by, for Flemish University of Ghent, 122; developments in platforms of, 123
Maximilian of Habsburg, Archduke, 18
Maximilian I, mausoleum of, 267
Mayombe district, 337
Mechlin (Mechelen): ecclesiastical capital, 9; Catholic Congress at, 98, 222, 224; Catholic university at, 241
Meit, Conrad, 266, 279
Memling, Hans, 259, 261
Mémoires of Royal Academy, 254
Menapians, 6
Mendicant Orders, 277
Mercier, Cardinal, 65, 224, 228
Mérode, F. de. *See* Flemalle
Metternich, 45, 95
Met Tijd en Vlijt, 110
Meuse (Maas): marks southern Belgium, 4; Liége on, 9; Prussia desired right bank of, 23; Germany requested Belgium fortify, 51; only obstacle from Verdun to Maastricht, 53; Americans occupied, sector, 62
Minimalists, 118, 123, 126
Ministerial Council, 89
Minne, Joris, 273
Minne, Georges, 272, 273
Minne, Richard, 298
Minorities, 277
Misner, E. G., "The Agriculture of Belgium," xi, 148–166
Missions, Christian, in Congo, 401–403
Mockel, Albert, 308, 309, 310, 312
Moens, Wies, 124
Mombasa, British expeditionary corps in, 63
Mone, Jean, 266, 280

Moniteur, 113, 120; *Belge,* 144
Mons (Bergen), 9–10, 58
Montalembert, 93, 98, 222
Monte, Philippe de, 323–324, 333
Moratorium, 134
Morlion, Felix, "The History of Christianity in Belgium," xv, 217–225
"Most favored nation" clause: Belgium advocated, 177; basis of Belgium policy, 185
"Movement of the 'Eighties," *De Nieuwe Gids*), 292, 293
Multatuli (Eduard Douwes Dekker), 292
Muséon, Le, 235
Music: school of religious, 219; polyphonic, 219, 318; religious atmosphere in compositions, 224, 318; great period of, 318; Bach's style dominated century, 318; fifteenth and sixteenth century, based on ancient liturgical modes, 319; early period in, 319–324; composition for three voices popular, 320; Motet of the Passion one of greatest forms, 321; principle of imitation in, 321; art of harmony, 321; influence of Nordic musicians, 322, 323; Venetian school of, 322–323; transformation of language of musical sounds, 323; in Italy, 323; modern period in, 324; vogue of virtuosity benefited, 327; Flemish composers, 330–331; new perspectives in musicology, 331
Mutalités, 193
Mystère de la Nativité, 315

Namur (Namen): higher plateau of, 4; fortifications at, 51, 55; forts at, crushed, 56
Nancy, 18
Napoleon: Belgian Provinces under, 22–23, 221; escaped from Elba, 23; plan of, for canal, 210; Concordat of, 221; pension to Grétry from, 326
Napoleon III, 41; dangers in reign of, 42
Nassau, Prince of Orange lost, 26
National Bank: Van Zeeland vice-governor of, 74; reorganized, 75
National Benefit Fund, 193

National Congress: assembled, 24; reforms for election of, 31; deputies for, 32; basic decisions of 32; general outline by national section of, 83
National Renaissance party, 104
Nationalist movement: progress in Flanders, 75–76, 223–224; revolution in, 75; Belgian bishops condemned, 224
Neckar, canalization of, 205
Nervii, 6
Netherlands, The, 200
Ngiri River, 341
Nijlen, Jan van, 296, 297–298
Nijmegen, Treaty of, 20
Nile, 337, 338, 340
Nivelles, 120; church at, 274
Norbertines, 277
Northern Provinces (modern Netherlands), William the Silent protector of, 19
"Note on Walloon Literature," by Jan-Albert Goris, 314–317
Notger, Bishop of Liége, 274
Nothomb, J. B., 83; unionist Cabinet of, 96
Nova Belgica, 171

Obrecht, Jacob, 319, 320–321, 333
Okeghem, Johannes, 319, 320–321, 322, 333
Ombiaux, Maurice des, 304, 305
Opsomer, I., 72, 271
Orange, Prince of (son of William I): popularity of, 29; abandoned Brussels, 29; offered concessions, 31; rival of Leopold I, 37
Oslo Agreement, 143, 185, 208, 433
Oslo Group: conference of foreign ministers of, at Copenhagen, 144; at Brussels, 144; *rapprochement* between Netherlands and Belgian-Luxemburg Union, 208
Ostayen, Paul van, 298
Ostend (Oostende): harbor works at, 70; market gardening region near, 156; world trade of, thwarted, 200
Ouchy Agreement: concluded, 141, 143; England opposed, 143; mentioned, 185, 208, 433
Ourthe River, 9

Palais des Beaux-Arts, 332–333
Palestrina, 319, 321, 323, 324
Palmerston, Lord, 35, 95
Paris, Treaty of, 81
Parmentier, Léon, 230–231
Parti du Mouvement, 34
Parties, political: profitable coalition of, 68; Catholic-Democratic-Socialist combination, 70; beneficial effect of, 90; history of, 93; two, 93; government by, 97 ff.; new Socialist, 100; coalition government, 103–104; most Flemings loyal to traditional, 119. *See also* Catholic party, Flemish nationalists, Labor party, Liberal party, Rexists, Socialists
"Passivists," 116
Pasture, De la. *See* Weyden, van der
Pavia, Battle of, 18
Pays Reel, Le, 106, 423
Peasant War, 221
People: supported national existence, 3; heritage of, of common sense, 3; two ethnic groups of, 3–4, 6, 49; early, 6, 15–16; language frontier, 6; description of, 6–7; population distribution, 7–8; per cent of, in agriculture, 8; industrial proletariat in southern provinces, 10; stability of, 10; emigration, 10–11; political awareness of, 11; evaded unpopular laws, 11; pride of, in past glories, 11; characteristics of, from Franks, 16; rights of, 21, 83-84; equality of, in various provinces, 23; all able-bodied men in army, 60; religious spirit driving force of, 225; realistic and persevering character of, 245
"Peoples and Cultures," (Congo), by Melville J. Herskovits, xxiv, 353–365
Permeke, Constant, 72, 272–273
Philip II of Spain, 19; patron of Bosch, 265; repressions by, 280
Philip IV of Spain, 20
Philippart, Georges, "Architecture," xix, 274–285
Philosophy, a stepchild, 7
Picard, Edmond, 307, 308
Piccard, August, 72, 247
Pierlot, Hubert, 104

Pirenne, Henri: in German prison, 64; greatest historian, 64, 230; quoted on Constitution, 94; leadership of, 233–234; *Histoire de Belgique* by, 233, 312; at University of Ghent, 236; Francqui prize to, 237
Pirmez, Octave, 302, 310
Plantin, Christopher, 219, 239, 280
Plisnier, Charles, *Prix Goncourt* to, 76
Polders, region of, 157
"Political Parties," by René Hislaire, viii, 93–107
Poot, Marcel, 330, 331
Poperinghe section, 158
Population, 31–32; density of, 41; losses in war, 67, 178, 179, 191; in agriculture, 148–149, 180; rapid increase in twelfth and thirteenth centuries, 168; peasant emigration, 168; Flemish colonies, 168; halved by sixteenth-century wars, 171; mass emigration, 171; 1930, 179–180; industrial, 180–181, 188
Potter, Louis de, 93, 94
Poullet, P., 70; Cabinet, 103, 104
Poupliniere, La (The Farmer-General), 325
"Pragmatic Sanction," 19
Prés, Josquin des, 319, 321–322, 323
Primitives, Flemish, school of, 7
Printing, of first polyglot Bible, 219. *See also* Plantin, Christopher
Prussia: established in Rhineland, 23; insatiable desires of, 26; on left bank of Rhine, 26; objected to defensive line against Holland, 41; attempted to absorb Belgium, 42
Pygmies: relation of, to other tribes, 355–356; language of, 356–358; mode of life of, 358–359

Queen Elizabeth Foundation, 330
Quellin, Arturus the Elder, and the Younger, 270
Quetelet, Adolphe, 242, 243
Quinet, Fernand, 330–331
Quoilin, Maurice, 308

Railroads, 71, 175–176, 202, 248; Congo, 344, 373, 387–391 *passim*
Ramillies, 21

Reeder, General, 11

Regensburg, Truce of, 20

Relief, Commission of, 53, 64, 247; became Educational Foundation, 229; material support by, in many fields, 235

Religion: Catholicism unites conservatism and democracy, 8; Christianity introduced, 15, 217–218; provisions for freedom of, in Treaty of Eight Articles, 27; violent campaign by clergy, 27; monolithic in unity, 44; influence of, issue in Church-State quarrel, 45; freedom in, under Constitution, 84–85; wars of, in sixteenth century, 171; Crusades, 218; school of Flemish mystics, 218; religious strife in struggle against Spain, 220

Renaissance; rise of Antwerp marked opening of, 220; definition of, 286; composers of French, 332

Renaissance d'Occident, La. See Gauchez, Maurice

Renkin, Jules, 102, 104, 143

Rerum Novarum, 97, 102, 223

Revolution of 1830: some Flemish support for, 109; factors in, 109; modern Belgium result of, 109

Rexist party: created, 105; Degrelle founder of, 105; negative action in Parliament, 106; subsidized by Mussolini and Hitler, 107; relation with Flemish nationalists, 124; collaborators from, 125, 423; to protect from sabotage, 125; fascist movement of, 224; Belgian bishops condemned, 224

Reynard the Fox, 110; masterpiece of Dutch literature, 288

Reynolds, Robert, quoted on Scholarship, 233

Rhine: fortified as bulwark against France, 25–26; traffic, 199, 204; regularization of, 203, 204; -Herne canal, 205; issue of canal from Antwerp, 206; "truce" concerning traffic, 209; future status of, 209; -Meuse-Scheldt system, 210

Rhineland Pact. *See* Locarno Pact

Rhodesia, Northern, 342

Richelieu, natural boundary theory of, 20

Riemens, Hendrik, 200

Rijswicjk, J. van, 111

Rijswijk, Treaty of, 21

Rodenbach, Albrecht, 112, 308

Roelants, Maurice, 298, 299–300

Roey, Cardinal van, quoted on Nazism, 423–424

Rogier, Charles: signed armistice with Chassé, 31, 94; Liberal Cabinet of, 96, 97–98; new Liberal Cabinet of, 98–99; wise course of, 99

Rolin, Henri E. A. M., "Constitution and Political Structure of Belgium," vii, 81–92

Romanists, 262, 263–264

Rotterdam: important port, 198; Strasbourg traffic with, 208–209; coöperation with other seaports, 209

Rowntree, Seeboom, quoted on factory legislation, 187

Ruanda-Urundi: mandate of, 68, 337, 378, 386; drainage of, 340; government of, 345; cultural ties of, 353–354; former German mandate, 378; population of, 386; trade of, 395

Rubber: "red rubber" exactions, 392; output, 395, 396, 397

Rubens, Pieter Paul, 260, 264, 265, 267–268, 270, 273, 280; influence of, in spreading Baroque style, 281, 286

Rudolph II, 264

Ruimte, 298, 299

Ruwenzori Range, 339, 341

Ruysbroeck, Jan van, 219, 260, 278

Sadowa, Battle of, 42

Saedeleer, Valerius de, 272, 273

Sainte-Aldegonde, Marnix de, 289, 301

Sainte-Claire, Deville, 245

St. Elooi, cited, 218

St. Germaine-en-Laye, Treaty of, 390

St. Gertrude of Nivelles. *See* Illuminated manuscripts

St. Martins-Laethem, 272

St. Remigius, quoted, 217

St. Thomas, 219, 220

St. Vith: to Prussia, 23; returned to Belgium, 133

Salian Franks, 6, 217–218

Sambre River, 159, 162, 205

Samuel, Adolphe, 330, 331

Schaerbeek, railway yards at, 70
Schebesta, Father Paul: quoted on Pygmies, 356, 357; cited, 359
Schelde, De, 124
Scheldt (Schelde): made navigable, 4; polders reclaimed from, 4; closed, 21; legal control of, object in revision of 1839 Treaty, 140; closed by Treaty of Westphalia, 172, 200; common estuary with Rhine and Meuse, 201; "free," 201–202; statute of, below Antwerp, 206; Netherlands dominant position on, 211
Schollaert, F., 103
Schouteden, Henri, 251
Science: practical fields in, 7; flowering of, in Renaissance, 239–240; depression in, 240, 241; men of, self trained, 241; rapid development of, after middle of nineteenth century, 241; mathematical, 242 ff.; physics, chemistry and engineering, 244–248; biology and natural history, 248–253; research in, 253 ff.; scientific institutions, 253–254
"Science in Independent Belgium," by Jean Timmermans, xvii, 239–255
Sculpture: increasing French influence in, 261; of town halls, 261; altar retables, 261–262, 266; sixteenth century, 266; influence of Rubens on, of seventeenth century, 269–270; eighteenth-century pulpits, 270; wooden confessionals, 270; neoclassical movement in, 270; nineteenth century, 273; Bushongo statuettes, 363
"Second Mannerism," 264
Sedan, disaster at, 99
Sens du pays, le, 9
Seraing: iron works at, 175; Albert's speech at, 229–230
Seventeen Provinces, 17
Severin, Fernand, 311
Sicambers. *See* Salian Franks
Sleeping sickness, 404–405
Small Tradesman party, 104
Smet de Naeyer, P. de, 103
Smuts, Jan, 63
Snieders, August, 111
Socialist party: gained, 49; Walloon proletariat, 50; gained in 1914 elec-
tions, 68, 223; for social legislation, 68; founded, 100, 223; conducted workers' education school, 190
Social legislation: social equality promised after war, 68; humanitarian optimism, 69; progressed normally, 70; disregarded, 96; first recognition, 97; beginning of coöperative movement, 100, 101; workers' unions, 100; demands of Labor party, 100; Parliament recognized need of, 101; bills passed, 101, 103; low standard of living for factory workers, 181, 191; significant factor, 185; labor conventions for, ratified, 187–188; law of May 1921 permitted trade unions, 189; minimum wage, 191–192; benefit funds, 192–193; subsidies to fraternal organizations, 193–194; unemployment insurance, 194; old-age insurance, 194–195; workmen's compensation, 196; eight-hour day, 196–197; measures for women and children, 197; labor-management committees, 197; development of civil liberties, 218–219; public health legislation, 252–253
"Social Legislation," by Max Gottschalk, xiii, 187–197
Solvay: process, 177; Ernest, 246–247; Armand, 247; Institute of Physiology, 253
Souris, André, 330, 331
Southern Provinces (Belgium), 19; twelve cities of, to France, 20; eight cities of, to Holland, 21
Spaak, Paul-Henri, 103; address by, 138
Stanley, H. M., 251; explorations of, 367–368; collaborated with Leopold II, 367–368; signed treaties with chieftains, 368–369; insisted on railroad, 373; listed export products, 395
Stas, Jean Servais, 244–245, 253
States General: recognized Charles of Habsburg as sovereign, 18; of Southern Provinces signed Pacification of Ghent, 19; founded Confédération des Etats Belgiques Unis, 22; equal representation under union, 28; voted separation, 30

Strasbourg, 203–206 *passim;* agreement about traffic to, 208–209, 210
Stravinsky, 330, 332, 333
Stresemann, Gustav, 133
Streuvels, Stijn, 292, 293–294, 295
Surlet de Chokier, Erasme, 24
Swarts, Fréderic, 245, 247

Tabora, victory of, 63
Tanganyika, Lake: Germans attacked, 62; offensive south of, 63; geography of, and of Tanganyika territory, 338, 339, 340, 343; first station established by International African Association, 367
Tapestry weaving: fifteenth century, 170; in Brussels and Audenarde, 260; cartoons for, by great artists, 260
Teirlinck, Herman, 292, 295
Teniers, 12, 269
Tervueren: School of, 271; Belgian Congo Museum at, 354, 363
Textiles, 170–171; expansion after First World War, 182
Theunis, Georges: "In the First World War," v, 53–65; Prime Minister, 103; presided over economic conference, 143
Theunis Cabinet: problem of, 69; accomplished reconstruction, 70; crisis over trade treaty, 70; deflationary policy of second, 74
Theux, B. T. de, Cabinet of, 96, 99
Thierry of Alsace, 218
Tholen, Island of, 210
"Three Glorious Days," 29
Thyrse, Le, 308
Tilly, Joseph Marie de, 243, 253
Timmermans, Felix: "Science in Independent Belgium," xvii, 239–255; represents Flemish literature abroad, 296–297
Today and Tomorrow (Van Nu en Straks), 112
Tongeren: churches at, 217, 218, 274; Flemish diocese of, 219
Tournai: oldest town, 9; cession of, 18; religious independence of, 274; place of pilgrimage, 274–275; Cathedral of, 275, 276–277; influence of, as architectural center, 275

Towns: development of, important in economic expansion, 169; brought urban emancipation, 169; charters, 169; political and cultural expansion in, 169
Trade: success in foreign, before World War, 142; never recovered, 142; economic treaty with U.S., 143; import foodstuffs, 191; export labor, 191; Rhine traffic, 205–209
Trade Union Commission of Belgium *(La Commission Syndicale de Belgique),* 189
"Transaction of Augsburg," 18
Treaty of 1839: terms of, confirmed, 52; ended Belgian-Dutch conflict, 53; Article 8 of, 53; "scrap of paper," 54–55; revision of, between Belgium and Netherlands, 130, 140; object of revision of, 140–141; separation of, 142
Trier, churches at, 217, 218
Trooz, J. de, 103
Twenty-four Articles, Treaty of, 35
Tumba, Lake, 341

Ubangi River, 343, 344
Unionism: formula of, basis of Revolution and of government, 43; internal cohesion of, weakened, 43; until 1847, 94–95, 222; Congress of Liberals ended, 97; Industrial Revolution during, 200; dissolution of Union, 201
Union of the Opposition, 28, 29
Unions: Le Chapelier Law prohibited, 189; law of May 1921 permitted, 189; basis of, 190; leadership in, 190; political and social force, 191; wage elements, 191–196; subsidies to fraternal organizations, 193–194; Christian and Socialist, 223
University Foundation, 255, 324. *See also* Relief, Commission of
Upper Katanga, 338
Utrecht: Treaty of, 21; Peace of, 200

Valkhoff, Marius, 314; quoted, 317
Vallée-Poussin, Louis de la, 230
Vandervelde, Emile, 64, 70, 103
Van Dyck, 267, 268

Van Nu en Straks, 292, 293, 295, 296, 298
Varlez system, 194
Verdun, Treaty of, 16
Verhaegen, Théodore, 96
Verhaeren, H. A., 270, 310, 311
Vermeylen, August, 112, 292
Versailles, Treaty of: universal disenchantment result of, 68; freed Belgium from war debt, 69, 130–131; article 31 of, on status of Belgium, 129; Germany confirmed stipulations of, 133; stabilized situations in western Europe, 134; article 40 of, ended customs agreement of Luxemburg and Germany, 141; repudiated obligations about Rhine, 207
Verviers, woolen industry at, 173, 174
Vesalius, Andreas, 220, 239
Veurne, 11
Victoria, Lake, Belgian troops reached, 63
Vienna, Treaty of: ignored Belgium's struggle for independence, 24–25; sanctioned Kingdom of Netherlands, 26; edifice built by, crumbled, 28; *Parti du Mouvement* questioned basis of, 34; ruling of Congress of, on Rhine navigation, 201; Germany repudiated, 207
Vieuxtemps, Henri, 327, 331
Villeroy, François, bombarded Brussels, 21
Virres, Georges, 303–304
Vleeschauwer, Albert de: "Administrative Structure" (Congo), xxvi, 380–385; quoted on trade policy, 390
V.N.V. (*Vlaamsch Nationaal Verbond*), 124, 125
"Von Bissing University," 105
Vondel, Joost van den, 290
Vooriut (Forward), 100, 113
Vreuls, Victor, 329–330
Vriendt, Cornelis de, 266, 280
Vyvere, A. van de, 104

Waal River, 201, 207, 209, 210
Wadelai, 338
Waes, soil of, 4
Wagemakere(s): Domien de, 279; architectural dynasty of, 279

Wall, Constant van de, "Art in Belgium," xviii, 256–273
Wallonia: imports steel and copper, 10; socially conscious element in, 10; collaborators from, 125; economic expansion in, 176
Wallonie, La, 308
Walloon language: described, 314; four dialects in, 314; distinct from Roman language in twelfth century, 314; history of, 315; survived in Liége, 315; humorous verve in lyrics in, 315; burlesque comedies in, 316; success of *Société liégeoise* for, 316; lyric poets of, 316; encouraged by government, 317
Walloons: close contact with Flemings, 3–4; Romanized Celtic, 6; description of, 6–7; gifted in arts, 7; supported Dutch Constitution, 28
Walschap, Gerard, 299, 300
Waterloo, Battle of: fixed fate of Belgium, 23; collapse of French Revolution at, 25
Wauters, Arthur, "Belgium under the Occupation," xxix, 415–428
Wellington, 27, 35
West Flanders, dunes country of, 156
Westphalia, Treaty of, 20; closed Scheldt, 172
Weyden, Rogier van der (De la Pasture), 259, 260, 261
Wildeman, E. de, 250, 251
Willems, Jan Frans, 110
Willemsfonds, 113
Wilhelmina, Queen, 141; offer of mediation, 146
Willaert, Adrian, 219, 319, 322–323
William of Orange, on English throne as William III, 21
William the Silent: protector of Northern Provinces, 19; tolerance under, 200; Union of Seventeen Provinces maintained under, 200; assassination of, 200
William I, King of Holland: Belgian territory to, at Congress of Vienna, 23; failed through lack of understanding, 24; lost Nassau, 26; sovereignty of, recognized, 26–27; used hostility of two parties, 93; did not

William I (*Continued*)
recognize decisions of Congress of London, 95; accepted decisions, 97; established banking corporation, 176; Industrial Revolution during reign of, 200–201; antiliberal navigation policy of, 201

Wilmotte, M., 312; quoted on Walloon language, 314, 316–317

Wilson, Woodrow, 131, 132

Woeringen, victory at, 17

Woestijne, Gustave van de, 273

Woestijne, Karel van de, 9, 292, 293, 296, 299

Woodbridge, Benjamin Mather, "French Literature in Belgium," xxi, 301–313

Workers' party, reorganized underground, 425

Young Plan, 134

Ypres (Ieper), 17; Battle of, 60; second Battle of, 61; producing center, 169

Ysaye, Eugène, 327, 328

Ysaye, Théo, 329

Yser: Battle of, 59; Valley flooded, 59; minimum motor lorries at, 60; front active, 61; Albert's headquarters near, 64; army four years on, 64

Zeebrugge, 204, 206

Zeeland, Paul van, 74; Flemish nationalists fought Cabinet of, 76; left office, 76; mentioned, 104; bold policy of, government, 106; opposed Degrelle, 106–107; "Belgium in the Postwar World," xxx, 429–442

Zollverein, 42, 202, 203

Zype, Gustave van, 312

Date Due

MAR 25 '60			
MAR 30 '61			
MAR 27 '61			
APR 19 '61			
RESERVE			
MAY 6 '64			
MAR 30 '65			
APR 20 '70			
FE 16 '84			
FEB 2 '87			
GB	PRINTED	IN U. S. A.	